CARS IN THE UK

Volume One: 1945 to 1970

CARS IN THE UK

A survey of all British-built and

officially imported cars available

in the United Kingdom since 1945

Volume One: 1945 to 1970

GRAHAM ROBSON

MOTOR RACING PUBLICATIONS LTD
Unit 6, The Pilton Estate, 46 Pitlake, Croydon CR0 3RY, England

First published 1996

British Library Cataloguing in Publication Data

Robson, Graham, 1936–
    Cars in the UK : a survey of all British-built and officially
    imported cars available in the UK since 1945
    Vol. 1: 1945 to 1970
    1. Automobiles – Great Britain
    I. Title
    338.3'4'2'0941

ISBN 1899870156

Typeset by Richard Clark, Penzance
Printed in Great Britain by
Hartnolls Ltd, Bodmin, Cornwall

Contents:

Introduction

How many times have you searched for a car's top speed, then not known how much it cost? Or looked for an engine size, but not known what was the car's top speed? Wondered which Ferrari was fastest? Which car was made over the longest period? Or tried to equate length with weight, and body options – and failed? That's right – often, and so have I.

This book, I hope, will solve all – or at least most of – your problems, for it sets out to list, summarize and describe every production car made, or sold, in the UK from 1945 to the end of 1970. A companion volume will cover the period 1971 to 1995.

Because I have a large library at home, I know I am very lucky, but I've always been irritated by the lack of an all-can-do book to save me the hours of digging around for information. Some time ago, more than 40 years after I bought my first motoring magazine, I decided to do something about it.

CARS in the UK sets out to provide you with all the facts, without any flowery opinions – and hopefully without any prejudice. There are tens of thousands of 'what's, 'when's, 'how fast's and 'how much's in these pages – and I *hope* I have covered every production car sold in the UK. Because of the way sales *and* prices have changed so radically over the years, I have also included tables to help you work out what is cheap by 1970 standards – or costly by 1945 standards.

When I first approached my publisher, John Blunsden, he thought I was about to propose yet another 'Centenary Book' (for the book appears for the first time in the British motor industry's centenary year, 1996), but when he saw that my intention was to cover only the post-Second World War period, but to do so in great detail, he became enthusiastic.

Originally, the intention had been to produce one vast volume covering the first 50 postwar years, but as the project progressed we both realized that if it were to do every subject justice, such a book would almost certainly be a lot too large for the reader to handle comfortably, as well as colossally expensive. We therefore decided to cover the same period in two matching volumes, to be published in quick succession, which would neatly and tidily split at the end of 1970, halfway through my target of 50 postwar years.

Ground rules

From the very first day that work started on this project, I was determined to conform to carefully selected rules as regards content and structure, and subject to my informants/information being correct, here they are:

Firstly, I decided to treat the subject by calendar year rather than by individual make, so that the way the UK motoring scene developed and changed could be seen more clearly.

I also decided to describe new cars in the year in which they were officially revealed, which was not necessarily the year in which they went on sale. As far as British cars were concerned, it usually was, but many overseas cars were announced a year (or even more, in some cases) before they were first sold in the UK. (Naturally, this means that there is a slight overlap between 1970, where this Volume ends, and 1971, where Volume 2 begins, but I am sure the reader will understand the necessity for this.)

I have included, by family, every basic car, whether British or imported, which has been sold in the UK fully built-up, by a factory or import concessionaire since 1945. Any cars missed must have slipped into these islands undetected by either newspapers or motoring magazines – in which case they deserve their place in the shadows!

As far as possible I have tried to sift out what I call the 'Motor Show Specials', which appeared, flared briefly, but were never heard of again, and were probably never sold to customers. How many French Hotchkiss or Russian Zaporozhet cars, for example, survived after Earls Court's doors finally closed?

I have omitted cars made in the UK which were sold entirely for export – the DeLorean DMC-12, which might otherwise have appeared in Volume 2, being a perfect example. Nor have I included 'grey imports' (ie personal imports, such as some 1990s exotica), or the import of one-offs.

Also, I have omitted cars which were only ever sold as do-it-yourself kits – which explains why there is no Lotus 6, or Duttons, or several other marques.

Where engine options were available, I have only included those which were ever listed for sale on British-market cars. In particular, cars imported from Japan or Europe were often sold in the UK with only a limited proportion of the home-market engine ranges.

I decided to include as much data as possible in a massive specification chart, which has been trimmed only insofar as I have only quoted the length of the shortest derivative, and the lightest weight, and only the price of the car when introduced: otherwise, the chart would have been quite unwieldy. For cars launched before the end of 1970, and made for many years afterwards, I have included every derivative: the first-generation Porsche 911, which was built from 1964 to 1989, is an example of this.

(If a particular feature is missing from the specification chart, please forgive me – there simply wasn't space for anything more!)

Controversially, I decided to include the most believable set of production figures in every case: you would be amazed how these seem to change, over the years, and from authority to authority.

Lastly, I accepted that I was most certainly fallible, and that inevitably and inadvertently there would be a few omissions. However, I am not blessed with second sight, and if I could find no record of a particular car in my researches, it has not been included!

On this occasion, I hope I may be allowed to end by quoting that great personality, Sir Winston Churchill, who once wrote:

'Writing a book is an adventure. To begin with it is a toy and an amusement. Then it becomes a mistress, then it becomes a tyrant. The last phase is that just as you are about to be reconciled to your servitude, you kill the monster and fling him to the public.'

I know what he meant, for in writing this book I went through all those phases. Here it is, then – a monster which I am delighted to have defeated.

GRAHAM ROBSON
Burton Bradstock
March 1996

Acknowledgements

If I tried to write down every name, publication, source and influence which has gone into the preparation of this book, it would be a colossal Appendix all on its own.

Everything I have ever read, written, learned, or observed has helped, in one way or another, to provide the facts listed here. Which means that I would like to thank:

Every editor who has helped to produce 50 years of motoring magazines since 1945.

Every publisher who has commissioned a motoring book during the same period – British, European or North American.

Every industry press officer, past and present, here or overseas, who has provided facts, figures and other reference material.

Every club enthusiast, individual and fully-paid-up car 'buff' who has helped me over many years.

Because they all provided paper, reams of it, this proves something that my wife has always complained about – that I rarely throw anything away!

GRAHAM ROBSON

Influences

The 1930s and the war years

If you were to be transported back into the 1930s, you would find a very different British motoring scene, one almost unrecognizable from that of the high-tech, cosmopolitan 1990s. Far fewer cars were on the road, the habit of 'Buying British' was ingrained and accepted, and the general pace of motoring life – and of life in general – was much more gentle.

Although British cars were smaller, simpler and a lot slower than they are today, they were still relatively expensive, yet sold into a different market place. Purely for economic and social reasons, the motoring habit had still not spread very far. Quite simply, the vast majority of Britons could scarcely afford to run a car – any sort of car, even a worn-out old banger.

With new car sales peaking in Britain at less than 400,000 a year in the late 1930s, and a car population which had only reached 2,000,000 by 1939, British motoring was still a middle and upper-class pastime; the average working man was not well paid, and usually could barely afford even to run a motorcycle.

Although every market town – and many villages – had franchised dealerships for most makes of British car, these were mostly small and very limited in their scope. Multi-franchise outlets were quite normal, as was the oft-seen garage slogan: 'Any make of new car supplied'.

Except in specialized market sectors, foreign cars were still relatively unknown, such imports as there were coming mainly from North America, France, Germany and Italy. The Japanese industry was still tiny, its cars backward in the extreme, and they were totally unknown in the UK. The total market share of imports rarely reached 5 per cent, and was considerably less than this in the early 1930s. Even later in the decade, if it hadn't been for fascinating little machines such as the Fiat 500 *Topolino*, or the cheap-and-cheerful Opel Olympia, the import figure would have been even smaller.

Amazingly, when Government ministers urged the population to 'Buy British', they put patriotism first and did just that. To back up this strategy, motoring magazines often carried industry-sponsored adverts which urged readers to 'Buy a car made in the United Kingdom'.

Worldwide free trade may have been seen as a desirable concept, but it was not always practised. Britain's motor industry – the country's whole manufacturing economy even – was well protected by tariffs and Imperial Preference (which meant favouring British and Empire-made goods and services) was dominant and ensuring that British or British-blessed products were usually cheaper than their foreign rivals.

Was it any wonder, therefore, that the British motor industry could best be described as complacent in its attitudes and about its achievements? Except for supplying the traditional Empire markets (especially Canada, South Africa, Australia and New Zealand), British car-makers took little notice of the rest of the motoring world, or of its desires. It was almost as if the entire British motoring scene was settled in a cosy, self-satisfied little time warp, sure that outside influences would never intervene.

Although Britain built the world's most successful sportscars and the best expensive limousines, most British cars were technically behind the times. By 1939 observers had already noted that American and European cars were well ahead of the British in innovation – all-steel bodywork and synchromesh gearboxes from North America (with automatic transmission just over the horizon), independent suspension and unit-construction bodyshells from Europe.

Similarly, in motorsport the UK's activities were restricted, parochial and inward-looking. Bentley had long since withdrawn from motor racing and there were no top-line teams to challenge the French, Germans and Italians in Grands Prix. It was only in Britain (at Brooklands, particularly) that handicap races were held in order to give everyone an equal chance.

Compared with today, in fact, British motor racing was a very small business, for there were only three purpose-built race tracks (Brooklands, Crystal Palace and Donington Park). Most

competitive racing cars were imported because, apart from ERA and one or two even smaller companies, there was no British concern able to satisfy this specialized demand.

War clouds gather

Then came the Second World War, which caused a rapid and massive upheaval in the British motor industry's factories. During the conflict, companies which had been used to building family cars had their factories rapidly converted to produce tanks, trucks, guns, aircraft and their components, and military equipment of all types.

Then six years later came peace, the realization of the country's dire economic straits, and the need to trade out of those difficulties. High prices, high taxation, 'Export or Die', steel quotas, shortages of material and restrictions on home market deliveries all helped to cause a revolution for the industry. Although the shape of British motoring had been well-settled by the late 1930s, after the fighting all that had to change – and fast.

Britain – Europe's largest car-builder

Although the Depression of the early 1930s had hit the UK's motor industry very hard, it had made a strong recovery. At its lowest point, in 1931, only 158,997 new cars were built, but output had soared to 379,310 in 1937 and would have risen further if re-armament and a general increase in motoring taxation had not got in the way.

Those were the days when Britain regularly built more cars than any other nation except the United States, which enjoyed a much larger market into which no fewer than 4,000,000 cars a year were being built and sold. By comparison, other European countries' peak production figures were 289,000 (Germany) and 201,000 (France), while the Italians never bought more than 40,000 cars a year. On that basis, perhaps, the British could be excused for their complacency about their motor cars – especially as nearly 80,000 of them were being exported every year.

During that period, not only was

almost every new car sold in the UK British-built, the vast majority of them came from one of the Big Six car-makers. Sales were very strongly influenced by two financial factors – there was no taxation of any type on new car purchase (although annual licencing costs – based on a notional engine 'horsepower' rating – were high) and most of the Big Six offered a full and carefully-priced line-up of models.

Whereas today all cars are subject to the same annual licence fee, in the 1930s the principle of taxation by horsepower was well-established. Under what was known as the RAC Rating, or Treasury Rating, every car was taxed according to the piston area of its engine, the long-term effect being to minimize ratings by encouraging the design of small-bore/long-stroke power units.

For years the tax had been levied at the rate of £1 per 'RAC' horsepower, but in 1935, in an effort to boost car sales, this had been slashed to the equivalent of 75p (15 shillings in old, predecimalized, money) per horsepower. It therefore cost £6 to licence a £120 Morris or Ford 8hp for the year; today's equivalent would be an annual licence fee of £500 on a £10,000 Escort!

Accordingly, when taxation had to be boosted in 1939 to help pay for re-armament the RAC tax was once again raised to £1/hp, with the threat of a further rise to £1 5s (£1.25) in 1940. Predictably enough, this caused car buyers to look for smaller-engined cars, and even if there had been no war, overall car sales would certainly have declined in 1940.

As now, the mass-production groups dominated the sales charts, the taxation changes mentioned above making this situation even more marked. Because the keeper of Britain's motoring statistics, the SMMT (Society of Motor Manufacturers and Traders) holds only sketchy records from those far-off days, few authors have been able to reveal how powerful were the Big Six – Austin, the Nuffield Organisation, Ford, the Rootes Group, Standard and Vauxhall. In fact many of the proud and independent marques were only hanging on precariously, with fine reputations but very limited activity.

Although many component makers were located in the West Midlands – particularly in Birmingham, Wolver-hampton and Coventry – there was no single centre of the motor industry, the Big Six being well spread at Long-bridge (Birmingham), Cowley (Oxford), Luton, Dagenham and Coventry. With the exception of Dagenham, all the largest car factories were old, much-modified, and becoming increasingly less efficient as mass-producers.

Because of the different ways companies reported their achievements (some by calendar year, others by differing financial years), some of the following figures should be considered as only very close approximations. However, these production figures (for 1936) tell their own story:

Total production of British cars
      367,237 (100 per cent)
Which included the following:
Morris   circa 90,000 (25 per cent)
Ford   74,998 (20 per cent)
Austin   70,458 (19 per cent)
Rootes   circa 40,000 (11 per cent)
Standard circa 30,000 (8 per cent)
Vauxhall   17,640 (5 per cent)
– a total of approximately 323,000

This means that all the other manufacturers, some prestigious, but some struggling to stay alive, held only about 44,000 units – a mere 12 per cent of the market – between them. Also, as at this time Rover was building 10,000 cars a year, SS-Jaguar about 3,000, MG about 2,000 and Riley and Triumph about 1,500 each, the rump is reduced to only 26,000 cars.

But what a rump! Here, for interest, is the list of active British marques which existed when *The Autocar* produced its price list for all current models on September 1, 1939, the day that Hitler's tanks drove across the border into Poland, thus precipitating the Second World War:

AC	Frazer Nash
Alta	Hillman
Alvis	HRG
Armstrong	Humber
Siddeley	Jensen
Aston Martin	Jowett
Atalanta	Lagonda
Austin	Lanchester
Bentley	Lea-Francis
British Salmson	MG
Brough Superior	Morgan
BSA	Morris
Daimler	Railton
Ford	Riley

Rolls-Royce	Sunbeam-Talbot
Rover	Triumph
Singer	Vauxhall
SS-Jaguar	Wolseley
Standard	

So 36 marques were still active at the end of 1939. When the developing economic climate is considered, several of them would certainly have died rapidly if war work had not come their way. Even with that unwonted windfall to prop them up, several would not make it beyond 1945.

For the postwar years, therefore, Britain's battered motor industry comprised no more than 31 marques, less than 20 of them being commercially significant. A handful of optimistic entrepreneurs – Sydney Allard among them – were ready to join in, but there would be no serious attempts to destroy the *status quo* for many years to come.

The war effort

Despite the long and looming build-up – and at least one narrow escape in the Munich crisis of September 1938 – the outbreak of war seemed to take Britain by surprise, and until the very last moment motor companies were preparing to launch their 1940 models. Cars like the new Austin 12hp and the 1940-model SS-Jaguars and Sunbeam-Talbots were stillborn, but one major new model, the Phase I (monocoque) Hillman Minx, was actually announced *after* that fateful day, September 3, 1939. Except for Wolseley, which showed and promised a new 8hp model 'when times are once again normal', everyone closed down their forward-planning files and motoring enthusiasts were little the wiser.

Amazingly rapidly, Britain's largest car-makers wound down their assembly of private cars, tore up the production lines, and prepared to build military machinery as soon as suitable contracts were placed. This took months rather than weeks, especially as the last of the purely civilian-specification cars were rapidly commandeered for military, Government or other official use. By mid-1940, though, almost every trace of 1939-style peacetime motoring had gone – and purchase tax, introduced in October 1940, would be applied to car purchase anyway.

Although the motoring magazines tried to keep up appearances for a time, there was precious little private (or, as it was called, non-essential) motoring left to be enjoyed. Branded petrols were banned, and a unified Pool substituted. Strict petrol rationing was introduced within weeks, and the supply of spare parts and – particularly – tyres rapidly became critical. Rationing gradually became more severe, and by the spring of 1942 the average private buyer had to make do with four or five gallons *a month*, then on June 30, when *all* private motoring was banned 'for the duration', there were few freedoms left to be abandoned.

Attempts to find alternative fuels centred on producer gas installations, which required voluminous gas bags, either on the roof or carried in two-wheel trailers, but few could be bothered with this, and the number of private cars on the road plummeted, the survivors all (theoretically, at least) being on Government business.

Three years before the outbreak of war, the Government had decided to increase its military aero-engine building capacity, and it was this move which eventually helped the motor industry to expand into more modern buildings.

Rather than expanding existing military plant, and to minimize the risk of enemy bomb damage, the Government chose to set up a series of 'shadow' factories in other parts of the country, with new workforces to be trained up. Shadow? Not because it was hoped to keep them secret – they were far too large for that – but because their efforts were expected to shadow those of the original factories.

Although Government finance paid for the buildings and all the machinery installed in them, Britain's car-makers were invited to set up and run the new factories on a fee-paying basis. Although most major companies eventually took up the challenge (Lord Austin chaired the entire scheme), there still seemed to be little urgency for rearmament in 1936, and there was surprisingly little enthusiasm for such schemes at first.

But eventually most of the industry's tycoons were persuaded to join in (is it cynical to suggest that the flow of knighthoods and peerages which eventually followed were all part of the bargaining process?), and by 1938 the Midlands was dotted by vast new factories. Perversely-inclined as usual, however, Lord Nuffield would have nothing to do with the scheme at first as he was in acrimonious dispute with the War Ministry over a Wolseley aero-engine project which they did not want!

Several shadow factories were erected close to existing car assembly plants: Austin ran a factory built near Longbridge, Standard had one in its own factory grounds at Fletchamstead South, and Rootes ran one behind its own complex in Stoke Aldermoor.

A second and even larger programme of shadow factory construction followed in 1939/40 and once again the motor industry was invited to run the plants. Eventually these had an even bigger influence on the motor industry's development, for some would later be taken over for the postwar building of cars.

Rootes ran a vast complex at Ryton-on-Dunsmore (near Coventry) and another at Speke (on Merseyside), Ford operated a plant at Irmston (in Trafford Park, Manchester), Rover operated similar buildings at Solihull and Acocks Green, Jaguar and Daimler ran factories alongside their own premises in Coventry, and Standard ran a huge enterprise at Banner Lane, Coventry. Daimler also ran a new free-standing factory at Browns Lane, in Allesley, Coventry.

Lord Nuffield, individual to the last, was finally persuaded to build and run a massive Spitfire-building plant at Castle Bromwich, near Birmingham, but he soon developed running disagreements with the Minister of Aircraft Production, Lord Beaverbrook, and eventually ceded control in mid-1940.

Weapons of war

Once the Government had taken complete control of Britain's manufacturing industry, production of military machinery soared. Not only did the motor industry convert its own factories and run shadow factories at the behest of Whitehall, but it was soon encouraged to operate many other far-flung enterprises into the bargain. By any standards, this was a period of which the entire industry – and its hugely burgeoning workforce – could be proud.

Some firms continued to make cars and trucks, but all for military purposes. Austin seemed to make most of the smaller saloons and utility models (the famous 'Tillys'), Rootes produced many Humbers as staff cars and Austin and Vauxhall (Bedford, really) churned out trucks in unprecedented quantities, but in many cases there was a complete upheaval.

Ford produced vast numbers of V8 engines (well over 250,000 by 1945) and masses of Merlin aero-engines at Irmston (using jigs supplied from Switzerland). Daimler produced scout cars and armoured cars, Rootes built engines in Coventry and aircraft (Blenheims at first, Lancasters later) at Speke (this was a factory later taken over by Dunlop), while Standard built Beaufighter and Mosquito fighter-bombers. Vauxhall-Bedford also produced thousands of Churchill tanks and Austin built aero-engines as well as Battle, Stirling and Lancaster aircraft. The MG sportscar factory worked on aircraft centre-sections and tanks, Vanden Plas produced wooden aircraft sections for Mosquito aircraft and Morris built Tiger Moths and huge quantities of aero-engines. SS-Jaguar produced sidecars for motorcycles and thousands of light trailers, Alvis produced aero-engines, Riley built SU carburettors and Wolseley built tanks instead of cars. Then there were shells, mines, bombs, bullets, helmets, gun chassis, petrol cans...the list seemed endless.

Workers who had been used to making trim for cars found themselves building fabric-covered fuselages for aircraft. Machinists used to working on car gearboxes became used to making aero-engine components instead. Redundant cotton mills in Lancashire turned to building aero-engines for Rover and hosiery factories in Leicester came under car industry control.

All in all, the shadow factory scheme, and the motor industry's own efforts backing it up, produced 45 per cent of all the bombers delivered to the RAF, a remarkable achievement. But there was a cost. None of these factories could be kept secret, or hidden from the air, and before Britain regained control of its own skies in 1941 a great deal of bombing damage was suffered.

Almost every car factory was bombed at one time or another, particularly in 1940, and some, including the original Alvis buildings in Coventry, were obliterated. Although temporary repairs were speedily made in most cases, the industry which survived to face up to the challenges of peacetime might have been proud, but it was in a tatty, patched-up, scruffy and run-down state, with camouflaged walls and blacked-out windows.

Meanwhile, to the delight of all who wanted to read about motoring, cars and personalities during those dark years, Britain's two principal motoring magazines – *The Autocar* and *The Motor* – miraculously had managed to stay in print, never missing an issue, and always contriving to cram a deal of information, comment and sheer golden-glow nostalgia into their much-reduced issues.

Even by 1944, when the tide had turned in the Allies' favour, there were only 16 to 18 editorial pages per issue – but how precious it all seemed. *The Motor*, in particular, used this time to carry out much historical research, amongst which a series of detailed technical studies of older racing cars by Laurence Pomeroy and his illustra-tor L C Cresswell were truly significant.

In order to save paper, all such publications were meant to be offered for salvage after being read, but a number of complete runs have survived, along with indices, to make fascinating reading half a century on.

For years, however, private motoring virtually ceased to exist, though there was enough time to look ahead, plan and hope for what peacetime motoring would be like. The fact, however, would be very different from the fantasy…

Men of Influence

Donald Healey

Born in Perranporth, Cornwall, in 1898, Donald Mitchell Healey first made his mark in British motorsport in the 1920s as a trials and rally driver, then went on to win the 1931 Monte Carlo rally in a 4½-litre Invicta. Moving to the Midlands in 1933, he worked briefly at Riley, then moved to Triumph, where he soon became technical director.

Under his control, Triumph not only produced the successful Gloria, Vitesse and Dolomite ranges, but there was also time to dabble with the supercharged Dolomite Straight Eight of 1934. Although he was financially hard-hit by Triumph's unprofitable flounderings in the late 1930s, he stayed with the company until 1939/40.

As an eminent engineer he then joined the Rootes Group (Humber Ltd) in Coventry to work on wartime automotive projects, but along with a handful of friends and colleagues he also used his spare time to design a new range of sporting cars for launch after the war.

When Triumph's owners refused to back him in this project, he persuaded Victor Riley to supply engines and transmissions, raised £50,000 of private capital and set up the Healey company, from where the original Riley-powered Westland and Elliott models were launched in 1946. These cars, with top speeds of more than 100mph, were Britain's fastest cars in the immediate postwar period.

Working from very basic premises in Warwick, using the absolute minimum of production tooling and building only small numbers of high-priced cars (most of them for export, especially to the USA), Healey often found it difficult to stay in business, and without a fortunate link-up with Nash of the USA (the Nash-Healey was the result) his company might not have survived into the 1950s.

His big breakthrough came in 1952, when his Healey 100 project was taken up by Len Lord at BMC, the result being the birth of the Austin-Healey sportscar. For the next two decades, Healey did the engineering, BMC the production and marketing of Austin-Healeys, an arrangement which finally ended in 1970, a result of the growth of British Leyland.

Although the birth of the Healey car gave Donald Healey much pride and satisfaction, it was the Austin-Healey name which confirmed his name worldwide. In the 1970s he was also involved in the takeover of Jensen, and in the Jensen-Healey project, and was active until the 1980s.

He died in January 1988.

1945

As the New Year dawned, the world was still at war, Britain was thoroughly war-weary, and more than five years after hostilities had broken out the end was not yet in sight. Although the Axis powers had suffered reverse after reverse, and Italy had capitulated soon after the first Allied invasion in September 1943, Germany, despite having been badly knocked about by Allied bombing, was still almost entirely unoccupied.

Britain's motor industry, on the other hand, now securely protected from enemy bombing by blanket fighter cover and able to carry on uninterrupted by air raid alerts, was at the peak of its output. The Allies' largest problem was no longer to acquire the *materiel* it needed, but to find somewhere to store it all. In theory, if not in practice, there was still no time for Britain's car firms to think about private-car work.

Things were very different in the car factories of France, Italy and Germany, which had all been targeted by British and American heavy bombers. The Fiat, Renault, VW, Ford-Germany, Opel and Mercedes-Benz plants had all been plastered by bombing, and there was no way that they could possibly be rebuilt quickly when the fighting stopped.

When the Mercedes-Benz directors convened again in 1945 they observed gloomily: '...for all practical purposes Daimler-Benz has ceased to exist...' As for VW, historian Bernard Hopfinger wrote that in 1945 its brand-new Wolfsburg factory: '...stood crippled, its roof gone, its halls shattered, its interior battered behind windowless walls, its machines idle and corroding in six inches of water.'

The chaos was less complete in France and Italy. Renault's Billancourt works, however, had been severely damaged in 1942 and 1943, and when the Allies arrived in August 1944 they discovered a plant with 10,000 broken windows, no roof, no coal in the bunkers and all work at a standstill. As historian Edouard Seidler commented: 'The Renault works were like a body drained of its lifeblood... Some 4,000 machines had been destroyed, and most of the remainder were obsolete.'

As Michael Sedgwick later observed,

Fiat was rather more lucky, though the ageing Lingotto plant had been gutted and Mirafiori was also damaged. Alfa Romeo's Portello works, home to aero-engine building and the production of jeep-type vehicles, was pulverized in February 1943, the destruction being completed in August of the same year. Lancia, too, was badly mauled.

Early in 1945 the Allied forces began their long-expected final push into Germany, Russian forces beginning their major assault in January and the Allied crossing of the Rhine following in March. Except for a fanatical defence of their capital, Berlin, German resistance then speedily came to an end, and early in May 1945 it was all over. VE (Victory in Europe) Day was greeted with rejoicing and relief.

Although the Far East war would not be brought to an end for another three months – in mid-August, following the emphatic message delivered by the dropping of two atom bombs – Britain, her people and her industries looked on VE day as the day when *their* war was over. Now, at last, Britain's motor industry could get back to its chosen business.

Aftermath

Until the Government gave the all-clear for postwar planning to go ahead, the motor industry had been told to forget all about private cars and to concentrate on winning the war. But if war work was 'business', and the development of new cars was 'pleasure', most directors and top managers found ways of combining the two. In fact it was not until September 1944 that the Board of Trade gave limited agreement for the development of postwar models.

This was never publicized at the time, but we now have innumerable memoirs and interviews to back up the suspicion that Britain's car enthusiasts spent their spare time (and sometimes a bit of 'stolen' working time as well...) on postwar research. Well-known examples abound:

Armstrong Siddeley: The company was so far advanced with the design of its postwar Lancaster and Hurricane models that it was able to release pictures of completed prototypes in the same week the European war ended.

Austin: Asked to design a new four-cylinder engine to power a proposed 'British jeep', the company did just that, then made sure it could be fitted into a new private car, the Austin 16hp, which was actually previewed in October 1944.

Healey: The marque was really born during the war when Donald Healey and a handful of associates spent their spare time working away at the design of a new sportscar. Some work was undoubtedly done at Humber Ltd, where Healey, 'Sammy' Sampietro and Ben Bowden were employed at the time, though the first body styles were reputedly sketched out on Bowden's dining room walls!

Jaguar: Planning of its postwar cars and engines began in 1943, much detailed design work being carried out in those now-legendary fire-watching sessions at the factory between then and 1945.

Jowett: The company previewed the new Javelin in 1945, having recruited Gerald Palmer from the Nuffield Organisation as early as 1942 so that he could start formulating the new model. As far as Palmer was concerned, there was no war work for him to do at Idle in the meantime.

Lagonda: With W O Bentley at the technical helm, the company already had a prototype twin-cam 2.6-litre engine running in September 1945. Design work had been going ahead for some time before the war ended.

Morris: With Sir Miles Thomas now in charge, the design of the future Morris Minor was initiated in 1942, though the car would not be ready for sale until 1948.

Riley: The company's brand-new RM models were revealed in August 1945, but because these cars had completely new chassis *and* coachwork, the design must have been started no later than 1944.

Rolls-Royce: By 1945 work was well-advanced on what would become the Mk VI Bentley, and soon all car assembly facilities were moved to the ex-Merlin aero-engine manufacturing plant at Crewe in preparation for building postwar cars.

Standard: Having bought the bankrupt and bombed remains of **Triumph** in 1944, by early 1945, well before VE Day, the company was able to announce what its postwar policy was to be.

But all this work, though commendable, was meaningless until the industry was *officially* allowed back to peacetime work. Meanwhile, as the war ended, hundreds of thousands of motorists made haste to bring their cars to life. It was estimated that up to 1,500,000 cars were in store – but a goodly number of these were probably beyond economic revival by 1945. All of them were six years older than when last used regularly, so the probability of corroding bodywork and perished tyres was ever present. Many cars, left alone for years, were found to have cracked cylinder blocks, and almost everything seemed to be gummed to everything else.

Although the basic petrol ration, which was good for about 120 miles per month, was restored from June 1, 1945, the public thought it to be both long overdue and far too little. By ignoring the hard facts – that every gallon of crude oil for distillation into petrol had to be brought into the UK by tanker, over U-boat infested seas – there had been repeated calls for 'Basic' to be reintroduced in the autumn of 1944. Certainly, once the threat of German occupation of the Russian and Iranian oilfields had been averted, crude oil supplies were plentiful, but the dangers of transporting well-head supplies to refineries remained.

Prices, taxation and supplies

Well before the first postwar models were announced, it was clear that prices would be a lot higher than they had been in 1939. It also became clear, soon after the General Election had seen the Labour Party installed with a huge parliamentary majority, that austerity would be a way of life for years to come.

Throughout the 1930s prices had remained remarkably stable, and because wages and salaries had tended to rise gradually, most people had felt increasingly prosperous. In 1939 Ford 8hp prices started at £115,

a 3½-litre SS-Jaguar sold for £445 and a beautifully-bodied Rolls-Royce Wraith retailed for perhaps £2,000. There was no taxation on car purchase and the average price of a gallon of petrol had been about 1s 3d (6p).

Subsequently, there had been severe inflation as military spending inexorably increased and, worse still, purchase tax had been introduced in October 1940 on a whole range of so-called luxury items. By 1945, therefore, not only would the same cars cost a lot more than they had in 1939, but buyers would also be taxed for the privilege of buying them. For comparison, for the Standard Flying Twelve, which had cost £219 in 1939, prices in 1945 started at £480 (this figure including the already-hated 33⅓ per cent purchase tax) – if, that is, a permit could be gained to buy such a car!

Because of the need to export as many cars as possible, there was strict control over all home market deliveries; one could not simply walk into a showroom, view a car and buy one. First one had to convince a faceless official that there was an essential need – which usually meant that one had to be a doctor, high official, or similar dignitary – then take delivery of the precious licence. Only then could a car be ordered. Even so, waiting lists blossomed and months, if not years, would elapse before the car arrived. One result was that the value of secondhand cars soared, and many postwar fortunes were based on the foresight of some entrepreneurs who had bought up cheap cars during the war and stored them away for just such an eventuality.

Meanwhile, membership of the AA, which had reached 730,000 in 1939, but plummeted to a mere 316,000 in 1945, quickly rose again with the return of private motoring and passed the 500,000 mark in 1946.

In one respect Britain's car-makers were in complete unison – the hated 'RAC' horsepower-rated tax would have to go. For years the industry's designers had known that this cylinder bore-based impost stultified the development of engines with more efficient bore/stroke ratios; what could be more ludicrous, for instance, than the 1938 Standard Flying Eight, the new side-valve 1,021cc engine of which had a bore of 57mm and a stroke of 100mm?

In a study published as early as June 1944, the SMMT began to lobby for a change, pressing for a simple annual tax based on the engine's cubic capacity and pointing out that the proposed tax change could also make British cars more saleable in export markets, where the postwar sales emphasis would be directed.

Then the horse-trading started all over again, for tycoons with an interest in large-engined cars objected to an engine-size tax, suggesting instead that an *ad valorem* tax (one based on the car's retail price) would be better. There was much more of this argument to come – in modern terms, it would run and run...

In December 1944, Britain's Chancellor of the Exchequer announced that a 'cubic capacity' tax was being planned, that he was not seeking to levy more tax overall than the RAC rating had raised, and that he would reveal all at the next Budget in April 1945, the new rates to take effect in 1946 on newly-built cars.

Naturally, the makers of large-engined cars (Rootes with the 4-litre Humber Super Snipe, for instance) were appalled and protested very loudly. Then, with the end of war imminent, decisions as to the rate of the duty to be applied and the starting date were both deferred.

Once the war machine began to wind down, there was a great surplus of fuel, rubber for tyres and many other raw materials, but drivers who expected these to be rapidly redirected towards building British cars were soon disappointed.

Because of the provisions of the United States' Lend-Lease programme, in order to equip its armies the British had borrowed billions of US dollars. Now, in the fullness of time, the nation would be obliged to pay it all back – and the easiest way to earn such hard currency was by trading with the USA. Right from the start, therefore, it was made clear that car-makers could only be guaranteed supplies (especially of sheet steel) if they would direct most of their production to export markets, and particularly towards North America.

It goes without saying that there were no cars imported into the UK in 1945, except for a handful of captured German machines brought in for inspection. The VW Beetle project was hawked around the industry, who could have taken it up as war reparations, but there were no takers. Invited to study the car by the British authorities, Britain's Rootes Commission commented that the Beetle 'couldn't possibly stay popular for more than two or three years'; the Commission concluded that it would never be competition for British cars. There would be red faces over this judgment in future years, particularly when the Beetle passed Ford's famous Model T to become the world's highest-selling car...

Although many established late-1930s marques did not immediately relaunch their new products in 1945 – these included AC, Alvis, Aston Martin, Bentley, Daimler, Frazer Nash, HRG, Jensen, Jowett, Lagonda, Lea-Francis and Rolls-Royce – all had ambitious plans to rejoin the fray in the years to come.

Motoring in austerity

The recovery from a strict wartime regime was patchy and frustratingly slow. Roads which had been battered by trucks and damaged by tanks would be patched up, but otherwise remained unrepaired for years, and signposts taken down in the invasion scare of 1940 would sometimes be re-erected at the wrong junction.

The gradual deletion of black-out regulations seemed to take far too long; for example, lights could be shown from windows or trains months before cars were once again allowed to use unmasked headlamps. But the last of the regulations was deleted in December 1944 – a real Christmas present for those who had been groping their way around in the gloom for so long – followed in 1945 by the raising of the night-time 20mph speed limit in built-up areas. At a stroke, road accidents, particularly involving pedestrians, were sharply reduced. With the prospect of a return to some semblance of private motoring, a million cars were being registered by May 1945 compared with just 734,000 in mid-1944.

The meagre basic petrol ration reintroduced soon after VE Day was increased by 25 per cent in September 1945, but it was still Government-controlled Pool of quite execrable quality and cost about 2s 0d (10p) a gallon; several years would pass before branded fuel returned.

New models, new alliances

There were very few entirely new cars in 1945, the most significant being the Armstrong Siddeley, Lanchester and Riley offerings. The rest, almost without exception, were 1939/40 models, mildly improved in the light of wartime experience and all using existing tooling which had been dug out of storage:

Armstrong Siddeley: Pictured in May 1945 with smart body styles, including flush-headlamp front ends, the Lancaster (six-light saloon) and Hurricane (drop-head coupe) models went into production later in the summer, but with technicalities not revealed until the autumn. Both models shared the same all-new channel-section chassis-frame, which had torsion-bar independent front suspension, and were powered by a development of the late-1930s six-cylinder engine, this time in 1,991cc form. There was a choice of synchromesh (by Rootes) or Wilson-type preselector transmission, while a new-type hypoid-bevel rear axle was fitted. Because these cars were expensive they never sold as well as they otherwise deserved.

Additional versions with further style variations – Typhoon and Whitley – would follow in future years.

Austin: The very first postwar car to be previewed, in October 1944, was the new 16hp model. Its premature launch caused a real stir and a great deal of complaint amongst Austin's rivals, but deliveries were not in fact made until the summer of 1945. The new model, in fact, was little more than a combination of the 1939 Austin 12hp (which had been launched a week before war broke out!) with a new 2.2-litre ohv four-cylinder engine.

Evolved from an existing 3.5-litre six-cylinder truck unit, this was the first overhead-valve engine to be put on sale by Austin, and eventually it would be modified to power the Austin-Healey 100 of 1952. As early as November 1944 Austin also revealed its other postwar range of cars – the 8hp, 10hp and 12hp saloons – all being mildly updated versions of the 1939/40 models. This, in fact, set the trend for most postwar model announcements.

Bristol: The aero-industry company took a tentative step towards the automotive world by acquiring a financial stake in Frazer Nash. Although this deal would eventually be dissolved, it helped Bristol to get its hands on the prewar BMW engine design and redevelop it for its own purposes.

Ford: The 1940-style Anglia and Prefect models were put back on sale. Old-fashioned when new, they looked even more ancient in 1945, but sold at remarkably low prices – £293 for the Anglia, £352 for the Prefect.

Hillman: Part of the Rootes Group, the company relaunched the monocoque Minx, which originally had been seen in September 1939; by 1942 several thousand had been produced for military and official use. The Minx was soon followed by other Rootes cars from Sunbeam-Talbot and Humber.

Humber: The upmarket part of the Rootes Group introduced a four-model range – Hawk, Snipe, Super Snipe and Pullman. The Hawk was actually a mildly revised Hillman 14 of 1939, the other models all being thoroughly familiar to Rootes buyers.

Jaguar: This marque name took over from the former SS-Jaguar, the 'SS' part of the prewar title being dropped in view of the horrifying reputation built up by the German SS (*Schutzstaffel*) during the war.

By September it was ready to relaunch the 1939/40 SS-Jaguar models with a choice of 1½-litre, 2½-litre and 3½-litre engines. These later became known, unofficially, as Mk IV models.

Jowett: The company stated that 'an entirely new car from stem to stern' was already being designed – and the car, the new Javelin project, was previewed in 1945 with a single side-on picture, but no technical details, though first deliveries would be delayed until 1947.

Kendall: This Grantham-based project need not be treated very seriously. Previewed in November 1944 and projected to be sold at the ludicrously impractical price of £100, it was supposedly meant to be tooled for 100,000 units to be built, which would have out-gunned anything which Austin, Morris or Ford had ever achieved! There always seemed to be an element of sleaze surrounding the enterprise. The original prototype was an air-cooled 595cc rear-engined car, but Kendall also proposed to make the new *front*-drive Gregoire car under licence. By the end of 1945 deliveries were being promised for mid-1946, but these never occurred. Company liquidation followed in 1947.

Lanchester: The new LD10 model had completed its development in 1939, but had never been seen in public. With a new chassis incorporating independent front suspension, a 1,287cc four-cylinder engine and Daimler-type fluid-flywheel transmission, it was the smallest Lanchester for a decade and was once described as 'modernized retired-colonel transportation'. Styling was really traditional Daimler, and bodyshells were to be produced by Briggs Motor Bodies.

MG: The TC Midget was launched, being no more than a slightly-widened 1939-type TB, which had been the first MG to use the 1,250cc XPAG engine.

Morgan: The Malvern-based firm showed off the postwar 4/4, looking identical to the 1939 car, but now to be fitted with a special, overhead-valve version of the Standard Flying Ten engine. Strangely enough, this unit would never be used by Standard or the Triumph subsidiary.

Morris: The 8hp Series E and 10hp Series MO models were reintroduced, virtually unchanged from 1939.

Riley: The 1½-litre RM-series model was previewed. Except for the improved late-1930s twin-high-camshaft four-cylinder engine, this was an all-new machine, a car with quite startlingly sleek and attractive styling. There was a new chassis, allied to torsion bar independent front suspension and rack-and-pinion steering (both of which, at the time, were expensive novelties). Bodies (four-door saloons only at first) were long, low and rakish, with fabric-covered roof panels and partly faired-

in headlamps. Deliveries began before the end of the year, though Riley did not release full details until 1946.

Rover: The company announced its intention to abandon its Coventry works and build cars at the ex-shadow factory at Solihull. Soon it relaunched the 10hp, 12hp, 14hp and 16hp models.

Singer: A three-model programme was announced, all being virtually unchanged 1939/40 models – the Nine Roadster and the Super Ten and Super Twelve saloons. All used unchanged styling, existing leaf-spring chassis with beam axles, four-cylinder overhead-camshaft engines of familiar Singer type and, except for the engines, they were strictly conventional machines.

Standard: Its immediate postwar programme, announced in May 1945, concentrated on just two lightly-modified 1939/40 Flying models, the 8hp and the 12hp types. The 8hp received a four-speed gearbox, but this was virtually the only innovation.

Sunbeam-Talbot: Rootes, on reintroducing the Ten and 2-Litre models, announced at the same time that the graceful 3-Litre and 4-Litre models of 1938/39 had been abandoned.

Vauxhall: GM's British subsidiary revealed a rationalized range – the 10hp, 12hp (H-types, as Vauxhall knew them) and 14hp (J-type) versions of the 1939 models, almost unaltered.

Wolseley: Three revived models were revealed – the 12/48, 14/60 and 18/85 saloons. All were pure-1939 except in detail, with traditional 'leafy-lanes' styling.

It took longer for car manufacturers to get back into their stride in continental Europe. However, in neutral Sweden **Volvo** previewed its original PV444 saloon in October 1944, though it was not yet ready to start series production. Although this probably counts as the first postwar European (ie non-British) model, Volvo sales would not begin in the UK until 1958.

By the end of the year, 15 British marques were in production again, with output going ahead as fast as supplies could be found.

Industrial developments

Although all the significant British motor manufacturers in 1939 survived, six of the 'tiddlers' – Alta, Atalanta, British Salmson, Brough Superior, BSA and Railton – failed to reappear. Geoffrey Taylor, who *was* Alta, concentrated on hand-building racing cars, BSA did likewise on motorcycles, British Salmson's links with the French Salmson concern had lapsed, and the other two concerns merely faded away.

But new names were destined to appear. Bristol was preparing to join the British motor industry, though we did not know it at the time.

Healey was set up by Donald Healey and a small group of backers in the Coventry/Warwick area. Healey himself had been Triumph's technical chief from 1933 to 1939, had spent much of the war working for the Rootes Group in Coventry, and after trying fruitlessly to persuade Triumph's temporary owners, Thos W Ward Ltd, to back his new designs, decided to go it alone. The first Healey sportscar would be unveiled in 1946.

The most controversial newcomer was the aforementioned Kendall, of Grantham, whose founder was the local Member of Parliament, W D Kendall. Unhappily, despite the high hopes and the bombast, reams of fine words and the takeover of a large ex-military factory, no cars were ever delivered and losses totalled £450,000.

Triumph, bankrupt in 1939, had been in hibernation throughout the war, its factories blitzed in 1940. Standard then took over the remains in November 1944 (paying £75,000 for all the rights – there were virtually no factories, parts or other hardware remaining), enabling it to be reborn as a new upmarket prestige label.

Even before the end of the war, Standard's Sir John Black announced that it was proposed to produce 'a 10hp Triumph of 1,300cc and a 15hp model of 1800cc'. There would be nothing 'old Triumph' about these cars, for both were to be based on Standard components.

Truly this was the start of something big – in retrospect, it was the British motor industry's most important *commercial* move of 1945 – for within 15 years the Triumph marque would be much bigger than Standard, which would itself die in 1963.

Later in 1945, too, Standard announced that it had struck an agreement with Harry Ferguson to build Ferguson tractors in the vast shadow factory at Banner Lane, on the outskirts of Coventry.

Car production was rapidly getting back to normal – although only 508 were produced in June, 1,822 followed in October and no fewer than 6,163 in December – but it was still too early to see the definitive shape of Britain's postwar motor industry, although the picture would be a lot clearer by the end of 1946.

Men of Influence

Sir David Brown

Although he was already a successful businessman by the 1940s, David Brown was still unknown to motoring enthusiasts when he took control of Aston Martin *and* Lagonda in 1947.

Born in Huddersfield in 1904, the grandson of the founder of the David Brown Gear Company of 1897, he joined the family firm as an apprentice in 1920. By 1932, when he was still only 28 years old, David Brown 'The Younger' became managing director of the company, then saw it grow much larger and more influential in the next four decades. Along the way he had a short-lived relationship with Harry Ferguson over tractors, quarrelled with him (which was very easy, apparently), and set up David Brown Tractors as a very successful rival concern.

He also found time to get involved in motorsport, making superchargers for Raymond Mays' TT Vauxhall and racing a similar car on Southport sands. Even so, once he had become MD of the David Brown Gear Company he turned his back on motor racing – until the late 1940s.

Seeing an advertisement in *The Times* in 1946, he responded, finally buying the very small Aston Martin company from its current owner, Gordon Sutherland, in 1947. Months later he also annexed Lagonda, which had just gone into liquidation. As a rich man, in later life he claimed to have bought both firms 'to have a bit of fun' – and that, indeed, is what he did until 1972!

Although both companies had promising new projects on the road, neither had the financial backing to put them into production. David Brown's immediate strategy was to merge them, putting the Lagonda into production and using the Lagonda's new Bentley-designed twin-cam engine into a new generation of Aston Martins.

For the next 25 years the David Brown Aston Martins (all carrying the DB initials as part of their titles) were fast, beautiful and successful sportscars, while the Lagonda name, to a lesser extent, became a notable brand of Grand Touring machine.

David Brown always made sure that Aston Martin Lagonda, which moved to Newport Pagnell in the mid-1950s, was commercially separate from the rest of the David Brown group, and he always made it clear that it was never a profitable enterprise.

Although he was a great motoring enthusiast and a frustrated racing driver (at one time he proposed to race a works DB2 in the Le Mans 24 Hours race, but was refused a competition licence by the RAC), his philosophy was to let others manage the business, while he influenced design as much as possible.

In the 1950s he financed an extremely successful sportscar racing programme (Aston Martin won the World Sports Car Championship in 1959), and even dabbled briefly with Formula One racing. As a businessman he always had so much to do (he bought the Vosper shipbuilding business, developing Vosper Thorneycroft, in the 1960s) that Aston Martin inevitably remained a sideline.

Knighted in 1968, he then sold out both David Brown Tractors and Aston Martin Lagonda in 1972, for he had despaired of ever making money from the car-making concern. Having cut all links with Aston Martin (and having seen his DB initials speedily removed from the cars) he rapidly fell away from the motoring limelight.

Once Vosper Thorneycroft was nationalized in 1977, he left the UK and lived in Monte Carlo from 1978. Many years later Aston Martin's new owners, Ford, elected Sir David honorary president for life of his old company, which apparently gave him great joy.

He died in 1993, at the grand old age of 89.

1946

This was the start of the lengthy period during which the British motor industry could sell every car that could be made. There was such an intense worldwide demand that a car's quality was thought to be less important than its availability. However, to quote one distinguished historian: '...the attitude of "make what you can – somebody's bound to want it" was short-lived, even though the country was riding a seller's market as late as 1952.'

To bolster the British motor industry's artificial advantages, all car imports were still officially banned – though statistics now show that 63 cars (most of them for assessment by British concerns) were brought in during 1946, and rather more followed in the next couple of years. This ruling would apply until 1953 – though in 1946 Citroen overcame the problem by beginning to assemble *traction avant* models in Slough from imported kits.

Much political hot air was vented on the subject of a British 'national car' – the suggestion being that all individual models should be dropped in favour of one new and rationalized design, to be assembled by several major concerns and then exported to earn US dollars – but this 'Stalinistic' nonsense was speedily shouted down by the industry.

Later, it was also suggested that each manufacturer should follow a one-model policy in order to maximize its output and reduce complication, but few firms took this seriously either.

With so many new cars going for export (though not as many as some imagined – just 38 per cent of production), there was a great shortage of deliveries in the UK, only 14,340 cars being registered between January and March. This, and the high prices commanded by well-kept prewar models, rapidly led to the development of a 'black market' in nearly-new examples. Some individuals took delivery of a new car, drove it for a few days, then sold it on for a large profit. Clearly this was immoral, and the Government was forced to act.

From mid-July 1946, new-car buyers had to sign a legally-binding document – a Covenant – which stated that they would not re-sell a car until they had owned it for at least six months, or they would have to face legal proceedings for breach of contract. That six-months rule would be stretched to a year in 1948, then subsequently to two years, before being abandoned in 1953.

Even so, by the spring of 1946, Britain's on-the-road car population had risen to more than 1,500,000 – still well below the 1939 figure, but increasing all the time, and probably up to more than 1,800,000 before the end of the year, even though driving test examinations were not reinstated until November that year!

Although British car production increased rapidly throughout the year (6,046 were produced in January, but as many as 26,767 in October), there was great industrial discontent (not to say anarchy) in the various factories, this exploding in a series of strikes in the spring. The main issue, on the surface at least, was pay, but there was also evidence of left wing-orientated unions looking for nationalization, or workers' control – a direct result of the way the country was now being run by a Labour Government.

In January 1946 the Chancellor of the Exchequer announced that a new type of annual licence duty would be introduced on January 1, 1947 for new cars registered from that date; for the time being, existing cars would continue to pay the long-established 'horsepower tax'. The new duty was to be calculated at £1 per 100cc of engine size, which meant that Morris 10 owners would pay £12, while Bentley Mk VI buyers would pay £43. That, however, was just a sighting shot, for much more controversy about this measure would follow...

In spite of a barrage of criticism, both from the press and from opposition politicians, petrol rationing continued, though from March there was a slightly increased allowance – equivalent to about 180 miles per month – and it was then raised by a further 50 per cent from August. Minister of Fuel, Emmanuel Shinwell, was deaf to all barbed comments that there was plenty of petrol in the world – or that once-devastated European countries had already scrapped a rationing system, so why couldn't we? There were even some dark suggestions that rationing might be made a permanent fixture, in an effort to control the mobility of the public.

This was also the year in which the British motor industry elected to celebrate its Golden Anniversary – the origins being found in Coventry where Daimler had begun assembling German-designed cars under licence in 1896. There were massive commemorative cavalcades later in the year, where hundreds of cars, including veterans and just-launched factory prototypes, turned out.

New-car prices began to rise, an inexorable process which has never ended. Standard made postwar history by becoming the first company to do this, they and their rivals rightly blaming the increased steel prices and the way that labour costs had crept steadily upwards.

Although there was no action to back up their fine words, the Government had finally started to plan a series of new roads – 'once essential maintenance and repairs of existing highways are completed'. First to be placarded was a new trunk road from Swansea to Cardiff, on to Newport and across the Severn estuary and up to the Midlands.

Then came the publication of the 'Grand Plan', which included many new Motor Roads (motorways), and the complete reconstruction of other strategic routes. It was easy, of course, to draw lines on paper and to issue maps, but much more difficult to find the money to invest in highways. That plan, viewed against today's high-speed road network, looks extremely familiar, for all the radial motorways were sketched out, along with what would eventually become the M5, the M62, and a completely rejuvenated A1 to the North. The only change, in later years, was to nominate the A303 as a main route to Exeter in place of the A30 through Salisbury.

Unhappily, there was no prospect of seeing a start to any of these major new highways until Britain's economic health improved. Work started again on the Dartford Tunnel approach roads, but was soon abandoned again until the late 1950s.

New models

In the second wave of new-model announcements, a series of true post-war designs appeared, though these were all from the smaller concerns.

Large-scale manufacturers were still struggling to get new components – particularly chassis – finalized and tooled, and the first of their new cars would not appear until 1947, the big wave following in 1948. Meanwhile, the most important announcements came from:

AC: The Thames Ditton company's postwar model, unimaginatively titled the 2-Litre, was previewed, this having a simple chassis layout with a beam front axle, the already-ageing overhead-camshaft six-cylinder engine (which had first appeared in 1919), and a smooth new body style – but AC admitted that it would not be ready to begin deliveries until 1947.

Allard: Motor trader Sydney Allard, whose South London premises had spent the war repairing army trucks, launched a range of hand-built sports-cars and tourers built around Ford parts. Although there was a specially designed ladder-style chassis, with pressings by John Thompson, and bodies were made from wood and aluminium sheet, the rest of the initial specification was not promising. Thirsty and old-fashioned Ford 3.6-litre side-valve V8 engines backed by three-speed gearboxes were fitted to chassis with transverse-leaf swing-axle front suspension, all hidden by bulbous bodywork – yet the cars found a small, but ready sale, and after Allard found supplies of enlarged, 3.9-litre Mercury engines, things looked up even further.

No fewer than five different body types were listed at first, though not all of them were ready to go on sale. The J1 was a competition two-seater, the K a longer-wheelbase version, the L a 112in-wheelbase tourer, the M a large drop-head coupe and the P a two-door saloon, but J1s were very rare, and deliveries of P-type saloons did not start until late 1949.

Alvis: Having lost their original car factory to enemy bombing – it had been totally destroyed in 1940 – there had been a year's hiatus before the company had relocated to its aero-engine buildings on the other side of the Coventry-Nuneaton railway track and was ready to relaunch the TA14 model. This was a modest update of the prewar 12/70, which featured a

slightly larger and more powerful version of the earlier (65bhp/1,892cc) engine, but few other changes. Alvis, in the meantime, was already working on a true postwar model (the TA21 3-litre), though this would not appear for a further four years.

Armstrong Siddeley: Having got the Lancaster and Hurricane models safely into production, the company added a third derivative – the Typhoon (a two-door sports saloon) – to the line later in the year. The Typhoon was basically a fixed-head coupe version of the Hurricane, with the same body structure below the waistline.

Aston Martin: Strangely, although Gordon Sutherland's company was not yet ready to show a postwar chassis and body design, it *was* ready to show a new 1,970cc engine, which featured conventional pushrod overhead-valve gear instead of Aston Martin's traditional 1930s chain-driven overhead-camshaft layout.

By the end of the year, with no postwar cars yet delivered, Aston Martin was already up for sale, and there would be big developments in 1947.

Austin: The company built its millionth car in June 1946, a cream 16hp model whose paintwork was signed by the entire workforce. This car still survives in the BMIHT collection, much faded, but because of the signatures on every panel there is no question of it being repainted or restored!

Bentley: A few weeks after Rolls-Royce had launched the Silver Wraith, it followed up with the Bentley Mk VI, a car which shared the same basic chassis and running gear (though with a slightly shorter wheelbase and a more powerful, twin-SU carburettor version of the new six-cylinder engine, featuring overhead inlet and side exhaust valves), and was assembled on the same tracks at Crewe. The chassis was a developed version of the 1939/40 Mk V, a model which had not survived the war.

The *real* novelty, however, was that this was the first Bentley *or* Rolls-Royce to be offered completely built-up, with a standard steel bodyshell erected at the factory.

The shell itself came from Pressed Steel at Cowley, but all painting, trim-

ming and finishing operations were carried out at Crewe. This handsome-looking four-door saloon, complete with semi-razor edge styling, became deservedly popular, and would be produced, in gradually-developed form, for the next nine years.

This was also the year when Bentley brought legal action against Lagonda, who had proposed to title its postwar car a Lagonda-Bentley: although W O Bentley was the technical director of Lagonda, the proposal had to be abandoned.

Bristol: Produced as a sideline by the Bristol Aeroplane Company, the original 400 saloon was really a careful and sophisticated crib of the late-1930s BMWs, from whom Bristol's associates, Frazer Nash, had procured designs, hardware and the services of an engine designer, Dr Fritz Fiedler, as unofficial postwar reparations. Carefully and painstakingly developed by Fiedler, there was BMW influence in every line, including a fine platform-style chassis with independent front suspension, a cross-pushrod engine and a smoothly-styled two-door shell. It was all very expensive and long-lasting – it would be developed continually, rather than replaced, over the next 50 years. Prices started at £1,854, which automatically limited sales.

Citroen: The famous French company, which had a small assembly plant on the Slough Trading Estate, west of London, introduced the *traction avant* (front-wheel drive) Light Fifteen model, virtually unchanged from 1939. Although the styling was already beginning to look out-of-date, it would be many years before the rest of Europe caught up with the advanced layout of the chassis, which included torsion-bar independent front suspension and rack-and-pinion steering.

Daimler: The prewar DB18 was relaunched with development changes including a new high-compression cylinder head. This car was a smart and well-equipped model with a Mulliners (of Birmingham) six-light body, and came complete with independent front suspension and fluid-flywheel preselector transmission. If it had not been so expensive (£1,183) it would have sold a lot faster.

The DE27 chassis, with a massive

1946

late-1930s style of 4-litre six-cylinder engine (as specially designed for Daimler armoured cars during the war!) was also put on sale, this being a middle-size car according to Daimler (a Straight Eight derivative would soon follow), but a very large car by anyone else's standards. In many ways it was the DB18 writ large, with a similar lay-out of chassis, suspension and prese-lector transmission. The chassis alone cost £1,400.

The DE36 chassis was basically the same as that of the DE27, but stretched by a further 9in to accommo-date a colossal and heavy 5.46-litre straight-eight engine. This was meant to be the very best Daimler the com-pany could make, and was aimed at royal and ambassadorial customers, company chairmen and the like. By contemporary standards it was the largest, most capacious, heaviest and – Daimler hoped – most desirable British limousine available.

Frazer Nash: The small Isleworth (Middlesex) company, which made most of its money in the late 1930s by importing BMWs from Germany, opened its postwar account by pre-viewing a fully-streamlined two-seater sportscar which used the same running gear as the Bristol 400, though in a higher state of tune. This, however, was a total false start, for there would be no deliveries before 1948, by which time the style had been modified. By then, too, all commercial links between Frazer Nash and Bristol would have been scrapped.

Healey: The design of this new car had been conceived during the war, but there were delays before Donald Healey could set up a factory in War-wick to make them. Fast, light and sporting, the first Healeys set a pattern for the next few years. The chassis incorporated trailing-arm front sus-pension, inspired by the prewar Auto Unions, while engines, gearboxes and rear axles all came from the 2½-litre Riley range. Healey had neither the facilities nor the finance to build its own bodies, so the Westland shell came from a Hereford coachbuilder, the Elliott from a business in Reading.

Until the Jaguar XK120 appeared in 1948, this was Britain's fastest produc-tion car, with a top speed of around 105mph. One detail – the prototype

carried the number VVV 214, which was entirely fictitious, Healey having found a pile of spare numbers in the corner of the workshops!

Hillman: Rootes offered a two-door drop-head coupe version of the mechanically identical Minx saloon, once again this being a derivative which had been planned in 1939.

HRG: The hand-built prewar-type sportscars were reintroduced, together with a new model, the Aerodynamic 1½-litre, which featured a new full-width sporty style atop the existing and rather narrow frame. There were no other novelties, the ultra-hard suspen-sion of the original types being retained – thus ensuring that the new shells would gradually shake them-selves apart!

Invicta: This was probably the bravest of all 1946 models in technical terms, for Invicta was a tiny concern, yet the new Black Prince included a totally-unique twin-cam 3-litre engine, all-independent suspension and an automatic transmission system by Brockhouse (called a hydrokinetic turbo transmitter). As it transpired, it was all too ambitious for such a firm; body-suppliers Charlesworth went bankrupt, there was endless trouble with the transmission, and the price (£2,940 initially) was double the equivalent Jaguar level. Only 25 cars were built before the money ran out, and Invicta finally folded in 1950.

Jensen: The West Bromwich-based concern introduced its PW (for Post War) model, a mostly-new machine complete with a straight-eight Mead-ows 3.9-litre engine. In fact it was based on the chassis of the prewar HC model. Always meant to be expensive and hand-built, it was literally that, for experience would show the Meadows engine to be unsatisfactory, so most of the 15 cars delivered before 1951 had either a prewar 4.2-litre Nash or a postwar Austin A135 engine instead. The original car was a four-door saloon, but not even a drop-head coupe (shown in 1948) could generate any demand. Jensen's days as series producers were many years ahead.

Jowett: The first brief and tantalizing details of Gerald Palmer's brilliant

design were revealed, though deliveries of the Javelin were not promised until 1947. All-new from end to end, it did, at least, retain the traditional Jowett feature of a flat-four engine. Smoothly styled and aerodynamic-efficient, with a unit-construction shell (to be produced by Briggs Motor Bodies at Doncaster), it also had torsion-bar front suspension and rack-and-pinion steering. After being previewed, how-ever, there was a long silence from Idle, Bradford, the first UK-market deliveries being long-delayed.

Lea-Francis: Two closely-related cars – 12hp and 14hp models – were revealed, these using developed ver-sions of the late-1930s models, which had used twin-high-camshaft four-cylinder engines designed by former Riley engineer Hugh Rose, in conven-tional beam-axle/leaf-spring chassis. Under the smooth new body styles, therefore, 1946 was 1939 all over again. The engines proved to be very adaptable to tuning, but as the cars were essentially hand-built they were expensive, and sales were restricted.

Renault: Although not yet ready for assembly at the British (Acton) plant, the all-new 4CV created a real stir in France when launched. Developed during the war and finalized after-wards, it was a real 'people's car', a tiny four-door four-seater monocoque with all-independent suspension, com-plete with new rear-mounted four-cylinder engine which was finally laid to rest in the late 1980s, after millions had been manufactured, its last 'cus-tomer' being the Renault 4 model. The 4CV itself would live until 1961.

Riley: Previewed in 1945, full details were finally given of the new RM-series cars. The 1½-litre model was described in February, the faster and even more graceful 95mph 2½-litre following in November. Both cars used developed versions of the familiar twin-high-camshaft Riley engine of the late 1930s, and shared a new chassis (in two wheelbase lengths) complete with torsion-bar independent front sus-pension, linked to rack-and-pinion steering (both being expensive novel-ties at the time). Bodies (four-door saloons only at first) were long, low and rakish, with part-recessed head-lamps.

Rolls-Royce: The first postwar Rolls-Royce, the Silver Wraith, was novel in many ways for the chassis was based on that of the stillborn 1939 Bentley Mk V and the engine was the first of the overhead-inlet/side-exhaust types which would be built until 1959; the chassis were assembled at Crewe rather than Derby (where jet aero-engine production now took precedence).

Replacing the prewar Wraith, the new type was intended as Rolls-Royce's flagship, and every car was supplied as a rolling chassis, ready to be bodied by an approved coachbuilder. Quite like old times, really – except that complete new car prices started at a whopping £3,802.

Standard: The company reintroduced the Flying Fourteen to its range as a sister car to the existing Flying Twelve on the home market; this had previously been confined to export deliveries.

Triumph: The first Standard-Triumphs were launched in 1946, sharing the same basic chassis design, but with totally different bodies. The chassis was built with tubular main members and used Standard Flying Fourteen suspension assemblies, there being 100in and 108in wheelbases, and all cars used the overhead-valve 1,776cc engine which Standard had originally developed for supply to (SS-)Jaguar for their 1½-litre saloon.

The bodyshell of the 1800 Roadster incorporated a fold-down dickey seat – probably the last to be seen from the British motor industry – and was built entirely by Standard at Canley, but the shell of the 1800 Town and Country saloon was a razor-edge style by Mulliners of Birmingham, having been inspired by Rolls-Royce and Bentley coachwork of the late 1930s.

Vauxhall: Only four months after announcing its postwar programme, the Luton company started to rationalize by concentrating on two instead of three variations of the standard shell. The medium-wheelbase monocoque of the Twelve was dropped, while the 12hp engine was then offered in the hull of the Ten, which meant manufacturing just one H-type and one J-type shell.

Wolseley: Two new cars, effectively 1939/40 models held over by the war, went on sale during the year, though by this time it was clear that all such machines were only being offered to hold the line until a new range could be developed.

The 8hp saloon, which had been previewed in 1939 without going on sale, was effectively an upmarket version of the existing Morris Eight Series E, fitted with a unique overhead-valve (33bhp) version of that car's 918cc engine, along with a characteristic Wolseley nose and grille.

The 10hp model was a mildly reworked version of the 1939 Ten, which meant that it had much in common with the Morris Ten of the period, including the monocoque bodyshell, and the engine was a detuned, underbored, version of the one more famously used in the MG TC sportscar. Both cars were assembled at Wolseley's Ward End premises in Birmingham, for the rationalization move to Nuffield at Cowley was still years ahead.

Industrial developments

Although postwar recovery proceeded rapidly, there still seemed to be no justification for holding a motor show, and as early as January the SMMT announced that it was looking ahead to at least 1947 for that first exhibition. In any case, Earls Court was unavailable as it was still being used by the Government, mainly as as 'demob' processing hall, where ex-servicemen were kitted out in civilian clothes before returning to private life.

The French, though, thought differently about their potential market, for the first postwar Paris Salon was held in October 1946, where the talking point of the entire show, naturally enough, was the new Renault 4CV, though quirky super-economy cars like the Rovin also gained much attention. Just to show that high style and good taste were still alive, there were brave showings from Bugatti (the Type 73), Delahaye (the 4½-litre) and coachbuilders like Franay and Figoni et Falaschi (perhaps inevitably, their English nickname was to become 'Phoney & Flashy'...)

Over in Germany, the Allied Forces had managed to weatherproof the damaged VW factory at Wolfsburg, and a trickle of VW Beetles, soon to become a stream, were being assembled.

Whilst several fledgling car-making businesses had appeared in Britain, the established Big Six companies preferred to concentrate on their existing activities rather than to innovate; Rootes elected to close down its ex-Talbot assembly lines at Ladbroke Grove, West London, and had moved all Sunbeam-Talbot assembly to Ryton-on-Dunsmore, Coventry, by 1947.

No fewer than 30 different marques were in production in the UK by the end of the calendar year, during which a total of 219,162 private cars had been built, of which 84,358 had been exported – but the big exporting push was yet to come.

1947

This was the year in which austerity Britain hit its lowest point since 1945, and rationing – which now included bread and coal – was even more severe than during the war itself. The country seemed to be in a desperate state, with no solution in sight. Not only did the worst winter for many years help to plunge the country into a coal shortage crisis, but the economic situation became so bad that the basic petrol ration was withdrawn completely before the end of the year. In contrast, war-torn France was freed of petrol rationing during the year...

For British motoring enthusiasts, this even meant the temporary loss of their motoring magazines, for early in the year there was often insufficient power to run the printing presses.

There were no immediate changes to motoring taxation at first, nor any easing of the shortage of new cars, for an even larger proportion of them were being exported. Yet despite the fuel shortage and other rationing problems, UK car production rocketed to 287,000 in 1947 – around 141,000 of these going overseas. By this time, people lacking undue influence had become reconciled to ordering new cars, knowing that the average waiting time would be about *five years* and that the model they wanted would probably have been replaced by then.

Then, on June 17, the Chancellor changed everything by announcing two far-reaching changes – to purchase tax and to licence duty. After less than a year of the latest form of £1 per 100cc annual duty he announced that it was to be swept away in favour of a new flat rate of £10 per year from January 1, 1948, regardless of a car's engine size. Further, the rate of purchase tax on cars carrying a basic price of £1,000 or more would be doubled from 33⅓ per cent to 66⅔ per cent.

The flat-rate licence proposal was received with acclaim, except among those running very small-engined cars, who stood to face a small penalty, but the massive hoist in purchase tax – which was instantly branded as a 'tax on luxury' due to the 'politics of envy' – was heavily criticized.

Companies like Jaguar, whose cars crept in under the £1,000 basic price mark, were unaffected, but it meant that Healey, for instance, had to charge £418 more on a car (say £8,000 at mid-1990s values) and even Austin was obliged to charge £279 more. Of the companies selling cars at or around the £1,000 divide (like Armstrong Siddeley) some were able to adjust their prices a little to bring them under £1,000 in order to limit the tax burden, but those unable to do so without facing bankruptcy soon realized that with a sudden marked reduction in home market demand they were probably facing it anyway!

The slide back towards grim wartime conditions began in August 1947 when it was announced that the basic petrol ration was to be reduced by one-third in October, as was the maximum amount of money that could be taken out of the country for travel. The excuse given, which was believed by very few people, was that improvements had to be made to the pound/dollar balance of trade, and it limited the average car to about 2,500 miles a year.

This proposal, however, lasted only a few weeks before it was decided to withdraw the basic ration completely, this being succinctly described as the persecution of the poor, defenceless, private motorist, and ensuring the existing Government's lasting unpopularity. National protest meetings and huge petitions had absolutely no effect, and the ban went ahead on December 1, 1947.

The effects on Britain's tourist trade and thousands of garage businesses was incalculable, but the Chancellor seemed neither to know or care about this, and all private cars were forced off the road. The basic ration would not be restored again until June 1948.

As *The Motor*'s editorial commented: 'On the face of things, this is all the more extraordinary since ample fuel for all United Kingdom requirements is produced within the sterling area...'

Even so, a few other aspects of motoring were – agonizingly slowly – getting back to normal, for Townsend finally reintroduced its cross-channel car ferry service, the Southern Railway's Autocarrier resumed shortly afterwards, and later in the year the overnight ferry services also reappeared.

Perhaps this was the year in which the personalized number-plate hobby began, too, for when HRH Princess Elizabeth took delivery of a new car she secured the number HRH 1 from the local authorities in Hull, where it had already been allocated to a local person. Apparently he readily waived his rights, but did he get an OBE or a knighthood in exchange? Who knows?

New models

AC: The company finally put the new 2-Litre on sale, a car which had been extensively previewed in 1946. In many ways this was a surprisingly backward-looking model, for the chassis used beam axles at front and rear, and the overhead-camshaft engine already had an amazingly lengthy heritage. AC, however, was (and would remain) a very small and privately-financed concern, and could not be expected to produce many technical novelties at that stage.

Austin: Its first series of true postwar models, the A40, was new from stem to stern, complete with a 1.2-litre overhead-valve four-cylinder engine (which would eventually grow up into the very long-running BMC B-Series family), a new chassis-frame incorporating independent front suspension (by a rather soft coil-spring system) and new body styles – two-door saloons being called Dorsets, four-doors Devons.

There was nothing sensational about these cars – chairman and *de facto* technical chief Leonard Lord having concentrated on a fresh postwar look and really low selling prices – but they were carefully and shrewdly aimed at worldwide sales, where they soon succeeded. At a stroke they replaced the old-style Austin 8hp, 10hp and 12hp models, but the bigger-bodied 16hp model would have to soldier on for a time.

Earlier, the closely related A110 (Sheerline) and A120 (Princess) cars had arrived, both being very large, spacious, heavy and frankly cumbersome beasts, and aimed mainly at the business, hire-fleet and mayoral markets. Sharing the same 119in-wheelbase chassis, these cars used refined versions of the 3.5-litre overhead-valve six-cylinder engines which Lord had originally commissioned for use in Austin trucks.

The Sheerline's body was a rather angular all-steel four-door saloon, but the Princess was given an altogether more graceful coachbuilt style by Vanden Plas. Although there was independent front suspension, which ingeniously used the arms of the lever-arm dampers as top wishbone joints, this had to be balanced against the use of a sloppy steering-column gearchange. Austin soon decided that these heavy cars were not fast enough, and in November announced larger 4-litre versions of their engines, which allowed the model names to be changed to A125 and A135.

Ford: The new V8-engined Pilot model, an old fashioned-looking and bulbous machine, was really nothing more than the prewar V8-62 chassis and four-door saloon body of the 1936–40 period, and was intended to be sold with a 2.5-litre engine, a developed version of the old side-valve V8 Ford unit.

It was bad enough that this car was afflicted with the ancient type of transverse-leaf spring suspension and beam axles which Ford seemed to have been using worldwide for decades, but the combination of 66bhp, a three-speed gearbox and an unladen weight of 3,200lb produced a slow, thirsty and unappealing machine which no-one – not even the car-starved British – seemed to like.

Within weeks, it seems, Ford had second thoughts and reinstated the familiar 85bhp/3,622cc version of the V8 from November 1947, which gave the Pilot a more acceptable performance, if a rather prodigious thirst. One bizarre chassis feature was a combination of hydraulic front and mechanical rear brakes, but vacuum-operated wipers (which stopped when the throttle was fully depressed, thereby killing the vacuum...) were retained.

How could Ford do this? What were they thinking of? Quite a lot, as it happened, but it would be 1950 – and the arrival of the Consul/Zephyr series – before anything modern came out of Dagenham.

Hillman: The existing Minx design was retouched, becoming Phase II with a new nose and, more significantly, by adding a steering-column gearchange, which was advertised as Synchromatic

and claimed to be an improvement. Everyone who drove one and compared it with the previous central-gearchange models instantly realized that it was not...

Humber: Like Hillman, Humber mildly updated its prewar engineering by fitting new gearboxes with a steering-column change, but there were few other improvements and no style changes.

Jowett: The much-promised Javelin model finally went into limited production at Idle just before the end of the year, where Jowett took delivery of the graceful fastback four-door monocoque bodyshells from Briggs Motor Bodies at Doncaster. In many ways this was an outstanding new medium-priced family car, a quantum leap ahead of all previous Jowetts, with which it shared not a single component.

Except that designer Gerald Palmer had elected to use a water-cooled flat-four engine (which drove the rear wheels through a newly-developed four-speed gearbox with steering-column control), there were precious few philosophical links with old-style Jowetts, so it was clear that the Yorkshire company had taken a huge financial gamble with this car.

By any 1947 reckoning it must have set new aerodynamic standards, and the many advanced chassis features included aluminium cylinder block and crankcase castings, torsion-bar independent front suspension, along with rack-and-pinion steering. At a British price of £819 (to those who could get their hands on one) it was cheaper than equivalent Rileys and Sunbeam-Talbots, though a lot more expensive than cars like the old-fashioned Austin 12hp models.

Lagonda: Its prototype 2.6-litre saloon was introduced, but it would not go into production before David Brown had injected much-needed finance into the company at the end of the year. Designed by a team led by W O Bentley, it was much smaller than late-1930s Lagondas and shared no features of any type, for there was a sturdy channel-section cruciform chassis-frame, with longitudinal steel rod reinforcements, and all-independent suspension, with swing-axles and long torsion bars at the rear.

The 105bhp twin-cam engine was a

technical masterpiece (and it predated the Jaguar XK unit, though it would never be made in the same quantities), and the prototype was equipped with the French Cotal four-speed epicyclic gearbox allied to a Newton centrifugal clutch, though neither feature made it into production at the end of the year.

The body of the prototype was a coachbuilt two-door saloon, panelled in aluminium, with semi-faired-in headlamps and smooth detailing. A top speed of 97mph was claimed. All in all, it was a brave technical effort, which could so easily have come to nothing if David Brown had not stepped in, for the imposition of double purchase tax threatened to send Lagonda into liquidation in August.

Lea-Francis: The launch of the Sports 12hp model could not have come at a worse time (it occurred after the announcement of the withdrawal of all private petrol supplies), so the impact of this nicely-styled two-seater was rather muted.

The new Sports used the same basic engine, transmission and chassis as that of the saloons which had gone on sale in 1946, which meant that its general character was still that of a hard-sprung 1930s machine. Compared with the saloons there was a little more power (64bhp, thanks to using a twin-SU version of the 1,496cc twin-high-camshaft engine) and the body style was a successful postwar update of prewar themes. Larger-engined, more powerful, and therefore faster versions would soon follow, but high prices always limited sales.

Lloyd: This totally independent Grimsby-based firm, founded in the 1930s, controlled by Roland Lloyd and completely unrelated to the manufacturer of the German Lloyd cars which followed some years later, announced a cheap but carefully detailed minicar, the 650 model. This clearly drew inspiration from the German DKW layout, but shared no components.

Even though Lloyd was a very small company, the 650 was technically advanced, though designed almost totally in-house in Lincolnshire. Powered by a transversely-mounted twin-cylinder two-stroke engine, it drove the front wheels through a three-speed gearbox, which was ahead of rather than alongside the engine, as one would expect to see these days. The chassis was a rugged but simple tubular backbone affair and there was all-independent suspension by coil springs.

A body style was not revealed at first, but was soon seen to be neat and small (the entire car was only 12ft 3in long), but Lloyd's problem was always how to bring prices down to the Ford Anglia/Morris Eight level – and to build up a reputation.

MG: The Y-type saloon was finally introduced, having been conceived well before the outbreak of war and intended for launch in 1940. Although the body was a modified version of the four-door Morris Eight Series E, the chassis was all-new, with a neat coil-spring independent front suspension allied to rack-and-pinion steering. In later years we learned that this had been designed by Alec Issigonis well before he had even started work on the Morris Minor (which, of course, was still a secret project at that stage); it was a system which would eventually find a home in the MG TD and TF sportscars, and in developed form in the MGA and MGB models which followed.

The Y-type's engine was a single-carburettor derivative of the TC's unit (with 46bhp instead of 54bhp), the gearbox and rear axle units also being based on that car's components. Although the Y-type, even then, was seen as a useful car with a fine chassis, it was much underpowered (the top speed was a mere 69mph), and little would be done to improve it during a six-year production life.

Morris: It was revealed that several all-new postwar models had already started prototype testing, including a small saloon coded the Mosquito, which was said to have a 50bhp flat-four 1½-litre engine. That was indeed so at the time, but before this car – which became, of course, the Morris Minor – was officially revealed in October 1948 the flat-four engine had been abandoned in favour of the old Morris Eight's side-valve 918cc unit.

Singer: The first official pictures of a new 1.5-litre SM1500 saloon model were issued, though few technical details were revealed, and it was made clear that cars would not be available

for sale before the autumn of 1948.

Standard: The totally-new postwar Vanguard model was previewed, with full technical descriptions, though the company warned that deliveries could not begin until the summer of 1948. With a body style rather dumpily based on the early-1940s Plymouths which Sir John Black had so often had seen parked outside the American Embassy in London, and with a lusty new 'wet-liner' overhead-valve engine which was already being fitted to Ferguson tractors, the new Vanguard was a real amalgam of influences.

Not a single component from the existing Flying Twelve/Flying Fourteen models had been used in the new car, which according to Sir John was to be his single new postwar model to cater for all markets for the foreseeable future – which was precisely what the Government was urging all Britain's car-makers to do. But this apparent resolve did not last long, for another mainly new car – the Triumph Mayflower – would be ready for launch only two years hence!

The name Vanguard came from Britain's latest (and last, as it happened) battleship, and there was no doubt that the car's simple but rugged construction was aimed squarely at success in export territories. The three-speed all-synchromesh gearbox had a steering-column control, there was a bench seat across the front, and the car had a short wheelbase, a tall roofline and a soft ride, which had been preferred to the firmer settings which would have given it fine handling.

In its initial form, the engine was a 1,849cc unit with an 80mm cylinder bore and a 60bhp power output, but before deliveries began a year later the engine would be enlarged to the familiar 68bhp/85mm bore and 2,088cc which persisted for so long at Canley.

Vauxhall: Having already reshuffled its tiny range once since the war, the company now elected to drop the 10hp completely, concentrating on 12hp and 14hp machines until the new range of cars became available in 1948.

Wolseley: Amazingly, all the prewar tooling for the vast 3.5-litre 25hp

limousine was dug out of store in Birmingham so that a limited number of such cars could be built. By any standards this was an antediluvian machine, for it weighed nearly 5,000lb, had only 104bhp, yet was expected to sell at £2,568, which was more expensive than Humber's Pullman and almost serious Daimler money.

It was a real period-piece, with beam-axle front and rear suspension, exposed headlamps and upright styling – yet it was one of the few limousines available to the hire-car and minor-borough markets. In view of the country's current economic state, it didn't deserve to sell at all – which was proved when Wolseley sold only 75 examples in a year. It was a real aberration, and one can only think that someone had discovered a stock of parts and decided to build them up for disposal.

Over in Italy, two important new high-performance cars – the original **Ferrari 125S** (complete with 1.5-litre overhead-cam V12 engine) and the **Maserati A6** – made their debut. Although notably anaemic by their own later standards, both would have been labelled supercars if that phrase had been invented in 1947! Neither marque, however, would send any new cars to the UK for at least another decade.

More significantly, **Saab** (the Swedish aircraft manufacturer) showed a prototype of its first-ever car, a twin-cylinder two-stroke-powered two-door saloon with a very smooth and aerodynamically-efficient shape. Once again, this was of no more than academic interest to British drivers as Saab imports to the UK would not begin until 1960.

Industrial developments

New car prices continued to increase (though some prices were occasionally slashed in an effort to stimulate sales), this trend eventually becoming so familiar that it no longer caused comment. To realize why this was inevitable, see Appendix D for year-on-year changes in Britain's Retail Prices Index.

Britain's car-makers suffered badly from a shortage of coal during the Arctic weather of February, some having to close down completely for a short period. Austin, for instance, made much of the loss to the country of its export earnings of £62,000 a day, while Nuffield pointed out that 10 per cent of annual production would be lost – thus harming the export drive. Everything from farm tractors with power take-offs, fun-fair generators and portable oil engines were used to keep some factories in production.

In the absence of an Earls Court motor show, British car-makers looking for exposure flocked to the first postwar show at Geneva, which was held in March in a country whose prosperity had never been affected by war. The first postwar 'Earls Court' had finally been promised for October 1948, and insiders knew that it would be a show absolutely crammed with brand-new models.

Even though he had reached 70 years old, Lord Nuffield (who had earlier promised to leave day-to-day running of his empire to his fellow directors) could not let go of the reins, usually choosing to interfere in a destructive fashion. In a crisis which boiled over and went public in November, the *real* dynamo of the Organisation, Sir Miles Thomas, was obliged to resign (he soon became a highly-successful chairman of the British Overseas Airways Corporation). R F Hanks, who had worked for Morris since 1922, took his place.

In what was almost the 'night of the long knives', a few weeks later Lord Nuffield also got rid of several other faithful and long-serving directors, including Victor Riley (of the Riley concern) and T C Skinner, of SU Carburettors. When Harold Seaward, the managing director of Morris Motors, also 'resigned' (which meant that he was pushed out), this brought the total of dismissals to eight, and Nuffield-watchers now agree that this harmed the Organisation so much that a merger with another group then became inevitable and only a matter of time.

Jaguar's Foleshill factory suffered a serious stores fire (estimated to have cost £100,000), though the damage was speedily put right. Compared with what would happen at Browns Lane in 1957, this was only a minor flare-up, and assembly of Mk IVs was not affected.

In February, industrialist David Brown took control of Aston Martin, whose small and sparsely-equipped factory was at Feltham in Middlesex. At this time Aston Martin had not even previewed its postwar model, though the latest 2-litre engine, designed by Claude Hill, had been shown in 1946.

Later, David Brown also bought Lagonda, but even before then there were upheavals in the Staines concern, where Alan Good (who had taken control in 1935) resigned to concentrate on other business activities. Shortly afterwards the factory was sold to Alan Good's syndicate, while David Brown bought up the rights and designs to the 2.6-litre and all the old cars. In September he took control, and the process of merging Lagonda with Aston Martin began. In the meantime, W O Bentley left Lagonda, setting up his own design consultancy.

However, if the Aston Martin/Lagonda tie-up was a marriage, Bristol and AFN (Frazer Nash) were divorced. The big aeroplane company and the tiny car-maker had found it difficult to work together, and although AFN continued to take supplies of engines and gearboxes from Bristol, that was the end of a short-term link.

Technical developments

By this time it was possible to see some British innovations being applied to new cars, though the pace of change was still gathering. The flood of unit-construction body/chassis units was yet to come (it took a great deal of time to complete the press and assembly tooling), but new chassis-frames were more rigid than before, with box-section side members usually taking over from channel-section members.

Most late-1930s British cars had been stuck with beam front axles, but many new cars were now being given independent front suspension, often of quite remarkable complexity. There was a surprising short-term trend towards using torsion-bar springs instead of coils (as later, torsion bars were expensive and difficult to package), and the first oil-filled telescopic dampers (by Girling) were seen. Only the new Invicta and Lagonda models (and, amazingly, the Lloyd minicar) had independent rear suspension.

Except where old designs were kept going with modifications (as with the latest Hillman Minx and Ford Pilot units, for instance), side-valve engines were gradually disappearing; new mass-production engines usually had ohv layouts. The pioneering Rolls-Royce valve arrangement (overhead inlets allied to side exhaust valves) was joined by a similarly equipped Rover engine at the end of 1947. In the event the Rover design would outlive the Rolls-Royce unit by eight years, being built in ever larger and more powerful private-car forms until 1967.

Twin-cam engines (like the Invicta and Lagonda units) usually came from tiny companies with big ideas, for these were still very expensive to manufacture in large numbers. Bristol, however, was delighted to be able to harness BMW engineering, which combined efficient part-spherical combustion chambers with (complicated) overhead pushrod valve gear.

Although automatic and other 'easy-change' transmissions were becoming known in the USA, there was still little evidence of such features being taken up by British companies. The Brockhouse system (in the Invicta) was a non-starter, and the complex Cotal installation, which still required its gears to be changed by hand, did not attract any significant orders.

1948

At long last the British motoring scene was beginning to look more promising. By the end of the year, not only had a basic ration of petrol been restored, but the first postwar Earls Court Motor Show had been held and a positive bonanza of important new models had been introduced; if only there had not still been a five-year waiting list for them…

Before the restoration of a petrol ration for every car owner from June 1, 1948, Britain's motorists had been forced off the road for a total of six cold, wet and totally miserable months, and even now, with the fuel allowance only a third of that which had existed in mid-1947, no-one was likely to be driving very far.

Britain's first postwar Earls Court Motor Show opened its doors on October 27, and such was the pent-up demand for a return to true peacetime motoring conditions it could not have failed to be a huge success. There had been no British motor show since 1938, and no fewer than 11 major new models – most of them aimed squarely at the family man – were on display.

But how times have changed! The admission cost on opening day was just 10s (50p), and 5s (25p) on all other days; naturally, the show remained closed on the Sunday. It was still possible to park (with some difficulty) close to the exhibition hall, and most manufacturers had demonstration cars parked behind the hall which could be driven around the streets of London by aspiring buyers!

Predictably, the show attendance was colossal and the crush enormous. It would be many years, in fact, before Earls Court became 'just another show', and the subterranean queueing galleries which linked the Tube station with the exhibition centre itself regularly looked like wartime air-raid shelters. A total of 562,954 people attended over the 10 days – more than double the figure for any previous show (in 1938, for instance, it was only 233,000).

There was mixed news on the production and delivery fronts, for although British car assembly surged ahead to 334,000 and exports leapt to a record 224,000, home-market deliveries had fallen considerably from 147,767 in 1947 to 112,666 in 1948.

The Government was continuing to stress the 'export or perish' philosophy, and backing up its exhortation with dictatorial control over most material supplies.

Although there were no changes in vehicle taxation, controversy continued to rage over estate cars. Although these were very few and far between at the time (the first great estate car surge would not occur until the 1950s), they were still seen as commercial load-carrying vehicles and consequently were free of purchase tax – but on that basis they were also limited to 30mph. Any owner wanting to cruise along at more normal speeds was obliged to pay the purchase tax, whereupon the estate became a private car!

On the holiday front, crossings by air, instead of by ferry, of the English Channel became available for the first time. Silver City Airways bought a small fleet of twin-engined front-loading Bristol Freighter aircraft, which could take two and sometimes three (depending on their length) cars across the Channel between Lympne in Kent and Le Touquet in France.

For the next 20 years this would be a very fast (20 minutes from terminal to terminal), noisy, draughty, rather clubby and also quite expensive way of getting over the water, a series of larger, four-engined car-ferrying aircraft being added in 1962.

New models

Alvis: The TA14 sports tourer, based on the existing TA14 saloon chassis, was truly a very strange device indeed, completely outside the traditions of the Alvis company – which may explain why hardly anyone bought one! British magazines carefully described its looks as 'striking', which was a diplomatic way of saying 'ugly'. It had more power than the saloon, weighed a little less, had a reduced frontal area, but otherwise had very little to commend it.

Aston Martin: Following its rescue by industrialist David Brown, this tiny company was finally ready to show its postwar car, later retrospectively known as the DB1 (DB = David Brown). It featured a rigid multi-tube chassis-frame, made up principally from square-section tubing, and was powered by the new 2-litre engine which had already been previewed.

Clearly, the car was intended to be slowly, carefully and almost entirely assembled by hand, for there was much labour content in such features as the trailing-arm coil-spring front suspension and the construction of the chassis.

Austin: The Len Lord-inspired rejuvenation of the entire product range continued apace with the old (1944/45) 16hp model being swept away during the winter of 1948/49. In its place came two new cars which shared the same chassis, independent front suspension and four-speed gearbox with steering-column change. In general the layout was similar to that of the A40 of 1947, though entirely different in detail, and with a substantial cruciform bracing member under the cabin. The A70 Hampshire was the more conventional of the duo, a rounded style of four-door saloon using the 2,199cc engine from the old 16hp model and selling for only £608, while the A90 Atlantic was a strange-looking two-door machine (a drop-head coupe in the first phase) with an enlarged and more powerful version of that engine, which would later find fame in the original Austin-Healey 100; the car was priced at £953 in the UK.

Lord entertained high hopes for the A90 in the USA, hence the Atlantic model name, but the car is now seen as an enormous failure, one of the few big mistakes he ever made. Complete with its electrically-operated soft-top and door window lifts, it was supposed to be irresistible to North Americans, but they stayed away in droves, reasoning that their domestic cars were cheaper, faster and better-looking.

Bond: By no means in the mainstream of British motoring, but still interesting in a rather cash-strapped market, the original Bond three-wheeler was a Villiers motorcycle-engined machine and would continue to be built in Lancashire until the 1960s, when the first Triumph Herald-based sports coupes appeared.

Bristol: To supplement the 400 model, Bristol added two more body styles – the 401 being a two-door saloon and the very rare 402 a two-door cabriolet version along similar lines.

Even though it still looked somewhat BMW-like around the nose, the 401 shape had started life as a Carrozzeria Touring project, but the Filton design staff had modified it, shown it to their wind-tunnel and produced an altogether more pleasing style. It was considerably roomier in the cabin and had more glass area than the 400, and along with the later 403, which was a direct development of it, the 401 would become the best-selling of all Bristols. But it was always an expensive car – £3,214 in 1948, which was a lot more money than similar-sized Daimlers, for instance, and three-quarters of the way to rarified Bentley levels. The 402, despite being an extra-special, hand-built soft-top model (reputedly with a rather flexible bodyshell) was priced exactly the same as the 401, yet strangely it proved almost unsaleable.

Citroen: Although the long-wheelbase six-cylinder version of the famous *traction avant* model had been launched in France before the war, it was not until 1948 that small-scale assembly (from kits) began at the British Citroen factory in Slough, where the cars took shape among the more familiar four-cylinder-engined Light Fifteen saloons.

The Six was always the rarest of these types (it was much more expensive), and it had a smooth but none too sporting 76bhp/2.9-litre engine. In all other major respects – front-wheel drive, torsion-bar suspension, three-speed gearbox, impeccable roadholding, long, low and totally unmistakable styling – it was the mixture as before. Surprisingly few of these fascinating cars seem to have survived to the present day.

Daimler: Wishing to inject a little excitement into its otherwise staid range of middle and upper-class cars, the company announced the Barker-bodied DB18 Sports Special, which was as powerful (and as special) as the similarly named Special Sports of 1939, which was really its prototype.

Except that the 2.5-litre engine had twin SU carburettors and an aluminium cylinder head, the chassis and running gear were almost pure DB18 saloon. The body, however, was a graceful if rather heavy two-door drop-head coupe style, with provision for three-abreast seating up front and a single sideways-placed seat behind it. In four years, during which a Hooper saloon version would be added, only 608 examples were to be sold.

Ford: Except that the Prefect model was mildly facelifted, with new front wings and flush-fitting headlamps, there were no changes to the British range, which was still singularly unbalanced – there being a yawning gap between the 1,172cc-engined Prefect and the 3,622cc-engined Pilot.

Incidentally, the first postwar Ford-Germany car was not built until the summer of 1948 – it had taken three years to clear up the chaos of the fighting and re-equip the factory in Cologne. By the 1970s, however, Ford-Germany would be larger than Ford-UK...

Frazer Nash: More details were given of the new high-speed sportscar which had been previewed in 1947, but although the chassis details were entirely accurate the body style shown would be altered considerably before the end of 1948, when what passed for series production at AFN began. The first car, shown in February 1948, was a mildly-modified BMW Mille Miglia racecar shell from 1940, and must have inspired William Lyons in some ways in the shaping of the XK120.

There were no links with prewar Frazer Nash models, the traditional chain-drive layout having been abandoned. The chassis, by ex-BMW engineer Fritz Fiedler, was a crib of various late-1930s BMW features. There was a sturdy large-diameter twin-tube chassis (BMW 328-style) with transverse leaf-spring independent front suspension (in some ways rather like that used in the BMW 327) and rear suspension by long torsion bars along the lines of the BMW 326, while Frazer Nash's agreement to take its engines and transmissions from Bristol still stood, even though all financial links with that company had been dissolved.

The original car was said to have a 120bhp 2-litre engine, which made it phenomenally efficient, and the claimed top speed was well over 110mph. Healey, whose sportscars only had 100bhp, were initially very worried by this, but when Frazer Nash announced prices starting at £2,250 the rival began to relax.

Healey: The little Warwick-based company had a quiet year mechanically, but added another body style – the Sportsmobile – to the existing chassis. This was a four-seater drop-head coupe with a rather angular full-width body, but it did not appeal to many customers, only 23 cars being built.

Hillman: More than three years after the war, Rootes was finally ready to reveal a new-style Minx, this Phase III model being a brand-new monocoque four-door, four-seater, the styling of which had been initiated by the Loewy studios.

The fresh, rather angular, but neatly-packaged bodyshell hid coil-spring independent suspension for the first time on a Minx, but many of the other mechanical features were familiar, the side-valve engine and 'four-on-the-tree' gearchange having been lifted from the previous Minx. In fact, the Minx engine had reached its 17th birthday, but there was still a lot of life in it. Technically this was a simple car, and in packaging terms it was aimed squarely at the lower-middle class market throughout the world.

Most significantly, it was a very important 'building block' for Rootes, who would produce many more of these cars than any other model or badge during the next few years. In addition to the four-door saloon, a two-door drop-head coupe was announced, and several more derivatives (including the short-wheelbase Husky) would soon follow.

Humber: The new-generation Hawk, like the new Hillman Minx, was an uncompromising postwar shape by Loewy, with four passenger doors, a bluff nose and flush-mounted headlamps. Under the skin was a new chassis-frame, still with old-fashioned channel-section side-members, but at least the ancient type of transverse-leaf suspension had been discarded in favour of a new coil-spring layout.

To open the lofty bonnet was a disappointment, for the same old 1.9-litre side-valve 'four' (which had its design roots in the early 1930s) had been retained, along with the four-speed gearbox with steering-column change of the previous model. The new Hawk, in other words, was a thoroughly conventional if technically backward machine, but it seemed to be what a lot of middle-income buyers wanted. Priced at £799, it would be a steady seller, in gradually developed form, for the next nine years.

There was also a new Super Snipe Mk II in September, taking over from both the early-postwar Snipe/Super Snipe types. Although the wheelbase was 3.5 inches longer than before, the wheel tracks were wider and the front-end style had been completely reworked (again with much input from the Loewy studio) with flush-mounted headlamps and a shallower front grille over which the bonnet loomed. But under the skin this was still a late-1930s car, most recently modified in 1947. The front-end style, of course, shared all its main cues with the Pullman (below) which preceded it by a few months.

It was not that Rootes did not want to produce a thoroughly modern Super Snipe – simply that investment in the Hillman Minx took precedence, allied to the fact that current-generation big Humbers continued to sell strongly. If only the public had realized it, the new Hawk (above) had forecast the shape of the next-generation Super Snipes *four years* ahead.

The vast (4,500lb) Pullman, an eight-seater limousine aimed fairly and squarely at the hire-car/ceremonial/business sector, was launched in May as a direct replacement for the 1945–48 model and was the first of a flood of new Rootes cars to appear over a period of six months.

The chassis, with its 131in wheelbase, represented conventional Rootes large-car thinking, as did the torquey 4.1-litre side-valve engine, all the novelties being confined to the body, which was modified from the obsolete type, a mixture of traditional (vestigial running-boards) and modern (flush-fitting headlamps and a steering-column gearchange). Tests showed that it was a surprisingly fast car, with a respectable 78mph maximum speed – good for its size and pedigree. Gentlemen, however, did not talk about fuel consumption, which was probably just as well…

Jaguar: While the new XK120 sports-car, complete with its new XK twin-cam engine, was the sensation of 1948, it

was another car, the Mk V, which was commercially the more important.

By any standards, the new XK engine was amazing, unexpected, beautiful, powerful – and in 1948 rather difficult to believe in. No other car-maker was making twin-cam engines in quantity, but here was a relatively small British concern proposing to do just that. William Lyons saw this new design as the cornerstone of all Jaguar's new models for the next decade and more, and was laying down production machinery on that basis.

Many people forget that originally there were to be both six-cylinder and *four*-cylinder versions of this mould-breaking unit. However, the four-cylinder engine, though previewed and used to help Major Goldie Gardner set record speeds on the Belgian Jabbeke road during the summer of 1948, never went into production.

Although the XK engine was primarily destined for use in Jaguar saloons, in 1948 it was confined to the prototype XK120, which used a much-shortened version of the Mk V chassis (below) and was clothed by a beautiful two-seater roadster bodyshell. Lyons originally foresaw the XK120 as a limited-production car (apparently a total run of only 200 was envisaged), which explains why the first cars had wooden body framing and aluminium skin panels.

Production of 125mph XK120s did not even begin until the summer of 1949, and an all-steel version of the bodyshell was speedily commissioned, taking over from the aluminium cars in 1950. The so-called XK100, with its 95bhp 2-litre four-cylinder XK engine, was never put on sale.

Although no-one realized it at the time, the Mk V was an interim car, which would be replaced by the Mk VII after only two years. Its all-new chassis-frame was a rock-solid item with box-section side-members and torsion-bar independent front suspension, the design of which had been influenced by what Citroen had invented for the *traction avant* model in the 1930s.

As we were later to discover, the chassis was originally intended to house the XK engine in a new saloon bodyshell. But because this shell could not be completed in time, Jaguar decided to use the existing, long-proven, overhead-valve engines – in 2.7 and 3.5-litre forms – in an interim

saloon body to be assembled by the company itself. In many ways the Mk V's shell showed a graceful link between the now obsolete 1930s-style cars (often subsequently referred to as Mk IVs), and the forthcoming Mk VII. For traditionalists, the bonus was that Jaguar was also able to offer a sumptuously-trimmed two-door drop-head coupe version, complete with extra hood frame bars and a fully-padded soft-top.

Jowett: The company revealed a rather ungainly two-door drop-head coupe derivative of the Javelin (complete with three-abreast seating and a dickey seat) though this car never actually went into production.

Lagonda: Following the company's rescue in 1947, development of the new 2.6-litre model was completed. After one major change – the substitution of a David Brown manual gearbox for the complex French Cotal design – the graceful but heavy new saloon and drop-head coupe types finally went on sale.

Land-Rover: In April Rover launched the original Land-Rover, an all-can-do vehicle originally conceived as an agricultural machine, but which rapidly found use in virtually any environment, for it had four-wheel drive, stiff suspension and an 80in wheelbase, which allowed it to surmount almost any obstacle where a modicum of grip could be found.

Obviously it had been inspired by the ubiquitous American military Jeep, but years would pass before it became known that the early prototypes had actually been built around Jeep chassis, using many Jeep components…

The first production machines – delivered in July 1948 – used the new 1.6-litre Rover 60 engine, and almost all the original batch went overseas. Except for a few components, the bodyshells were made completely from aluminium sheet, which rendered them virtually rotproof; in old age, indeed, it was usually the chassis-frames which rotted away! Nearly 50 years later, direct descendants of this model – much larger, more powerful and even more capable, and latterly called Defenders – were still being made.

In October the original seven-seater estate car version of the Land-Rover was shown, but because this was subject to purchase tax whereas the basic working Land-Rover was not, the price was quite uneconomic (at £959, more than twice that of the base model), so it was very speedily withdrawn.

Lea-Francis: Still struggling to cope with the heavy burden of double purchase tax on their cars, the Coventry firm introduced a new chassis with independent front suspension (but only for export under its saloons), while the sportscar was given the 1,767cc engine which it had always deserved.

MG: The Abingdon concern carried forward its TC and Y-type models for another year, but also launched another new model – the YT. Never to be sold in the UK, the YT was a rather strange, backward-looking design, for although it used the Y-type's rolling chassis and the more highly-tuned TC engine, it was equipped with an old-fashioned late-1930s style of four-seater open body, constructed by the Morris Bodies Branch in Coventry. Perhaps the British market was not missing much, for only 877 of these cars were made.

Morris: If the Jaguar XK120 was the most glamorous car at the 1948 Earls Court Motor Show, the Morris Minor was certainly the most important. Here, for the first time, was a small, low-priced, British family car which not only looked good and had a great deal more cabin space than its predecessor, but steered and handled extraordinarily well.

Alec Issigonis, who had masterminded the layout, had designed a remarkable machine with wide tracks, great stability and a totally engaging character. All its technical elements had been seen before, but the combination of torsion-bar front suspension, inch-accurate rack-and-pinion steering and a supple ride in an up-to-the-minute package was irresistible: not only that, but it had a decisive central gearchange. Within months, saloons, tourers and estate car (Traveller) types would be available, while vans and pick-ups were also being developed for commercial use.

Few people were aware at the time that Issigonis' original creation had been somewhat narrower and had used a brand-new flat-four engine, nor

did anyone know that the Minor (reviving a famous name from the past) would become a British best-seller and remain in production for more than 20 years. Shortly after the car's launch, Issigonis received a well-deserved promotion, becoming chief engineer of Morris Motors.

Now here's a puzzle. Viewed from a range of nearly 50 years, the Morris Oxford (Series MO), introduced alongside the Minor, is not considered to have been successful – yet nearly 160,000 of them were sold in less than six years. Of course, it *should* have been a success because in almost every way it was the Minor writ large. Every major component – monocoque, engine (a new 1.5-litre side-valve) and suspension items – was different, but the same general layout had been followed throughout except for the steering-column gearchange. Even the general proportions and styling were similar.

The Morris Six, on the other hand, was not nearly as coherent a design. Combining the same basic hull as the Oxford, but with a 13in longer wheelbase and a 65bhp version of the six-cylinder engine from the new Wolseley 6/80 (below), it was afflicted with cam-gear steering and was a heavy and somewhat lumbering car. Because it was launched at the same time as the 6/80, which was faster, better-looking and better-equipped, the Six did not stand much chance of success, and only 12,400 would be built in five years.

Murad: Here was a real oddity, puzzle and mystery. From an Aylesbury-based company with no previous track record (except for making machine tools), nor any obvious financial backing or high-profile engineers, came a 1.5-litre four-door saloon prototype looking rather like an immediate postwar Vauxhall Twelve with a different nose. It was not easy to make a close study of the prototype – by all accounts only one car was built – but it had an all-steel body, which would have demanded expensive press tooling, and even the four-cylinder engine appeared to have been specially designed. The project disappeared almost as mysteriously as it had been revealed, and little was ever heard again of the founder, although he continued to live in the UK and was briefly interviewed by puzzled 'classic car' writers in the 1980s.

Riley: Although the new three-seats-abreast Riley RM Roadster was at first described as being for export only, it received a great deal of attention by the British press. Mechanically almost identical to the existing 2½-litre saloon chassis, and with the same front-end style, it had only one row of seats (made practical by the use of a steering-column gearchange) and a long and shapely tail. The doors were sharply cutaway, and there were detachable side curtains for use when the weather was poor.

Before the end of the year, the three-seater was also listed in the UK market, while Riley had also introduced an elegant two-door, four-seater, drop-head coupe version of the 2½-litre chassis. Neither of these cars would ever sell in large numbers, even though they were not priced much above that of the saloons.

Rover: The Solihull-based company had a very busy year, not only launching the graceful P3 saloons in February, but in April also revealing the Jeep-like Land-Rover described above.

The P3, built as a 60 and a 75, was a car which looked very similar to the transitional models of 1945–48, but it had a brand new chassis and a novel type of engine. The chassis was a sturdy box-section affair which stopped short of the line of the rear axle (the rear leaf springs, therefore, were hung from brackets on the bodyshell in the extreme tail), while there was a new, massively-detailed, coil-spring independent front suspension.

There was a choice of new engines – four-cylinder and six-cylinder derivatives of a new design – which featured overhead inlet and side exhaust valves, the camshaft and rockers being so placed that the combustion chamber was shaped between the piston, the flat cylinder head face and the exhaust valve only. As on all recent Rovers, too, a freewheel was incorporated in the transmission. The P3 was an ambitious new design which strangely was to have a very short life, for yet another range of new Rovers would appear before the end of 1949.

Singer: Having struggled for more than three years, not only to get back into series production of its older cars, but to find the investment for a new model, Singer eventually launched the

SM1500, which was a very austere-looking four-door saloon having a rather nondescript nose devoid of any Singer 'identity'.

The all-steel body hid a new separate chassis-frame, with pierced box-section side-members and independent front suspension (this was a 'first' for Singer), all being powered by a familiar type of overhead-camshaft engine, but with unfamiliar dimensions. Oddly, although the bore was larger and the stroke shorter than before, Singer originally chose a size of 1,506cc, putting the car just outside the 1.5-litre limit which was important in some countries.

Although Singer dealers welcomed the car, it was difficult for anyone to work up much enthusiasm for what, after all, was one in the Hillman Minx/Morris Oxford/Austin A40 class, but selling at a 50 per cent premium.

Standard: The Vanguard, fully described when it was previewed in 1947, finally went on sale in the summer of 1948, by which time the engine size had been increased to the subsequently so familiar 2,088cc; rugged though not beautiful, it was expected to sell well overseas. It was very keenly priced – British prices started at £544 – but it was a compromise in so many ways and many pundits would never forgive its wallowy handling, vague steering-column gearchange and semi-transatlantic touches. However, those who wrote that it fell between stools were surely being uncharitable because it made very healthy profits for Standard for several years.

In paying lip-service to the Government's urge for a 'one-model' policy, once the Vanguard was into production Standard swept away all the older Flying Standard models – the 8hp, 12hp and 14hp. Commercially this was very stupid as few of the hundreds of thousands of motorists looking to buy an 8hp car could possibly be interested in the large (and more costly) Vanguard. Even so, it was five years before Standard closed the gap that Sir John Black had created.

Incidentally, although there was only a four-door saloon at first, before the end of the year an estate car and a utility pick-up had also been added to the range.

Sunbeam-Talbot: Among the flood of postwar models from the Rootes Group was a handsome quartet of Sunbeam-Talbots – the 80 and 90 models as four-door saloons or two-door drop-head coupes. Although their body styling was identical, their running gear was very different. The cynical way to describe them (though not in the 'establishment' motoring magazines) was as Hillman Minxes and Humber Hawks in party frocks, though much more was involved than that.

Except that the saloons used a type of pillarless construction around the trailing edge of the rear passenger doors, as the prewar Sunbeam-Talbots had done, there was little resemblance to older models. Rootes designers later admitted that they had been influenced by wartime aircraft shapes when designing the new Sunbeam-Talbots, which certainly had a style which lived gracefully for almost a decade.

Amazingly for cars launched in 1948, these cars used old-fashioned separate chassis-frames with beam-axle front suspension. On the other hand, both were fitted with overhead-valve versions of existing Rootes engines – that of the 80 being based on the Hillman Minx unit, that of the 90 on the Humber Hawk design. Like all other new-generation models from Rootes, both these cars were afflicted by very imprecise steering-column gearchanges, which were most unsuitable for what were meant to be elegant sports saloons.

Although there was a healthy demand for the 90s, the heavy and underpowered 80 was never popular and was dropped after only two years. The 90s, on the other hand, would become famous as rally cars, the works teams doing great things for Rootes' image.

Triumph: As part of Standard-Triumph's rationalization policy (around the new Standard Vanguard), the quirky Roadster was re-engined to become the 2000 Roadster.

All the running gear of the old-style 1800, which had been borrowed from the Standard Flying Fourteen, was swept away in favour of the Standard Vanguard's engine and three-speed gearbox, complete with a horrid right-hand steering-column gearchange. Prices were unchanged.

Vauxhall: The General Motors-owned company (much lower in the British pecking order than it has since become) announced a new range of saloons with unit-construction bodyshells which were actually clever updates of the old (small) H-type structure. Described by Vauxhall specialist Michael Sedgwick as: 'Really only the H-type with stream-lined front end, projecting boot, concealed spare wheel and alligator bonnet, plus disc wheels and column shift', they looked dated from the day they were revealed.

Called the Wyvern (four-cylinder) and Velox (six-cylinder), the cars shared the same shell, wheelbase and overall dimensions, while their engines were long-stroke overhead-valve units, updated from those which had been in production at Luton since the 1930s.

Except for their very low prices (£448 for the Wyvern, £550 for the Velox) and weight, these were disappointing cars by almost any standards, for they were neither modern, fast, nor good-looking. More than three years after the end of the war, Vauxhall had done no more than work over the prewar designs, and potential customers knew it. Compared with what other members of the Big Six were doing, this was a giant step backwards and it would be 1951 before a really new shape emerged from Bedfordshire.

Not satisfied with this design in 1948, Vauxhall would tinker with it a year later, offering modified front wings (and larger headlamps), along with different steering gear, but the design was essentially unchanged.

Wolseley: Following trends established back in the mid-1930s, Wolseley was able to announce new models as derivations on a Morris theme, the new 4/50 and 6/80 models being better, faster and more complete versions of the Morris Oxford and Six models, respectively.

The 4/50 was a little more special than one might have expected. Although it shared the same basic monocoque with the Oxford (Series MO), the 4/50 had a 5in longer wheelbase (which was unique to this sub-model in the entire family) and the engine had an overhead camshaft and 51bhp, compared with 41bhp and side valves of the Morris. However, the steering was a Bishop cam item, which meant that the 4/50 did not handle as well as the Oxford, but at least its engine *sounded* better, as well as offering a performance bonus. Yet the car was a sales flop, with less than 9,000 sold in five years.

The 6/80, now affectionately remembered for all its police car versions, was a much better statement of the Morris Six theme, for the engine was rather more powerful, the front-end style was impressive, and the interior looked as good as Wolseley customers had come to expect. It sold well, too – 24,886 over a five-year period.

If only it had been known at the time, there were two very important births in Europe during 1948. One came at the Paris Salon, where **Citroen** showed off a prototype of its 2CV economy car, which would eventually stay in production for more than 40 years. At the other end of the performance and desirability scale, the prototype of the **Porsche** sportscar – a mid-engined roadster, was unveiled at Gmund, in Austria. The lines, though new and striking at the time, would become very familiar indeed during the next 15 years or so, during which the VW Beetle underpinnings of the original type would gradually be replaced by special components.

Behind the Iron Curtain – a new phrase coming into common use – the first postwar Russian cars were taking shape. First to show was the Pobieda, the second being the original Moskvich (itself derived from the prewar Opel Kadett, whose tools had been 'liberated' from Germany as war reparations).

Industrial developments

The main motor industry talking point in the autumn of 1948 was that Austin and Nuffield (meaning Leonard Lord and Lord Nuffield) had agreed to get together, not in a complete merger, but in a rather unspecific co-operative deal which would pool all manner of technical, production, purchase and costing details. For the time being, it was stressed, there was no question of new joint models being developed, but there was every chance of components being shared.

This move was both unexpected and

astonishing, and outside the two boardrooms there was great doubt that it could ever be made to work. Nor could it, and by July 1949 the deal was off, and intense rivalry had resumed, to the great relief of rival tycoons like Sir John Black and Sir William Rootes, both of whom could see (even if Lord Nuffield could not) what such co-operation could do to them!

The reluctance to co-operate, it seems, came mostly from Nuffield, and the breakdown made Austin's Len Lord even more determined to complete a proper merger – which would eventually take place in the winter of 1951/52.

There was one other significant piece of news from Nuffield – that Wolseley assembly would shortly be transferred from its factory at Ward End, Birmingham, to the Morris Motors factory at Cowley. Tractor assembly would take its place.

When Brooklands was sold off, much was made of the closing down of a motor industry test track (though, in truth, its usage had decreased in the late 1930s). Finally, in 1948, the Motor Industry Research Association (MIRA) secured the lease of a redundant military airfield at Lindley, immediately north of the A5 road and close to Nuneaton. At the time it was amply large enough for the industry's needs – the perimeter track totalled 3 miles and the longest runway measured about 2,000 yards – but ambitious plans for development included the provision of a banked outer circuit and many special surfaces and facilities.

The Rootes Commission's disdain of the VW Beetle project when they examined it rapidly began to look foolish when the 20,000th car was built early in 1948, a figure which would have leapt to 40,000 by the end of the year and 80,000 by the end of 1949!

Technical developments

General trends, reinforcing those already seen in 1947, were easy to identify, being centred around the adoption of unit-construction body-

work where production rates permitted it, overhead-valve instead of side-valve engines, and independent front suspension instead of old-fashioned beam axles.

Unhappily there was far too strong a tendency for steering-column gear-changes (allied to bench front seats) to be fitted to any car which might possibly be exportable: the trick was to try to convince people that three-abreast passenger carrying was possible, even though most owners did not even consider this when drawing up their needs.

Technically, the side-valve engine was in retreat, which made it all the more surprising that Nuffield introduced a brand-new side-valve engine for the new-generation Morris Oxford (MO Series) and elected to keep a side-valve 918cc unit for the Morris Minor when an overhead-valve version of that unit had already been developed for the Wolseley 8hp. The reason, it seems, is that an ohv-engined Minor would have out-performed an sv-engined Oxford!

Apart from the Jaguar XK engine, the outstanding technical innovation of the year was the original type of Rover automotive gas-turbine engine. This pioneering unit, designed by Frank Bell and a youthful Spencer King, had been running since early 1947, but was not made public until mid-1948.

Called T5, it was a 100bhp machine whose compressor turbine ran at speeds up to 55,000rpm (an unheard-of figure in those days), but it was extremely profligate in its use of kerosene. It was a thoroughly practical engine, being small and 200lb lighter than the existing Rover P3 75 piston engine, but although it was bench-tested, the world's first automotive gas turbine was never fitted to a car.

In fact, Rover was already planning to build a bigger and better unit to be fitted into a car, and it would produce some sensational performance figures when it appeared in 1950.

A minor point, perhaps, but sunroofs were rapidly falling out of fashion, for whereas most of the transitional prewar/postwar models had them, when these were dropped the replacement models invariably had a solid roof; not until the 1970s would the once so-popular sunroof make a comeback.

1949

After all the excitement of 1948 – reintroduction of a basic petrol ration, the announcement of so many new cars, and an extravagantly-staged Earls Court Motor Show in which to inspect them, 1949 seemed certain to be an anticlimax, and so it proved. Not only was there little improvement in the British motoring scene, but the flow of new cars almost dried up.

The majority of them were still being sent overseas to earn precious foreign currency, while the hated Covenant (which ensured that in Britain the first owner kept his car for at least 12 months), was extended to foreign visitors who bought their new cars in the UK.

Although the petrol ration was increased slightly during the summer months (a shrewd politician's move intended to encourage people at least to use their cars to go on holiday), there was still no sign of this restriction on motoring being lifted, even though there seemed to be plenty of oil and petrol in the world. After the French proposed to abandon all rationing during the year (while raising the price of petrol to damp down demand), *The Motor* ran an opinion column in which it was suggested: 'It appears fairly probable that Great Britain is about to become the last civilized nation to be burdened with petrol rationing.' (In fact, rationing was reintroduced in Australia for a short time in the autumn, but rescinded again for 1950.)

Thanks to the deletion of petrol rationing in Europe, intrepid tourists could roam much wider than before – if they could find funds from their limited travel allowance. This was the first postwar year when it was once again possible for tourists to visit Germany – to discover that four years after the war there was still much devastation to be cleared up.

The first so-called 'zebra' pedestrian crossings appeared on our roads in 1949, and rapidly spread all over the country, and to indicate that in one respect, at least, things were getting back to the 'good old days', the British motor industry finally beat the previous all-time production record by building 412,290 cars. Exports, at 257,250,

were also at an all-time high, but the good news for British buyers was that nearly 150,000 were also released for sale on the home market.

That most of the exports were going to North America, however, was a complete myth, as the following official figures for 1949 exports make clear:

Australia	84,670
Canada	31,213
South Africa	18,584
Belgium	11,628
New Zealand	11,553
Brazil	7,882
Ireland (Republic)	7,183
USA	6,716
Holland	6,376
Switzerland	5,285
All others	66,832

The hoped-for late-1940s bonanza in USA sales, in fact, had never materialized, and once postwar American cars became freely available the demand for British models virtually collapsed – as Austin had found to its cost.

Although theoretically there was still a ban on the import of foreign cars, SMMT statistics show that 1,868 machines were registered in the UK during the year. Some, for sure, were kit-built Citroens and Renaults, but clearly others were genuine imports, even though throughout the year there was still no price listing for imported European cars in any of the motoring magazines.

Not that this deterred the many manufacturers who opted for the 'Grand Gesture' in October: Buick, Cadillac, Chevrolet, Chrysler, Citroen, Delahaye, De Soto, Dodge, Fiat, Ford-USA, Hotchkiss, Hudson, Kaiser, Lancia, Lincoln, Mercury, Packard, Panhard, Peugeot, Plymouth, Pontiac, Renault and Studebaker all took stands at Earls Court, increasing greatly the variety of the occasion. Yet precious few of them could hope to sell new cars to British subjects because of the stringent import regulations of the day.

To remedy the country's economic situation, which was still well out of balance, in September 1949 the Government was obliged to devalue the pound against the American dollar by 30 per cent, from $4.03 to $2.80. This had the immediate effect of making British car exports cheaper, and therefore easier to sell, but of course it also

lifted the price of imports (including oil for the distillation of petrol) by the same amount.

New models

AC: A graceful drop-head coupe version of the 2-Litre was added to the range, without technical changes. Later in the year it was also joined by a five-seater sports tourer version of the same design.

Allard: For owners looking to use their two-seater cars in motorsport, the company made a larger V8 engine available as an aftermarket fitting. This Ford-USA (actually Mercury) unit measured 4,375cc, and fitted with Allard's own light-alloy cylinder heads it produced 115bhp.

Later in the year the first of the 'coil spring' cars was announced – this referring to the new front suspension layout of the J2 sportscar and P1 saloon models. The J2 was a simple but purposeful machine, nominally fitted with the 4.37-litre V8 engine, though a number of American customers bought their car without engine and chose one of the massively powerful Cadillac V8s instead.

The P1 saloon, previewed as early as 1946, finally went on sale with the same basic front-end style as other Allards covering a 3.5-litre Ford V8 engine, and with a four-seater, two-door cabin. Allard could not offer a great deal of refinement and grace, but it did offer truly effortless performance, although it would be 1952 (when Sydney Allard won the Monte Carlo rally in one of his own cars) before this model really hit the headlines.

Armstrong Siddeley: The Coventry company developed the existing range even further, principally by introducing an enlarged 75bhp/2,309cc engine and adding yet another derivative of the style, a four-door, four-light Whitley saloon.

Aston Martin: A new DB2 model was being developed with the Lagonda-type 2.6-litre twin-ohc engine. The first official news of this car came when pictures were released of what were coyly described as 'prototypes' which would race at Le Mans.

Even so, there was still no evidence of these as road cars at the Earls Court Motor Show in October.

Austin: Evidence that the A90 Atlantic was not selling well came when the British price was reduced and a cheaper version with a manually-operated soft-top was put on sale. Later in the year a sports saloon version was added, using the same basic style with a steel roof. It was a bold marketing move, but it failed to boost the car's appeal, even after a specially-prepared car had taken a series of high-speed endurance records (up to seven days duration at average speeds of around 72mph) at the Indianapolis race track in the USA.

Daimler: The existing range carried on for 1950, the major innovation being the new Consort six-light saloon, initially for export only, but listed in Britain by the autumn. The 2.5-litre Consort ran on the latest version of the DB18 chassis, but used a discreet new body style by Mulliners of Birmingham. As ever, the Daimler fluid flywheel/pre-selector transmission was standard.

Frazer Nash: Because the postwar chassis was so new, there were no basic changes for 1950. However, after a fine sporting performance during the year, the existing competition two-seater was renamed the Le Mans Replica. There was also a new Mille Miglia model, a road car with full-width two-seater sportscar styling on the same basic chassis.

Healey: The stark, much-lightened and totally sporting Silverstone version of the existing Healey chassis was put on sale. Although it never sold in large quantities, it became one of the most desirable of 'classic' Healeys. Compared with the other models, it had a very basic bodyshell, complete with cycle-type front wings and a spare wheel/tyre so mounted that the tyre actually operated as a rear bumper.

Hillman: Surprisingly, the Rootes Group made very little fuss about the enlargement of the engine in the Minx, which therefore moved from Phase III to Phase IV. The increase – from 1,185cc/35bhp to 1,265cc/38bhp – was the first since the engine had been launched back in 1931.

Humber: The only additional model was the Imperial, which was actually a saloon version of the Pullman. Normally this vast seven-seater would be kitted-out as a limousine, with a division, but this was deleted for the Imperial, though the fold-down occasional seating was retained. From 1949 to 1954 there would always be an Imperial version of Pullman models.

Jaguar: The company demonstrated the pace of the new XK120 sportscar by taking it to Belgium's Jabbeke highway, folding down the screen and unleashing it along the flat straight with R M V 'Soapy' Sutton driving, where it recorded a two-way speed over a mile of 132.596mph. Those who had not been impressed by the car as a static exhibit were now amazed by its obviously immense performance.

Jensen: The company finally admitted that the Meadows straight-eight engine had been a failure, and henceforth the Austin 4-litre engine would be fitted instead. Of more importance, though, was a preview of the new Interceptor range (originally a cabriolet, but later also to be available as a hardtop), whose smart new body style hid a modified Austin chassis into which a 3,993cc A135 engine and gearbox had been squeezed. Although not quite ready for production, when available it sold faster than the hapless PW model had ever done.

Austin's gift of the A70 chassis for this car had not been without strings – these being that Jensen would develop a similar (but smaller) style for a proposed Austin A40 Sports, the bodies for which would also come from Jensen! The A40 Sports, however, would not be launched until 1950.

Jowett: A new sports coupe called the ERA-Javelin was shown at Earls Court, though the car never went into production. It used a tubular chassis which had been designed at ERA by Professor Dr Ing Eberan von Eberhorst (of Auto Union GP car design fame) and would eventually form the basis for a new Jowett sportscar to be called the Jupiter – though this would not be revealed until 1950.

Mechanically, the ERA-Javelin was almost pure Javelin saloon, and the prototype as proposed was to have a smooth but rather anonymous two-door fixed-head coupe body.

Lanchester: Although there were no changes to the LD10's chassis, the original Briggs all-steel bodyshell was dropped in favour of a new (and more expensive) four-light coachbuilt saloon shell from Barker. This change was undoubtedly inspired by Briggs, who had become reluctant to supply such a limited number of all-steel shells.

Lea-Francis: A new 2½-litre engine was offered for both a six-light saloon, based on the style of the model which had been exported for some time, and for the existing sportscar. The sportscar was also given the torsion-bar front suspension of the latest saloon, as was the 14hp saloon, though for the time being the station wagon derivative kept its old half-elliptic springing.

Rolls-Royce: The company launched the Silver Dawn, while making it clear that it was for sale in export markets only (it would not become available in the UK until 1953). Except that it sported the usual patrician radiator grille and badge, the Silver Dawn was effectively a detuned version of the Bentley Mk VI, with a single-carburettor (Stromberg) version of the 4¼-litre engine, and it had a steering-column gearchange. The facia/instrument panel layout was also different from the Bentley's. [Before the Silver Dawn reached its first British customers it would receive a longer-tailed body, an automatic transmission option and the benefit of four years more development.]

Rover: The launch of a brand-new saloon – the P4 – came as a surprise so soon after the retro-style P3s had been put on the market, but after a production life of about 18 months the P3s were swept away and replaced by the definitive postwar Rover. At first it was only available as a 2.1-litre six-cylinder 75 model, which meant that there was no four-cylinder Rover currently available, thus breaking the tradition of several decades.

Soon christened 'Auntie' because of its gentle and rather matronly habits and character, the P4 had an entirely new full-width, four-door saloon body style, an immediate and obvious recognition point being the centrally-mounted 'Cyclops' driving lamp between but below the level of the main headlamps.

Under the skin there was yet another new chassis-frame – unlike the P3 frame this was conventional, with box-section side-members sweeping over the line of the back axle to the tail – though the front suspension, steering, engine and transmission were all as in the P3.

The P4 was commercially important, not merely because of its looks, but because of its implications to Rover. Having spent so much investment capital on a new all-steel shell from Pressed Steel, the company was then obliged to keep it going for some years. What no-one realized at the time was that this shape (modified a little over the years) would be around for the next 15 years, with several different engines, and that more than 130,000 examples would be produced.

Singer: Having so recently launched the SM1500 saloon, the only significant change made for 1950 was to fit the latest four-speed gearbox to the 9hp Roadster. At the same time the old Ten and Twelve models (1930s machines, really) were finally laid to rest.

Triumph: Early in the year the company leaked the news that it was developing a new small-engined model, but first official details of this machine, the Mayflower saloon, were held back until September. It was an intriguing mixture of old and new – new unit-construction two-door shell by Fisher and Ludlow, but old-type razor-edge styling, new independent front suspension, but old-type Standard side-valve engine. Clearly it was going to cost a lot more than the Standard 8hp car which had disappeared a year earlier, and a quick study showed that the chassis was distinctly over-engineered in some parts. [Three years into the future, the front suspension and rear axle would both be used in the Triumph TR2 sportscar.]

The styling was, let us say, controversial, for though it was meant to have visual links with the existing big Triumph saloon (soon to be renamed Renown) these sat awkwardly on a car with only an 84in wheelbase. One cynic described it tersely as 'Queen Anne front, Mary Anne sides'… The little four-cylinder engine, apart from a slightly smaller bore, was pure Standard Flying Ten, complete with side valves, though its power had been boosted a little since the late 1930s when that unit had been current. Strangely, Standard-Triumph does not seem to have considered using the overhead-valve version of this engine, which was already being supplied to Morgan.

Although not admitted at the time, the gearbox was from the Standard Vanguard, while the steering-column change was just awful. The Mayflower was not yet ready for sale, though, as the tooling was not complete – deliveries would begin in mid-1950.

In yet another step towards rationalization at Canley, Standard-Triumph also started building razor-edged Triumph saloons fitted with the Vanguard engine and three-speed gearbox (instead of the old 1.8-litre Standard Flying Fourteen unit), thus a short-lived car called the Triumph 2000 was born – the Renown name would not be adopted until the end of the year.

The Renown, in fact, used a totally different chassis-frame and suspension – a lengthened version of the Vanguard's chassis, which meant that there was now something approaching full rationalization of running gear at Canley.

In Sweden, **Saab** finally put the twin-cylinder 25bhp front-wheel-drive 92 model into production – though Saab cars would not be sold in the UK until 1960.

Industrial developments

After the extravagant new-model launches and displays of 1948, this was a relatively quiet year for Britain's car-makers. Because there were few new shapes there – among the family cars the Rover P4 and the Triumph Mayflower took most of the attention – Earls Court was a quieter place than it had been in the bedlam of 1948, attendance falling from 562,954 to 355,486.

Perhaps it was not thought important at the time, but in February Daimler's chairman, Sir Bernard Docker, married Lady Norah Collins. Later, Lady Docker would have great influence on Daimler's products – and their resultant publicity – which indirectly would inspire big changes at Daimler in the mid-1950s.

The new MIRA proving ground at Lindley airfield, near Nuneaton, was officially opened and instantly became a great success for the motor industry, for none of the Big Six had test tracks of their own – not until the 1960s would any of them take this big step.

Proof that Austin's ambitious push into North American markets had failed came with the news that 1,000 cars were to be shipped back to the UK for reconditioning and sale elsewhere. After all the fine words which had regularly poured out of Longbridge over the years, this was intensely embarrassing.

Renault became the second overseas manufacturer to restart the assembly of its cars in the UK. Kits of parts for the rear-engined 4CV model were sent over from Paris to the Renault-UK plant at Western Avenue, Acton, near London, where they were assembled. The only British content of these cars were the trim items.

Technical developments

Although 1949 was essentially a year of technical evolution rather than innovation, there was one important launch. Laycock introduced its new Laycock-de Normanville overdrive installation, a two-speed device intended for attaching to the back of any company's gearbox.

The importance of this installation, which had already been under test for some time, was that it would allow clutchless gearchanging, up or down, due to the use of an epicyclic chain of gears and a cone clutch. Operation of the clutch was hydraulic, though actuation was by an electric solenoid.

Testing began on a Standard Vanguard during the year, and although little was said about it, it was assumed that Standard-Triumph would be one of the first to offer this very important item as an optional extra.

1950

This was the year when motoring finally broke free of the after-effects of war. For British drivers the year's big news, of course, was the easing and finally the abandonment of petrol rationing, though this had to be tempered by a big rise in the excise duty on petrol, while for those wanting to go overseas on holiday the currency allowances were still very limited. All in all, though, the motoring atmosphere lightened considerably.

The excise duty on a gallon of petrol had been unchanged at 9d (3.75p) since 1938, but in his Budget speech of April 1950 the Chancellor, Sir Stafford Cripps, doubled it to 1s 6d (7.5p), which raised the price of a gallon to 3s 0d (15p). However, as a sop to the private motorist he also proposed to increase the petrol ration, effectively doubling it, although even this would only let drivers do about 180 miles per month.

The Government, despite having recently been re-elected, albeit with a tiny majority, was deeply unpopular, and this must have been a factor in the sudden announcement on May 26 that petrol rationing was to end immediately; there was no warning and no transitional period. Nor was there any improvement to petrol quality – everyone was still obliged to use the Government-imposed Pool petrol, whose octane rating was a mere 70–75; late in the year, a Government spokesman said that it was 'not possible' to raise the octane level to 80.

Except for one short period in 1956–57, this was the end of petrol rationing in the UK. First introduced in September 1939, and leading to a complete ban on private motoring between July 1942 and June 1945, it was always a totally inadequate ration, and there had even been a six-month peacetime period in 1947–48 when it had been withdrawn once again.

The motorists' media was both ecstatic and scandalized by the manner in which rationing had ended – if it could end so suddenly, why had not more supplies been made available earlier? The good news for the motor industry was that it was bound to increase the demand for new cars; the bad news for customers was that it was

going to make waiting lists longer than ever, and of course used car values jumped immediately. Not surprisingly, attendance at the Motor Show recovered sharply – for no fewer than 475,326 visited Earls Court in October.

In another sop to the hard-pressed car-makers, the double purchase tax (66⅔ per cent) which had been introduced in 1947 for cars whose basic price was £1,000 or more, was dropped in the 1950 Budget. There was no effect, of course, on the cost of the typical family car – it was the Daimlers, Healeys, Aston Martins and Bentleys which benefited most.

The Government insisted that once again home-market supplies of new cars would have to be limited in 1950, setting a maximum allocation of a mere 110,000, though in the event production boomed so much that almost 135,000 would be registered. The final disappointment of the year was that the period of the Covenant (which legally obliged new-car owners to keep their machines for a minimum period after purchase) was doubled from one to two years.

The industry set yet another production record, 522,515 cars being produced – more than 10,000 a week – of which nearly 400,000 went overseas. Much of the export boom was a direct result of British prices being lower after the devaluation of the previous year. Once again official imports of new cars were not allowed, apart from the locally assembled Citroens and Renaults from imported kits.

Obstacles still faced foreign travel, adults being restricted to £50 of foreign currency and children £35 – the extra allowance for the use of a car being a miserable £10, later raised to £15. It was being promised that for 1951 the £50 allowance would be doubled.

New models

Allard: Continuing the process started with the J2 and P1 models in 1949, the small London company introduced the second-generation tourer, the K2, using the new coil-spring front-end. At the same time an Ardun-headed version of the V8 engine was previewed, though very few cars fitted with it would ever be delivered.

Alvis: The company was finally ready to introduce its postwar model, the TA21 3-litre saloon. Although new in every detail – the overhead-valve six-cylinder engine, transmission, chassis-frame (complete with coil-spring independent suspension) and handsome if traditionally-styled four-door bodyshell – there was nothing technically exciting in its design, and many observers wondered why it had taken five years to get it to the showrooms.

The engine was a nicely-detailed in-line 'six' which at first was very conservatively rated at 86bhp, or a mere 29bhp/litre, and clearly Alvis was in no mood yet to press it further. The same engine in progressively developed form would be used on every new Alvis until the last car was built in 1967 – by which time it was developing no less than 150bhp.

Described even then as a modern classic, the 90mph TA21 was an elegant and refined gentleman's carriage, and it was sold at a price level which ensured that it remained rather exclusive, too!

Later in the year, the company combined this new chassis with a development of the TB14 sports tourer's bodyshell (though with a much more graceful front-end style), to produce the TB21 sports tourer. Like the obsolete TA14, this car was so far out of character with Alvis' developing image that demand was virtually non-existent.

Aston Martin: The long-awaited DB2 finally went into production during 1950, an event which had been forecast ever since prototypes of this sleek machine had raced at Le Mans in 1949.

By gathering together the assets of both the Aston Martin and Lagonda businesses which he had bought in 1947, David Brown had inspired his engineers to produce a fine new car. The multi-tubular chassis was a development of that used in the very limited-production DB1, while the 2.6-litre twin-cam engine and gearbox were as already used in the Lagonda models, but the smart two-seater fastback coupe was unique to this car.

At £1,915 (compared, for instance, with the £1,263 asked for the faster Jaguar XK120) the handbuilt DB2 was clearly an expensive proposition, but it had such an appealing combination of modern technology, good looks and a capable chassis that everyone who could afford one made haste to order one.

The coil-spring/trailing-arm front suspension was like that of the Healey in concept, though not in detail, while the whole of the front of the body hinged up (from the nose) to let mechanics get at the nicely-styled twin-cam engine. Surprisingly, a steering-column gear-change was offered at first (but how many DB2s have you seen with one?).

This model family was important to Aston Martin and destined for a long life, for there would be no new chassis to replace it until 1958.

Austin: Although the hapless A90 Atlantic continued, the A70 Hampshire was shelved after only two years, being replaced by the A70 Hereford. This used the same basic chassis and 2.2-litre engine, but with a roomier and more rounded body, which was available as a four-door saloon or a two-door drop-head coupe.

Austin also announced the A40 Sports, a car with a much less sporting character than its name and looks implied. The four-seater open-top body, styled and built by Jensen, hid nothing more exciting than an A40 Devon chassis with a slightly more powerful (46bhp) version of the 1.2-litre engine.

During this period Austin was clearly out of touch with what sporting motorists wanted; it would be two years before Len Lord made his historic deal with Donald Healey to invent the Austin-Healey marque.

Early in the year the prototype of a new military-market 4x4, dubbed the FV1800, was previewed. This would eventually go into production at Long-bridge, and in the mid-1950s a few civilian versions, called Austin Champs, would be sold.

The FV1800 had a strange 4x4 layout, with the front-mounted engine driving the rear axle through a normal propeller-shaft, while a separate long propeller-shaft linked the front and rear axles. There was no central transfer box of the type that are now commonplace on four-wheel-drive vehicles.

Ford: Without a doubt, the new Consul/Zephyr models vied with Jaguar's Mk VII for the title of Star of the Motor Show – and commercially there was no doubt they were the runaway winners.

More than five years after the war Ford had finally launched their definitive postwar family saloons. Although their styling was directly influenced by the latest Ford-USA models, there were no shared parts, and they were packed full of innovation. Except that they had different wheelbase lengths, the Consul (four-cylinder) and Zephyr (six-cylinder) saloons shared the same unit-construction four-door bodyshell. The engines were from a brand-new overhead-valve family, the gearboxes were new three-speed assemblies with steering-column change, and there was MacPherson-strut independent front suspension.

Although the facia layout was distinctly ordinary, and slippery bench front seats were standard, they were clearly very capable machines. Even though they soon acquired a reputation for being tail-happy (particularly the Zephyrs, which were more nose-heavy than the Consuls), they still handled better than any previous Ford had ever done.

These cars replaced the elephantine old V8 Pilot models and technically were a quantum leap ahead of them. Rivals shuddered when they realized that Ford was now building such advanced machines, having recovered at a stroke all the lost ground of the last two decades.

Keenly priced (£544 for the Consul), these cars were immediately competitive on value, looks and specification. Production took a while to begin, but within two years the cars would transform Dagenham, Ford's British dealerships and the company's market share.

Humber: The Hawk, still only two years old as a basic design, was given a larger engine of 2,276cc, but still with side valves.

Jaguar: By almost any standards the new Mk VII was an astonishing car. Although its chassis was a modified version of the Mk V, which the new car replaced, and the XK engine was already being used in the XK120 sportscar, the vast four-door saloon bodyshell was brand-new and the overall effect was stunning.

Not only was this a very fast car (top speed comfortably over 100mph), it was roomy, graceful by any reckoning and, as usual with a Jaguar, it was

being offered at a remarkably low price – £1,276. William Lyons had taken pains to produce a massive shape which was easy on the eye from all angles, one that was quite clearly evolved from the themes of the Mk V and XK120 and would definitely appeal to buyers in overseas markets.

The Mk VII was the first of a whole series of big Jaguars, for this shape would persist until 1961 – a production life of 11 years.

Jowett: Having shown the new tubular chassis at the previous Earls Court Motor Show, Jowett revealed the definitive Jupiter in March, abandoning the idea of building a coupe and instead offering the car as a smart three-seater open roadster with wind-up door windows and a two-piece windscreen.

The Jupiter's chassis-frame was a stiffened-up derivative of that shown in 1949, with further rearward extensions, but the running gear was otherwise pure Javelin. Although constructed from aluminium pressings on a tubular framework, the bodies were virtually hand-built, which meant a high price, this being one reason why sales were so restricted in what was to be only a three-year career.

Eight years later the 'frogeye' Austin-Healey Sprite would copy two of the features introduced on the Jupiter – the use of a massive one-piece lift-up bonnet/front wings assembly, and the omission of a separate bootlid. Access to the luggage area had to be by way of folding down the seats in the cockpit.

Lanchester: This Daimler-owned marque produced a neat, though somehow staid and rather old-fashioned middle-class machine – the Fourteen – which, unknown at the time, was something of a market-tester for the Daimler Conquest which would follow in 1953.

The motoring press called it all-new, which was almost correct except that the traditional type of Daimler pre-selector transmission was specified. Certainly it had nothing in common with the current (and much smaller) Lanchester LD10, nor even with the Daimler DB18/Consort models which were also being built at Radford at the time.

The chassis-frame was a sturdy box-section item, there was torsion-bar independent front suspension with laminated bars, and the engine was a 2-litre four-cylinder unit, the first example of a four/six-cylinder family which would be used on many new Lanchester and Daimler cars in future years.

The original six-window body style was a Barker coachbuilt four-door saloon (with wooden framing as the basis of the structure), but when export models, called Ledas, were put on sale they were equipped with all-steel lookalikes. But, as one sage later remarked, don't get excited – both varieties rust!

Marauder: The small Dorridge (Birmingham) company of Wilks, Mackie & Co introduced a heavy three-seater roadster based on the shortened chassis of the Rover 75 saloon. Of the three people involved in the design of this car, Peter Wilks was a nephew of S B Wilks, the chairman of Rover.

Mechanically, the Marauder was almost pure Rover P4, though a high-compression engine was fitted, and although the rear-end body style looked like that of the P4, the shell (by Richard Mead) was mostly unique. On the original car, a special overdrive by H & A Engineering, of Surrey, was fitted.

At £1,333 this was an expensive car, and because it cost more than a Jaguar XK120 and was much slower it could not be expected to sell in large numbers. In the end only 15 of the very graceful machines would be built – almost all of them surviving into the 'classic' 1990s.

MG: The launch of the new TD Midget was very important to MG as the TC model which it replaced had been looking technically obsolete for some time. Developed in double-quick time, the TD effectively used the existing TC engine and transmission in a reworked Y-type chassis layout, all topped off with a new, but still square-rigged, two-seater body.

Although it was simple to describe the TD in this way, quite a lot more was involved. Compared with the Y-type, of course, the wheelbase was shorter and the engine more powerful, and this was the first MG production sportscar to use independent front suspension, rack-and-pinion steering – and disc wheels.

Commercially, too, the TD was

important as the first MG sportscar to be offered with left-hand as well as right-hand steering. Sales of the TC to North America had been encouraging enough, but this was always with right-hand-drive cars; now, with an LHD option, more Americans would surely be tempted to buy?

Morgan: The original 4/4, whose roots were in 1936, was finally abandoned in favour of a new Plus 4 model, which looked virtually the same, but was different in many ways.

The Plus 4 had a longer wheelbase, but it retained the traditional Morgan features of sliding-pillar front suspension, rock-solid rear springs and a wooden-framed body in a style which was already looking old-fashioned, but which the company insisted was 'typically Morgan', steadfastly refusing to be bounced into making changes for fashion's sake.

The engine came from the Standard Vanguard, the separately-mounted gearbox was built by Moss, and the overall character of the car was much as before, but larger, heavier, faster, more costly – and more capable. Morgan never did anything in a hasty manner, so the Plus 4 was destined for a long and successful life – after 18 years, four body derivatives, several engine tune-ups and myriad development changes, its successor would still look very similar to the Plus 4!

Paramount: A small Derbyshire-based concern previewed a four-seater convertible using Ford running gear, with a bodyshell somewhat influenced by the current Sunbeam-Talbot models. Its chassis featured independent front suspension by transverse leaf spring, and power was by Ford's side-valve 1,172cc Prefect unit.

Although the body was panelled in aluminium, this car's problems were its lack of performance and its relatively high price. It was difficult for drivers to get excited about its very humdrum specification, so the Paramount had a great deal of difficulty in establishing a market.

Rolls-Royce: The first of a very limited number of Phantom IV models, complete with 5.7-litre straight-eight engine and an H J Mulliner limousine body, was delivered to HRH Princess Elizabeth. Rolls-Royce never intended to put

this chassis into series production, preferring to limit supply to royalty and to foreign heads of state.

Technically, the chassis was a stretched version of the Silver Wraith, while the engine was also a close relative of the rationalized R-R/Bentley six-cylinder design. Prices were never released...

Singer: The company continued to tinker, this time rejigging the 1930s-style Roadster with a chassis featuring independent front suspension, this being a development of that used in the SM1500 saloon.

Standard: Laycock overdrive became optional on the Vanguard – a 'world first' for the company, shared with the Triumph Renown, but it cost a lot of money – nearly £64 (about £950 at mid-1990s values).

Sunbeam-Talbot: Having dropped the underpowered 80 model, Rootes introduced the much-improved 90 as a Mk II version. Although it looked virtually the same as before (you had to be a real rivet-counter to notice that the headlamp height had been raised...), there was a brand-new chassis-frame under the skin, complete with independent front suspension, while the engine had been enlarged to 2,276cc, a capacity which would be used on Sunbeams and Humbers for the next 17 years. Not only did this make the 90 a more saleable proposition, it helped to make the works rally cars even more successful than before.

Triumph: Laycock overdrive became optional on the Renown – at the same price as applied to the Standard Vanguard.

There were two new models at the Earls Court Motor Show, neither of which went into series production. The Mayflower drop-head coupe was a good idea which proved to be too expensive to build in small numbers; after a mere 10 cars had been 'knife-and-forked' during the winter of 1950/51 it was abandoned.

The TRX Roadster, theoretically a replacement for the old 2000 Roadster which had been abandoned a year earlier, might have looked super-modern, but would also have been too costly to make in series. It was based on a Standard Vanguard chassis, though with a twin-SU carburettor/ unique cylinder head version of that car's engine, and a four-speed gearbox with overdrive. It had a swoopy-styled bodyshell with concealed headlamps, wind-up windows, but no dickey seat, and was stuffed with a variety of electro-hydraulic features to operate things like headlamp covers, seat adjustment, window lifts and soft-top folding and unfurling.

Body engineer Walter Belgrove had been given his head with this project, but Sir John Black must surely not have been looking, for this was an utterly impractical car. The complicated gizmos always seemed to give trouble (one car reputely disgraced itself on the Motor Show stand in front of VIPs!), and once the cost accountants had run their sliderules over the specification it was speedily consigned to the 'waste-of-time' bin. Two of the three proto-types have survived.

Industrial developments

At the end of the year came the interesting news that Jaguar had acquired the lease on a 600,000sq ft factory at Browns Lane, Allesley, Coventry and proposed to move its entire car-making business into this former aero-engine plant as soon as possible.

Although Jaguar's existing factory in Swallow Road, Foleshill, Coventry had been expanded enormously since the first SS cars had been built in 1931, it was too small for what William Lyons had in mind for the future. Although Jaguar was currently producing about 6,600 cars a year, the boss already had plans to add another product line to his range and wanted to increase annual output to well over 20,000.

The move from Foleshill to Allesley would not be complete until 1952, but it was done progressively. For a time, parts of Jaguars were being made in two different factories, but amazingly there seemed to be virtually no loss of production.

Invicta, whose complex and expen-

sive Black Prince car had sold very slowly indeed, finally closed its doors after only 25 such cars had been delivered. Shortly, AFN (who built Frazer Nash cars) would buy the remnants of the company from the Receiver, but they never attempted to build Invicta cars again.

According to AFN historian Denis Jenkinson, the Aldington family who owned AFN were much more interested in the plant and machinery and: 'This acquisition kept AFN supplied with nuts, bolts and spring washers for many years to come!'

The American Nash company had started looking around for a European car-maker to help it build a new very small model for supply to the North American market. This car would eventually mature as the Nash Metropolitan, made by BMC at Longbridge, but during 1950 there were extensive negotiations with Standard-Triumph, with a view to using Triumph Mayflower running gear in a Nash-styled and engineered shell.

Soon afterwards those negotiations petered out, and it became known that Fiat was also trying to get Nash's business. What no-one knew then was that this saga had much longer to run before any contracts would be exchanged.

Technical developments

Although it would never have a significant effect on production cars of the future, the most exciting technical launch of the year was the demonstration of Rover's original gas-turbine car (later to be registered, and always known as JET 1).

Based on the chassis of the new P4 model and using the same nose and general proportions (the original car used the Cyclops nose of the P4 saloons), JET 1 was styled and constructed as a two-seater tourer with neither hood nor sidescreens, and it had its 200bhp gas-turbine engine mounted behind the driver (but ahead

of the driven rear wheels).

In many ways JET 1 was a real mongrel or paradox, with a space-age engine mounted in an extremely stodgy chassis, and with 'Auntie Rover' styling, but even so everyone became excited about this new concept when it first appeared. In March 1950 the press watched as it was demonstrated at Silverstone by Rover's principal governing directors, Spencer and Maurice Wilks, plus designer Spen King and even – briefly – Mrs Spencer Wilks.

Rover was at pains to emphasize that JET 1 was merely a research project, a car which currently was colossally costly to build and with a great thirst for kerosene, but there was no doubt that it was seriously hoping to turn this into a commercially viable machine.

From Ford, of all people (who hitherto had been renowned for making positively old-fashioned cars), came the very first use of a new type of independent front suspension known as MacPherson strut, named after its inventor, the American Erle MacPherson. Totally familiar these days, it was new, mysterious and very strange-looking in 1950.

The secret of the strut was that the wheel's kingpin, or kingpost, as it was generally known, was integrated with the long coil-spring/damper unit, which was fixed to a turret high up in the body monocoque. The wheel's location was ensured by a single transverse link and the swinging arm of the anti-roll bar, which also acted as the forward member of a 'bottom wishbone'.

Not only was this simple and therefore cost-effective to use, it also spread the loads – and the noise paths – widely around the shell, thus cutting down on any incipient noise and vibration problems. Within 20 years it would have become virtually the industry's standard for front suspension layouts.

Lucas also broke away from the habits of a generation by introducing double-dipping headlamp bulbs and lenses to match. This might look minor today, but it certainly seemed (and was) significant at the time.

1951

This was a pivotal year for motoring and the motorist. Although restrictions on pleasure motoring were as severe as ever, there were forecasts of fun, prosperity and the ready supply of cars and petrol in the near future; all this in a year when purchase tax on cars shot up and BP's largest oil refinery, in Iran, was nationalized and expropriated by that state!

At the beginning of the year, the hard-pressed British motor industry had been told that it could only allocate 80,000 new cars to the British market (later that restriction would be dramatically loosened, for 138,000 were actually sold before December 31), but there were greater shocks to follow in April.

In his Budget, the Chancellor, Hugh Gaitskell, announced what the media of the day called two vicious anti-motorist measures: excise duty on a gallon of petrol was raised from 1s 6d (7.5p) to 1s 10½d (9.4p) and purchase tax on *all* new cars was doubled – from 33⅓ to 66⅔ per cent.

Although politicians assured anyone who would listen that this impost was meant to be 'temporary', no-one believed them. Instead, people gritted their teeth, realized that motoring was still much more of an expensive toil than a pleasure, and carried on saving harder.

Doubling the tax had this effect on several popular cars:

	Old price	New price
Morris Minor 2-door	£426	£520
Austin A40 Devon	£537	£655
Ford Consul	£544	£663
Rover P4 75	£1,164	£1,417

– while this was how elite cars suffered:

Bentley Mk VI	£3,674	£4,474
Daimler Consort	£1,764	£2,148
Rolls-Royce Silver Wraith	£5,246	£6,387

This was a shattering blow, which did nothing to sustain the popularity of the administration, and after several Government defeats in the House of Commons it was almost inevitable that another General Election had to be called. *The Motor's* editorial called the Budget 'Dangerous Folly' and wrote: 'It is inconceivable that...a responsible Government can remain unaware of the damage done.' – which was a sentiment with which everyone agreed.

The General Election finally took place on October 25 and resulted in a tiny swing, which returned a Conservative Government to office. Would a change from left-wing to right-wing politics bring big changes for motorists? Would the new Chancellor, R A Butler, be more sympathetic than Hugh Gaitskell had been? It didn't look like it, for one of the new Chancellor's first actions was to cut back the foreign travel allowance from £100 to £50 per person – and there was worse to come.

Even so, it wasn't all bad news, for Esso's huge oil refinery at Fawley (near Southampton) finally went into full production (it had been officially opened by the Labour Prime Minister, Clement Attlee, in September), while a vast new sheet steel works at Margam, near Port Talbot, in South Wales, also came on stream. With petrol and sheet steel supplies looking up, could real motoring freedom be far behind?

Meanwhile, things were getting back to near-normal in Germany in more ways than one. Most of the wartime damage to roads and bridges had been repaired, which meant that long stretches of autobahn were once again open. The first postwar Frankfurt motor show was held, while Mercedes-Benz also introduced its first true postwar models, the tubular-chassis six-cylinder 300 family.

The UK market remained totally reserved for British cars, imports of foreign cars still being forbidden. Frequently, interesting foreign cars would be described by the motoring media, but only as a technical exercise, with a bit of 'wouldn't it be nice...?' comment attached. British car production, in fact, was slightly down compared with 1950 – entirely due to material shortages – while home deliveries remained static.

In spite of the continuing import ban, no fewer than 31 foreign marques were exhibited at the Earls Court Motor Show, and a total of 3,723 foreign cars were registered in the UK during the year. Many of the Earls Court exhibits were American machines, and mainly of interest to US servicemen stationed in Britain or on the mainland of Europe.

Taking one's car to the Continent by air had become very fashionable and Silver City Airways was booming. A new route – Southampton to Cherbourg – was opened as an alternative to Lympne–Le Touquet, while other routes, notably Southend–Ostend, were also being considered; the Southend route would be inaugurated in 1952. Silver City ordered six of the latest long-nose Bristol aircraft, which would allow three of almost any type of cars to be carried.

New models

Austin: The most important car at the Earls Court Motor Show (though deliveries would not begin until May 1952) was undoubtedly the all-new Austin A30 – or Austin Seven, as the company tried to title it during the first few months of its life. This was one of those very rare products – a car that was all-new from stem to stern, including engine, transmission and monocoque, and moreover one set to be a deadly and cheaper rival to Nuffield's Morris Minor.

Austin dealers were delighted to welcome this tiny saloon, especially at such a bargain price, as the company had not been in the 'small car' business sector since the old Austin Big Seven disappeared in 1939.

Designed to take advantage of Austin's brand new and ultra-modern car assembly building (CAB1), which had been completed in 1951, the A30 was a short, narrow and distinctly marginally-sized four-seater model, initially sold only as a four-door saloon, but with a two-door version already on the way. Coil-spring independent front suspension incorporated a lever-arm damper as its upper member.

The overhead-valve engine – it would eventually become known as the A-series – was totally new, and although it only produced 30bhp from 803cc at this time, tuners soon found that there was a lot of built-in stretch – and potential. Even though there were only five cylinder head ports for four cylinders (siamesing was rife) Harry Weslake had had a hand in shaping the combustion spaces. [That engine, in much-developed guise, was still being built at Longbridge more than 40 years later, latterly for fitment to the Mini.] Backed by a tiny new four-speed gearbox and hypoid-bevel axle, this had been a massive investment on which Austin planned to capitalize during the 1950s.

Provisionally it was priced at £520, a figure which no doubt horrified Nuffield's sales force, whose equivalent four-door Minor cost £632, or 22 per cent more – a huge gap in marketing terms. No doubt they breathed a sigh of relief when the BMC merger erupted, bringing the realization that the two cars would, after all, be in reluctant harness.

Bentley: In mid-year it was announced that Mk VIs would henceforth be built with 4,556cc instead of 4,257cc six-cylinder engines, though as ever the power and torque outputs were not revealed. The same change was also made to current Rolls-Royce models.

Daimler: Postwar expansion continued with the (rather premature) launch of the 3-litre Empress model, which proved to be the first of a whole range of modern six-cylinder Daimlers culminating in the Majestics of the early 1960s.

Here was a brand-new 114in-wheelbase, box-section chassis-frame with coil-spring independent front suspension, hydro-mechanical brakes (these wouldn't last indefinitely), the usual Daimler preselector transmission and an overhead-valve engine which was the six-cylinder version of the Lanchester Fourteen's 'four' and was a thorough redesign of the Consort's layout.

The style, in general, looked like that of the Lanchester Fourteen, though there were no common panels. In its initial form it was a big and spacious four-door, five-seater saloon, with a walnut facia and, naturally, the preselector's control lever in a quadrant on the steering column.

The Regency was an expensive machine, designed to slot in above the Consort and to take over from the bigger, heavier, more old-fashioned DE27 (4-litre) which had just been dropped. Daimler also exhibited a Hooper-bodied DE36 Straight Eight at Earls Court, whose only function was to show off the gold-plated metalwork and the star-spangled treatment on its side panels. This had been done as an indulgence for Lady Docker, and it

attracted mountains of national newspaper publicity.

Ford: Less than a year after the new Consul/Zephyr range went into production, the company produced a much more satisfactory facia for it, which incorporated grouped instruments and a full-width parcel shelf. At the same time a convertible version of the Zephyr was launched, with bodies assembled by the soft-top experts, Carbodies of Coventry.

Healey: The Nash-Healey sportscar, exclusively for sale in the USA, was put on show for the first time at the Chicago Auto Show in February. In October, by permutating its resources as much as possible, Healey also produced the Sports Convertible or 3-litre. This combined the existing chassis with a modified version of the original Nash-Healey body style, but was powered by the latest Alvis 3-litre six-cylinder engine. With a similar price to existing Healey production cars, this should have sold better than it did – but in any case Healey was far too busy producing Nash-Healeys to send to the United States for this to be a problem!

Jaguar: With the all-steel body for the XK120 now settled into production, Jaguar next added a curvaceous fixed-head coupe version to the range. Mechanically there were no changes, but the new type – for export only at first – had a deeper V-screen, a bubble-top steel roof, wind-up door windows, a wooden facia board and a nicely-trimmed interior. As expected, it had an even higher top speed than the open roadster, but was as docile and flexible as the original type.

After a winter of changeover to the Mk VII, the last Mk V was produced.

Jensen: A saloon (really a hardtop) version of the existing Interceptor cabriolet was announced, this being achieved without changing either the running gear or the seating space of the car.

Lanchester: A smart drop-head coupe version of the Fourteen, with coachwork by Carbodies, was introduced, though very few appear to have been sold. As with the saloon, this was a forerunner of the DHC style

to be offered on the larger-engined Daimler Conquest in a few years' time. This was also the year in which the last of the 'retired Colonel' LD10 models was built.

Morris: The revised, high-headlamp front-end style of the Morris Minor, which had been used on export models for some time, was finally standardized for cars delivered to British customers.

Rolls-Royce: As with Bentley, Rolls-Royce began fitting the 4,556cc version of the six-cylinder engine in place of the original 4,257cc unit.

Singer: By rejigging its existing resources, the company produced yet another version of the long-established Roadster, the new SM1500 Roadster having the latest independent front-end AB-type chassis-frame with the SM1500's engine, though the styling was not changed. It was not immediately available on the home market, and was never listed in 1951.

Interestingly, the stroke of the engine was made slightly shorter so that the displacement measured 1,497cc to bring it within the 1.5-litre category; soon after, the tiny reduction of 9cc was also made to SM1500 saloons.

Triumph: By lengthening the Standard Vanguard-based chassis by 3 inches and totally rejigging the detail of the Renown's razor-edge style, the company produced a more exclusive and expensive Limousine version. At first glance the two bodies looked identical, but there were subtle differences in most panels. Apart from lengthening the propeller-shaft and stiffening the suspension there were no mechanical changes.

In 1952 the Renown saloon would also adopt the Limousine's chassis length and structure, so there was considerable rationalization in the last two years of this range's life.

Vauxhall: 1951 was a very important year for the Luton-based company, which launched a new range of E-type Wyvern/Velox saloons, the first with all-postwar bodywork. Although these retained the old-style engines and three-speed transmissions from the obsolete L-types, the new range had totally fresh, transatlantic-styled four-door saloon monocoques and (for the first time on a Vauxhall) coil-spring independent front suspension.

Although no heavier, the E-types were larger and considerably more roomy than the old L-types with their late-1930s-style cabin dimensions; the new cars' shape was clearly inspired by the 1949 Chevrolets, with perhaps a hint of the first-generation Australian Holdens. They would remain in production for six years (new-generation engines were being developed and would follow in 1952) and would sell widely. Unhappily, they soon earned a reputation for premature rusting, and very few have survived.

Industrial developments

On November 23, 1951 came news that Austin and the Nuffield Organisation were preparing to merge. This momentous announcement would lead to the foundation of the British Motor Corporation (BMC) and was really the first step along the very tempestuous road to the formation of British Leyland in 1968.

To quote Graham Turner's excellent book *The Leyland Papers*:

'Lord once remarked that they [Austin and Morris] were like two Second Division teams trying to play in the First Division. Altogether, there seemed to be a good deal of logic in a merger: the only trouble was that Nuffield and Lord had not been on speaking terms for a long time.'

[We now know that it was Lord Nuffield's personal secretary, Carl Kingerlee, who eventually brought the two tycoons back together again, but that was in 1950, and all merger proposals were vetoed by the Nuffield board at the time. Lord then said that he would have to put the new A30 into production, and that this would be bad news for Nuffield. The final series of successful talks did not take place until a year later...]

Although Lord Nuffield was nominated as chairman of the new combine and Leonard Lord became deputy chairman and managing director, it was always clear that Lord would be the policy-forming executive while Lord Nuffield would become the elder statesman; Lord, after all, was only 55 years old while Nuffield was already 74.

News of the merger (which was a merger, for no shares, cash or other capital changed hands in either direction) came as a complete surprise to the motoring world, the City of London and, most especially, the 42,000 workers who made up the combined workforce of the new combine. So the Big Six became the Big Five when BMC formally came into existence on March 31, 1952, by which time a good deal of forward-planning, particularly regarding new models, had already taken place.

Just before this, the Nuffield Organisation had made much of the production of the 2,000,000th Morris car, which was carefully stage-managed to leave the assembly lines at Cowley on Lord Nuffield's 74th birthday!

Jaguar, in the meantime, steadily transferred its entire business – department by department – from Swallow Road to Allesley, and still found time to build up a racing team and win Le Mans at its first attempt!

There were two interesting personal promotions during 1951, which eventually would have far-reaching effects on two of Britain's car-makers. Alick Dick (who had been Sir John Black's personal assistant for some time) became Standard's deputy managing director, while Peter Morgan became deputy governing director of the family-owned Morgan Motor Company.

Later that year (although this was not made public for many years), Standard tried to take over Morgan, but were rebuffed, this being one of the major reasons why Sir John Black then authorized work on a new Triumph sportscar – the TR2. When Sir John's erratic management methods finally became too despotic in 1953/54 it would be Alick Dick who would lead the directors' coup which unseated him.

Technical developments

The most notable advances of 1951 came in motor racing, where Jaguar's new XK120C (which soon became known as the C-type) not only featured a multi-tubular chassis-frame, but also had a very smooth body shaped to provide low wind-resistance rather than a recognizable Jaguar style. This was only the start of the aerodynamic revolution which would sweep through British motorsport – and eventually through the ranks of road-going sportscars – in the next decade or so.

1952

Although the whole nation was saddened by the unexpected death of HM King George VI in February, there was general delight at the opening of what Fleet Street began to call 'The New Elizabethan Age'. In many ways the beginning of a new reign also signalled the beginning of a happier and more prosperous period in British history.

First indications, on the other hand, were that the recent change of Government was going to do little for the British motorist, though later in the year the atmosphere lightened considerably.

In February, the Chancellor stated that he would only authorize the delivery of 60,000 cars to the home market during 1952. With orders known to exceed 1.25 million, clearly this was a ludicrous suggestion, and in the end the politicians had to make a complete turnabout, and treble the intended number were eventually delivered.

The change of heart came in mid-summer (by which time 50,000 of the original 60,000 had already been delivered!), when the Ministry of Supply initiated a rather flexible quota system instead, and for the first time since 1945 waiting lists began to fall, albeit slowly.

In mid-summer the much-criticized Covenant restrictions were partly lifted. A list of 19 marques was freed from this restriction of the movement of new cars to their second owners. Almost all the names on the list were small independent concerns, or selected models from the Big Five which were slow sellers...

The process then accelerated later in the year, and by September, more than half of all British cars listed had been freed from the Covenant, including several popular models such as the Austin A70 and the Humber Hawk. Weeks later, more cars, including all Bentleys and Rolls-Royces, MGs, Standard Vanguards and the Wolseley range, were also freed, and soon only the fast-selling products of the Big Five were still affected. Then the Covenant period on these remaining cars was cut from two years to one; the end of this much-hated scheme (but one which had proved gratifyingly easy for the Government to enforce) seemed to be in sight by the end of the year.

In another move to contain car-buying demand, hire purchase restrictions were imposed for the first time – requiring a 33⅓ per cent deposit, with the balance to be paid off within 18 months. This was the first of many different regulations which would apply to hire purchase in the next three decades.

The foreign touring spending allowance was slashed once again – this time to a mere £25 – and the car expenses allowance also came down, from £25 to £15. The intention was to save on foreign currency by making it economically impossible for people to take their holidays abroad – and as a strategy this worked very well.

Only a few weeks later, in the Budget, the Government once again increased the excise duty on petrol – this time to a total of 2s 6d (12.5p) a gallon, which brought the average price of the gallon to about 4s 2½d (21p). At least the tax 'take' then stabilized for a time, for with one temporary exception (in 1956–57) there would be no further changes until 1961.

At the same time, though, the annual licence fee was raised to £12 10s (£12.50) on all but the smallest cars, this being the start of a creeping tax increase which has continued ever since.

New models

Allard: The new Safari estate car was produced, on the basis of the latest chassis, this being the first really new style and body assembly from Allard since the marque had come into existence in 1946. The final X-type chassis of the big Allards was used in de Dion rear suspension guise. Although still a two-door machine, with smoother front-end detailing (in which the radiator air intakes were shaped like an A (for Allard) it was a big and heavy device, with wooden bracing to the estate car bodyshell, and a claimed 45 cubic feet of storage capacity behind the rear seats.

Before the end of the year the saloon type had been brought technically into line and dubbed Monte Carlo, after Sydney Allard's famous rally victory, while a new body style of three-seater tourer (the K3) was also added, but the time for technical innovation was past, and Allard's reputation began to slide.

The all-new Palm Beach sports models, with a choice of Ford Consul (four-cylinder) or Zephyr (six-cylinder) engines, were launched in October, but although these tubular-chassis cars were smart and neatly styled, they were far too expensive to have a chance of selling against the two major new sportscars (Austin-Healey 100 and Triumph TR2) previewed at the same Motor Show.

The Allard marque, in fact, was already slipping rapidly towards extinction. In the late 1940s, when there was a shortage of new cars on the market, they sold steadily, but as the supply situation eased they struggled against much cheaper and better-engineered machinery.

Armstrong Siddeley: Six years after the original postwar range had gone on sale, the Coventry company reshuffled its body styles, dropping the original Lancaster six-light saloon and replacing it by a six-light version of the more recent Whitley. The chassis, complete with its 2.3-litre six-cylinder engine and (on most cars) the preselector transmission, was unchanged. By Motor Show time the cheapest of these graceful cars cost £1,557.

To join them, and soon to take over, the all-new Sapphire was introduced in October, a big, graceful and potentially fast car which gave Jaguar great cause for thought for some time. Having tried, then abandoned, a twin-cam engine designed on its behalf by W O Bentley's consultancy team, the Coventry firm chose to develop its own new 120bhp 3½-litre six-cylinder unit, one which combined pushrod overhead valves with part-spherical combustion chambers in what was technically a very elegant layout.

The chassis, with a separate frame and coil-spring independent front suspension, was conventional enough, but the engine was backed by a choice of manual and (Wilson-type) preselector gearbox assemblies, and there was to be a choice of four-light or six-light saloons with semi-razor-edge styling, the bodies being produced in-house at Parkside by Armstrong Siddeley itself.

This time, at least, there should have been no problems with the price, for Armstrong Siddeley matched Jaguar's Mk VII at first – the Sapphire cost £1,728 compared with £1,775 for the

Mk VII. But was this an 'introductory offer', and could the Sapphire possibly be profitable at that level?

Austin: Although the all-new A30 (or Austin Seven) had been previewed in October 1951, it actually went on sale in May 1952. In fact only about 4,000 cars (a drop in the ocean compared with what was to follow) were to be built before the end of 1952, which meant that the Morris Minor's market leadership was barely challenged at first.

The new A40 Somerset was a direct replacement for the A40 Devon, using the same chassis and wheelbase, but with a wider, roomier and altogether more bulbous four-door saloon body style. It brought the A40's looks into line with those of the A70 Hereford, and both cars had that characteristic 'flying Austin' badge/mascot on the bonnet. So that the heavier new A40 would not be slower than the old model, there was slightly more power from the 1.2-litre engine (which used the same head as that of the A40 Sports) and, in a retrograde step, there was a steering-column gearchange instead of a floor change. Later in the year a two-door drop-head coupe derivative was added to the range.

The little-loved A90 Atlantic dropped out of production, which made the planners even more anxious to find more customers for the modern 2.66-litre engine which had powered it.

Before the end of the year the Champ 4x4 model, first launched in 1950, and originally built only for the British Army, was put on the civilian market. The four-cylinder Rolls-Royce engine was continued, but for civilian purposes there was also the option of a detuned Austin A90 power unit (Len Lord was determined to get rid of that surplus capacity somehow!). Originally sold only to export markets, the limited-production Champ was eventually sold in very small quantities in the UK.

Austin-Healey: The car which arrived at Earls Court in October badged as a Healey 100 left it a few days later as the new Austin-Healey 100, thus founding a marque which would bring great credit to Donald Healey and BMC in the next 18 years.

The prototype evolved around Healey's desire to replace the original chassis (which dated from 1945/46) by a new one which would be cheaper,

lighter and able to sell in larger numbers. There was a rugged and simple chassis-frame to which the basic body was welded on initial assembly. Power was by an Austin A90 engine (supplies were plentiful now that the A90 had been dropped...), and A90 suspension and transmission components were also used, while the prototype shell had been built by Tickford.

Even today, few realize just how different that prototype was from production cars, for it had a four-speed gearbox, with optional overdrive, and 16-inch steel wheels. These would change during development, and the first cars would be ready for delivery in the spring of 1953.

Bentley: The sleek, graceful and formidably fast Continental coupe model was previewed in February, though first deliveries did not take place until June. For the first few months there were no home-market deliveries either. The prototype, registered OLG 490, was inevitably christened 'Olga', and has survived to this day.

The Continental used the R-type's chassis (it was therefore the original user of that chassis), but it had more horsepower, unstated by Bentley, and higher overall gearing.

'Olga' had a smooth style by H J Mulliner of London, who would provide most of the shells for production cars, though in the next three years four other coachbuilders were allowed to build two-door coupes on this formidable base.

Although the R-type Continental was a large and heavy (3,700lb/1,678kg) car, it was also very fast, with a top speed of around 115mph. Everyone yearned after one of these gorgeous cars, but at the original price of more than £7,500 (when a Morris Minor only cost £582!) the wish was always much stronger than the ability to pay for one.

Later in the year the familiar Mk VI saloon was replaced by the R-type (or B7) model, this effectively being a long-tail version of the existing Mk VI style with enhanced equipment. The 4.5-litre engine was continued, but a new feature was the use of the four-speed GM Hydramatic automatic transmission. Optional rather than standard at first, this soon came to be fitted to almost every new Bentley, and by the mid-1950s the manual gearbox had become extinct.

Citroen: As ever, these long-wheelbase front-wheel-drive types were assembled at Slough, and for 1953 the existing Light Fifteen and Six models were joined by a new derivative, the Big Fifteen. This combined the longer wheelbase of the Six with the engine of the Light Fifteen, and had a boot bustle, where the entire wraparound panel lifted up to give access to the luggage.

Citroen's problem at this time was that although the *traction* chassis was still technically advanced, the style was now looking old-fashioned, and UK prices were too high. UK sales, accordingly, were always limited.

Daimler: The on-off, dribs-and-drabs Regency saga continued for a further season, for although very few of the original saloons had been delivered, Daimler now added a smart two-door drop-head coupe derivative to the range, a car whose general lines were like those of the existing Lanchester convertible.

This, however, was the only new-model activity from Daimler, as more effort was being put into the latest Lanchester range – and a new and smaller Daimler (the 1953 Conquest) was in preparation.

Ford: The Zephyr convertible was finally ready for production and went on sale, but no other significant changes were made during the year. The reason was that Ford was bracing itself to introduce a new Anglia/Prefect range in 1953 – new body, new suspension, new style and all.

Frazer Nash: As well as rationalizing its range of limited-production Bristol-engined sportscars, all of which were built around the same narrow tubular chassis-frame, the company also showed an incomplete Austin A90-engined prototype at Earls Court. However, once it became clear that Donald Healey's rival A90-engined project had gained the approval of BMC, Frazer Nash speedily lost interest in this project, especially as it was found not to handle very well. In any case, at a projected price of £2,335 it would not have sold in significant quantities.

Healey: Only a year after it had been announced, the US-market Nash-Healey model was given a thorough facelift in February. Instead of a British body style (which was retained for the Healey 3-litre convertible), there was a new open-top style by Farina of Italy, who were already contracted to Nash for much styling work. This meant that the Nash-Healey was now to be built by shipping rolling chassis to Italy, where the bodies were added, after which they were shipped direct to the USA for sale.

Humber: The Rootes-controlled marque only tinkered with the Hawk design (which was just four years old and not yet due for replacement), but this was soon joined by a new large car.

The major new-model announcement of the year came in October, when the radically new Super Snipe was launched. Although this car clearly used the same cabin and centre structure as the Hawk, it had a much longer wheelbase, longer nose and tail structures, and was powered by a brand-new overhead-valve six-cylinder 4.1-litre engine.

This was a big step forward for Rootes as the rugged old side-valve engine replaced by this unit had its roots in a 1930s design and was well overdue for replacement. In addition, coil-spring independent front suspension took over from the old Evenkeel transverse-leaf type; in general, by early-1950s standards, the Super Snipe had become a thoroughly up-to-date model.

At about the same time, Pullman and Imperial prices were reduced by no less than £319 to make them more competitive in the UK market.

Jowett: Minor changes were made to the slow-selling Jupiter, turning it into the Mk 1a model. Most notably, this saw the existing style given an opening rear bootlid, and there was more stowage space than the miserably tiny locker provided on the original cars.

Lanchester: Having introduced the Fourteen for the British market with a Barker coachbuilt body, in April the company offered an identically-styled car, but with an all-steel bodyshell (produced by the Pressed Steel Co Ltd) for export markets, calling it the Leda. First deliveries were made in April.

This was very confusing, but as Barker was a Daimler-controlled operation, and presumably needed the business, there were no overt mutterings at the time. One reason given for not sending coachbuilt shells overseas was that Daimler-Lanchester was worried about the effects of heat and humidity on the wooden structural sections of the Barker shell. Very strange – especially as the coachbuilt shell must have cost considerably more to build, so why not use the all-steel shell on all models? Daimler-Lanchester, though, was not always a logical-thinking company at that time... In any case, the same all-steel saloon shell would find another use – in the six-cylinder-engined Daimler Conquest of 1953.

MG: Improvements were made to the Y-type saloon, including the use of a hypoid rear axle, a front anti-roll bar and leading-shoe brakes, the latest car becoming known as the YB.

Morris: Less than a year after the BMC merger was formalized, Nuffield's Morris Minor became a Series II with the fitment of a lightly-modified A-series (Austin A30) engine and gearbox, first to the four-door saloon, then progressively to other models in the range. By April 1953 this consigned the original Minor's Nuffield 918cc side-valve unit to the spare parts bin, and was the first of many such rationalization moves to affect Nuffield's new products in the next few years.

Although the new overhead-valve engine was more powerful than the ousted side-valve unit, the overall gearing of the Minor was actually *dropped*, which turned the car into a rather gutless screamer: it was fortunate that the new engine seemed to like high revs as most enthusiasts seemed to use all of the revs, all of the time...

Riley: Although there were no visual changes, Riley fans noticed with some dismay that the RM-series cars were made somewhat more orthodox for 1953, abandoning the torque-tube rear suspension in favour of a new 'corporate' hypoid-bevel rear axle and conventional half-elliptic leaf springs. The effect on roadholding was much less significant than diehards expected.

Rolls-Royce: As with the Bentley, Rolls-Royce also made the GM Hydramatic automatic transmission optional on its Silver Dawn (export only) and Silver Wraith models.

Rover: Improvements to the P4 75 model, announced in March, included abandoning the Cyclops front-end style in favour of a more conventional grille, moving the spare wheel to a separate compartment under the boot, adding even more insulation to the suspension members, and making various improvements to the furnishings.

Singer: This cash-strapped manufacturer was beginning to suffer, mainly because of its inability to invest in new models. Yet again no new shapes were offered during 1952, which meant that the 1930s-style Roadster was beginning to look very ancient indeed.

Even so, the tinkering included enlarging the rear window and adopting a new facia style for the SM1500 saloon, and offering a more powerful (58bhp instead of 48bhp) twin-carburettor version of the well-known overhead-cam engine, which became optional on both models.

Standard: Early in the year the company revealed that it was developing a new small car. This was the SC project, which became the Standard 8hp/10hp range, but it would not be put on sale until the autumn of 1953. Presumably the announcement was made so that traditional Standard buyers did not desert the company to buy a new A30.

Triumph: The prototype sportscar (the 20TS, sometimes wrongly named TR1 in later years) which was shown at Earls Court in October, was totally undeveloped, and on its first showing it was not thought likely to be a success.

But here was an ugly duckling which was rapidly to be turned into a swan. In the next nine months, a fierce and intensive redesign, not least with a more rigid chassis-frame and more power being extracted from the engine, saw it turned into the TR2 – and we all know what happened after that.

Although the 20TS was recognizably the ancestor of the TR2, it had a short tail with an exposed spare wheel, a modified Standard Nine chassis-frame, and its 2-litre (Vanguard-based) engine produced only 75bhp. No car of this type would ever be sold to the public.

Vauxhall: After less than a year of production of the new E-type Wyvern/ Velox models, a completely new range of overhead-valve engines was introduced. This was overdue as the original engines dated from the late 1930s. It meant that the 'long-stroke' E-types had been in production for a mere eight months.

The new units – closely related four-cylinder and six-cylinder types – were sturdy over-square units, significantly more powerful and higher-revving than before. They had 30 per cent more piston area, but were rated only 10–15 per cent more powerful, and clearly there was much more to come when it was needed.

Interestingly enough, although there was no connection between the two makes, these engines used exactly the same bore (79.4mm) and stroke (76.2mm) dimensions as those of the latest Ford Consul/Zephyr models – surely a case of Great Minds...

Wolseley: The new 4/44, previewed in October, was a smart, almost Italianate, four-door saloon, which bore the first fruits of designer Gerald Palmer's work in the Nuffield technical office. The four-door monocoque was all-new and very attractively shaped, and was powered by the same engine as found in the MG Y-type saloon, which was also a detuned version of the MG TD's unit.

Some people thought it a pity that the staid Wolseley badge had been applied to what might have been a spirited sports saloon, but connoisseurs of product planning thought they knew what was brewing: was an MG version of this car on the way? Indeed there was, but it was not even previewed for another year – by which time the MG engine ancestry had been lost!

Industrial developments

A major surprise (but not, perhaps, to insiders) came in December 1952 when Lord Nuffield decided to step down from the chair of BMC after only one year in office and become the Corporation's honorary president. He was succeeded as chairman by Leonard Lord, who was already BMC's chief executive, and then rapidly withdrew from the business.

He was 75 years old and had been involved with the Morris/Nuffield side of the business for 40 years – the original bullnose Morris having been conceived in 1912. As one of Britain's motoring magazines commented: 'No man has better earned his retirement.'

In October, Austin (for which, read BMC) was chosen by Nash of the USA as the European company to build its projected new NXI light car. Nash announced the actual deal like this:

'The Austin Motor Co Ltd and Fisher and Ludlow Ltd, both of Birmingham, England, will produce the cars for Nash Motors. Fisher and Ludlow will build the bodies and Austin will provide the engine and chassis complete, and do the final assembly...A name for the new car, which has a definite sports-car appearance, has not yet been selected.'

Len Lord of Austin/BMC confirmed that the A40 engine would be used, and it was also made clear that the entire production of the new car would be shipped to the USA, no supplies being available for the British market. This, then, was the start of the Metropolitan project; the car itself would not be revealed until March 1954.

Lord, indeed, was very busy at this time, having joined forces with Donald Healey, taking over the new Healey sportscar design and inventing the Austin-Healey marque, and arranging to have this smart new car built at Longbridge in place of the A40 Sports.

Once the Morris Minor inherited the Austin A30 engine and gearbox, the first effects of BMC's proposed rationalization plans became clear, though the major move to reduce the number of different engines and transmissions in the vast range would become more obvious in 1953/54.

Jaguar finally completed its gradual move from Foleshill to Browns Lane, Allesley, at last occupying their permanent home which still builds Jaguars in the 1990s.

Technical developments

Rover, having quietly developed the original gas-turbine car, JET 1, and smoothed out the nose with the latest P4-style nose, fitted a highly-tuned version of the turbine engine, this time developing about 200bhp, and took it

to the famous Belgian Jabbeke highway for maximum-speed tests. Sometimes with intrepid designer Spen King at the wheel, and sometimes with Marauder designer Peter Wilks driving, JET 1 achieved a series of startling standing-start acceleration figures. Then it completed a stupendous day by setting a two-way maximum speed of no less than 151.196mph – all in one gear, for this machine used the characteristics of the gas-turbine engine as its own torque converter *and* transmission!

Not only did Rolls-Royce (and Bentley) start using American-made automatic transmissions, but the Laycock overdrive found several new customers (with many more on the way), and various easy-change British transmissions started prototype testing. Development continued on the Hobbs automatic transmission (it was fully described in the technical press and would shortly be adopted by Daimler for a new model), while Automotive Products (the Lockheed parent company, of Leamington Spa) showed prototypes of the Manumatic system, which was intended to offer a clutchless change to manufacturers' existing manual transmissions.

They were not yet ready to put this system on sale, but a careful reading of the technical details – which involved lots of vacuum switches, electrical relays, gear-lever knob switches, a centrifugal clutch and combinations of all these – promised a very complex and rather expensive installation. Not everyone awaited this system with bated breath, or even with enthusiasm...

Jaguar was the first British concern to race a car (the XK120C) with Dunlop disc brakes, and before the Earls Court Motor Show Girling and Lockheed also showed off their prototype disc brake installations. The Dunlop system was intended for use in large, heavy and powerful cars, whereas the Girling and Lockheed systems were meant to be simpler, cheaper and for more run-of-the-mill models. It would be three or four years before either type was ready for quantity-production.

Another Jaguar innovation – a modified body style on the C-type – failed ignominiously at Le Mans, when all cars overheated and had to retire.

The use of a complex multi-tube spaceframe and the appearance of gullwing doors on the Mercedes-Benz 300SL racing sportscar caused a real stir, though as both looked like being very expensive to use in series production there were doubts about their technical significance. The 300SL, incidentally, was *the* outstanding new racing sportscar of the year.

John Cobb, already the holder of the Land Speed Record, announced that he was planning to attack the Water Speed Record on Loch Ness in Scotland with a new jet-propelled De Havilland Ghost-powered speedboat called *Crusader*. This craft had been designed and built by Vosper Ltd, of Southampton. Unhappily, when this new craft attacked the record in September it broke up at more than 200mph and the hapless driver was killed after being thrown violently into the water.

Having made his name at the Nuffield Organisation, Alec Issigonis joined Alvis during the year, though little was ever announced about the purpose of this move. It was not for many years, well after he had moved on to BMC at Longbridge, that enthusiasts learned of an all-new and technically advanced saloon car which he and his team had designed. It was never put into production, and no pictures of the prototypes were ever released.

As a direct result of Issigonis leaving Nuffield, Gerald Palmer took his place. As we now know, Palmer was to be responsible for the mid-1950s range of Nuffield-BMC saloons including the Wolseley 4/44, MG Magnette, Riley Pathfinder and related models.

Men of Influence

Sir John Black

It was John Black's successor, Alick Dick, who summed up this dictator best of all: 'No-one hit it off with John Black really…you either hated him or loved him. I alternated between the two fairly often…!'

In many ways John Black was a British parallel to Italy's Benito Mussolini – bombastic, unfeeling, ruthless, efficient, and full of self-importance – in other words, a real dictator. Like all such dictators, he was eventually unseated by his subordinates, but not before he had been at the helm of Standard (and, later, Triumph) for 20 years.

Born in Kingston-on-Thames in 1895, John Black fought with the Tank Corps in the First World War, then as Captain Black joined the Hillman Motor Company in Coventry. Having wooed and won one of William Hillman's daughters, he moved out of Hillman when the Rootes brothers moved in.

Joining Standard, at Canley, as general manager in 1928, and becoming a director by 1930, he became sole managing director in 1934 when Standard's founder, R W Maudslay, died. By that time, Black's master plan, to expand Standard from a company making only 7,000 cars a year in 1930, to one of the Big Six making 50,000 a year by 1939, was well under way, and he was already running the company with great dynamism. It helped to keep on the right side of him, for anyone who crossed or disappointed him was first vilified, then shortly sacked, so his senior colleagues made sure that he received regular dollops of unstinting praise.

Having seen Standard join the Government-inspired shadow factory scheme in 1936, and run the massive Banner Lane complex, he became Sir John during the Second World War. During 1944 and 1945 he not only absorbed Triumph, but agreed to make Ferguson tractors (for Harry Ferguson) at Banner Lane.

For Standard-Triumph the first postwar decade was extremely successful, although Sir John seemed to became increasingly capricious and impulsive as the years passed by. Alick Dick, who became his personal assistant, then his deputy, saw respected colleagues dismissed on a whim, and became increasingly unhappy with developments.

The crunch came at the end of 1953, when the schizophrenic Sir John not only signed a long-term deal with Ferguson over tractor manufacture (which his board of directors had not even discussed, let alone endorsed), but also proposed to sack his technical director Ted Grinham, for no sensible reason. Standard's board therefore rose up in revolt, confronted their boss and demanded his resignation, which came in January 1954. As far as the public was concerned, the excuse was illness following a recent car crash (in a Swallow Doretti), but the industry was not fooled.

Except that Sir John then dabbled with the deputy-chairmanship of Enfield Cables, he was no longer involved in industry. He retired to Wales, to farm near Harlech, where he died on Christmas Eve 1965, aged 69.

There was a huge attendance at his memorial service in Coventry, though one mordant wit insisted that this was: 'Because they all wanted to see that he had *really* died…'.

1953

For British motorists, the industrial and social scene brightened considerably during the year, with car production rocketing and UK deliveries exceeding 300,000 for the first time. The ban on foreign imports was also lifted in the spring, though this had only a limited effect at first.

There was good news for drivers in the April Budget when purchase tax on cars was reduced from 66⅔ to 50 per cent – still a high level, but at least a step in the right direction, which reduced the total price of a Morris Minor by £52, a Hillman Minx by £66 and a Jaguar Mk VII by £159. Since income tax was cut by 6d (2.5p) in the pound at the same time, motorists began to feel positively bullish about the future.

British car production soared to nearly 600,000 – yet another record – and although exports remained static at around 300,000, the number of cars delivered in the UK soared to 301,354, which did a lot to cut waiting lists.

The overseas travel allowance was also boosted from £25 to £40 and the motor car expense allowance from £15 to £20 – this at a time when average petrol prices in Europe were still less than 5s 0d (25p) a gallon in UK terms.

There was also another way in which cross-channel travel became easier. After a great deal of discussion, planning and delay, the new drive-on/drive-off facilities in Dover's Eastern Docks were finally opened, matched by similar facilities in France. Although the crossing itself, between Dover and Calais or Boulogne, still took 90 minutes (the sea crossing is still 75 minutes in the mid-1990s), the speed of loading and disembarkation was cut dramatically compared with when cars had to be individually slung aboard or put ashore.

Helped by their flexible design, Dover's 'floating bridges' which linked ships to shore could cope with a tidal rise and fall of 22 feet, which was considerably more than the port ever experienced.

Meanwhile, the alternative and much faster air ferry service run by Silver City Airways had prospered. During the summer, when celebrating its fifth anniversary of operation, Silver City claimed to hold 25 per cent of the cross-channel traffic in cars, motorcycles and bicycles, though of course the aircraft were too small to carry trucks or coaches. The company was already planning to move from Lympne airfield, near Hythe and Folkestone, which had grass runways, to the newly-built Romney (later to be renamed Lydd) airfield, a few miles to the south-west, which would have concrete runways; the move was forecast for mid-1954. Tourism was obviously very important in this part of Kent, and what was claimed to be Britain's first American-style motel was opened at Newingreen, which was near to Lympne, Folkestone and Dover.

February 1, 1953 was the glorious day when branded fuels once again became available in the UK, along with higher-octane premium grades. Pool petrol, sometimes of dubious quality with an octane rating of just 72, had been in use since September 1939; now it was time for the brightly-coloured petrol pump globes, supported by aggressive advertising campaigns, to reappear. As now, Esso and Shell were the dominant marques, with BP not far behind, but famous 1950s fuels such as National Benzole, Regent and Clevecol have all since disappeared. There was, of course, a price to be paid – the higher-octane premium fuels retailing for 3–4d (1.25–1.67p) a gallon extra.

As a result of the long-standing ban on car imports being lifted, several much-respected European models became available for the first time since 1939, including BMW, Borgward, Ford-France, Mercedes-Benz, Peugeot, Porsche and VW. Several others, including Fiat, Lancia and Simca, were poised to join in during 1954. No wonder British motorists felt so confident and up-beat about the future, or that the attendance at the Earls Court Motor Show was an all-time record; during the 10 days in October 613,000 people fought their way to the exhibition halls by tube, bus or even private car, beating the previous record of 565,000 set in 1948.

Britain's first 'reversed' registration numbers were issued in June, Middlesex County Council being the first to run out of the well-known 'XYZ 123' type of numbers; the first of its reversed types was 1000 H.

Britain's first parking meters were forecast to arrive in Leicester – and the spread of these money-hungry machines has not ceased since!

New models

AC: After years of desultory production of the old-fashioned 2-Litre models (which continued, unchanged, into 1954), AC startled everyone by unveiling a prototype of a new two-seater sportscar to be called the Ace. It was not yet ready for sale, and the first deliveries were to be made in April/May 1954.

Although this revived a famous 1930s AC name and used yet another development of the old AC overhead-camshaft six-cylinder engine, the rest of the car was new. By AC standards the Ace's engineering was quite startlingly advanced. The company had bought in an existing racing sportscar chassis design from John Tojeiro, modified it with the sole intent of making it more practical for road use, then announced it to judge the public's reaction.

Based around a simple but rugged large-diameter tube chassis, the Ace used transverse-leaf independent suspension at front and rear. The 2-litre engine developed 85bhp at first, and was concealed by a smoothly-styled two-seater Barchetta-style body in light alloy. Even in this guise its top speed was more than 100mph. This was to be the start of a hectic period for AC, when its cars would become both fashionable and successful in motor racing, and would lead to the birth of the ferocious AC Cobras of the 1960s.

Alvis: A higher-performance version of the 3-litre model, the TC21/100, was introduced. Not only did this car have a 100bhp engine, it was also available with centre-lock wire-spoke wheels. Alvis made much of the 100mph top speed, though it needed half a county for the last few mph to be achieved.

Armstrong Siddeley: Only a year after the Sapphire had been launched, a 150bhp twin-carburettor version of the engine became optional, making the Sapphire a genuine 100mph car, and theoretically (if not in the showrooms) a formidable competitor of the Jaguar Mk VII.

Aston Martin: The DB2 theme advanced a stage further for 1954 with the launch of the DB2-4, a sexy new sports coupe which retained the DB2 chassis with many new features and a much-modified body style. It was a direct replacement for the DB2.

The existing twin-cam 2.6-litre engine had been tuned to give 125bhp (a 2.9-litre version was under development and would appear as an option within 12 months), while the new car's cabin featured 2+2 seating and a lift-up hatchback (though no-one called it that in those days!). The DB2-4 was an expensive car – £2,622 at launch – but because of its immaculate road manners, high performance and graceful style it was always a favourite with well-to-do enthusiasts.

Austin: BMC introduced a two-door saloon version of the A30, with the same general style, running gear and performance as the continuing four-door saloon. [As a personal reminiscence, in 1959, a year-old A35 two-door saloon was the first modern car I ever owned...]

A facelifted version of the A135 Princess, dubbed Princess III, was also introduced in October, though the general dimensions of the cabin, and the car's performance, were unaffected.

Austin-Healey: Development and tooling of the Healey 100 was completed in double-quick time. The production car featured wire-spoke wheels, and a three-speed gearbox with overdrive on top and intermediate gears as standard. First deliveries of Warwick-built cars were made in March 1953 (most of the early cars going to the USA), and once the car's 100mph-plus top speed had been confirmed by the motoring magazines the customers queued up to buy.

Four-cylinder versions would be built until the summer of 1956, after which heavier six-cylinder versions with longer-wheelbase chassis and 2+2 seating would take over.

BMW: The prestigious German company, which had struggled to re-establish itself in the chaotic aftermath of the Second World War, made its first post-war appearance in Britain, showing the 501 at Earls Court.

Except that a 65bhp version of the familiar 1930s 326-type BMW 2-litre six-cylinder engine was retained, the 501 was a new design, big, bulbous and technically complex. Launched in Germany in 1951, though deliveries did not begin until October 1952, it had a massive tubular chassis-frame, the gearbox was separated from the clutch by a short propeller-shaft (there was a very complex steering-column gear-change, too!), while the steering gear was unique, with a heavy but beautifully machined sector-and-pinion layout.

The original body style was a four-door, six-light saloon with the familiar kidney-shaped BMW grille dominating the front, a style which would be seen in several guises and with both six-cylinder and V8 engines for another 10 years.

At £2,480 for the first UK-market cars, the 501 was hardly likely to break any sales records, but it was important historically as the first of a still-expanding flood of BMW models to reach the UK.

Borgward: The first imports of 1800s and 2400s from Bremen, in north-west Germany, began in the autumn of 1953. The Hansa 1800 was a conventional, almost Volvo-like, five–six-seater with a choice of petrol or diesel engines, while the Hansa 2400 had an 82bhp six-cylinder engine. Both were too costly (the 2400 was listed at £2,424) to make more than a marginal impact on British sales.

Bristol: It was not easy to tell them apart, but the 403 which took over from the 401 was a significantly better car. Still with the inspired-by-BMW chassis and the same wind-tunnel-tested two-door saloon shell, the 403 had more power (100bhp), better brakes, improved suspension and detail improvements to the heater and interior appointments. Bristol motoring, however, was still for the rich, for this car retailed at £2,976.

The short-wheelbase 404 coupe, also introduced in 1953, was instantly titled the 'Businessman's Express', but was so expensive and had such a small two-seater cabin that it never sold in appreciable quantities. The chassis was a short version of that first seen under the 400 (and carried forward under the 403), the engine was either a 105bhp or a 125bhp version of the established six-cylinder 2-litre, but the style was all new and incorporated tiny fins on the rear wings. Within a year the 404 would be joined by a much more sensible new Bristol, the 405, which stretched the 404's style to practical lengths on a longer wheelbase and incorporated four passenger doors and seats.

Citroen: The company announced that the quirky, but technically-advanced, 2CV was to be assembled at the Slough factory alongside the *traction avant* models. Introduced in France in 1948, the 2CV was already legendary for its abilities and versatility.

Sometimes described as a mobile chicken shed (the corrugated panels had much to do with this), it featured a platform chassis with an air-cooled flat-twin engine and front-wheel drive. Independent front and rear suspensions were interconnected, springing and damping were incredibly soft, and because there was only 9bhp this was a quite amazingly slow machine with a natural cruising speed of only about 35mph and a top speed in the low-40s.

Trim and furnishing were so simple as to be virtually non-existent, which is what Citroen had always intended, for this was meant to be the first mechanically-powered car a French peasant would choose when he was ready to abandon his horse-and-cart. The simple seats, which featured stretched rubber for their support, were light, simple and effective. They could be removed, if needed, and there was a canvas roof which could be rolled back – not just to let in the sun, but to allow oversize packages (or even animals!) to be carried.

Daimler: Ahead of the launch of the new Conquest, Daimler sharply reduced the price of the old Consort models to move existing stocks out of the show-rooms before the new model took over. The new Conquest combined the chassis and basic body style of the Lanchester Leda (though with a Daimler radiator, of course), with a newly-developed short-stroke six-cylinder engine, which owed something to the layout of the Consort unit, but was totally different in detail and considerably lighter. With independent suspension by laminated torsion bars, and the new higher-revving engine matched by the usual Wilson-type preselector gearbox, this was an appealing combination. Although the first cars had only 75bhp, they could exceed 80mph. There was a 100bhp engine on the way, to be announced in 1954. Like the Lanchester Leda, four-door saloon and two-door drop-head coupe versions were available. The Conquest's basic price was £1,066 – but did the price or the title come first?

There was a surprise in October when the two-seater Conquest Roadster was revealed, this being a sports-roadster type of a variety never before put on sale by the staid and dignified Daimler company. It was said that the design had been executed and the prototype built in a mere six weeks – and some cynics suggested there was plenty of evidence of this!

Using the same chassis and running gear as the Conquest, though in the 100bhp tune which predated the 1954 Conquest Century model, the Roadster had a long (178in) two-seater body style by Carbodies with a wraparound windscreen, removable sidescreens and tailfins on the rear wings.

The body was built up of aluminium panels on a framework of aluminium castings – technically exciting but intrinsically cheap to tool up for limited-series production. Opinion about this new machine was universal – it was thought to be striking, technically brave, risky in marketing terms, and perhaps too expensive (at £1,673 more costly than a Jaguar XK120, for instance) to sell well.

Unlike other sporting cars previewed at Earls Court in 1953, this model at least went into production, though as predicted the demand was very limited. Even so, it would remain in Daimler price lists for several years in this and a revised form.

The last of the Type DE36 models, with their gargantuan 5.5-litre engine, was made in 1953, bringing to an end the use of straight-eight engines on British cars.

Fiat: British sales were ready to start again in 1953/54 with the long-established 500C *Topolino*, the new 1100 model and 1400/1900 types.

The 1400 had been launched in 1950, a plain-Jane four-door monocoque saloon with undistinguished roadholding and strange gear ratios. The 1900 of 1953 was a larger-engined, five-speed-transmission version of the same car, faster but still not dynamically attractive. Even though there was still a new-car shortage in the UK at the time, neither car sold in significant numbers.

Except for its engine and gearbox, the 1100-103 was an entirely new and more enterprising design, coming complete with a four-door monocoque bodyshell, flexible coil-spring independent front suspension and a surprisingly agile chassis. Tuners already knew this to be a very free-revving engine, the result being that well-prepared 1100s soon shone in rallies.

In Britain, of course, the 1100 had to sell against cars like the Austin A40, where it was at a price disadvantage, but it was always extremely popular in Italy, and the 1100 family would remain in production for nearly 20 years.

Ford: The new and very closely-related Anglia and Prefect (100E) models were the most significant new British cars of the year as they signalled Ford's completely new approach to small-car design. At long last a break had been made from the 1920s-style separate frames and transverse leaf-spring beam-axle layouts of the ancient Anglias and Prefects, for until 1953 all small British Fords had been based on the Model Y layout of 1932.

Although a much-modified side-valve engine and a three-speed gearbox were retained, here, for the first time, were mass-market small Fords with up-to-the-minute unit-construction styles and MacPherson-strut independent front suspension allied to a conventional half-elliptic rear suspension.

Surprisingly, Ford claimed that the 100E's side-valve engines were mainly new, though the age-old bore, stroke and 1,172cc capacity were retained. The 100E Anglia would always use this engine size, for the old-type 933cc unit had been abandoned.

In many ways the new Anglias (two-door) and Prefects (four-door) were Consuls writ small, though of course there were no common parts. Roomier and better-equipped than the old types, they were also very keenly priced and sure to be strong competition to cars like the A30, Minor and Standard Eight.

The most surprising Ford new-model launch, though, was of a technically-obsolete car, the 'new' Popular actually being a stripped-out version of the 1,172cc export Anglia of the late 1940s/early 1950s and remarkably priced at a mere £391, making it much the cheapest British car of the period.

Never mind that it had the ancient transverse-leaf-spring chassis of the

Anglias which had just been ousted by the new 100E models, or that it struggled to beat 60mph. Nor was it even economical (there was nothing remarkable about Ford's small side-valve engine) – its attraction was that it was incredibly cheap, and for that reason there was always a healthy demand. Originally built at Dagenham, and latterly at the ex-Briggs factory in Doncaster, the Popular would stay in production for six years before being replaced by *another* Popular for the 1960s.

By comparison, the arrival of a more lushly trimmed, but mechanically unchanged version of the Zephyr, called the Zodiac, was almost ignored. Two-tone paintwork and upholstery colours and other decorative gizmos were all that distinguished one big Ford from the other, but there was a healthy demand for both.

Ford-France: Think of a car developed in the USA, but built in France, with styling rather similar to that of the current Ford-UK Consuls and Zephyrs, but with a choice of 2.1-litre (Vedette) or 3.9-litre (Vendome) side-valve V8 engines, and the layout of these French Fords becomes clear. Imported for the first time at the end of 1953, they were very rare indeed on British roads. This was a very short-lived enterprise in Britain, for Simca soon bought up Ford-France (in 1954) and brought UK sales to an end.

Frazer Nash: Still shuffling its options, though not changing the simple-to-make tubular chassis, the company produced yet another version, this being a closed Le Mans coupe with the racing-type de Dion rear axle. Other models, all hand-built to special order, were continued, and it was stated that the de Dion rear end could be supplied to existing Frazer Nash cars as a conversion.

Hillman: Although the existing Minx had already been in production for five years by 1953, Rootes continued to develop it. The Mk VI, launched in February, featured front-end style changes but, most importantly, there was also the arrival of the Californian model, which was effectively a hardtop version of the existing convertible. The Californian was the precursor of a whole series of two-door Rootes coupes which, in future years, became known as Sunbeam Rapiers. Further minor changes were made in October, when the latest cars were dubbed Mk VII types, though the mechanical and marketing mixture was as before.

HRG: The small Tolworth company announced a new twin-overhead-camshaft conversion of the Singer engine, which it proposed to use in future HRG models. In the event this engine would never go into series production in HRGs, whose sales had fallen away almost to zero, but limited numbers of twin-cam-engined Singer cars *would* be built before that company was bought by Rootes in 1955/56.

Humber: To bring the old-shape Pullman and Imperial models into line with the latest big Humbers, Rootes fitted the latest overhead-valve 4.1-litre engines. These cars, however, were looking old-fashioned and would only remain in production until mid-1954.

Jaguar: The third derivative of the already-famous XK120 was added to the range – this time a smart and well-trimmed drop-head coupe model. Compared with the original roadster, there were no mechanical changes, but above the waistline there was a larger windscreen, drop windows and a padded and fully trimmed fold-back soft-top.

Early in the year, Borg-Warner (Type DG) automatic transmission became optional on export-market versions of the Mk VII saloon, and eventually would also be offered on British-market versions.

Jensen: A prototype of a new four-seater, two-door coupe, called the 541, was previewed at Earls Court, though this car was not yet ready to go into production.

By Jensen's standards, the 541 would dramatically increase the company's sales – from a mere handful in 1953 to the dizzy heights of around 60–80 cars a year in 1955! Using a new type of chassis-frame incorporating 5in diameter longeron tubes braced by box-sections and flat floor members (the effect being a rather rudimentary platform structure), along with Austin-type wishbone front suspension, there was the usual 4-litre Austin power unit (in 130bhp or 140bhp guise) and its related gearbox.

Production cars would use a glass-fibre bodyshell, which incorporated a moving flap (controllable from the cockpit) to open or close the air intake for the radiator. Altogether lower, smoother and sleeker than the Interceptor, here was a Jensen which could justifiably call itself a Grand Touring car. Put on sale in 1954, it would be built in many different forms (latterly as the C-V8) until the mid-1960s.

Jowett: With the company's financial troubles well-known by the autumn, it was a real surprise to see a new Jupiter sportscar prototype – the competition-based R4 – shown at Earls Court. In the event, the R4 never went into production, but Jowett-lovers still coo over its specification, and talk about 'what might have been'.

Influenced by the work which had gone into producing Jupiter race cars for the Le Mans 24 Hours race, the R4 was built around a short-wheelbase chassis-frame (84in instead of 93in as in existing Jupiters), which was newly designed, with box-section instead of tubular side-members and reinforcements. A 65bhp version of the existing 1.5-litre flat-four engine and its related transmission were retained. Strangely, the rack-and-pinion steering was abandoned in favour of a less accurate Bishops cam-and-lever.

The real novelty was in the stubby two-seater body style, which had the minimum of front and rear overhang and lacked a windscreen in the form shown at Earls Court. Because of the company's parlous financial state, nothing further was ever heard of these cars.

Lagonda: Although the well-known cruciform chassis layout was retained, the Lagonda 3-litre model looked and felt even newer than it was. The twin-cam engine had been enlarged from 2.6 to 2.9 litres, while Tickford had developed a smart new body style – a smooth-flanked four-seater with two large passenger doors, available in saloon or drop-head coupe layouts. Expensive, and therefore exclusive, this new Lagonda would be built by hand until 1958.

Lancia: UK imports of these Italian-made machines were about to begin at the end of 1953, the initial range including the Appia and Aurelia models.

The original Aurelia, launched in 1950, was a complex front-engine/rear-wheel-drive car with a 1.75-litre V6 engine, rear-mounted gearbox/final-drive unit and semi-trailing-arm swing-axle rear suspension. Saloons were soon joined by smart Farina-styled fastback GT coupes, engines grew to a sturdy 2.5 litres and a de Dion/leaf-spring rear suspension was also adopted. Technically interesting, but expensive, these cars sold in only tiny numbers in the UK.

The Appia was all-new in April 1953. Taking over from the much-loved Aprilia, the stubby but conventional body style hid a front-engine/rear-drive layout which featured a front-mounted 20-degree V4 engine. It was a sturdy, but by no means fast car, which would be built in several guises in the next few years.

Mercedes-Benz: Imports from Germany began before the end of the year, the ranges listed being the pre-war Type 170SD (diesel), the brand-new Type 180 and the expensive but highly-specified 300 models which had made their debut in 1951.

The design of the W136 Type 170s actually dated from the late 1930s, the cars having been revised, updated and then put back into production in Germany in 1949. Based on a tubular backbone-style chassis-frame, with all-independent suspension (swing-axles at the rear), these cars were built with a variety of side-valve four-cylinder petrol and overhead-valve diesel engines.

By the early 1950s they had been joined by a 220 model, which used a 2.2-litre six-cylinder unit, but all types had a dated appearance, with separate free-standing headlamps and front wings.

The new Type 180, the first of the vast W120 family, was launched in 1953 and immediately christened the Ponton (German for pontoon) because of its rigid bridge-like structure. Although the coil-spring independent suspension and choice of engines were familiar, this square-rigged saloon was the first Mercedes-Benz model to use a unit-construction body/chassis unit.

Although the first variety – the 180 – had an established 52bhp 1.77-litre side-valve engine, over the years there would be myriad other engines and options, the last cars of this type being produced as late as 1962.

The 300 range, first shown in 1951, was a magnificent statement of Daimler-Benz's determination to recover from the war by producing cars of superb engineering and quality. Based around a tubular backbone-type chassis, with all-independent coil-spring suspension (the general layout being similar in many ways to the prewar W136/Type 170 models), this car used a brand-new 3-litre overhead-camshaft six-cylinder engine and related transmissions. The engine and running gear had already featured in much-modified form in the gullwing 300SL racing sportscars, production versions of which would be launched in 1954.

The original 300 had a conservatively-rated 115bhp engine and a massive, rather bulbous, six-light saloon shell, but exotically special coupes and cabriolets would also become available in future years. Once again, this was a range with a long life, for the last would be delivered in 1962.

MG: It was all-change time at Abingdon, for both of the existing models – the TD sportscar and the YB saloon – were swept away in favour of two new models – the TF and the Magnette.

Although MG's designers had wanted to put an all-new sportscar into production, BMC had refused permission, so what would become the MGA was put back on to the back-burner for a couple of years. Instead, the hastily-developed TF sportscar was really no more than a major facelift of the TD, for it retained the same rolling chassis, 1.25-litre engine and body centre-section. The TF's shell, though, while retaining traditional steel-on-a-wood-frame construction, had a lowered nose with a semi-sloping radiator shell and partly-recessed headlamps, while there was a more rakish tail, still with an exposed, slab-type fuel tank.

If BMC had not seen this as purely a holding operation until a brand-new design could be produced, it was soon obliged to do so as the TF's reception was lukewarm at best. Although it looked better than the TD, it was no faster than before, and no cheaper either.

The Magnette ZA saloon, on the other hand, was a real advance. The old YB saloon had looked and felt prewar in concept, but here was a truly smart four-door sports saloon to take its place. Designed at Cowley in paral-

lel with the Wolseley 4/44 (which had gone on sale at the end of 1952), the Magnette shared the same basic unit-construction bodyshell, suspensions and general layout, but was powered by BMC's new rationalized B-series 1.5-litre engine and its related transmission units.

Although there were significant differences in style from the 4/44 (not only the front grille, but the sills and some other panels were different), this was the same sleek and curvaceous offering. The engine, though not technically exciting, was more powerful and torquey than that fitted to the Wolseley – and, if we had known it, was also destined for use in the next MG sportscar of 1955 – the MGA.

Traditionalists moaned about the Nuffield/BMC influence on this car (but there was nothing new, surely, in this at Abingdon?), but seemed to like the octagonal treatment of instruments, the stubby and sporty feel to the gearchange – and, above all, the well-balanced handling of the car itself.

Originally priced at £915, which made it an attractive proposition, Magnette deliveries did not begin until 1954, when they immediately outstripped anything achieved by the Y-type models. Dealers, BMC accountants *and* customers were all delighted.

Morris: A Traveller (estate car) version of the Morris Minor was launched to add to the existing saloons and tourers. This had the 'Olde Worlde Tudor Cottage' type of wooden construction which would become so familiar on Morris Minors in the next 20 years.

Panhard: Just prior to UK sales beginning, Panhard revealed the new Dyna 54 model, a front-wheel-drive machine using many of J A Gregoire's principles. The smoothly-shaped four-door saloon hid a front-wheel-drive chassis, a flat-twin air-cooled engine and a monocoque hull in which most panels – including structural ones – were pressed from aluminium rather than steel.

Peugeot: Imports of 203s began before the end of 1953, this being an ultra-conventional four-door saloon car with a front-mounted 1.3-litre engine, very solid construction and excellent reliability.

Already familiar to British tourists dri-

ving through France (the French police bought fleets of them), these would be sold in small numbers in the UK for some years to come.

Porsche: The VW Beetle-based, rear-engined, air-cooled Type 356 sports-car from Germany had been in production since 1950, but the first tentative British imports did not begin until the summer of 1953. At this time, 1.3-litre and 1.5-litre models in coupe or convertible guise were listed, prices starting at £1,842.

These cars, identifiable today by their V-windscreens, were carefully built and (considering their small and untuned engines) remarkably fast, but the handling was always tricky. No amount of pro-Porsche propaganda could hide the fact that one needed lightning reactions to tame the early cars' sometimes vicious oversteer, and most of these machines were spun or crashed at least once in early ownership. Their handling improved, but was never tamed, in the years which followed.

Renault: Once the import of French-built cars was authorized, Renault put the Fregate on sale in Britain, though it was only delivered in tiny quantities. Announced in France in 1952, this was an altogether larger and more conventional car than the 4CV, for it had a front-engine/rear-drive layout, rounded but essentially plain four-door styling and pedestrian performance. The only advanced technical feature was its independent rear suspension, though the roadholding was by no means outstanding.

Riley: The new Pathfinder replaced the 2½-litre RM-series model. Previewed in October, but not ready for deliveries to begin until 1954, it was first 'BMC' Riley, in fact the first new Riley chassis since 1946. Riley traditionalists complained that the only real Riley part of the car was the engine, though chief designer Gerald Palmer had certainly tried very hard to give this big, smoothly-detailed, four-door saloon an identity all of its own.

Based on a new box-section perimeter-style chassis, the Pathfinder retained many existing Riley traditions, including the famous Big Four engine (now producing 110bhp) and torsion-bar independent front suspension, though rack-and-pinion steering had been abandoned. The rear suspension of the beam axle was by coil springs, angled radius-arms and a Panhard rod, while the gearchange lever was placed outboard of the driver's seat, tucked in close to the door sill.

In its general shape, the style was really a larger version of Palmer's Wolseley 4/44-MG Magnette ZA shape, which is to say that there was a vertical front grille, but a sloping tail.

Naturally, British enthusiasts dubbed this new car the 'Ditchfinder', and although some cars were sold to the British police, it was never a big seller. The Wolseley 6/90, which would appear in the autumn of 1954, was a close relation.

At the same time, the remaining RM-series model, the 1½-litre, was given a final facelift, this featuring the use of helmet-type front wings and the removal of the running-boards under the doors, though there were no significant changes to the chassis. This, however, was enough to keep RM-series demand afloat until 1955.

Rover: The P4 range of saloons was expanded by adding 60 and 90 derivatives to the existing 75. There were no styling changes and virtually no difference in trim and furnishing standards of these 'Auntie' Rovers.

All types used the same layout of overhead-inlet/side-exhaust engines. The new 60 had a four-cylinder 2-litre type (shared with the latest Land-Rover), the 75 retained its 2.1-litre six-cylinder, while the 90 had a 2.6-litre version of the 'six'. All types used a gear-lever which was adjustable for alignment and there was a new hand-brake layout.

At the Earls Court Motor Show Rover also showed a Farina-styled (and built) convertible prototype on the P4 chassis, though this was never put into production.

Simca: Aronde models, still relatively new in France, were imported to the UK from the autumn of 1953. Like their domestic competition (the Peugeot 203 and Renault Fregate), they were conventional front-engine/rear-drive cars, with four-cylinder engines, that of the 1953/54 model being a 45bhp 1.2-litre example.

Singer: The introduction of a glassfibre-

bodied SMX Roadster fell into the 'high hopes' category, for Singer was not ready to build such a car, nor was there the demand for it.

Based on the chassis of the 1.5-litre 4AB Roadster, the SMX had a new and more modern body style, still a four-seater with detachable side-screens, but with a more pleasing and up-to-date look than before. Its problem was that it could not compare with cars like the TR2 in performance, style or value for money, and since Singer had no established sales network in the USA it was always likely to have an uphill task ahead of it. Singer's directors presumably realized this because the SMX was abandoned after a few prototypes had been made.

Standard: The Coventry concern had an extremely busy year, not only launching the all-new Eight saloon and the Phase II Vanguard, but also ushering the fully-developed Triumph TR2 into series production.

The long-awaited Eight arrived in September as a direct competitor to the Austin A30 and Morris Minor. Although it carried the same name as previous small Standards, there were no carryover parts, nor was anything shared with the Triumph Mayflower, dropped to make space for the new car.

This was one of those rare machines which was all-new from end to end – new unit-construction shell (from Fisher and Ludlow), new engine, new transmission and new suspension units. The original version of the car was a very sparsely trimmed and furnished four-door saloon, with no external access to the boot (which had to be reached by folding down the rear seat squabs) and with sliding rather than wind-down door glass. For a few short weeks – until Ford's Popular appeared – the Eight was Britain's cheapest 'real' car.

It was no wonder that Standard's Sir John Black privately christened it the 'Belsen line', or that larger-engined and more fully-equipped versions were already being planned. Although the new SC engine was not as long-lived as BMC's rival A-series, it would be a Standard-Triumph mainstay for the next three decades.

The Phase II Vanguard combined a new body style with the existing roly-poly chassis, for there were no changes to the basic running gear, or the rather transatlantic handling char-

acteristics. Compared with the six-year-old original Vanguard, the new style was a notchback rather than a fastback, with much larger rear doors than before and a little more rear-seat space. As before, an estate version was also available, and although there had been a weight increase there appeared to be no significant change to performance or fuel economy.

Standard, who were already building a 2.1-litre diesel engine for the Ferguson tractors it assembled on behalf of Harry Ferguson, also announced that it would be launching a diesel-engined Vanguard in 1954, but as this engine would only have about 40bhp, compared with the petrol-engined car's 68bhp, no-one could get very excited about the prospect.

Sunbeam (and Sunbeam-Talbot): During the year Rootes decided to tinker with its marque names, allowing a new Sunbeam-Talbot model to be called a Sunbeam, thus paving the way for the Talbot half of the title to be dropped altogether at the end of 1954.

The new Sunbeam Alpine was effectively a two-seater tourer version of the well-established Sunbeam-Talbot saloon, with the same front end and very similar body lines, though with more power from the 2.27-litre engine.

Although it was heavy and retained a steering-column gearchange, the Alpine was soon pressed into service as a works rally car, where heroic drivers like Stirling Moss and George Murray-Frame achieved success against all the odds. In the same week that it was launched, timed high-speed runs on the Jabbeke road in Belgium, and on the Montlhery track in France (where the same car achieved 120mph) did great things for its reputation.

Triumph: During the winter and spring of 1952/53, the production-specification TR2 sportscar was developed and the first deliveries were made in July/August 1953. By the end of the year several hundred had left Canley, and this shape of Triumph sportscar was established for a further nine years.

Compared with the abandoned 20TS prototype, the definitive TR2 had an all-new and more sturdy chassis-frame, a 90bhp version of the 2-litre 'wet-liner' engine and a lengthened and squared-up tail. Many more options and accessories would be introduced in the years to come.

Volkswagen: Imports of the now-legendary Beetle began in July 1953, with cable-braked 1.1-litre cars selling at prices from £650 to £773. Before long a 1.2-litre Export model had been added, and at about the same time the 500,000th Beetle rolled off the assembly lines at Wolfsburg in West Germany. In those days the design was still not well-known, but before long the platform chassis, rear-engined layout, air-cooled flat-four engine and cruising-speed-is-top-speed behaviour would all become familiar, as would the car's ugly looks, its famous high build quality – and the vicious tail-happy handling characteristics which caught out many a novice…

Industrial developments

In August, BMC announced that it was bidding to take control of Fisher and Ludlow, which was one of Britain's two largest bodyshell or monocoque manufacturers (the other being the Pressed Steel Company). Its principal factory was at Castle Bromwich, east of the centre of Birmingham, in premises originally erected to build Spitfire and Lancaster aircraft in the Second World War [by the 1990s this factory complex had moved into the control of Jaguar].

Although this takeover bid came as a surprise to the rest of the British motor industry, the only non-BMC company to be significantly affected was Standard-Triumph, who at the time were taking Standard Vanguard, and shortly Standard Eight shells from the same source.

The takeover was finalized within weeks – a move which encouraged Standard-Triumph to build up its own alternative body supplies, though that strategy would not become clear until mid-1954.

Even before launching the monocoque Anglia/Prefect models, Ford began an inexorable expansion process by buying up Briggs Motor Bodies, its major supplier of bodyshells. Briggs, with factories in Dagenham and Doncaster, was soon obliged to cut off the supply of bodies to other companies (notably Jowett), and before long it no longer operated independently.

Jowett stumbled rapidly towards closure in September, bringing car-building to an end for good. Although body-supply difficulties were blamed at the time, in truth there were already stacks of unsold Javelins at the Yorkshire factory, a situation brought about by big problems with the reliability of engines and transmissions, and consequently in bolstering up the car's reputation.

The plain fact was that Jowetts were selling very slowly, the business was no longer profitable and the directors could see no way out of this dilemma. Briggs refused to build Javelin hulls at a much reduced rate, which meant that closure was inevitable. Although a new type of Jupiter sportscar – the R4 – would be shown at Earls Court in October, the Jowett marque was already moribund and the business would rapidly be wound up. Before long the production lines were cleared, and the factory was eventually taken over by the International Harvester company, this offer going public in mid-1954.

One of Britain's 'tiddlers', Paramount, the Derbyshire-based marque which had been launched in 1950 but had never made money for its sponsors, was rescued by Camden Motors of Linslade, Buckinghamshire, but this was always a risky enterprise based on a technically boring car, and little more was ever heard of it.

Standard-Triumph's chief executive, Sir John Black, was badly injured in a road accident when Ken Richardson (driving a prototype Swallow Doretti sportscar – to be officially revealed in 1954), hit another car outside Standard's Banner Lane factory. Forced to spend weeks away from his desk, he then returned in December, seemingly even more embittered than usual towards the world in general and his workforce in particular; Sir John was never the same man again. The consequences – and his abrupt exit from the company which he had controlled for 20 years – would follow in January 1954.

Technical developments

It may sound routine today, but after several years of development, Dunlop caused quite a sensation when it announced its first tubeless tyre. Such technology had already been pre-viewed by B F Goodrich in the USA, and would be rapidly adopted by other tyre manufacturers in the 1950s.

In Britain, at least, where foreign cars began to appear in numbers for the first time since the war, one of the main talking points was the number of new, advanced and technically brave rear suspension systems being used on imported cars. British cars were still notoriously conservative in this respect, but designers should, at least, have noticed that independent rear suspension was being used by companies like Lancia, Mercedes-Benz, Renault and VW, while Lancia had adopted a de Dion system for its latest Aurelia GT.

A major road-building programme

Just before the end of the year, the British Government announced the start of a major road-building programme, which would start slowly, but build up into a flood of new construction in the late 1950s and throughout the 1960s and 1970s.

After years of total road-building famine, this was almost too good to be true, so most observers were sceptical that high hopes would ever be turned into new roads. This time, though, the Government was serious, though it took several frustrating years for some of the schemes to be turned from drawings into asphalt, bridges and junctions.

Among the many schemes mentioned at the time, the major plans listed for attention in the next few years included (today's road numbers are used to identify them):

A48 Port Talbot bypass
A465 Heads of the Valleys road, South Wales
M50 Ross Spur motorway
A4 London, Cromwell Road extension
A20 Ashford bypass in Kent
Dartford Tunnel, the first tube
M6 Preston bypass
M6 Lancaster bypass

Work on the Dartford Tunnel, a Maidenhead bypass (now part of the M4), the Cromwell Road extension and the A20 Ashford bypass had already been started, then frozen out by capital expenditure cuts, so there was every incentive to start these up again.

On the other hand, the Government was not yet prepared to authorize expense on the proposed Severn or Forth road bridges, and it was interesting to note that in 1953 there was still no mention of what would become Britain's first long continuous length of motorway, the M1 from the St Albans area to the Coventry/Northampton region. Clearly there was a lot of planning and horsetrading to be done in the next year or so.

Men of Influence

Walter Hassan

This was a period of time when a noted engineer, having dropped out of the limelight, was about to have an even greater influence on the future of Britain's motorsport industry. It was after Walter Hassan had left Jaguar, to join Coventry Climax.

Born in London in 1905, Walter Hassan joined Bentley Motors of Cricklewood in 1920 as an engineering apprentice, the 14th employee to arrive at a company which had still not yet delivered its first production car. Once out of his apprenticeship, the young Hassan became a service engineer, then a motorsport mechanic, with the famous works team, acting as riding mechanic to several of the drivers.

After Bentley closed down, he went to work for Woolf 'Babe' Barnato, in Sussex, where he designed and built the Barnato-Hassan Bentley special which raced so successfully at Brooklands. Later in the 1930s there was a short sojourn with ERA, in Bourne, before he returned to work with Thomson & Taylor at Brooklands in 1937 (being involved with building John Cobb's Railton Land Speed Record car).

Then, in 1938, he moved to Jaguar, in Foleshill, as chief experimental engineer, spent a couple of wartime years with the Bristol Aeroplane Company in Bristol, then returned to Jaguar to concentrate on the design and development of the new twin-cam XK engines, along with the new chassis and suspensions to which they were to be matched.

Invited to move to Coventry Climax in 1950, he became that company's chief engineer (later technical director), where he supervised the design not only of new fire-pump and other industrial engines, but also of a series of fine racing power units including the stillborn FPE V8, the four-cylinder FPF, the World Championship-winning FWMV V8 and the fascinating but also stillborn flat-16 FWMW type. He was, above all, a consummately practical engineer, rather than a head-in-the-clouds boffin – but no other engineer's racing units at that time were as powerful or as reliable.

Following Jaguar's takeover of Coventry Climax in 1963, Hassan soon moved back to Jaguar to take control of power-unit design and development, where he oversaw development of the legendary 5.3-litre V12 power unit. Even after retiring in 1972 he found time to consult with BRM about the improvement of their 3-litre V12 F1 engines, and he was still actively involved in engineering work until his late eighties.

As recently as 1990 he upgraded a 1920s Bentley racing engine for Fayed Majzub, which proved to be considerably more powerful than the original.

He lived on into his 90s, that milestone birthday being celebrated affectionately in the Midlands by an enormous number of friends and acquaintances. He died in 1996.

1954

Although the British Government made no further fiscal concessions to motorists in 1954, optimism and what these days is often referred to as the 'feel-good' factor was on the increase. The motor industry produced almost 770,000 cars, yet another record, and no fewer than 395,000 of these were delivered to British buyers.

However, although restrictions on foreign car imports had been swept away, still very few were actually being sold, and incredibly their market share was little more than 1 per cent – no wonder the British motor industry was accused of complacency!

1954, in fact, was the last year in which sizeable waiting lists for new cars still existed; quite suddenly, the motor trade had to change from being an easy-going order-taking business to one which actively had to go out and sell cars against widespread competition. This was also the year when the Government brought forward a new Road Traffic Bill, one of the most controversial proposals in which was to authorize experimental parking meter schemes, initially in the West End of London. At the same time, the first proposals for testing old (meaning 10 years old) cars were discussed.

Overseas touring continued to grow steadily. Helped along by the modern roll-on/roll-off facilities at Dover, more cars used the ferries, but air-ferry competition was still growing, especially after Silver City's new Ferryfield airfield at Lydd, on the Dungeness peninsula, came into use. This new field, 72 miles from central London, brought car-ferry flights within 20 minutes of Le Touquet in France, and since fares started at a mere £7 5s (£7.25) for short cars, with passenger fares at £2 10s (£2.50), business was brisk.

Silver City, in fact, was still expanding, for a new Southend-Calais service also opened, and more new routes would radiate from the Essex airfield in future years. The shipping companies based on Dover and Folkestone were definitely worried at this stage, though in the end they would win a battle which raged for another two decades.

More local authorities were beginning to cater for motorists. In Scotland, a new car ferry came into service across the River Clyde between Gourock and Dunoon. Other existing car ferries in Scotland would be replaced by larger craft in the next few years, though the building of new bridges to replace them would not be tackled until the 1970s and 1980s.

New models

AC: Having brought the exciting new Ace sportscar into production, AC then announced another version of the same design, this time with a sleek fastback/hatchback body, and called it the Aceca. As with the Ace of 1953, this car was previewed long before it was ready for sale, deliveries not beginning until 1955.

Alfa Romeo: The first of the 1.3-litre-engined Giuliettas, a Bertone-styled coupe, was exhibited at Earls Court, though production had only just started in Italy.

The unit-construction Giulietta range, which would soon include a four-door saloon and eventually encompass all manner of spiders (sportscars) and specially-bodied coupes, was new in every respect, including a small, high-revving, twin-cam engine, transmissions to match, coil-spring independent front suspension and accurate and careful location of the back axle beam.

Armstrong Siddeley: The relatively new Sapphire was developed even further, GM Hydramatic automatic transmission (as used on Rolls-Royce and Bentley cars) now becoming an option. At the same time brakes were increased in size and vacuum-servo assistance provided.

Aston Martin: Because the 2.9-litre twin-cam engine had already found a home in the latest Lagonda, Aston Martin enthusiasts hoped that it would soon be made available in the DB2-4. In August their patience was rewarded when a 140bhp/2,922cc derivative was announced for British-market cars. This made a splendid car even better, for the enlarged DB2-4 could now reach almost 120mph. But how many people could afford £2,728? Not many, it seemed.

Austin: There was a bonanza of new models from BMC, led by two major

ranges of Austins, both of which used rationalized corporate components. The new A40 and A50 Cambridges which replaced the old A40 Somerset were rather narrow, craggily-styled unit-construction cars fitted with 1.2-litre or 1.5-litre B-series running gear. Unhappily, the chassis, with soft springing and woolly steering, were even less accomplished than the A40 Somersets' had been – but as the cars were cheap and looked new they began to sell in large quantities.

[It was at the launch of these cars that the now-knighted Sir Leonard Lord announced BMC's intention to make 600,000 vehicles a year within two years.]

The second new range replaced the A70 Hereford (and the already dead A90 Atlantic) and was dubbed the A90 Westminster; although this six-cylinder car looked very similar to the new A50, almost every panel was different. Naturally, the A90 had a longer wheelbase and more cabin space, and it was powered by the all-new but technically unadventurous BMC C-series engine, a six-cylinder 2.6-litre unit which was eventually to be used in many other new BMC models including Austin-Healeys and light commercial vehicles.

As previewed in the A90, it was smooth but heavy, rated at 85bhp (which was less than the old A90's 2.66-litre 'four' had delivered six years earlier) and had almost criminally inefficient inlet manifolding, with angular ports actually cast into the cylinder head itself. Nevertheless, at £792 it offered good value – the 2.2-litre Ford Zephyr was only £37 cheaper – and, after all, *anything* was likely to be more successful than the old A70/A90 range.

Austin-Healey: After an intensive racing programme with what were called special test cars, Austin-Healey was ready to put the very special 100S model on sale. Although it was based on the 100/4, the 100S was much more specialized and intended for sportscar racing.

There were styling changes, the body was entirely clad in aluminium, there were no bumpers or windscreen, there was a totally new cylinder head (designed for BMC by Harry Weslake) and Dunlop disc brakes were fitted to all four wheels. With 132bhp instead of 90bhp in a lighter structure, this was a formidably fast sportscar, though most were sold abroad and very few were used as normal road-going transport. Only 50 would be built in 1954 and 1955, for this was a short-lived 'homologation special'.

Bentley: With remarkably little fuss, Bentley phased-in a 4.9-litre version of its well-known IOEV six-cylinder engine, though for the time being it was only available on Continental models. As ever, power and torque figures were not published.

BMW: The 2.6-litre V8-engined 502, which shared the same chassis and rounded body style as the 501, made its first appearance in the UK. This large and robust overhead-valve unit was BMW's first new engine since the war. Although not very familiar here, it would be used in a variety of BMW models, and would remain in limited production until the early 1960s. At this stage, imports were still in left-hand-drive form, although right-hand-drive models would be available from 1955.

Borgward: A new medium-sized two-door saloon, the 1½-litre Isabella, was introduced in June, British sales beginning towards the end of the year. This was a spacious and relatively conventional machine, though with all-independent suspension. Over the years the engine was made progressively more powerful, so much so that late-model Isabellas achieved some success in saloon car racing.

Bristol: The subsidiary of the aerospace company produced the new 405 four-door saloon (and a closely related drop-head coupe, whose body was by Abbott of Farnham), which looked totally different from the old 401/403 types, being a lengthened version of the style already seen on the 404 model. The 114in-wheelbase chassis was virtually the same as on the 403, though the six-cylinder engine was rated at 105bhp, and for the first time Laycock overdrive was fitted behind the existing four-speed gearbox.

An interesting feature was the stowage of the big 16in diameter spare wheel in a body recess behind one front wheel, a matching recess on the other side of the car housing the battery and other accessories.

Daimler: The Conquest Century was added to the successful new Conquest range; it was virtually the same car, but fitted with the 100bhp twin-carburettor 2,433cc engine already previewed in the Conquest Roadster. To match the higher performance there was a more completely equipped dashboard and bigger and more powerful brakes.

Daimler was so enthusiastic about this model's prospects that it approved a limited works motorsport programme, and for a short time the Century was used in International rallies and saloon car races. A hardtop version of the Conquest Roadster was also promised, though such a car never went into production.

At the top of their range, Daimler reshuffled the pack considerably. Having cleared out the old DE27 and DE36 types, there was space to extend the Regency model range upmarket. Accordingly, the original hand-built Regency was dropped in favour of lightly facelifted Regency IIs with longer and more squared-up tails and larger luggage trunks. One version had the same 3.5-litre engine as before, another using a 4.6-litre version of the same power unit. Thus the Regency style edged towards the shape of the later 104 and (finally) the Majestic which carried this range into the 1960s.

In addition, Daimler also revealed the Sportsman, which had a much-modified Regency structure (the style included a wraparound rear window) and a highly-tuned 3.5-litre engine producing no less than 140bhp. Then, to top off the range, a new razor-edge style by Hooper was dropped on the 4.6-litre version of the chassis, this being the Regina limousine. A careful look will reveal definite style links between the Regina of the late 1950s and the Daimler limousine of 1968...

Delage: The D6 model was listed for sale in the UK for 1954, but was almost non-existent on the roads. This French machine was a descendant of the noted prewar *Grand Routier* type, with a 3-litre ohv engine backed by the Cotal gearbox, but time was running out for Delage, and the cars were really obsolete.

Delahaye: Like the Delage, this French marque made a belated appearance into British price lists,

though production was just about to end in its native country. The 135/235 range were really final statements of a 1930s theme, topped by smart though rather over-blown coupe and saloon bodies. In British marketing terms they were totally insignificant.

DKW: Imports of this newly-developed two-stroke-engined front-wheel-drive car, the Sonderklasse (or Three-Six, as the concessionaires tried to name it) began in 1954, initially being handled by AFN of Isleworth, the manufacturer of Frazer Nash sportscars.

The Sonderklasse chassis, which was built in a variety of closely-related body styles, was a lineal development of one put on the road in the 1930s. In its latest form there was an in-line three-cylinder engine of only 896cc, but although this sounded too small to provide a respectable performance in a 1,900lb car, the results were impressive. Not only could this car beat 75mph, but it also handled well, the only let-down being the use of a steering-column gearchange.

In short, this was an impressive effort – so much so that Saab, having studied the design of 1930s-type DKWs very closely before settling on the layout of its first front-wheel-drive cars, adopted the Sonderklasse layout for its 93 models of the mid-1950s...

Frazer Nash: There was still room for developing the existing chassis, so a smart and curvaceous open two-seater called the Sebring was introduced. Even lighter than the Targa Florio, it had de Dion rear suspension and race-bred roadholding; in the event, only three would be sold.

Hillman: What would now be called a three-door car, the short-wheelbase Husky estate, was unveiled in October. In effect this was a shortened-wheelbase (by 9in) version of the existing Hillman Minx estate car platform with only two passenger doors; mechanically it was just the same, the old-type 1,265cc side-valve engine being fitted (it would be retained until this original Husky was dropped in 1957).

The introduction of an entirely new small four-cylinder engine for the Minx, with overhead valves and a capacity of 1,390cc, was an extremely significant commercial move. Intended to replace the ancient side-valve unit (which had been designed for the original Hillman Minx of 1931), it was at once more powerful and had a great deal of in-built stretch for the future.

The first ohv Minx power unit produced 43bhp, compared with 38bhp for the last of the side-valve types, but this was only the beginning of a long and gradual improvement and tuning process, at which Rootes was adept. Further developments of the new type would eventually displace 1,725cc, and would be built until the late 1970s in Britain, and for even longer overseas.

Hotchkiss: The French firm listed high-performance British-market cars in 1953–54, but as all Hotchkiss production was about to end this was a futile gesture. Theoretically these 1930s-engineered 3.5-litre six-cylinder machines were available as 686 or even faster 2050 derivatives – but few if any were seen.

Humber: Rootes continued its policy of upgrading all its models by giving them overhead-valve engines. For the latest Hawk, the Mk VI, neither the style nor the basic chassis engineering was changed, but the old 58bhp side-valve engine was swept aside in favour of a 70bhp version of the 2,267cc unit already found in the Sunbeam-Talbot 90. Laycock overdrive became optional, so although this was by no means a sporting car, it was at least faster, potentially more economical, and alto-gether more versatile than before. This shape of Hawk, although basically six years old, still had another three years to run.

Jaguar: In January the Mk VII became the latest British car to be offered with Laycock overdrive as an optional extra, but this was only a holding operation for what was to fol-low in October. At that juncture, both the existing ranges were substantially modified and uprated:

The XK120 was dropped in favour of the XK140, which looked similar except for a different radiator grille and the use of more sturdy front and rear bumpers, but had more powerful versions of the XK engine, rack-and-pinion steering, an optional overdrive, more completely-equipped cockpits and – in the FHC and DHC versions at least – more cabin space. A 210bhp engine with 'C-type' head was avail-

able as an option.

A great car had been made even better – even if by modern standards the steering was a lot too heavy and the brakes not up to the same stan-dard as the engine.

The Mk VII gave way to the Mk VIIM, a massive and curvaceous saloon which still looked the same except for a few style changes at the front, and had the same uprated engines as the XK140s. Basic, overdrive and auto-matic transmissions were available, and with a 105mph-plus top speed these were very saleable cars. This shape of big Jaguar still had a long way to go, for the last of all (by then titled Mk IX) would not be built until 1961.

[Although somewhat outside the scope of this book, Jaguar announced that the sports-racing D-type was also to be put into limited production for sale to selected competitors all over the world.]

Lagonda: Persevering with the 3-litre model, the company added a similarly-styled four-door saloon alternative to the two-door version announced a year earlier.

Lanchester: Shown at the October 1954 Earls Court Motor Show as a prototype, the new Sprite was a chunky, square-rigged four-door saloon with a four-cylinder 1.6-litre version of the Daimler Conquest's six-cylinder engine.

It was the first Lanchester to use a unit-construction body/chassis unit, and the first car in the world to adopt the Hobbs four-speed automatic trans-mission. It was also the first newly-designed Daimler-Lanchester model for some years to use coil-spring inde-pendent front suspension (laminated torsion bars had been very fashion-able for a time).

This was a clear attempt to replace the LD10 and fill the production lines at Radford with a new Lanchester, for the last of the Ledas was built during the year, leaving only the Daimler Conquests in volume production for the time being.

However, at the end of 1954 the Sprite was still not ready for produc-tion, the body style was clearly provi-sional and a lot more development work was necessary before the pro-posed production version was intro-duced in October 1955.

Lancia: The Italian company, which never liked to leave its designs alone for long, began importing 2.3-litre ver-sions of the Aurelia saloon instead of the earlier Type B22 2-litre type, and even found a few buyers for the smart fastback 2.5-litre/de Dion rear-sus-pended Aurelia GT coupes.

Mercedes-Benz: Two new sporting models were introduced, the excitingly-specified 300SL and the less-powerful but still technically interesting 190SL. Both went on sale in the UK as soon as series production began late in the year.

The 300SL was a productionized and further-developed version of the cars which had been raced so success-fully in 1952, and it bristled with inno-vation. Not only was there a complex tubular spaceframe chassis and pas-senger doors which lifted upwards in what became known as the gullwing style, but the engine was the world's first petrol-powered unit to use direct fuel injection.

By any standards the 240bhp 300SL was formidably fast (though claims of a 165mph top speed with the appro-priate gearing were certainly exagger-ated), but its high-pivot swing-axle rear suspension meant that the handling could be very tricky indeed. Neverthe-less, it was a very desirable, albeit expensive car.

Because the unit-construction 190SL was based on a shortened version of the 180's chassis platform, it had a much more conventional specification. The 1.9-litre overhead-camshaft engine guaranteed more than 100mph, and the all-independent suspension gave a supple ride. It was typical of the Ger-man concern that wind-up windows and a properly-engineered fold-back soft-top had also been provided. Somehow, though, the 190SL was more sporting than outright sports, and it rarely figured in motorsports events. Both these cars – or developments of them – would remain in production for the next nine years.

MG: Deliveries to the USA of TF1500s – TFs fitted with an enlarged (63bhp/1,466cc) engine – began during the summer, though the existence of such a model was only revealed to the British in November, cars for the home market becoming available during the winter.

Morgan: As soon as supplies could be obtained, Morgan upgraded the performance of the Plus 4 by making the 90bhp Triumph TR2 engine available as an option to the 68bhp Standard Vanguard unit. As the price increase was only £20 (basic), demand was high.

Morris: During the summer, two closely related new models – the new-generation Oxford and Cowley – were introduced; they replaced the Morris Minor-shape Oxford MO, which had been in production for nearly six years. Sharing the same rounded style of four-door saloon shell, they used the newly developed BMC engines and transmissions first previewed in the MG Magnette in late 1953, this signalling that true volume production of B-series equipment had begun just over two years after the British Motor Corporation had been founded.

In the first phase the Cowley used a 1.2-litre engine (which was very similar to that of the Austin A40), while the Oxford used a 50bhp/1.5-litre version. Both cars had a wide cabin and a sweeping facia/instrument panel set well forward from the bench seat, but used an offset steering wheel and a steering-column gearchange. Their chassis (designed at Cowley, not Longbridge) was surprisingly advanced, with torsion-bar independent front suspension and rack-and-pinion steering.

Rover: Shuffling the pack of its P4 four-door saloon range even further, from the autumn of 1954 Rover began fitting the 75 with a different, large-bore/short-stroke, version of the six-cylinder engine. Whereas the original 75 had a 2,103cc/75bhp engine, the 1955 model had the latest 2,230cc/80bhp derivative which was effectively a short-stroke version of the 90 unit.

Singer: Eight years after it had first been previewed, the SM1500 was upgraded and named the Hunter (some years later, Singer's new owner, Rootes, would adopt the name for a new medium-sized Hillman). Mechanically there were virtually no changes, but the front was given a traditional style of vertical grille, and on the first cars some of the surrounding panels were in glassfibre, though this material was later abandoned because of fit and quality problems.

Standard: As forecast, a Ten version of the Eight went on sale in March, this effectively being a larger-engined (33bhp/948cc) and better-equipped derivative of the original type. Apart from the increased power, torque and flexibility of the Ten, the new car also had an opening bootlid providing proper access to the luggage stowage area, wind-up windows in the doors and much more complete trimming and furnishing of the interior.

Customers' choice, therefore, was between paying as little as possible (£481) for minimal motoring, or £100 extra (£581) for an altogether more lively and better-equipped derivative of the design. For years, that choice was to be finely balanced, for both cars sold extremely well.

The choice was made even more difficult in mid-year when an Eight De Luxe appeared, this having most of the Ten's equipment and selling for £538. A few months later an estate car (Companion) version of the Ten also made its debut.

A 40bhp/2.1-litre diesel engine was introduced as an option for the Standard Vanguard, though in the event this only sold in tiny numbers. The engine was totally different in every way from the Vanguard's usual petrol unit, and had originally been developed for use in the Ferguson tractors which Standard assembled. Rugged, reliable, but noisy and gutless, it was not really a private car engine at all, as all who drove behind it confirmed. Two years later, when the Phase II Vanguard had been dropped in favour of the monocoque Phase III, this diesel engine was abandoned.

Sunbeam: In a final change to the design which dated from 1948, Rootes turned the Sunbeam-Talbot 90 Mk IIA into the Sunbeam Mk III (this model still being built as a saloon or a drop-head coupe). The new designation was justified by a minor front-end facelift, changes to the facia (with a rev-counter in the middle), a power boost to 80bhp, and offering Laycock overdrive as an option. In this form, but at a slowly decreasing rate of production, the Mk III would be built until 1957. At the same time, Laycock overdrive was standardized on the Alpine sportscar, though this car had less than a year to live before being dropped in mid-1955.

Swallow: The Walsall-based Swallow Coachbuilding Company, which was a distant descendant of Jaguar from the 1930s, introduced a brand-new two-seater sportscar, the Doretti. Even while it was still under wraps this car had received unwanted publicity, for it was the crash of a prototype in 1953 which had injured Standard's Sir John Black so badly.

Although the Doretti used a unique ladder-style chassis-frame and had a very smart body style in the 'barchetta' shape with the steel shell panelled in aluminium alloy, the engine, transmission, rear axle and suspension units were all lifted from the Triumph TR2 (with that company's approval). Compared with the TR2, however, the Doretti had a 7in longer wheelbase, a wider front track – and cost considerably more at £1,102 when sales began, compared with £887 for the current TR2.

Triumph: Optional overdrive, hard-top and wire-spoke wheels, and a rejigging of the door/sill structure all helped turn the TR2 into an even more practical proposition than before. Sales increased – and MG's TF1500 looked even more outmoded.

Vauxhall: Like Ford, Vauxhall was intent on moving its cars gradually up-market, so the launch of a Cresta as a more luxuriously-equipped Velox was no surprise. Except for slight upgrading of engines to take advantage of premium fuel, there were no significant mechanical changes on these cars for 1955.

Wolseley: The 6/80 of 1948 vintage was finally laid to rest and replaced by the entirely different 6/90 model. Best described as a BMC C-series-engined, rebadged version of the Riley Pathfinder, the 6/90 was a perfect example of the way BMC intended to make two, three or even more derivatives of every new model where possible.

Like the MG Magnette–Wolseley 4/44 relationship, there were enough differences to allow the two cars their individuality, for although they shared the same chassis, suspensions and basic shells, the Wolseley had more pronounced body sills, a smoother engine – and a steering-column instead of a right-hand floor-mounted gearchange.

Industrial developments

The biggest upheaval of the year came in January when Standard's controversial chief executive, Sir John Black, abruptly retired. At the time it was said to be due to ill-health following the Swallow Doretti crash of autumn 1953, but in fact he was ousted following a boardroom coup.

Sir John had been Standard's managing director since the 1930s and had only just taken on the additional task of chairman. It was his capricious behaviour and schizophrenic character which finally caused his board to turn against him.

In his place, 37-year-old Alick Dick became Standard's managing director, with engineering director Ted Grinham as his deputy. Completing these changes, the Second World War hero, Marshal of the Royal Air Force Lord Tedder, became Standard's chairman in the middle of the year.

One of Alick Dick's first moves was to begin merger discussions with Rover, though these came to nothing and were abandoned. Incidentally, a repeat approach in 1959 also foundered, for both companies wanted supremacy in a merged business and neither at that time was desperate enough to accept a partner.

Leonard Lord, the chairman of BMC, was knighted and became Sir Leonard – not that this altered the way that most of his associates thought of him. As the thrusting and workaholic supremo of Britain's largest car-maker, this accolade was well-earned.

The Nash Metropolitan project, which he had masterminded with the American company in 1952, finally came to fruition in 1954 when production of 1.2-litre Austin A40-engined cars began at Longbridge. All cars were sent to North America at first, and the Metropolitan (unbadged, in Britain) would not, in fact, go on sale in the UK until 1957, by which time the engine would be bigger and external access to the boot added (none was provided on the original model).

When BMC purchased Fisher and Ludlow in 1953, Standard began to worry about the future security of its own body supplies (both the Eight/Ten and Vanguard types were built by F&L). During 1954 Alick Dick moved swiftly

to counter this by securing a long-term body supply and first-priority agreement from Mulliners of Birmingham. At the time, Mulliners were already suppliers of TR2 shells and many Eight/Ten and Vanguard derivatives.

There was something of an outcry from other manufacturers, for shells such as the Aston Martin DB2-4, Daimler Regency and Sunbeam Alpine sportscar were also being sourced from Mulliners. However, this was not yet a takeover (although one would follow four years later) and Mulliners gave their other clients a lot of time to find alternative supplies.

The consolidation of Britain's car-making industry continued when BSA Ltd (who already owned Daimler-Lanchester) also absorbed Carbodies, the Coventry-based manufacturer of bodyshells. Since much of Carbodies output was already devoted to Daimler and Lanchester bodywork, this merely tidied-up an arms-length arrangement into something more definite.

At the end of the year David Brown completed the purchase of Tickford Ltd, the famous Newport Pagnell-based coachbuilding concern. Like the BSA-Carbodies deal, this made a great deal of business sense because Tickford was already supplying many shells to Aston Martin-Lagonda. However, as with the Standard-Mulliners accord, it meant that other clients (in this case including Alvis) would soon have to make alternative arrangements.

The announcement of a large proposed expansion in Vauxhall's production facilities passed virtually unnoticed, though in 1957 it became clear that this had been to allow a second range of cars – the new Victors – to be added to the existing Wyvern and Velox models. Expansion at Luton (and later at Ellesmere Port) has continued ever since.

This was the year in which the last series-production Lea-Francis cars were built. The Coventry-based company, which had already spent much of the 1930s in hibernation, had been revived in 1938 around an efficient new range of Riley-like four-cylinder engines, but found that its postwar cars rapidly became dated, and because no capital was available to develop new designs or even new body shapes, production had to end when demand for the old 1940s-style cars finally dried up. There would be two abortive attempts to revive the name – one in 1960 and one in the

1980s – but both were fruitless.

It was also the end of the road for Sunbeam-Talbot, a marque which Rootes had invented, in any case, in 1938. Future cars of this type were always badged as Sunbeams.

Allard, though on its last legs as a car-maker, soldiered on for another year or so, but would soon follow Lea-Francis into history.

Technical developments

Several years after the start-up of the MIRA (Motor Industry Research Association) project, the proving grounds at Lindley, near Nuneaton, were officially opened. The laboratories (still visible from the A5 road) and the banked outer circuit had been completed, along with a useful variety of special surfaces.

In those days, almost every Midlands-based car-maker used these grounds (for none had a proving ground of its own), and each company was expected to keep itself to itself, without prying into the opposition's prototypes (they were surprisingly honest about this, too). Only Ford and Vauxhall, who each had their own rudimentary facilities, did not make much use of MIRA.

Although Rover pressed ahead with gas-turbine engine development, it was clearly not close to putting such a car on sale. However, in addition to JET 1, the open-top car first shown in 1954, Rover had now completed another prototype with its gas-turbine engine in the tail of a P4 saloon, exhausting its gases out of an enormous tunnel built up behind the car's rear window.

This was also the year in which BMC first ran an experimental gas-turbine-engined car, though as this was a case of mating an industrial project with a vast Sheerline chassis and body it was not treated quite so seriously by the pundits. BMC soon lost interest in this combination, in fact, and little more was ever heard of it.

After a great deal of discussion and testing, flashing direction indicators became road-legal on UK-market cars; previously all cars had been obliged to use semaphore indicators. This technical battle had once been summarized as the 'wink or wave' choice...

1955

With the economy improving steadily, Britain and its motorists looked set for a very contented year – until November, when the Chancellor suddenly increased purchase tax on new cars from 50 to 60 per cent. This was meant to dampen down the booming demand, and as a strategy it certainly succeeded: within a year several of Britain's car-makers would have introduced short-time working!

Before this, though, new-car production shot up once again to nearly 900,000, and home-market deliveries breached the 500,000 mark, though exports were still rather disappointing; Britain's cars were being outclassed by more technically adventurous machinery from France, Germany and Italy.

Even so, there was every incentive for the British to buy cars. Not only had waiting lists virtually disappeared, but purchasing power was up as income tax was reduced by 6d (2.5p) in the pound, which was the second such reduction in two years.

Even though the country was hit hard by newspaper and dock strikes, the sense of euphoria grew apace, and in the British General Election, the reigning Government was returned with an increased majority.

Once again the Government dabbled with restrictions on credit. For hire purchase transactions, customers now had to put down a minimum deposit of 15 per cent, then pay off the balance within 24 months.

Airborne car ferries were more popular than ever, for Silver City announced new services between Stranraer and Belfast, and between Birmingham and Le Touquet, the latter run 200 miles long and timed to take 90 minutes – serious stuff in the draughty and noisy Bristol Freighters. A Liverpool–Belfast service was also added during the year, then a Lydd–Basle route for the winter, using what Silver City hastened to add were 'heated' Bristol Freighters!

The thin end of the parking meters wedge appeared when the Government set the first rate at a mere 6d (2.5p) an hour for the first trials in London. At the time, even that was thought to be dangerously expensive, yet everyone expected the rates to be increased before long...

New models

Note: Starting in 1955, a growing number of imported American cars were listed for UK sale, although some of these do not appear to have been delivered in significant numbers. They are recorded below and on future pages at the time when they first became officially listed in the UK.

Alvis: The old traditionally-styled TC21/100 model was dropped, and in its place came the first of the Graber-styled coupes, the original type being known as the TC 108/G.

Except that the engine had been further boosted to 104bhp, there were few mechanical changes to the 3-litre chassis. The new two-door body style was smart and distinctive. Alvis' only problem was that neither Tickford nor Mulliners (its previous suppliers) could take on manufacture of the new body, and the company had not secured an alternative source when the car was launched. Eventually the contract was placed with Willowbrook of Loughborough (who were really bus body-builders), but assembly was always very limited.

Alvis had abandoned development of an all-new V8-engined car on which Alec Issigonis had been working for more than three years. The result was a considerable waste of time and money for Alvis – and it led to Issigonis joining BMC, where the Mini and other front-wheel-drive cars were to emerge.

Armstrong Siddeley: Yet another version of the graceful Sapphire appeared, this being a long-wheelbase limousine which carried the same basic styling lines as the saloon, but had a more spacious cabin. The wheelbase had been stretched by 17in, there were three rows of seats and the roof was significantly higher than that of the saloons, so the car was considerably heavier. Power-assisted steering by Girling became optional in August, the company pointing out that this was the very first British car to have that feature.

The closely related 234 and 236 models were brand-new models with box-section chassis on a 111in wheelbase and with a choice of engines – one refined, one coarse and sporting – and with rather awkward body styling. There was a story at the time that the

directors had ordered that the roof of prototypes be raised to give more headroom, but had not authorized any other style changes to balance it; it showed...

The 236 used the final development of the 2.3-litre six-cylinder engine which had originated in the 1930s as a 2-litre and was smooth, if not very powerful. The 234, on the other hand, used a highly-tuned four-cylinder 2.3-litre which was effectively a chopped-down Sapphire engine. Powerful but not very refined, it gave the 234 an enterprising performance, but somehow the result was most 'non-Armstrong Siddeley'.

The 234/236 models had one major problem; it was called Jaguar 2.4. The new Armstrong Siddeleys were introduced at the same time as the new Jaguar, but looked less attractive and cost considerably more. Unhappily for them, this meant that they struggled to establish any sort of following, and they would only remain in production for three years.

Austin: It was a year for tinkering, with automatic transmission as a new option on the big Princess limousines and Borg-Warner overdrive becoming optional on the A90 Westminster.

Austin-Healey: The 100/4 was given a four-speed C-series gearbox, complete with overdrive, in place of the odd three-plus-two-overdrive ratios of the original type, and thus became known as the BN2.

At the same time the 100M was introduced, this being a tuned-up version of the 100/4, complete with a 110bhp engine, a louvred bonnet panel and a leather strap to hold it down. The 100Ms were supplied either as complete cars (the conversion from a 100/4 being carried out by the Healey factory in Warwick), or suitable kits were supplied to dealers to do the conversion on their own premises.

Bentley: The new S-type, taking over from the R-type, was nearly identical to the new Rolls-Royce Silver Cloud described below.

Later in the year the first of the new-generation S-type Continental coupes was launched. Because it was based on the new S-type chassis and therefore could use a larger and more spacious body, a Continental S was different in almost every way from a Continental R. With the larger (4.9-litre) engine and weighing considerably more, it was faster than before, if not as nimble, but for those who could afford one it was still an attractive machine; for the first time there was a convertible body on offer, this time from Park Ward.

BMW: The West German company took over the manufacture of the Isetta bubblecar, which was originally an Italian design, and soon brought it to the British market.

The first of a number of such machines, the Isetta was probably the best (and best-known) of the bunch. Philosophically it was more of a motor-cycle grown up rather than a car made smaller. The basis was a simple tubular chassis with a mid-mounted, air-cooled, single-cylinder motorcycle type of two-stroke engine mounted behind the seats, actually in the mid-engine position as defined for racing cars. Twin rear wheels were mounted very close together, there being no need for a differential.

Access to the seats was by opening up the front (and only) forward-facing door, which was hinged at one side, the steering wheel and column being arranged to swing to one side at the same time.

The Isetta was a simple, crude, but somehow endearing little 'car', with marginal performance, only just over 7ft long, with creditable agility and park-anywhere ability.

During the year BMW also increased the engine of the 502 to 3.2 litres, then introduced two very different sporting cars at the Frankfurt show – the 503 coupe/cabriolet and the 507 roadster. By British standards, both were extremely rare and very expensive.

The 503 used the same basic chassis as that of the 501/502 saloon, but was powered by a 140bhp/3.2-litre version of the V8 engine. Under the very smart 2+2 body style the four-speed gearbox was separate from the engine and (oddly, this, for a sporting car) there was a steering-column gearchange. The style was by Count Albrecht Goertz, who had also penned the 507. Altogether, the 503 was a big, heavy and rather ponderous car for which demand was always limited. Four years later, when the chassis had been updated (with an integral gearbox and central change) it was dropped after only 412 cars had been built.

The 507 was much smaller than the 503, for although it used the same basic chassis-frame and running gear, the wheelbase had been reduced by no less than 16in. Styling of the curvaceous two-seater was also by Count Goertz, and was apparently aimed at sales in the USA, where initially it was priced at a whopping $9,000.

Although it could reach 120mph, it never had the handling, or poise to match its straight-line speed, and its high price hurt it very badly wherever it was put on sale. Only 253 cars would be built in four years.

Buick: Century and Super models were newly listed.

Cadillac: The V8-engined Special, Eldorado and Fleetwood models were all newly listed.

Chevrolet: The Bel Air, One-Fifty and Two-Ten models were newly listed.

Citroen: For the last season of its life the big six-cylinder-engined front-drive Six was equipped with self-levelling oleopneumatic suspension, but only at the rear. The same feature was later added to other *traction avant* models for the remainder of their production run, which would end in 1957. At the time this looked to be an odd market-ing move, but when the DS19 was introduced, it became clear that it had been a proving trial of what was soon to follow.

To make the 2CV a little more practical and able to keep up with other traffic, its engine size was increased from 375cc to 425cc, this meaning a leap in peak power from 9bhp to 12hp.

The new DS19, which was 'wall-to-wall high-tech' apart from its old-style 1.9-litre engine, arrived in October and was as important in its own way as was the Fiat 600 in *its* class. The new car, which had taken several years to develop, would eventually take over from the *traction avant* models whose design roots were in the early 1930s, though both types would be built alongside each other until 1957.

Naturally the futuristically-shaped front-wheel-drive DS19 had a unit-construction shell, but it was one with a difference. Citroen called it a base unit structure, for every skin panel was a bolt-on item; this theoretically made accident repairs very easy and saved weight in many ways.

The engine was an updated version of the old 1,911cc long-stroke design, though with a new type of cylinder head, and in this application it provided hydraulic power to operate the brakes, clutch, gearchange, steering and suspension.

The DS19, in other words, was an amazingly complex machine with power-assistance for almost everything, including the all-independent oleo-pneumatic suspension. At rest, with the engine switched off, the big shark-nosed car sank down towards the ground, only returning to a normal level when the engine was fired up.

At speed the new car had a very soft ride and impressively tenacious road-holding. If there was cause for complaint it was that the engine did not live up to the rest of the design, this being a car which always *looked* much faster than it actually was. At first the new Citroen looked likely to be tempera-mental, in fact a plumber's nightmare, but everything worked well, the dealer chain soon became used to it, and nearly 1,500,000 of all types would be built in the next 20 years.

Daimler: There was a reshuffle of existing models and resources, and several new names, though shapes for 1956 would be broadly the same as they had been in 1955.

The Conquest Roadster and Con-quest Drophead Coupe were dropped, replaced by one new model, the Con-quest Sports Drophead Coupe, which effectively was a grown-up and more refined version of the Roadster with wind-up windows and a proper fold-up, padded-and-lined soft-top. Some-how, a sideways-facing extra seat had been placed behind the front seats, though with such restricted head and legroom that it cannot have been com-fortable to ride in.

The Regency Mk II, which had only been revamped as recently as October 1954, gave way to a new car called the 104, this using a further-modified Regency chassis and bodyshell, but with a considerably more powerful (137bhp) 3.5-litre engine with an alu-minium cylinder head.

There was also the ludicrously titled 104 Ladies' Model, surely one of final follies influenced by Lady Docker, which was no more than a standard 104 with extra upmarket equipment built in. It cost £312 more, and sank without trace or regret.

The other new model for 1956 was the DK400 limousine, a massive car built on the Regina's chassis, but with curiously rounded styling rather like that of the latest 104 models. Not surprisingly, sales were very limited.

Fiat: There's no doubt that the launch of the rear-engined 600 was one of the most important of the year. Not only was it Fiat's much-tested long-term replacement for the 500, or *Topolino* series, it was the most technically advanced private car the Italian giant had yet produced.

Every detail of the design was new from the tiny rear-mounted 633cc overhead-valve engine to the all-steel unit-construction monocoque and all-independent suspension. To those drivers used to the detail conventionalities of Austins, Morrises and Standards, the Fiat 600 was a startling machine, but until Alec Issigonis' Mini arrived on the scene four years later it was *the* standard-setter by which most other companies had to measure their efforts.

The 600s and their descendants would be built until 1970, and an entire sub-industry grew up in Italy where special, modified and unrecognizably altered versions and other cars using the engine/transmission units were all developed. The engine itself, or enlarged and improved versions of it, would have a mass-production life of nearly 40 years.

Ford: Borg-Warner overdrive was made available as an option on Zephyr Six/Zodiac models, though very few such cars seem to have been made before the first-generation model was discontinued in 1956.

In addition there were estate car versions of the Anglia and Prefect saloons, badged as Escort and Squire. Although a bit further upmarket than the first type of converted-van estates, these were still not as well-developed or equipped as later-generation load carriers would become.

Ford-Canada and **Ford-USA:** Customline, Fairlane and Thunderbird models were newly listed.

HRG: Sadly, the technically interesting Singer-HRG sportscar announced in

February was a commercial failure, for only four were ever produced. The new car used a ladder-style frame with large-diameter tubes, and the engine was a further-developed version of the twin-cam unit first seen in 1953 (two different states of tune were available). There was all-round independent suspension, using both transverse leaf *and* coil springs at each end of the car, and four-wheel disc brakes which had been developed for HRG by Palmer, already producers of such systems for aircraft.

Topped off by an aluminium shell in what has been described as a rather 'gawky' style, this car seemed to have a promising specification. HRG, however, was not a company with an established dealer network, and since their new car was set to be priced at £1,650–£1,750 (Jaguar XK140 prices), demand was almost non-existent.

Hudson: Rambler, Wasp and Hornet types were newly listed.

Humber: In what was the last significant update of these separate-chassis big Humbers before they were replaced in 1957/58, both Hawk and Super Snipe types were given more power for 1956, while Laycock overdrive became optional on the Super Snipe. In addition there was a short-lived estate car version of the Hawk.

Jaguar: The first unit-construction Jaguar saloon, the compact 2.4, was introduced in September. Compared with other Jaguars, this was a smaller car, with more rounded lines.

Powered by a 2.4-litre, short-stroke version of the famous XK engine, it was backed by the same transmission options (though there was no automatic transmission at first). Suspension layouts were all new – by coil springs and wishbones at the front and a solid axle with cantilevered half-elliptic springs, radius-arms and a short Panhard rod at the rear.

Two versions were available, but the better-equipped Special Equipment type accounted for the vast majority of the cars sold. In its original 112bhp form, the 2.4 was only just a 100mph machine. This was the first of what would become an impressive and wide-ranging family of compact Jaguars. A 3.4-litre version would follow in 1957, and then, after a restyle in 1959, a

3.8-litre car would be launched. Years after that, S-types and 420s would take the pedigree to its natural limits.

Automatic transmission became available on home-market versions of the Mk VIIM.

Kaiser: Special and Manhattan types were newly listed.

Lanchester: It was stated in October that the new Sprite, which had been previewed at the previous Earls Court Motor Show, was now ready for production, though in much-changed form. The original squared-up body style had been dumped in favour of a much more rounded four-door/six-light shape, which owed a lot to the Conquest for its general proportions, while the prototype's coil-spring independent suspension had been abandoned in favour of a torsion-bar layout.

All this, however, was in vain, for after only 13 pre-production cars had been built (none apparently reaching the public) the project was abruptly cancelled, leaving Daimler-Lanchester to pick up cancellation charges of more than £500,000. One car, at least, survives, as a curiosity.

Lincoln: Continental models were newly listed.

Mercury: The Montclair model was newly listed.

MG: Without fuss, the TF sportscar slipped into retirement in the spring. This brought to an end an entire generation of MG sportscars whose style had been settled in the early 1930s and changed only in detail over the next two decades.

The new MGA, the first all-new MG sportscar to be launched since 1936, went on the market in September 1955, though a trio of specially-prepared EX182 prototypes had already been raced at Le Mans in June.

In their racing guise the prototypes had aluminium bodywork and special Weslake cylinder heads, which used transfer port balance pipes to improve inlet breathing, while a prototype twin-cam engine (from Morris Motors) was also fitted for the Tourist Trophy race at Dundrod, in Northern Ireland.

The suitably detuned MGA production car which followed in September was based around a new and rock-solid box-section chassis-frame and had a sleek, full-width, two-seater sports tourer body, and was power by a tuned version of the now well-known BMC B-series 1.5-litre engine.

Even in its original form with 68bhp, the MGA was a 100mph car, which demonstrated how much more aero-dynamically efficient it was compared with the old-fashioned TF.

Morgan: Ever since the Plus 4 had taken over from the 4/4 in 1950, Morgan had persistently been badgered for a replacement. Finally, in October 1955, a new type of 4/4, to be known as the Series II, was introduced.

Using the same chassis, wheelbase, two-seater body and basic layout as the Plus 4, the Series II had a Ford side-valve 1,172cc engine and a three-speed gearbox.

Thus equipped, it might have handled like every Morgan should, but there wasn't much performance, not even as much as the pre-1950 4/4 had enjoyed. Later 4/4s, with more modern overhead-valve Ford engines, would become progressively better.

Morris: Viewed against the product-planning atmosphere which had developed so rapidly within BMC, the arrival of the new six-cylinder Isis model was almost inevitable. Effectively this was a long-nose/long-wheelbase version of the latest Morris Oxford, powered by the 86bhp/2.6-litre C-series engine. Overdrive transmission became optional from September. There was a four-door saloon and a two-door estate car with an exposed wooden bracing structure around the hind quarters.

Once again there was torsion-bar front suspension, but no rack-and-pinion steering (which would have made a difference), and none of this could help the car's handling balance, which was distinctly nose-heavy. Like the Morris Six which had been dropped a couple of years earlier, the Isis always struggled to make its reputation. After three short years, at least one major facelift and much mechanical attention to freshen it up, it was dropped.

Nash: The Rambler model was newly listed.

Oldsmobile: The 88 and 98 models were newly listed.

Packard: The Clipper and Patrician models were newly listed.

Peugeot: The conservative French concern introduced the 403 model, first sold in the UK as a saloon, using upgraded versions of the existing running gear (including a 1.5-litre derivative of the engine) in a larger, more spacious and pleasingly-styled unit-construction shape.

Like the 203, the 403 broke no new technical ground, but it was solidly built, proved to be extremely reliable and was also pleasingly fast on the sort of roads for which it had been developed – fast, sweeping, continental highways. Like the 203, too, the 403 would have a long life in the UK, for the last car would not be delivered until 1966.

Pontiac: These cars were listed for the first time.

Porsche: The charismatic rear-engined/air-cooled sportscars moved smoothly from Type 356 to Type 356A with slight styling changes (which included a curved one-piece screen instead of the V-screen) and a wider range of engines. For the first time the noisy, complex, but extremely effective four-cam flat-four Carrera engine was added to the range.

This was merely the latest of a whole series of product improvements which Porsche made during the 1950s. With each of these, the VW parentage became more blurred as ever more special Porsche parts were fitted instead.

Riley: The last of the 1½-litre RM-series cars was built during the year, and overdrive transmission became available from September on the Pathfinder model.

Rolls-Royce: Nine years after the first postwar Rolls-Royce/Bentley chassis had appeared there was a second new design, this being the basis of the Silver Cloud range and the *very* closely-related Bentley S-series cars.

Although the Silver Cloud was similar in layout to the Silver Dawn which it replaced, only the engine and transmissions were carried over. There was a new, larger, heavier and more sturdy chassis, this time with semi-trailing coil-spring independent front suspension, while the four-door bodyshell (provided by Pressed Steel) was larger, more spacious and only marginally less craggy than before.

The engine was the final 4.9-litre stretch of the familiar IOEV six, the GM-type automatic transmission was standardized (though a few cars were fitted with a manual gearbox in the first year or so) and the new car relied on the delicately engineered but definitely obsolete type of mechanical servo which Hispano-Suiza had invented all those years ago.

As usual, it was a pleasure to contemplate the fixtures and fittings of the bodyshell, which were of the highest standards, and there was much detail in the chassis (including the so-called Z-bar on the rear suspension, which was really a torque arm under another name).

However, this was a triumph of development rather than of new engineering, and it was a miracle that the Silver Cloud and the Bentley S-series equivalent went on to sell so steadily and so well for the next 10 years.

Rover: No major changes were made, but the P4 90 model received a new braking system, while Laycock overdrive became optional.

Singer: Determined to wring the last possible sale out of the long-running SM1500/Hunter range, the company launched the Hunter 75 at Motor Show time, this being powered by a detuned (75bhp) derivative of the very specialized twin-overhead-cam engine developed by HRG for its own Singer-powered sportscars. Not many people realized that the Hunter 75 used a cast iron cylinder head, whereas the HRG version had originally been designed in cast aluminium.

This was always likely to be a pricey and specialized Hunter, but at the time no-one knew just *how* rare it would be, for just as limited production was getting under way the company fell into the arms of Rootes, who speedily cut back on all such fripperies!

Skoda: After one or two false starts, these crudely-engineered Czechoslovakian cars finally went on sale in the UK. Although the original postwar type of 1200 was listed, it is doubtful if any were sold here, though the new-type 440 launched during 1955 had a little more success.

The 440 model was a very basically-trimmed front-engined people's car, built around a tubular backbone chassis-frame, which sprouted outriggers to support the bodyshell and to hold the transverse leaf-spring front and rear suspension. Although this was never a car which would excite great enthusiasm, it was rugged and reliable, so there was a small but noticeable demand from British buyers.

The first cars had a 1.1-litre engine with 40bhp, so a top speed of around 65–70mph was guaranteed. The 440s gradually improved and eventually were renamed Felicias (which was where the new 1995 model gained its inspiration) and were marketed in the UK for the next eight or nine years.

Standard: The smaller Eights and Tens were quite overshadowed by the arrival of the new Vanguard, and there were no mechanical changes. Earlier in the year the Family Eight replaced the original basic Eight, and was fitted with wind-up windows, though there was still no external access to the boot. Then, in October, for 1956, the more upmarket versions became Super Eight and Super Ten, with much improved trim and furnishing; three derivatives of the one design were now on sale.

The unit-construction Vanguard III took over from the Vanguard II in the autumn, whose chassis design had originated under the original Vanguard of 1948, though the same basic running gear was retained. The new Vanguard looked higher, squarer and certainly more 'transatlantic' than before, which was not surprising as it had been shaped by a North American styling consultant, Carl Otto.

The famous wet-liner engine, the robust three-speed gearbox and the rugged no-nonsense suspension were all as one might expect. Standard still thought this car could sell to 'the Empire' in large numbers, which explains why everything in the Vanguard tradition – the considerable ground clearance, the soft ride and the simple specification – had all been retained.

Studebaker: Champion, Commander and President models were all newly listed.

Sunbeam: It was not obvious at the time, but the original Rapier, new in

October 1955, was the first of what would be a very wide-ranging and successful group of Hillman, Singer and Sunbeam models in the next decade.

The Rapier's base was the platform and front end of the new-generation Hillman Minx (which did not appear until 1956), but with a two-door/four-seater body of what the Americans would call the hardtop coupe style. There was a pillarless side view, and the rear quarter-windows could be retracted.

The running gear was strictly-conventional Minx, which is to say that the new type of 1.4-litre ohv engine was specified, this time in 58bhp form. On the Rapier, though, the four-speed gearbox was backed by a Laycock overdrive as standard equipment.

Although the first of the Rapiers was not very fast (85mph was flat-out), the car would be improved considerably over the years, and it became an extremely successful rally car.

Triumph: The TR3 took over from the TR2, changes concentrating on a more powerful (95bhp instead of 90bhp) engine and a more robust rear axle (from the new Vanguard). Before long the engine would be modified still further to become rated at 100bhp.

Willys: Custom and Bermuda types were listed for the first time, but then dropped before the end of the year.

Wolseley: Overdrive transmission became available from September.

Industrial developments

Singer, which had been in financial difficulties for some time, accepted a takeover bid from the Rootes Group in December 1955, though not before other industrial groups had tried their hand.

At the time, Rootes' chairman, Sir William Rootes, made much of the fact that he was really 'coming home', as he had originally been apprenticed to Singer Motors. Behind the scenes, Rootes immediately began to clear out dead wood like the ancient Roadsters and kill off costly diversions such as the twin-cam-engined Singer Hunter 75. Work began at once on the develop-

ment of new 'Rootes-Singers', the first of which (the Singer Gazelle) would appear less than a year after the takeover was formalized.

Austin celebrated its Golden Jubilee. Up to that point the company's fortunes had only ever been directed by two men – Herbert Austin (later Lord Austin) until his death in 1941, then Leonard Lord, who had originally joined Austin as the heir apparent in 1938.

Technical developments

Aerodynamic aids made many headlines in motorsport, from the all-enveloping shell of the B-series Connaught GP car to the refinements applied to the works D-type Jaguars for 1955, but most especially with the lift-up airbrake fitted to the Mercedes-Benz 300SLR models in the Le Mans 24 Hours race.

Cheating the air by streamlining body shapes was already well understood, though aerodynamicists from the aircraft industry (such as Frank Costin) were often consulted on the finer points. His work on the latest Lotus sports-racing cars was particularly successful: this, allied to Colin Chapman's ultra-light (and sometimes fragile!) chassis designs meant that Lotus were real trendsetters, soon to be consulted by BRM and Vanwall, whose chassis were by no means state-of-the-art.

It is interesting to note that although the D-type was much praised at the time, indeed analyzed carefully by technical writers, its drag coefficient was actually rather high at nearly 0.500 (and its ground clearance considerable), though it seemed impressive at the time.

Power-assisted steering, already common in North America, was beginning to make an appearance in Europe. In Britain, Cam Gears produced a system known as Hydrosteer, which would soon be adopted on several British models. Marles was also working on its own new system, which would be adopted by Rolls-Royce for the Silver Cloud in 1956, while Girling had one under development, Armstrong Siddeley becoming their first customer later in the year, and so did Automotive Products – everyone, it seemed, was looking for the same business!

Overdrive certainly won the 'optional equipment of the year' award, many new and existing cars being offered with it; Laycock, from Sheffield, and Borg-Warner, from Letchworth, split this growing business between them.

Cars by train

For the first time since the war, British Railways introduced special cars-by-train services on June 19, 1955, initially as an overnight run between London King's Cross and Perth; it was the start of what became known as a Motorail service, with cars being carried in special vans or wagons behind passenger sleeper coaches. When Britain's roads were so awful (there were no motorways in 1955, of course, and the A1 Great North Road was already a disgracefully overcrowded highway), a Motorail service, though expensive, was a great attraction.

The return fare was £15 for car-plus-driver, with an extra £4 10s (£4.50) return fare for each adult passenger. A sleeper berth was included in this fare. By the 1990s, though, demand had fallen, and the last Motorail services were run in 1995.

More new roads – a serious programme

After being under pressure for years, the Government finally laid out a serious road-building programme, costed at £212 million, with a commitment which would last well beyond the 1950s. So all those schemes which had been announced back in 1946 had not been forgotten after all.

The most significant schemes, to be completed before the end of the 1950s, were the first stretch of the M1 motorway from the St Albans area to Crick (Junction 18) and along the M45

spur towards Coventry, plus a series of major bypasses along the A1. Work on the Dartford Tunnel was finally to be restarted (it would not be finished until the early 1960s), and work began on dualling the A74 between Carlisle and Glasgow. A start was also being made on several major bypasses, in a ring round Manchester (this work would still be going on in the mid-1990s) and on planning for the Forth road bridge (though a tunnel was mentioned, too, at this stage!).

This programme was revealed just two weeks after an even more ambitious £1,240 million plan to modernize British Railways had been announced.

Incidentally, to put this spending proposal into perspective, in 1955, the dollar equivalent of £18.5 *billion* of interstate highway construction in the USA was approved by President Eisenhower in a 12-year programme involving building 40,000 miles of new roads! In the end this took a lot longer than 12 years, but all of those roads have been brought into use.

Men of Influence

Sir William Lyons

Along with William Walmsley, Blackpool-born William Lyons had founded the Swallow sidecar-building business in Blackpool, later made special bodies for cars, then turned to manufacturing SS cars in 1931, before becoming sole proprietor of the company in 1935. That year he invented the Jaguar model name, saw it become world-famous after the Second World War, and was 'Mr Jaguar' until the day he retired in 1972.

During his working life William Lyons, who seemed to have a faultless eye for a line, despite his lack of formal training, shaped every Jaguar production car except the E-type of 1961 (which was a direct evolution of the wind-tunnel-inspired D-type racing sportscar). This ensured that there was always a recognizable connection between one Jaguar and the next, and it meant that 'the Jaguar look' was always instantly identifiable all over the world.

In the late 1940s designers could see obvious visual cues linking the Mk V with the SS-Jaguars of the 1930s, and even with the original SS1 of 1931. Mr Lyons even insisted that the new twin-cam XK engines should not only be very powerful, but should also *look* powerful (and glamorous), too.

Knighted in 1956, Sir William would always be respected by his workforce, though not actually loved, as he was reputedly a very hard taskmaster. He liked to keep a formal atmosphere in his business, calling even his closest colleagues by their surname, and keeping them personally at arm's length.

William Lyons was not only an accomplished and successful stylist, but also an astute businessman and a talented chooser of staff. It was no accident that SS Cars, and later Jaguar Cars, grew steadily during the 1930s and 1940s while rival marques such as Alvis, Armstrong Siddeley, Daimler and Riley all struggled to survive.

The launch of the sensational XK engine was merely one phase in the building of the Jaguar master plan, which was later to include sleek new saloons like the Mk VII, a move to a new factory in Allesley, Coventry, and the development of racing cars which won the prestigious Le Mans 24 Hours race five times during the 1950s.

Sir William stayed at the helm of Jaguar until 1972 (when he was already 70 years old), and he kept in touch with the business for at least the next decade.

He died in 1985, when 84 years old.

1956

This was a year in which Britain's motoring euphoria evaporated rapidly. On the one hand the Government tightened a fierce credit squeeze, and on the other the Suez war and the subsequent oil supply crisis hit petrol supplies very hard for a time.

The Government's squeeze on the motor industry, which had started at the end of 1955, continued apace with restrictions on hire purchase and by increasing purchase tax on car prices.

In February, bank rate was increased to a (then) unprecedented 5½ per cent and there were further financial restrictions including the requirement of a hefty 50 per cent deposit to be paid on cars being bought by hire purchase: HP deals declined dramatically as soon as this impost was applied.

An early effect came when Austin put its workers on to a four-day week, and later Standard also introduced short-time working, to be followed by Ford and Vauxhall before the end of the year.

The result was that UK car production slumped to 707,594 cars – 190,000 fewer than in the previous year, and home deliveries dropped by more than 100,000. Privately, some politicians were delighted that their fiscal policies seemed to have worked, but workers on short time, with reduced wages, did not share their glee.

Following the success of the pioneering Motorail service from London to Perth in 1955, British Railways announced plans to link Newcastle and Stockton-on-Tees with Dover; Newcastle and Stockton-on-Tees with Exeter; York with Inverness; and London (Paddington) with St Austell in Cornwall during 1956. A Manchester–Dover service was also promised for motorists planning to take their cars abroad.

The move towards the introduction of parking meters dragged slowly on, and in 1956 came the first news about the traffic wardens who would administer them and the parking of motorists' cars in surrounding streets.

For the first time, what were known as 'intermediate' speed limits of 40mph were proposed for outer built-up areas.

Britain entered the motorway building age in June with a start being made on the Preston bypass, which eventually became an integral part of M6. It would be opened at the end of 1958.

The Institute of Advanced Motorists (soon to be nicknamed 'The Great I AM'...) came into being.

The last months of the year (and the first few of 1957) were totally dominated by the Suez crisis, the subsequent oil shortages and the rationing of petrol, which quickly followed in Britain and several other European countries.

Allied forces invaded Egypt at the end of October, and within days the British Government announced defence regulations which covered the imposition of petrol rationing from December 17, which returned Britain's motorists to the dismal situation last experienced in 1950. However, the supply situation would improve so much that rationing would be abandoned before the middle of 1957.

The first ration books contained coupons for four months, their quantities varying according to the size of car owned. Cars of up to 1.1 litres were granted 6 gallons' worth a month, while those over 2.4 litres had 10½ gallons a month – the intention being to allow drivers about 200 miles of motoring each month.

Even before then, what was described as a 'temporary' tax increase was slapped on petrol, which went up by a whopping 1s 5d (7.1p) a gallon. This would eventually be withdrawn during 1957, to the great relief of all concerned.

New models

AC: In a very low-key announcement, the company stated that the Bristol 2-litre engine was now to be optional on Ace and Aceca models. Thus, with the minimum of fuss, the Ace-Bristol and Aceca-Bristol models were born, and would soon dominate the scene at Thames Ditton.

Alfa Romeo: With the Giulietta saloon safely launched in Italy during 1955, the first UK imports followed. Prices, however, were extremely high for the performance and product quality offered, so sales were always strictly limited. Saloons and Sprint types were both available and the special derivatives of each would follow in the next few years.

Allard: The London-based company revealed that they would now only build cars to special order, which was a diplomatic way of admitting that their business had contracted so much that series production was no longer justified. By this time, in fact, assembly of V8-engined cars had ended and sales of Palm Beach types had all but ceased.

Austin: BMC began a programme of upgrading their entire model range – Austin to Wolseley – and to reflect the arrival of premium fuels all models were given higher-compression engines.

The A30 was turned into the A35 by fitting a larger (948cc) engine and a remote-control gearchange. The A50 was given smaller wheels to lower the ride height, along with Manumatic semi-automatic transmission as an extra, Borg-Warner overdrive having been made optional earlier in the year. There were bigger changes for the six-cylinder cars, which were given longer tails and revised front-ends. The A90 became the A95, an estate car body option was introduced, and this and the A105 models were offered with automatic transmission as an extra.

The original-shape A105 had been a new arrival in May as a more powerful version of the A90 Westminster. Not only did the A105 have a 102bhp twin-SU 2.6-litre engine (the same unit, in fact, as was to be fitted to the Austin-Healey 100-Six), but Borg-Warner overdrive was standard equipment, the ride height was lower and there were extra fixtures and fittings in the cabin, along with a two-tone colour scheme.

Although it was only a very slow seller, the new Princess IV model was technically interesting, being an advance on previous Princess/Sheerline models. The separate chassis now supported a 150bhp version of the long-established 4-litre engine, while automatic transmission was standard. There was power-assisted steering, a new Vanden Plas style to the saloon body, and all the same mechanical improvements were applied to limousines from the same stable.

Austin-Healey: Against the wishes of the Healey family, BMC decided to 'modernize' the 100 model by making it longer, heavier and fitting it with the six-cylinder BMC C-series engine; the result was the 100-Six, a car which was no better than the 100/4 it replaced.

There were good and bad points to the new model, which needed more power (road tests showed that the first cars were slower than the 100/4), and overdrive was no longer standard equipment, but its cockpit was somewhat more roomy, with tiny '+2' seating added. This was the BN4, but within 18 months BMC would acknowledge their error — by that time a more lusty engine would have been developed and a two-seater style reintroduced.

Bentley: Power-assisted steering, which was so desperately needed, became available, while all cars were given 13 per cent (unquantified) more power than before.

Berkeley: The Biggleswade-based caravan-maker introduced a tiny new sportscar, the design of which was credited to Laurie Bond, who had earlier designed the cheap-and-cheerful Bond three-wheeler.

The new Berkeley had a front-mounted two-stroke motorcycle-type engine and transmission driving the front wheels, the chassis was an aluminium-and-glassfibre moulded platform, and the bodywork was also in glassfibre.

Although this was almost a motorcycle on wheels, the Berkeley was so light and nimble that it created quite a demand, but many people were put off by its relatively high price, obvious crudities and lack of refinement.

In the next few years the Berkeley would gradually grow up, always by using motorcycle engines, the 322cc engine of the original eventually giving place to altogether larger and brawnier four-stroke types.

Citroen: The process of filling out the 'Goddess' range proceeded with the launch of the ID19, a simplified version of the DS19 with a less-powerful (62bhp) engine and conventional (ie non-hydraulic) clutch and gearchange operation. The braking system, too, was conventionally hydraulic instead of high-pressure-powered, as in DS19 types, and there was no power-assisted steering.

Daimler: Scratching away to improve its existing range of cars, the company finally made Borg-Warner automatic transmission optional on its 2.4-litre and 3.6-litre models — this being the first break from the fluid-flywheel/pre-selector tradition which Daimler had established 25 years earlier.

At the same time the DK400 limousine was greatly improved, not only by a revised style to eliminate any family resemblance with Regency and 104 types, but by fitting the 4.6-litre engine with an aluminium cylinder head, which liberated a creditable 167bhp.

Fairthorpe: The first Electron sportscar was shown, this being a two-seater with a tubular chassis-frame and a stubby but distinctive open-top two-seater glassfibre shell. At first the 1.1-litre overhead-camshaft Coventry Climax engine was used, along with a proprietary (Moss) gearbox, but in later years Electron derivatives would be powered by one or other of the small Standard-Triumph units.

Fiat: The Multipla, a remarkable forward-control derivative of the tiny Fiat 600, was previewed in January and went on UK sale later in the year. This, in retrospect, was the very first 'people carrier', for in a very compact and ingenious package, modestly powered by a rear-mounted 633cc engine, it could carry six people in three rows of seats. Except for the blunt 'barn-door' front of the car, much of the design was common with the 600 saloon.

Ford: The Mk II Consuls, Zephyrs and Zodiacs took over from the original types during the spring, the latest cars being larger, with bigger and more powerful engines, and more passenger space.

The Mk I range had been so successful that there had been no need to change the marketing approach with their replacements. Once again the styling had been conceived in Detroit, and estate car derivatives were approved for the first time as part of the official range (as distinct from being conversions). As before, there were bench front seats and a steering-column gearchange was standard, while MacPherson-strut front suspension continued to give a very soft ride. Automatic transmission became optional from the autumn. These cars would remain in production for six years.

Frazer Nash: Although it would never go on sale, the BMW V8-engined Continental model looked promising when first launched in October 1956. Still using the well-known postwar-type Frazer Nash chassis, and with an engine reduced to 2.5 litres, it was a very capable looking product, but as demand for *all* Frazer Nash sportscars (which were always hand-built and very expensive) had collapsed, the Isleworth company never actually delivered any of this model.

Goggomobil: This was a short and stubby minicar from West Germany, a car whose styling looked almost the same from the front as from the rear. The chassis was tubular, the tiny air-cooled two-stroke engine (of 293cc) was in the tail, and somehow there was space for four passengers in a wheelbase of only 71in.

Production was at a factory in Dingolfing, later to be noted for producing Glas models, and since the late-1960s being part of the BMW empire.

Hillman: The new-generation Minx — a commercially vital new model — took over from the old range, which had been in production since 1948, and would be Rootes' major production car for the next decade.

Based on an entirely new unit-construction platform (already seen in the Sunbeam Rapier which had been launched late in 1955), it was to be built in saloon, estate and convertible guises. There would also be a van for commercial use and, after a suitable interval, there would also be a new short-chassis Husky type. [In 1959, the Alpine sportscar would also use the elements of the same underframe and running gear...]

Powered by Rootes' modern 1.4-litre overhead-valve engine, the Minx was a thoroughly conventional car, which was certain to be modified and improved in many ways in the years to come. For the record, though, the first such Minx had less than 50bhp and cost a mere £748.

Jaguar: The Mk VIIM saloon evolved into the Mk VIII, which was a further-modified version of the design that had started life in 1950. The Mk VIII was slightly restyled, with a different grille and one-piece windscreen, along with duotone colour schemes and a more powerful and torquey engine. The Mk VIIM remained on the market for another season, though its sales gradually fell away.

Jensen: The 541 became the first British production car (though admittedly only a limited production) to have four-wheel disc brakes as standard, these being by Dunlop. The same installation would find its way onto most Jaguar models in the next two years.

Mercedes-Benz: The company continued the steady expansion of its mid-sized Ponton range of four-door saloons with the launch of the 190, 219 and 220S models.

The 190 was the first saloon to be powered by the new-generation four-cylinder overhead-camshaft engine which had been previewed in the 190SL of 1954, the 219 was really a budget version of the six-cylinder 220 model, while the 220S was a considerably more powerful derivative (100bhp instead of 85bhp) of this popular type. Other versions of the Ponton range would follow, and it takes a Mercedes-Benz expert to relate exactly how all of them became intertwined and evolved, one from the other!

Although the gullwing 300SL had been a great success, the company clearly divined the demand for an open-top version. In November, the first official pictures of a 300SL Roadster were circulated, though the official launch was delayed until 1957.

Metropolitan: Although still only being built by BMC for sale in the USA at the time, this car was upgraded to have the larger A50 1.5-litre engine. Before the end of 1956, however, BMC announced that the car would also soon become available on the home market.

MG: The smart bubble-top MGA fixed-head coupe, complete with wind-up windows, was announced and at the same time the MGA's horsepower was slightly increased.

Meanwhile, the Magnette became the ZB type, complete with a facelift, an enlarged rear window, and Manumatic transmission as an optional extra.

Morris: Like the Austin A30, the Minor was upgraded with a more powerful

948cc engine and a remote-control gearchange, along with a one-piece front screen and larger rear window: the result was the birth of the Minor 1000.

The Cowley evolved into the Cowley 1500, and was thereafter a slightly stripped-out version of the Oxford (so why bother?). The Oxford, on the other hand, was given a front-end/rear-end facelift, a revised facia layout, a higher-compression engine, and options of Manumatic transmission and a rather dubious duotone paint scheme.

The slow-selling Isis received the same visual changes as the closely-related Oxford, overdrive or automatic transmission as options and, of all things, a right-hand gearchange lifted from the existing Riley Pathfinder layout.

Oppermann: Since it was launched at almost exactly the time the Suez crisis erupted, the tiny two-seater Unicar seemed to have a promising future. Like the Berkeley, it had been designed by Laurie Bond, and used the same intriguing basic type of aluminium and glassfibre monocoque for its structure. Also like the Berkeley, there was an Anzani (later, Excelsior) two-stroke engine for motive power, this time in the tail and driving the rear wheels.

The shell was a rounded, two-seater coupe (sometimes rather unkindly described as 'one step up from an invalid carriage'...) in glassfibre, the seating being of the same stark variety as used in Citroen 2CVs.

The Unicar's day, however, was over almost as soon as it had begun, for the factory at Borehamwood only produced about 200 examples before sales dried up completely.

Peugeot: An estate car version was added to the 403 range.

Renault: The smoothly-styled new Dauphine was introduced, intended to be an eventual replacement for the 4CV, though in fact it was larger, heavier, faster and more highly priced. The two types would co-exist for several more years.

The new car shared the same rear-engined layout with the old, allied to soft coil-spring independent suspension all round, but although the 4CV's engine had been enlarged from 747cc to 845cc, there was still only a three-speed gearbox at first. The new car

had four passenger doors and was very lightly built.

In looks and Gallic character, the Dauphine had great charm, but the cars had unpredictable handling characteristics, especially in side winds, where the tail could prove to be remarkably unwieldy, and experience would show that they nearly all suffered from heavy premature rusting. Nevertheless, more than 2,000,000 would be built in 12 years, making the Dauphine a huge commercial success.

Riley: As with several other BMC cars of the period, the Pathfinder was upgraded, Borg-Warner overdrive becoming optional.

Rolls-Royce: Power-assisted steering became available on the Silver Wraith, and soon would also be offered on Silver Clouds.

Rover: For 1957 the 60, 75 and 90 models were altered in detail, most noticeably with front-end style changes to the wings and the addition of overdrive as an option on all three types, which meant that the long-established freewheel mechanism was abandoned (the two items occupied the same space in the driveline).

On the eve of the Earls Court Motor Show, however, Rover sprang a real surprise by launching the twin 105S and 105R models. The shape, style and general character of these cars was like the existing P4s, but both had a more powerful (108bhp) version of the 2.6-litre engine.

The 105S (S for sporting – surprisingly for Rover!) used a manual-plus-overdrive transmission, while the 105R (at first no-one explained what the R meant, but later it was defined as Roverdrive) incorporated Rover's own idiosyncratic idea of automatic transmission. This, in fact, combined a torque converter, a conventional clutch, a two-speed-and-reverse gearbox and a Laycock overdrive in a lengthy, heavy and complex ensemble. The net result was a rather sluggish and expensive car, which only ever sold in small quantities.

Simca: New during 1956 was the Vedette model, the result of Simca's takeover of Ford-France. In effect this was the old Ford-France V8 model suitably tarted-up, but still only available with the ancient design of 2.35-litre Ford V8 side-valve engine. It made virtually no impact in the UK, and the less powerful (1.2-litre Simca-powered) Ariane model which evolved from it was never even listed.

Singer: Less than a year after Rootes had taken control of the business, the new Gazelle was announced. This new model, which was effectively a new-type Hillman Minx with an overhead-camshaft Singer Hunter engine and a restyled nose, had been developed in double-quick time, yet was an immediate success.

Priced very deftly between the Hillman and Sunbeam lines of this versatile range, the Gazelle was a marketing coup, for which Rootes deserved to succeed; it did, recouping its investment handsomely in the next 11 years.

Standard: Adding to the complication of its small-car range, Standard revealed the Family Ten, which was really the stripped-out, no-external-boot-access Eight, but fitted with the 948cc engine.

The arrival of an estate car version of the Vanguard III was expected and widely forecast, but the launch of the Vanguard Sportsman was a real surprise. Years later it became clear that this car *might* have been badged as a Triumph Renown (a proposal dropped at a late stage, which was wise as this was neither a sporting nor an elegant car).

The Sportsman was really a Vanguard III with a more powerful (90bhp) twin-carburettor engine and a Triumph-like front grille. Overdrive was standard, the suspension was stiffened up somewhat, and there was better equipment and insulation – but this was not a combination which appealed to the buyers: less than 1,000 such cars would be sold.

Sunbeam: Rootes made haste to improve the Rapier's performance, giving it a twin-carburettor R67 version of the 1.4-litre engine only a year after the model had originally been announced. Rootes-watchers knew that this was likely to be an ongoing process – as would be confirmed less than 18 months later with the first facelift!

Triumph: Girling disc brakes were standardized at the front of the TR3

sportscar, this therefore becoming the first British quantity-production car to have discs (the Jensen 541, with its new Dunlop discs, was really only a hand-built machine).

Turner: The first of these capable little two-seater sportscars, built in Wolverhampton, was delivered. Produced for almost a decade in small numbers, each Turner was based on, or progressively modified from, the initial design, which had a tubular frame, Austin A30 (A35 from the autumn of 1956) running gear and front suspension and a glassfibre body. In size, performance and general layout it predated the Austin-Healey Sprite by more than two years.

Vauxhall: Two different estate car conversions were approved for the Velox – one from Grosvenor, the other from Martin Walter. The E-type range, however, only had one more year to run, so these derivatives would always be extremely rare.

Volvo: Later in the year the first few Volvos were brought in from Sweden, although serious importation did not begin until the end of 1958.

Although the limited-production P1900 sportscar was exhibited at Earls Court, it was never sold in the UK. Initial imports were of the PV444 saloons, the latest version of the beetle-backed cars which had been previewed as long ago as 1944, and the new Amazon range.

Amazons (later more accurately known as 120-series models) used the same basic running gear as the PV444s, which included a rugged and reliable four-cylinder engine up front, driving the rear wheels through a beam axle. The body style of the 120-series was smooth but anonymous, and before production ended in the 1960s it would be sold in various two-door, four-door, estate, single-carb and twin-carb guises.

Wolseley: The 15/50 model took over from the outwardly identical 4/44 saloon, the principal change being the fitment of the 1.5-litre BMC B-series engine and gearbox (with a central change) instead of the MG-type powertrain previously used. With this change the 15/50 fell into line with BMC's rationalization policy, and was

virtually a detuned version of its sister car, the MG ZA/ZB Magnette. Manumatic transmission became optional from the autumn of the year.

The 6/90 was given its mid-life revision, complete with overdrive or automatic transmission as options, and with the same right-hand gearchange as the Riley Pathfinder (its sister car) and the Morris Isis.

Industrial developments

Standard took over Beans Industries, thereby guaranteeing its own in-house supply of major castings. Managing director Alick Dick's strategy was to build up his empire in this way, while at the same time looking around for a new partner to underpin the future.

There was upheaval at Daimler at the very top level when the chairman, Sir Bernard Docker, was sacked. A somewhat turbulent era, which had included a great deal of direct influence on cars and policies by his wife, Lady Docker, thereby came to an end. Almost immediately there was a return to more businesslike policies, waste was eliminated, and some of Daimler's obvious fripperies (such as ludicrously over-specified Earls Court show cars) were discarded. One of their first marketing moves was to reduce prices in an attempt to increase demand.

In Sir Bernard's place, John Sangster became chairman, with Edward Turner (who was already a noted designer of motorcycle engines) also joining the board. One result was that Daimler's parent company, BSA, set up a new Automotive Division, in which Turner was made responsible for co-ordinating all Daimler, Lanchester and Carbodies activities. In effect this meant getting the best out of Daimler and Carbodies, for Lanchester, as a marque, had already been killed off when the Sprite project had been cancelled.

BMW granted a licence to Dunsfold Tools Ltd to assemble Isetta bubblecars in the UK. The intention was to use a redundant railway facility in Brighton, which would be ready during 1957.

Citroen continued to assemble cars at Slough (in premises which would later become part of the Mars confectionary complex), announcing that the futuristic DS19 had finally gone into production in Britain.

In the New Year's Honours List, Jaguar's founder was knighted, becoming Sir William Lyons: rarely, it seemed, had there been a more popular accolade.

Even though it was made available with a 1.5-litre engine, the Paramount project staggered to its conclusion when Welbeck Motors of London bought up the remaining stock of unsold examples, advertised them for sale at £795 (a considerable reduction) and cleared the decks during the year.

Technical developments

In Britain there was great excitement when 100-octane (later referred to as '5-star') fuel finally became available, though this was no great technical breakthrough as higher-octane fuels had been used during the Second World War more than a decade earlier in fighter aircraft and similar fuels had been on sale in the USA for some time. Shell and BP were the British pioneers, though Esso and National Benzole were not far behind.

One popular theme among new models was the launch of optional two-pedal control for cheaper cars.

Such systems, though complicated, were not automatic transmissions, but provided clutchless gearchanges. Standard used a system known as Standrive, which was really Newton-drive, while Lockheed's Manumatic transmission found a home in many BMC cars and light commercial vehicles.

In the case of Newtondrive, there was a centrifugal clutch to allow easy take-up from rest, and all gearchanging was controlled by microswitches in the gear-lever knob, which disengaged the clutch when the lever was moved from slot to slot. The Manumatic system was laid out in a similar manner.

The arrival of disc brakes in production quantities was another British 'first'. Discs had been used on limited-production sports-racing cars for a couple of years – Jaguar and Lotus sportscars, for example – but Citroen's DS19 had been the first *European* car to specify front-wheel discs as standard.

From the autumn of 1956, Girling's discs went into the Triumph TR3, while Dunlop's four-wheel discs were fitted to the Jensen 541 (and would be adopted in 1957 for the new Jaguar XK150). Lockheed, with yet another version of the layout, would not be far behind.

Lucas also revealed its pioneering fuel-injection installations, which were successfully used on works Jaguar D-type sports-racing cars at Sebring, Le Mans and other circuits during the year. The system was still complex and somewhat prone to problems, but Lucas was determined to turn it into a production system – eventually, Maserati would be the first to take it up, on the 3500 model.

Rover's new T3 gas-turbine car caused a real stir, not because there was much chance of it ever reaching production (most observers *and* the Rover company seem to have accepted that this was not yet economically possible), but because it was such an integrated and well-thought-out design.

This, in fact, was the first new-from-end-to-end Rover gas-turbine car, in which the 110bhp engine was mounted in the tail. There was de Dion rear suspension, independent front suspension and four-wheel drive, along with disc brakes. The whole of this intriguing two-seater chassis was covered by a neatly styled coupe body. The new T3 project had been conceived, designed and managed by Spen King – from whom a lot more would be heard during the next two decades.

Men of Influence

Dr Dante Giacosa

Perhaps it was not yet time for the cult of the 'personality engineer' to erupt, but in due course Fiat's Dante Giacosa certainly qualified. He had a phenomenally successful career at Fiat. Armed with a degree in mechanical engineering, his working life began in 1928. Much involved in all of Fiat's most notable 1930s and wartime products, he became director of engineering in 1946, and was then totally responsible for every new Fiat developed until 1970.

Today the idea of such a high-profile, publicity-worthy, engineering figure would be abhorred by modern management, but Fiat – and Giacosa – were delighted to see so much limelight directed their way. The combination, in any case, was entirely successful. Giacosa was a great hands-on designer, not merely an administrator, and his excellent book *Forty Years of Design with Fiat* lists an enormous number of projects.

Like most enthusiastic Italian engineers, Giacosa liked sporty cars, and above all he liked innovative engineering. Cars like the Fiat 600 and *nuova* 500 established his reputation for ever, but he was also much involved with cars as various as the 1800/2100 saloons, the Fiat Dino, the front-wheel-drive 127s and 128s, the mid-engined X1/9 and the mass-production 124s and 125s.

The 1100-103 was a typical example of his practical, 'can-do', approach to new-car design, for although the engine was old, the rest of the car was new. Although the style was distinctly ordinary, the handling and character were sporting. Like the man himself, the 1100-103 was versatile and successful in almost everything it did.

Am I alone in thinking that after he retired there was never as much technical enterprise – 'spark' – at Fiat, at least until the mid-1990s? Dante Giacosa died, aged 91, in 1996.

1957

In spite of the gloom brought about by petrol rationing, Britain's automotive output began to rise again and the short-time working introduced in 1956 was progressively abandoned in the first half of 1957. Output almost recovered to the pre-squeeze levels of 1955, though most of the extra cars went overseas; exports, at more than 424,000, were at a new record. Just to keep things in check (or so the Government insisted), British bank rate was raised to an unprecedented 7 per cent in September.

By April the worst of the world's petrol shortages were over and all European countries except France and Britain had abandoned petrol rationing. Predictably, Britain lagged behind everyone else; 1s (5p) of the emergency tax on petrol was removed during April, and the ration was increased by 50 per cent from April 17, but rationing was not formally lifted until May 14. Further small price decreases followed during the year. Official statistics claimed that initially rationing had saved 30 per cent of normal fuel consumption, though this figure dropped as drivers began to use up hoarded coupons.

At long last there was a definite start to a road-building programme, the line of the M1 being fixed, the Lancaster bypass and many A1 schemes started and the Ashford (A20) bypass completed.

East of London, too, the talking ended and the digging began when a start was made on driving the bore of the Dartford Tunnel in March. The tunnel would eventually open in 1963, well before it was incorporated as part of the M25 motorway; almost instantly it became overloaded, leading to a parallel tunnel and a high-level bridge having to be built as well.

During the year UK highway authorities introduced double white line road markings after carrying out experiments on lengths of the A3 and A20 main roads, and 1957 also saw the first successful prosecution of a British motorist caught speeding by the use of a radar detector. The location was Lancashire, the fine just £3. On a lighter note, the AA celebrated the enrolment of its 2,000,000th member – the second million people having joined since 1950.

New models

AC: The Ace/Aceca range was further improved with front-wheel disc brakes becoming optional at £52 extra.

Armstrong Siddeley: The Armstrong Siddeley 234 and 236 models were dropped, only two years after launch (though a number of unsold cars were registered in 1958), because they had been unsuccessful and had cost the company a lot of money.

Aston Martin: The third derivative of the DB2 design, later to become known as the DB Mk III (*not* the DB3), was introduced; initially for export, it was also available in Britain before the end of the year.

Mechanically the main changes were to the 2.9-litre engine, for which two higher ratings – 162bhp and 178bhp – were available, and to the chassis, where Girling front disc brakes were fitted and overdrive became optional. Visually, the front-end style was altered, though the car's basic outline and the cabin remained unchanged.

A brand-new twin-cam engine was seen in the first of the DBR2 sports-racing cars. There were few clues as to its real purpose at this stage, but in the autumn of 1958 it surfaced again, this time as the power unit of the new DB4 road car. The 'Marek-six' would power all the most famous Aston Martins and Lagondas of the 1960s.

Austin: The A55 model displaced the A50, this being a heavily facelifted (or, perhaps, tail-lifted) version of the original, with a longer and smoother style around the rear quarters, though there were no significant mechanical changes.

Austin-Healey: The launch of a more powerful version of the 100-Six came in November, several weeks after the British Motor Show. This was very important to the marque following the criticism of the 100-Six for being slower than the 100/4.

The latest version of the BMC C-series engine had a completely new cylinder head, this time with a separate and much more volumetrically efficient inlet manifold, and larger (SU HD6) carburettors. Peak power went up from 102bhp to 117bhp and the car felt much more lively thereafter.

Bentley: There were no changes to mainstream models (which were being overshadowed by Rolls-Royce Silver Cloud sales), but a four-door saloon version of the Continental, the Flying Spur, was added. This had a coach-built aluminium body by H J Mulliner and was much faster than the steel-bodied S-series saloon.

Berkeley: The ambitious little sports-car manufacturer added a new type to the range, this being powered by a more lusty three-cylinder Excelsior motorcycle engine.

BMW: The appealing little (British-built) Isetta bubblecar was made more attractive with an enlarged engine (though still of only 298cc!) and a top-end restyle. The chassis and quirky two-seater accommodation was not changed, but there was more glass area and a slightly different roof profile.

To join the Isetta, BMW introduced the altogether larger 600 model, a compact four-seater car which was mechanically totally different. Once again there was a simple rear-engined chassis and bubblecar styling, which included both front *and* side doors for access to the seats, but the engine was an air-cooled flat-twin descended from the company's motorcycle designs.

Bristol: A special Beuttler-bodied version of a new chassis, dubbed the 406E, was introduced for export only, this having a stretched 2.2-litre version of the familiar six-cylinder engine. This car was never put on sale in the UK, and a very different home-market version of the 406 would appear during 1958.

Citroen: The ID19 model, previewed at the Paris Salon in October 1956, finally went into production in May, with British sales of Slough-assembled cars beginning later in the year. Meanwhile, one of the most famous trend-setting cars of all time, the Citroen *traction avant* (originally launched in 1933) was finally discontinued.

Edsel: What would turn out to be Ford-USA's greatest financial disaster, the new Edsel marque, was put on sale and was almost immediately price-listed in the UK, though very few cars were ever sold here. Early Edsels had hideous styling and overblown detailing, and were really no more than dressed-up, heavily disguised versions of existing Ford and Mercury models. Their chassis, complete with ultra-soft suspension, big and thirsty V8 engines and lamentable brakes, were equally uninspiring.

Facel Vega: The latest big and powerful Chrysler V8-engined coupes from France were price-listed in the UK, though they were always extremely rare. All Facel Vegas had massive tubular frames carrying bodyshells styled and produced in-house and were among the fastest, as well as the thirstiest, of all French cars.

Fiat: Anyone who thought that the 600 of 1955 was the smallest possible four-seater car had to think again when Fiat introduced the even smaller 479cc-engined 500 model. With a length of only 106in and a mere 13bhp from its rear-mounted air-cooled engine, the 500 offered truly marginal motoring.

In spite of the rock-bottom price (it was by far the cheapest car on sale in Italy for many years), it was always mechanically well-specified, with all-independent suspension and most ingenious packaging. It would remain in production for 20 years until effectively displaced by the larger and squarer 126 model.

Later in the year the new 1200 model arrived, this being a redesigned, restyled version of the 1100 using the same platform and suspension layouts, but with a 55bhp 1.2-litre version of the famous engine and a squared-up body style with much more glass than before. UK deliveries would begin during 1958.

Ford: There were no major changes, though a two-pedal gearbox option was added to the Anglia/Prefect range.

Ford-Germany: Although a few cars had already arrived, the first official deliveries into the UK of the Cologne-built Ford Taunus models 12M, 15M and 17M began at the end of the year. In some ways looking rather like their British counterparts (Ford-Germany also took its orders from Ford-USA...) and using similar MacPherson-strut front suspension, these cars mainly used their own variety of overhead-valve four-cylinder engines. Few observers could see the wisdom of these cars being imported to sell in competition with Ford-UK products. Neither, it seemed, could the public, for sales were strictly limited.

Hillman: A five-door estate car derivative of the new-generation Minx was added to the range, the shell shortly to be shared with the Singer Gazelle. Later in the year the range progressed to Series 2, with minor mechanical and appearance changes.

Humber: For the first time since 1948, Rootes introduced an all-new Humber, this being the unit-construction Hawk saloon. Although it retained the existing Hawk's 2.3-litre four-cylinder engine and related transmissions, the structure and suspensions were novel.

Bodyshells were pressed and assembled at the BLSP works in Acton, West London, and to make space for this the Sunbeam Mk III shell had to be taken out of production. An estate car derivative of the new Hawk followed in the autumn.

Jaguar: The new XK150, introduced in May, was a second and final reworking of the original XK120 sportscar design, and was a direct replacement for the XK140. Two body types – fixed-head and drop-head coupes – were available at once, while the two-seater would arrive in 1958.

The XK140's chassis was updated by providing more powerful derivatives of the XK engine and fitting Dunlop disc brakes to all four wheels, but it was otherwise very familiar. Although some XK140 body panels were retained, these were all hidden, for the entire skin was new, being smoother, with a higher waistline and a wraparound windscreen. Many observers suggested that the XK150 had suffered some middle-aged spread, which was quite true as this was a more bulky (and more spacious) car than before.

The 3.4-litre saloon, which had been forecast from the day that the 2.4 appeared in 1955, was finally introduced, initially for sale primarily to North America, but later becoming freely available throughout the world, including Britain. The mechanical specification, with a 210bhp 3.4-litre version of the XK power unit, was predictable enough, though eyebrows were raised at the use of drum brakes on what was sure to be a 120mph car.

Within months, however, a four-wheel Dunlop disc brake kit became optional, along with centre-lock wire-spoke wheels, and after that the majority of 3.4s seemed to have at least one of these options fitted. At this point the 2.4's front-end style was commonized with that of the 3.4 with its wider grille; henceforth the only way to identify one from the other was by the badging.

In addition, early in 1957 there was the short-lived XKSS project, the idea being to convert unsold D-types into stark but relatively practical two-seater road cars. This involved cutting an extra door into the side of the D-type's centre-section, then adding a full-width screen and a rather rudimentary soft-top.

The result was a 150mph two-seater, practical if a little draughty, but any long-term hopes for this model were dashed when several cars were consumed in a major fire at Jaguar's factory. Less than 20 were made, though several were 'created' in the classic car boom of the 1970s and 1980s.

Jensen: Introduced the 541R, a 150bhp-engined version of the 541, with a claimed top speed of 125mph. Not many 150bhp versions were made, but the 541R would stay in production until the early 1960s.

Lancia: The Flaminia, Lancia's direct successor to the Aurelia, went on sale in the UK. The basis of the range was a handsome, rather square-rigged, saloon, complete with a V6 engine; even more handsome, but expensive, coupe and sporting versions would follow in the next few years.

Land-Rover: A 2-litre diesel engine was added to the range, which was already complex, for by this time there was a choice of wheelbases and several body types. At this stage, however, the ubiquitous Land-Rover's career was nowhere near its peak.

Lloyd (West Germany): Not to be confused with Lloyd of Grimsby, which had already ceased operations, *this* Lloyd was a wholly-owned subsidiary of Borgward of West Germany, the cars being made in Bremen.

Although there were smaller LP models, it was the 596cc-engined LP600 which was first to be listed for sale in the UK. Priced at £586 at first, it should have been competitive with British marques, but there was no distribution network, so its impact on the British market was tiny.

Looking rather like a Borgward Isabella which had shrunk in the wash, the LP600 was a small (11ft long) two-door saloon with a front-mounted two-stroke engine driving the front wheels. By mid-1950s standards it was a reasonably roomy four-seater for this class of car, if rather crudely and basically trimmed. It remained tentatively on the British market until 1959.

Lotus: The first prototype of the new Elite road car was shown, though series-production would not get under way until 1959. This sleek two-seater coupe was technically brilliant, though clearly undeveloped at that point.

Not only did the car have unit construction, but this was in glassfibre, reinforced only lightly at strategic points by steel members. Power was by the 1.2-litre Coventry Climax FWE unit and there was soft, long-travel, all-independent suspension. The door shape was such that the side windows had to be removed, not wound down, if more fresh air was needed.

This was Lotus' first practical road car (the 1953 Lotus Mk 6 did not really count), and almost 1,000 of them would be sold before the Elan arrived in 1962.

The Elite's appearance caused such a stir that the launch of the Seven, a new statement of Lotus' lightweight, multi-tube-frame, cycle-type front-winged, open-top sportscar theme, went almost unnoticed. Nearly 40 years later, developed versions of the Seven (called Caterham Super Sevens) were being made in larger numbers than ever before...

Meadows: This long-established industrial engine-building concern linked up with businessman Raymond Flower and stylist Giovanni Michelotti to announce the tiny new Frisky model, which was in the bubblecar mould, with a mid/rear-mounted Villiers two-stroke engine. The tiny tubular chassis featured Dubonnet-type independent suspension using rubber in torsion, though the chain-driven rear axle was solid, with no differential.

The first cars were shown with closed bodies including upward-lifting gull-wing doors for the two-seater cabin, but these were discarded before deliveries began. Friskies sold to the public were either saloons or Sport models with conventional doors and closed or open-top styles. This was a brave effort, but like all such noisy, motorcycle engine-powered creations, its vogue was short, and at £484 for the open-top Sport model it really wasn't cheap enough to establish a new market.

Mercedes-Benz: The side-valve four-cylinder engine which had been fitted to so many smaller models since the 1930s was finally dropped, all such cars henceforth being fitted with the latest overhead-camshaft units.

The prestige 300 model was given a 4in longer wheelbase, while the latest type of fuel injection was standardized, the gross power rising to 180bhp.

The easy-change transmission habit spread yet further when the two-pedal Hydrak system became optional on six-cylinder 219 and 220 models.

As previewed at the end of 1956, the 300SL Roadster took over from the 300SL gullwing model, with the same basic running gear except that low-pivot rear suspension was specified to improve the car's roadholding characteristics. Under the skin the multi-tube spaceframe had been redesigned, particularly in its centre, to allow shallow but nevertheless conventional passenger doors to be fitted.

At first only a folding soft-top version was available, but by the end of 1958 a detachable hardtop had also been developed.

Metropolitan: The BMC-built US-market car, initially sold only by Nash/Hudson on the North American market, finally went on sale in Britain. By this time the specification included the familiar 1.5-litre B-series engine, but with a *three*-speed gearbox.

Even though the front track was quite narrow, the heavily-spatted front wheelarches restricted the lock a little, there was a peculiar dropped waistline along the doors, and rather too much of what was called transatlantic trim, furnishing and colour schemes. Soft-top or hardtop versions were available.

Morgan: The company slightly

changed the frontal aspect of their traditional styling and increased the cockpit width. At the same time a Competition version of the side-valve 4/4 Series II was added to the range.

Morris: The only significant change of 1957 was the addition of an all-steel five-door estate car version of the Morris Oxford, which would only have a limited life as the Farina-styled Oxfords would be launched less than two years later.

NSU: The noted German motorcycle manufacturer entered the car market with a small four-seater called the Prinz. This, like a whole family of new NSU models which would appear in the next decade, had a unit-construction shell and an air-cooled engine (a twin-cylinder unit in this case) mounted in the tail. British sales were always limited, for this car seemed to have no extra appeal over the VW Beetle.

Peerless: The prototype of the GT model was shown, though production cars would not be available until 1958. The Peerless was a four-seater, two-door closed coupe with a multi-tubular chassis-frame, a glassfibre body and Triumph TR3 engine and transmission.

Although too expensive and not refined enough to attract a lot of orders, it was a very capable machine, which struggled on for a couple of years before financial problems overwhelmed the Slough-based concern. It would enjoy a very short renaissance in 1960 as the Warwick GT.

Princess: BMC invented a new marque by deciding to hive off the Princess models from the Austin franchise, making them Princess cars in their own right; this enabled them to be marketed through any of the dealer chains in the BMC group, not just the Austin network.

Renault: The two-pedal/easy-drive fashion spread to France, where the Fregate was equipped with Transfluide as an option.

Riley: The Pathfinder's chassis layout was changed, the rear axle now being located by half-elliptic springs in place of the original coil-springs-and-radius-arm layout; the new arrangement was simpler and apparently cheaper to build.

Later in the summer the Pathfinder model was dropped and replaced by the Two-Point-Six. Although visually similar to the old Pathfinder, the new car was an even closer clone of the Wolseley 6/90 than before because it was powered by the BMC C-series six-cylinder engine instead of the unique Riley 'four' (which had been dropped).

Predictably, there were protests from Riley diehards about this change, but there was even more controversy when the One-Point-Five (1.5) appeared in November! This was a more powerful (twin-SU, B-series engine) version of the Wolseley 1500, kitted out with a Riley grille, more complete instrumentation and a rather gaudy two-tone colour scheme inside and out. The 1.5 should have become a very desirable sports saloon, but somehow its performance never lived up to its promise. At £864 it was only £68 more expensive than the Wolseley 1500, but it never sold as well.

Rolls-Royce: A longer-wheelbase (by 4in) limousine version of the Silver Cloud was added to the range, complete with style changes and a six-light side aspect.

Singer: The Gazelle took on the same development changes as the Hillman Minx, which meant that an estate car derivative was also launched in October.

Standard: Development and tinkering of the Eight/Ten range continued, overdrive becoming available on the Eight in February, while at the same time peak engine power crept up from 30bhp to a 'Gold Star' 33bhp. The exterior bootlid found on most other models was finally standardized across the range.

The Pennant was added later in the year, really as a much-facelifted version of the Ten. The basic unit-construction shell, platform and running gear were all the same as before, but there were longer and more aggressively shaped front and rear body panels and duotone colour schemes. The most significant mechanical change was the addition of a remote-control gearchange, this being inspired by the same fitting applied to Austin A35/Morris Minor 1000 types a year earlier.

There was also a new Ensign, which was really a stripped-out, cheaper (£900) version of the Vanguard III, but with a 60bhp/1,670cc derivative of the Vanguard's engine. This was the first of the family to have a four-speed gearbox, while automatic transmission was added to the Vanguard range as an option.

Sunbeam: The last of the Mark III saloons were produced, leaving the Rapier as the only Sunbeam still in production.

Vauxhall: Although the new FA-type Victor was a very important car for Vauxhall to introduce in 1957, no-one ever forgave the company for making it look so awful. The car's layout – smaller, lighter and more compact than the E-type Wyvern it was meant to displace – was logical enough, but the quasi-Chevrolet looks, complete with dog-leg screen, heavy sculpting on the flanks and the traditional Vauxhall spears also on the sides of the car, were awful.

But anyone who could bear to look at a Victor before getting into it and could withstand the taunts of neighbours found a car which matched Ford's Consul for performance and handling. Perhaps Vauxhall got it right after all, because most customers seemed to ignore the style and buy the package for what it was. Priced at £729 (the old Wyvern, which would soon disappear, cost £804), it was an interesting and ultimately successful family car.

Well ahead of the October launch of the new P-type Velox/Cresta models, the existing six-cylinder engine was improved and made more powerful in the existing (old-type) E-type models before being carried over to the new types. At the same time the three-speed gearbox was upgraded to provide synchromesh on all forward ratios.

The new P-type Vauxhalls had a large (178in long) unit-construction four-door body with very smooth and rounded lines and many obvious influences from GM in Detroit. Except for minor transatlantic over-decoration and the use of steeply dog-legged screen pillars, this was an extremely smart new style. In one year, therefore, Vauxhall had completely renewed its product range, ditching the six-year-

old E-types and introducing two brand-new types, the Victor and the Velox/Cresta.

Vespa: Although designed by Piaggio of Italy, this neat little two-seater convertible coupe was always built in France. It sold in only small quantities in the British Isles (mainly in the Channel Islands, where its small size was appealing), but it was successful elsewhere in Europe, 34,000 being produced in four years.

The specification was adventurous, with integral body/chassis construction, all-independent suspension and an air-cooled rear-mounted twin-cylinder 393cc engine. Build quality was surprisingly high, but with a cruising speed of little more than 45mph it did not attract many people. It faded away in 1961.

Wolseley: BMC launched the new 1500, which had started life as a proposed replacement for the Morris Minor but had changed a lot during design and development. This was the first of the Riley 1.5/Wolseley 1500 duo to be revealed. The new car's underpan and suspension layout were similar to the Morris Minor 1000, but there was a new four-door saloon cabin.

The BMC B-series engine and transmission were all familiar 'building blocks', but the overall gearing was high and there was a good deal of wooden veneer and leather inside the cabin to justify a relatively high price.

Changes, mainly cosmetic, were also made to the 6/90, turning it into the Series III.

Industrial developments

BMC announced that in future all sportscar assembly would be concentrated at the MG factory in Abingdon. This not only freed up a lot of space at Longbridge, which in 1958 BMC would fill with a new 4x4 Gipsy model, but it also meant that a new small Austin-Healey (the Sprite, also to be launched in 1958) could be produced at Abingdon.

There was an overlap of 100-Six assembly at Longbridge and at Abingdon, but the change was completed by the end of 1957. One consequence was that Riley assembly was displaced from Abingdon, some models going to Longbridge, others to Cowley.

During May, Alec Issigonis was appointed as BMC's chief engineer, with J R Stansfield (Austin) and Charles Griffin (Nuffield) as his local chief designers. This was the start of an amazingly fruitful period for BMC engineering, for the first front-wheel-drive cars were already being designed. [Shortly after this, Stansfield left BMC to join Fisher & Ludlow.]

Controversy, bitterness and much confusion surrounded Standard and its erstwhile industrial partners, Massey-Harris-Ferguson, during the year. Since 1946, Standard had been producing tractors, first for Harry Ferguson Ltd, then for the enterprise to whom the Irishman sold out in the mid-1950s.

Behind the scenes there had been a great deal of talk about co-operation and future strategy, but during 1957 the large Canadian concern decided to mount a complete takeover of the Standard Motor Company Ltd.

Although not public knowledge at the time, Standard had been in merger talks with the Rootes Group and had only turned to M-H-F when these discussions foundered. At first, chairman Lord Tedder and managing director Alick Dick agreed to recommend their shareholders to accept the M-H-F proposal as it fell into line with their long-term strategy of seeking a partner for the business. Then the atmosphere soured (M-H-F had been stockbuilding without telling Standard — a move

which would be quite illegal these days), share prices moved in the wrong direction and the entire deal was called off in October in some acrimony. From that point Alick Dick decided that he would have to break all ties with M-H-F, even to the extent of walking away from the profitable tractor assembly deal, but this move would not be achieved until 1959.

On the evening of February 12, a large part of Jaguar's Browns Lane factory was destroyed by fire, which reputedly started in one of the stores departments. At least a quarter of the main assembly building was destroyed and 270 new cars (including a handful of D-type and XKSS models) were consumed.

Jaguar, however, bounced back remarkably quickly, the first cars being delivered from a shortened assembly line within two days, complete 'post-fire' cars within four weeks and a complete new extension opened by the summer. In total, it seems, the damage cost Jaguar's insurers more than £3 million.

During the year David Brown decided to concentrate the manufacture of Aston Martins and Lagondas at the erstwhile Tickford body-manufacturing plant at Newport Pagnell, the process being complete by the time the new DB4 was ready for launch in 1958.

The BMW Isetta factory in Brighton, a conversion of the redundant locomotive-building works close to the railway station, finally opened its doors. At the

same time the owner of the business, Dunsfold Tools, changed its name to Isetta of Great Britain.

The only access to public roads was by a flight of 100 steps, which meant that all parts to build Isettas had to be delivered by rail, while completed cars were removed in a similar way! The existing railway line, linked to the main approach line into Brighton station, was therefore retained. Although this was a most awkward manufacturing arrangement, it persisted for several years, for Isettas were small enough to be moved easily by rail.

Lord Hives, at the age of 70, retired from the chairmanship of Rolls-Royce, the company he had joined as a mechanic in 1908.

Technical developments

Although this was a year of consolidation, disc brakes and two-pedal control systems continued to spread throughout the industry. There was no doubt that disc brakes were a real advance, but years later it was difficult to see the merit behind some of the two-pedal installations, especially the cheaper ones for smaller cars. Although these eliminated the clutch pedal, they often did so at the expense of gearchanging precision; the changes were often jerky, and many operating and reliability problems were found when they went into service.

1958

This was a year when the atmosphere for motorists progressively lightened. What Prime Minister Harold Macmillan identified as the 'never had it so good' era was blooming; there seemed to be more money to spend, and spirits were high.

Although there were some purchase tax increases in the Budget, these did not apply to cars. There were no major pro-motorist Budget changes, but everything was helped by bank rate falling to 6 per cent in March, 5 per cent in June, and 4 per cent in November. The really good news came in October, when all restrictions on hire purchase were lifted.

The improvements were reflected in the motor industry's output figures, which showed remarkable resilience. For the first time total output beat the million mark – in fact it soared to 1.05 million – this figure being matched by two more record figures: 566,319 home-market deliveries and nearly 500,000 cars exported.

Even so, car imports were still lagging, for only 10,940 were imported from all sources: their market share, in other words, was still only a fraction over 1 per cent.

Not only did Britain's first stretch of motorway – a mere 8.5 miles of the Preston bypass (now a part of the M6) open on December 5, but work also began on building the first major length of the M1 motorway in March, with John Laing winning a contract to construct 53 miles – and to have it ready in a mere 19 months. The race was on, with opening promised for October 31, 1959.

The road-building programme, in fact, was exploding into action, with a start on the M50 motorway, the Maidstone bypass, the Forth road bridge and many other schemes. After more than a decade of criticism for not building any new highways, the Ministry of Transport could now point to a great deal of activity, which has continued ever since.

On the other hand, the first 'No waiting' yellow lines were introduced in London, and after several years of talking and delay, Britain's first parking meters came into use on July 10 in the Grosvenor Square area of London. In those days the charges were 6d (2.5p) an hour for up to a maximum of two hours.

The popularity of taking one's car to France by air, instead of by ferry, continued to increase, and Silver City Airways celebrated the 10th anniversary of this unique service during the year; 170 cars had been carried in 1948, 34,361 in 1957, and all the signs were than 60,000 would make the journey in 1958. Rising fares had been balanced by better facilities at Lydd (Ferryfield) and Southend, and Silver City's fleet of short and longer-nosed Bristol Freighters was up to 22 aircraft at one point.

By 1958, the retail price of petrol had finally returned to its pre-Suez level – with average prices of around 4s 1d (20.5p) a gallon.

The first proposals for the compulsory testing of older cars were made in Parliament, for enactment in 1959; initially they were confined to a very simple check of brakes, lights and steering, and then only on cars which were at least 10 years old. In fact this law was delayed until 1961, the first compulsory testing beginning on February 15 of that year. Over the years, of course, the requirements would steadily be tightened, by reducing the age qualification to three years and adding many check points to the testing procedure.

New models

Abarth: As a real indulgence, one or two British drivers bought the Zagato 750GT, a car based on the platform of the Fiat 600, but with a 44bhp/747cc version of the engine. The Zagato body style was a tiny two-seater coupe, with a double-bubble cross-sectional profile (the better to provide some semblance of headroom!).

The Zagato's problem was not that it was very small, but that it was expensive. At £2,248 it cost more than twice as much as a Triumph TR3A, for instance.

Alfa Romeo: The first of the 2000 models were shown in the UK, these being replacements for the long-running 1900 range. Engines were enlarged versions of the 1900's 'four', the platforms were new, and there would eventually be a choice of square-rigged saloon and altogether more graceful coupe and convertible types. Early in the 1960s the six-cylinder 2600 would evolve from these 2000s, though few of any type were ever sold in the UK.

Alvis: The announcement that the Graber-style bodyshells for the latest TD21 3-litre models were to be produced by Park Ward Ltd, in London, ensured that many more such cars would be built in future, production of cars with Willowbrook bodies having always been severely restricted.

The definitive Park Ward-bodied Alvis was shown in October, this having a larger cabin with more space (especially for rear-seat passengers), a brand-new facia/instrument layout, along with the addition of automatic transmission (as an option) and disc brakes.

Armstrong Siddeley: Unable to afford the time or capital expenditure to develop an all-new model, the Coventry company produced a much-modified version of the Sapphire 346 (which continued), calling it the Star Sapphire.

Under the virtually unchanged four-door body style there was a 4-litre version of the Sapphire's engine, power-assisted steering, front-wheel disc brakes and Borg-Warner automatic transmission (as standard), all for the first time on this range.

Aston Martin: The new DB4, introduced but not yet ready for production, was Aston Martin's first all-new model for a decade. It was based on a new steel platform chassis and powered by a brand-new 3.7-litre twin-cam 'six' that had originally been seen in the DBR2 sports-racing cars of 1957.

The almost-four-seater fastback coupe body style was by Carrozzeria Touring of Italy, whose *superleggera* type of construction (shaping by many small-diameter tubes, with body skins laid over and welded to the framework) was also adopted.

0–100–0mph in less than 30 seconds was claimed, and duly backed up by tests at MIRA, when the average figure of several runs was found to be 27.2sec! Compared with the DB Mark III, which would not drop out of production until the end of 1959, the DB4 was a much larger, heavier and more expensive car. For comparison, at the end of 1958, when the two cars still overlapped – just – the DB Mark III cost £3,076 compared with £3,976 asked for the DB4.

The DB4 was the first of a family whose chassis platform would spread, improve, change and evolve for the next 30 years, for there were still some elements of the old chassis design in the V8-engined cars being built in the 1980s.

Austin: The most important arrival of the year was the A40 model, the first BMC car to be styled by the Italian Farina coachbuilding concern. Underneath its sharply-fashionable lines, the A40 ran on modified A35 running gear – engine, transmission, front suspension and back axle – but the shell was a practical two-box shape (no separately-contoured boot area) which was really halfway to being an estate car. At the rear, however, the rear window was fixed, and there was a conventional let-down bootlid: the rear seat could be folded forward to enlarge the space for luggage.

BMC also entered the small 4x4 market by introducing the new Gipsy, which was assembled in the same corner of Longbridge which had previously been occupied by the Austin-Healey sportscar.

Like its obvious rival, the Land-Rover, the Gipsy had a sturdy separate chassis, and there was a choice of petrol or diesel four-cylinder engines, though at first there was no choice of wheelbases. Unlike the Land-Rover, there was independent suspension all round, by Flexitor trailing-arm plus rubber-in-torsion members, and the bodyshells were in steel rather than aluminium sheet, making them more prone to rotting.

BMC decided to use the Vanden Plas label more than before, introducing a much-gilded version of the A105 which carried it. Production, it was said, would be 'strictly limited because of hand finishing'...

Austin-Healey: BMC introduced a new small sportscar, the Sprite, which had been designed by the Healey concern. It used modified versions of the engine, transmission and front suspension of the Austin A35 and Morris Minor models, and the unit-construction bodyshell featured a lift-up 'alligator-style' bonnet, with protruding headlamps, so it was almost immediately nicknamed the 'frogeye' model.

There was no exterior bootlid on this version, and the rear axle was sprung on cantilevered quarter-elliptic leaf springs. It was brisk, though not very fast (83mph top speed), and was extremely good value at £679. However, items like the heater, rev-counter, front bumper, windscreen washers and several other desirable fittings were all optional extras.

This was the first of long line of Sprites and (from 1961) badge-engineered MG Midgets, of which the last would not be built until 1979.

BMC also introduced a two-seater version of the larger sportscar, the 100-Six, initially as a direct replacement for the earlier 2+2 type. This move, however, proved to be misguided, the result being that the 2+2 was re-introduced later in the year, and both body derivatives were then catalogued for the next few seasons.

Berkeley: For such a small concern, the enterprise was astonishing, for at the 1958 Motor Show a longer-wheelbase version of the front-wheel-drive sportscar, the Foursome, was introduced and made available in open-top or coupe form, but it was not to prove a success.

Bristol: Although it had been previewed in 1957, not only with an export-only body style by Beuttler, but with a picture of the definitive prototype being sampled by HRH the Duke of Edinburgh, the new 406 was not officially revealed until August 1958.

The 406 was a direct replacement for the 405, and was based very closely on it. The chassis platform and suspension was much as before (except for the use of Watts linkage location to the back axle), the engine had been stretched to 2.2 litres (by increasing both bore and stroke), the overdrive transmission was retained, while there was a new two-door saloon body style in place of the 405's four-door layout.

Like previous Bristols, this was a fast and graceful car, but as before it was a very expensive, hand-built machine, prices beginning at £4,494.

Citroen: An extremely practical estate car version of the ID19 was introduced, which had a longer wheelbase and could therefore swallow a cavernous amount of luggage.

DAF: The first of this intriguing family of Dutch cars was introduced, though sales did not begin until 1959. Originally known as the Daffodil, it had a front-mounted air-cooled engine, the transmission being a unique form of automatic, with final drive by belts which were squeezed between conical pulleys. Different ratios were provided by arranging for the split pulleys to draw closer together or move further apart, which allowed the belt to take up a large or small radius around the driveshaft.

In spite of the ridicule heaped on this system by those who had not tried it (belt drive, it was said, had disappeared in the 1920s because it was unreliable....), the DAF transmission system was very durable and was to be used on many more models in the next 15 years.

[DAF would eventually be taken over by Volvo, and the last to bear that badge would be produced in the mid-1970s.]

Daimler: The new Majestic model was added to the range in mid-summer. This was yet another derivation of the Regency II/104 family, with more power and a revised style.

The chassis layout was virtually unchanged from the 104, but the engine had been enlarged to 135bhp/3.8 litres, while Borg-Warner automatic transmission was standard equipment: for the first time in many years on a Daimler, there was no preselector transmission on offer. Four-wheel Dunlop disc brakes (as used by Jaguar) were also standard.

The style had been altered along the flanks, with the deletion of a rear wingline crease on the rear doors and wheelarches. Instead, the body had been widened and smoothed out, this being a facelift which really was prettier than the original, resulting in a fast, dignified and well-balanced car – and there was still another variation to come. That car, the Majestic Major, would appear in 1959 when a new V8 engine was made ready.

During 1958, company leaks mentioned another new V8 engine, and a new sportscar design, but enthusiasts had to wait until the spring of 1959 to see what this was all about.

Elva: The Sussex-based racing car constructor launched a new two-seater sports road car. In some ways rather like the Turner, it used a (large-diameter) tubular chassis-frame and had a glass-fibre bodyshell. Power was by BMC (the MGA engine and transmission), and the new Courier could be supplied built-up, or in kit form.

Facel Vega: In France, the small but prestigious maker of vast *grand routier* models began fitting larger, 5.9-litre, Chrysler engines, which produced 360bhp (gross). HK500 and Excellence (four-door saloon) models were both available.

By this time Dunlop disc brakes were available on Facel-Vegas, in fact all British imports seemed to have this feature.

Fairthorpe: The Electron was evolved into the Electron Minor, with the same basic design, structure and style, but with a 38bhp/948cc Standard Ten engine – and a much lower price.

Ferrari: For the first time, this famous Italian marque was put on sale in the UK, though the original impact of the 250GT road car was totally insignificant. Mike Hawthorn's Tourist Trophy Garage, in Farnham, tentatively held the concession, which was almost immediately transferred to Col Ronnie Hoare's Maranello Concessionaires.

In the next three years just two 250GT cabriolets and nine 250GT berlinettas would be imported – it was not until the launch of the 2+2 250GTE of 1960 that the numbers would start to increase.

Fiat: A more powerful version of the tiny 500, with 499cc and 22bhp, was added to the range.

Goggomobil: The 'Supergog' (more accurately known as the T700) was launched, this being a much more orthodox car than the original tiny Goggomobil which was already on sale in the UK. The T700 had a front-mounted flat-twin air-cooled engine driving the rear wheels, and had near-conventional styling, with a two-door four-seater saloon body.

There was also a T600, which was never marketed in the UK.

Hillman: A new-generation Husky estate car took over from the original type at the beginning of the year. Though still a short-wheelbase three-

door estate car, the latest Husky was based on the bodyshell of the modern-generation Hillman Minx and initially had a 40bhp version of the 1.4-litre overhead-valve engine. The changeover from old-type to new-type Minx-family production at Rootes was now complete.

At the end of the year the Minx was given another update, becoming Series III, this time with an enlarged, 49bhp/1.5-litre version of the engine, along with a new facia/instrument panel lay-out.

Humber: The new-generation Super Snipe arrived, being virtually a more upmarket version of the latest monocoque Hawk fitted with an all-new 2.6-litre six-cylinder engine.

That, at least, is what Rootes tried to tell the world. In fact the new engine had been designed in close collaboration with Armstrong Siddeley, and bore a very strong family resemblance to the existing Sapphire 346/Star Sapphire design, down to the layout of the valve gear, the part-spherical combustion chambers, the opposed valves and the crossflow breathing.

[What we did not know then, but learned later, was that Rootes was involved in another deal with Armstrong Siddeley, who were about to take on the manufacture for Rootes of a new sportscar, the Sunbeam Alpine of 1959.]

Jaguar: Two new versions of the XK150 were added, one being the two-seater roadster (which restored the range to its familiar three types), the other a higher-powered 250bhp S version of the same car, with a new cylinder head casting and three 2in SU carburettors.

The Mk VIII saloon was upgraded to become the Mk IX, powered by a 220bhp (gross) 3.8-litre version of the XK engine and fitted with four-wheel disc brakes and power-assisted steering. This was the first use in a Jaguar production car of the 3.8-litre engine size already seen in D-type racecars.

Land-Rover: Within weeks of the launch of the new Austin Gipsy, Land-Rover introduced its own Series II model. The style was similar to the Series I, but a little more rounded at the edges than before, and the technical mixture was also much as before, with a choice of 88in and 109in wheelbase lengths and petrol or diesel

engines. The Series II, however, had a new, purpose-built, 2.3-litre petrol engine – more powerful, more torquey and much more durable – to replace the game old Rover 60 unit.

Meadows: The stark, purposeful, but not-very-practical Frisky Sprint was previewed, this using the existing Frisky chassis, but powered by a rear-mounted 34bhp/492cc three-cylinder Excelsior motorcycle engine, all covered by a stark two-seater sportscar shell.

This car was forecast to be built by the aircraft manufacturer Vickers-Armstrong at its Swindon factory, but in the face of negligible interest it never went into production.

Mercedes-Benz: Not only was fuel-injection made available on 2.2-litre six-cylinder models, but there was also a new overhead-camshaft diesel-engined car, the 190D.

Messerschmitt: The odd, but extremely effective, Tiger 500 version of the 'cabin cruiser' went on sale in the UK. This was a tiny four-wheeler version of a three-wheeler which looked just like the fuselage of an aircraft (access was by tipping up the Perspex top and side and climbing in!), the 500cc engine was in the tail, and steering was by handlebars rather than a wheel. It was quick, and not expensive at £651, but almost totally impractical. As one wag also commented: 'Add wings and, there you are, a new Luftwaffe!'

MG: After several years of sometimes difficult engine development, MG was finally ready to introduce its excitingly-specified MGA Twin-Cam models (roadster and GT coupe). Although looking almost the same as the original pushrod-engined cars, the Twin-Cams had a brand-new 108bhp/1.6-litre twin-overhead-camshaft engine, there were four-wheel Dunlop disc brakes, while centre-lock knock-off steel wheels, looking like those used on Jaguar D-types and other racing cars, were also standard.

Naturally, the Twin-Cam was much more expensive than the conventional MGA – £1,266 compared with £996 – but with a top speed of nearly 115mph it was also a much faster car. Unhappily, this model soon earned a reputation for engine problems, sales never lived up to expectations, and it would be dropped in 1960, less than two years after launch.

Morgan: The annual changes to Morgan cars were always small, this time there being no mechanical changes, though the rear-end of the bodies was smoothed-out, the spare wheel of the two-seater being partly recessed into a more rakish line. The Vanguard engine option was finally laid to rest, all Plus 4s henceforth being supplied with TR3A power units.

NSU: To follow the Prinz saloon, NSU now introduced the Sport Prinz, which used the same platform, but had 37bhp and used a pretty fastback coupe body style by Bertone. Production actually began early in 1959.

Oppermann: The Borehamwood-based concern was still trying to make its mark, adding a new sporting coupe model, the Stirling, to the Unicar. Once again designed, or inspired, by Laurie Bond, the Stirling featured a rear/mid-mounted Excelsior engine, this time of 424cc, but demand was very limited and these cars would disappear by 1960.

Peerless: Deliveries began of this TR3-engined 2+2 sports coupe.

Porsche: The first few 1.6-litre four-overhead-camshaft Carreras were produced as a direct (and more powerful) replacement for the original 1.5-litre cars. Peak power was up from 105bhp to 115bhp, the engines still being extremely complex and expensive to own and service.

Renault: The Floride, a smart two-door coupe or convertible built on the rear-engined Dauphine's platform, was previewed at the Paris Salon, though production (and deliveries to the British market) would not begin until 1959.

Rover: The P5 3-litre saloon was the first new shape to come from Rover since the arrival of the P4 in 1949. An additional model, it was an altogether larger machine and was always ripe to be nicknamed 'Great Auntie'.

Underneath the staid but elegant four-door monocoque was a massive front-end subframe supporting a 3-litre version of the famous Rover six-cylinder engine, and there was a choice of manual, overdrive, or fully automatic transmissions. Surprisingly, the new car had four-wheel drum brakes, but that shortcoming would be rectified within a year.

Like the latest P4s, the P5 had a beautifully equipped and tastefully decorated cabin, and would shortly be adopted by many company chairmen, politicians and dignitaries who could not afford, or did not want to flaunt themselves in, a Rolls-Royce.

The arrival of the P5 led to the death of the 105R (which had never sold well), and at the same time the 105S was renamed simply 105.

Singer: Rootes rationalization progressed one stage further when the Gazelle was given a 56bhp/1.5-litre version of the Hillman Minx engine, listed as optional to the existing Singer overhead-cam unit, although the last of the 'Singer-engined Singers', in fact, would be produced immediately after this announcement.

Standard: Standard-Triumph was holding its breath, almost ready to launch the expansive new Herald project in 1959, so 1958 was a 'treadwater' year for the company. The ill-fated Vanguard Sportsman was dropped in the spring of the year, shunned by almost everyone.

Helped along by deft retouching from the Italian stylist Michelotti, the Vanguard III became the Vignale Vanguard. There were larger front and rear windows, less aggressive taillamps, a different grille and a general upgrading of the interior. The Ensign picked up the same bodyshell changes.

Sunbeam: The Rapier reached Series II with a major facelift which included the use of a new grille and prominent tailfins, plus a convertible option, all with an enlarged, 68bhp/1.5-litre version of the engine. The new car came immediately after Peter Harper's fine drive into fifth place in the Monte Carlo rally in a Series I: using a new Series II, he then went on to win the RAC rally of 1958.

Triumph: The facelifted TR3A, complete with wide-mouth grille, took over from the TR3 with very few mechanical changes. This would become Triumph's best-selling sportscar for the next four years. The larger 2.2-litre version of the engine was blooded by works cars on the French Alpine rally, and would be made optional on production cars from 1959.

TVR: A new Blackpool-built sports coupe with a multi-tubular frame, all-independent (VW Beetle front end-type) suspension, a glassfibre body style and a choice of Ford or Coventry Climax engines, was shown for the first time. It was the first of a long line of open or closed sportscars which would pour out of Blackpool in the next 40 years.

Vauxhall: There was more variety in the still-new Victor range, first with the launch of an estate car, then with the option of two-pedal transmission control, using the Newtondrive system.

Volvo: The long-established PV444 gave way to the PV544, which was essentially the same car with a body facelift, including a one-piece screen, deeper rear window and a revised interior. A serious import plan for these cars was laid at the end of the year.

Wolseley: At the end of the year, this BMC marque became the first to reveal its own version of what became known as the 'B-series Farina' range, with the 15/60. It was a direct replacement for the 15/50, so in effect a Nuffield Wolseley had been replaced by a BMC equivalent. The Corporation had decided to renew its entire mid-size family car range – Austin, MG, Morris, Riley *and* Wolseley – by developing one new commonized unit-construction shell, which would then be badged, equipped and decorated in different ways, sometimes with more powerful B-series power units.

From the end of 1958 until 1971 (when the last Morris Oxford was produced), the same basic car was churned out in large and (for BMC) very profitable numbers. None of the cars were exciting, all had very ordinary engineering and roadholding, yet the general public seemed to like what it saw.

The 15/60 used the single-carburettor 55bhp version of the 1.5-litre engine, and there was a traditional Wolseley grille, matched by a good deal of wood and leather inside the cabin. For the time being there were no transmission options to the basic four-speed gearbox.

Industrial developments

Standard, having concluded a 'priority supplier' agreement with Mulliners, the Birmingham-based body manufacturers, in 1954, mounted a successful takeover bid for them during the year.

It was as a result of this bid that Massey-Ferguson (previously Massey-Harris-Ferguson) tried once again to take over Standard, but again were firmly rebuffed. Alick Dick now realized that he would have to secure

another partner as rapidly as possible, and started talking to Rover again. There would be more upheavals to come in the next three years...

Car production at the old Singer factory in Coventry came to an end: this was all part of the Rootes rationalization process, for the plant would eventually be used for making components.

George Goodall retired, so Peter Morgan, son of the founder, became managing director of the Morgan Motor Company Ltd and would direct its fortunes for the next 30 years and more.

Ford-USA sold its minority-interest shareholding in Simca (15.2 per cent of the capital) to Chrysler, the shareholding having been acquired when

Simca took over the Ford-France business in 1954. This was Chrysler's first move towards taking control of Simca and its first move into Europe. Its gradual takeover of the Rootes Group would eventually follow.

The death was announced, in Spain, of the Pegaso supercar, which had only ever been built in tiny numbers. Henceforth Pegaso would concentrate on building its main profit-earners, which were trucks and buses.

In the UK, the Lagonda car was also laid to rest, or rather put into suspended animation. Certainly the 3-litre model had dropped out of the Aston Martin-Lagonda range, and there would be no more Lagondas until the Rapide arrived in 1961.

Men of Influence

Keith Duckworth

No-one with a flippant manner or a butterfly's mind ever got Keith Duckworth's attention, for this Blackburn-born engineer only ever treated people seriously if they took him, or his subject, in the same way. Perhaps more than any other engineer of his day, he applied sheer, devastating, logic to every problem and every project which he tackled, the result being that his company, Cosworth Engineering, produced a whole series of peerless racing engines.

Born in 1933 of prosperous mill-owning parents, then educated at Giggleswick school and Imperial College, London, he joined Lotus as a gearbox development engineer in 1957, where he rapidly forged a friendship with Mike Costin. He soon became frustrated with Colin Chapman's cavalier attitudes at Lotus, so he left to form his own company in partnership with Costin.

Starting in a mews garage in West London in 1958, then rapidly expanding the business through premises in Friern Barnet and Edmonton, Duckworth developed a series of race-winning Ford-based Formula Junior engines, then tackled the design of the SCA F2 unit. After taking the big step to build a new factory at Northampton in 1964, he then secured a large contract from Ford, first to design the 1.6-litre FVA F2 racing engine, to be followed by the phenomenally successful 3-litre V8 DFV F1 power unit. With these two designs he refined the combination of twin overhead camshafts, four valves per cylinder and a narrow angle between the

opposed valves, none of this entirely new, but never before made so devastatingly efficient.

The DFV won its first race, first time out, in Jim Clark's Lotus 49 at the 1967 Dutch GP. Other teams soon secured supplies, and for the next 15 years the DFV was the standard-setter in Formula One; by the time it was outdated it had secured no fewer than 155 World Championship successes.

Duckworth, in the meantime, had inspired the birth of many more great Cosworth engines, including the Ford BDA, the Cosworth-Vega, the Ford GA V6, the Opel Ascona/Manta 400 unit and a new 16-valve engine for Mercedes-Benz. In the mid-1980s, too, he also inspired his staff to produce the extremely successful YB-type Sierra Cosworth/Escort Cosworth turbocharged unit, the short-lived but extremely powerful 1.5-litre V6 F1 turbo unit and the normally-aspirated F1 V8s which followed. All these engines were as powerful as any of their rivals, and usually much more reliable, for under Duckworth Cosworth was a very dedicated and painstaking business.

Although he ceded financial control of Cosworth to UEI in 1980 (who were later absorbed by Carlton), his health continued to betray his own high standards, and after a second heart attack, followed by open heart surgery, he decided to retire from executive management in 1988, though he continued to dabble with many engineering matters at his home near Northampton for some years after that.

1959

There was great joy among motorists, car manufacturers and especially the motor trade when the Chancellor reduced purchase tax on cars from 60 to 50 per cent in his April Budget. It was not a massive price reduction, but at least it reversed the increase which had been imposed in 1955.

It meant that the price of a Morris Minor 1000 was reduced from £625 to £590, a Ford Zephyr from £916 to £865 and a Rover 90 from £1,539 to £1,456. There was also a general reduction in income tax (cynics said that this was all being done ahead of a General Election, and in October they were to be proved right!) so people had a little more money to spend on their motoring.

After a period of financial stringency, the Government was easing the pressure, and the three-year credit squeeze came to an end with the dropping of all credit controls. Not surprisingly, at the General Election the existing Government was returned with an increased majority.

This was also the year in which all remaining import restrictions on foreign cars were removed, although they still had to bear an import duty of 30 per cent. The move was to boost sales of foreign cars in the years ahead.

British car production was still on the increase, with nearly 1,200,000 produced during the year. Home sales rose again to more than 650,000, but the most significant leap was in the sales of imported cars, which moved up to nearly 27,000 – a trivial figure today, but in 1959 the first sign of a truly free motoring market developing. The biggest problem facing concessionaires was finding the right type of dealers – and enough of them.

This was a year well-provided with motoring interest. Apart from the launch of three brand-new British small family cars – the BMC Mini, Triumph Herald and Ford Anglia – there was the arrival of a new V8 engine from Rolls-Royce and a new sportscar (the SP250) from Daimler. From West Germany, too, came rumours of a strange new type of engine, the Wankel.

Even so, one of the year's most important British motoring events was the opening of the first long stretch of the M1 motorway on Monday, November 2. This spanned the St Albans bypass to the M45 spur towards Coventry, which instantly returned the narrow old A5 road to its status of a country highway, and cut journey times from the heart of the motor industry – Coventry – to London by at least an hour. Suddenly it was possible to travel from the Midlands to the West End in less than two hours.

Relatively undeveloped at first (the service areas were not yet complete, and the extension south around the Watford bypass did not open for another six weeks), this new six-lane highway was initially very fast and relatively uncrowded. Point-to-point average speeds of 100mph were achieved by Jaguar owners, magazine road-testers checked out cars' maximum speeds along it, and the Minister of Transport, Ernest Marples, expressed himself appalled by the speeds he witnessed on that first day. For better or for worse, this was the true start of Britain's motorway age.

New models

AC: Another new sporting coupe, the Greyhound, was previewed, this having a family resemblance to the Aceca, but featuring an altogether larger, 2+2, fastback coupe style.

There was a new design of multi-tube chassis-frame, with a longer wheelbase, powered by the 105bhp Bristol engine. Not only was Laycock overdrive to be available as an option, but there was coil-spring independent front suspension and a new type of semi-trailing wishbone rear suspension (to allow space for the rear seats).

The Greyhound's launch was premature (deliveries would not, in fact, begin until 1960) because of the need to redesign the original chassis and make it stronger, from square-section tubing. Able to carry four people (just) and with a tendency to oversteer when fully loaded, this was an expensive car which was destined not to sell well. Only 82 were sold.

Amazingly, AC's venerable own-brand six-cylinder overhead-camshaft engine (first seen in 1919) was developed still further for the Ace and Aceca models. In its final state of tune, for 1960, it was fitted with three SU carburettors and rated at 102bhp at 5,000rpm.

Alvis: Only months after getting the Park Ward-bodied cars into production, Alvis upgraded them with a more powerful 120bhp engine (helped along by a new head casting), and with Lockheed front wheel disc brakes as options.

Armstrong Siddeley: The move up-market, from Sapphire to Star Sapphire, was completed with the launch of the Star Sapphire Limousine, which combined the existing Limousine's style with the Star Sapphire's 4-litre engine and automatic transmission. Although the latest car's wheelbase was 2in longer than before, this was achieved without changing the rear style.

At the time, few people suspected that this was the start of Armstrong Siddeley's final model year in the car-making business.

Aston Martin: With the DB4 only recently on sale (though launched in October 1958, the first deliveries had not been made until well into 1959), an important derivative, the DB4GT, was also announced. This featured a shorter-wheelbase version of the DB4's platform chassis and body style, fitted with an even more powerful (302bhp) version of the 3.7-litre engine, and having a claimed top speed of around 150mph. This time, the 0–100–0mph party trick was achieved in a mere 20sec. Understandably, it was considerably more expensive than the DB4, the two prices being £4,534 (DB4GT) and £3,755 (DB4).

Austin: The most important Austin of the year – of the generation, some say – was the tiny Mini, or 'Se7en', as BMC tried to call it for the first two years or so of its life! As soon as production began, the A35 saloon model was dropped.

Conceived by Alec Issigonis' team, it was the first truly new approach to family-car design for many years. Not only was it a very small four-seater (just 10ft long), but it had front-wheel drive, all-independent suspension by rubber in compression, and a transversely-mounted A-series engine with the four-speed gearbox mounted 'in the sump'.

Everything was new except for the engine (and even that had a unique bore/stroke combination), and the little car bristled with innovation and cost-saving details. Door windows slid rather than wound down, the battery was in the boot to allow sufficient under-bonnet space, the cooling radiator was at the side of the engine bay, pushing air out into the wheelarch, and this was also the first British car to run on 10in wheels and tyres.

After the inevitable teething problems had been overcome (most of which were down to poor build quality rather than technical defects), the new Mini began to sell in very large numbers. Close relatives of the design, looking almost exactly the same, were still in production in the mid-1990s, more than 35 years later!

Even at this early stage, BMC also revealed a stark open version called the Moke, which was already being assessed by the British Army: however, it would be years before a civilian version called the Mini-Moke was put on sale.

In 1959, the new-generation A55 was the second of the versatile BMC 'B-series Farinas' to be introduced. Mechanically it was identical to the Wolseley 15/60 which had been introduced a few weeks earlier, though the grille was different, and the general level of the interior was rather less lavish. Later in the year it would be joined by new MG Magnette, Morris Oxford and Riley 4/68 types.

Meanwhile, the third Farina-inspired shape from Austin to make its appearance was the A99, a massive 2.9-litre saloon which took over from the five-year-old A95/A105 range. The A99, which shared its monocoque with the Wolseley 6/99 and the Vanden Plas Princess 3-litre, was a solidly-engineered but strictly conventional six-seater which used upgraded derivatives of BMC C-series hardware.

The engine was larger than before, there was a new type of three-speed gearbox (mated with Borg-Warner overdrive), while the four-door body bore a strong family (ie Farina) resemblance to the A55 which had arrived just a few months earlier.

One year after the original type had been launched, a Countryman version of the A40 'Farina' went on sale. Technically and visually this looked the same as the original, except that there was now a fully opening rear end, provided by upper and lower doors.

Austin-Healey: The 100-Six gave way to the 3000 (Type BN7), this being a lightly re-engineered car with a 124bhp/2,912cc version of the C-series engine and front-wheel disc brakes.

Auto Union: By this time the DKW marque had been swept back under the wing of the parent company, which explains why the latest larger-engined DKW Sonderklasse was now known as an Auto Union 1000! The final versions of that car were given a wraparound screen in the autumn of the year.

There was also a new and smaller model, still with front-wheel drive and a two-stroke engine, but based on a new and rather sharply-styled two-door monocoque. This was a 34bhp/741cc-engined car known as the Junior. All these cars were produced at Ingolstadt, in Bavaria, the future home of larger and altogether more upmarket Audis, which would arrive in the 1960s.

Bentley: The brand-new V8 engine (see Rolls-Royce, below) was also adopted for all Bentleys, saloons and Continentals. A top speed of 120mph was claimed for the Continental S2.

Berkeley: Pushing the design of its tiny sportscar to the limit, Berkeley revealed the B95 (and later the B105) models, which used 692cc four-stroke parallel-twin Royal Enfield motorcycle engines instead of the smaller two-strokes of earlier cars.

To ensure adequate cooling, there was a new snout, with a squared-up grille and larger air intake, the raised bonnet profile being needed to clear the cylinder head of the bulkier engine.

This turned the Berkeley into a much faster, but less refined car, with sparkling performance. The problem was that it was by no means smooth enough for most prospective customers, and even though it was faster than BMC's new Austin-Healey Sprite and no more expensive – it sold for £628 compared with the Sprite's £632 – that proved to be an insuperable obstacle.

Berkeley also produced a three-wheeler version of their sportscar, this being powered by the 328cc twin-cylinder Excelsior engine.

BMW: The German company produced a smart new model in a most unusual way, upgrading its rear-engined 600 chassis with a larger 748cc version of the engine, and clothing it in a smart new 2+2 coupe body style, a lot of the shaping influence having come from Michelotti of Italy.

Even so, these were very difficult times for BMW, whose finances were in disarray. For a time there were even rumours that it would be obliged to merge with Mercedes-Benz.

Borgward: The northern Germany company previewed a new and larger model, the 2.3-litre Grosse saloon. This car used a six-cylinder engine derived from the four-cylinder Isabella unit, and had fascinating chassis features such as all-independent suspension incorporating pneumatic units. However, it would be short-lived as Borgward ceased building cars altogether in 1961.

Chevrolet: In the USA, GM's largest division announced a startlingly different type of car. Built for the newly-fashionable 'compact' category, the Corvair was totally different from any previous Chevrolet.

Not only did it have all-independent suspension and a rear-mounted engine, but the engine was a horizontally-opposed, air-cooled, flat-six. To cynics it looked as if Chevrolet had decided to out-Beetle the VW Beetle, though with an altogether larger car.

Limited UK sales began during 1960, when the car's oversteering tendencies and other crudities were rapidly exposed. In the USA, self-appointed safety crusader Ralph Nader soon got his claws into the Corvair, publishing a notorious book titled Unsafe at Any Speed.

Citroen: The Bijou was a British project, the rebodying of the 2CV chassis. The new style was in glassfibre, apparently with identical mouldings for one front wing and the rear wing on the opposite side of the car. However, although it was of technical and commercial interest, it never sold well, only 211 cars being delivered over the next three years.

Daimler: Previewed in the spring, but not going on sale until October, was the new SP250 sportscar, the first of what the management hoped was a new generation of more sporty Daimlers.

First labelled the Dart, until trademark problems (Dodge had the rights) got in the way, the SP250 used a chassis which was a clear (and close!) copy of the Triumph TR3A unit, but was powered by a powerful, smooth and high-revving 2.5-litre V8 engine.

There were disc brakes all round, automatic transmission was an option, and the rather strange body style was made in glassfibre – the first time this material had been used by Daimler on a private car.

The style was always controversial, but all would no doubt have been well if build quality had been better. In the event, the SP250 always struggled to make its mark, the Jaguar takeover (see 1960) didn't help its cause, and it would be dropped within four years.

There was also a new version of the Majestic saloon, the Majestic Major, which used the 'other' new V8, a 4.5-litre unit which was visually similar to that of the SP250, but much larger. Daimler was not really equipped to make this engine in quantity, which was a pity, as it produced no less than 220bhp, making the Majestic Major one of the fastest (and most sure-footed) large saloons available.

Elva: The Courier sportscar went on sale in the British market, fitted with the latest, enlarged, 1.6-litre BMC B-series engine, in MGA 1600 tune.

Facel Vega: After several years of building vast and expensive Chrysler V8-engined cars, the French company surprised everyone with the arrival of its own much smaller in-house design. Whereas previous Facel Vegas had been supercars, the new Facellia was meant to be an affordable, MGA-size, 1.6-litre model.

The style and general engineering layout were familiar enough, there being a choice of disc or drum brakes (but since no-one ordered drums these were soon abandoned!), but the engine – a four-cylinder twin-overhead-camshaft unit – was all new. Various British specialists (Harry Weslake among them) had been involved in the layout.

Although this all looked very promising, Facel Vega struck endless troubles with the engine, which meant that sales lagged far below estimates.

Fairthorpe: The Zeta combined the chassis and style of the existing Electron/Electron Minor with a 137bhp version of the 2.5-litre Ford Zephyr Six

engine. There were front disc brakes to keep this potentially lethal combination in check, but even so no-one seemed to like it. At £1,482 for the open two-seater, who could blame them?

Fiat: The Italian giant produced an entirely new range of six-cylinder cars, effectively to replace the long-running 1900 type. The 1800 and 2100 models were derivatives of the same saloon car, which had sharp-edge styling.

Engines were brand-new, with polyspherical combustion chambers, but overhead-valve operation rather in the Armstrong Siddeley/Humber Super Snipe manner, while the chassis featured longitudinal torsion-bar front suspension, and beam axles suspended on a combination of cantilever leaf springs and coils, the leaf springs also acting as radius-arms.

Ford: Along with the BMC Mini and the Triumph Herald, the new-generation Anglia 105E was one of three fascinating small family cars to be introduced during the year. Compared with the other two cars, however, the new Anglia's mechanical layout was conventional – and with hindsight we also know that it proved to be much the most profitable to build.

But it was not too conventional: although there was a familiar type of steel monocoque and Ford-type front and rear suspensions, the styling was different, as was the layout of the engine.

The saloon's style, complete with reverse-slope rear window, had been influenced from Ford-Detroit, where such features had already been seen on the company's Lincoln-Mercury models. Ford tried to talk-up this layout with all manner of practical advantages, but in truth there were none apart from the use of a larger bootlid!

The engine, however, was a real innovation for Ford-UK, for whom it was their first small overhead-valve unit. Very 'over-square' in this guise (the stroke was a mere 48.41mm), it was the first of a whole family which, in much-modified and developed forms, would power myriad Fords over the next two decades. On the Anglia it was backed by a slick-action four-speed gearbox, once again a novelty from Ford in this price class.

Rounding off the reshuffle, there was also a 'new' Prefect 107E, this actually

being the old Prefect 100E fitted with the 39bhp overhead-valve engine and four-speed gearbox from the new-generation Anglia.

As a back-up to this very important launch, Ford also replaced one Popular with another! The old 1930s-style model was finally abandoned (27 years after the original basic design had appeared), the new Popular being a simplified version of the Anglia 100E, which had just been superseded by the new 105E.

The 'new' Popular, therefore, had the familiar 36bhp/1,172cc side-valve engine and the three-speed gearbox, both of which had been rendered obsolete, but as the car was to be sold for only £494 it was still a saleable proposition. As with the old-style Popular, this was Britain's cheapest car.

Early in the year, the Consul/Zephyr/Zodiac range was retouched, with a flatter roof style and a smarter interior, but few other improvements to an already very successful design.

Ford-Germany: Like the British, the Germans retouched the design of their mainstream car, the Taunus, and for the first time set out to market them seriously in the UK. The latest versions had a flatter roof design and trim/interior changes. Although the 12M was listed and marketed in the UK, it was always quite overshadowed by the domestic models.

Hillman: For 1960 the Minx was given a more powerful 1.5-litre engine, the Manumatic transmission option was dropped, while there was the new option of the latest Smiths Easidrive transmission, a complex new piece of kit which included magnetic powder rather than hydraulic couplings to transmit torque to the transmission, and electric control of gearchanging. This was a technically brave, but almost impossibly complex, alternative to the conventional type of automatic transmission. Power losses proved to be more severe than with fluid couplings, and customer demand was very low.

Humber: Only a year after it had been launched, the Super Snipe was considerably modified, with a 121bhp/2.96-litre version of the six-cylinder engine and front-wheel disc brakes. For the time being there were no styling changes.

Jaguar: The smart new Mk 2 range took over from the original 2.4/3.4 saloons, featuring a major restyle and a wider choice of engines.

Although the same basic unit-construction shell was used, there was a major increase in glass area, helped by the use of half-frame doors, and a much wider rear window. Under the skin there was now a choice of 2.4, 3.4 *and* 3.8-litre versions of the XK engine, Dunlop disc brakes had been standardized on all types, and there was a wider rear track to help improve the roadholding. The 2.4-litre engine had been made more powerful – 120bhp instead of 112bhp – which ensured 100mph on all examples rather than merely those whose engine was in top form.

The 3.4-litre 250bhp XK150S engine was also made available on fixed and drop-head coupe versions of this chassis early in the year, but it became obsolete in October when a 265bhp/3.8-litre version of the engine took over instead. Thus equipped, an XK150S could reach nearly 140mph.

Mercedes-Benz: For the first time in some years, the German company produced an entirely new unit-construction body style, which because of its rear shape was soon nicknamed the Fintail by Mercedes-watchers. As with previous types, this car was always meant to be produced in a variety of forms, with four-cylinder and six-cylinder engines.

The first type to be announced was the 220 range, one of which (the 220SE) combined the existing 2.2-litre six-cylinder engine with Bosch indirect fuel injection. This injection system was very different from that previously used in the 300SL sports model.

Under the skin, Mercedes-Benz had persisted with all-independent suspension, including swing-axles at the rear, but this was of the low-pivot type, as first seen under the 300SL Roadster in 1957.

Metropolitan: The 1.5-litre-engined 'British car for America' was withdrawn from the British market as a current marketing agreement expired. It would not be reintroduced until the summer of 1960.

MG: The new-generation Magnette was the third of the five new B-series Farinas to appear, and was a great disappointment to everyone except BMC's accountants! The old ZB Magnette had been smart, fast and nimble, whereas the new-generation car was – well, merely an A55 with more power, different trim, and new front and rear-end styling. This was the first of the new series to have a twin-SU engine, which developed 64bhp.

Although it was not as inspiring, nor as capable, as the car it replaced, the new-type Magnette sold much better, which tells us a lot about British tastes at the time – and perhaps about the narrow views of British motoring writers of the day as well.

The successful MGA was upgraded to become the MGA 1600. Looking almost precisely the same as before, it had a more powerful 1,588cc version of the BMC B-series engine, along with front-wheel disc brakes.

Morgan: Continuing its slow and methodical upgrading of what was already an old design, Morgan added front-wheel disc brakes as options to the Plus 4 models. Later in the year, too, it widened the cockpit of the 4/4 model.

Morris: The new Morris Mini-Minor was almost exactly the same car as the Austin Se7en (or Austin Mini), the only differences being in the radiator grille, the choice of colours, the fact that it was built at Cowley rather than Longbridge and that it was sold through Morris rather than Austin dealerships.

The new-generation Oxford was the fourth of the B-series Farinas to appear. In all respects except badging and decoration, it was the same car as the Austin A55 – but sold through the Morris dealer network.

Moskvich: The first of the Russian cars to be marketed in the UK was announced. This was the Type 407, a model from one of the Soviet state's vast car-making concerns, with strictly conventional front-engine/rear-drive engineering.

Moskvich had developed its cars from prewar Opel designs, the tooling for which having been 'liberated' by the Russians as part of postwar reparations.

Porsche: Once again the design of the rear-engined 356 was improved, rather than replaced. Ten years after it had gone on sale, the third variation of the design – 356B – was introduced. The main improvement was the addition of an even more powerful 90bhp version of the 1.6-litre flat-four engine, and there were minor style changes around the nose, including more vertical headlamp lenses and raised front winglines. By this time, almost every trace of VW parentage had been eliminated. However, it would still be another four years before an entirely new shape came from Porsche.

Renault: The first UK deliveries were made of the Dauphine-Gordini, whose engine had been breathed upon by Amedee Gordini's business to produce 38bhp at 5,000rpm instead of 30bhp at 4,250rpm. There was also a four-speed gearbox, but the rear-engined chassis' quirky cornering behaviour was not changed!

Riley: The new 4/68, a Farina-styled MG Magnette clone, was introduced in April, the last of the five different models to be squeezed out of the one new design. Like the Magnette, it had 64bhp and a twin-carburettor engine, and by a small margin over the MG it was the most expensive of this quintet.

Rolls-Royce: After many years of testing, Rolls-Royce finally introduced a new 6.23-litre V8 engine. Widely rumoured to have been copied from the best of American V8 design (Cadillac and Chrysler in particular), the new engine used aluminium castings for the block and heads, but had conventional pushrod overhead valves. It was wider, shorter, but apparently no heavier than the six-cylinder unit which it immediately replaced. At the same time a new air-conditioning system was standardized, and with these changes the Silver Cloud became S2.

The launch of the new engine quite overshadowed the arrival of the vast new Phantom V, a limousine with a 12ft wheelbase which took over from the Silver Wraith at the end of its 12-year career. This was the sort of car bought by royalty, the gentry, and luxury-seeking businessmen for whom a Daimler was not enough.

The Phantom V used a long-wheelbase version of the Silver Cloud II's chassis, but it had its own choice of coachbuilt bodyshells, most of the cars being built by H J Mulliner. This car, and its slightly-modified successor of 1968, the Phantom VI, would be built in gradually decreasing numbers for the next 30 years.

Rover: Ten years after it had been launched in 1949, one might have expected the P4 range to be dropped. Rover, however, had no such plans. Instead, the design was rationalized, though the same basic style, engineering and character were maintained. The old 60, 75, 90 and 105 derivatives were all dropped, being replaced by newly-developed 80 and 100 models.

The 80 was powered by the latest four-cylinder 2.3-litre Land-Rover engine, while the 100 used a new version of the familiar IOEV six-cylinder power unit, this effectively being a destroked version of the Rover P5 3-litre's engine, displacing 2,625cc. Both cars had front-wheel disc brakes and overdrive.

After only one year on the market, the modern P5 3-litre was given front-wheel disc brakes as standard.

Simca: In a very odd 'belt and braces' engineering move, Simca changed the rear suspension design of its Arondes, fitting coil springs above the leaf springs. At the same time there was a facelift to the style, which took on more glass, but retained the same 'chassis', underbody and engine/transmission layout.

Singer: The Gazelle took on the changes intended for the near-identical Minx, including the larger windscreen and the new remote-control gearchange, while the engine was improved by the fitment of twin downdraught carburettors, Rapier-style.

Sunbeam: The new-generation Alpine appeared during the summer, this new sportscar being a subtle amalgam of available Minx/Rapier/Husky hardware, all clothed in a smart, befinned, two-seater sports style with wind-up door windows.

As with all Rootes medium-sized cars of this period, the platform was based on that of the Hillman Minx, or more precisely on the short-wheelbase Husky, though there were extra cruciform members under the floor, and stiffening tubes in the engine bay.

The running gear was mainly modified Sunbeam Rapier – 78bhp/1.5-litre engine and four-speed-plus-overdrive

transmission – though the aluminium cylinder head was new (the Rapier would soon adopt it), as were the disc brakes and the 13in wheels. The gear ratios were closer and more sporting than before.

Except that the Alpine was rather heavier than the MGA, it provided worrying competition for the BMC sportscar, and in the USA it also took some sales from the Triumph TR3A. The Alpine and its successors would remain on the market until 1968.

A few weeks later Rootes also introduced the Rapier Series III, which also adopted the new aluminium cylinder head, the closer-ratio gearbox and the front-wheel disc brakes which had been revealed in the Alpine sportscar. All this, without a price increase, made the Rapier more saleable than before, and it was an even more promising rally car.

Triumph: Except for its engine and gearbox, which were modified versions of those fitted to the Standard Ten/Pennant range, the new Herald really *was* all new. In a complete change of marketing approach, here was a small/medium-sized Triumph, ready to take over from the small Standards (Eights, Tens and Pennants). This, in fact, was the beginning of the end for the Standard marque.

Unfashionably, the new Herald had a separate chassis-frame, a choice of body styles built up by bolting (not welding) together large sections of bodywork, and it also had sharp-edged and flamboyant styling by Michelotti. Initially the coupe was more powerful than the saloon, but the twin-carburettor engine was soon made available on the saloon as an option.

Standard-Triumph stated that the separate chassis was really used so that CKD assembly in other countries would be simplified. Maybe so, but another major reason was that neither Fisher and Ludlow, nor Pressed Steel, had been able to build an all-new monocoque at this time.

Technical novelties included a truly tiny, taxi-like turning circle of around 25 feet, independent rear suspension by transverse leaf spring and swing-axles, and the ability to make several different styles available when necessary: saloon and (twin-carb) coupe versions were available at once, a convertible would soon follow, and in later

years there would also be estate car and van derivatives.

If the product quality had been better from the start, the Herald would have sold better than it did; it only truly came of age in the 1960s, with larger and more torquey engines, and with the corporate backing of Leyland Motors.

Vanden Plas: Having dabbled with the Princess marque, BMC settled on Vanden Plas instead, the first product being the new 3-litre model, which was a well-trimmed and equipped version of the Austin A99/Wolseley 6/99. All this shuffling of names confused the buying public, who were never really convinced – tending to call the cars Austin Princesses anyway!

Mechanically, these cars were identical to the A99/Wolseley 6/99 saloons, but there was an entirely special interior, completed at the Kingsbury (North London) works, with special instruments, seating and trim materials. Outside the car there was a new type of grille (any resemblance to a Bentley was strictly intentional!) and a duotone colour scheme.

Vauxhall: Only two years after launching the Victor, Vauxhall reacted by giving the car a thorough facelift, particularly along the flanks, where the original creases were abandoned. There were no important technical changes. Those who understood tooling cycles realized that the change must have been authorized within six months of the car originally going on sale; a case of second thoughts!

Even so, Vauxhall claimed that 145,000 of the original Victors had been sold in the first two years, and the first 250,000 were completed by the end of 1959, so the 1.5-litre car already counted as a commercial success.

Velox and Cresta estate cars, as conversions by Friary Motors, were added to the big Vauxhall range.

Volga: The M-21 saloon was the second and larger Russian car to be marketed in Britain (the Moskvich being the first). Like the Moskvich, the engineering was sturdy and conventional, rather than adventurous, for power was by an 80bhp/2.4-litre 'four', there were drum brakes and a beam rear axle, and ground clearance could be described as 'generous'.

Although these cars would be price-listed in Britain for years, they were never sold in large numbers.

Volvo: A new sports coupe, the P1800, was previewed, though there were few details at first. The cars, it was stated, used Amazon (120-series) running gear, would have their bodyshells built in the UK by Pressed Steel, but would not be available until the end of 1960. The news that Jensen would also assemble the complete car at first was not yet ripe for release.

Wolseley: The new 6/99, revealed during the summer, was simply an upmarket version of the Austin A99, though with its own traditional radiator grille and with wood, leather and deep carpets in the cabin. Over the years, mechanical improvements made to this car would always track those being made to the Austin.

Industrial developments

Once again Standard was in the news, this time as a potential partner with Rover (the same manoeuvre had been forecast in 1954). Once again, talks went a long way, but foundered as neither company seemed to be willing to surrender its independence.

We now know that each company learned that the other was planning an all-new 2-litre 'executive' saloon model. Then, as for the next 20 years, the two companies would be rivals.

Later in the year Standard finally broke away from Massey-Ferguson, handing back the tractor-making facility and the Banner Lane factory to the Canadian concern. In return, Standard gained £12,500,000 – of which £4,000,000 was returned to shareholders, the rest of the money being put to its own expansion programme, which included buying up body manufacturers and erecting a new assembly hall at Canley.

Slowly but surely Chrysler of Detroit was on its way to gaining a foothold in Europe. Having bought a minority share in Simca of France, it now agreed to part-assemble Simca Aronde

cars for the UK in its factory at Kew Gardens, Richmond, this plan being put into operation before the end of the year.

The very last Allard car was produced – though series production of these cars had ended as long ago as 1956.

The Meadows Frisky motor car project came to a sad end when the Frisky Cars business was wound up, revealing a large financial deficit. The remains of the business were bought by Frisky Cars (1959) Ltd, who turned the design into a three-wheeler and continued to sell the tricycle until 1964.

Hooper closed down its coachbuilding business in London, transferring all its remaining activities to the Daimler plant in Coventry. The Hooper building, on the A40 road in Acton, was soon to be taken over by Standard-Triumph for use as its London service centre.

Sir William Rootes became Lord Rootes in the New Year's Honours List.

In the United States, the Edsel was laid to rest, little more than two years after it had been born, having proved to be one of Ford's most expensive mistakes.

Technical developments

Preliminary news came of a radical type of rotary engine which had been designed by Dr Felix Wankel. Having sold his ideas to NSU, Wankel was also working with several other companies, and at this stage the idea of a smooth, high-revving, rotary unit without pistons, connecting rods and valves was seductive. Even so, few details were published at first, and no Wankel-engined car would be ready to go on sale until the end of 1963.

For years, Michelin had held master patents on the use of radial-ply tyres, and with the exception of Pirelli no other manufacturers had produced rival tyres. In 1959, however, after much testing and use in International rallies, Dunlop revealed the steel-braced radial-ply Durabands, which were soon available in many sizes.

Rally teams soon adopted them, not only for their better grip, but for their

longer life when pushed very hard, but these Durabands were not initially meant to be mass-production products, for they were neither cheap to build, nor yet (in their on-the-limit behaviour) 'idiot-proof'.

Front-wheel drive – the big breakthrough

Without a doubt, the launch of the BMC Mini was the most important technical innovation of the year.

Although there was nothing startlingly new about front-wheel drive (Citroen and DKW had built many thousands of such cars in the 1930s), except in very isolated cases it had always been associated with cheap and relatively unsophisticated machines.

The now-legendary BMC/Issigonis Mini combined front-wheel drive with transverse mounting of the engine, all in a very small and space-efficient package, with newly-designed GKN driveshafts having universal joints which did not tug when the wheels were locked well over.

On the Mini the transmission was actually underneath the engine, effectively in the sump, and although this was hailed at the time, it proved to be a technical blind-alley, and would later be dropped in favour of 'end-on' transmissions.

Once British drivers got their hands on the new Mini, they soon realized that this car's front-wheel drive offered truly remarkable roadholding and handling characteristics, but those who had already driven Citroens, Saabs and DKWs knew this already.

For the moment, the rest of the world's automotive designers looked, studied, took notes and learned as much as they could, but were not yet ready to follow Issigonis' lead. Soon, though, the packaging lessons, the handling benefits and the many advantages offered by placing the engine sideways to reduce a car's length, were all learned, and a flood of next-generation FWD cars would be revealed from the mid-1960s onwards.

1960

Convinced by all the press comment on the 'You've never had it so good' election of 1959, Britain's motorists went on a spending spree until restrained later in the year. With waiting lists for cars long gone, they could order what they want and take delivery of it within weeks.

The result was a year where all previous records were shattered. No fewer than 1.35 million cars were made in Britain, and a huge 820,000 were sold in the UK – 170,000 more than in 1959 and a massive 45 per cent increase on 1958. However, sales fell away towards the end of the year, when stricter hire purchase controls were introduced, and several concerns found themselves with too much capacity.

There was a surge of imports – to 57,309, which was more than double the 1959 figure – but this proved only temporary as demand and deliveries both fell back again in 1961.

All of which made it difficult to understand how Standard-Triumph fell into so much trouble. During the year its sales (mainly of Heralds) plunged, and before winter the company's plant was on a three-day week. Without Leyland's intervention bankruptcy could only have been weeks away.

Catering for people on the move, the first Little Chef roadside diner was opened at Tilehurst, on the Oxford–Reading road, in June. In contrast, the M1 motorway had been open for nine months before the first service area cafeterias opened for business at Newport Pagnell and Watford Gap. When a similar delay occurred with the new Oxford–Birmingham M40 motorway in the early 1990s there were major complaints – as if it had never happened before!

The motorway programme expanded significantly, and among many other projects started were bridgeworks and advance preparation for the M6 between Preston and the West Midlands, and on two major suspension bridges – the Forth and the Severn.

New models

Aston Martin: At the Earls Court Motor Show, Zagato showed a new lightweight body style on the basis of the DB4GT chassis. More powerful than the regular DB4GT, and with flimsy coachwork intended for use in motorsport, the Zagato version would only be available to a few, at a very high price.

Austin: Having announced a van derivative of the Mini earlier in the year, which had a lengthened version of the front-wheel-drive platform, in September BMC revealed a three-door estate version on the same longer wheelbase; there were no other mechanical changes.

At almost the same time, an estate car version of the A55 was put on the market.

Berkeley: To supplement the existing motorcycle-engined sportscars, the Ford 105E-engined Bandit was previewed, though as Berkeley closed down almost immediately afterwards it never went into production. It was a fascinating technical effort, but a blind alley. Racing-car designer John Tojeiro had developed a steel platform chassis, topped off by a glassfibre shell, and there was all-independent suspension and front-wheel disc brakes. Unhappily, no-one got the chance to discover if it was as good as it looked.

Borgward: The British Hobbs automatic transmission was introduced as optional equipment on Isabella and 2.3-litre models. However, this was only a short-lived success for Hobbs as the German manufacturer would go out of business in 1961.

Bristol: Previewed in 1959, but available in 1960, the 406 Zagato used the existing 406's chassis, but was fitted with an ultra-light two-door coupe body style by Zagato; 450lb was saved, it was claimed. Engines were tuned to give 130bhp, and a top speed of 120mph was possible.

These were not attractive cars, and they proved a commercial failure. Even though UK prices were cut sharply in 1961 (bringing them down to normal 406 levels) the car was virtually unsaleable and died, unlamented.

Citroen: The Chapron-bodied four-seater convertible version of the DS19/ID19 family was unveiled in France. British deliveries, while severely limited by the high prices, began a few months later.

Fairthorpe: Led by Air Vice-Marshal Donald Bennett, this tiny company continued to improve its Electron models. For 1960 these were given independent rear suspension, along with style changes to the glassfibre bodywork.

Fairthorpe was nothing if not inventive, for another new model was the Electrina, which was called a saloon but in reality was a Triumph Herald-engined Electron Minor with 2+2 seating and a permanent glassfibre roof.

Ferrari: Although purists were not enthusiastic at first, Ferrari knew what it was doing with the launch of the 250GTE, the first ever 2+2 model from that company. The chassis and running gear, complete with the already-famous V12 3-litre engine, was like that used in the 250GT Berlinetta, and included four-wheel disc brakes, but there was a more spacious body style by Pininfarina.

By Ferrari standards, this car would become something of a best-seller – 950 would be made in three years, of which 47 originally came to Britain.

Fiat: Ever-enterprising, the Italian company produced what had to be the world's smallest estate car, the Giardiniera version of the 500 model. Still with a rear-mounted engine, but with the twin-cylinder unit laid on its side, it was a tiny three-door car measuring only 10ft 5in long.

The 600 range was extended with the launch of the 600D, which had a bigger, 767cc, engine.

Ford: Front-wheel disc brakes became optional on the Consul/Zephyr/Zodiac models, but this was a very quiet year for the Dagenham giant.

Ford-Germany: A new style of 17M Taunus model was announced, this having a much smoother and more flowing style than the Zephyr-like shape which had been on sale since 1957. There were no styling similarities to anything from Ford-UK, though artists could see definite family resemblances to the latest big Galaxies and Thunderbirds being produced by Ford-USA.

Technically there were few changes, and although these cars were to be marketed persistently in the UK, they did not sell in large numbers.

Gordon: An interesting Chevrolet-powered prototype, which in technical terms was almost 'son of Peerless GT', was revealed at the Geneva motor show, but could not be put into production at that time because of a lack of financial backing.

Entrepreneur John Gordon had persuaded Jim Keeble to design a multi-tube chassis, while Bertone had developed a two-door four-seater GT style. No more would be heard of the Gordon for some time, however, but years later it would go into limited production as the Gordon-Keeble.

GSM: The smart little Delta sportscar was put on sale in October. Originally produced in South Africa, it would have a precarious four-year existence in Britain, being built in Kent. There was a tubular ladder-style frame with a glassfibre body moulded around it on initial assembly, power coming from Ford's ubiquitous 105E unit.

Hillman: The short-wheelbase Husky moved on to become Series II, complete with detail styling changes, and the remote-control gearchange which was gradually being standardized on all Minx/Gazelle/Rapier cars as well.

Rootes also revealed plans to build a new small Hillman model by 1962/63, which would be assembled in a brand-new factory adjacent to the Pressed Steel body plant at Linwood, in Scotland. This was the first public reference to the car which would become the Hillman Imp, but it would not go on sale until May 1963.

Humber: The Super Snipe was face-lifted (only two years after its original release), with a four-headlamp nose, becoming the first British production car to have this feature. At the same time, front disc brakes were added to the Hawk sister car.

Jaguar: Power-assisted steering became optional on Mk 2 models.

Jensen: The existing 541 models were dropped and replaced by the 541S, which used the same basic chassis and body except that it had been chopped down the middle and widened by 4in. [Reliant would go one

better than this with a mid-life change to the Scimitar GTE in the 1970s – that car being both widened *and* lengthened by similar means!]

The 541S retained the familiar three-carburettor BMC 4-litre engine, though for the first time there was an automatic transmission option – by GM Hydramatic, as used on current Rolls-Royce and Bentley models.

Lancia: The new Flavia saloon was literally all-new, with front-wheel drive, a flat-four 1.5-litre engine, a four-speed gearbox/transaxle, and independent front suspension by transverse leaf spring.

Although rather a square-rigged, stolid-looking model and a little too heavy at first, it handled very well and was clearly the first of a new family of middle-size Lancias, all of which would be marketed in the UK. Coupe, Zagato coupe, and convertible models would all eventually spawn from this design.

Lea-Francis: Star prize for 'Lemon of the Year' went to the Lynx sportscar, which was a totally abortive attempt to relaunch this Coventry marque.

Unlike any previous Lea-Francis, the Lynx had a tubular ladder-style frame, power by a tuned-up version of the Ford Zephyr six-cylinder unit, and awful styling of a 2+2-seater body for which nobody was ready to claim responsibility. Three cars were built, but Lea-Francis never received a single order, so the project (and Lea-Francis) died rapidly.

Metropolitan: After an 18-month absence, the Metropolitan was once again re-introduced to the British market, improved this time by the fitment of a bootlid (the original car having had no external access to the stowage space behind the seats).

MG: After the MGA Twin-Cam was dropped in March, BMC found itself with many surplus chassis, suspension and brake kits from this model, which resulted in the arrival, little advertised, of the MGA 1600 De Luxe, which was effectively the Twin-Cam fitted with a pushrod engine. Several hundred of these cars would be produced in the next two years.

Morgan: The 4/4 model became Series III by the use of the modern Ford

105E overhead-valve engine and its related four-speed gearbox. These replaced the side-valve engine/three-speed gearbox combination from the old-style 100E Ford Anglias, which were now technically obsolete.

Also new was a Super Sport version of the TR3A-engined Plus 4, this having a LawrenceTune-prepared engine giving 116bhp. It featured twin side-draught dual-choke Weber carburettors and a free-flow tubular exhaust manifold.

Front-wheel disc brakes were now standardized on all TR-engined Plus 4 models.

Morris: *(See Austin, above, for Mini and A55/Oxford additions.)*

Peugeot: The new 404 was revealed, this being a sharply-styled four-door saloon, which had been styled by Farina for the French company. It was generally agreed that this shape was altogether more graceful than the broadly similar style applied to BMC's B-series saloon cars.

The 404 was a conventional front-engine/rear-drive medium-size machine which would eventually replace the existing 403, although the two cars would sell alongside each other, in large numbers, for some years yet. Power was by a 1.6-litre version of the 403 unit.

Rolls-Royce: HM The Queen took delivery of a very special Phantom V limousine model, which not only had a much higher roof than the standard version (if there was any such thing as a standard Phantom V!), but where the rear section of the roof (above and behind the rear seats) was in clear plastic, which could be obscured if necessary with lay-on aluminium panels. That car, meticulously maintained and periodically updated, was still in use in the Royal Mews in the 1990s.

Rover: The P5 3-litre was further developed, with power-assisted steering becoming optional.

Saab: The Swedish company, really an aerospace business which had only been car-making for a decade or so, revealed the new 96 model. This saloon, and its closely related 95 estate car, would shortly go on sale in Britain, the first time Saab had exported cars to the UK.

Like its ancestors, the latest Saab had a unit-construction two-door saloon style, aerodynamically shaped with a smooth nose and a fastback, tapering, tail. Power was by an in-line three-cylinder two-stroke unit driving the front wheels. Although not very fast in standard form, this was an extremely nimble machine, as heroes like Erik Carlsson would prove so convincingly in rallies.

Simca: Although the Aronde's styling was not changed, for 1961 the car was given a new, five-main-bearing version of the existing 1.3-litre engine.

Standard: The new Vanguard Six was an interesting technical mixture which sold very slowly – an old car with a brand-new six-cylinder engine. Closely related to the existing Herald unit, the new 2-litre 'six' was conventional but smooth, and in this guise it used twin semi-downdraught Solex carburettors. The engine would be developed, enlarged and used in many other Standard-Triumph models during the next two decades, including the Triumph 2000, the Vitesse and the TR6. Nice engine, shame about the car...

Sunbeam: Rootes turned the Alpine sportscar into a Series II version, complete with 1.6-litre engine.

Tornado: This small specialist manufacturer from Rickmansworth made a determined attempt to build mainstream sportscars, launching the Thunderbolt and closely-related Tempest models. They shared the same chassis, a sturdy channel-section affair, and a curvaceous coupe style in glassfibre. Thunderbolts were powered by a 100bhp TR3A engine, while the Tempest made do with a 39bhp Ford Anglia 105E unit. Unhappily, the prices were too high and the build quality poor, and the Thunderbolt was totally unsaleable (only one was produced, apparently).

Triumph: Less than a year after the original car had been launched, Triumph added a convertible body style to the Herald range, this car also having the twin-carburettor version of the engine (as fitted to the Herald Coupe). Early deliveries all went for export, but home market sales began in August.

TVR: The still-tiny Blackpool-based company announced a new version of the Grantura sports coupe, this time with the current MGA engine and transmission as standard, though options also included the 997cc Ford 105E engine and the 1,216cc Coventry Climax unit.

Vauxhall: Overdrive became optional on the six-cylinder Velox and Cresta models before mid-summer, but the biggest change came in August with the arrival of a larger (2.65-litre) and more torquey version of the straight-six cylinder engine. Although superficially similar to the earlier 2.2-litre type, this was a more bulky engine in all respects – and in later years Vauxhall would expand it further, to 3.3 litres. The development process continued, for only weeks later GM Hydramatic automatic transmission became optional.

Victors exported to Canada were given new noses and new names – Envoy saloons, and Sherwood estate cars – but these were never sold in the UK. In August, British-market cars were slightly retouched, with a new radiator grille and larger rear windows, along with a new instrument panel.

Volvo: Pre-launch information about the new P1800 coupe continued to emerge – though it was still not ready to go on sale – with the news that Jensen would build the cars from bodies supplied by Pressed Steel's Linwood factory, but that initial deliveries would probably be held back until 1961.

Warwick: The Warwick GT was effectively the Peerless GT reborn, though it now had a complete lift-up body front-end, and its sponsors claimed an 80lb weight-saving. The Peerless business had collapsed financially, and this was an attempt to get the TR3A-engined 2+2 GT project on the road again. However, only a few cars would be built before it all ended again in 1962.

Industrial developments

It was takeover time in the British motor industry, with Ford-USA buying up various minor shareholdings in Ford-UK, Jaguar buying Daimler and Leyland Motors buying Standard.

The Ford bid was mainly administrative, for Ford-USA already held majority control of its own subsidiary, but there was a 45.4 per cent shareholding to be mopped up. At the time there were ritual political protests, but otherwise the £129 million takeover went ahead with the minimum of fuss.

Jaguar took control of Daimler at the end of May 1960, when Daimler's parent company, the BSA Group, accepted an offer from Jaguar's Sir William Lyons. Commercially this made a lot of sense to both sides, for Jaguar needed space to expand, whereas Daimler's factories were currently too large for their business.

At the end of the year, Standard, which had been losing sales – and lots of money – for some months, finally accepted a takeover bid from Leyland Motors, the Lancashire-based truck manufacturers. This corporate move, in fact, would not be finalized until the early spring of 1961, but it undoubtedly saved Standard.

This was Leyland's first move into the car-making business since the very limited-production Leyland Eight had been built in the 1920s. It was also the first move along a road which would lead to the foundation of British Leyland in 1968.

The Bristol car-making business was bought from the aerospace company by George White and Anthony Crook in what nowadays would be referred to as a management buy-out.

Production of lightly-modified BMC cars began at the Innocenti factory in Milan, Italy. Over the next few years, the Italian-built BMC products would become progressively more distinctive, notably the specially-styled Sprite sportscars and, later, the totally restyled Minis.

This was also a fashionable year for the industry to announce expansion away from its traditional bases, such moves being forced on various businesses because of Government policies forbidding further development 'at home'.

Ford announced that it was to build a brand-new factory at Halewood, on the Eastern outskirts of Liverpool. The first stage was set to be a completely integrated assembly plant, capable of producing 200,000 cars a year: in fact, it came into use in 1963, and soon became the home of the Anglias, followed by the Escorts. A massive transmission-making plant would be added later.

Shortly afterwards, Standard-Triumph also announced major expansion on Merseyside, first by purchasing the Hall Engineering plant at Speke, then by planning an entirely new factory close by. The second phase, in fact, was delayed by several years because of the company's takeover by Leyland.

Vauxhall also decided to build a new factory, on an abandoned airfield on the other (south) side of the Mersey, at Hooton, hard by Ellesmere Port. Although originally intended for commercial vehicle manufacture (Vauxhall said it wanted to expand car production into the existing commercial plant in Dunstable), this factory would eventually become the home of the Viva and its descendants.

Rootes, too, announced that it was to build a new factory, literally across the road from the Pressed Steel plant at Linwood, just west of Glasgow. This was to be dedicated to the new small Hillman which we later came to know as the Imp.

After less than two years of somewhat precarious and always turbulent existence, Peerless Cars Ltd plunged into bankruptcy. This meant the end of the Peerless GT model, although it would be revived, albeit very briefly, as the Warwick GT.

After less than two years, the MGA Twin-Cam was dropped. Serious engine unreliability problems had cost large sums to meet warranty claims, and just as the major problem (piston burning) was being solved, BMC pulled the plug on the project.

Armstrong Siddeley announced the imminent end of car production in June, and the last of these cars was produced later in the summer. Henceforth the only private cars being built on the Parkside, Coventry, site were Sunbeam Alpine sportscars for the Rootes Group.

Berkeley closed down at the end of the year, which meant that the promising new Bandit sportscar never went on sale.

Technical developments

The most interesting technical changes of the year came in the USA, where the fashion for 'compacts' was blooming fast. The second wave included a new family of Pontiac, Buick and Oldsmobile cars.

Not only did the Pontiac Tempest included a slant-four front-mounted engine which had been developed by chopping a V8 in half, but there was also a rear gearbox layout and all-independent suspension, these being linked by what became known as 'rope drive', in which a slim, curved, propshaft was supported on centre bearings.

This was also the year when GM introduced a new 3.5-litre V8 engine which had aluminium alloy cylinder heads *and* cylinder block. Amazingly, GM fell out of love with this engine after only three years and sold the manufacturing and development rights to Rover. The engine would first be fitted to a Rover (the P5B) in 1967, and it was still being built for Range Rover, TVR and other cars in the mid-1990s.

Although there had not been time for any rival to make a response to the Issigonis-inspired Mini, Lancia revealed a new front-wheel-drive car, the Flavia. In fact, 1959/60 signalled the start of a wholesale move towards front-wheel-drive cars.

Men of Influence

Sir Alec Issigonis

Born in Smyrna, Turkey, in 1906, where his father was a marine engine designer, Alec Issigonis travelled to Britain in 1922 in the aftermath of the war with Greece. Here he studied at the Battersea Polytechnic (but failed to matriculate), worked briefly in London, then joined the design department of Humber Ltd, in Coventry.

Having worked on front suspension design for two years, he then joined the Nuffield Organisation in Cowley to do the same thing, where his most important early work was the independent front suspension later adapted for the MG Y-type saloon and many later MG models.

During the Second World War he was encouraged to start work on a new small car, the 'Mosquito', which matured as the Morris Minor, then from 1952 to 1956 he moved to Alvis, in Coventry, where he was asked to design an all-new 3½-litre V8-engined, all-independent saloon, which the directors then declined to put into production.

Nuffield having been subsumed into BMC, Issigonis then returned, this time to a dedicated and small design centre at Longbridge, where he speedily developed the revolutionary Mini-Minor layout. It was not that the new car, coded ADO15, had front-wheel drive, or that it had a transversely-mounted engine, or that it was small – it was that *all* these features were brought together in such a technically elegant and effective manner.

If Issigonis had retired at that point, his technical reputation would have been secure for ever (for most of the world's cars adopted a similar general layout in the next generation or so), but he had much more to offer to BMC before he eventually retired at the end of 1971 on his 65th birthday.

After the Mini there was the BMC 1100/1300 family, then the 1800/2200 cars and finally the Maxi, but he was effectively sidelined after BMC had been absorbed into British Leyland. Knighted in 1969, and allowed to follow his own whims as a research engineer, he 'retired', only to be re-employed as a senior statesman.

His 'retirement present' was a No 10 Meccano set, complete with a steam producer and an electric power unit, and his final dabbling was into steam-powered cars and advanced transmissions. In old age he did not so much stop work as gradually slow down. He died in 1988.

1961

After a brief period of happiness, British drivers were once again hit by a financial squeeze on motoring costs. For businessmen there was a restriction on capital allowances, which from July were only allowed on cars costing less than £2,000 (equivalent to about £22,500 at mid-1990s levels).

The Chancellor also included a 'regulator' clause, which allowed him to increase petrol duty at any time in the future without needing a formal Budget to announce this, while the annual licence fee was increased from £12 10s (£12.50) to £15 (equivalent to £170 at mid-1990s values).

In July, the mini-Budget duly invoked the new regulator by increasing the purchase tax on cars from 50 to 55 per cent, adding £17 to the price of a Ford Anglia and £24 to the cost of an Austin A55. At the same time, 3d (1.25p) was added to the price of a gallon of petrol. This was greeted with howls of rage from the motor industry, the motor trade and from motorists.

At the same time, Bank Rate was increased from 5 to 7 per cent and hire purchase interest charges soon followed – upwards. The net result was to take money out of consumers' pockets and make cars and motoring more costly.

As The Autocar's leader writer commented: 'Sour medicine of this sort is usually taken to do one good...How can a manufacturer succeed – when struggling to increase exports and to balance production programmes...if factors completely outside his control can upset most of his calculations overnight...'

It was immediately obvious that car sales would suffer still further, and so it proved, especially when world markets also began to sag. By the end of the year British manufacturers had built 350,000 fewer cars than in 1960 and new registrations were down by 70,000. Sales of imported cars were particularly badly hit.

Welbeck Motors, in London, took advantage of new regulations by buying a fleet of Renault Dauphines and setting up as mini-cab operators. Predictably, there were many protests from the licenced 'black cab' profession, and (behind the scenes at least)

all manner of skullduggery took place. The service was inaugurated in June, but unhappily for Welbeck, not only were there the inevitable protests, but the Dauphines were none too reliable, so this was a relatively short-lived experiment.

Britain's first automatic car washing plant was opened in London in June. Relatively speaking, this was expensive for its day at 10s (50p) for a large car (about £5.70 in mid-1990s money).

When Channel Air Bridge unveiled the prototype four-engined car-carrying Carvair aircraft in the middle of the year, holiday flights to Europe promised to be even more attractive than before. The Carvair was a converted DC4 airliner, arranged to have front-end loading for up to five medium-sized cars, with seats for up to 23 passengers in the tail. The cockpit and controls had all been moved upwards into a bubble, to the position later made familiar on the Boeing 747 Jumbo jet.

Channel Air Bridge planned longer-distance flights with this aircraft, choosing Strasbourg, Geneva and Basle for its original destinations. The first scheduled services began in April 1962.

Testing of 10-year-old cars became compulsory during the spring, the testing deadlines being phased according to the age of the cars. However, no sooner had British drivers got used to this than seven-year testing was proposed. Legislation was introduced so rapidly that the first such tests could not be carried out until November, yet all seven-year-old cars theoretically needed an MoT certificate by January 1, 1962! Later, an allowance was made, but by July 15, 1962 the proposals were finally made law.

New models

AC: The Ace/Aceca 2.6s arrived as additional versions of the long-running sports models, which meant that AC, Bristol and Ford engines were now available to choice. The 2.6 was fitted with the 2.55-litre Ford Zephyr engine, with a choice of five engine tunes from Ruddspeed.

Aston Martin: Laycock overdrive became optional on the DB4 model during the summer and a smart drophead coupe version was introduced in October.

Austin: The arrival of the new 998cc twin-carb Mini-Cooper caused quite a stir, for with 55bhp and tiny front-wheel disc brakes this was a near-90mph version of the popular little Mini, with even more verve and character than before.

The A40 'Farina' became Mk II, with a more powerful engine, and a 3.5in longer wheelbase under a lightly retouched version of the estate car-like body style.

BMC carried out a major facelift on all five of its B-series Farina models in October. The A55 gave way to the A60, which had chopped-back tailfins, wider wheel tracks, a longer wheelbase and a 61bhp/1,622cc version of the familiar B-series engine. The new Borg-Warner Type 35 automatic transmission became optional.

The A99 was dropped to make way for the A110, which used the same basic design, for which the engine had been tuned to give 120bhp, while there was also a longer wheelbase and some suspension improvements.

Austin-Healey: The Sprite II took over from the original frogeye in mid-year, with a comprehensive restyle. Although the basic centre-section and chassis platform was retained, the cheeky, lift-up bonnet/wings assembly of the frogeye was abandoned, as was the rounded rump, and in its place was a rather squared-up and conventional style, where the headlamps were in the corners of the front wings, and there was a more capacious rear end with a separate bootlid. The story goes that the front-end and rear-end styles were conceived in different factories, though the result was harmonious enough.

At the same time the 948cc engine was made more powerful – it was henceforth rated at 46.5bhp – and the entire design of the car was also lifted by BMC, rebadged and put on sale as the new MG Midget.

The 3000 model also became Mk II, with the fitment of a 132bhp/triple SU carburettor version of the 2.9-litre engine.

BMW: The most important prototype of the year was a new BMW 1500 four-door saloon at the Frankfurt show. This was effectively BMW's future, for the conventional (Michelotti-influenced) style hid MacPherson-strut front suspension, semi-trailing-link rear suspension and a brand-new overhead-cam four-cylinder engine.

It was the engine and basic chassis principles, rather than the styling, which laid down BMW's markers for the rest of the 1960s – for the company's great leap forward was about to occur. The 1500, as such, was not to be sold in the UK until 1964, by which time the 1600, which evolved from it, was ready to join it.

At the same time the Bertone-styled 3200CS four-seater coupe took over from the 503 model, complete with 3.2-litre V8 engine, though this machine was never sold in the UK.

Bristol: There was a major change at Bristol, where the old 406 models, complete with the familiar six-cylinder engine, were finally dropped. In their place came a new 407 model which, although it used basically the same chassis as before, was now powered by a 250bhp/5.1-litre Chrysler V8 engine, backed by Torqueflite automatic transmission, while the front suspension now featured coil springs instead of a transverse leaf spring. The two-door saloon style was virtually the same as that of the ousted 406, but of course the performance was dramatically improved.

Citroen: The oddly-styled new Ami 6 filled a corner of the big gap in Citroen's range between the 2CV and the ID19. Based on the same platform as the 2CV, and using the same basic flat-twin/front-wheel-drive mechanical layout, the Ami 6 had a 22bhp/602cc engine and a somewhat bizarre four-door body style.

DAF: The little Dutch company was maturing well, its belt-drive variable-ratio automatic transmission having proved very reliable. For 1962, the original 600 model was dropped, replaced by the 750/Daffodil types, which had larger 746cc engines.

Daimler: The company continued to reshuffle its resources, this time introducing the DR450 Limousine, which was effectively a marriage between the existing long-wheelbase chassis of the DK400 model, the latest Majestic Major V8 engine, and a smart seven-seater limousine style which was similar in some ways to the Majestic Major saloon.

Compared with the Majestic Major, the wheelbase was 24in longer and its overall length was no less than 18ft 10in, but the vast machine was surprisingly nimble. With 220bhp, automatic transmission and four-wheel disc brakes, it was a much more appealing prospect to many buyers than the rival Austin 4-litre Limousine, and 864 of them would be sold in the next seven years.

Facel Vega: The French builder of large and heavy supercars added another version of the Chrysler-engined chassis to its range in October, this being the two-door fixed-head coupe Facel II. Lower, more angular and somehow more overtly aggressive than the HK500 which it replaced, the Facel II had a 6.3-litre Chrysler V8 and was an impressively fast (if thirsty), but extremely expensive machine. It was marketed in the UK, but few cars were sold.

Fiat: The new 1300 and 1500 models took over from the 1200 (the old 1100-103 type was soon to be dropped), both being based on the same new engineering and style except for using different sizes of engines, these being four-cylinder versions of the six-cylinder family already seen in the 1800/2100 Fiat range.

Styling was in the modern squared-up fashion, complete with a ribbed 'bath rim' emphasis around the car at waist-level, though the engineering of the car was strictly conventional.

The 1800/2100 range was also thoroughly revised, becoming the 1800B and 2300 models instead. The existing 1800 engine was improved and made more powerful for the 1800B, while a larger (2,279cc) engine powered the 2300 which replaced the 2100. Both cars were given a new and simpler rear suspension, which used half-elliptic leaf springs, along with four-wheel disc brakes.

Later in the year Fiat also launched a 2300S Coupe, based on the running gear of the 2300 saloon, but with a striking two-door 2+2 coupe body style by Ghia. Although marketed in the UK, it was expensive and never sold in large numbers.

Ford: The new Consul Classic saloons were gap-filler models between the Anglia and the Consul/Zephyr/Zodiac

ranges. Like the Anglia, the Classic featured a reverse-slope rear window, and an enlarged (54bhp/1.34-litre) version of the Anglia's overhead-valve engine was fitted. The rest of the chassis was typical Ford, with a MacPherson-strut front-end, soft half-elliptic rear leaf springs and recirculating-ball steering, but with the real advance of front-wheel disc brakes.

Two-door and four-door versions were available – and a coupe called Capri would follow months later. This used the same platform, rolling chassis and front-end body pressings, but was a two-door fixed-head coupe with '2+rear shelf' seating and a vast boot.

A three-door estate car version of the Anglia 105E was introduced in October.

Front-wheel disc brakes, previously optional on Consul/Zephyr/Zodiac models, were standardized from May.

Hillman: The Singer Vogue (see below) came first, in July, but the Hillman Super Minx, announced in October, was the lower-priced basic version of the design from which that car was developed. Compared with the Vogue, which looked similar except for its nose and the interior trim, the Super Minx was less glossily equipped, though it shared the same 62bhp/1.6-litre engine and choice of manual or Easidrive transmissions. Drum rather than disc front brakes were standard, but otherwise, despite the lower price of the Super Minx, the two cars were very similar.

The continuing smaller-bodied Minx (class of 1956, but periodically updated since then) was brought into line with other medium-sized Rootes cars by the fitment of a 1.6-litre engine.

Jaguar: Car of the Year – and of the decade, probably – was the fabulous new Jaguar E-type, which was introduced at the Geneva show in March. Wickedly attractive, with lines conceived by Malcolm Sayer rather than Sir William Lyons, here was the lineal descendant of the D-type racing sportscar, but thoroughly practical as a very high-speed road car.

A monocoque centre-section combined with a multi-tubular front-end, the 3.8-litre XK engine was rated at 265bhp (gross), and there was soft all-independent suspension and four-wheel disc brakes to round off the mechanical package. Open roadster or fastback (hatchback, really, because of the layout of the bootlid) coupe versions were available.

Road tests showed that a coupe in excellent (some said, super-excellent!) health could reach 150mph. With prices starting at a mere £2,098, it was an irresistible bargain for thousands of enthusiasts. UK-market deliveries began in July.

One major new Jaguar model in a season would have been thought enough for Jaguar, so the arrival of the gargantuan Mk X saloon, the biggest Jaguar ever put on sale, was a real surprise.

The Mk X was a low, wide, but sleek monocoque four-door, six-seater saloon which replaced the last of the Mk IXs, cars which in any case drew their basic chassis engineering from the Mk VII of 1950. There was an all-new type of coil-spring front suspension, but the rear suspension was almost like that of the new E-type, though with a much wider track. The engine, gearbox and rear axle, too, were all the same as those used in the E-type, which more or less guaranteed that the 265bhp Mk X could reach 120mph. Mk Xs, and their descendants, would remain on sale until 1970.

Lagonda: The new Rapide model made its debut, this being a four-door saloon quite unrelated to any previous Lagonda model. Although it had a much longer wheelbase – 114in instead of 98in – the chassis platform/underside of the Lagonda was similar to that of the Aston Martin DB4, with the important difference that it had a de Dion/torsion-bar rear suspension. The engine was a 4-litre version of the Aston Martin's 3.7-litre twin-cam 'six', producing 236bhp, with a Jaguar-type Borg-Warner automatic transmission as standard.

Big, impressive and undeniably highly-specified, the Lagonda was also highly-priced (£5,251), and first deliveries were not even promised until the spring of 1962. In the event, this was not to be a popular model, and only 54 would be sold in three years.

Lancia: The British concessionaires, based at Alperton in north-west London, announced a considerable expansion. For the first time this was to include right-hand-drive versions of the Flaminia saloon and Zagato GT coupe models:

the Farina coupe had been available with RHD for some time.

The new Flavia became available with right-hand drive from May, and a smart 2+2 fastback coupe version of the design, styled by Pininfarina, made its debut at the Turin motor show in November.

Land-Rover: A new 2.3-litre diesel engine replaced the original 2-litre diesel from September 1961, the new unit sharing the same bore and stroke dimensions as the existing petrol unit.

Mercedes-Benz: The large, heavy, but graceful 220SE coupe joined the relatively new Fintail range of medium-sized models from Stuttgart in February, the convertible version arriving in September. The coupe was the first Mercedes-Benz model to be fitted with disc brakes as standard – the 300SL (nearing the end of its long run) following suit a few weeks later.

The new-generation 300SE was also based on the now-ubiquitous Fintail body structure, though powered with a modernized version of the existing 3-litre, six-cylinder engine, which was fitted with indirect (port-type) fuel injection. There was also a brand-new four-speed automatic transmission, a 'building block' which would feature on many different Mercedes-Benz models in future years.

This, in fact, was a car full of innovation, for all-round disc brakes were fitted, as was a new own-brand type of air suspension. In many ways, therefore, Mercedes-Benz had set standards for other high-price manufacturers to try to match.

Other cars added to the Fintail range at the same time were the four-cylinder 190 and 190D (diesel) models.

MG: Shortly after the Austin-Healey Sprite Mk II appeared, BMC also launched a new MG Midget, this being identical to the Sprite in all ways except for minor badging and trim differences. At the time, the new Midget cost £670, the Sprite Mk II £641.

Simultaneously, BMC also gave the MGA a final upgrade, to 1600 Mk II, complete with a 90bhp/1,622cc version of the familiar B-series engine and a minor front-end facelift.

Like other B-series saloons, the Magnette was upgraded and became Series IV, with wider wheel tracks, a

longer wheelbase and an enlarged, 68bhp/1,622cc version of the engine.

Morgan: After only one year, the 4/4 Series III was dropped, being replaced by the 4/4 Series IV, this car having the enlarged 1,340cc version of the Ford overhead-valve engine, along with front-wheel disc brakes.

Morris: The new Morris Mini-Cooper was exactly the same as the Austin Mini-Cooper except for the grille and badging (see above).

The Morris Oxford became Series VI, with the same changes as the Austin A55 to A60 transformation (see above).

NSU: To replace the original, rather gawky, rear-engined Prinz, NSU now revealed the Prinz IV, which had a 'bathtub' body style very much like that of the Chevrolet Corvair: clearly this car had been the inspiration for the style, though the new car's chassis, complete with its rear-mounted twin-cylinder air-cooled engine, was much as before.

Ogle: There were high hopes for the new 1.5-model, which had been styled by David Ogle, of whom the British motorist knew little at the time. Later, of course, his styling work on Reliant cars would be widely praised.

The 1.5 used the basic underpan of a Riley 1.5 model, much-modified with a multi-square-tube frame behind the seats, all topped off by a fastback 2+2 glassfibre coupe body style.

The 1.5's problem was that it was expensive – it was priced at £1,574 when the equivalent Riley 1.5 donor car cost only £816.

Peugeot: The French company became only the second European manufacturer (after Mercedes-Benz) to offer fuel-injection on a petrol-engined road car, with the launch of the 404 Injection model. The installation was by Kugelfischer.

Later in the year, a smart drop-head coupe version of the 404, styled and engineered by Pininfarina, was added to the range.

Porsche: To upgrade the fierce four-cam Carrera models, Porsche introduced a 2-litre version of the same engine, with 145bhp (gross), and fitted disc brakes.

Reliant: The Tamworth-based company had been producing stark, crudely-detailed three-wheelers for some years, but the Sabre 4 of October 1961 was not only the company's first sportscar, but its first four-wheeler car of any type for the UK market.

The Sabre 4 was a real amalgam of existing resources, which included an LMB-type chassis, complete with swing-axle front suspension, a 1.7-litre Ford Consul four-cylinder engine, a ZF gearbox, and an oddly-styled glassfibre open-top body style with a long nose incorporating moulded-in front over-riders.

It was an ungainly machine which deserved to fail – and it did so! Not even the later six-cylinder Ford-engined model (the Sabre 6) could rescue much of its reputation.

Renault: The arrival of the new Renault 4 caused a real stir in France and elsewhere, as this represented serious competition for the Citroen 2CV in an altogether visually more acceptable, five-door, estate car style. This was the first Renault private car to have a front-engine/front-wheel-drive layout – with the engine behind the line of the front wheels and the gearbox ahead of it – the engine being yet another version of the famous 4CV/Dauphine design, and the gearbox/transaxle a descendant of that used in the modern Estafette delivery van.

Like the 2CV, there was soft, long-travel, all-independent suspension with large wheels. The stage was set for a long-term battle between the two types – which would eventually favour the Renault, though not for some years to come.

Riley: The Elf was basically a BMC Mini fitted with a lengthened box-shaped tail, a distinctive nose, and a more fully trimmed interior. Except for its nose and badging, the new Wolseley Hornet was the same car as this.

At the same time, the 4/68 gave way to the 4/72, which picked up the same mechanical changes as the MG Magnette, including the 68bhp/1,622cc engine.

Simca: The rear-engined four-door 1000 model was the first mainly-new Simca to be revealed by that company for some years. Influenced in many ways by the Fiat 600 (Fiat had held a shareholding in Simca for many years), the 1000 was a squared-up machine with many Fiat-like features, including transverse-leaf front suspension and semi-trailing-arm rear suspension.

The 944cc engine was a short-stroke derivative of the existing Aronde unit and, with its cast iron cylinder block, gave the car a pronounced rear weight bias, which did nothing for the handling.

For 1962, also, some of the existing Aronde models were given more powerful (70bhp) versions of the 1.3-litre engine.

Singer: The Vogue was the first of a new generation of medium-sized Rootes cars to be launched (the future Hillman Super Minx and Humber Sceptre models would be built on the same base).

Like the existing Minx/Gazelle ranges, which continued, the Vogue had a conventional four-door saloon monocoque structure, this time being powered by a 62bhp/1,592cc version of the familiar Rootes overhead-valve engine. There was coil-spring independent front suspension, a leaf-spring rear and front-wheel disc brakes – in other words, a very conventional package.

During the week when the Vogue was revealed, the Gazelle was also upgraded, being given a 53bhp version of the same 1.6-litre engine and a central gearchange as standard.

Skoda: Mid-1990s buyers of modern Skoda Felicias should be reminded that the *original* Felicia was a four-seater convertible version of the Octavia, which became available in the summer of 1961.

Sunbeam: The Rapier progressed to Series IIIA, with a 75bhp/1.6-litre version of the familiar overhead-valve engine. Although this was not a production-line model, there was a lot of factory support behind the Sunbeam Harrington Alpine, which added a smoothly pro-filed fastback hardtop to the Alpine's existing shell. Various engine tune-up kits were also provided, in association with George Hartwell Ltd.

Tornado: Having failed miserably with the Thunderbolt and Tempest models, the Hertfordshire company tried again with the Ford Classic-engined Talisman, which was much more successful.

The mixture, if not the detail, was as before, there being a ladder-style chassis-frame, a glassfibre body, independent front suspension and – this time – a neat 'almost four-seater' body style. Nearly 200 would be made before 1964, when Tornado finally ceased trading.

Triumph: The most interesting new Triumph of the year was the Michelotti-styled TR4 sportscar. Designed as a direct replacement for the TR3A (though a TR3B continued, for USA sale only, during 1962), the TR4 used the same basic chassis, though with an enlarged 2,138cc engine, wider wheel tracks and rack-and-pinion steering.

The bodyshell not only featured wind-up door windows, but there was face-level ventilation on the dashboard, and an optional 'surrey top' feature when the hardtop was ordered, which really predated Porsche's Targa top by some years.

With sales of normal-price Heralds flagging, the new stripped-out Herald S saloon (priced at £664) was introduced in the spring. This had the 948cc engine, which was retained even after the new 1200 appeared a few weeks later.

The Herald 1200 range appeared in April, replacing the original range of 948cc-engined Heralds which had only been on sale for two years. Although the technical layout and style, which included the separate chassis and swing-axle independent rear suspension, was not changed, all versions of the car now shared a new and more torquey single-carburettor 39bhp/1,147cc version of the SC engine, and all cars had higher overall gearing.

An additional model, the 1200 Estate, was added to saloon, coupe and convertible derivatives from May 1961.

Vanden Plas: The Princess 3-litre picked up all the technical changes given to produce the Austin A110 (see above) and Wolseley 6/110 types.

Vauxhall: Less than five years after first putting the Victor on sale, Vauxhall introduced the second-generation (FB) type. This used virtually the same underpan/platform/chassis engineering as before, but was topped by a much smarter and more acceptable body style; there was also an estate car version.

The mainstream cars used the same lightly-tuned 1,508cc engine, and there was an all-synchromesh gearbox with a choice of three or four forward speeds. However, at Motor Show time in October, the company previewed the first VX4/90 model, which had a twin-carb/71bhp version of the same engine, a four-speed gearbox and front-wheel disc brakes. There was a more completely-equipped facia and stiffened-up suspension.

At the same time Vauxhall began to show some interest in works rallying, the VX4/90 being a useful basis for cars to be built for such a team.

Front-wheel disc brakes also became optional on Velox/Cresta models.

Volkswagen: The giant Wolfsburg-based concern released its first new-style model for many years – the 1500 saloon and estate car types, along with a Karmann-Ghia coupe on the same platform.

Like the Beetle, which continued to be built in enormous quantities (and on which the 1500's chassis platform was based), the new 1500 had a flat-four/air-cooled engine mounted in the extreme tail. The styling was simple and squared-up, and by careful design of the engine it was possible to provide two luggage boots – one up front, the other in the rear, effectively above the engine.

Volvo: The P1800 coupe, complete with its Pressed Steel Company bodyshell, and with final assembly concentrated at Jensen Motors in West Bromwich, finally went on sale in Europe and the USA, in left-hand-drive form at first, though right-hand-drive types soon followed.

Already extensively previewed, this was an all-steel two-door fixed-head coupe with Volvo 122S-type running gear, which included a 100bhp/1.8-litre engine, Laycock overdrive as standard and front-wheel disc brakes. British-market deliveries began in March 1962.

In the meantime, development changes to the 122S saloons, some of which helped to commonize the specifications, included the arrival of a 90bhp/1.8-litre engine in place of the earlier 85bhp/1.6-litre unit, and front-wheel disc brakes.

Wolseley: The new Mini-based Hor-net was essentially the same car as the Riley Elf (see above) apart from trim details.

The 16/60 took over from the 15/60, complete with all chassis and engine (1,622cc) changes introduced on Austin A60/Morris Oxford Series VI models.

The 6/110 replaced the 6/99 with the same technical changes as introduced for the Austin A99.

Industrial developments

BMC announced the building of the 1,000,000th Morris Minor with a series of a rather luridly painted 'Minor Million' saloons. This, it was stressed, was the first time that a million of any British car had been made. Almost exactly half of that total had been sold overseas – Australia having taken more than 100,000. Surprisingly, well over 50,000 had gone to the USA and 30,000 to Canada.

Later in the year – in November – BMC's founding genius, Sir Leonard Lord, decided to retire from the chairmanship, handing over to his long-time deputy, George Harriman. Sir Leonard remained on the board and became BMC's vice-president.

Another important appointment at BMC was announced at the same time, Alec Issigonis becoming technical director of the entire corporation. Charles Griffin became his chief engineer.

Leyland's takeover of Standard-Triumph was formalized in April, with a previously little-known (to private car drivers) salesman called Donald Stokes joining the board. Leyland's Sir Henry Spurrier became chairman. The corporate blood-letting began almost at once. Many middle managers lost their jobs, then in August there was a wholesale shake-up of directors. Managing director Alick Dick lost his job and was replaced by Stanley Markland, from Leyland. Six other Standard-Triumph directors also lost their seats on the board. Thereafter Leyland was firmly and totally in control.

Rootes suffered a very damaging strike at its British Light Steel Pressings plant in Acton, West London, where Humber Hawk and Super Snipe bodyshells, plus many other pressings, were normally manufactured. The strike dragged on for 13 weeks. Having made £6.8 million in 1960, Rootes plunged to a £2 million loss in the financial year covered by the BLSP strike. This, and the colossal expense of setting up the new Linwood factory in Scotland, meant that thereafter Rootes always struggled to stay afloat.

In Germany, Borgward, one of the top five car-makers in that country (Borgward also produced Hansa and Goliath cars), got into serious financial difficulties. Even though the State of Bremen took over in February, assuming responsibility for all debts, this was just a last-ditch holding operation, for all car assembly ended a few months later. BMC dabbled with the idea of taking over Borgward, but decided against it.

Berkeley Coachwork, the sportscar-makers who had ceased trading in December 1960, were found to have a deficiency of £332,938, and there was no chance of the cars ever being put back into production.

The final Ford Prefect (100E with 105E-type engine) was produced in mid-year, since when the name has not been used by Ford.

After seven eventful years, the BMC-built Nash Metropolitan (plain Metropolitan for British buyers) was dropped.

Technical developments

Harry Ferguson Research startled the technical world, not only by revealing its latest four-wheel-drive installation, but showing it in a front-engined, four-wheel-drive single-seater racing car, the P99 model. As shown at first, the car had a Coventry Climax FPF engine, and Dunlop disc brakes with Maxaret anti-lock control. Clearly this was not purely a research vehicle, though there never seemed to be any serious attempt at a regular racing programme.

In May, Harry Ferguson Research had also shown one of its road-car prototypes, this being a four-door saloon with proportions (but not detail styling) rather like that of a Jaguar 2.4, with a horizontally-opposed engine and four-wheel drive.

Rover showed what would turn out to be its final gas-turbine project, the T4 four-door saloon. This was a smartly-styled four-door saloon, with swing-axle rear suspension and a front-mounted 140bhp gas-turbine engine. Unknown at the time, the basic body/structure of the T4 was that of the piston-engined Rover 2000 road car, which would not make its public appearance for another two years – in October 1963.

Borg-Warner introduced a new and versatile three-speed automatic transmission, the Type 35, which at the time was smaller and more compact than any other. It was specifically designed for fitment to cars with engines as small as 1.5 litres – and before long many British cars would pick it up as optional equipment.

It was originally to be manufactured at Letchworth, north of London, and in later years, after being upgraded, and particularly with a different torque converter, the Type 35 box was used widely on much more powerful cars than those for which it had originally been intended.

Men of Influence

Sir Leonard Lord (Lord Lambury)

Millions of words have been written about Leonard Lord, many of them critical of his manner, but most of them complimentary of his business achievements. Born in Coventry in 1896 (*not* in Yorkshire, as some biographies have stated), he was originally apprenticed to Courtaulds before joining Hotchkiss & Cie, the Coventry-based engine manufacturer.

After Hotchkiss was bought by William Morris, Lord rose rapidly in that company, building a formidable reputation as a production engineer. Morris sent him to Wolseley in 1927 to modernize that business, then installed him at Morris Motors in the early 1930s (as managing director) to develop the Nuffield Organisation.

Lord's rough and abrasive manner produced results, but made him few friends at Cowley, and after one final bitter quarrel with Lord Nuffield he stormed out of the business. Returning to the motor industry with Austin as works director in 1938, with Lord Austin's agreement he rapidly assumed responsibility for new-product design as well.

After Lord Austin died, Len Lord became Austin's joint managing director in 1942, then chairman and managing director in 1945. From then on until the early 1960s he was the engine, the dynamo, behind everything which Austin (and later BMC) did.

With a merger in mind, his first approach to Lord Nuffield came in 1948, but this was rebuffed, as was a further move in 1950. The successful approach, joining Austin with Nuffield to form BMC (the British Motor Corporation) came in the winter of 1951/52.

Although this might have looked like a straight merger of equals at first, Len Lord was always determined that Austin (and he!) should be dominant. Within a year, Lord Nuffield stepped down from the business, becoming BMC's honorary president, which allowed Len Lord to become the outright boss of the entire BMC empire.

Just as all the early postwar Austins had been directly inspired by what Lord wanted (that influence even stretched to styling preferences), so all the first-generation BMC cars bore his stamp.

After being knighted in 1954, Sir Leonard went into partial retirement in 1956, but did not step down from the BMC board until 1961, when he became Lord Lambury. He died in 1967.

Throughout his long motor industry career he was always known (behind his back) as Len. Not even in later life did he mellow – much. He was a real rough diamond, an organizing genius, a compulsive designer and a vibrant, combative personality who usually chose to call a spade a bloody shovel.

1962

Less than a year after the Chancellor increased purchase tax on cars, the tax was reduced in the April 1962 Budget from 55 to 45 per cent on cars and many other consumer items, giving a saving, for example, of £30 on a Mini and £59 on a Vauxhall Cresta. There was no reduction in the duty charged on petrol.

Then, to every motorist's delight – and amazement – purchase tax was slashed further in November, from 45 to 25 per cent. Mini prices now started at £448, which was a further reduction of £62, while the Rolls-Royce Silver Cloud III became £754 cheaper.

Naturally, this greatly stimulated the demand for new cars, putting smiles back on the faces of manufacturers and the motor trade; it was the most heartening news Britain's motor industry had received since the formal end of fuel rationing more than 10 years earlier. Of course, this all came too late to have much effect on British car sales in 1962 (which rose modestly), but the big surge which followed in 1963 led to more than a million cars being registered in the UK for the first time.

Compulsory testing of older cars progressed rapidly, the six-year rule being applied from November 1. There was still a long way to go, however, before the familiar three-year rule was applied.

Britain's motorway network continued to expand, with the first long stretch of the M5 opening (to link up with the M50), work on most of the M6 nearing completion (nearly 40 miles of it now open) and a start to pushing the M1 northwards towards Yorkshire. By the mid-1960s, indeed, there would seem to be road-building activity all round the nation.

New models

AC: The Ford V8-engined Cobra was unveiled at the New York Auto Show in May, series production deliveries beginning later in the year. The Cobra combined Ford-USA engine power with a modified AC Ace chassis and body style, along with four-wheel disc brakes, wider wheels and tyres and a beefed-up transmission. The first few cars used a 4.2-litre (260cu in) engine, but this was soon displaced by a more powerful 4.7-litre (289cu in) unit.

For the time being this car was only sold to North American customers, being delivered, without engine/transmission, from Thames Ditton to Carroll Shelby's factory in Los Angeles for completion.

Alfa Romeo: During the summer, the first of a new generation of small/medium-sized saloons – the Giulia TI – was announced. Bulkier and altogether more craggily-styled than the Giulietta (which remained in production for the time being), the Giulia used a 1.6-litre version of the Giulietta's twin-cam engine, allied to a five-speed gearbox.

The underbody and suspension layout of the new car was similar to the old, with a complex linkage locating the rear axle, and for the present four-wheel drum brakes were still being specified.

Shortly after this the Giulietta Sprint and Spider models were equipped with the new 1.6-litre engine/five-speed gearbox assemblies, though these were strictly interim models, as newly-styled 'proper' sporting Giulias were already on the way.

Released at the Geneva show, but on sale in Britain later in the year, the 2600 range was really a re-engineering of the existing 2000s. In place of the old four-cylinder engine there was a new 2.6-litre twin-cam 'six'. These were the first-ever Alfas to use disc brakes.

Alfa Romeo GB also promised that all cars would be available with right-hand drive from the spring of 1963.

Alvis: The TD21 became the TD21 Series II, with a facelifted nose, and most importantly with four-wheel disc brakes. A five-speed ZF gearbox soon became optional.

Aston Martin: The Vantage engine, with three SU carburettors, was added to the DB4 range, offering 266bhp instead of the 240bhp of the original model.

Austin: BMC finally bowed to public opinion and allowed the Mini to be called – the Mini!

The Mini-Moke was officially previewed as a small, open-top, cross-country version of the Mini saloon, but at this time it was still intended for military use and was not ready for civilian sale.

The new-generation BMC diesel engine, a 40bhp/1.5-litre unit, was made available to special order in the A60 model.

More than four years after launch, the 4x4 Gipsy was considerably redesigned. There had been problems with the original Flexitor rubber suspension, so two new types were made available – one with a beam axle and half-elliptic leaf springs at the rear, the other with beam axles and half-elliptic leaf springs all round. At the same time the old (Austin A70-type) engine was boosted from 62bhp to 72bhp, though the diesel alternative was not changed.

The new 1.1-litre A-series engine was adopted for the A40 model.

Austin-Healey: The 3000 became the 3000 Sports Convertible (which, in future years, became known unofficially as 3000 Mk IIA), with a considerably upgraded and redesigned cockpit, and engine modifications. The latest car had wind-up door windows, a curved windscreen and a fully foldback soft-top, while the engine reverted to a twin-SU carburettor set-up with the nominal loss of 1bhp at peak.

At the Earls Court Motor Show the Sprite was shown with the latest 1.1-litre engine, rated at 55bhp, along with front-wheel disc brakes – all just in time to match what was on offer in the new Triumph Spitfire.

Bentley: *See Rolls-Royce, below.*

Citroen: The ID19/DS19 family had been continually improved, in mechanical detail, since its launch in 1955. Now, for 1963, there was a front-end facelift and an aerodynamic clean-up which was said to be worth 6mph in top speed.

Daimler: The arrival of the 2½-litre saloon was the first evidence of the way Jaguar was planning to develop its ownership of Daimler. This car, in effect, used a lightly-modified and facelifted Jaguar Mk 2 shell and chassis, but with the Daimler SP250-type V8 engine and Borg-Warner automatic transmission standard, no manual transmission option being offered (though this would follow some years later).

Faster than the Jaguar 2.4 Mk 2, but

even more expensive than the 3.8 Mk 2, this new Daimler was meant to appeal to a different type of customer. As a concept it proved highly successful, almost outselling the sum total of *all* previous postwar Daimlers. There would be many more 'Daimler-Jaguars' in the coming years.

Fairthorpe: Still more variations on the Electron/Zeta theme came with the introduction of the Rockette, which was like the Zeta, but with the Triumph Vitesse's 1.6-litre six-cylinder engine.

Ferrari: The beautiful 250GT Lusso – a thoroughly practical two-seater coupe road car – was launched at the Paris show and immediately displaced all previous 250GT types, including the road-race type of 250GT Berlinetta. Using the familiar Ferrari tubular chassis, but still with beam-axle rear suspension, and with a 280bhp/3-litre V12 engine, this was a magnificent machine, which in later life became an adored and valuable classic for any Ferrari fanatic who could afford one.

Fiat: In a quiet year by their own frenetic standards, Fiat upgraded the twin-cam-engined sportscar from 1.5 to 1.6 litres, calling it the 1600S. This was a smart, 100mph-plus machine which was never strongly marketed in the UK.

The 1100D, a much improved and more sharply-styled version of the nine-year-old 1100, appeared before the end of the year.

Ford: It was a big year for Ford with the launch of two brand-new models – Cortina and Zephyr/Zodiac Mk III – and the upgrading of several others.

The first Cortinas were revealed in September, to the surprise of many observers, as they appeared to be in the same size class as the Classics, which continued. The Cortina, however, was a much lighter car, and initially was fitted with a smaller (1.2-litre) version of the engine attached to a new all-synchromesh gearbox. Surprisingly, a steering-column gearchange was still available as an option to the central floor-change.

Two-door and four-door saloons were immediately available, though Ford made it clear that many other versions would follow in the next year or so.

Although it was only 18 months old, the Classic/Capri range was upgraded

with the latest 1.5-litre version of the modern overhead-valve engine, along with the Cortina's new all-synchromesh gearbox. Not only was the engine larger than before, but it had a more rigid bottom-end, complete with a five-bearing crankshaft.

In a similar upgrading exercise, there was also a new version of the Anglia, the Anglia 1200, which had the Cortina's 1.2-litre engine and all-synchromesh gearbox.

A new range of larger models, christened Zephyr 4, Zephyr 6 and Zodiac – always more familiarly known as Mk IIIs – went on sale in the spring. These replaced the old Mk IIs, and the Consul name was temporarily laid to rest.

As before, these cars shared a new monocoque four-door saloon structure and had MacPherson-strut front suspension and front-wheel disc brakes. The new cars were significantly larger than before, still with definite transatlantic styling themes, but the Zodiac now had 109bhp, giving it a top speed of more than 100mph – the first European Ford to breach that barrier. Estate car versions, converted by Abbott, joined the range later in the year.

Ford-Germany: The new-generation Taunus 12M (originally coded Cardinal) was Ford's first front-wheel-drive car. Outwardly a rather ordinary two-door saloon, which Ford later acknowledged to have been styled, designed and partly-developed in North America, the new 12M had a 1.2-litre 60-degree V4 engine.

In size, market aspiration and price it was almost a straight competitor for the new Ford-UK Cortina, so it never sold in Britain in any numbers.

Hillman: An estate car version was added to the Super Minx range, and a few weeks later a four-seater convertible version joined it. Then, only 18 months after launch, the Super Minx became Series II with front-wheel disc brakes standard and automatic transmission as an option.

Humber: Rootes never let an Earls Court Motor Show go by without changing the Hawk/Super Snipe models. This time there were changes to the roof/rear quarter/rear window shape, along with a more powerful (by 3bhp) six-cylinder engine, and slight changes to the transmissions.

Iso: The Italian company, which was already famous for building scooters, motorcycles and bubblecars, announced the first of a new family of what historian Michael Sedgwick would have called 'Anglo-American Sports Bastards' – these being supercars in every way except that they were powered by down-to-earth North American V8 engines.

The Iso Rivolta was a two-door 2+2 coupe styled by Bertone, with a 340bhp 5.3-litre Chevrolet Corvette V8 engine. Designed by Ing Bizzarrini, whose last triumph had been the Ferrari 250GTO, the Rivolta was in direct competition with the biggest Ferraris and Maseratis.

Jensen: After only two years in production, the 541S was pushed aside in favour of yet another variation on the existing chassis/glassfibre body, the C-V8. This used a 305bhp/5.9-litre Chrysler V8 engine and related transmissions (manual or automatic), while there were further modifications to the front and rear styling, the front including four headlamps mounted slant-style. Clearly this was a much faster car than the 541S, but it was expensive (£3,861 at launch), so the C-V8 would only ever sell in small numbers.

Jaguar: The Mk X finally went on sale in the UK in March – five months after it had been launched.

Lotus: At the Nurburgring in May, Jim Clark raced a new type of sportscar, the Lotus 23, which was fitted with a newly-designed Lotus twin-cam engine. A few months later the significance of this new unit would become obvious – it was intended to power a new Lotus road car, the Elan.

The Elan was previewed in October, actually as the Elan 1500, the twin-cam engine being based on the bottom-end of the latest five-bearing 1.5-litre Ford power unit. The Elan was the first of several new Lotus road cars, all of which would have a twin-cam engine, pressed-steel backbone chassis-frame, softly-sprung all-independent suspension and a lightweight glassfibre body.

The Elan was tiny and light – initial figures showed a length of 145in and a weight of only 1,290lb; by the time quantity production began the engine would be enlarged to 1,558cc and the car badged as an Elan 1600. However, unhappily for Lotus, reliability was not good; this was the period when Lotus became a cynic's acronym for 'Lots Of Trouble, Usually Serious'!

Mercedes-Benz: Using the mix-and-match approach for which the company was increasingly famous, the new 300SE's chassis and running gear were matched to the 220SE's Coupe and Convertible structures, with modifications to the front-end style, to create the 300SE Coupe/300SE Convertible models.

MG: The 100,000th MGA was produced in the spring, but this was shortly before the end of the car's long career as it was about to be replaced by the new-generation MGB.

The new sportscar was launched in September on what would prove to be an 18-year life, during which more than 500,000 would be made. The MGB had a rock-solid unit-construction shell, with wind-up windows and a two-seater roadster style. The engine, at 1.8 litres, was the final stretch of the familiar BMC B-series power unit, while the gearbox, back axle and suspension were all further-developed versions of the MGA assemblies.

The new MG 1100 was a compact front-wheel-drive saloon, closely based on the design of the Morris 1100 (see below), but with a 55bhp/twin-SU version of the 1.1-litre engine. There was a traditional type of MG front grille and, at first, a rather horrid veneer-type dashboard and strip speedometer.

In October, the Midget inherited the 55bhp/1.1-litre engine and front-wheel disc brakes, and was therefore still mechanically identical to the lower-priced Austin-Healey Sprite.

Morris: The new Morris 1100, introduced in August, was the first of another big badge-engineered family of BMC models, really a restatement and improvement on the Mini theme. The same type of transverse engine/gearbox-in-sump/front-wheel-drive layout was used, along with similar suspension geometry.

The engine, however, was a new, long-stroke, 48bhp/1,098cc development of the A-series theme, while instead of rubber springs there was a new-fangled Hydrolastic system, where a combination of rubber springs and a water/alcohol mixture, with front and rear suspension units linked by transfer piping, gave a much softer ride than

that of the Mini, as well as a degree of self-levelling. Front-wheel disc brakes were standard, and the driving position was much more comfortable than that of the Mini – indeed, this was a much better thought-out car than the Mini and it soon began to outsell it.

The structure was all new, considerably larger than that of the Mini, with a choice of two or four passenger doors and crisp sharp-edged styling by Pininfarina (the name by which the former Farina company was now officially known).

The new-generation BMC diesel engine, a 40bhp/1.5-litre unit, was made available to special order in the Oxford.

From January, the Morris Mini-Minor officially became the Mini, which is what most enthusiasts had been calling it for a long time! (For Mini-Moke details, see Austin, above.)

The new 1.1-litre engine was also standardized in the Morris Minor 1000, though to prevent any confusion the car's title was not changed.

Ogle: To follow the 1.5 model, Ogle now introduced the Ogle-Mini, a rather egg-shaped coupe with a glass-fibre bodyshell attached to the Mini's platform and running gear. Was this a new marque, or just a special? Ogle was adamant that it was not merely a rebodied Mini…

Peugeot: The 404 Coupe, which was a very close relation of the 404 Convertible, went on sale, with bodyshells produced by Pininfarina in Italy.

Reliant: Not only did the ugly-duckling Sabre gain a new, shorter and altogether smarter nose style, but it was also given the option of the latest six-cylinder Ford Zodiac engine. The more conventional bonnet was only available on the Sabre 6 at first, but Sabre 4s would fall into line in mid-1963. Both cars, though, proved something of an acquired taste. The first truly successful Reliant (the Scimitar) was still two years into the future.

Although it was not yet available in a four-wheeler car, the company introduced a new 600cc four-cylinder water-cooled engine for use in its three-wheeler models. Because of the strict weight limits imposed on three-wheelers, this engine had aluminium cylinder block and head castings, and steel 'wet' liners.

Renault: The new R8 was likely to be another million-plus best-seller. Effectively a grown-up, faster and larger version of the Dauphine, it retained the same basic rear-engined layout, with swing-axle rear suspension. This time, however, the styling was much squarer (and therefore a little roomier in the cabin), while there was a totally new type of four-cylinder engine with 956cc and five main bearings, and disc brakes were fitted to all four wheels. UK sales began in September.

The new version of the Floride, complete with a four-seater version known as the Caravelle, had a restyled cabin roof providing more usable 2+2 accommodation. The new car's 956cc five-bearing engine, four-wheel disc brakes and all related chassis fittings arrived on the market in March, well ahead of the R8 saloon from which they were lifted, and consequently were the subject of great interest as a preview of the R8.

Rolls-Royce: The Silver Cloud and Bentley S range became SIII models, with new four-headlamp noses, lowered bonnet lines and an (unstated) 7 per cent power increase – perhaps 15bhp extra. In due course the various special-bodied cars using this chassis also took up the four-headlamp nose motif.

Rover: Although the P4 and P5 models were continued, Rover reshuffled the pack. The P4 80 and 100 models were dropped, replaced by the 95 and 110, these both having 2.6-litre six-cylinder engines, of 92bhp and 115bhp respectively.

The P5 3-litre was given a more powerful (121bhp) engine, thanks to advice from Weslake, the engine consultants. There was a new and additional Coupe body style, which was the same as the saloon below the waistline, but with a lowered and more rakish roof style and half-frame doors. There was now a remote-control gearchange rather than the original direct-action lever.

Saab: The 96 Sport was introduced, a 52bhp version of the existing 96 model with three downdraught carburettors.

Singer: An estate car version of the Vogue became available: structurally and mechanically this was almost identical to the Hillman Super Minx estate car. Note, however, that no convertible version of the Vogue was ever put on sale. These cars became Series II in the autumn, with minor improvements and automatic transmission as an option.

Standard: The Ensign De Luxe replaced the Ensign, with a 75bhp/2.1-litre version of the wet-liner engine instead of the 1.67-litre engine of the earlier Ensign.

Triumph: After a very rapid development period, Triumph introduced the new Spitfire sportscar, a Michelotti-styled two-seater with a backbone chassis-frame, which used modified versions of the Triumph Herald 1200 engine, transmission, suspension and steering. Aimed directly at the market previously held by the Austin-Healey Sprite/MG Midget, the Spitfire was a prettier and roomier car than its rivals, but would need to work hard to build itself an image.

Front disc brakes, 90mph-plus performance and excellent engine bay access all helped, but the Herald's swing-axle remained (though lowered and somewhat stiffened), and testers would soon discover the limits of its roadholding.

This was the first of a whole family of Spitfires (and later GT6s) which would be built for the next 18 years.

The combination of a stiffened type of Herald frame and suspension and modified body, powered by a 1.6-litre version of the Standard Vanguard Six's engine, formed the basis of the new Vitesse 1600. The Vitesse had front disc brakes as standard, but retained swing-axle rear suspension, which was already being criticized by many Herald owners. Saloon and convertible bodies were available.

TVR: Although the exterior style was virtually unchanged, the Grantura Mk III had an entirely new multi-tubular chassis and suspension. The old-type trailing-link/torsion-bar layout had been abandoned in favour of a coil-spring-and-wishbone layout at both ends, with rack-and-pinion steering for the first time on a TVR.

Vauxhall: The new PB-series Velox/Cresta models took over from the five-year-old PA-type, using the same basic floorpan, 2.6-litre engine and running

gear, but with a new and squarer body style which bore a distinct family resemblance to current FB Victor models – in fact the door pressings were the same.

Late in the year the company confirmed that a new small (Ford Anglia-sized) car was under development. This proved to be the new Viva, but it would not be introduced for a further 12 months.

Volvo: A five-door estate car was added to the 120/Amazon family of cars.

Industrial developments

In January, BMC and Rolls-Royce announced that they were 'examining the feasibility of technical collaboration in the field of motor car engineering'. However, it was made clear that results of such talks were not expected for some time.

No less than 11 months later the two companies announced that they now had no plans to merge any part of their interests. Exchanges of technical information would continue, along with possible swops of major components. Rolls-Royce already supplied automatic transmissions to BMC (for the Princess 4-litre limousine), but we would have to wait until 1964, and the launch of the Vanden Plas Princess R (complete with Rolls-Royce engine) to see any noticeable effect.

Having recently retired from the chairmanship of BMC, Sir Leonard Lord was raised to the peerage in January 1962, taking the title of Lord Lambury.

After many years at the helm, Spencer Wilks stepped down from the chairmanship of Rover at 70 years of age. His place was taken by his brother, Maurice Wilks, who had been Rover's managing director since 1960. William Martin-Hurst became managing director in his place.

The Elva Courier project was taken over by the Lambretta-Trojan group of companies, which allowed production to be transferred to a factory in Croydon.

Having failed to find any buyers for the Lynx, or the other car projects with which it then dabbled, Lea-Francis went into receivership, owing £130,000 to its bankers.

Technical developments

Although turbocharging was well understood in aircraft engines and for trucks, it was still novel for road cars. Chevrolet's Monza Spyder Turbo was the first turbocharged engine to go into series production, being put on sale in April 1962. The normally-aspirated 2.4-litre flat-six air-cooled Corvair engine produced 80 or 102bhp (depending on its state of tune), but the turbocharged unit produced no less than 150bhp.

BMC's new Hydrolastic suspension, as fitted to the new 1100 saloons, was an interesting further development of the rubber suspension fitted to Minis. Although rubber remained as the principal suspension medium, the front and rear units were interlinked by hydraulic pipes containing a water/alcohol mixture under high pressure.

When compressed, the rubber took most of the strain, but the liquid was then transferred from one end of the car to the other, through two-way rubber damper valves, giving secondary resistance. This meant that when a front wheel rose over a bump, it transferred liquid to the rear, raising the rear suspension just before the rear wheels hit the same bump.

Although various combinations were possible, BMC arranged interconnection merely between a front and a rear wheel on the same side of the car. Naturally, there were teething troubles (loss of pressure meant loss in ride height, for instance), and some passengers found that the rather floaty, bouncy, ride made them queasy, but Hydrolastic was generally hailed as a great advance.

The Lotus 25 F1 car, with which Jim Clark won three World Championship races during the year, was said to be the world's first monocoque single-seater. Within a few years, monocoques would displace multi-tube framed cars completely.

Safety belts were still not yet a compulsory fitting on British cars (though the bodyshell mountings *were* already required). Up to this time, all available belts had been fixed-length static types, but during 1962 three different inertia-reel belts of the modern variety were previewed – one each by Brooks, Irving and Britax.

1963

After the sharp cut in purchase tax which had been made in November 1962, the inevitable boom in the demand for new cars proved to be even greater than forecast. British factories churned out no fewer than 1,600,000 cars – a new record by a long way – and while British registrations passed the 1,000,000 mark for the first time, exports also reached an all-time record while – most significantly – sales of imported cars sales boomed from 28,000 to 48,000. This was the start of an inexorable rise in car imports, which would not peak until the end of the 1970s.

That was the good news. The bad news was that in the first week of the year Britain's winter was one of the most severe ever recorded, and certainly the most severe of the motoring 20th century.

A series of interesting figures published this year showed that estate cars were still rarities in the late 1950s and early 1960s. In 1958 only 8.1 per cent of new British cars had been estates, and the figure had risen to just 10 per cent by 1963.

By mid-November, 87 miles of M6, from south of Stafford to the north end of the Preston bypass, were open for traffic, which finally got rid of the misery of having to fight one's way north or south through industrial Lancashire. The M2 motorway (in Kent) opened in mid-year – Britain's motorway network was enlarging all the time.

The Dartford Tunnel – at that time a single tube for two-way traffic – also opened in November. Today, of course, there are two tunnels *and* a high-level bridge crossing the Thames at that point, all forming part of London's M25 ring motorway.

One of the least popular of all so-called safety measures ever imposed on British motorists was enacted over the August Bank Holiday weekend when a general 50mph speed limit came into force on open roads. This only lasted for three days during summer weekends and was widely ignored. One of the most popular slogans of the day was aimed at the current Minister of Transport, Ernest Marples: 'Marples Must Go!' (but it took a change of Government in late 1964 to

send him on his way).

The first batch of a new type of British registration numbers – the fabled XYZ 123A, or A-plate series – appeared. In this case the final A showed that the car was originally registered in 1963. Age-related plates were only used in a proportion of council areas in 1963, but by 1965 their usage was universal.

For the first time since the 1930s, a new, larger and much clearer system of road signs and route marking was proposed. This new generation of signs, recommended by the Worboys Committee, gradually came into use over the next decade, though some remnants of old-type signing remained on isolated (mainly country) roads into the 1990s.

Membership of the AA passed the 3,000,000 mark in mid-year, an indication of the pace at which British roads were filling up. The motorways had arrived in the very nick of time!

New models

[*Although separately-badged Austin and Morris Minis continued to be made until 1969, they were always identical apart from badging. For that reason, and to avoid unnecessary duplication, I have now 'invented' the Mini marque, six years before British Leyland did so…*]

Alfa Romeo: The 1.6-litre engine had already been fitted to the erstwhile Giulietta Sprint GT, but permutations on the 1.6-litre/Giulia theme continued at the Geneva show when the Bertone-styled Giulietta SS also inherited the larger engine.

The most important new 1.6-litre-engined car of the year, however, was the excellent Bertone-styled Sprint GT. In its original form it had a 106bhp version of the engine which, in conjunction with a five-speed gearbox, four-wheel disc brakes and remarkably attractive 2+2 coupe looks, made it successful in many countries.

Alvis: The familiar Graber-styled 3-litre car advanced to TE21 Series III specification with a more powerful (130bhp) version of the engine, along with a four-headlamp nose – the pairs of lamps being mounted vertically.

Amphicar: This unique German-made machine, a car-cum-boat, finally

went on sale in the UK. Powered by a Triumph Herald 1200 engine in the tail, the four-seater open-top Amphicar not only had rear-wheel drive, but also a drive propeller which could be clutched into engagement to propel the car on water. The doors could be clamped to ensure water-tightness, the result being a device which could be used as an amphibian, though it was wise not to try to do this in heavy seas.

The Amphicar was heavy, ungainly and strangely styled. In reply to cynics who suggested that it was not a very good boat, the accepted reply was that it wasn't a very good car either… It was expensive, and therefore difficult to sell in the UK.

Aston Martin: The 4-litre DB5 took over from the DB4 range, which had been on sale since 1959. The first DB5 was a lineal development of the final DB4, with the same enclosed-headlamp nose and choice of coupe or convertible styles, but with an enlarged (3,995cc) engine in 282bhp tune – and with the promise of more power to come.

There was a choice of a four-speed gearbox (David Brown), a five-speeder (ZF – not the same as used in the latest Alvis TD/TE models, but common with the Maserati 5000GT design), or Borg-Warner automatic transmission.

Austin: The front-wheel-drive 1100 appeared, being identical to the Morris 1100 (*see 1962*) except for badging and facia design.

BMW: The 1500/1600 models had established themselves well, so at Frankfurt in September BMW introduced an 1800 version of the same car. Except for details, the style was not changed, but there were 90bhp and 110bhp versions of the enlarged engine, and a five-speed gearbox was optional on the most sporting version. This was the first of a fleet of different overhead-camshaft four-cylinder BMWs to be launched over the next few years.

Bond: The Preston-based maker of three-wheel minicars announced its first four-wheeler, the sporting Equipe GT. This, the result of an alliance with Standard-Triumph, was a mixture of Triumph Herald and Spitfire parts, with some Herald bodywork under the skin, all topped off with Bond's own glassfibre coupe body style and 2+2 seating. The Herald chassis-frame and suspension used the 63bhp/1,147cc Triumph Spitfire engine, while the cabin included a wooden facia and bucket seats.

This was a great opportunity for Bond, as Standard-Triumph agreed to back the Equipe with a normal factory warranty, and the car was also marketed through the Standard-Triumph dealer chain.

Bristol: The 408 took over from the 407, the latest car being a development of the old, with a restyled nose.

DKW: The German company modified its existing Junior/800S range to produce the F12 model by lengthening the wheelbase, retouching the lines of the cabin, enlarging the two-stroke engine to 889cc and fitting inboard disc brakes at the front.

There seemed to be no end to DKW's faith in the two-stroke engine, as the launch of the F102 proved in August. Yet another, larger, derivative of three-cylinder two-stroke was provided, along with front-wheel drive, to power the newly-styled, larger and more roomy car. Right-hand-drive cars did not reach the UK until 1965, and then only in small numbers.

The F102, however, was even more significant than this, for in the mid-1960s it would prove to be the ancestor of the Audi motor car, for the original Audi 70 would use the same basic structure with a new four-stroke engine.

Facel Vega: Humiliated by the engine problems encountered in the Facellia sportscar, the French company announced a new and re-engined version of it, the Facel III, which was fitted with a Volvo P1800 type of engine with 108bhp/1,780cc.

Fiat: Continuing to upgrade its existing models, Fiat changed the 1200 Cabriolet into the 1500 Cabriolet by installing the engine from the latest 1500 saloon, along with the front disc brake installation from the same car.

In another permutation, the engine of the 1500 was fitted to the structure of the larger 1800 saloon, the result being the little-known 1500L. Although this was price listed in the UK from 1964, it was a virtually unknown derivative.

Ford: Many people were astonished by the somewhat premature launch of

the Lotus-Cortina, an acknowledged 'homologation special' with which the company wanted to win in production saloon car racing.

Based on the two-door Cortina shell, the new model used the 1,558cc Lotus-Ford twin-cam engine from the Lotus Elan and the same car's close-ratio gearbox. Lotus had totally redeveloped the rear suspension, the springing being by combined coil-spring/damper units, the axle then being located by radius-arms and an axle-mounted A-bracket, an arrangement that was destined to give a lot of trouble in service. Assembly was to be at the Lotus factory in Cheshunt, north London, and all cars would be finished in white with Lotus-green side spears and tail flashes.

Launched at the same time, the Cortina Super, with its 1.5-litre five-bearing overhead-valve engine, received very little press coverage, though clearly it was commercially much more important. In fact, 1963 was developing into the 'Year of the Cortina', for more derivatives, including an estate car, arrived in the ensuing months.

The Cortina GT, which appeared in April, combined a 78bhp version of the 1.5-litre Cortina engine (the camshaft and manifolding having been developed by Keith Duckworth of Cosworth Engineering), with front-wheel disc brakes and larger-section tyres. Two-door or four-door versions were available, and soon this car was selling very rapidly indeed.

Another new car from Ford was the Capri GT, which combined the engine of the Cortina GT with the fastback coupe Classic Capri body. This car, in fact, was revealed a few weeks ahead of the Cortina GT.

The new Corsair appeared in October as a replacement for the Classic saloon (though the Capri derivative of that car continued for the time being). Based on the lengthened platform, suspensions and running gear of the Cortinas, the Corsair had a larger, smoother-styled body which bore more than a passing resemblance to the current sharp-nosed Ford-USA Thunderbirds. Immediately available in two-door, four-door and GT forms, it was assembled at the new Halewood factory on Merseyside.

Ford-Germany: Only months after launching the new 1.2-litre front-

wheel-drive 12M, the 1.5-litre 12M TS appeared, this having 62bhp and a claimed top speed of around 84mph.

Hillman: In May, Rootes revealed the reason for its major investment in Scotland with the launch of the all-new Imp saloon. This square-rigged little car had all-independent suspension, a Coventry Climax-cloned 875cc overhead-cam engine mounted in the tail and, in spite of a rearward weight balance, it was a car which handled extremely well.

Nice touches included the opening rear window, which allowed luggage to be stowed behind the rear seat but ahead of the engine, and on the original cars there was pneumatic throttle control.

If build quality and product reliability had been better (blowing head gaskets and failed water pumps were endemic at first) the Imp family would have been more successful. In the event, the Linwood factory, designed to produce up to 150,000 cars a year, was never busy enough to make a profit.

This was the first of a whole family of Imps, badge-engineered with different styling or mechanically modified, which would arrive in the next few years – the last Imp of all would be produced in 1976.

Later in the year the Minx family became Series V (missing out Series IV completely) with front-wheel disc brakes standard, Borg-Warner instead of Smiths Easidrive as an optional automatic transmission, 13in instead of 15in wheels and a restyled nose and cabin roof; the wraparound rear window had been discarded and there were new-shape rear quarters.

The Husky became a Series III with the same front-end facelift as other Minx-type cars and was given more power, though it kept the 1.4-litre version of the engine, the price going up to £587.

Humber: The new Sceptre was really a much-modified Hillman Super Minx or Singer Vogue, though it also had a modified roof line with a wraparound front screen. The nose looked rather like that of a four-headlamp Sunbeam Rapier (it had actually been developed as a Rapier until a late stage...), there was a complex new facia/instrument panel and the 1.6-litre engine was in the 80bhp/twin-carb tune as found in the Rapier.

Disc front brakes, an overdrive transmission and a well-trimmed interior all helped to make it the most upmarket of the Super Minx family yet to be launched.

Jaguar: The S-type saloon, produced in 3.4-litre and 3.8-litre XK-engined forms, was a further development of the Mk 2 theme, though with independent rear suspension of the E-type/Mk X variety, and with a longer tail.

It was more expensive than the existing Mk 2 models, which remained in production, but it pointed the way that Jaguar's technical trend was moving as the 1960s progressed. Some observers did not like details of the new car's looks, thinking that the hooded headlamps were messy, but there were few arguments with its ride, and the performance was as exhilarating as ever.

Lamborghini: The first prototype of a new supercar marque was shown in Italy, first as a bare chassis and later with a two-seater fixed-head coupe body style. Ferruccio Lamborghini was determined to match everything which Ferrari could offer, so even the first Lamborghini outstripped Ferrari's best – offering twin-cam instead of single-cam cylinder heads, 3.5-litre V12s instead of 3-litre V12s, and all-independent suspension instead of a live rear axle.

There was never any doubt about the Lamborghini 350GT's performance. All that had to be done, thereafter, was to establish a reputation for reliability and build quality, which did not take long.

Lancia: The new Fulvia arrived in March, an ambitious and technically-modern front-wheel-drive saloon from Italy. Following the Lancia tradition, this was to be the first of a whole new family of cars, with sporty coupes and Zagato-styled sports models to follow.

Like the bigger Flavia, the Fulvia had a rather stodgily-styled four-seater saloon body. The new engine was a narrow-angle (13deg) V4, canted well over to one side of the car, initially a 58bhp/1.1-litre unit and incorporating two overhead camshafts in a common, full-width, light-alloy cylinder head. A 72bhp twin-carburettor (Fulvia 2C) version soon followed.

Valve gear operation, by rockers, was complex, but as there were part-

spherical combustion chambers, this was clearly an engine with a great deal of tuning potential. Four-wheel disc brakes and a light 'dead' beam axle completed an interesting technical specification.

Later in the year, the company's famous 'improve, mix, match and confuse' strategy went a stage further with the release of 1.8-litre derivatives of all Flavias and 2.8-litre V6 versions of the Flaminia, while keeping the original 1.5s in production; the British concessionaire must have found it almost impossible to provide parts and service for all these cars.

Mercedes-Benz: The 230SL sports tourer was an emphatic statement of the way that the German company's marketing approach to fast sporting cars had changed. Taking over at Sindelfingen from the 190SL *and* the 300SL (though how could any such car take over from the magnificent 300SL?), the 230SL was much more 'tourer' than 'sports'.

Based on the body platform and suspensions of the existing 220SE Fintail model family, though with a shorter wheelbase, the 230SL used an enlarged version of that car's six-cylinder engine. There was the option of a smart removable hardtop, which was so styled that it was almost instantly christened the 'pagoda' roof: Mercedes-Benz later pointed out that this style was not meant to lower the roofline, but to raise the sides! The car, in various guises and with a succession of three different engines, would remain in production until 1971.

The Grosse 600 was launched as a confident statement of how good a vast, high-priced, top-quality car could be, and it immediately made every likely competitor (including anything from Rolls-Royce and Cadillac) look seriously obsolete.

Every component and layout of this complex machine was new. There were two wheelbases for this enormous car – long (126in) and colossal (153.5in) – as derivatives of the same squarely-styled unit-construction shell, and even the lightest variety weighed nearly 5,400lb. Power was by a 6.3-litre overhead-cam V8 engine, backed by a sturdy new four-speed automatic transmission. All-independent suspension was by air springs, with self-levelling, and naturally there were disc brakes

all round. Also, there was a complex hydraulic system powering everything from brakes to seat adjustment, and from window operation to bootlid lock release.

Even though production was to be limited to a few hundred cars a year, there were saloons and limousines (one or two landaulettes would later be built, to special order), six-light or eight-light cabins, and four or even six passenger doors. A well-preserved 600 was apparently a magnificent, super-refined, magic carpet – but in later life older examples could be nightmares to maintain. Tycoons and dictators of African and Middle East nations loved them.

MG: Overdrive became available on the MGB in January, almost instantly becoming a very popular option.

Mini: The first of the Cooper S types appeared in April, this being one step up on the Mini-Cooper, with a special and more robust oversquare version of the A-series engine, of 70bhp/1,071cc, and with larger disc brakes. This car was specifically built with motorsport in mind, and there would be other even more specialized Cooper S models in 1964.

Morgan: The Plus Four Plus was a very controversial new Morgan, which would turn out to be a flop. Riled by constant criticism of the ageing style of traditional Morgans (a style that was still to be in evidence more than 30 years afterwards, with the cars selling better than ever!), Morgan clothed the existing chassis in a smooth but somehow gawky full-width coupe body style.

Glassfibre was used, and there was a small bubble-top covering the two seats, with wind-up windows in the doors, but beneath the skin the ride was as harsh and the character as uncompromising as ever. Only 26 of these cars would be made.

Once again the 4/4 was updated, becoming the Series V, this time with the latest 1.5-litre Cortina engine in either 60bhp or 78bhp tune.

NSU: The launch of the single-rotor Wankel-engined car called the Wankel Spider vied with the Porsche 911 as the most interesting new machinery on show in Frankfurt in September.

The Spider's engine was mounted in

the extreme tail, where NSU's conventional air-cooled piston engines would normally be situated. The rest of the chassis was conventional and predictable, for it was merely a neat open-top derivative of the existing Sport Prinz, once again with styling by Bertone. Thus, there was all-independent suspension, disc front brakes and a rearward weight bias. The first authoritative tests of the Spider would not appear until 1964/65.

NSU also continued to develop, evolve and enlarge its range of rear-engined cars with the introduction of the 1000 model. This looked similar to, but was longer than, the Prinz IV, and was fitted with a new overhead-cam air-cooled four-cylinder 1-litre unit. Surprisingly, it was nowhere near ready for sale, for production would not begin until May 1964.

Porsche: The famous 911 series was previewed at the Frankfurt show in September, though at that time it was called a 901, and again was not yet ready for production.

Porsche had been building VW-based 356 models since the late 1940s, and were heavily involved in secret design work for VW, but this new-generation sports coupe was really overdue. Not only were there no common components with the old 356 types, which continued, there were no VW parts, either. The 901/911 kept to the same basic layout as the 356 had always used – a rear-mounted air-cooled engine, all-independent suspension and a wind-cheating shape – but this time there was an all-new flat-six overhead-camshaft power unit and a five-speed transmission. The original car had a 2-litre/122cu in engine, rated at a mere 130bhp – Porsche flat-six engines have certainly come on a long way since then!

Almost swamped by this launch was the news that the long-running 356B series had advanced to 356C, the principal change being the adoption of disc brakes all round (previously these had only been found in Carrera 2-litre models). The Damen 60bhp model had disappeared, the two choices now being of 1.6-litre 75bhp or 95bhp types.

Renault: The nationalized French company continued its inexorable drive upmarket. A new version of the

still-new 956cc engine appeared, this time with 1,108cc, along with a new-generation all-synchromesh gearbox, these being fitted first to the sporty Caravelle. There was a great deal more stretch built into this wet-liner design, which would eventually reach 1.4 litres by the 1980s.

Riley: In March, less than two years after launch, the front-wheel-drive Mini-based Elf was updated with a 38bhp/998cc version of the A-series engine (this was the first use of this particular size) instead of the original 848cc unit.

Rover: The all-new P6 2000, which had been under development for a very long time, was finally revealed in October, and the 'battle of the 2000s' (for the Triumph 2000 appeared just seven days later) was joined.

The P6 was new from stem to stern, with a unit-construction base unit covered by bolt-on body skin panels (even the roof), with independent front suspension, de Dion rear suspension, four-wheel disc brakes and a four-cylinder overhead-camshaft engine. The ride was 'long' and soft, but the chassis extremely capable.

Sales of this 90bhp machine began at once, though the P6 would initially be outsold by the Triumph 2000: even so, these two cars would continue to fight, head to head, for the next 14 years.

Simca: The long-running Aronde range was finally dropped and replaced by a new, conventionally-engineered, but very smart 1300/1500 range in March 1963.

The existing 1,290cc engine was joined by a 1,475cc version, there was an all-synchromesh gearbox, the body style being neat, subtly rounded and a great advance on the old Aronde types. British sales began later in the year, with right-hand-drive supplies following early in 1964.

Singer: Copying its parent car, the Hillman Minx, the Gazelle adopted all the same changes for 1964.

Skoda: The Octavia/Felicia models became available with the larger, 1.2-litre, version of the existing engine.

Sunbeam: The Alpine sportscar

became Series III, with major improvements to the packaging, a new hard-top and – in general – a complete mechanical makeover.

The 1.6-litre engines were little changed (though for the fixed-head GT there was actually a power reduction), while a telescopic steering column was standardized, as were reclining front seats, while twin fuel tanks were fitted (one on each side of the boot space) instead of the original single tank. The Alpine III was a better-equipped and better-looking car than the Alpine II it replaced, but it would only have a life of one year as the Series IV model would appear in 1964.

Similarly, the Rapier became Series IV in the autumn, with a more powerful engine, smaller (13in instead of 15in) wheels and an adjustable-length steering column.

Rumours began to spread about the development of a Ford-USA V8-engined Sunbeam Alpine, though this was all a bit premature as the production car – the Sunbeam Tiger – would not be launched until April 1964.

Triumph: The new 2000 took over from the old Standard Vanguard Six, but was a completely different type of car. Longer, lower, better suspended and altogether more refined than any Vanguard had ever been, the new 2000 was an instant success. Power was by a 90bhp version of the Vanguard Six's 2-litre engine, there was independent front and rear suspension, and the attractive long-nose/short-tail style was by Giovanni Michelotti.

The Triumph 2000 did not reach the showrooms until January 1964, but it immediately started to outsell its brand-new rival, the Rover 2000. Both cars had a lot to offer, the Triumph's major advantages being its smooth six-cylinder engine and its more roomy interior.

The Herald 12/50 was an upmarket derivative of the 1200, complete with a 51bhp version of the 1,147cc engine, with front-wheel disc brakes and a slide-back sunshine roof as standard.

TVR: Having survived a recent bankruptcy and yet another change of management, the Blackpool company modified the Grantura Mk III by fitting the latest 1.8-litre MGB engine, and rearranging the facia/instrument panel.

Vanden Plas: The Austin 1100-based Princess 1100 was previewed, being a completely retrimmed and refurnished version of the already-familiar front-drive Austin/Morris 1100 model, with lots of wood, carpet and leather seating, complete with a Vanden Plas type of front grille.

Although this might sound like and unattractive way of gilding the lily, it paid off well, for the 1100 (and later the 1300, with an enlarged engine) would sell extremely well in the next 10 years.

Vauxhall: The all-new Viva, launched in September, gave Vauxhall a small family car to sell in the important Mini/Anglia/Imp/Herald class. Similar in many ways to the Opel Kadett, which had been introduced a year earlier, the Viva was an ultra-conventional car, with front-engine/rear-drive, but very 'Plain-Jane' styling, whose main selling points were low first cost and simplicity in service. Nevertheless, it would be a big seller, and there would be Vivas in the Vauxhall range for the next two decades.

The four-cylinder engines used in Victors were enlarged from 1,508cc to 1,594cc, which provided both power and torque improvements. Front discs became available on normal Victors, as well as being standard on VX4/90s.

Volkswagen: The process of refining the familiar rear-engined, air-cooled designs continued. A new version of the 1500, the 1500S, appeared with twin carburettors and a 10bhp power increase.

Wolseley: Like its sister car, the Riley Elf (see above), the Hornet was given a 998cc engine.

Industrial developments

In March, Jaguar surprised everyone by taking over Coventry Climax – even some of Coventry Climax's directors knew nothing of this in advance! There was no immediate change of policy by either concern, the first major step being that Climax's technical director, Walter Hassan, shortly moved back to Jaguar to oversee all engine design and development work in the group.

The shake-up of Standard-Triumph by Leyland continued. At the end of the year Stanley Markland stepped down from the managing director's position and at about the same time Donald Stokes took over as the Leyland Motor Corporation's managing director, and as chairman and chief executive of Standard-Triumph. During the next 12 years he would become even more important and influential...

Chrysler took a majority financial stake in Simca of France, thus developing its long-term plans for a European presence. This takeover would have little effect in Britain, though when Chrysler later bought a stake in the Rootes Group (in 1964), other British rivals began to sit up and take notice.

Ford-USA spent weeks negotiating to buy Ferrari, but although Enzo Ferrari originally encouraged the idea, the scheme eventually collapsed. As a direct reaction to the rebuff, Ford decided to set up its own team of racing sportscars, the Le Mans programme and the Ford GT of 1964 being the result.

In Germany, Porsche took over Reutter, the long-established bodyshell and seat manufacturers in Stuttgart. One component of Reutter, which produced Recaro seats, remained independent. This move not only guaranteed Porsche's body supplies for the future, but it also gave the sportscar maker more valuable assembly space.

Ford-UK's new assembly plant at Halewood started production during the year, the first cars being Anglia 105Es, Classics and Capris. The Corsair (announced in the autumn) soon joined it, displacing the Classic. One consequence was that Ford decided to run down car assembly at its ex-Briggs Motor Bodies factory in Doncaster, Anglia estate car assembly being transferred to Dagenham.

When the Ensign and Vanguard models were replaced by the new Triumph 2000, the Standard marque disappeared for good. At Standard-Triumph, the move from badging its cars as Standards to Triumphs had been in progress for some years, with the launch of the Triumph Herald in 1959 really signalling the beginning of the end.

Standard would still be around for a year or two on the group's light commercial vehicles, and there would still be some pensioned-off Standards in some overseas territories, but the Standard name was never seen again on a British car.

After a long and distinguished life, the Mercedes-Benz 300SL was finally discontinued. It had always been a costly car to build, and especially to maintain and repair, though it had always done great things for Mercedes-Benz's high-performance and technological image.

Technical developments

The much-vaunted Wankel engine was finally put on sale in a private car, the NSU Wankel Spider. In that form (described above), it was only a single-rotor engine, with which NSU was hoping to gain production car experience before launching more complex two-rotor engines later in the 1960s.

There had been much speculation about a Wankel engine's durability when the new technology was still at the prototype stage, most of this centring on tip seal wear, and how accurately the complicated rotor chamber would have to be machined.

Glas of West Germany introduced a new engine in which the overhead camshaft was driven by an internally-cogged belt: this was a technical 'first', whose popularity would rapidly spread. The traditional, long-established chain-makers were not impressed.

It may have been part-marketing, part-technical, but the arrival of two medium-sized 'executive' cars to compete in the 2-litre business car class was significant. Although the Rover 2000 and Triumph 2000 were technically quite different, both were aimed unerringly at a category which had not been properly served until that time. Within two years they were selling at the rate of 40–45,000 cars a year in total, and other makers were rushing to join in.

The most fascinating racing car of the year was the gas-turbine-engined Rover-BRM which appeared in the Le Mans 24 Hours race. This rather lumpily styled (or perhaps it should be unstyled) two-seater was a mid-engined machine, the combination of a widened 1961-vintage BRM F1 car's chassis and a 2S/150 Rover gas-turbine unit.

Except that it made excellent publicity for Rover *and* for BRM, this was not a very serious motor racing project as it was by no means fast enough to challenge for the lead in the race – nor could it actually compete as there was no gas-turbine category at the time! In 1963, when driven by BRM's con-tracted drivers Graham Hill and Richie Ginther, it completed the 24 hours at an average of 107.84mph, and would have finished eighth overall if classified.

Although Rover had virtually given up on gas-turbine engine development for cars, Chrysler of Detroit was still enthusiastic about this technology. The latest fourth-generation car – a smart two-door four-seater coupe – was shown, Chrysler promising to build 50 replicas for extended public trials.

Men of Influence

Lord Nuffield

When the BMC merger had been formalized and the dust had settled, it was clear that the Nuffield Organisation was always likely to be the junior partner. However, for the first year, Lord Nuffield was the group's chairman, but since he was already close to his 75th birthday he seemed to be ready (relieved, even) to step down at the end of the year, to become BMC's honorary president. By that time he had already been in the motor industry for 40 very successful years.

Born in 1877 in Worcester, William Richard Morris came to Oxford with his parents a few years later. At 14 years of age he became an apprentice bicycle repairer, set up his own business at Cowley in 1892, and soon began making pedal cycles. Motorcycles followed by 1900, and in 1902 his business was also beginning to service, repair and sell cars.

The Morris Garage was set up in 1910, and the first Morris Oxford car was shown in 1912. Starting from the nucleus of a redundant school building in Cowley, he then went on to build up a vast and sprawling factory complex, assembling more and more cars. During the 1920s the 'bullnose' Morris outsold every other British car, after which Morris not only developed a wider range and agreed to the development of MG (Morris Garages) sportscars, but bought control of companies like E G Wrigley (which became Morris Commercial), Hotchkiss (Morris Engines) and the Wolseley company.

All this had been achieved with his own personal finances, but in the 1930s he turned Morris into a public company, the resulting Nuffield Organisation becoming larger and more complex, but remaining equally as profitable. In 1938 Nuffield also rescued Riley from bankruptcy, but its further development was held back by the outbreak of war.

William Morris was knighted in 1929, became Lord Nuffield in 1934 (taking his title from the area of Oxford in which he had settled) and became a viscount in 1938. He never had children, and during this time he set about giving away large sums (totalling £30 million) to deserving causes. His last was to set up Nuffield College in Oxford.

Always a kindly, though gruff, uncommunicative man, he found it difficult to delegate authority to his subordinates, which explains why he quarrelled catastrophically with capable managers like Leonard Lord and Sir Miles Thomas, never giving them enough elbow room to develop a business which he increasingly neglected on long sea voyages taken 'for his health'.

After two false starts he finally struck an agreement with Len Lord to merge Nuffield with Austin, but he retired at the end of 1952. Thereafter, a somewhat lonely man, he used an early postwar Wolseley Eight to commute between Nuffield Place and his old office at Cowley (which has been preserved, in its entirely, latterly in the BMIHT collection at Gaydon), to look after his personal and charitable affairs.

He died in August 1963, just weeks before his 86th birthday.

1964

After 13 years of Conservative rule, the Labour Party took control, narrowly, at the General Election held in October. Although this had not been expected to make much difference to motorists at first, almost immediately there was a Budget in November which increased taxes and therefore reduced spending power. The same Budget added 6d (2.5p) to the price of petrol, which was widely criticized in the motoring press. [The average British weekly wage in those days was only £16.75.]

The result was that car sales, which had been roaring ahead throughout the year, abruptly peaked and began to decline. All-time records of 1.87 million cars produced and 1.22 million registered on the British market would not be matched again until the early 1970s.

The British and French Governments reached an agreement, in principle, to build the Channel Tunnel, costed at a mere £160 million, and construction work began later in the year. With the country's financial situation worsening, however, the digging would stop in 1965 and there would be no more progress until the late 1980s.

The Forth road bridge came into service in September. By the mid-1990s, 30 years after its inauguration, it was already overcrowded and a second bridge was being proposed.

We wondered what all the fuss was about at the time when a works AC Cobra, being prepared for the Le Mans 24 Hours race, was taken on to the M1 motorway at dead of night, where its driver waited in a service area for a lull of traffic (there were such things in those days!) before setting off and achieving 183mph. However, questions were asked in the House of Commons, and the resulting furore must have been one of the first steps along the way to imposing overall speed limits on British roads.

New models

AC: The Cobra was price-listed in the UK from the autumn at £2,454, though very few cars became available as Shelby American continued to take almost the entire output.

Alfa Romeo: The Giulia range continued to expand with the launch of the Giulia 1300 saloon, which used the Giulietta-sized 1,290cc engine. This one was easy to spot for it had two instead of four headlamps.

At the same time the Giulia Spider was given a more powerful (112bhp) version of the 1.6-litre engine, and there were more permutations on the Giulia theme still to come.

Alvis: At Earls Court Motor Show time power-assisted steering became optional on the TE21 models.

Aston Martin: From October 1964 there was a new and optional Vantage engine tune for the DB5, with a triple twin-choke Weber carburettor installation and a claimed 325bhp.

Austin: The third-generation Issigonis front-wheel-drive design, badged as an Austin 1800, was introduced. Later it would be joined by Morris and Wolseley (but no MG) versions. Like the Minis and 1100s, the 1800 featured a transverse engine with the gearbox in the sump, along with all-independent suspension.

For the 1800, however, the engine was a five-bearing version of the long-running B-series unit, while the suspension was by Hydrolastic units of almost the same type as those used in 1100s, though the front-end installation was totally different.

The A110 Westminster was given a mid-life makeover, complete with a four-speed (instead of three-speed) gearbox and trim improvements.

Austin-Healey: The 3000 Mk III arrived in February, being similar to the Mk IIA, but with a more powerful (148bhp) 2.9-litre engine and with a revamped interior including a wooden facia panel and revised storage/occasional seating in the '+2' area.

The Phase II 3000 Mk III did not appear until later in the year, for the tooling required had not been ready at first. Phase II incorporated revised main chassis side members, swept further down under the rear axle to allow more axle movement, along with the fitment of twin radius-arms to help locate the axle.

A few weeks later the Sprite became Mk III with a new rear suspension (half-elliptic instead of cantilever quarter-

elliptic leaves), wind-up windows and a larger windscreen, all topped off with a more powerful (59bhp) version of the 1.1-litre engine. The equivalent Midget was upgraded at the same time.

Bedford: The Beagle estate car was a conversion of the small Bedford van, which was itself a version of the Vauxhall Viva saloon which had been introduced in 1963. Although this was all too obviously a van conversion, it was very cheap (£620 when new) and would sell steadily for several years.

Bond: After little more than a year, the original Equipe was joined by the Equipe GT4S, which not only had a slightly roomier cabin, but was given a four-headlamp nose and a tail spoiler.

Facel Vega: The Facel 6, yet another derivative of the original Facellia design, was fitted with an Austin-Healey 3000 engine and gearbox, the engine being reduced in size to 2.8 litres for fiscal reasons. That, at least, is what the publicity material said – but BMC records show that engines supplied to France for fitment to this car were of the normal 2,912cc size! This particular Facel Vega was never officially marketed in the UK.

Ferrari: The most important new Ferraris of the year (there were several new model announcements) were the 275GTB Coupe and the closely related 275GTS Spider. Not only were these the first Ferraris to have 3.3-litre V12 engines, but they had combined five-speed gearbox/transaxle units and independent rear suspension. The GTB was a long, low, sleek, closed coupe, the GTS a more conventionally-styled open car.

The successful 3-litre 250GTE was dropped, to be replaced by the 330GT, which had effectively the same chassis and body, but with a 300bhp/4-litre V12 engine and a facelifted nose incorporating four headlamps.

Fiat: The new 850 saloon was really to the same formula as the existing 600 range, for there was a rear-mounted engine, independent front suspension by transverse leaf spring and semi-trailing/coil-spring rear suspension. But it *was* new, larger, and one more model in Fiat's increasingly large range. Why change a winning formula?

Ford: Early in the year, Borg-Warner automatic transmission became available on all 1.5-litre Cortinas and Corsairs except for Cortina GT and Lotus-Cortina models.

From October, all Cortinas were given a new type of ventilation with face-level vents and outlets in the rear quarters. Called Aeroflow, this was a real advance at family car level. At the same time, the Cortina received a mid-life facelift, with a different nose and yet another facia design.

Ford-Germany: There was a new range of 20M and 20M TS models, these being front-engined/rear-drive saloons powered by a series of closely-related V4 and V6 engines. Neither type had any relationship to engines which Ford-UK would announce a year later, but they would be an integral part of Ford-Germany's various ranges for many years to come. Indeed, the pushrod V6 engines – much enlarged and improved – still used to power Ford Scorpios in the mid-1990s were direct descendants of these power units.

Styling of the new 20M types was similar to that of the existing Ford-Germany front-drive models, though naturally much larger and somewhat smoother.

Ford-USA: The Mustang 'ponycar' made its phenomenal debut, and went on to sell at an amazing rate for the next two or three years. Although it was technically ordinary – the platform and suspensions being from the Falcon compact and the engines lifted straight out of Ford-USA's existing 'parts bin' – the Mustangs' long-bonnet/short-tail styling appealed greatly to young buyers in the USA. Indeed, the Mustang invented a new category all of its own, which GM and American Motors would hasten to join. British deliveries (of left-hand-drive cars) began later in the year.

Gordon-Keeble: Although the prototype Gordon GT had been seen as early as March 1960, it did not go on sale, as the Gordon-Keeble, until early 1964. In some ways this was the Peerless/Warwick GT approach grown-up, for Jim Keeble had designed the chassis, and the Bertone-styled body was constructed in glassfibre. Complete

with Chevrolet V8 engine, it went on sale for £2,798, which was certainly not enough to guarantee profitability, and it was built at a factory at Southampton Airport.

Hillman: Along with all other medium-sized Rootes cars, the Minx and Super Minx models inherited a new all-synchromesh gearbox. For 1965, too, the Super Minx had a cabin restyle, with flatter rear windows and no wraparound corners.

Humber: In what would turn out to be the final change to this long-running family, the Hawk/Super Snipe cars received a major facelift, which gave them a new roofline and six-window cabin, all atop the same basic shell as before. In addition, there was a new top-of-the-range model called the Imperial, which was really a better-equipped and furnished version of the Super Snipe.

The Hawk's engine was unchanged, but the Super Snipe/Imperial six-cylinder engine was tuned to produce 128.5bhp instead of the previous 124bhp. On the Imperial, automatic transmission was standard.

The Sceptre gained the same all-synchromesh gearbox as other medium-sized Rootes cars.

Jaguar: Three years after its successful introduction, Jaguar upgraded the already-famous E-type by giving it a 4.2-litre version of the XK engine, along with a new all-synchromesh gearbox, which had much more effective synchromesh than the previous box which Jaguar had been using for so many years. There were no styling changes.

The Mk X saloon also became a 4.2-litre car, again with the all-synchromesh gearbox, but there were many more modifications in this package. Marles Varamatic power-assisted steering was standardized, there were double-circuit brakes with a suspended vacuum servo, along with Borg-Warner Model 8 automatic transmission (where ordered as an option) in place of the old DG type.

Maserati: Though both models had previously appeared at European motor shows, the Quattroporte and the Mistrale were both new to the UK.

The Mistrale was a descendant of the 3500/3500GTi/Sebring family, with

Frua-styled two-seater bodies (coupe or convertible) and 3.7-litre fuel-injected engines.

The Quattroporte was much the largest Maserati so far to be put on sale, with a long-wheelbase four-door, five-seater body style and a front-mounted 4.2-litre V8 engine. These early cars were fitted with de Dion rear suspension, though a change to a conventional beam rear axle would follow a year or so later.

MG: The Midget became Mk II with the same changes as the Austin-Healey Sprite Mk III (see above).

Although the MGB looked to be technically unchanged for 1965, it was given a five-bearing version of the B-series 1.8-litre engine to bring it into line with the new Austin 1800.

Mini: The Cooper S range was fleshed-out with two extra engines – the short-stroke 65bhp/970cc version and the long-stroke 76bhp/1,275cc derivative. The 970cc-engined cars, in fact, did not become available until the end of the year, but the 1275S soon became the most popular Mini-Cooper S type of all.

After several years of previews, trials and leaks, the Mini-Moke finally went on sale, badged as an Austin or a Morris and fitted with the standard Mini 850 engine, transmission and suspension units. Though based on the Mini's layout, the open-top structure was unique, with four seats, very low sides and no doors. A rudimentary hood was provided, but there were no side curtains. Clearly this machine was only suitable for dry-weather territories, but it also achieved a brief fashion in 'trendy' London. By 1968, though, it would be withdrawn from British production, though later it was revived in Australia, and later still in Portugal.

From October, all Mini passenger cars were given the BMC 1100-type Hydrolastic suspension in place of the original rubber cone-springs, and there was a price increase of £21 to match this. This was not a totally successful move, and five years later it was to be reversed to rubber cone-springs again!

Moskvich: The latest-generation Moskvich, the Type 408, was shown at the Earls Court Motor Show in October, though British deliveries were not expected to begin until 1965. Visually more to European tastes than its predecessor, though still rugged and durable rather than plush and seductive to drive, the Type 408 had little to offer over British and Western European competition. Smaller than the current Cortina, but quite significantly heavier, the latest Russian car had a 55bhp/1.4-litre engine and strictly conventional chassis engineering.

Porsche: Previewed in 1963 as the 901, the new 130bhp flat-six-engined 911 finally went into production; 911-family machines have been on sale ever since. Soon it was to be joined by the 912, a strictly interim model, being a clever (and successful) amalgam of the new 911's structure with the 90bhp flat-four pushrod engine from the not-yet-obsolete 356C model. Even in this form it was a 120mph car.

Reliant: The smart new Scimitar GT took over from the Sabre models and was an instant success. There was a separate steel chassis, with Triumph TR4-type front suspension, and with the rear axle located by leading and trailing arms, sprung on coils. The engine was a 120bhp version of the 2.6-litre Ford six-cylinder unit.

Styling of the glassfibre body was by Ogle Design, and based closely on a special Daimler SP250 exhibited briefly at an earlier Earls Court Motor Show. There was an upholstered shelf behind the front seats, but this was not really a 2+2 model.

At the same time, the new small Rebel four-seater was also introduced, using many existing chassis items from the current Reliant three-wheeler, including the light-alloy 27bhp/598cc engine, along with Scimitar-type front suspension. The small (11ft 6in long) four-seater saloon style was in glassfibre.

Renault: Having introduced the Caravelle 1100 in 1963, Renault then launched the larger-engined R8 1100 in February 1964, along with an all-synchromesh four-speed gearbox.

A new type of car, the R16, was previewed, but would not go on sale, or be fully described, until January 1965. At this stage Renault merely revealed that the 16 would have front-wheel drive and that it had a sharply-styled hatchback structure.

The R8 Gordini was a purposeful high-performance derivative of the R8, complete with a 95bhp version of the 1,108cc engine, which included a totally new cylinder head with part-spherical combustion chambers. All such Gordinis came in French blue, with white striping kits which could be fitted, or otherwise, by the customer after taking delivery.

Simca: The smart Bertone-styled 1000 Coupe went on sale in the UK in left-hand-drive form.

Singer: The Vogue was updated alongside the Hillman Super Minx to become Mk III, with a restyled roof and an all-synchromesh gearbox. The Gazelle also received the all-synchromesh box.

The new rear-engined Chamois was no more than a slightly more upmarket version of the Hillman Imp.

Skoda: The Czechoslovakian company introduced a brand-new model, the rear-engined 1000MB, which was to be its mainstay for more than a decade, and would help give rise to countless Skoda jokes in many countries.

Structurally, though, it was no joke, for clearly it had drawn on cars like the Renault Dauphine/R8 for its layout. The four-door monocoque style hid a new type of 1-litre pushrod engine (complete with wet liners) mounted in the tail, and although there was all-independent suspension, this was the limit of technological advance, for the trim and fittings were spartan, the build quality variable, and the roadholding was also suspect in certain conditions. However, it was extremely cheap, and since it had a captive market in Czechoslovakia, its long-term future was assured.

Sunbeam: Early in the year, after less than 12 months of life, the Alpine Series III gave way to the Series IV, which was changed visually with slight alterations to the nose and a major reduction in the height of the tailfins. An automatic transmission option (by Borg-Warner) became available for the first time on this range.

The Tiger made its debut in April, with all the style changes already phased in for Alpine Series IV, but with a 4.2-litre Ford-USA V8 engine, a Ford-USA gearbox and a Salisbury back axle. Rack-and-pinion steering

with very strange geometry was fitted, while the rear-axle movement was kept partly in check by a Panhard rod. For the time being, all Tiger deliveries were aimed at the USA – British sales would begin in the spring of 1965.

In October, the four-cylinder Sunbeams – Alpine and Rapier – both inherited the new Rootes all-synchromesh gearbox.

Vanden Plas: The introduction of the Princess 4-litre R was the only evidence of any lasting links between BMC and Rolls-Royce, which had been founded with such optimism in 1962. The 4-litre R was effectively no more than a re-engined Princess 3-litre with styling changes, the engine being a 3.9-litre six-cylinder Rolls-Royce type developing 175bhp (gross).

Although there were modern details in the engine, it was actually based on 1940s technology, for the valve gear and other details were all closely related to the obsolete six-cylinder engine which had been fitted to Rolls-Royce/Bentley models from 1946 to 1955.

Styling changes included smoothing-out the tail to eliminate the fins of the 3-litre, there was a different roofline, and Borg-Warner Model 8 automatic transmission was standard. The 'R' part of the Princess R name was never explained – R for Rolls...Royce...Royal? Who knows?

Although this car received a warm reception (it cost £1,994 when new), demand collapsed after two years and the model would be withdrawn early in 1968.

Vauxhall: The third-generation Victor and VX4/90 – known officially as the 101 Series – appeared in October with the same basic mechanical equipment, floorpans and running gear as before, but with smoother body styles. By this time the Victor was almost unrecognizably different from the awkwardly styled original of seven years earlier, and was considerably more popular for that reason. Competent if not exciting, these cars went on to sell in large quantities before finally being made obsolete in 1967.

The Velox/Cresta range was given newly-developed 3.3-litre engines with 115bhp, and although a three-speed gearbox was still standard, a four-speed box now became optional for the first time.

Wartburg: British imports of this two-stroke-engined front-wheel-drive car from East Germany began in May. Although these were not technically advanced, nor well-equipped cars, they were low-priced and would sell steadily until the early 1970s, when the public tired of buying smelly two-stroke machines.

Wolseley: Like the Austin A110, the Wolseley 6/110 was given a four-speed gearbox.

Industrial developments

Having suffered big losses after the BLSP strike of 1961 and in setting up the Linwood factory in Scotland, Rootes was rumoured to be looking for a richer partner. In June, Chrysler-USA bought a major financial stake in the Rootes Group – 30 per cent of the voting shares and 50 per cent of the non-voting stock; later in the year this investment was valued at £12.5 million.

Except that Chrysler's involvement underpinned the future of Rootes, there was no immediate effect on the company, or its products. Straight-away, though, cynics could see the potential embarrassment of Chrysler having a stake while the Sunbeam Tiger used Ford-USA V8 engines.

Facel Vega finally stopped making cars, for their business had never recovered from the traumas of producing Facellias with unreliable engines.

Technical developments

Although the Autobianchi Primula was never to be sold in the UK, it qualifies as showing the most important technical advance of the year. For Autobianchi, of course, read Fiat – for this was a subsidiary of the Italian giant.

As we now know, Fiat had used the Primula as a mass-production testbed for its own ideas on front-wheel drive. Technical guru Dr Dante Giacosa had studied the Issigonis/Mini formula, found it wanting in some respects, and developed his own layout. The Primula, therefore, was the very first car to have its transverse engine offset to one side, and with its gearbox 'end-on' rather than underneath or behind the cylinder block.

Even so, it took years for Fiat to digest the information gained – the *next* such Fiat layout to be launched was the 128, which would not appear until 1969.

Men of Influence

Sir William (Lord) Rootes

When he absorbed Singer in the winter of 1955/56 and inspired the birth of the Singer Gazelle, Sir William ('Billy') Rootes had not only added to his business empire, but had annexed the company where he had been apprenticed before the First World War. Certainly he made much of this 'return to base' in public pronouncements at the time.

Born in Hawkhurst, Kent, in 1894, to a family whose father owned a small cycle shop, William Rootes began running the Maidstone branch of that business in 1913, served in the RNVR during WW1, then joined forces with his younger brother Reginald to build up Rootes Ltd, a garage business which started life in Maidstone.

Rapid expansion in the 1920s saw Rootes become Britain's largest motor trade distributors, based at Devonshire House, in London's Piccadilly. Having bought Thrupp & Maberly (a London coachbuilder), with backing from the cash-rich Prudential Assurance Company, Rootes moved on to take stakes in Hillman and Humber, which would soon merge, with Rootes having taken control, thus founding what is now known as the Rootes Group. Once Rootes had introduced the all-new Hillman Minx, then taken control of Sunbeam and Talbot (both members of the moribund and financially chaotic STD combine), the Group had become very important indeed, controlling more than 10 per cent of UK car production. Then, and for the next 30 years, William Rootes was always at the helm, latterly as company chairman.

Having joined the Government's shadow factory scheme in 1936, bought a further pressings company (BLSP, in London), and run two further vast Government factories – at Ryton-on-Dunsmore and Speke – 'Billy' became Sir William in 1942, and pressed on to the future.

For Rootes, the next 20 years saw almost continual expansion, for after Singer was purchased Rootes output rose steadily to 150,000 cars a year by 1960. Unhappily, Rootes then had to face a 13-week strike at BLSP in 1961 (which it won, by sacking the workforce then rehiring those it wanted...), and was then persuaded to expand into Scotland to build its new small car, the Hillman Imp, where the Linwood project was never profitable.

Sir William, who became Lord Rootes in 1959, was finally obliged to sell a stake in his business to Chrysler of the USA. This move was finalized in the autumn of 1964, but he died only a few weeks later, in December 1964, aged 70.

His eldest son Geoffrey succeeded to the hereditary title, while his younger brother, Reginald, took over as chairman of Rootes.

1965

This was the first full year for British motorists under a Labour administration since 1950: due to the higher taxes introduced near the end of 1964, sales of new cars in 1965 were slightly down over the record previous year. However, in the April Budget, the only extra tax on motoring was an increase in the annual licence fee from £15 to £17 10s (£17.50).

With the opening of the elevated section of the M4 into Chiswick in March, Heathrow airport was much more closely connected to central London. This was the first British motorway to reach closely towards the centre of a big city.

As in 1964, there was an overall 50mph speed limit on Britain's roads during the busiest holiday weekends, but again this was widely ignored (and not actively policed). Although Government sources insisted that accidents fell, it did not persist with this experiment. On the other hand, permanent 50mph speed limits were applied to many specific sections of road.

The biggest blow of all, though, came in December, when a so-called 'experimental' 70mph upper speed limit was applied to all main roads, including motorways. Imposed on the flimsiest of excuses following a series of motorway accidents in thick fog, this limit would subsequently be reviewed and made permanent. Never again would Britain's motorists be able to drive at speeds comfortable to themselves – they would have to go abroad for that.

New models

AC: At Earls Court in 1965, the Frua-styled 428 was previewed, though at this time it was called the AC 427! Basically, this was a long-wheelbase version of the 7-litre Cobra's chassis and running gear, all topped off by a modern two-seater convertible body style by Frua of Italy. It was not yet ready to go into production, but eventually a two-seater fixed-head coupe version would also be made available.

Alfa Romeo: The Giulia Super was yet another version of the Giulia range, having the usual four-door saloon body, but a more powerful (98bhp) version of the 1.6-litre engine. A convertible (the GTC) was shown in Italy at the same time, but was never imported to the UK.

Aston Martin: The DB6 took over directly from the DB5, though the old type of convertible model carried on for a while. Compared with the DB5, the DB6 had a 3.75in longer wheelbase and a significantly enlarged cabin which offered more genuine '+2', or 'almost four-seat' accommodation.

Structurally and technically it was virtually the same as the DB5, though as it was heavier it was not quite as fast through the gears.

Audi: Now that VW was in control of the Auto Union Group, one of its famous names – Audi – was revived. The new Audi 70 was effectively a re-engined and modified DKW F102, the engine being a brand-new four-stroke 1.7-litre unit which had been designed by Mercedes-Benz, and was distinguished by a very high compression ratio of 11.2:1 at first.

The new front-wheel-drive 70 had torsion-bar independent front suspension, with the engine mounted ahead of the line of the transaxle. It set the standard for a range which would grow considerably in the next few years, for the last of this type would not be built until 1972.

Austin: The AP automatic transmission (see Technical developments, below) became optional on 1100s.

Bentley: Except for its badges, the new T-series, introduced in October, was exactly the same as the Rolls-Royce Silver Shadow, details of which are given below.

BMW: The 2000CS was a smart two-door Karmann-bodied coupe version of the established 1600/1800 platform, this time with a 120bhp/2-litre version of the modern overhead-camshaft engine. Although the four-cylinder-engined coupe would only be built until 1968, it was the first of a long line of cars developed around this basic style.

Bristol: Only two years after the 408 had been introduced, it was displaced by the 409, which was basically the same car, though now with a slightly enlarged engine and a Dunlop all-disc braking installation.

Citroen: It was time for a shake-up of the DS/ID range, which was already 10 years old. For 1966 the old long-stroke engine was confined to ID19-type models. For DS models there was a new short-stroke engine with a five-bearing crankshaft and opposed valves in part-spherical combustion chambers (some of the chambers also being in the crown of the pistons); the engine was being built in 1,985cc and 2,175cc sizes.

At the same time an all-synchromesh transmission was specified. With the new larger engine, these cars became DS21s or (in the highest possible state of tune and equipment) DS21 Pallas.

(For a short period, British-assembled cars used slightly different names – DE referring to ID19-type cars, DLs having the new short-stroke 2-litre engine. British assembly, however, ended during 1966.)

Daihatsu: The Compagno, which was a total marketing failure in the UK, goes down in history as the first-ever Japanese car to be price-listed in the UK.

With a separate chassis, torsion-bar front suspension and a cramped four-door cabin, the Compagno's small overhead-valve engines (795cc or 958cc were both available in Japan, but only the smaller unit was marketed in the UK) could hardly get this Oriental misfit up to 70mph. A curiosity value machine at the time, it is even more so today.

Fiat: There were two new models, both developed from the still-new 850 saloon and retaining the saloon's platform and tuned versions of the engine. The 850 Coupe was a conventional-looking 2+2 closed coupe by Fiat's own styling studio, whereas the 850 Spider was a Bertone-styled open two-seater. Both these cars were available in right-hand-drive form before the end of 1965.

In the final change made to this model before it gave way to the 124 Spider, the 1600S Tourer was given a five-speed gearbox, which was being consumer-tested ahead of its use in much higher quantities on future Fiats.

Ford: The innovation of the year was the arrival of the Corsair V4/Corsair GT models, which meant that the existing Corsair had been re-engined with two versions of a brand-new type of V4 engine – in 1,663cc and 1,996cc forms. Although the new engine was not as smooth as the straight 'four' which it replaced, and did not share the same top-end breathing characteristics, there was more torque than before.

Along with the addition of Aeroflow ventilation, this helped to distance the Corsair from the Cortina on which its platform was based.

In mid-year, without fanfare, the Lotus-Cortina's troublesome coil-spring rear suspension was dropped and replaced by a Cortina GT-like leaf-spring and radius-arm set-up. At a stroke, reliability was transformed, and no-one ever complained about a change to the roadholding. Also at a stroke, the Lotus-Cortina became a sturdy and viable rally car.

Early in the year the Zodiac Executive, a top-of-the-range version of the existing Zodiac, was added to the range, mechanically unchanged, but with acres more wood, leather and a higher price of £1,303.

Gordon-Keeble: After a short and unprofitable production career, the GK1 Grand Tourer project failed. Although the business was sold to new sponsors, little could be done to revive it. Only 99 cars were sold.

Hillman: Along with all other derivatives (Humber, Singer and Sunbeam) of the Minx/Super Minx models, there was an enlarged 1,725cc engine, complete with a five-bearing crankshaft.

Later in the year, to back up a motorsport programme, the very limited-production Rallye Imp was announced. This was effectively a conversion of the existing Imp, with a 998cc engine producing 65bhp, along with revised suspension and a few other equipment upgrades.

Humber: The Sceptre received a facelift which really revolved on it using the same front-end pressings as the Hillman Super Minx (previously, unique pressings had been used), along with the latest 1,725cc engine (see Hillman, above). Automatic transmission was a new option.

Iso: The short-wheelbase two-seater Grifo, a close mechanical relation of the Rivolta, was added to the range. Although still Chevrolet-engined and therefore not 'pure-bred' as far as some diehards were concerned, the Grifo was a 160mph car, offering genuine competition for the front-engined Ferraris and Maseratis of the day.

Jensen: The C-V8 became Mk III in mid-summer with a slightly revised body style and interior changes.

At the Motor Show, a four-wheel-drive prototype, the FF, was displayed, though the new chassis was hidden by C-V8-style bodywork. This car did not go into production, but it was the forerunner of the new-generation FF, which would be launched a year later.

There was also a new open-top Interceptor prototype at Earls Court, but once again this was a one-off which did not go on sale.

Lamborghini: At the Turin show, a one-off chassis was shown, having a mid-engined/rear-drive layout and using a 4-litre version of the already famous V12 engine. This was the genesis of the legendary Miura, though the complete car would not be shown until the Geneva show of March 1966.

Lancia: The Fulvia Coupe had been forecast since the original Fulvia saloon had been introduced, but when it appeared in 1965 it was seen to be even more attractive than expected. The Fulvia's chassis platform was shortened, but the 1.2-litre engine was in a higher state of tune (80bhp) than those fitted to 2C saloons.

Lotus: The Elan Coupe appeared, three years after the launch of the original Elan. This was a neat bubble-top version of the sportscar, with near-identical styling, but higher overall gearing, and was still only a snug-fitting two-seater.

Mercedes-Benz: Wholesale changes were made to the German company's model line-up in the autumn. Some of the long-established Fintail models continued, in four-cylinder and small-capacity six-cylinder forms, while there was a new type W108 S-class, with a larger, wider, flatter, body style and originally with carburetted and fuel-injected 2.5 and 3-litre engines. The Type W108

would have a seven-year life, with all cars featuring all-independent suspension and four-wheel disc brakes. The 2.5-litre engine was largely new, with a seven-bearing crankshaft, though the 3-litre was one of the last of the long-running family which had first appeared in the early 1950s.

MG: The MGB GT of October 1965 was an extremely smart coupe/hatchback derivative of the MGB sportscar, which would have a long and extremely successful career.

With a style retouched by Pininfarina, this was almost a small saloon and was fitted with what turned out to be quite useless 'occasional' rear seats.

Mini: AP automatic transmission (see Technical developments, below) became available on Minis from the end of the year. Although this sounded incongruous at first, it was actually a very attractive package, and in further developed form was still optional on such BMC-derived cars 30 years later.

The 1,000,000th Mini was built at Longbridge in February. BMC was very proud of this, but did not like to admit that the Mini was still a long way behind the VW Beetle, and falling further behind every day. The Mini would still be in production in the mid-1990s, with total sales then well over the 5,000,000 mark.

Morris: The new AP automatic transmission (see Technical developments, below), became optional on 1100s.

NSU: Two more derivatives of the Prinz 1000 appeared, both with a larger, 1,085cc version of the existing rear-mounted four-cylinder engine. The Typ 110 was the mainstream model, while the 1000TT was a more highly tuned version, with front-wheel disc brakes as standard and larger-diameter wheels.

Peugeot: It had been a long time since this French company had announced a new model, never mind a totally-new one like the 204, which was introduced in March. It was a conventionally-styled four-door, front-wheel-drive saloon with a transverse engine, but with its gearbox behind rather than beneath the line of the crankshaft. The engine itself was a newly-designed overhead-cam 1.1-litre 'four', there was all-independent suspension, front disc brakes and the promise of a typically supple Peugeot ride. British imports, in right-hand-drive form, were expected to begin before the end of the year.

Porsche: Already the 911 range was expanding, for the Targa version (complete with removable roof panel) was previewed at the Frankfurt show.

Reliant: Without fuss, the Scimitar's chassis layout was changed so that the rear axle was henceforth to be located by a conventional twin-radius-arm and Watts-linkage system.

Renault: The all-new R16 broke every previous Renault passenger-car mould. Although it was not the French company's first front-wheel-drive vehicle (there was already such a commercial vehicle on French roads), it was the first front-wheel-drive Renault car.

Soon to become familiar as a Renault layout, the engine/transmission unit was in the 'north-south' mode (in-line rather than transverse), with the engine behind the line of the front wheels and the transmission ahead of it. The engine was totally new, with aluminium cylinder head and block, along with wet-liner construction, and was set to have a very long life at the *Regie*. There was long-travel all-independent suspension by torsion bars all round, and the sharply-styled five-seater body included a hatchback in the tail. Not only for Renault, but for the rest of Europe, the new R16 was an extremely significant car.

In mid-summer, most R8 models (but not the Gordinis) were facelifted, with lengthened noses and tails, but with no chassis changes.

Riley: The new Kestrel, introduced in October, was an upmarket version of the front-wheel-drive Austin/Morris/MG 1100 design, and the Wolseley 1100 (*see below*) was its near-identical clone. Structurally and mechanically, Kestrels were identical to the twin-carb 55bhp MG 1100, though with their own distinctive radiator grilles and facia/instrument/furnishing styles. They were only available in four-door saloon guise.

Rolls-Royce: By any standards, this was the most important new-model launch which Rolls-Royce had ever

tackled. Except that the V8 engine and the GM Hydramatic gearbox of the old Silver Cloud car were retained (though the gearbox, too, would shortly be displaced by a new three-speed transmission), everything was new.

This was the first Rolls-Royce to use a unit-construction bodyshell, the first to have all-independent suspension (with self-levelling), and the first to use disc brakes. With a large but sensibly-proportioned four-door saloon style, it looked modern, but not outrageous, and as usual there had been a great deal of detailed development to get the feel and operation of all controls absolutely right.

Compared with the Silver Cloud, the Silver Shadow was nearly 7in shorter, 4in lower and 4in narrower. Because it was better-shaped and lighter than the Silver Cloud series, which was now obsolete, it was a faster car, though fuel economy (at around 12mpg) was still awful.

Deliveries did not begin until the first quarter of 1966, when the Silver Shadow was found to have an ultra-soft ride, and the handling was something of a disappointment.

The Silver Shadow would continue in production until 1980, after which the Silver Spirit (which was based on the same basic platform and suspension layouts) took over.

Singer: The Gazelle and Vogue models received a 1,725cc engine (*see Hillman, above*).

Sunbeam: The Ford V8-engined Tiger went on UK sale in March, priced at £1,446. In the autumn, the Alpine and Rapier models both received the enlarged 1,725cc engine (*see Hillman, above*).

Toyota: Although the Daihatsu Compagno (*see above*) was the first Japanese car to be marketed in the UK, the Toyota Corona was the first serious contender from that country.

Priced at £777, this was another ultra-conservative front-engined, rear-drive car, which did not seem to pose any problems for British models. That, at least, might have been true in 1965, but Toyota went on to become one of the most significant Japanese importers, would set up its own production plant in Britain, and by the 1990s was Japan's largest car manufacturer.

Triumph: The 1300, previewed in October, was Triumph's first front-wheel-drive car. However, technically it was simpler than the fashionable Minis and 1100s. The 1.3-litre engine was an enlarged, eight-port version of the Herald/Spitfire unit, and in this car it sat in line, above the final-drive unit which fed power to the front wheels. In this ingenious package, the four-speed transmission was below the clutch, behind the final-drive.

The four-door style, by Michelotti, was really a small version of the 2000, and was trimmed to similar standards, with a wood-trimmed facia. Like the Mini/1100 layout, the engine sat rather high in the engine bay, but the handling did not seem to be much affected. Along with all-independent suspension, front-wheel disc brakes and the upmarket interior, this was an appealing car, which finally went on sale in January 1966.

The TR4A sportscar took over from the TR4, looking almost the same, but with an entirely new chassis underneath. Engine power was only up slightly – to 104bhp – but the new chassis incorporated independent rear suspension, very similar to that used in the Triumph 2000 saloon.

At the same time the Spitfire advanced to Spitfire 2, with a slightly more powerful (67bhp) version of the 1,147cc engine.

At the end of the year, the 2000 estate car was introduced, this being a well-trimmed and successful version of the 2000 saloon.

Vauxhall: New in October, the Viva SL90 was a more powerful version of the original Viva, with 10bhp more from a twin-carburettor engine.

In mid-year the Velox/Cresta range was given a change of automatic transmission option – GM Powerglide instead of Hydramatic – along with a new option of power steering.

Powerglide also became available on Victor 101 and VX4/90 models.

Then, in October, a new-generation Cresta was launched to take over from the 1962–65 variety. Mechanically it was much as before, with a torquey 3.3-litre six-cylinder engine, a choice of transmissions and a very roomy five-seater cabin, but there was a new and rather smoother style. As before, door pressings and a few other details were shared with the current Victor, this time the 101 model.

The old Velox name was dropped.

Volkswagen: In preparation for the 1966 model year, there were several new models. For the already-old Beetle, there was more power for the 1200 model, along with the alternative of a new 1.3-litre-engined model. At the same time this engine became available for the Karmann-Ghia coupe/convertible models.

The notchback 1500 models were displaced by the 1600TL, which was a fastback with a 54bhp/1.6-litre engine and front-wheel disc brakes.

Wolseley: The new 1100 arrived on the same day as the Riley Kestrel (*see above*) and was really the same car with different badging.

Industrial developments

BMC took over the Pressed Steel Company in mid-year, which made much industrial sense for them, but put some of Pressed Steel's other customers – notably Rootes, Rover, Triumph and Rolls-Royce – into a quandary. In fact this spurred on the search for alternative body supply sources, and was just one more instance of the way in which Britain's motor industry was beginning to consolidate.

Rover took over Alvis, but there was no immediate change in policy by either company. This was an agreed rather than a contested merger, the main commercial advantages being to bring the two companies' military vehicle interests together and to give Rover a little more factory space. Rover-Alvis, in fact, would only be independent until the winter of 1966/67, when Leyland Motors put in an offer for the combined business.

Triumph announced that it had agreed to manufacture a new engine for Saab, but gave few other details. In fact this was the start of the slant-4 overhead-camshaft engine programme. The engine would first be fitted to the Saab 99, which went on sale in 1968, and the first Triumph to use it would be the Dolomite 1850 of 1972.

Jaguar continued to build its empire by buying Henry Meadows Ltd of Wolverhampton. This company, once famous for producing proprietary engines for cars, now concentrated on the larger commercial vehicle diesel-engine market, so the Jaguar purchase had no implications for its car-building strategy.

Lotus announced that it had outgrown its factory at Cheshunt, in Hertfordshire, and had decided to moved to Hethel Airfield, south of Norwich. The move, it was suggested, would not be made until the end of 1966 – in the event it was not completed until 1967.

Citroen concluded its takeover of Panhard (it had held a 45 per cent stake since the mid-1950s), but apparently had no plans to rejuvenate the Panhard range. The extra factory space acquired was much more attractive to Citroen, which had outgrown its own Paris headquarters.

Also in Europe, Volkswagen took financial control of Auto Union (which included DKW and the soon-to-be-announced Audi), which hitherto had been supported by Mercedes-Benz. Although this was not spelt out at the time, VW and Mercedes-Benz also agreed not to compete with each other in the same market sectors.

Technical developments

Looking back, the arrival of the Renault R16, complete with its hatchback style, was a technical milestone. Before this, cars were usually either saloons (or notchbacks, as the North Americans would call them), coupes, or estate cars. Although the R16 was not the first car with a hatchback body – there was one on a late-1930s Citroen, and of course another on the Aston Martin DB2/4 of 1953 – it was the first to use a full-size rear door in conjunction with such a versatile interior, including fold-down seats. As such, it established the trend, although it would be 1969, with the arrival of the Austin Maxi, before it would have a competitor in Britain.

AP's new four-speed automatic transmission was a real breakthrough, not merely because it was meant for use in small, low-powered cars, but because it was specifically developed to fit into a BMC Mini or 1100 in place of the existing manual gearbox. At the time, no other automatic transmission was as small, or as delicately packaged.

By the standards of 1965, Ford's introduction of a new family of 60-degree V-engines was technically adventurous. At first only the V4 (for the Corsair) was revealed, but it was common knowledge within the industry that a V6 version would soon follow. To minimize vibration problems, the V4 had a counter-rotating counter-weighted shaft.

NSU began co-operation with Citroen over Wankel rotary engine developments and revealed a twin-rotor power unit which, they said, would be available in two years' time. We now know that this engine was earmarked for the NSU Ro80, but there would never be a series-production Citroen car with rotary power.

1966

As the New Year opened, Mrs Barbara Castle – a non-driver – took over from Tom Frazer as Minister of Transport, then in March there was another General Election, which saw the existing Government returned with an increased majority, now up to 96, which meant that the politicians were secure to implement whatever policies they wanted.

However, a credit squeeze was shortly forced upon them and a pay and prices freeze for 12 months was applied from mid-year. In the main this held, but relations with trade unions were permanently soured, one result being an outbreak of unofficial strikes over pay, the most serious being a series of stoppages at BMC.

Purchase tax was increased from 25 to 27.5 per cent, which was not too depressing as it hoisted Mini prices by just £8 and Jaguar Mk X prices by only £38. But the foreign travel allowance was slashed from £250 to a miserable £50 per person, hire purchase restrictions were tightened and petrol prices were pushed up by 4d (1.6p) a gallon, the inevitable result being that car production and sales sagged.

Nevertheless, more than 1,000,000 British cars were sold during the year, and imports hit a new high at 66,793 to claim a still-modest market share of 6 per cent – about a tenth of what would be achieved in the heady days of the 1980s.

BMC was still Britain's largest car-making group, the SMMT's summary of British production in 1966 revealing:

BMC	604,348
Ford	466,177
Vauxhall	172,777
Rootes Group	171,904
Triumph	121,212
Rover-Alvis	39,676
Jaguar-Daimler	22,958
All others	4,627
Total:	1,603,679

Among the 66,793 imported cars, only 654 came from North America, of which 135 were Ford Mustangs with a whole variety of engine and body types and around 200 were Ramblers. Fewer than 100 were Chryslers, the rest being from General Motors.

Later, the SMMT revealed that the BMC 1100 was Britain's best-selling car, but this was after combining the sales recorded under all the six marque-badges. The individual best-seller was the Ford Cortina, with 127,037 registrations.

The British road-building programme continued apace – though Government cutbacks on expenditure didn't help – and while M1 continued to march northwards towards Sheffield and Leeds, the M4 Severn Bridge was finally opened.

The disgraceful farce surrounding the imposition of a national 70mph speed limit continued when, after a so-called four-month 'experiment' to assess its effects (during which statistics disproving the worth of the limit were blatantly ignored), the Government extended the trial period for a further two months and later pushed it even further forward towards a review date in September 1967. By this time few people expected the 'anti-motoring' politicians ever to abandon the 'experiment', and so it proved; the limit has been with us ever since.

Meanwhile, tourism and the movement of cars was getting easier. Hover-lloyd opened the first regular cross-channel hovercaft service in April, linking Ramsgate and Paris. British Railway's car-carrying service (which finally came to an end in May 1995) was rationalized in 1966 with the opening of the new Motorail terminal at Kensington Olympia station, on the West London Line, alongside the well-known exhibition halls. In spite of protests from local residents, all existing services were concentrated on this site for some years, which meant that trains for the north had to start their journey with a serpentine passage of the tracks in North London.

Roadworthiness testing of older cars continued to tighten, with a 'four-year' test being introduced during the year.

New models

Alfa Romeo: The most important new model of the season was the short-wheelbase open-top Giulia Spider, subsequently named Duetto. This had the shortest-yet version of the Giulia's platform, topped by Pininfarina two-seater styling which featured deep scallops along the side and a long and rounded tail. Previewed at Geneva in March 1966, it went on sale during the summer.

Yet another derivative of the boxy Guilia saloon was the new 1300 TI, which used the old-size 1.3-litre Giulietta engine with 83bhp, matched to a five-speed gearbox and with the existing Giulia soft-sprung chassis components. It went on sale in the UK later in the year.

In the same type of equipment shuffle, the elegant Giulia Sprint became the GTV, along with a more powerful (109bhp) version of the 1.6-litre twin-cam engine. Then, in September, the 1.3-litre engine was also applied to the 1600 GTV body, the result being the 1300 GT Junior.

Alvis: The TF21 of March 1966 replaced the TE21 types, and although there were no style changes of this Graber-shaped machine, there was a more powerful 150bhp version of the 3-litre engine. As it transpired, this was the last new Alvis model to be announced.

Aston Martin: A Volante (convertible) version of the DB6 was introduced in October, having the DB6's squared-off tail and a power-operated soft-top.

Audi: During the summer, the German 1.7-litre front-wheel-drive saloons were imported into the UK for the first time. Sales were small at first – but they would increase steadily in the years ahead.

Austin: The 1100 estate car was an obvious evolution on the front-wheel-drive 1100 theme.

Austin-Healey: The Sprite advanced a stage further with the adoption of the 65bhp/1,275cc version of the BMC A-series engine, along with a more civilized type of foldaway soft-top for the cockpit. There was also a similar MG Midget (see below).

Bentley: (See Rolls-Royce, below.)

BMW: The new two-door 02 series – originally just one 1.6-litre model badged as the 1600 – was introduced in March as a smaller and additional model. Although the monocoque shell was entirely different from that of the existing 1800 and 2000 saloons, under the skin the overhead-camshaft engine, the choice of transmissions and the basic suspension layouts were all the same.

This was the first of an ever-enlarging model family, which would be BMW's best-seller for a decade before it finally gave way to the first of the 3-series cars. British sales would begin in mid-1967.

The latest derivative of the ever-widening saloon car range, the 2000 and 2000TI types, were revealed in Germany and went on sale in the UK later in the year. Except that there was a smoother front-end, with rectangular headlamps, the basic four-door style was little changed, and the enlarged (1,990cc) engine produced either 100 or 120bhp.

For a short time, starting in the autumn of 1966, the TI version of this car was given a special badge (but no other changes) and sold as the Frazer Nash-BMW, though this arrangement would be abandoned by the end of 1968.

Chrysler: Rootes, having forged links with Chrysler, announced that it was to make stronger efforts to market Chrysler Valiants in the UK, these being Australian-built versions of a Detroit design. Although theoretically several different models were available, including a 180bhp/4.5-litre-engined example, sales were extremely limited. British and American tastes, it seems, were still chasms apart.

Citroen: Once again the French company continued to develop the long-running Goddess (DS/ID) range, finally abandoning the old three-bearing long-stroke 2-litre engine in the ID19 in favour of a 78bhp 2-litre version of the latest crossflow five-bearing unit.

DAF: The new Michelotti-styled 44, revealed in September, was only the second new shape to come from this Dutch concern. Although larger and more roomy than the original Daffodil type, the 44 was still a front-engine/rear-drive car, with an 844cc version of the air-cooled flat-twin engine and the infinitely-variable automatic transmission featuring drive by cogged belts and expanding pulleys. Right-hand-drive deliveries were scheduled to begin in the UK early in 1967.

Daimler: The Daimler Sovereign was a badge-engineered version of the Jaguar 420 (see below).

Ferrari: Yet another variation on a V12 theme – the 330GTC – was introduced in March at the Geneva show, this being a 2+2-seater closed coupe with a 330bhp 4-litre engine and five-speed gearbox, but still with the old beam-type rear axle.

Later in the year, with very little fanfare, the 275GTB became 275GTB/4, complete with a more powerful (300bhp) four-cam version of the 3.3-litre V12 engine.

Fiat: After more than a decade in which the well-known 1100-103 was succeeded by the much-modified 1200, Fiat finally started again from scratch with a brand-new Cortina-sized car called the 124. Although this was very much the same size and type of car as the 1950s-generation 1100, it was new in almost every way.

The basic style of the 124 would still be in production 30 years later (for the car was taken up by the state-owned Russian motor industry for the Lada model). Originally this four-door saloon was powered by a high-revving 1.2-litre overhead-valve engine.

Except for the use of four-wheel disc brakes, the new 124 was technically conventional, though the rear axle beam was sprung on coils and located by radius-arms and a torque-tube. The engine, clearly, was at the very beginning of its development, and before long twin-overhead-camshaft versions would appear.

Before the 124 was revealed, the long-running 1100 model was thoroughly revised to become the 1100R. Not only did the existing platform receive a much smoother version of the four-door body style, but the familiar engine reverted to its original 1.1-litre size, and front-wheel disc brakes were standard.

Although neither car was officially catalogued for sale in the UK, a number of 124 Sport Spiders and Dino Spiders eventually arrived on the market (and the later coupe versions of these models sold here in higher numbers).

The 124 Spider was based on the shortened under-platform of the 124 saloon, but had a 90bhp/1.4-litre twin-cam engine which had evolved from the 124's unit, backed by a five-speed gearbox. Covered by a smart MGB-like Pininfarina body style, this was a very saleable car whose main market was always intended to be the USA.

The Dino was a technically more ambitious car, for its unique new underpan was powered by a 2-litre Ferrari Dino four-cam V6 engine, which had been productionized and would be manufactured by Fiat itself. The gearbox was a modified 2300 type, and there was a simple beam rear axle located on half-elliptic springs and radius-arms. The swoopy body style was again by Pininfarina. Here was a 130mph car whose reason for existence was to enable the engine to be homologated as quickly as possible for Ferrari to use in F2 single-seater racing.

Ford: After more than a million of the original Cortinas had been built in four years, the model was displaced by the completely restyled Cortina Mk II models. Using the same basic platform as before, though with a slightly larger, heavier and more roomy body, the new Cortinas had 1.3-litre (in place of 1.2-litre) and 1.5-litre engines, along with a 78bhp GT version of the 1.5-litre.

Two-door or four-door saloons of the new style were available at first, with an estate car sure to follow shortly, but for the time being there was no Lotus-engined version.

A new Mk IV range of Zephyrs and Zodiacs took over from the Mk IIIs. Featuring very long noses and short tails, these were new models in every detail. Not only was there a totally different four-door monocoque, complete with all-independent suspension and four-wheel disc brakes, but the old in-line four and six-cylinder engines had been abandoned in favour of a family of new 60-degree V4 and V6 units. There were also new four-speed manual and three-speed (American-made) automatic transmission options.

The V4 had already been revealed in the latest Corsairs, but for the time being the V6s were only used in the Zephyr 6/Zodiac models. Big, heavy, but lusty, these were the so-called Essex engines, which would be one of Ford-UK's major 'building-blocks' for the next decade or so.

Estate car versions arrived in October, and a top-of-the-range Zodiac

Executive also arrived later in the year, complete with wood, leather and carpets in profusion.

An estate car version of the Corsair was put on sale from March.

Ford-Germany: A rebodied range of front-wheel-drive Taunus 12M and 15M models were introduced, with sharper-edged styling than before. The smallest V4 was now to be a 1.3-litre unit. These cars were only ever of marginal interest to British drivers.

Gilbern: To replace the long-running GT Coupe, Britain's only Welsh carmaker introduced the Genie in October. This followed the same basic layout as before, which is to say that there was a multi-square-tube chassis-frame, a glassfibre coupe body style, and proprietary running gear. This time there was generous 2+2 seating, and power was by a 3-litre Ford V6.

Glas: Although various Glas models were price-listed in the UK during 1966, and a British importer was appointed, no evidence seems to exist of cars ever being delivered to British customers, and contemporary trade guides make no mention of them. In any case, after BMW absorbed Glas towards the end of the year, no more was heard of plans to produce right-hand-drive cars, and the marque soon disappeared.

Hillman: As a replacement for the Super Minx, the new Hunter was the first of a comprehensive family of 'Arrow'-designated cars to be launched by the Rootes Group, with a Singer Vogue version soon joining in and estate cars, Minx and Singer Gazelle types all set to follow in 1967.

In many ways the Hunter was a Cortina-copy in that it was lighter and more obviously cost-conscious than previous Minx/Super Minx cars had ever been. The style was simple, but neat, hiding a conventional Rootes Group engine/transmission driveline. This, however, was the first Rootes Group car to use MacPherson-strut front suspension.

Honda: This was the third Japanese company (after Diahatsu and Toyota) to arrive on the British scene, though this was a very tentative beginning for the future major shareholder of and

collaborator with British Leyland/Rover.

The S800 was a tiny two-seater sportscar with a separate chassis-frame, whose four-cylinder twin-cam engine had started life at 360cc, but had finally been enlarged to 791cc/70bhp (gross) for export sale. Although meant to be a Sprite/Midget and Spitfire competitor, the S800's problems were that the cockpit was too small, the engine too high-revving and potentially expensive to maintain, while at £779 it was £105 more costly than the Sprite.

Jaguar: After a lengthy development period, the long-wheelbase 2+2 E-type Coupe was finally revealed in March. Mechanically it was the same as the original-style 4.2-litre two-seaters, though this time Jaguar had altered the floor pressings to allow for the option of automatic transmission.

The wheelbase was 9in longer, and to give the best possible 2+2 seating without destroying the famous style, the roof had been raised by 2in and there was a larger but less gracefully-shaped windscreen. Although not as 'pure' in looks as the two-seaters, the 2+2 went on to sell steadily, and in 1971 its longer wheelbase would also be adopted for the Series III V12-engined Roadsters.

The new 420 saloon, introduced in October, was the final development of the long-running Mk 2 theme. Developed from the S-type cars (which meant that it had independent rear suspension and the lengthened tail), the 420 had the 245bhp/4.2-litre version of the XK engine, along with a squared-up four-headlamp nose. It was the only model derivative in this Jaguar class to use the 4.2-litre engine.

At the same time, the Mk X became the 420G, with no more than minor decorative changes.

Jensen: A new family of Italian-styled Interceptors (rear-wheel drive) and FFs (four-wheel drive) took over from the C-V8s at West Bromwich, and would sell very well for the next 10 years. The FF, in fact, was the world's first four-wheel-drive production car, using a transmission system developed by Harry Ferguson Research, the same as had been previewed at Earls Court in October 1965. As with that prototype, Dunlop Maxaret (aircraft-type) anti-lock braking was also specified.

The new car's chassis was a devel-

oped version of that used in the C-V8, as was the big Chrysler V8 engine and choice of transmissions. The body style, however, was no longer in glass-fibre, but in steel. Initial supplies came from Superleggera Touring, but series production was ensured by building the shells at West Bromwich.

To accommodate the four-wheel-drive system – especially the front axle – the FF's wheelbase was 4in longer than that of the Interceptor. The cabin was a two-door 'almost four-seater', with an enormous lift-up rear window/tailgate.

Lamborghini: Sensation of the Geneva show was the launch of the first complete mid-engined 4-litre V12 Miura – the rolling chassis having been previewed four months earlier in Turin. Sales of this 170mph supercar began later in the year, the first cars arriving in the UK within a year.

Almost lost in the torrent of comment which followed the arrival of the Miura, the 400GT was launched to take over from the 350GT. Although the basic style of this front-engined coupe was much as before, there had been many detail changes, and with an engine enlarged to 3.9-litres (like that of the Miura), the 400GT was claimed to have a 165mph top speed.

Lotus: In December 1966, to celebrate its move to a new factory at Hethel, just south-west of Norwich, the company previewed the new mid-engined Europa. At first, all deliveries were earmarked for export to Europe, and the first British deliveries would not take place, in fact, until 1968.

Like the existing Elan, the Europa had a steel backbone frame, but this was different in every respect. Power was by a tuned version of the Renault 16 engine (78bhp instead of the standard car's 59bhp), there was a four-speed Renault gearbox and all-independent suspension, but disc brakes only on the front wheels.

The body style, in glassfibre, was an ultra-low two-seater closed coupe, with virtually no space for luggage. As expected, roadholding was excellent, though there was disappointment over the performance, which naturally could not match that of the 105bhp front-engined Elan.

Maserati: The front-mounted V8-

engined Ghibli, whose chassis was a shortened version of that of the Quattroporte saloon, made its debut at the Turin show. The style was a magnificent two-seater fastback coupe (a Spider would eventually follow) by Ghia, and top speed was reputed to be well over 150mph. The first British deliveries followed in 1967.

Mercedes-Benz: The latest derivative of the recently-launched S-class, the 300SEL, was first delivered in the UK, complete with a 4in longer wheelbase than other S-class cars, all-independent air suspension and automatic transmission as standard.

MG: The Midget inherited a 1,275cc engine (see Austin-Healey Sprite, above).

Morris: In another fit of badge-engineering, BMC introduced the Morris version of the Austin 1800, this being mechanically, structurally and visually (apart from grille and badging) identical to the original type.

The 1100 estate car (also joined by an Austin version) was an obvious derivative of the successful front-wheel-drive 1100 theme.

Porsche: The long-term development of the 911 model began with the introduction of the 160bhp 911S, for which a top speed of 140mph was claimed, though absolutely nothing had been done to improve the tail-happy handling characteristics.

Reliant: After only two years, the Scimitar GT's design was significantly changed. Instead of the old 2.6-litre Ford straight-six-cylinder engine, there was now a 3-litre V6 Ford, offering more power and torque than before.

Riley: The Elf became the first Mini-based car to be given wind-up door windows. The same changes were also made to the Wolseley Hornet.

Rolls-Royce: In March, the H J Mulliner, Park Ward coachbuilding concern (which was financially controlled by Rolls-Royce), revealed a smart two-door four-seater coupe version of the new Silver Shadow saloon, to be built in Rolls-Royce and badge-engineered Bentley guises. Prices started at £9,789.

For the first five years these cars would be known only as specially-bodied Silver Shadows, but from 1971 they would be slightly modernized and christened Corniches. This basic shape, in fact, would then stay on the market until the early 1990s, latterly with the Bentley Continental name.

Rover: The 2000TC, launched in March 1966, was a desirable variation of the 2000, for it had a twin-carburettor 2-litre engine developing 114bhp (net), which boosted the top speed to a claimed 110mph. Sales were confined to export markets at first, though British deliveries began in September.

Saab: Recognizing that its two-stroke engines were technically out of date, the Swedish firm introduced the 95 and 96 V4 models, with four-stroke power by courtesy of Ford-Germany's 1.5-litre 60-degree V4 engine, which produced 65bhp and made the familiar Saab a much faster car than before.

Simca: The 1300/1500 range was given a major facelift, with a longer tail and smoother front, becoming the 1301/1501 series, all without raising British prices.

Singer: The new-generation Vogue was a clone of the Hillman Hunter (see above) except for the use of rectangular headlamps.

The Chamois Sport was similar to the Sunbeam Imp Sport (see below).

Sunbeam: The Imp Sport arrived in October, this being a 50bhp twin-carburettor version of the Hillman Imp, with a near-90mph top speed and a rather more upmarket interior. The Singer Chamois Sport was a near-identical clone.

Triumph: Like BMC, Triumph was increasingly adept at mixing and matching engines, chassis and body styles. Launched in October, the GT6 was effectively a fastback/hatchback coupe version of the Spitfire sportscar, but fitted with a tuned version of the 2000's six-cylinder engine.

In some ways the GT6 looked rather like the Jaguar E-type, and it also had a smooth and seamless six-cylinder engine. The all-synchromesh gearbox was brand new, a great improvement on the 'crash-first' assembly which it displaced. There was much criticism of the handling at first, not only because of the swing-axle rear suspension, but also because the GT6 was an altogether softer car than the Spitfire, this apparently having been influenced by USA-market requirements.

At the same time, the Vitesse 2-litre took over from the Vitesse 1600, this being another model cocktail combining the existing Vitesse's chassis, body and suspension with the 95bhp 2-litre running-gear of the new GT6.

Vauxhall: After only three years, the original, rather basic Viva HA was displaced by an altogether smarter and more curvaceous car, the Viva HB. The latest model had an enlarged (1,159cc) version of the engine, and as before was available in normal or '90' tune. There was coil-spring independent front suspension instead of a transverse leaf, along with coil-spring/radius-arm location of the rear axle and, for the first time on a British car, rectangular headlamps were standard – the similarly equipped Singer Vogue arriving a few days later.

The Viscount, launched in June, was a top-of-the-range derivative of the latest Cresta, and was clearly aimed at the Ford Zodiac, Wolseley 6/110 market. Mechanically the same as the Cresta, the Viscount had a much-improved and well kitted-out interior, including a wooden facia and reclining front seats: prices started at £1,373.

Volkswagen: The Beetle was developed a stage further, this time with the adoption of a larger 1.5-litre version of the air-cooled flat-four engine, along with front-wheel disc brakes for the first time, and changes to the swing-axle rear suspension which included a supplementary anti-roll torsion bar.

Volvo: The 140-series models made their debut in mid-summer, though UK deliveries of right-hand-drive cars would not start until the beginning of 1967.

The rather angular style featured a six-light saloon, and very shortly an estate car would be added, this hiding a familiar Volvo powertrain of 1.8-litre engine, four-speed transmission (with optional overdrive or automatic transmission) and a beam rear axle. There were two engine ratings at first – 75bhp or 100bhp (nett), and disc brakes were fitted to all four wheels.

In March the 1800S was further improved, with a more free-flowing exhaust system and a power increase from 108 to 115bhp, though the UK price was unchanged at £1,814. Because this was so much more expensive than – say – the £998 MG MGB GT, sales of 1800Ss were always limited.

Wolseley: *(For changes to the Hornet, see Riley Elf above.)*

Industrial developments

In July, BMC sprang an enormous surprise by announcing an agreed merger with Jaguar. Sir William Lyons of Jaguar, it seems, had not been willing to retire and hand over to a successor in his own organization as long as it remained independent. Instead, he wanted to merge Jaguar with a larger company provided that it would allow Jaguar to keep its technical and marketing independence.

To administer both BMC and Jaguar, a new holding company, British Motor Holdings, was created, but except that Sir William joined the BMH board, there seemed to be few immediate implications for Jaguar.

In the meantime, BMC's merger operations continued when, in May, Pressed Steel Fisher was formed by grouping all four of its bodybuilding businesses – Pressed Steel, Fisher & Ludlow, Morris (Bodies Branch) and Nuffield Metal Products – into one.

At the time, BMH stated that it had 120,000 employees, 30 UK factories and a production capacity of 1.1 million cars. The tragedy was that its sales never came close to reaching that capacity, and its market share soon began an inexorable slide, though it would be some years before Ford could claim market leadership.

Just before the end of the year, Leyland made a bid for control of Rover (which therefore would also mean control of Land-Rover and Alvis). When this was speedily accepted and formalized in the first weeks of 1967, it meant that henceforth Rover and Triumph would be partners, however reluctantly, rather than competitors.

The Rootes Group bought the former Pressed Steel factory next door to the Linwood plant, which had always supplied it with Hillman Imp bodies. This was a big step along the way to making Rootes independent of Pressed Steel, which had been taken over by BMC in 1965.

Only months later the imminent closure was announced of British Light Steel Pressings (which had been the scene of the financially crippling strike of 1961), and soon afterwards came news of the imminent demise of the Thrupp & Maberly business in Cricklewood, indicating that the Rootes business was becoming ever more concentrated on two sites – Coventry and Linwood.

Citroen, which had been running down its commitment to assembly in the UK for some time, finally closed its Slough factory early in 1966. Henceforth all UK-market Citroens would be produced in France and shipped over complete and ready for delivery.

After a decade spent only as an engineering company (for car production had ceased in the mid-1950s), HRG finally closed its doors.

Technical developments

Lucas unveiled its production-type fuel-injection installation, developed for use in four-cylinder and six-cylinder engines, though there were no applications for the moment. Lucas made it clear that it was looking for OE (Original Equipment) business, but the first customer, Triumph, would not be ready to show the Lucas-injected TR6 sportscar until the autumn of 1967.

Men of Influence

Sir Donald (Lord) Stokes

History will rightly see Lord Stokes (as he became in the 1970s) as the man who brought British Leyland into existence – and as the man who also axed several of the marques thus gathered together. In theory, when Leyland joined forces with British Motor Holdings, it was to be a straight merger, but from day one Leyland ideas and philosophies were imposed on BMH and its subsidiaries.

Although he was born in Kent, in 1914, Donald Gresham Stokes joined Leyland Motors, in Lancashire, as an apprentice in the 1930s, concentrated on the sales side after the Second World War, joined the board of Leyland in 1953 and became sales director of Standard-Triumph (following its takeover by Leyland) in 1963. After becoming chairman of Standard-Triumph in 1964, he was knighted in 1965, masterminded the merger with Rover in 1966/67, then inspired the link-up with BMH in January 1968.

On its formation, Sir Donald became British Leyland's chief executive (BMH's Sir George Harriman was chairman at first), but following Sir George's retirement he became the corporation's chairman from the end of 1968. One of his first acts at British Leyland was to announce a wide-ranging review of new-model policy; along with John Barber, his closest associate in the early 1970s, he imposed a new and corporate approach on BLMC.

This resulted in the importance of marques being downgraded, and eventually to the disappearance of several of them – notably Austin-Healey, Riley and Wolseley.

Lord Stokes remained as chairman until 1975, but after British Leyland was nationalized he stepped down, becoming honorary president, before leaving the Corporation completely in 1977.

1967

Until the end of the year, this was very much a 'marking time' period for British motorists, with few major innovations and no new taxes hitting their wallets. Then came a rash of new cars in the autumn, including signs of real technical advance from Vauxhall, followed by the shock of the devaluation of the British currency in November.

The truly awful news was that the so-called 'experimental' 70mph speed limit on British roads, which had applied since the end of 1965, was made permanent from mid-July 1967. No convincing statistics to support claims of accident reductions were ever published, and in spite of many later suggestions from police forces that the limit should be raised, this was never done.

It was a year during which Sweden took a brave decision, changing over from driving on the left (British-style) to driving on the right (European-style). It involved a great deal of planning, a close-down during the changeover weekend in early September, and draconian speed limits being applied in the first weeks after the change. Suggestions that such a changeover might be considered for the UK were firmly dismissed.

The British motorway network continued to expand, with the M1/M18 motorway from London to Doncaster being completed in December. The full extension of M1 to Leeds would be ready by the end of the next year.

This, too, was the year in which the British star rating was introduced for petrol – the best grade being 5-star.

The currency devaluation – which reduced the pound sterling's nominal value from $2.80 to $2.40 – arrived with shattering suddenness in November. Its immediate effect was limited, but once the motor industry had done its sums it was clear that the price of all imported cars would have to rise.

On the other hand, Britain's exports became cheaper – a fact which led to an additional 170,000 British cars being sold overseas in 1968. It was not before time, particularly in North America, where sales had been sagging very badly. In 1967, for instance, only 81,577 cars – mostly sportscars like the MGB and the Triumph Spitfire –

were sent across the Atlantic.

Britain's best-selling car was the Ford Cortina, with 165,300 registrations, sales of the BMC1100/1300 suffering from lack of availability due to strikes and slumping to 131,382.

The police started breathalyser tests from October, after which it became illegal for the driver to have more than 80mg of alcohol in 100ml of blood.

New models

AC: By the end of the year the Cobra was about to drop out of production, AC proposing to concentrate on the 428 Coupe and Convertible models instead. Although these were technically similar to the last Cobras, with power from a massive 7-litre Ford-USA V8 engine, they were longer and heavier cars, with bodies by Frua of Italy. Production was always very limited.

Aston Martin: In a very discreet launch in January, a brand new 5-litre four-cam V8 engine was previewed, this being described as a new racing engine; no-one was supposed to know that it was an early development of an engine which would soon be adopted for Aston Martin road cars – though the first production cars to use it would not be introduced until the end of 1969.

In the meantime, sales of DB6 models were slow, so the company announced major price reductions – more than £1,000 a car in 1967 currency – which did the trick. Unhappily, this meant that the cars were being sold at a loss, but David Brown was used to that...

In September the new DBS model was introduced, being an altogether larger – longer, wider and heavier – car than the DB6, though it was not a replacement for it. Styled by William Towns, the DBS was always meant to be powered by the new V8 engine mentioned above, but for the first few years it used the 325bhp (gross) version of the existing 4-litre six-cylinder unit instead. It was enough to provide a 140mph top speed, but Aston Martin enthusiasts asked for more...

The platform chassis was largely new and featured a de Dion rear suspension, while the cabin was the closest to a genuine four-seater that Aston Martin had yet offered. If this car had been badged as a Ferrari, no doubt it would

have been received with acclaim, but because it was an Aston Martin it was received without much comment. When the V8 version appeared in 1969, however, it was a different story...

Audi: Steady expansion of the range continued, and by mid-summer, 70, 80 and 90 versions of this front-wheel-drive car had become available and an estate car had been launched.

Austin: Although previewed at the Earls Court Motor Show in October, the ADO 61 3-litre saloon was not yet ready for series-production, which actually began in the summer of 1968. The new 3-litre was a replacement for the A110, which was soon to be discontinued (as was the equivalent Wolseley 6/110 model).

Based on the centre-section of the 1800 model, the 3-litre was a front-engine/rear-drive car using a heavily-modified, seven-bearing, in-line version of the 2.9-litre C-series engine, along with an all-synchromesh four-speed gearbox and Hydrolastic all-independent suspension, which included self-levelling at the rear. The front-end style, complete with rectangular headlamps, was not liked, and would be changed before deliveries began.

In a general reshuffle of the 1100 range, a 1300 derivative with a 58bhp/1,275cc engine, allied to a new all-synchromesh gearbox, was announced in October and, along with detail style changes, the 1100s and 1300s became Mark IIs.

Bentley: (See Rolls-Royce, below.)

Bond: The Equipe GT model was updated by the fitment of the latest 75bhp/1.3-litre Triumph Spitfire engine instead of the original 1,147cc unit.

In the autumn, the new Equipe 2-litre GT went on sale. This followed the same mix-and-match Triumph-based formula as before. This time there was a Vitesse 2-litre chassis, complete with 95bhp six-cylinder engine, along with some Herald/Vitesse inner panels, but there was a new body style in glassfibre, very sharply detailed and still with 2+2 seating. As with the four-cylinder-engined Bond, this car carried the full Standard-Triumph mechanical warranty.

Bristol: The 409 gave way to the 410, with minor changes.

Citroen: Yet again the DS range was updated, this time with a four-headlamp nose in which inner lamps were linked to the steering gear, swivelling from side to side as the front wheels were turned.

The big Citroen news of the year, however, was the introduction of the Dyane, which was really a 2CV chassis fitted with a more powerful version of that car's engine, and with a four-door saloon body.

DAF: The 33, introduced in the autumn, was an updated version of the original Daffodil/750 range, so for 1968 there were 33 and 44 models in the range.

Daimler: In the spring, manual transmission became optional on the 2½-litre saloon, which in the autumn became the V8-250, with trim and equipment changes and a different type of power steering, but with no changes to the performance.

Dino: Ferrari showed the first of the mid-mounted and transverse-engined Dino sports coupes. This was the first mid-engined road car from Maranello, but because it was so small, and only fitted with a V6 engine, it was officially badged as simply a Dino, not a Ferrari.

At least, that is what the company intended, but from the very first day every enthusiast talked about Ferrari Dinos, which is the way I intend to treat this marque during its short life.

With a tubular frame, all-independent suspension and a sinuous aluminium-panelled body styled by Pininfarina, the Dino 206GT was typically Ferrari, and mouthwateringly attractive. Except in tiny detail, the engine was identical to that used in front-engined Fiat Dinos (and was made by Fiat), but it was matched to a new five-speed transaxle.

British sales – extremely limited – began in 1968, before the steel-bodied 246GT took over in 1969.

Ferrari: The 365GT 2+2, a replacement for the 330GT, was introduced at the Paris show, being a large, heavy, though graceful four-seater coupe with a front-mounted engine and gearbox. The single-cam 4.4-litre V12 produced 320bhp and there was independent rear suspension and self-levelling control.

Fiat: Only a year after introducing the 124 family car range, Fiat launched the 125 in 1967. However, although this car looked remarkably like the 124, it was based on the floorpan and suspensions of the 1500 model (which it made obsolete), had 124 doors, roof and glass, but unique front and rear panels, and was fitted with a 1.6-litre version of the twin-cam engine which had been seen for the first time in the 124 Sport Spider and Coupe. As with the 124, this was just the start of a wider 125 range.

Following the successful launch of the 124 Spider and Dino Spider models in November 1966, Fiat introduced 124 Sport Coupe and Dino Coupe versions in March. Both were mechanically like their open-top cousins, but had longer wheelbases and 2+2 seating. The Fiat's style was an in-house shape, while that of the Dino was by Bertone, who also built the shells.

Ford: The Lotus-Cortina Mk 2 arrived in March, this being a logical update of the original theme. As with the last of the recently discontinued Mk 1 type, it was really a re-engined Cortina GT. This time, however, assembly would be at Dagenham instead of at the Lotus factory. There were no aluminium panels on the standard production type, but these, and a mountain of other items, were optional extras.

The 2-litre V4-engined Corsair 2000E, launched in January, was a much-improved development of the Corsair GT, which it replaced. Not only was there a higher standard of trim and finish, along with a more powerful engine, but this was the first Ford to use what became known as the 'Corsair 2000E' gearbox, whose ratios were much better chosen than before.

As promised, the estate car derivative of the latest Cortinas arrived in February.

Only a year after the Cortina Mk 2 range had been launched, it was given a much-revised range of pushrod overhead-valve engines, the now-legendary Kent crossflow four-cylinder units. At the same time the 1.5-litre engine was dropped in favour of a longer-stroke 1.6-litre, this becoming one of the standard Kent units for the next decade or so.

An extra niche model, which few people thought important at the time, but which subsequently has achieved genuine 'classic car' status, was the new Cortina 1600E, a combination of Cortina GT running gear, Lotus-Cortina-style suspension and a totally retrimmed interior. It sold beyond Ford's wildest dreams for the next three years.

Ford-Germany: After a life of only three years, the 17M/20M range was completely revised, with a reshuffled pack of V4 and V6 engines and more stylish bodies. These would have a three-year life, to the summer of 1970, before being replaced by another generation of Cortina-based Taunus types.

Hillman: The new-generation Minx appeared in January, being a Hunter-based model taking over from the previous Minxes built from 1956. Compared with the Hunter, the new Minx had smaller and less powerful engines and simpler trim and appointments, but was otherwise structurally, mechanically and visually almost the same. Estate car versions followed a few weeks later.

The Imp Californian was a smart, lowered-roof, fastback coupe version of the Hillman Imp, still with two doors and the same single-carburettor engine. In this case the rear window was fixed, not hinged, and there was less headroom in the rear seats, but this was an interesting little niche model which sold well. A much more powerful version of it, the Sunbeam Stiletto, would be announced later in the year.

The new-generation Husky was a small and boxy estate car on the basis of the rear-engined Hillman Imp, the miracle being that the loading floor was above the engine, yet still at a practical height. There was also a Commer van version of this shape.

Honda: The Japanese company began importing small numbers of the tiny N360/N600 minicars, which were smaller than Minis, though with tiny, transversely-mounted, air-cooled twin-cylinder engines driving the front wheels.

Although they were competitively priced against the BMC Minis, they proved to be too noisy and too frantic to appeal to many British drivers.

Humber: Early in the year Rootes announced that the Hawk/Super Snipe/Imperial models would be dropped during the summer of 1967, marking the end of 'Big Humber' production.

Henceforth, the only Humbers to be price-listed would be Sceptres, which were really heavily modified Hillman Super Minxes, and later Hunters.

The new-generation Sceptre appeared in September, being a Hillman Hunter-based four-door saloon car with a Sunbeam Rapier driveline (see Sunbeam, below), and a more upmarket interior, which included a wooden facia panel and reclinable front seats. There was a special front grille and wheel trims, but in general character this car was pure Hunter.

Iso: The third model in Iso's expanding range was the new four-door, four-seater Fidia, which used the same basic Chevrolet-engined chassis as other Iso models, but featured a style by Ghia.

Jaguar: Although not known at the time, Jaguar was preparing to introduce the XJ6 (in the autumn of 1968), so at Motor Show time there was merely a reshuffle to the existing compact Jaguar range.

The original Mk 2 models were dropped and replaced by very similar 240 and 340 models, though there was no longer a 3.8-litre type. Both cars had simplified trim and furnishings, though the 240 had more power (133bhp gross) than before, and Borg-Warner Type 35 replaced old-type DG as the automatic transmission option.

Along with price reductions for S-types, and the appearance of a revised Daimler 2½-litre derivative, this was a major shake-up of the existing cars. The 420, 420G and E-type models continued largely unchanged.

Lancia: A major reshuffle and update of the Fulvia range saw 1.2-litre engines being used in the saloons and 1.3-litre units in the Coupes, with more power and torque. The most desirable of these cars were the Rallye 1.3 (Coupe), 1.3HF (Coupe) and special-bodied Zagato Coupe.

During the year, too, the Fulvia saloon was given a front-end facelift, with much more carefully integrated headlamps, grille and body contours, though the cabin and platform were not changed.

Land-Rover: The 2.6-litre IOEV engine was offered on the entire long-wheelbase normal-control Land-Rover

range from April, the existing four-cylinder (petrol and diesel) engines being continued. With only 83bhp, the 2.6-litre engine was much less powerful than those versions fitted to previous P4 saloons.

Lotus: The Elan Plus 2, introduced in September, used the same basic chassis engineering as the two-seater Elan, but had a 12in longer wheelbase and 7in wider wheel tracks. The twin-cam engine was uprated to 118bhp, and the glassfibre coupe body enclosed 2+2 seating, though there was very little space in the rear seats due to the restricted headroom.

The Lotus range now comprised four model families – Seven kit-car, mid-engined Europa, Elan two-seater and the 2+2-seater Elan Plus 2. Except for development changes and updates, this range would remain unchanged until 1973.

Marcos: Development of the wooden-chassis coupe began with the addition of the 1650 model, with a Lawrence-tune derivative of the Ford Cortina engine. Although this car had 120bhp, it was short-lived as Ford introduced an entirely different type of cylinder head at the end of 1967, thus making the basic engine obsolete, and the Marcos 1500 and 1600 took over instead.

Mazda: The Japanese company announced its intention of selling cars in the UK in September 1967, starting with the space-age Cosmo coupe, along with the 1.5-litre Bertone-styled 1500 saloons and estates.

Although this Japanese company would eventually make its name in the UK by selling conventional small and medium-sized family cars, its first import was the Wankel-engined 110S Coupe. Not only did this front-engined/rear-drive sports coupe have odd styling and de Dion rear suspension, but it was the world's first twin-rotor Wankel-engined production car, beating the NSU Ro80 by a few months.

For Mazda, this car was really an attention-raiser rather than a long-term project, which explains the complexities of the new-fangled engine and the high price. Very few of them were brought into the UK, but they caused comment wherever and whenever seen.

Mercedes-Benz: The 230SL gave way to the 2.5-litre-engined 250SL, though this would turn out to be a one-season model as the 280SL would be launched in 1968. In the meantime, Mercedes-Benz was gearing itself up for a truly major launch of 'New Generation' cars in January 1968.

MG: The MGC arrived in October, looking almost the same as the MGB except for the use of 15in diameter wheels and having a bulge in the bonnet. Under the skin was a 150bhp version of the Austin 3-litre's 2.9-litre engine (which was very different from the old Austin-Healey 3000 unit), an all-synchromesh gearbox and torsion-bar independent front suspension.

Although the MGC was meant to take over from the Austin-Healey 3000, it had neither the same character nor the same handling characteristics, and only 10,000 of them would be produced in the next two years.

At the same time the MGB became Mk II, mainly with the new all-synchronmesh gearbox and other structural changes to commonize as far as possible with the MGC.

During the summer, BMC made a single-carburettor (58bhp) version of the latest 1,275cc A-series engine optional in the MG 1100, but did not change its name! However, by the end of the year it had become known officially as the MG 1300.

Mini: The famous BMC range became Mk II, with the choice of 848cc or 998cc engines and with minor style changes to identify them in the showrooms and on the road.

An all-synchromesh gearbox was announced for the Mini-Cooper S (and later, by inference, for other Mini models), but in true BMC fashion this was a premature announcement of a development which was not actually completed until the summer of 1968.

Morris: (For 1100 changes see Austin, above.)

NSU: After much carefully contrived leaking of pictures, the amazing twin-rotor Wankel-engined Ro80 was put on sale during the autumn. Not only was the engine advanced, but it was placed ahead of the line of the front wheels, matched to a three-speed semi-automatic transmission, and the car had front-wheel drive, all-independent suspension and four-wheel disc brakes.

The four-door saloon shell had a very aerodynamic shape and the ride and handling soon proved to be excellent, but the price was high, and there were still many (justified) doubts about the engine's longevity. Within a year its tendency to wear its rotor tip seals was well-known, and NSU had already embarked on an expensive warranty programme.

The latest derivative of the Prinz range was the 1000TTS, which was effectively a Prinz 4 shell with a tuned-up version of the NSU 1000's engine, and clearly this was aimed directly at the Mini-Cooper/Renault R8 Gordini market.

Opel: General Motors announced that the German Opel range was to be put on sale in the UK for the first time since 1939 and that first deliveries would take place in the autumn. Opel was the German counterpart of Vauxhall, so the Kadett was really the equivalent of the obsolete Viva HA (1963–66 type), while the four-cylinder Rekord was a much more technically advanced equivalent of the Victor. The latest Opels were the Olympias and Commodores, the Olympias being larger-engined upmarket Kadetts, the Commodores using the Rekord structure, but having in-line six-cylinder engines.

Kadetts and some Olympias used simple overhead-valve engines, while Olympias, Rekords and Commodores used advanced cam-in-head engines; these were not true overhead-camshaft engines, for the valves were driven from the camshaft by tiny pushrods and rockers.

Reliant: The Scimitar GT also became available with the 2.5-litre Ford V6 engine. Although this still had a top speed of 111mph (compared with nearly 120mph for the 3-litre), it was not a popular model and was soon dropped.

Riley: The 1,275cc engine became available in the Riley Kestrel (see MG 1100, above).

The Elf received the same modifications as the Minis in the autumn (see Mini, above).

Rolls-Royce: To join the special-bodied

Mulliner, Park Ward coupes which had gone on sale in 1966, the company now introduced the convertible version of the same style, which Rolls-Royce proudly claimed took 20 weeks to be completed. There was also a Bentley version of the same car: this Rolls-Royce cost £10,511.

Rover: After years of painstaking development, Rover released the 3.5-litre light-alloy V8 engine which it planned to use in so many future models. In the beginning, this engine had been designed and manufactured in large numbers by General Motors in the USA, but after only a few years Rover had bought the manufacturing rights, but not the tooling. Except that cylinder heads *and* block were cast in aluminium, this was a conventional 90-degree overhead-valve V8, which Rover originally rated at 161bhp. In much-developed and enlarged (4-litre and 4.6-litre) forms it would still be used to power Range Rovers in the mid-1990s. Specialist builder/converters such as TVR pushed the capacity out to a full 5 litres and extracted more than 300bhp from it.

The first new model to use the V8 was the 3.5-litre (or P5B), which was really a re-engined version of the P5 3-litre car, a chassis which had already been on the market for eight years. As before, four-door saloon and lowered-roof coupes were available.

With this move, the old six-cylinder engine was pensioned-off, though it continued to power versions of the Land-Rover for some time.

Saab: The Swedish company announced the 99 model, which was only its second all-new model in 20 years, all previous Saabs having been developments of the original two-stroke 92 layout.

Although the new 99 was still a front-wheel-drive machine, it was larger, faster and totally different from the existing 96 models, which continued in production. The engine was a brand-new 1.7-litre overhead-camshaft unit with an aluminium cylinder head, which had been designed and was being manufactured by Triumph in Coventry. This was an engine which would later be used in Triumph Dolomites and TR7s of the 1970s.

The front-wheel-drive layout was unique, for the in-line engine was

effectively mounted back-to-front, with the clutch near the nose, the gearbox being under the engine and ahead of the line of the front wheels.

This launch was premature, as series-production was not scheduled to begin until the summer of 1968, and first British imports were not made until the autumn of 1969.

Simca: To add spice to the rear-engined 1000 range, the company redesigned the previous Coupe, giving it a 1.2-litre version of the engine, a revised front-end of the Bertone shape and calling it the 1200S Coupe.

The new 1100 was the first transverse-engine/front-wheel-drive Simca and was available as a three-door or a five-door hatchback. The engine was yet another derivative of the Simca 1000 layout, which was itself a version of the old 1950s-style Aronde engine.

As might be expected from such a French machine of the period, the 1100 had soft, long-travel suspension, versatile seating arrangements, and was aimed at the same market sector as the Peugeot 204, though neither Renault nor Citroen had anything in the same bracket.

Singer: As expected, a new-generation Gazelle (like the new-type Hillman Minx) and Vogue estate car (like the latest Minx/Hunter) joined in Rootes' renewal of its medium-sized range.

Sunbeam: The Tiger II took over from the Tiger I, though entirely for export at first (very few, indeed, would ever be sold in the UK). The mechanical update included a 200bhp/4.7-litre Ford V8 engine and detail style changes including a honeycomb-pattern front grille. This was a very short-lived model, for the Tiger range was killed-off later in the year.

The Stiletto, introduced in October, was a mixture of Hillman Imp Californian styling and Sunbeam Imp Sport engineering, all with a more upmarket interior, which included a special facia layout and reclining front seats.

The most important new Sunbeam of 1967 was the new-generation Rapier Coupe. Although this used the platform of the new Hillman Hunter, there was an entirely fresh two-door four-seater fastback body style, and the engine was similar to that of the Alpine sportscar, a twin-carburettor 76bhp

(DIN) version of the 1,725cc power unit. The top speed was more than 100mph, and the engine was immediately shared with the new-generation Humber Sceptre (see above).

Toyota: The gradual build-up of this Japanese marque's range for UK sale began when the original-generation 1.1-litre Corolla went on sale alongside the Corona. This was a conventional (Anglia/Viva) type of small saloon, with a claimed top speed of 87mph, and it was originally priced at £700.

Triumph: The new TR5 sportscar, announced in October, was the first TR to use a six-cylinder engine, this being a 150bhp Lucas-injected 2.5-litre version of the 2000's power unit. In most other respects, the TR5 was a re-engined TR4A, whose old wet-liner four-cylinder engine had finally been discontinued, though marques such as Morgan continued using it for a time.

In 'Rest of the World' form, the TR5 was much faster than any previous TR, with a 120mph top speed, but for export only to the USA Triumph marketed the TR250 instead, with a 106bhp carburetted version of the same power unit, which was never sold in the UK.

The Spitfire became Mk 3 from March, with an enlarged (1.3-litre) engine and slightly altered styling, which included the 'bone-in-the-teeth' front bumper position.

Launched in the spring, the 1300TC was a 75bhp (Spitfire 3)-engined version of the front-wheel-drive 1300 saloon, with a 90mph top speed.

Also new was the Herald 13/60 range – saloon, estate and convertible – which was an update of the 1200 design, but with the 61bhp/1.3-litre version of the engine. Front-wheel disc brakes were standard. The Herald 1200 continued unchanged.

TVR: The evolution of the tubular-framed sports coupe continued with the Mk IVs giving way to the Vixen 1600, which was effectively a re-engined version of the old car, this time using the new crossflow 1.6-litre Ford Kent engine.

Vanden Plas: The Princess 1100 gained an optional 1,275cc engine (see MG 1100, above).

Vauxhall: The old type of Victor 101

and VX4/90 models were dropped, replaced by a totally new generation of Victors. Not only were these cars larger than previous Victors, they had more curvaceous styling and were powered by a new type of overhead-camshaft engine, which was available in 1.6-litre or 2-litre form. Estate versions would appear in mid-1968.

There was rack-and-pinion steering, the coil-spring rear suspension was new, and as usual with Vauxhall there was a wide choice of manual or automatic transmissions. If only the build quality had lived up to the technical specifications, these cars would have been more successful.

A Brabham conversion of the Viva HB was approved by the factory – this giving 69bhp on the 1.2-litre engine – while automatic transmission became optional on other Vivas. Viva estate cars appeared later in the year.

Volkswagen: A new large range of estate cars – Microbuses, later to be generally known as Transporters – were introduced, with an even more boxy style than the original, but still with a 1.6-litre version of the familiar flat-four air-cooled engine in the tail. More than 1,800,000 of the original Type 2 cars had been built.

The launch of the new Microbus quite overshadowed the arrival of an automatic transmission option for larger-engined Beetles and the 1600 range. At the same time these cars were given a significantly redesigned rear suspension, known as the double-jointed axle, but really with a fundamentally different geometry which cut down (though it could not entirely eliminate) the tail-happy swing-axle effect.

Volvo: Power outputs were increased in all engines fitted to 120-series cars, though the rest of the design was left alone. Volvo spent 1967 getting their newer 140-series cars into world markets.

Wartburg: The first UK imports were made of the two-stroke-engined front-wheel-drive Knight saloon from East Germany. In many ways this car was a lineal development of older DKW models and it produced 45bhp from its 1-litre engine. Square-rigged styling was not easy to like, and at £612 the Knight was not particularly cheap, but

UK sales would be slow and steady until the early 1970s.

Wolseley: The new 18/85 was an upmarket derivative of the Austin/Morris 1800 front-wheel-drive saloon. Mechanically it was modified, with power-assisted steering as standard and the option of automatic transmission (the first such fitting on a BMC 1800 model).

The Wolseley 1100 was given an optional 1,275cc engine (see MG 1100, above). The Hornet received the same modifications as the Minis in the autumn (see Mini, above).

Industrial developments

Ford of Europe was formed to co-ordinate and eventually merge all activities carried out by previously independent Ford companies in Britain, Germany and France. Within five years the product range would be totally integrated.

Following its capital injection of 1964, Chrysler achieved a controlling financial stake of the Rootes Group early in the year and soon set about integrating the operations of its new subsidiary with Simca of France. Even so, it would not be until 1970 that the company's name would change to Chrysler United Kingdom Ltd.

In the new regime, Chrysler controlled 67 per cent of the voting shares, while the British Government controlled 13 per cent. Sir Reginald Rootes stepped down from the chairmanship, his position being taken by Lord (Geoffrey) Rootes.

The first rumours of a merger between BMC and Leyland began to circulate, but were immediately denied. Sir Donald Stokes of Leyland would only admit that the two companies were: '...discussing the possibility of working together in an overseas market where their interests did not clash...'

Series-production of Austin-Healey 3000 models ended, bringing to an end 15 years of 'Big Healeys'. This car (theoretically at least) was replaced by the MG MGC, though that car would only have a two-year life.

The last Alvis private car, a TF21, was produced in mid-summer, after which this famous car marque disappeared. Since then, Alvis has concentrated on producing military vehicles.

Technical developments

In the USA, the first moves were made to impose exhaust emission controls on engines, and later a whole series of laws about crash safety and prevention would come into force. The enforcement of emission controls had an immediate effect on British car-makers sending models to the USA, and as these regulations tightened over the years, an element of panic, followed by depression, enveloped engineering and sales departments. This, in fact, signalled the beginning of the end for many companies' presence in the North American market.

In the UK, the introduction of an overhead-camshaft engine from Vauxhall and the preview of an overhead-camshaft engine from Triumph (although for the time being it was to be manufactured solely for the Saab), plus the launch of Britain's first fuel-injected road car (the Triumph TR5) signalled the start of a technical advance by Britain's largest manufacturers. It was not before time.

Men of Influence

Walter Hayes

Ford's phenomenally successful F1 engine programme was apparently founded on a chance remark Walter Hayes made at a board meeting in 1965. At the end of a long session, under 'Any Other Business', Walter casually told the directors: 'Harley Copp [at that time Ford-UK's technical director] and I would like to do a Grand Prix engine.'

Cosworth, and Keith Duckworth, were given the contract, which cost Ford £100,000. The result was the birth of the 3-litre V8 DFV engine, which went on to become the most successful F1 engine of all time. What a bargain...

Before he became one of Ford's most important personalities, Hayes had already been a successful newspaper man. Born in Harrow in 1924, he joined the *Daily Graphic* in 1939, gradually moving up through the ranks to become the editor of the *Sunday Dispatch*, before moving on to the *Daily Mail*.

Head-hunted to manage Ford of Britain's public affairs department in 1962, he soon built up a massive motorsport programme, and by the end of the 1960s Ford was not only in F1 and F2 (becoming dominant at both levels), but had produced the Le Mans-winning GT40, the Lotus-Cortina racing saloons, and the first of the Escort rally cars.

Hayes was also responsible for attracting team manager Stuart Turner (see 1966) out of motorsport retirement in 1969, and for encouraging the establishment of the Advanced Vehicle Operation factory at South Ockendon. Wherever there was motorsport or sporting cars at Ford, Hayes was sure to be involved, either as the prime-mover, or as the major influence behind the scenes.

Moving ever onwards and upwards, he became a Ford of Europe vice-president in 1968 and its vice-chairman in 1976. Moving to Ford-USA in 1980, he became its vice-president of public affairs, as well as No 1 confidante to Henry Ford II and a major influence behind the revival of Ford's motorsport programme in the USA. Returning to Europe in 1984, he once again became vice-chairman, Ford of Europe, and until 1989 it is often said that he, more than any other personality in the business, made sure that exciting sporting Fords like the Sierra RS Cosworth, the RS200 and the Escort RS Cosworth made it from 'good idea' status to the showrooms.

After retiring, or so he thought, in 1989, Ford soon drafted him in to Aston Martin, first as a director, then as chairman, where one of his most important executive decisions was to promote the design, development and launch of the Aston Martin DB7.

Only then was he able to retire properly – or would there be even more 'emeritus' duties ahead of him?

1968

In spite of what social and economic historians might say, this was a period in which the 'Swinging Sixties' meant a lot to the British people. BMC adverts linked the Mini car to the mini-skirt (using a series of striking pictures to make their point!), and manufacturers including Ford made their cars available in some quite astonishing hues. John Lennon, of *The Beatles*, even bought a dignified Rolls-Royce Phantom V limousine and had it repainted in psychedelic colours.

Even so, this was once again a year in which the tax burden on British motoring increased. In the Budget of March 1968, purchase tax on cars was raised from 27½ to 33⅓ per cent, another 4d (1.7p) was added to the tax on a gallon of petrol, and the annual road fund tax rocketed from £17 10s (£17.50) to £25.

Even that was not the end for 1968, for purchase tax was raised yet again in November, this time to 36⅔ per cent. It was almost as if the Government was trying to discourage private motoring altogether as a long-term policy, and yet another 4.5d (1.9p) was added to the price of petrol. For the first time, petrol now cost more than 6s 0d (30p) a gallon, and this hurt badly. The heady days of the early 1960s, when motoring taxes seemed to come *down* in most years, now seemed so very far away...

Yet even now there was more to come because from November hire purchase regulations were tightened still further, with the minimum deposit going up from 33⅓ to 40 per cent and the maximum payment period coming down to two years.

According to Government economists, all this was being done to damp down demand, which was thought to be too high. They had a point, for this was a year in which no fewer than 1,144,770 cars were sold in Britain, of which 102,276 were imports. Both these were records – and in fact this was the first year in which more than 100,000 imported cars had been sold in Britain.

To add to drivers' go-anywhere euphoria, Britain's motorway network continued to expand steadily. The M1 motorway reached Yorkshire, the M5 and M6 roads gradually crawled towards a meeting north-west of Birmingham, and M6 construction reached Penrith and Carlisle. Government ministers were adamant that the first 1,000 miles of British motorway would be open by the early 1970s – and for once this was a promise which was kept!

New models

Alfa Romeo: Only five years after the Giulia family had been started, Alfa Romeo now produced yet another all-new four-door saloon monocoque, rather plainly-styled but larger than the Giulia. This was powered by a 1.8-litre version of the Giulia's twin-cam engine, backed by the same five-speed gearbox and rear axle.

At the same time the existing GTV Coupe and Spider (no longer called Duetto) were also uprated with the same 122bhp 1.8-litre engine.

Later in the year, too, the 1.3-litre version of the engine was offered in the GT Coupe model (and the Spider soon followed suit). In the next few years, in fact, it was going to be difficult to keep track of the different engine/bodyshell/specification combinations which Alfa Romeo wrung out of this single basic platform and running gear.

Audi: At the end of the year, a new 100 range was unveiled, having a sleek new four-door body style, but retaining the (enlarged) engine, transmission and front-wheel-drive installation of the original Audi, which carried on in production for three further years.

The new 100 was much longer and lower than the original DKW-based Audi, with a bigger cabin, and although it only had a 1.76-litre engine it was a genuine contender for the 2-litre class.

The existing 70-80-90 range was extended further, at the bottom of the range, by the launch of a smaller-engined (1.5-litre) version of the model, to be known as the Audi 60.

Austin: The front-wheel-drive 1800 model became Mk II, with more power (86bhp nett), 14in road wheels and slight restyling of the rear quarters. At this stage, though, there was a pause at Austin as the all-new Maxi (to be launched in 1969) was nearing pre-production status.

BMW: In October, BMW introduced a range of new six-cylinder-engined models. The four-door saloons used brand-new unit-construction bodyshells, with MacPherson-strut front suspension and semi-trailing rear-ends, powered by 2.5-litre and 2.8-litre engines. The engines were evolutionary developments of the successful four-cylinder types already found in other BMWs.

As a supplementary to this launch, the 2000CS coupe was replaced by a new 2800CS coupe, this car using a much-modified version of the 2000CS bodyshell, but fitted with the new engine and front suspension from the 2800 saloon.

The 2002 appeared, this being the modern two-door 1600 model into which the 100bhp 2-litre engine had been shoehorned. It was a very capable sports saloon, and yet more powerful versions were already being planned.

Later in the year, in a change made more for production convenience than for technical reasons, the 1.8-litre engine's bore and stroke were changed. Instead of 84 x 80mm, giving 1,773cc, the latest unit was 89 x 71mm, for 1,776cc: this was to standardize the cylinder bore with the 2-litre version of the same engine.

Bond: The Preston-based company added a convertible version of the 2-litre GT Coupe to its range.

Citroen: All ID/DS models received development changes in October, which included increases in power for most models. The Ami 6 also received a power boost, and there was a 602cc version of the Dyane, which became known as the Dyane 6.

DAF: The new 55 model, unveiled in January, used a modified version of the DAF 44 body (though with torsion-bar front suspension), but was fitted with a 1.1-litre Renault engine. Not only was this the most powerful DAF car so far put on sale, it was also the first to have a bought-in engine, the first to have four cylinders and the first to be water-cooled.

Daimler: The first new model to be introduced from the British Leyland combine was the Daimler DS420 Limousine. Replacing the stately (but fast) V8-engined DR420 limo, this 18ft 10in long car was an interesting amalgam. The platform (with all the running gear) was a lengthened version of the Jaguar 420G (ex-Mk X), the style was a joint effort by Daimler and Sir William Lyons of Jaguar, with bodyshell manufacture by Motor Panels of Coventry and all final assembly, trim and furnishing by Vanden Plas in North London.

This limousine was ideal for use by embassies, business tycoons, dignitaries and wedding/funeral businesses. Sales were always slow but steady, and the last of more than 4,200 machines was not built until 1992.

Ferrari: The most desirable sporting supercar of the year was the 365GTB4, more familiarly known as the Daytona, which was first shown in October. Using a developed version of the 275GTB/4's chassis, complete with rear-mounted five-speed gearbox, the Daytona had a 354bhp/4.4-litre four-cam V12 engine, a claimed top speed of more than 170mph and a quite beautiful body style by Pininfarina.

Until it was displaced by the mid-engined Boxer in the early 1970s, the Daytona was certainly the most desirable Ferrari of all time. To many people, it still is.

The Daytona overshadowed another new-Ferrari announcement of 1968/69, which saw a less powerful (320bhp) version of the 4.4-litre engine dropped into the 330GTC (which had 2+2 styling), this model therefore becoming the 365GTC. Deliveries in the UK did not begin until 1969.

Fiat: In March, both the popular 850 sporty cars – the Coupe and the Spider – were improved by the fitment of more powerful 903cc versions of the existing overhead-valve engine. There were rear-end styling changes for the Sport Coupe, but the Spider looked the same as before.

Later in the year the 124 range was boosted by the arrival of the 124S, which had a larger overhead-valve 1.4-litre engine and a new four-headlamp nose.

In a similar move, the 125S, with 100bhp, joined the existing 125, also having a five-speed gearbox.

Ford: The Escort range of two-door saloons was introduced in January, taking over from the Anglia 105E; estate car derivatives were added from March, and automatic transmission options in May. This was the first version of a small-medium series which has been in production ever since. All cars were based on the same simple monocoque shell, which featured MacPherson-strut front suspension.

All mainstream models used one or other of the latest Kent engines – 1.1-litre (a newly-developed size), 1.3-litre or 1.3GT – and were backed by a brand-new light-duty four-speed transmission.

At the same time the Escort Twin-Cam 'rally-special' was previewed, this effectively being a reinforced Escort bodyshell into which all the Lotus-Cortina running gear – twin-cam engine, gearbox, back axle and all – had been crammed. Production of this car was very limited at first, the works race and rally teams starting their programmes before any private cars had even been delivered.

Honda: The N600, a larger-engined version of the N360, finally went on sale in the UK.

Jaguar: Without doubt, the Car of the Year was Jaguar's new XJ6, which was introduced in September. Although the original cars were powered by 2.8-litre and 4.2-litre versions of the famous XK six-cylinder engine, it was already known that V12 engines were being designed for this car, though in the event the V12 would not be seen until 1971 – and then in the E-type Series III. As everyone expected, all-independent suspension and four-wheel disc brakes were standard.

The new four-door saloon shell was a graceful structure, larger and more capacious than the old S-type and 420 models which it displaced, though significantly smaller than the 420G, which continued in production. Sales began at once, and such was the demand that there was soon a considerable waiting list.

At the same time the E-type became Series II, with changes to the facia, the equipment and the slope of the screen on the 2+2 model, together with the adoption of exposed headlamps (which had previously been behind glass fairings) to meet new USA legislation. Except that power-assisted steering and steel disc wheels became optional extras, there were few mechanical changes.

Lamborghini: Using the existing hardware to widen the range further – 3.9-litre V12 engine, five-speed gearbox, chassis-mounted rear final-drive and coil-spring all-independent suspension – two more Lamborghini supercars appeared.

The Islero was really no more than a rebodied 400GT, with a 2+2 closed coupe style with rather angular lines which had been shaped by Lamborghini itself.

The Espada, a wide, flat, almost-four-seater two-door saloon, was styled by Bertone and was an altogether more startling machine. Whereas the Islero only had a short life, the Espada would be built, in gradually developed form, until the late 1970s.

Lancia: The Fulvia range was further developed, principally with the introduction in November of the 1.6HF Coupe, which not only had a larger (1.6-litre) version of the famous V4 engine and a five-speed transmission, but also many light-alloy body panels and a simplified interior. Later, just to confuse matters, Lancia would also market the same running gear in a normal-weight/normal-trim coupe.

Lotus: The mid-engined Europa, now known as S2 due to detail engineering and production changes, was finally made available on the British market; previously, all Europas had been sent for export.

The newly-launched LV220 16-valve twin-cam 2-litre engine, which used a Vauxhall Victor 2000 cylinder block, gave a few hints about the company's possible future, for it was a much larger and potentially very much more powerful engine than the existing eight-valve twin-cam. Even so, the LV220 would only be used in Lotus racing cars until 1972; then, fitted with its own specially-designed cylinder block, it would be used by Jensen to power the Jensen-Healey.

Mercedes-Benz: A totally new generation of smaller-size saloons appeared to take over from the long-running Ponton models. These, in Stuttgart-speak, were the W114/W115 models, whose styling was rounder and more aerodynamically efficient than the Pontons, and distinguished by the use of vertical headlamp/sidelamp/turn indicator units in the wings.

Semi-trailing-arm independent rear suspension was used for the first time on a Mercedes-Benz car and there were disc brakes all round, along with a large (and initially confusing) range of four-cylinder and six-cylinder petrol engines; diesel-engined types would be added later.

Later in the year a smart, under-stated, two-door coupe version of this new design was also revealed, with a choice of carburetted or fuel-injected six-cylinder 2.5-litre engines. No four-cylinder coupes were ever to be produced.

At the same time the S-class was rationalized, the original 250SE and 300SE models being dropped in favour of new 280S (carburetted) and 280SE (fuel-injected) types. Incidentally, if you *really* wanted to be confused, the 300SEL was continued, with the same title but a 2.8-litre engine...

To take advantage of all this engine reshuffling, the SL sportscar became the 280SL, which meant that the ousted 250SL had been on sale for less than a year.

The introduction of the 300SEL 6.3, where a 300bhp Type 600 V8 engine was somehow persuaded to fit into the engine bay of a 300SEL bodyshell, was one of the most audacious engine transplants of all time. The first UK deliveries of this near-140mph super-saloon were made before the end of the year. [At about this time a German magazine published a cartoon of development engineer Erich Waxen-berger trying to force a V12 aero-engine, as supplied for the Messer-schmitt Bf109 during the Second World War, into the same bonnet...]

MG: The front-wheel-drive 1300 gained a 65bhp twin-carb engine in mid-year, then became Mk 2, with twin carburettors and even more power than before (70bhp), in October. This, in fact, demonstrated three important series of changes to this car in the previous 12 months – something symptomatic of the way BMH, and later British Leyland, went about its business.

Monteverdi: Previewed in 1967, but on sale in tiny numbers in 1968, this was a new (and as it transpired, short-

lived) motoring marque. The cars were Swiss, and inspired by Peter Monteverdi, but they had to rely on engines supplied from Chrysler and body styles and shells by Frua of Italy.

The original type was the 375 High Speed coupe, a Maserati-like supercar with a tubular chassis-frame, a 7-litre Chrysler V8 engine and a choice of bodies ranging from a two-seater cabriolet to a 2+2 coupe. Monteverdis were persistently listed in the UK until the early 1970s, though sales were extremely limited.

Morgan: The long-running Plus 8 (which would still be on sale in the late 1990s, getting on for 30 years after its launch) was introduced in September, taking over from the Plus 4, which had had an 18-year career. Although the basic chassis-frame, suspension and two-seater body style all looked famil-iar, they were actually slightly enlarged to make space for the Rover V8 engine.

The wheelbase was 2in longer than before, the track was wider and there was a little more space in the cockpit. Cast alloy wheels were standard. This was by far the fastest and most expen-sive Morgan so far put on sale.

At the same time, the 4/4 was updated by the fitment of the latest 1.6-litre Ford Kent engine: its specifi-cation was now settled, and 4/4 1600s of this type would be built with only minor changes until the 1980s.

Morris: The 1800 became Mk II (see *Austin, above*), and later in the year an 1800 Mk IIS, complete with 96bhp/twin-carburettor engine, was added to the range.

Opel: The new two-seater GT was previewed and would eventually go on UK sale (but only in left-hand-drive form). Clearly, its style was derived from that of the latest Chevrolet Corvette (Opel and Chevrolet both being GM marques, of course).

The GT's platform and suspension was that of the latest Kadett/Olympia types, and there was a choice of engines in Europe, although the only one avail-able in the UK would be the 1.9-litre Olympia/Rekord four-cylinder unit.

Neat but stylish, and complete with rotating rather than flip-up headlamp pods, the GT was always expensive in the UK, and its left-hand drive was a real deterrent to sales.

Porsche: The first major update of the 911 design was introduced in Septem-ber. Not only was the rear-engined car's wheelbase increased (by 2.25in) and the rear track widened, but fuel injection was introduced for 911E and 911S models, resulting in increased power outputs. There was a lot more detail improvement to come in future years.

Peugeot: The 504 appeared in Sep-tember, a more modern statement of Peugeot's design for middle-size, middle-class machines. With an entirely new four-door saloon style, for which Pininfarina had advised, and with inde-pendent front *and* rear suspension, the new 504 was powered by an enlarged, 1.8-litre, version of the familiar four-cylinder engine from the 404.

Carburetted or fuel-injected versions were available, four-wheel disc brakes were standard, and tests soon showed that this was a most refined package. An estate version was already in prepa-ration, and the existing 404 range continued unchanged.

Reliant: The Scimitar GTE arrived in October to establish an entirely new class of sporting car, which became known as the sporting-estate. Based on a separate chassis-frame, which was longer and wider than that used in the Scimitar GT (which continued in production), but with the same front and rear suspension systems and the same Ford 3-litre V6 engine, the GTE featured a smart and practical 2+2 body style in glassfibre, into which had been integrated a large lift-up glass hatchback.

In the summer, the Tamworth com-pany enlarged its own-design four-cylinder unit to 700cc, which meant that the latest Rebel was faster and more torquey than before.

Renault: The R6 was yet another gap-filler in the big Renault range, effec-tively being a developed version of the R4 chassis and front-wheel-drive running-gear, along with a new and somewhat R16-like five-door hatch-back body. Because this car looked more conventional, and certainly was more upmarket than the R4, it sold very well.

The 16TS, introduced in March, was a much more powerful version of the original 16, with a slightly enlarged engine, complete with new crossflow cylinder head and producing 83bhp instead of 55bhp.

In the autumn, the R8S model appeared, to supplement other R8 types, really as a boy-racer's R8 Gordini. The 1.1-litre engine was more powerful and there was a four-head-lamp-nose version of the short-nose body, but in most other respects the basic layout was unchanged.

Riley: The Kestrel 1300 was updated twice (see MG 1300, above).

Rolls-Royce: With no more than a series of development changes, the Phantom V limousine became the Phantom VI limousine from October 1968.

Rover: The 3500 (which Rover insisted on calling 'Three Thousand Five' for a time...) was new in April. Based on the successful P6 2000 model, it used the new light-alloy 3.5-litre V8 which had first been seen on the larger and older P5 model in 1967.

Available only with automatic transmission at first (a manual-transmission version would follow in October 1971), what became known as the P6B was a 115mph four-seater which soon became popular as a chase or 'intervention' car with Britain's police forces.

Saab: During the year the last two-stroke Saab 96 model was sold in the UK, though the model carried on in production in Sweden for a time. Saab was clearing its decks, ready to move upmarket when the 99 model became available in 1969.

The new 99 went into volume-production, but only for left-hand-drive markets: British deliveries would not begin until 1969.

Sunbeam: The Rapier H120 was introduced at the Earls Court Motor Show, using a Holbay-tuned version of the Rapier's 1.7-litre engine, featuring two twin-choke Weber carburettors. Visual changes included a spoiler on the bootlid and stripes along the flanks.

Early in the year the smart 100mph Alpine two-seater sportscar was dropped, bring to an end the production of sportscars by the Rootes Group. Although more than 80,000 such cars had been sold in eight years, Rootes later insisted that the programme had never been profitable.

Toyota: Expansion in the UK market continued with the launch of the 2.3-litre Crown model, which had a single-overhead-camshaft six-cylinder engine and a high level of equipment. Toyota's strength in the UK was with smaller cars, so the Crown was never a major player in the range.

Triumph: The new 2.5PI saloon was Britain's first fuel-injected saloon, being an intriguing combination of Triumph 2000 body structure and suspension units with a detuned version of the fuel-injected 2.5-litre TR5 engine. Sales began at once, but this was to be a short-life model as a radically facelifted body style would follow in a year's time.

Only two years after launch, the GT6 sports coupe and Vitesse 2-litre models became Mk 2 with the introduction of a much-improved lower-wishbone independent rear suspension, which replaced the original swing-axle layout. At the same time the 2-litre engine was given the TR5's cylinder head and more power – 104bhp instead of 95mph.

Vauxhall: The new Ventora was a mixture of Victor and Cresta engineering. The 3.3-litre six-cylinder engine of the Cresta had been squeezed under the bonnet of the existing Victor bodyshell, backed by a choice of manual, overdrive or automatic transmissions, all supported by the latest Victor suspension. Trim, furnishing and equipment were all boosted, putting the Ventora at the top of the new FD-type Victor range.

The Viva GT, introduced in March, was another mix-and-match model, this time by inserting a 104bhp version of the new Victor 2000 engine into the Viva HB two-door bodyshell. This was a 100mph car, not really in direct competition with Ford's new Escort Twin Cam, but having the same sort of character.

In June, the huge gap between 1.2-litre and 2-litre Vivas was filled with the arrival of the Viva 1600, this using the 1.6-litre Victor engine in untuned form. Four-door saloon types followed in October, so completing the Viva range after two years of evolution.

Volkswagen: The new Type 4 appeared in August, attracting great waves of disinterest and criticism, for it was yet another statement of the hack-

neyed rear-mounted air-cooled engine theme to which only VW was now committed.

Novelties included a conventional unit-construction bodyshell, along with MacPherson-strut front suspension and coil-spring/semi-trailing-arm rear suspension, but there was still a flat-four, air-cooled engine in the extreme tail. This, of 1.7-litres, would later be used in the VW-Porsche 914 sportscar and in VW light commercial vehicles. The style was neat and understated, for the car was a fastback whose cues were clearly descended from those of the 1600TL.

Volvo: The 164 made its debut in the autumn, with first British deliveries taking place in 1969. The new car was based closely on the 140-series, but had a longer front-end enclosing a new straight-six 3-litre engine producing 130bhp (net). The front-end style incorporated a big square grille, but the cabin was recognizably the same as that of the 140-series saloon.

At the end of the year, both the 140-series saloons (which were only two years old) and the 1800S sports coupe were given enlarged 2-litre versions of the well-proven four-cylinder overhead-valve engine. This was the final stretch for that power unit, though an overhead-camshaft conversion would follow in the 1970s.

In advance of this, the 140-series family had expanded further with the launch of a square but capacious estate car.

Wolseley: The 1300 was updated to twin carburettors and 65bhp during the year, and except for failing to get yet more power, took the other changes applied to MG 1300 and Riley Kestrel 1300 models in October.

Industrial developments

The most important British merger of the decade came in January when BMH got together with Leyland to form British Leyland. Sir George Harriman became chairman, and Sir Donald Stokes chief executive, but Sir Donald was always seen as the vibrant personality in this so-called partnership. Within months Harriman retired, and Sir Donald became the outright chief of the vast combine, which then had more than 40 per cent of all UK car sales, much more than any other British concern. In 1968, it was announced subsequently, British Leyland built no fewer than 1,001,105 vehicles, of which 807,067 were private cars.

At a stroke, this brought together Austin, Austin-Healey, Daimler, Jaguar, MG, Morris, Riley, Rover, Triumph, Vanden Plas and Wolseley, and there was huge duplication of models, engines, transmissions, factories and management.

Clearly, major rationalization was needed – of products and factories – but this was not properly tackled for

some time, though the Austin Gipsy, MG Magnette, Vanden Plas 4-litre, Vanden Plas 4-litre R and Austin A110 models disappeared almost straight away.

Reluctance to go further than this in 1968 led to the traumas which eventually destroyed British Leyland in 1975, only seven years later.

In the autumn, Lotus was floated as a public limited company, its shares being very popular and almost immediately soaring to a premium.

In Europe, Citroen took a controlling stake in Maserati, but the first jointly-designed model would not surface until 1970.

Technical developments

Harry Ferguson Research's work on four-wheel-drive installations evolved further, not only with a prototype installation in a Ford-USA Mustang, but with a contract to provide conversions for a batch of 20 Ford Zephyr police cars. This was Ferguson's first firm link with Ford's engineers, a collaboration which would eventually lead to the birth and development of four-wheel-drive production cars like the Sierra XR4x4 and rally specials such as the RS200.

Men of Influence

Spencer 'Spen' King

Britain's motor industry watchers had known all about 'Spen' King for many years before the Range Rover appeared, but it was the arrival of that impressive 4x4 which did so much to introduce him to the general public. By that time, in fact, he had already been connected with Rover (latterly British Leyland) for 25 years, his list of 'credits' including the pioneering Rover gas-turbine cars.

Charles Spencer King's mother was Rover chairman Spencer Wilks' sister, but for his first job (during the Second World War) he chose to be apprenticed to Rolls-Royce at Derby, where he rapidly became involved in pioneering gas-turbine aero-engine work. Joining Rover in 1946 (along with Frank Bell), he then concentrated on gas-turbine engine and car design and development work until the mid-1950s. He was not only a talented engineer, but also a brave driver – it was he who drove the first Rover turbine car, JET 1, at 152mph on the Jabbeke road in Belgium in 1952.

Both the engine and the advanced chassis layout of the rear-engined 4WD T3 turbine car were to his credit, and from 1959 he move up to head Rover's technical forward-planning team. In the next decade he and his engineers installed the light-alloy Rover V8 engine in many different cars, designed two attractive Rovers which were cancelled at the prototype stage – one the mid-engined P6BS coupe, the other the big 'Grosser' P8 passenger car – then conceived the Range Rover.

Not only did King and his associate Gordon Bashford

lay out the chassis and running gear of the Range Rover, they also sketched out and had built the first prototype bodyshell. Although the shape was subsequently refined, the basic 'King-Bashford' style of 1967/68 was retained on production Range Rovers for the next generation.

King and Bashford both had a healthy desire to overturn accepted practice, which is why they insisted – so successfully – that the Range Rover could have a supreme cross-country performance, but a remarkably soft ride, and be suitable for elegant on-the-road transport as well. Some say that their efforts were not equalled until the new-generation Range Rover was launched in 1994.

Although Spen always insisted that he was happier designing new cars than running a management team, steady promotion forced him to become a senior manager. Drafted in by British Leyland to be Triumph's technical director in 1968 (to replace Harry Webster, who had gone to Austin-Rover) he then became technical supremo of Rover-Triumph in 1972 and of the entire Leyland Cars technical operation in the late 1970s. From 1979 he became BL Technology's deputy director, before retiring from the company in 1986.

Ten years later, still tremendously active in spite of his advancing years, he was continuing to consult with various engineering companies in the Midlands and resisting any suggestion that he should retire!

1969

Economically it was not a happy time for the British nation, for Government policies piled on extra taxes, and at the same time unemployment began to climb, reaching around 600,000. Today, no doubt, everyone would be happy with that figure, but it caused real concern in 1969.

Once again there was an increase in motoring taxation in the April Budget, for in its drive to eliminate a borrowing deficit the Government added extra charges to many items. There was an extra 2d (0.8p) on a gallon of petrol, which meant that in the five-year life of this administration petrol taxation had soared by 1s 9d (9p), which was a considerable impost at 1960s price levels.

From May 1 all cars over three years old had to be tested and to earn an MoT Certificate of Roadworthiness, a situation which has persisted ever since.

New models

Alfa Romeo: The Italian company reshuffled its pack, making the most it could out of existing four-cylinder twin-cam engines and body styles; with the 2600 now out of production, the 1750 saloon was now the top-of-the-range car.

At the end of the year the Spider models were relaunched, with modified Pininfarina body styling incorporating a much shortened tail with a sharp cut-off.

Aston Martin: The DBS-V8 was finally launched, two years after its 'base car', the DBS (henceforth familiarly known as the DBS-6), had been put on sale.

The principal novelty, of course, was the 5.3-litre V8 engine, which had aluminium alloy cylinder heads and blocks, twin-overhead-camshaft cylinder heads and Bosch fuel injection. Aston Martin chose to keep its power and torque figures to itself, but this was about a 320bhp engine.

The engine was to have a very long and distinguished life, with more powerful Vantage versions following in the late 1970s and four-valve versions being developed in the late 1980s for a new range. It was still being built (sometimes in twin-supercharged 6.3-litre guise) in the mid-1990s.

To commonize it as much as possible with the new DBS-V8, the DB6 became the Mk II version, taking on the DBS's wheels and tyres, along with similar seat and trim styling. At the same time, Associated Engineering Brico fuel injection was made optional – but very few such cars were ever sold, and as all seemed to have given trouble, they were retrospectively converted back to a carburetted set-up in due course.

Audi: The 100S Coupe was a lineal development of the 100S, which had been introduced a year earlier. The engine, however, had been enlarged to 115bhp/1,871cc, and the style was a smaller and neat two-door four-seater fastback with a four-headlamp nose. UK deliveries began in 1970.

Austin: The first important new British Leyland model was the front-wheel-drive Maxi, badged as an Austin, which arrived in April 1969 and was greeted as having five of everything, for it had a five-door bodyshell and a five-speed gearbox.

Although looking somewhat similar to the existing 1800, it was different in almost every detail. There was a brand-new under-square overhead-cam 1.5-litre engine, while the gearchange linkage was by cable rather than by rods.

The all-independent suspension was by Hydrolastic, as with other front-wheel-drive BMC/British Leyland machines, and although the styling was Plain Jane, this was apparently much better than it had been when first seen by Leyland staff less than 18 months earlier.

Because of its stodgy character, and the poor quality of its gearchange, the Maxi was always a controversial car, sales falling well below what had originally been expected. Nevertheless, the Maxi family would remain on sale for more than a decade, the overhead-camshaft engine for even longer.

The 1800S version of the existing 1800 Mk II was launched in September, this being mechanically, structurally and functionally identical to the Morris 1800S which had been put on sale in 1968.

The Austin 1300GT was effectively a rebadged and slightly downmarket version of the MG 1300 which appeared in October.

Bentley: *(See Rolls-Royce, below.)*

Bristol: The Type 410 was dropped in the autumn and the very similar-looking Type 411 took over, the principal change being a much larger (6.3-litre) version of the Chrysler V8 engine which had powered all Bristols for some years.

Citroen: New for 1972 was a fuel-injected version of the 2.2-litre DS21, this unit having 139bhp (gross). At the same time there was a wholesale shuffle of engines, power ratings and specifications among other DS models, and just to add to the confusion, several names were changed! Citroen was nothing if not byzantine in its dealings.

The new Ami 8 was a semi-fastback derivative of the Ami 6, which it replaced, retaining the same 602cc air-cooled flat-twin engine, but having front-wheel disc brakes.

Daimler: The Jaguar 420-based Sovereign dropped out of production, and was instantly replaced by two XJ6-based models. Mechanically identical to the 2.8-litre and 4.2-litre XJ6 types, these cars had slightly different trim and badging, but were otherwise the same as the Jaguars.

Datsun: Japan's largest car-maker at the time (but not by the 1990s...) was still selling cars in the UK in only modest numbers. At the British Motor Show the new 1800 model – known in Japan as the Nissan Laurel – was put on sale, this being a conventionally-engineered Cortina-like car, though with all-independent suspension and a 1.8-litre overhead-camshaft engine.

In Japan, the parent company announced a smart sports coupe to be known there as the Nissan Fairlady, but would carry the designation Datsun 240Z in the UK, British sales beginning before the end of 1970. The 240Z was a spiritual successor to the Austin-Healey 3000, and in the USA it was a rival for (and an immediate winner over) the Triumph TR6.

Powered by a 150bhp version of the existing single-overhead-camshaft 2.4-litre Nissan/Datsun engine, it also had a five-speed gearbox and all-independent suspension. Except for a few plasticky features in the cabin, this was an attractive and capable proposition from the start and it would become a worldwide best-seller.

Dino (Ferrari): The much-liked mid-engined Dino became the Dino 246GT during the year, complete with a 2.4-litre iron-block version of the V6 engine and a slightly longer-wheelbase chassis. These became the standard Dino 246 types, which would be made until 1973.

Enfield: This was a make of which no-one in Britain had heard, and of which they would learn very little in the future. The Enfield was an electric car with a 4.65bhp engine and a bank of lead-acid batteries, with a range of only 30 to 40 miles between charges. Unsurprisingly, it was a complete failure: the miracle is that some companies are still trying to promote electric cars in the mid-1990s when there has been no fundamental breakthrough in battery technology.

Fiat: The new transverse-engined front-wheel-drive 128 model was probably the most important car to come from Fiat in a generation, for it was the first of a new generation of up-to-date designs which would flood out of Turin in the next few years. Many other new Fiats would stem from it.

The styling was square and mundane – the 128 was a saloon, not a hatchback – but there was an all-new overhead-camshaft four-cylinder engine, an end-on gearbox (rather than a box which was under or behind the crankshaft), MacPherson-strut front suspension and a transverse-leaf-spring rear.

The new, large, V6-powered 130 saloon was previewed in the spring, but did not actually go on sale in Italy until the end of the year. British sales, with the later 3.2-litre engine, would not begin until 1972.

The 130 was a more upmarket replacement for the 2300 model, which disappeared from the market. Not only did it have a brand-new Lampredi-designed 2.9-litre overhead-cam engine (which was no relation, incidentally, to the Fiat Dino V6), but there was MacPherson-strut all-independent suspension and a choice of manual or automatic transmissions.

The style was somewhat angular, and the build-quality only average – the 130 would not be a success, though the Coupe which followed in

1970 was a much more promising proposition.

Before the end of the year the two front-engined Fiat Dino models – Spider and Coupe – had been thoroughly revised. The 2400 models were equipped with an iron-block version of the Ferrari-designed 2.4-litre V6 engine, and received the 130-type independent rear suspension and five-speed transmission.

It was a very busy year for Fiat, for also at the Turin show were new 1.6-litre versions of the popular 124 Spider and 124 Sport Coupe models. The Spider's style was unchanged, but the Sport Coupe had a new and very neat four-headlamp nose. UK sales began during the winter.

Ford: 'The car you always promised yourself' was how Ford advertised the Capri coupe when it went on sale early in the year. With its long-nose, short-tail styling, cramped four-seater cabin and wide choice of engines, in many ways this was a European mini-Mustang.

The chassis, complete with MacPherson-strut front suspension, rack-and-pinion steering and front-wheel disc brakes, was typical of Ford-Europe passenger cars. At first, engines varied from a 52bhp/1.3-litre unit to a 93bhp/2-litre V4, with a 128bhp 3-litre V6 option promised for launch in October. It was also possible to order a car with a variety of trim packs – X-trim, L-trim, R-trim or combinations of all three.

Prototypes were shown with a brand-new Ford-Cosworth BDA 16-valve twin-cam engine, but were never put on sale: this engine, in fact, would first find a place in the Escort RS1600 which arrived in 1970.

Like the Mustang in the USA, the European Capri was an instant and colossal success, and nearly 1.9 million of all types would be sold over the next 17 years.

Gilbern: The Genie was discontinued, and the Invader took its place, though this was technically less important than it might sound. The same basic design of chassis and two-door glassfibre body was retained, along with the torquey 3-litre Ford V6 engine. Apart from the name, the principal changes were to trim and equipment.

Hillman: Nearly a year after winning

the London–Sydney Marathon with a tuned-up Hunter, Rootes made a belated marketing response with the launch of the Hillman GT, a car which was really a Hunter with the twin-carburettor Rapier engine and transmission, though with a rather stripped-out interior more closely related to the Minx.

Iso: The new Lele was a rather angular 2+2-seat closed coupe, which used the same basic Chevrolet-powered chassis as all other Iso models of the 1960s. With this model, Iso ran out of ideas and carried on building the existing range for some years before eventually fading away in the mid-1970s.

Lancia: The Flavia Coupe was extensively facelifted with a much more attractive nose style and a smoother tail, but retaining the same Ferrari-like cabin. For the first time there was a 2-litre version of the flat-four engine, which produced a claimed 131bhp (gross) and made this a near-120mph car.

Marcos: After several years of building sportscars with unique marine ply-wood chassis, the Wiltshire-based company abandoned this layout in favour of a more conventional square-section tubular chassis. This change was made not only to allow more cars to be produced, but with an eye to the proposed USA crash tests that the Marcos would have to meet.

By this time the Ford 3-litre V6 was available to join the existing 1.6-litre and 2-litre engine options.

Matra: The French aerospace giant, which also dabbled with sportscar manufacture, decided to enter the British market and put the new mid-engined M530A model on sale in the UK.

This car, which had odd, sharp-edged styling, was powered by a 73bhp/1.7-litre V4 engine from Ford-Germany. Because it was so expensive – £2,160 compared with the £1,063 asked for an MGB – sales in the UK were almost non-existent.

Mazda: The Japanese concern pushed a little harder to build up its UK sales by introducing the R100 fastback, which was a twin-rotor Wankel-engined 2+2 coupe whose engineering was otherwise conventional.

Mercedes-Benz: In September, the company launched a new 3.5-litre V8 engine, which initially was fitted to a variety of S-class models. Much more than the gargantuan 6.3-litre V8, this was a very important 'building block' for the German firm, for it was to be fitted into many cars in the years which followed and would be refined, developed and persistently redesigned. Direct descendants of the engine were still in use in Mercedes-Benz production cars in the mid-1990s.

The original 200bhp engine of this family had fuel injection as standard, a cast iron cylinder block and single-overhead-camshaft aluminium cylinder heads. Larger versions, though with no more specific horsepower, would follow in the early 1970s.

In addition to the important new V8 engine there was also the new mid-engined C111 research sports coupe. Not only did this car have a chassis as advanced as that of any racing car of the period, it also had a 280bhp triple-rotor Wankel engine.

Since there was no intention to race or to put this car on sale in order to demonstrate its mighty technical skills, there seemed to be no reason for Mercedes-Benz to build it at all, so its true purpose was something of an enigma. In due course it would be shown with an even more powerful *four*-rotor Wankel engine, and in later years diesel-engined versions would be used to set endurance speed records.

MG: Only two years after it had been launched with such pomp, the 2.9-litre MGC was discontinued after less than 10,000 had been built.

Mini: At the British Motor Show there were additions to the Mini range – the long-nose Clubman and 1275GT models, structurally and technically similar to existing models, but with squared-up styling aimed at giving the decade-old basic design a new appearance.

The Clubman had a 998cc version of the transverse engine installation, with drum brakes all round, while the 1275GT was really a low-rent alternative to the Mini-Cooper, with a 59bhp single-carburettor version of the 1,275cc engine, and front-wheel disc brakes.

At the same time the Mini-Cooper, but *not* the Mini-Cooper S, was dropped from production.

Then, in November, the car was offi-cially 'debadged', becoming Mini in its own right, and at the same time the suspension of non-Clubman types reverted to rubber cone-springs, and wind-up windows were specified for the doors. The 2,000,000th Mini was built in June.

Monteverdi: The small Swiss builder of Chrysler-engined supercars took a stand at the Earls Court Motor Show, promising that UK deliveries would begin in 1970. They did, but few were ever sold to British customers.

Morris: Effectively, the 1300GT was a slightly-downmarket version of the MG 1300 and was identical in almost every way to the Austin 1300GT.

Moskvich: The latest model, the 412, went on to the British market, complete with an overhead-camshaft 1.5-litre engine. There were rumours that this was a fairly close copy of the BMW unit, but if so it was a pity that Moskvich had not also copied many other BMW aspects of roadholding and quality control...

NSU: The front-wheel-drive K70 was extensively previewed (sometimes with sneak pictures, at other times with official pictures from NSU) but then killed immediately before launch in March, when VW mounted a successful bid for the NSU company. The K70 would later be reborn, badged as a VW, in the autumn of 1970.

Peugeot: The new 304 of September 1969 was structurally similar to the 204, but with a longer and quite distinctive nose style. The engine was a 65bhp/1,288cc version of the 204's transverse unit, the suspension and steering being carried over from the 204 itself.

Only months after the arrival of the 504 saloon, Peugeot introduced smart Pininfarina-styled coupe and cabriolet models. These would eventually go on sale in the UK, though only in left-hand-drive form.

Porsche: At the Frankfurt motor show, the entire 911 range was given enlarged (2.2-litre) engines, ranging from 125bhp to 180bhp, depending on the individual model.

(For Porsche 914/6 details, see Volkswagen-Porsche, below.)

Renault: The new 12 model, introduced at the Paris show in October, was the first of a new range of mid-size Renaults, a front-engine/front-wheel-drive saloon which effectively took over from the rear-engined R8 and R10 models, though there was an overlap in production and in the showrooms.

Unlike the larger 16, the 12 had its engine ahead of the driving wheels and its transmission behind it, which meant that the *Regie* was currently building a bewildering number of different layouts. The engine was a further enlarged version of the 8 and 10 four-cylinder family. UK deliveries started in mid-1970.

From late in the year, the existing long-nose R8S-1100 was replaced by the near-identical-looking R10, which picked up the same enlarged 1.3-litre engine as the new 12. The 10 would be produced for two years and sell nearly 700,000 copies.

Rolls-Royce: A longer-wheelbase (by 4in) derivative of the Silver Shadow (and its very close relative, the Bentley T-series) appeared in May. It was available in saloon and limousine (with electrically-operated division) forms. In general it was almost impossible to distinguish from normal-wheelbase Silver Shadows except that all LWB cars had a vinyl-covered roof and smaller rear windows.

Saab: Two years after it was previewed, the Triumph-engined 99 finally went on UK sale, where it had 80bhp and was initially priced at £1,295.

Skoda: The S100L and S110L were 1-litre and 1.1-litre versions of the well-known rear-engined 1000MB design, complete with a restyle producing rather more curvaceous front and rear ends.

Sunbeam: Rootes reintroduced the Alpine model name, but on a most disappointing new car, the fastback Rapier, into which the less-powerful single-carburettor Hillman Hunter engine had been fitted. The interior was simplified, and even though this was a much cheaper car it was always a slow seller.

Toyota: The 1.9-litre Corona Mk II was added to the range, conventionally engineered, with front engine/rear drive, but being larger, faster and more costly than the original Corona, which remained on sale.

Triumph: In January, only 15 months after the fuel-injected TR5 sportscar had been put on sale, it was replaced by the TR6. Although the new type used the same chassis and basic inner body, it had a major front-end and rear-end restyle by Karmann. The power output and performance figures were virtually unchanged. The USA version was now titled TR6, too, so the TR250 title had only had a short life.

In the autumn, the 2000/2.5PI range was modified to become Mk II, complete with restyled and longer noses and tails. Though the four-door cabins were still the same size as before, they had new and more plush trim and furnishings, along with a new and very smart wood veneer-covered facia.

Vauxhall: The new-generation VX4/90 appeared in October and was a 104bhp version of the existing Victor 2000, though with the four-speed gearbox, overdrive and front-wheel disc brakes as standard.

A new generation of GM automatic transmissions was introduced, this being intended for use in the entire Vauxhall range.

Volkswagen-Porsche: Announced in the autumn of the year, with British sales due to begin early in 1970, the 914 model was a mid-engined sports coupe which had been engineered by Porsche, though it mainly had VW or Audi mechanical components, and was actually built by a new marketing organization. The flat-four, air-cooled, 411-based engine was in front of the line of the rear wheels and the styling was rather angular and gawky, but unlike other Porsches this was only a two-seater.

There was also a flat-six 2-litre Porsche-engined version, badged as the Porsche 916.

Wolseley: The front-wheel-drive 18/85 model became Mk II in the summer, complete with the mechanical improvements already made to the Austin and Morris versions of this car, and with a reworked and more luxuriously-trimmed interior.

At the same time an 18/85S, mechanically identical to the Austin and Morris 1800S types, was also added to the range.

Industrial developments

Reliant announced that it was taking over Bond, which meant that two of Britain's largest users of glassfibre bodies would now be under the same ownership. There were no immediate effects on model line-ups, and production continued as normal in Tamworth and Preston.

The Riley marque died in the summer, the first major British Leyland make to be killed off – but there would be others. In the mid-1990s, incidentally, after BMW bought British Leyland's descendant, Rover, there were rumours that the Riley badge would eventually be revived. British Leyland set up the Unipart parts supply subsidiary. Unlike some of their other enterprises, this was a great success and would eventually become independent in the 1980s.

Technical developments

Ford commissioned Cosworth to develop a 16-valve twin-cam conversion of the existing 1.6-litre Kent engine. This was previewed in January 1969, rated at 120bhp (or 75bhp/litre) and was intended to be a road-car engine which could be supertuned for motorsport use. It was *not* a detuned version of the FVA Formula Two engine, which was different in almost every detail.

Complete with cogged-belt drive to the camshafts, the BDA was the first modern-generation four-valve twin-cam to be built in series. Traditionalists, of course, pointed out that vintage Bentleys had used this layout in the 1920s...

One minor but useful innovation was the location of overdrive switches recessed into the top of gear lever knobs, instead of having their own separate stalks behind the steering wheel. Surprisingly, this attracted some resistance at first.

1970

This was a steady-as-she-goes year for British drivers, even though there was political upheaval in mid-year. Just before annoucing a dissolution of Parliament, the Government presented a Budget in which taxes were reduced. The Labour Party was widely expected to be returned to power, but in fact the Conservatives took over. Motorists hoped that this would mean a gradual reduction in taxes on new cars and petrol and in a lifting of hire purchase restrictions. In the main, they were to be disappointed.

Inflation was beginning to creep upwards in the UK, and most car prices began to increase. This news was received with horror at first, but this was only the beginning, and as inflation became worse, price increases were made not only annually, but at even more frequent intervals.

By 1970, car prices were already 250 per cent higher than 1946 levels had been, but the inflation/price/wages spiral would reach its height in the mid-1970s, the result, on average, being a 350 per cent leap during the 1970s alone. In 1970, for instance, a 998cc Mini sold for £675, but by 1980 the price for a virtually unchanged car would have leapt to £2,710.

Britain's motorway system became more of a network in May when the M5 (Birmingham to South West) and M6 (Midlands to Scotland) motorways were linked up in the West Midlands. Even so, that part of the network was not yet complete, for the connection from the West Midlands to M1 near Rugby had yet to be made.

BP announced that it had struck oil under the North Sea, establishing that there were huge recoverable reserves. This was later christened the Forties Field and was one of the largest of all such reservoirs which helped to make the UK self-sufficient in oil production by the mid-1980s.

New models

Alfa Romeo: The Montreal coupe, which first appeared in March, was a visual descendant of the special Bertone-designed project car seen at the Montreal Expo 67 exhibition of 1967. Like the Expo car, it was based on the front-engined Guilia/Sprint GT platform and suspensions, but in proposed production form it had a detuned version of the Alfa Type 33 racing sportscar's V8 unit.

For production, the engine was a 2.6-litre unit with 200bhp, and although the Montreal was no match for the performance of other Italian supercars, it was much faster than any other Alfa put on the market since the Second World War. British-market sales began before the end of the year, originally only in left-hand-steering form, though RHD would eventually follow.

Austin: Only 18 months after it had been launched, British Leyland made major changes to the Maxi model. The troublesome cable gearchange was abandoned in favour of a rod change, an enlarged (1,748cc) engine was added to the range, and the facia style was much improved. But it was all too late as the damage to the car's reputation had already been done in the first two seasons.

Bentley: During the year the V8 engine was increased from 6,230cc to 6,750cc, which liberated more power and torque, though once again peak figures were never revealed.

Chrysler: The new 160/180 model was a French-built big four-door saloon whose styling had definitely been influenced from the now-defunct Rootes Group *and* from Chrysler-USA, for this was the first of Chrysler-Europe's 'international' cars. As revealed there were 1.6-litre and 1.8-litre versions of a brand-new overhead-camshaft engine, but the chassis was otherwise conventional.

To be made by Chrysler-France (ex-Simca), this was always treated as something of a 'cuckoo' by the French company and was originally advertised (in France) as 'An American from Paris'.

The British Humber version (which would have used a new V6 engine and would have been built in the UK) had already been cancelled before launch. The 160 would never be marketed in the UK, but British sales of 180s would begin in 1971.

Citroen: The launch of the GS model was commercially very important to Citroen as it filled a yawning gap in the model range between the air-cooled flat-twin 2CV, Dyane and Ami types and the large DS models.

Like all other Citroens it was technically advanced, but whimsical in so many detail ways. The first GS types were fastback four-door models which looked as if they should be hatchbacks (that feature would follow a few years later), and the chassis platform was fitted with Citroen's well-proven hydro-pneumatic self-levelling suspension.

The engine was an all-new flat-four air-cooled unit which would eventually be fitted to other models. In its original form it was a 56bhp/1-litre unit, and because the car weighed nearly 2,000lb it was widely criticized for lacking power. Like the larger Citroens, however, the GS had excellent ride and handling characteristics, and soon began to sell in large quantities.

The arrival of the complex but technically fascinating SM coupe was the first evidence of co-operation between Citroen and Maserati (the Italian concern which it had controlled since 1968). The SM was a large 'almost-four-seater' coupe with front-wheel drive, Citroen-type hydro-pneumatic suspension and typically idiosyncratic styling. The engine was a 2.7-litre four-cam, 90-degree V6 which Maserati had developed very rapidly indeed, and was backed by a five-speed transmission.

Not only were four-wheel disc brakes and power-assisted rack-and-pinion steering standard, but the steering had power-operated self-centring to aid parking manoeuvres, while the SM had six headlamps, which were linked to the steering gear in the same way as on recent-model DSs. Unhappily for British enthusiasts, the SM was only ever built with left-hand steering.

Datsun: In Japan, the first Cherry model (actually badged as Nissan, which was Datsun's parent company) was announced, being a chunky transverse-engine front-wheel-drive car with a 59bhp (gross) 1-litre engine. The Cherry, which was the first front-wheel-drive Datsun to enter the UK market, replaced the old-style Datsun 1000. UK deliveries would begin in 1971.

Ford: The third-generation Cortina arrived in October, complete with a new platform and style, new suspensions and a new range of engines. Except for its outer style, the latest Cortina had much in common with the new-generation Ford-Germany Taunus models launched at the same time (though never available in the UK).

Slightly larger than before, with a 3.5in longer wheelbase (almost the same as the Corsair, which was discontinued ahead of the launch of this car), the new Cortina had coil-spring-and-wishbone front suspension with rack-and-pinion steering (becoming the first new Ford for 20 years not to have MacPherson struts), and coil-spring suspension of the rear beam.

The 1.3-litre and 1.6-litre versions used the familiar Kent overhead-valve engines, but there was an entirely new range of Pinto overhead-camshaft engines, these being produced in 88bhp/1,593cc and 98bhp/1,993cc capacities.

As ever there were two-door, four-door, estate car and various trim pack types in a 35-car range, which was as complex as usual.

The Escort RS1600 was previewed in January, but did not go on sale until later in the year. The first cars were built at Halewood, but from the end of the year assembly was moved to South Ockendon, in Essex.

Powered by a 120bhp version of the Cosworth-Ford 16-valve BDA engine, which had twin overhead camshafts and two twin-choke Weber carburettors, this was meant to be a 'homologation special' for use in racing and rallying. The RS1600 had a five-year life, and its successor, the RS1800, took over in 1975, both being phenomenally successful rally cars.

At the end of the year the new AVO plant started to build the Escort Mexico, which was really a re-engined RS1600. Instead of the complex 16-valve engine there was an 86bhp overhead-valve Kent unit – and the price, at £1,150, was much lower.

The Capri range was expanded even further with the launch of the 3000E, mechanically identical to the 3000GT, but with more upmarket trim and fittings. A Capri RS2600 was also seen in Europe, but this variety was built in Germany and never officially marketed in the UK.

Detail improvements to the four-cylinder Kent engines meant slightly more power for a variety of Escorts and Capris, starting in October.

Ginetta: The small Suffolk-based company showed prototypes of a new G21 model, which was a front-engine/rear-drive sports coupe of MGB GT size. At the time it was suggested that there would be a choice of 1.6-litre four-cylinder and 3-litre V6 Ford engines, but by the time the car actually went on sale in 1971 the small Ford engine had been replaced by a Rootes/Chrysler 1,725cc unit.

Hillman: The launch of the Avenger in February was the most important made by the Rootes Group for four years. Aimed at the Escort/Viva class, the Avenger was all-new – bodyshell, engine, transmission and suspension – and was produced at the Ryton factory. All cars previously built at Ryton were now being assembled at the Linwood factory in Scotland.

The Avenger's four-door body style was conventional, as were the overhead-valve four-cylinder engine and beam-axle rear suspension. Originally there was a choice of 53bhp/1,248cc or 63bhp/1,498cc engines, with automatic transmission only available with the larger of the two. Performance and character was stodgy, to say the least, but the 75bhp/1,498cc Avenger GT, which followed at the end of the year, was much better. Although these were not exciting cars, they made a good deal of commercial sense, and would be built behind Hillman, Chrysler and finally Talbot badges for the next decade.

Towards the end of the year the Minx and GT models were killed off, the Hunter range being revised. The same engines, transmissions and body styles were all still present, but names and trim/power/status combinations had been changed. It was little wonder that the Chrysler-UK image began to sag – for no-one really seemed to know what was on offer from one season to the next.

Jaguar: The vast old 420G (ex-Mk X) model was finally dropped to make space for yet more production of XJ6 types. New engines were forecast, but although Jaguar admitted that these were on the way, they were not promised until 1971.

Lagonda: It was all a false alarm – for four years, anyway – but in January, a prototype of a new four-door

Lagonda was seen on BBC TV. This was a larger and more spacious version of the Aston Martin DBS-V8, with the same basic platform chassis and running gear, but it would not be seen again until 1974.

Lamborghini: There was great excitement in Italy when the mid-engined P250 Urraco model was launched. This car, with styling by Bertone, had a unit-construction shell, a transverse engine position and a brand-new 2.5-litre V8 engine with single overhead camshafts per bank. It was an obvious head-to-head competitor for the Ferrari Dino 246GT, but it was not yet ready for production and in the end would never establish the same sort of reputation.

Lotus: The Series 4 Seven appeared in March to a barrage of criticism from all fans of the earlier types. The Series 4 car was new in most respects, with a revised multi-tubular chassis-frame and a rather angular glassfibre body style which was a less-pure pastiche of the original.

As with previous Sevens, wet-weather protection was minimal, there was a wide choice of four-cylinder engines, ranging from the standard Ford 86bhp 1600GT to a 135bhp Holbay-tuned version of the Lotus-Ford twin-cam.

Marcos: At first for export only, but later put on the UK market, was yet another version of the familiar sports-car style. This particular machine used the 130bhp/3-litre straight-six Volvo engine and its related gearbox: in performance this almost paralleled that of the Ford V6-engined version of the same car.

In September, the inexplicably ugly Mantis model was launched, this being totally different from any other Marcos. Technically it was familiar in that it had a fabricated steel-tube chassis, a glassfibre coupe body, independent front suspension and a rear axle beam suspended on coil springs, but detail execution was different.

Power was by the 150bhp fuel-injected 2.5-litre six-cylinder Triumph TR6 unit, and the body style of this 2+2-seater could best be described as unmistakable.

Not even Marcos' owner, Jem Marsh, could really justify why the Mantis looked as it did, but there were very few customers – only 32 were sold and the model died within a year.

Mercedes-Benz: The latest C111 Wankel-engined research car appeared in March 1970, this time with a 350bhp four-rotor engine and styling changes. As described in the 1969 section, this was not proposed for production, but merely showed the technical prowess of the German concern.

Monteverdi: The Swiss car-maker revealed the mid-engined (Chrysler V8) Hai 450SS supercar, which had a very simple square-tube chassis and was quite obviously undeveloped when first revealed.

Although it was claimed to have 450bhp and a mountainous 490lb ft of torque, not forgetting a colossal top speed of around 180mph, little further was ever heard of this car, and in later years it was revealed that no orders had ever been taken and just two prototypes had been built!

Opel: Towards the end of the year there were two important new models – the Ascona saloon and the Manta coupe, both based on a brand new unit-construction platform. These cars filled the large marketing gap between the small/medium Kadett and the large Rekord/Commodore models. The Ascona took over from the Olympia range.

Both these cars had conventional front-engine/rear-drive layouts, using 1.6-litre and 1.9-litre versions of the well-known cam-in-head four-cylinder engines. Coil-spring front suspension, coil-spring/beam-axle rears, front-wheel disc brakes and a choice of manual or automatic transmission made up a predictable package.

The Ascona was officially launched at the Turin show in November, offering two-door or four-door saloon and estate car derivatives of the new body style with the two sizes of engine.

The Manta had smart, curvaceous, two-door, almost-four-seater coupe styling – and was actually the first of this range to be announced.

Peugeot: Convertible and coupe versions of the 304 models were introduced, sharing their styles with existing 204 coupe/convertible types.

At the start-up of the 1971 model year, the company simplified its old 404 range around the 1.6-litre engine. However, the same engine was enlarged to 2 litres for the 504, there being carburetted or fuel-injected versions, as before.

Renault: The 16 range was revamped, the 16/16TL models being given an enlarged and more powerful engine – 67bhp/1,565cc instead of the 55bhp/1,470cc unit of the original types.

The smaller hatchback in the Renault range – the R6 – was also uprated with a 45bhp/1,108cc engine.

Rolls-Royce: During the year the size of the V8 engine fitted to all models was increased from 6,230cc to 6,750cc, the increased power and torque values remaining unquoted.

Rover: The Range Rover made its first appearance in June, immediately setting new standards for a 4x4 car. Bigger, more capable and faster than previous Land-Rovers, it established a new leisure-vehicle class in Europe which was still expanding in the 1990s. There were no mechanical links with the Land-Rovers, which stayed in production.

The Range Rover had a sturdy 100in-wheelbase chassis, long-travel suspension by coil springs, and four-wheel disc brakes, with power by a detuned version of the light-alloy 3.5-litre V8, which was already being used in other Rovers (and in the Morgan Plus 8 sportscar).

The body style was a simple, rather angular, three-door layout, with much more load-carrying steel than in the earlier Land-Rovers, though many skin panels were aluminium alloy pressings.

Compared with later versions, which went progressively more upmarket, the furnishing was much more simple. At this stage Rover thought that the Range Rover would be used mainly as a working vehicle, so most of the trim surfaces were washable, and there were rubber mats rather than carpets on the floor.

All that would change in the years which followed, and the original-shape Range Rover, heavily developed, would still be in production in the mid-1990s after a new generation had finally been developed.

In the autumn, the P6 range – 2000 and 3500 models – were treated to a front-end facelift, and there was also a new and more gracefully detailed facia style for all but the basic 2000 model.

Saab: Evolution of the 99 model began, not only by the arrival of an enlarged 1.85-litre version of the Triumph-built overhead-camshaft engine, but also a fuel-injected version. At the same time Saab announced that it would soon be able to manufacture its own engines in a new factory in Sweden: when this happened, many of the original Triumph features were seen to have been changed by Saab, and these would never be seen in Triumph-type engines.

Simca: The 1204 Special was a high-performance version of the front-wheel-drive 1100, complete with a 75bhp/1.1-litre engine.

Skoda: The S110R Coupe was a two-door fastback version of the existing S110 saloon, still with a rear-mounted engine, this time tuned to give 52bhp.

Sunbeam: Following the death of the Singer marque, the Sunbeam Sport took over from the identical Singer Chamois Sport, while the short-lived Sunbeam Vogue (only built in 1970) replaced the Singer Vogue. These were both temporary expedients to keep dealers and customers happy for a time.

Triumph: The Stag was a brave attempt to take on Mercedes-Benz and BMW in the large-engined/open-top/sporting/GT category, which eventually failed because of engine unreliability problems.

The Stag was based on a much-modified and shortened underpan from the Triumph 2000/2.5 model and had a smart 2+2-seater body style by Michelotti. The transmission, suspension, steering and brakes were all developed versions of the 2000/2.5 models, but the engine was a brand-new 3-litre V8, complete with aluminium heads and overhead-camshaft valve-gear.

This engine, in fact, was a blood relation of the slant-four unit already being supplied to Saab for the 99 model, and shared much of the same production machinery. Sales began in the autumn.

Although the 1300 and 1300TC models were discontinued in mid-summer, there were two recognizable new derivatives of that old design. The first, the 1500 model, was still a front-wheel-drive machine, with the same transmission, but fitted with a 61bhp/ 1,493cc version of the four-cylinder engine.

The Toledo, on the other hand, was a major carve-up. Although the basic bodyshell was as before, it now had a front-engine/rear-wheel-drive layout, with a new all-synchromesh gearbox which would shortly be adopted for the Spitfire, and for the British market there was a two-door saloon, soon to be joined by a four-door saloon. The Toledo was the simplest of all such types, for it had a beam rear axle and four-wheel drum brakes in its most basic form. Yet more permutations of this design would follow in the next few years.

Immediately *after* the Earls Court Motor Show (thus emphasizing that export sales were much more important than the home market), heavily-revised Spitfire and GT6 sportscars were launched. Both had reskinned and smoother bodies, complete with sharply cut-off tails which were similar to those introduced on the new Stag.

The Spitfire was given new 'swing-spring' rear suspension, which eliminated the considerable camber change inherent in earlier rear suspensions, along with the new all-synchromesh gearbox recently launched for Toledo models.

Vauxhall: The Viva HC took over from the HB in October. This new range used the same platform, suspensions and basic line-up of engines as the HB, though there was no 2-litre GT version in the new line-up. The cabin style was less curvaceous than that of the HB, there being two-door and four-door saloons and three-door estate cars in the range.

Volkswagen: Well over a year after it had taken over the NSU business and killed off the new K70 model the week before launch, VW launched a new model – the VW K70! Modified only slightly from the original NSU design, but subjected to VW's usual quality audits and now to be built in the VW Salzgitter plant, the K70 was the first VW to have a water-cooled and a front-mounted engine, and the first with front-wheel drive.

With a chassis and passenger cabin closely based on that of the NSU Ro80, the K70 used a new type of 1.6-litre

four-cylinder overhead-camshaft engine (similar, in many ways, to other NSU units) and was close in performance, size and class to VW's existing air-cooled 411 model. British sales were not expected to start until 1971.

Fuel-injected engines were added to the rear-engined 411 range for the 1600TE Fastback and the 1600E Variant (estate car).

At the start of the 1971 model year, VW also made major changes to the incredibly successful Beetle, announcing a new Type 1302S Super Beetle derivative which had a 1.6-litre version of the flat-four engine, MacPherson-strut front suspension instead of trailing arms and torsion bars, and the semi-trailing-arm suspension previously only found on automatic transmission cars. At the same time the 1300 Beetle became the 1302, complete with a more powerful engine.

Volvo: The development of the 140 series continued, with fuel-injected versions of the 2-litre engine being added to the range. The 2-litre 1800E coupes were also introduced to the UK market during the year.

Industrial developments

From July 1, the Rootes Motors name disappeared and was replaced by Chrysler United Kingdom Ltd. Although this change seemed only cosmetic at first, it proved Chrysler's determination to integrate Rootes (which it already controlled) into its worldwide empire. Simca of France became Chrysler France at about the same time.

There was a great deal of industrial unrest at British Leyland, which caused many strikes, much loss of production, and bizarre demonstrations such as the one in London where Swiss businessmen marched through London complaining that they had been waiting for 14 months for Jaguar XJ6s to be delivered!

Ford opened a new Advanced Vehicle Operations (AVO) factory at South Ockendon, Essex, to build specialized high-performance cars. The first model to be launched was the RS1600, to be followed closely by the Escort Mexico.

Jensen, which had been controlled by various groups or companies in the 1960s, changed hands once again.

This time it was the American motor trader Kjell Qvale, along with the Healey family, who bought the business. Production of existing Interceptor and FF models continued – at an increasing rate – but plans were also laid to produce a new Jensen-Healey sportscar. The new Jensen-Healey would not actually appear until 1972.

Reliant announced that it was to close down the Bond assembly factories in Lancashire. A new Bond Bug three-wheeler (based on the Reliant three-wheeler) was announced, but proposals to build Bond four-wheelers at the Reliant factory were abandoned.

Although it was never officially revealed by British Leyland, the Austin-Healey marque was quietly killed off at the end of the year as the Healey business' royalty and consultancy agreement ran out. For 1971 the Austin-Healey Sprite became the plain Austin Sprite and the MG Midget carried on unchanged.

The Morris Minor, first launched in 1948, began its long goodbye, with production of saloons and convertibles ending during the year: the last Morris Minor of all would be built in 1971.

The Singer marque disappeared in the spring of the year. Rootes had bought Singer in the winter of 1955/56, and in the next 15 years had built many thousands of Gazelles, Vogues and Chamois models, all based on one or other of the Hillman range. However, Chrysler, having seen the steady decline of Singer sales, decided to drop the name.

Technical developments

This was the year in which the first Russian Ladas were assembled, these being re-engined and reworked versions of Fiat's 124. The co-operative design and production deal had been announced as early as 1966, but it had taken a full four years for the new factory to be built at Togliattigrad.

Anti-lock braking systems were still virtually unknown in motor cars (that used in the Jensen FF was really an aerospace system), but Mercedes-Benz showed the first of their prototype installations: it would still be some years, however, before what are now familiarly known as ABS systems became commercially available.

APPENDIX A

CARS in the UK: 1945 to 1970
Specifications and performance data

NOTES:

i) Cars listed are those which were officially sold in the UK, either by their manufacturers, or by official importers. Private imports, test cars, and (in a few cases) British models only sold overseas are not listed.

ii) With some limited-production models, many items of optional equipment were available. In those cases I have produced what was a 'typical specification'.

iii) Production figures are totals, not UK deliveries. In some cases, where models were introduced pre-World War Two, these figures include prewar production. Except where stated, these figures come from factory sources.

In some cases accurate figures are not available and are quoted as 'Est' (for estimated). N/A = not available. 'In prod' indicates that a car was still in production.

iv) 'Years built' refers to the production life of these cars, not necessarily the years in which they were sold in the UK. For example, a foreign car built from 1945–1954 may have been sold in the UK for only two of those years. Cars announced overseas in 1970 have been included even though they may not have gone on sale in the UK until 1971. For cars still in production at the time this book is published, dates are quoted like this: 1959–Date.

v) Body styles are those officially marketed by the factory. Some types were not available in the UK.

vi) Accepted engine positions are: F – ahead of the driving seat; M – behind the driving seat, but ahead of the rear wheels; R – behind the line of the rear wheels. In some cases engine tunes changed during the production run. Where possible, these are summarized in the tables.

vii) Quoted engine sizes and tunes are for such cars sold in the UK. Other sizes, types and power outputs which may have been available in other markets are not quoted.

viii) Prices quoted are total retail figures for the cheapest original version, including all purchase or VAT/special car taxes, and are

those listed when the car first went on sale in the UK. They do not include engine or transmission options, or other optional extras.

ix) Performance figures, where available, were those recorded by independent testers. In the tables these are quoted on the same line as the appropriate engine specification. Where such tests have not been found, factory-recorded figures are sometimes shown instead.

Abbreviations:

Body styles

Conv	Drophead/Convertible/Cabriolet
Cpe	Coupe
Est	Estate car
Htch	Hatchback
Limo	Limousine and Landaulette
Sal	Saloon
Spl	Special coachwork
Spts	Sportscar
Targa	Removable roof panels
Ute	Utility (especially 4x4s, etc)

Engine and transmission

F/F	Front-engine/front-wheel drive
F/R	Front-engine/rear-wheel drive
F/4	Front-engine/four-wheel drive
R/R	Rear-engine/rear-wheel drive
M/R	Mid-engine/rear-wheel drive
M/4	Mid-engine/four-wheel drive
R/4	Rear-engine/four-wheel-drive
IL	In-line engine
(Tr)	Transversely mounted
V	Vee-engine
HO	Horizontally-opposed engine
Rot	Rotary (Wankel) engine
AirC	Air-cooled
SV	Side-valve
IOEV	Overhead inlet/side exhaust valve
OHC	Single overhead camshaft per head
2OHC	Twin overhead camshaft per head
OHV	Overhead valves, pushrod-operated
2-Str	Two-stroke engine
Diesel	Diesel
Auto	Automatic transmission
SemiAuto	Semi-automatic
O/D	Overdrive
PreS	Preselector

Chassis

I	Independent
DD	De Dion
Beam	Beam axle
C	Coil springs
TrL	Transverse leaf spring
1/4E	Quarter-elliptic leaf spring
1/2E	Half (semi)-elliptic leaf spring
Tor	Torsion bar
Air	High-pressure air suspension
HP	Hydro-pneumatic (and Oleopneumatic) suspension
Rubber	Rubber springs
HydroL	Hydrolastic suspension
HydraG	Hydragas suspension
Disc	Disc brakes
Drum	Drum brakes
R & P	Rack-and-pinion steering
Worm	All other steering types
N/A	Not available/not known
N/Q	Not quoted by manufacturer

Cars from North America:

Except in isolated cases, it has not been practical to give details of North American cars price-listed in the UK since 1945. In many cases cars were listed but not stocked, the choice of engine, transmission and body options was enormous, and deliveries were only made against special orders. Cars seen at British Motor Shows, and subsequently listed, were often sold only in ones and twos – and then not always in the specification listed in British magazines at the time!

Many North American cars seen on British roads were originally imported for use by North American government departments, businesses, individuals and military service personnel. Although such cars were often registered in the UK, then sold on to British buyers in due course, in many cases these models and derivatives were not even price-listed as being for sale in the UK.

Individual specifications and performance details of North American cars tested by *Autocar*, *Autocar & Motor*, and *Motor* since the import ban was lifted in 1953 have been included and marked with stars: **

Make and model	Production Figures	Years Built	Body Styles	Mechanical Layout	Engine Make (if not own)	Capacity/(cc)/Layout/Valves	BHP/rpm	Torque (lb.ft)/rpm	Transmission gearbox/automatic transmission
Abarth									
Zagato 750	N/A	1957–1961	Cpe	R/R	Fiat	747/4IL/ OHV	44/6000	44/3500	4-spd/-
AC									
2-litre	1,284	1947–1958	Sal Conv Spts Conv	F/R	—	1991/6IL/ OHC	74/4500 85/4500	105/2750	4-spd/-
Ace/Aceca/ 2.6	1,059	1953–1964	Spts Cpe	F/R	—	1991/6IL/ OHC	85/4500 102/4500	105/2750 120/3000	4-spd (+O/D)/-
					Bristol	1971/6IL/ OHV	105/5000 125/5750	123/3750 122/4500	4-spd (+O/D)/- 4-spd (+O/D)/-
					Ford	2553/6IL/ OHV	90/4400 to 170/5800	133/2000 N/Q	
Greyhound	83	1959–1963	Cpe	F/R	Bristol	1971/6IL/ OHV	105/4700	129/3000	4-spd (+O/D)/-
Cobra/AC289	1,137	1962–1968	Spts	F/R	Ford-USA	4261/V8/ OHV	260/5800	269/4500	4-spd/-
	(Figures incl. Cobra 427 – which was not officially sold in the UK)					4727/V8/ OHV	300/5750	285/4500	4-spd/-
428	81	1965–1973	Cpe Conv	F/R	Ford-USA	7014/V8/ OHV	345/4600	462/2800	Auto/-
Alfa Romeo									
1900/TI	17,243	1950–1958	Sal	F/R	—	1884/4IL/ 2OHC	80/5000 115/5500	96/3000 116/3700	4-spd/-
1900 Sprint	1,796	1951–1958	Cpe Conv	F/R	—	1884/4IL/ 2OHC	100/5500 115/5500	104/3000 121/3700	4-spd/- 5-spd/-
Giulietta saloons	131,785	1955–1962	Sal	F/R	—	1290/4IL/ 2OHC	53/5500 74/6200	69/3000 69/3500	4-spd/- 5-spd/-
							63/6000	69/3500	4-spd/-
Giulietta Sprint	27,142	1954–1962	Cpe	F/R	—	1290/4IL 2OHC	80/6300 90/6000	72/3500 80/4500	4-spd/- 4-spd/-
Giulietta Spider	17,096	1955–1962	Spts	F/R	—	1290/4IL/ 2OHC	80/6300 90/6000	72/3500 80/4500	4-spd/-
Giulietta SS/SZ	1,366/200	1957–1962	Cpe	F/R	—	1290/4IL/ 2OHC	100/6000	83/4500	5-spd/-
2000 saloon	2,804	1958–1961	Sal	F/R	—	1975/4IL/ 2OHC	105/5300	112/3500	5-spd/-
2000 Sprint	700	1960–1962	Cpe	F/R	—	1975/4IL/ 2OHC	115/5700	112/3500	5-spd/-
2000 Spider	3,443	1958–1961	Spts	F/R	—	1975/4IL/ 2OHC	115/5700	112/3500	5-spd/-
2600 saloon	2,092	1962–1968	Sal	F/R	—	2584/6IL/ 2OHC	130/5900	148/3400	5-spd/-
2600 Sprint	6,999	1962–1966	Cpe	F/R	—	2584/6IL/ 2OHC	145/5900	156/4000	5-spd/-
2600 Spider	2,255	1962–1965	Spts	F/R	—	2584/6IL/ 2OHC	145/5900	156/4000	5-spd/-
Giulia saloons	836,323 (all Giulias)	1962–1974	Sal	F/R	—	1290/4IL/ 2OHC	82/6000 89/6000	77/4900 101/3200	5-spd/-
						1570/4IL/ 2OHC	92/6200 95/5500	108/3700 100/4400	5-spd/-
							98/5500	96/2900	5-spd/-
							102/5500	105/4400	
							112/6500	112/4200	
Giulia 1600 Sprint	7,107	1962–1964	Cpe	F/R	—	1570/4IL/ 2OHC	92/6200	108/3700	5-spd/-
Giulia 1600 Spider	10,341	1962–1965	Spts	F/R	—	1570/4IL/ 2OHC	92/6200	108/3700	5-spd/-
Giulia Sprint Speciale	1,400	1963–1965	Spts Cpe	F/R	—	1570/4IL/ 2OHC	112/6200	98/4200	5-spd/-
Sprint GT/ GTV family	210,495	1963–1975	Cpe	F/R	—	1290/4IL/ 2OHC	89/6000 96/6000	101/3200 101/3200	5-spd/- 5-spd/-
						1570/4IL/ 2OHC	106/1000 109/6000 115/6000	103/3000 103/2800 119/5500	5-spd/- 5-spd/- 5-spd/-
						1779/4IL/ 2OHC	122/5500	137/2900	5-spd/-
						1962/4IL/ 2OHC	132/5500	134/3000	5-spd/-
Duetto/1750/ 2000 Spider	N/A	1966–1993	Spts	F/R	—	1290/4IL/ 2OHC	89/6000	101/3200	5-spd/-
						1570/4IL/ 2OHC	109/6000	103/2800	5-spd/-

Suspension Front	Rear	Steering	Brakes (Front/rear)	Wheels/model Tyres	Length (in)	Weight (lb, unladen)	Performance Top speed (mph)	0–60mph (sec)	Standing ¼-mile (sec)	UK Total Price (£: at Launch)
ITrL	IC	Worm	Drum/drum	5.50-12	137	1232	95	15.8	20.0	£2248
Beam 1/2E	Beam 1/2E	Worm	Drum/drum	5.00-17 6.70-16	184	2688/ 2800	80	19.9	22.0	£1277
ITrL	ITrL	Worm	Drum/drum Disc/drum	5.50-16	153	1685/ 1840	103	11.4	18.0	£1439
ITrL	ITrL	Worm	Drum/drum	5.50-16	153	1845	108 (Est)	N/A	N/A	£2011
ITrL	ITrL	Worm	Disc/drum	5.50-16	153	1845	117	9.0	16.8	
IC	IC	R & P	Disc/drum	6.40-15 or 5.50-16	180	2240	104	11.4	18.9	£2891
ITrL	ITrL	Worm	Disc/disc	6.50-15 F/ 6.70-15 R	158	2100	138	5.5	13.9	£2454
IC	IC	R & P	Disc/Disc	205-15	176	3115	139	5.9	14.4	£4250
IC	BeamC	Worm	Drum/drum	165-400	174	2531	103	17.8	20.6	£2622 £2851
IC	BeamC	Worm	Drum/drum	165-400	173	2205	112 (Claimed)	N/A	N/A	£3543
IC	BeamC	Worm	Drum/drum	155-15	158	2017	87	N/A	N/A	£1726
IC	BeamC	Worm	Drum/drum	155-15	158	2079	95	17.7	20.8	£2191
IC	BeamC	Worm	Drum/drum	155-15	152	1897	101	13.0	18.9	£2261
IC	BeamC	Worm	Drum/drum	155-15	152	2100	113	11.8	18.4	£2919
IC	BeamC	Worm	Drum/drum	155-15	152	1860	112	11.8	18.4	£2116
IC	BeamC	Worm	Drum/drum Disc/disc	155-15	162/150	1730/1654	122	11.2	17.8	£2721
IC	BeamC	Worm	Drum/drum	165-400	186	2955	100 (Claimed)	N/A	N/A	£2832
IC	BeamC	Worm	Drum/drum	165-400	172	2650	109 (Claimed)	N/A	N/A	£3129
IC	BeamC	Worm	Drum/drum	165-400	177	2600	111	14.2	19.5	£3111
IC	BeamC	Worm	Disc/drum	165-400	186	3100	108	13.0	18.5	£2746
IC	BeamC	Worm	Disc/disc	165-400	180	3000	117	11.7	18.0	£2806
IC	BeamC	Worm	Disc/disc	165-400	177	2770	124 (Claimed)	N/A	N/A	£2979
IC	BeamC	Worm	Disc/disc	155-15	163	2152	97	15.3	19.8	£1225
IC	BeamC	Worm	Disc/disc	155-15	163	2240	106	13.1	18.9	£1659
IC	BeamC	Worm	Disc/disc	155-15	163	2307	108	11.3	18.3	£1599
IC	BeamC	Worm	Disc/disc	155-15	158	1995	107	12.2	20.5	£1650
IC	BeamC	Worm	Drum/drum Disc/drum	155-15	156	2065	107	12.9	18.8	£1729
IC	BeamC	Worm	Disc/disc	155-15	162	2094	124	12.0	18.0	£2382
IC	BeamC	Worm	Disc/disc	155-15	161	2046	102	13.2	19.1	£1749
IC	BeamC	Worm	Disc/disc	155-15	161	2117	102	13.8	19.6	£1649
IC	BeamC	Worm	Disc/disc	155-15	161	2090	112	10.6	N/A	£1650
IC	BeamC	Worm	Disc/disc	155-15	161	2286	113	11.1	17.7	£1950
IC	BeamC	Worm	Disc/disc	165-14	161	2180	115 (Est)	N/A	N/A	£2128
IC	BeamC	Worm	Disc/disc	165-14	161	2292	116	11.2	18.0	£2248
IC	BeamC	Worm	Disc/disc	165-14	161	2288	120	9.2	16.4	£2439
IC	BeamC	Worm	Disc/disc	155-15 or 165-14	167, later 162 from 1970	2181	106 (Claimed)	N/A	N/A	£1749
IC	BeamC	Worm	Disc/disc	155-15	167	2195	111	11.2	17.7	£1895

Make and model	Production Figures	Years Built	Body Styles	Mechanical Layout	Engine Make (if not own)	Capacity/(cc)/Layout/Valves	BHP/rpm	Torque (lb.ft)/rpm	Transmission gearbox/automatic transmission
						1779/4IL/2OHC	122/5500	137/2900	5-spd/-
						1962/4IL/2OHC	115/5500	119/3000	5-spd/Auto
							133/5500	134/3000	5-spd/-
							120/5800	118/4200	5-spd/-
1750 saloon	101,883	1967–1972	Sal	F/R	—	1779/4IL/2OHC	122/5500	139/3000	5-spd/-
2000 saloon	89,840	1970–1977	Sal	F/R	—	1962/4IL/2OHC/	131/5500	134/3000	5-spd/-
Montreal	3,925	1970–1977	Cpe	F/R	—	2593/V8/2OHC	200/6500	173/4750	5-spd/-

Allard

Make and model	Production Figures	Years Built	Body Styles	Mechanical Layout	Engine Make (if not own)	Capacity/(cc)/Layout/Valves	BHP/rpm	Torque (lb.ft)/rpm	Transmission gearbox/automatic transmission
J1	12	1946–1948	Spts	F/R	Ford/Ford-Canada	3622/V8/SV	85/3800	150/2000	3-spd/-
						3917/V8/SV	100/3500	N/Q	
K1/L/M	842	1946–1950	Spts Conv	F/R	Ford/Ford-Canada	3622/V8/SV	85/3800	150/2000	3-spd/-
						3917/V8/SV	100/3500	N/Q	
P1 saloon	559	1949–1951	Sal	F/R	Ford/Ford-Canada	3622/V8/SV	85/3800	150/2000	3-spd/-
						3917/V8/SV	100/3500	N/Q	
J2	90	1950–1951	Spts	F/R	Ford/Various	4375/V8/SV	120/3800	221/2000	3-spd/-
K2	119	1950–1951	Spts	F/R	Ford/Ford-Canada	3622/V8/SV	85/3800	150/2000	3-spd/-
						3917/V8/SV	140/3500	225/2500	3-spd/-
J2X	83	1951–1952	Spts	F/R	Cadillac	5420/V8/OHV	172/4000	N/Q	3-spd/-
M2X	25	1951–1953	Conv	F/R	Ford/Ford-Canada	3622/V8/SV	85/3800	150/2000	3-spd/-
						3917/V8/SV	100/3500	N/Q	
P2 saloon/estate (Monte Carlo, and Safari)	21	1952 only	Sal Est	F/R	Ford/Ford-Canada	3622/V8/SV	85/3800	150/2000	3-spd/-
K3	62	1952–1955	Spts	F/R	Ford/Ford-Canada	3622/V8/SV	85/3800	150/2000	3-spd/-
						3917/V8/SV	100/3500	N/Q	
Palm Beach	73	1952–1955	Spts	F/R	Ford-UK	1508/4IL/OHV	47/4400	74/2400	3-spd/-
						2262/6IL/OHV	68/4000	112/2000	3-spd/-
GT	6	1956–1959	Cpe	F/R	Jaguar	3442/6IL/2OHC	210/5500	213/4000	4-spd (+O/D)/-

Alvis

Make and model	Production Figures	Years Built	Body Styles	Mechanical Layout	Engine Make (if not own)	Capacity/(cc)/Layout/Valves	BHP/rpm	Torque (lb.ft)/rpm	Transmission gearbox/automatic transmission
TA14 saloon	3,311	1946–1950	Sal Conv	F/R	—	1892/4IL/OHV	65/4000	95/2750	4-spd/-
TB14/TB21 Sports	131	1949–1951	Spts	F/R	—	1892/4IL/OHV	68/4000	95/2750	4-spd/-
						2993/6IL/OHV	90/4000	150/2000	4-spd/-
TA21/TC21 saloon	2,074	1950–1955	Sal Conv	F/R	—	2993/6IL/OHV	90/4000	150/2000	4-spd/-
							100/4000	163/2000	4-spd/-
TC/TD/TE TF21	1,556	1956–1967	Sal Conv	F/R	—	2993/6IL/OHV	104/4000	163/2500	4-spd/Auto
							115/4000	152/2500	4-spd/5-spd/Auto
							130/5000	172/3250	4-spd/5-spd/Auto
							150/4750	185/3750	5-spd/Auto

Amphicar

Make and model	Production Figures	Years Built	Body Styles	Mechanical Layout	Engine Make (if not own)	Capacity/(cc)/Layout/Valves	BHP/rpm	Torque (lb.ft)/rpm	Transmission gearbox/automatic transmission
Amphicar	Est 2,500	1961–1967	Conv	R/R	Triumph	1147/4IL/OHV	38/4750	56/2500	4-spd/-

Armstrong-Siddeley

Make and model	Production Figures	Years Built	Body Styles	Mechanical Layout	Engine Make (if not own)	Capacity/(cc)/Layout/Valves	BHP/rpm	Torque (lb.ft)/rpm	Transmission gearbox/automatic transmission
Lancaster Hurricane/ Typhoon/ Whitley	12,470	1946–1953	Sal Cpe Conv Est Limo	F/R	—	1991/6IL/OHV	70/4200	95/3000	4spd/4PreS
						2309/6IL/OHV	75/4200	108/2500	4spd/4PreS

Suspension Front	Rear	Steering	Brakes (Front/rear)	Wheels/model Tyres	Length (in)	Weight (lb, unladen)	Performance Top speed (mph)	0–60mph (sec)	Standing 1/4-mile (sec)	UK Total Price (£: at Launch)
IC	BeamC	Worm	Disc/disc	165-14	167, later 162 from 1970	2292	116	9.2	17.1	£2199
IC	BeamC	Worm	Disc/disc	165-14 to 195/60-15	162	2291/2445	116	8.8	17.1	£2439
IC	BeamC	Worm	Disc/disc	165-14	162	2245	116	9.8	17.1	
IC	BeamC	Worm	Disc/disc	195/60-15	167	2444	118 (Est)	9.4	N/A	£15,950
IC	BeamC	Worm	Disc/disc	165-14	173	2447	116	10.8	17.5	£1898
IC	BeamC	Worm	Disc/disc	165-14	173	2447	113	9.1	17.1	£2026
IC	BeamC	Worm	Disc/disc	195-14	156	2794	137	7.6	15.4	£5077
ITrL	BeamTrL	Worm	Drum/drum	6.00-16	149	2240	85 (Est)	N/A	N/A	£1125
ITrL	BeamTrL	Worm	Drum/drum	6.25-16	168-182	2632-2968	(K)86 (M)82 (L)85 (Est)	13.6 15.2 N/A	N/A 20.5 N/A	£1151 £1125 £1259
IC	BeamTrL	Worm	Drum/drum	6.25-16	186	3024	85 (Est)	N/A	N/A	£1277
IC	DDC	Worm	Drum/drum	6.25-16	148	2016	(Cadillac)111	7.4	16.2	£1277
IC	BeamTrL	Worm	Drum/drum	6.25-16	168	2464	85 (Est)	N/A	N/A	£1277
IC	BeamTrL	Worm	Drum/drum	6.25-16	168	2689	101	11.6	18.1	£1868
IC	DDC	Worm	Drum/drum	6.25-16	148	2688	100	10.0	18.5	£1713
IC	BeamTrL	Worm	Drum/drum	6.25-16	190	3136	86	15.7	20.3	£1790
IC	DDC	Worm	Drum/drum	6.25-16	192	3248	85 (Est)	N/A	N/A	£2568
					192	3248	85 (Est)	N/A	N/A	£1946
IC	DDC	Worm	Drum/drum	6.25-16	177	2604	85 (Est)	N/A	N/A	£1713
IC	BeamC	Worm	Drum/drum	5.50-15	156	1850	85 (Claimed)	N/A	N/A	£1021
IC	BeamC	Worm	Drum/drum	5.50-15	158	2156	85	16.9	20.3	£1064
ITor	BeamC (or DDC)	Worm	Disc/drum	6.00-15	162	2856	120	9.6	17.1	£2409
Beam1/2E	Beam1/2E	Worm	Drum/drum	6.00-16	175	3136	74	22.2	N/A	£893
Beam1/2E	Beam1/2E	Worm	Drum/drum	6.00-16	174	2730	80	19.0	21.0	£1276
IC	Beam1/2E	Worm	Drum/drum	6.00-15	177	2830	95	N/A	20.5	£1598
IC	Beam1/2E	Worm	Drum/drum	6.00-15	182	3190	86	19.8	21.6	£1598
IC	Beam1/2E	Worm	Drum/drum	6.00-15	182	3346	100	16.5	20.5	£1822
IC	Beam1/2E	Worm	Drum/drum	6.00-15	189	3285	102	13.5	19.8	£2766
IC	Beam1/2E	Worm	Disc/drum Disc/disc	6.40-15	189	3450	104	13.9	19.6	£2827
IC	Beam1/2E	Worm	Disc/disc	6.40-15	189	3450	107	12.5	18.8	£2775
IC	Beam1/2E	Worm	Disc/disc	6.40-15	189	3450	120	9.9	17.8	£3225
IC	IC	Worm	Drum/drum	6.40-13	171	2315	70	42.9	25.4	£1275
ITor	Beam1/2E	Worm	Drum/drum	5.50-17	185	2968	75	29.7	N/A	£991
ITor	Beam1/2E	Worm	Drum/drum	5.50-17	185	3115	80 (Est)	N/A	N/A	£1247

Make and model	Production Figures	Years Built	Body Styles	Mechanical Layout	Engine Make (if not own)	Capacity/(cc)/Layout/Valves	BHP/rpm	Torque (lb.ft)/rpm	Transmission gearbox/automatic transmission
Sapphire/Star Sapphire	8,187 (all Sapphires)	1953–1960	Sal	F/R	—	3435/6IL/ OHV	125/4200	177/2000	4-spd/PreS/Auto
							150/5000	194/2000	4-spd/PreS/Auto
						3990/6IL/ OHV	165/4250	260/2000	Auto/-
Sapphire Limousine	381	1955–1959	Limo	F/R	—	3435/6IL/ OHV	125/4200	194/2000	4-spd/PreS/Auto
						3990/6IL/ OHV	140/4000	250/1750	4-spd/Auto
234/236	1,406	1956–1958	Sal	F/R	—	2309/6IL/ OHV	85/4400	118/2750	4-spd (+O/D)/ SemiAuto
						2290/4IL/ OHV	120/5000	139/3500	4-spd (+O/D)/-

Aston Martin

Make and model	Production Figures	Years Built	Body Styles	Mechanical Layout	Engine Make (if not own)	Capacity/(cc)/Layout/Valves	BHP/rpm	Torque (lb.ft)/rpm	Transmission gearbox/automatic transmission
DB1	15	1948–1950	Spts Conv	F/R	—	1970/4IL/ OHV	90/4750	108/3000	4-spd/-
DB2/2-4/ Mk III	1,725	1950–1959	Cpe Conv	F/R	—	2580/6IL/ 2OHC	105/5000	125/3000	4-spd/-
							125/5000	146/3500	4-spd/-
						2922/6IL/ 2OHC	140/5000	178/3000	4-spd/-
							162/5500	180/4000	4-spd (+O/D)/Auto
							178/5500	180/4000	
DB4	1,113	1958–1963	Sal	F/R	—	3670/6IL/ 2OHC	240/5500	240/4250	4-spd (+O/D)/Auto
							266/5750	255/4500	
DB4GT	81	1959–1963	Sal	F/R	—	3670/6IL/ 2OHC	302/6000	270/5000	4-spd/-
DB4GT Zagato (plus Second sanction of 4 cars in 1991/1992)	19	1961–1963	Cpe	F/R	—	3670/6IL/ 2OHC	314/6000	278/5400	4-spd/-
DB5	1,063	1963–1966	Sal Conv Est	F/R	—	3995/6IL/ 2OHC	282/5500	288/3850	4-spd (+O/D)/
							325/5500	290/4500	5-spd/Auto
DB6/ Volante/ Mk II	1,755	1965–1970	Sal Conv Est	F/R	—	3995/6IL/ 2OHC	282/5500	288/3850	5-spd/Auto
							325/5500	290/4500	5-spd/Auto
DBS-6	899	1967–1973	Sal Est	F/R	—	3995/6IL/ 2OHC	282/5500	288/3850	5-spd/Auto
							325/5500	290/4500	5-spd/Auto
DBS-V8/ AM V-8/ Vantage	2,666	1969–1989	Sal Conv	F/R	—	5340/V8/ 2OHC	N/QN/Q		5-spd/Auto
							N/Q (Vtge)	N/Q	5-spd/-

Audi

Make and model	Production Figures	Years Built	Body Styles	Mechanical Layout	Engine Make (if not own)	Capacity/(cc)/Layout/Valves	BHP/rpm	Torque (lb.ft)/rpm	Transmission gearbox/automatic transmission
60/70/80/90	416,852	1965–1972	Sal Est	F/F	—	1496/4IL/ OHV	55/4750	83/2500	4-spd/-
						1696/4IL/ OHV	72/5000	94/2800	4-spd/-
							80/5000	98/3000	4-spd/-
						1760/4IL/ OHV	90/5200	108/3000	4-spd/-
100	796,787	1968–1976	Sal Est	F/F	—	1760/4IL/ OHV	100/5500	111/3200	4-spd/Auto
						1871/4IL/ OHV	115/5500	117/4000	4-spd/Auto
100 Coupe S	30,687	1969–1976	Cpe	F/F	—	1871/4IL/ OHV	115/5500	117/4000	4-spd/Auto

Austin

Make and model	Production Figures	Years Built	Body Styles	Mechanical Layout	Engine Make (if not own)	Capacity/(cc)/Layout/Valves	BHP/rpm	Torque (lb.ft)/rpm	Transmission gearbox/automatic transmission
8hp	56,103	1939–1947	Sal	F/R	—	900/4IL/ SV	23/4000	N/Q	4-spd/-
10hp	55,521	1939–1947	Sal	F/R	—	1125/4IL/ SV	28/4000	N/Q	4-spd/-
12hp/16hp	44,132	1939–1947	Sal	F/R	—	1535/4IL/ SV	42/4000	N/Q	4-spd/-
						2199/4IL/ OHV	67/3800	97/2200	4-spd/-
A40 Devon/ Dorset	316,484	1947–1952	Sal Est	F/R	—	1200/4IL/ OHV	40/4300	57/2800	4-spd/-
A70 Hampshire	35,261	1948–1950	Sal Est	F/R	—	2199/4IL/ OHV	64/3800	96/2200	4-spd/-
A90 Atlantic	7,981	1948–1952	Sal Conv	F/R	—	2660/4IL/ OHV	88/4000	140/2500	4-spd/-
A110/A125 Sheerline	8,700	1947–1954	Sal Limo	F/R	—	3460/6IL/ OHV	110/N/Q	N/Q	4-spd/-
						3993/6IL/ OHV	125/N/Q	N/Q	4-spd/-
A120/A135 Princess/ Princess II/III	1,910	1947–1956	Sal Limo	F/R	—	3460/6IL/ OHV	120/N/Q	N/Q	4-spd/-

Suspension Front	Rear	Steering	Brakes (Front/rear)	Wheels/model Tyres	Length (in)	Weight (lb,unladen)	Performance Top speed (mph)	0–60mph (sec)	Standing 1/4-mile (sec)	UK Total Price (£: at Launch)
IC	Beam1/2E	Worm	Drum/drum	6.50-16	193	3472	91	15.5	20.0	£1728
IC	Beam1/2E	Worm	Drum/drum	6.50-16	193	3472	100	13.0	19.3	£1758
IC	Beam1/2E	Worm	Disc/drum	6.70-16	194	3920	100	14.8	21.1	£2646
IC	Beam1/2E	Worm	Drum/drum	7.00-16	212	4032	90 (Est)	N/A	N/A	£2866
IC	Beam1/2E	Worm	Disc/drum	7.60-15	212	4200	95 (Est)	N/A	N/A	£3150
IC	Beam1/2E	Worm	Drum/drum	6.40-15	180	2912	80 (Est)	N/A	N/A	£1657
IC	Beam1/2E	Worm	Drum/drum	6.40-15	180	2912	97	15.5	20.2	£1600
IC	BeamC	Worm	Drum/drum	5.75-16	176	2240	100 (Est)	N/A	N/A	£2332
IC	BeamC	Worm	Drum/drum	6.00-16	163	2660	116	11.2	18.5	£1920
IC	BeamC	Worm	Drum/drum	6.00-16	169	2632	111	12.6	20.3	£2622
IC	BeamC	Worm	Drum/drum	6.00-16	169	2772	119	10.5	17.9	£2622
IC	BeamC	Worm	Disc/drum	6.00-16	171	2947	119	9.3	17.4	£3076
IC	BeamC	R & P	Disc/disc	6.00-16	177	3000	141	8.5	16.1	£3980
IC	BeamC	R & P	Disc/disc	6.00-16	172	2800	152	6.4	14.0	£4530
IC	BeamC	R & P	Disc/disc	6.00-16	168	2700	153	6.1	14.5	£5470
IC	BeamC	R & P	Disc/disc	6.70-15	180	3200	141	8.1	16.0	£4249
IC	BeamC	R & P	Disc/disc	6.70-15	182	3250	140 (Est)	N/A	N/A	£4998
IC	BeamC	R & P	Disc/disc	6.70-15 8.15-15	182	3250	148	6.5	14.5	£4998
IC	DDC	R & P	Disc/disc	GR70-15	181	3760	140 (Est)	N/A	N/A	£5500
IC	DDC	R & P	Disc/disc	GR70-15	181	3760	148	8.6	16.3	£6897
IC	DDC	R & P	Disc/disc	GR70-15	181	3800	162 183	6.0	14.1	£6897
IC	DDC	R & P	Disc/disc	GR70-15	184	4001	170 (Est)	5.4	13.7	£20,000
ITor	BeamTor	R & P	Disc/drum	6.15-13	173	2080	86 (Claimed)	N/A	N/A	£1068
ITor	BeamTor	R & P	Disc/drum	165-13	173	2251	89	13.4	20.0	£1147
ITor	BeamTor	R & P	Disc/drum	165-13	173	2459	97 (Est)	N/A	N/A	£1096
ITor	BeamTor	R & P	Disc/drum	165-13	173	2184	100	12.8	18.7	£1194
IC	BeamTor	R & P	Disc/drum	165-14	182	2310	106	11.9	18.7	£1475
IC	BeamTor	R & P	Disc/drum	165-14	182	2340	109	9.9	17.6	£1876
IC	BeamTor	R & P	Disc/drum	185-14	173	2397	112	10.6	17.7	£2418
Beam1/2E	Beam1/2E	Worm	Drum/drum	4.50-17	149	1701	56	N/A	27.6	£326
Beam1/2E	Beam1/2E	Worm	Drum/drum	5.00-16	158	1975	60	N/A	N/A	£397
Beam1/2E	Beam1/2E	Worm	Drum/drum	5.50-16	171	2643	63	N/A	N/A	£531
Beam1/2E	Beam1/2E	Worm	Drum/drum	5.75-16	171	2995	75	25.1	22.9	£569
IC	Beam1/2E	Worm	Drum/drum	5.00-16	153	2100	67	34.8	24.4	£403
IC	Beam1/2E	Worm	Drum/drum	5.50-16	163	2688	82	21.5	22.2	£608
IC	Beam1/2E	Worm	Drum/drum	5.50-16	177	2698	91	16.6	20.9	£953
IC	Beam1/2E	Worm	Drum/drum	6.50-16	192	4340	80 (Est)	N/A	N/A	£1277
IC	Beam1/2E	Worm	Drum/drum	6.50-16	192	4340	81	19.4	21.9	£1277
IC	Beam1/2E	Worm	Drum/drum	6.50-16	192	4452	85 (Est)	N/A	N/A	£2102

Make and model	Production Figures	Years Built	Body Styles	Mechanical Layout	Engine Make (if not own)	Capacity/(cc)/Layout/Valves	BHP/rpm	Torque (lb.ft)/rpm	Transmission gearbox/automatic transmission
						3993/6IL/ OHV	130/3700	212/2200	4-spd/-
A40 Somerset	173,306	1952–1954	Sal Conv	F/R	—	1200/4IL/ OHV	42/4300	62/2200	4-spd/-
A40 Sports	4,011	1950–1953	Conv	F/R	—	1200/4IL/ OHV	46/4400	61/3000	4-spd/-
A70 Hereford	50,421	1950–1954	Sal Conv Est	F/R	—	2199/4IL/ OHV	68/3800	116/1700	4-spd/-
A30/A35	527,000 (approx, and incl. vans)	1951–1962	Sal Est	F/R	—	803/4IL/ OHV	30/4800	40/2400	4-spd/-
						948/4IL/ OHV	34/4750	50/2000	4-spd/-
Champ	1,200	1952–1955	Ute	F/4	Rolls-Royce	2838/4IL/ IOEV	80/3750	147/1750	5-spd/-
					—	2660/4IL/ OHV	75/3750	135/2000	5-spd/-
A40/A50/ A55	299,500 (approx, and incl. vans)	1954–1958	Sal	F/R	—	1200/4IL/ OHV	42/4500	58/2400	4-spd/-
						1489/4IL/ OHV	50/4400	74/2100	4-spd/SemiAuto
							51/4250	81/2000	4-spd/SemiAuto
A90/A95/ A105	60,400 (approx)	1954–1959	Sal Est	F/R	—	2639/6IL/ OHV	85/4000	124/2000	4-spd (+O/D)/-
							92/4500	130/2000	4-spd (+O/D)/Auto
							102/4600	141/2600	4-spd (+O/D)/Auto
Gipsy	21,208	1958–1968	Ute	F/4	—	2199/4IL/ OHV	62/4100	110/1500	4-spd/-
							72/4100	116/1800	4-spd/-
						2178/4IL/ OHV Diesel	55/3500	89/2500	4-spd/-
Princess IV/Limo	200/ 3,344	1952–1968	Sal Limo Land	F/R	—	3993/6IL/ OHV	150/4100	227/2400	Auto/-

[Princess was rebadged Vanden Plas Princess from 1959]

Make and model	Production Figures	Years Built	Body Styles	Mechanical Layout	Engine Make (if not own)	Capacity/(cc)/Layout/Valves	BHP/rpm	Torque (lb.ft)/rpm	Transmission gearbox/automatic transmission
A40 Farina	342,180	1958–1967	Sal Est	F/R	—	948/4IL/ OHV	34/4750	50/2000	4-spd/-
							37/5000	50/2500	4-spd/-
A55/A60	426,500 (approx)	1959–1969	Sal Est	F/R	—	1489/4IL/ OHV	52/4350	82/2100	4-spd/-
						1622/4IL/ OHV	61/4500	90/2100	4-spd/Auto
						1489/4IL/ OHV Diesel	40/4000	64/1900	4-spd/Auto
A99/A110	41,250 (approx)	1959–1968	Sal	F/R	—	2912/6IL/ OHV	103/4500	158/2000	3-spd (+O/D)/Auto
							120/4750	163/2750	3-spd (+O/D)/Auto
							120/4750	163/2750	4-spd (+O/D)/Auto

Mini – see **Mini** marque, below

Make and model	Production Figures	Years Built	Body Styles	Mechanical Layout	Engine Make (if not own)	Capacity/(cc)/Layout/Valves	BHP/rpm	Torque (lb.ft)/rpm	Transmission gearbox/automatic transmission
1100/1300	1,119,800 (approx)	1963–1974	Sal Est	F(Tr)/F	—	1098/4IL/ OHV	48/5100	60/2500	4-spd/Auto
						1275/4IL/ OHV	58/5250	69/3000	4-spd/Auto
							70/6000	74/3250	4-spd/-
1800	210,000 (approx)	1964–1975	Sal	F(Tr)/F	—	1798/4IL/ OHV	80/5000	100/2100	4-spd/-
							86/5300	101/3000	4-spd/Auto
							96/5700	106/3000	4-spd/-
3-litre	9,992	1967–1971	Sal	F/R	—	2912/6IL/ OHV	124/4500	161/3000	4-spd (+O/D)/Auto
Maxi	472,098	1969–1981	Htch	F(Tr)F	—	1485/4IL/ OHC	74/5500	84/3500	5-spd/-
						1748/4IL/ OHC	84/5500	105/3000	5-spd/Auto
							91/5250	104/3400	5-spd/-

Austin-Healey

Make and model	Production Figures	Years Built	Body Styles	Mechanical Layout	Engine Make (if not own)	Capacity/(cc)/Layout/Valves	BHP/rpm	Torque (lb.ft)/rpm	Transmission gearbox/automatic transmission
100/4	14,634	1953–1956	Spts	F/R	—	2660/4IL/ OHV	90/4000	144/2500	3-spd (+O/D)/-
							110/4500	143/2600	4-spd (+O/D)/-
100S	50	1955 only	Spts	F/R	—	2660/4IL/ OHV	132/4700	168/2500	4-spd/-
100-Six/ 3000	58,370	1956–1968	Spts	F/R	—	2639/6IL/ OHV	102/4600	142/2400	4-spd (+O/D)/-
							117/4750	149/3000	4-spd (+O/D)/-
						2912/6IL/ OHV	124/4600	162/2700	4-spd (+O/D)/-
							132/4750	167/3000	4-spd (+O/D)/-
							131/4750	158/3000	4-spd (+O/D)/-
							148/5250	165/3500	4-spd (+O/D)/-
Sprite I	48,987	1958–1961	Spts	F/R	—	948/4IL/ OHV	43/5200	52/3300	4-spd/-
Sprite II/ III/IV	79,338	1961–1970	Spts	F/R	—	948/4IL/ OHV	46/5500	53/3000	4-spd/-
						1098/4IL/ OHV	56/5500	62/3250	4-spd/-
							59/5750	65/3500	4-spd/-

Suspension Front	Rear	Steering	Brakes (Front/rear)	Wheels/model Tyres	Length (in)	Weight (lb, unladen)	Performance Top speed (mph)	0–60mph (sec)	Standing 1/4-mile (sec)	UK Total Price (£: at Launch)
IC	Beam1/2E	Worm	Drum/drum	6.50-16	192	4452	88	16.8	21.3	£2102
IC	Beam1/2E	Worm	Drum/drum	5.25-16	159	2156	69	31.6	24.3	£728
IC	Beam1/2E	Worm	Drum/drum	5.25-16	159	2520	78	25.6	23.2	£818
IC	Beam1/2E	Worm	Drum/drum	5.50-16	168	2716	81	21.4	22.1	£687
IC	Beam1/2E	Worm	Drum/drum	5.20-13	137	1484	63	N/A	25.3	£507
IC	Beam1/2E	Worm	Drum/drum	5.20-13	137	1484	72	30.0	23.5	£541
ITor	ITor	Worm	Drum/drum	6.50-16	144	3470	65 (Est)	N/A	N/A	£1100
ITor	ITor	Worm	Drum/drum	6.50-16	144	3470	65 (Est)	N/A	N/A	£750
IC	Beam1/2E	Worm	Drum/drum	5.60-15	162	2248	70 (Est)	N/A	N/A	£650
IC	Beam1/2E	Worm	Drum/drum	5.90-13	162	2248	74	28.8	23.2	£678
IC	Beam1/2E	Worm	Drum/drum	5.90-13	167	2325	75	31.8	23.3	
IC	Beam1/2E	Worm	Drum/drum	6.40-15	182	2912	86	18.9	21.0	£792
IC	Beam1/2E	Worm	Drum/drum	6.40-15	181	2975	90	19.8	21.8	
IC	Beam1/2E	Worm	Drum/drum	6.40-15	181	2975	96	15.4	20.2	£1110
IRubber	IRubber	Worm	Drum/drum	6.00-16	139	2912	63	N/A	24.7	£650
IRubber	Beam1/2E									
Beam1/2E	Beam1/2E	Worm	Drum/drum	6.00-16	139	3360	68	N/A	25.1	£680
IRubber	IRubber	Worm	Drum/drum	6.00-16	139	2912	60 (Est)	N/A	N/A	£755
Beam1/2E	Beam1/2E									
IC	Beam1/2E	Worm	Drum/drum	6.50-16	201	4590	99	16.1	20.6	£2517
IC	Beam1/2E	Worm	Drum/drum	5.20-13	144	1680	72	35.6	24.5	£639
IC	Beam1/2E	Worm	Drum/drum	5.20-13	144	1800	75	27.1	23.7	£657
IC	Beam1/2E	Worm	Drum/drum	5.90-14	178	2473	78	23.6	22.5	£802
IC	Beam1/2E	Worm	Drum/drum	5.90-14	175	2473	81	21.4	21.8	£854
IC	Beam1/2E	Worm	Drum/drum	5.90-14	175	2520	68	34.3	25.4	£922
IC	Beam1/2E	Worm	Disc/drum	7.00-14	188	3305	98	14.4	20.2	£1149
IC	Beam1/2E	Worm	Disc/drum	7.00-14	188	3470	102	13.3	19.4	£1270
IC	Beam1/2E	Worm	Disc/drum	7.50-13	188	3470	101	16.2	19.8	£997
IHydroL	IHydroL	R & P	Disc/drum	5.50-12	147	1780	78	22.2	22.7	£593
IHydroL	IHydroL	R & P	Disc/drum	5.50-12	147	1780	88	17.3	20.7	£672
IHydroL	IHydroL	R & P	Disc/drum	145-12	147	1900	93	15.6	20.0	£910
IHydroL	IHydroL	R & P	Disc/drum	175-13	164	2645	90	17.1	20.5	£769
IHydroL	IHydroL	R & P	Disc/drum	165-14	164	2645	93	16.3	19.9	£999
IHydroL	IHydroL	R & P	Disc/drum	165-14	164	2645	99	13.7	19.4	£1105
IHydroL	IHydroL	R & P	Disc/drum	185-14	186	3290	100	15.7	20.1	£1418
IHydroL	IHydroL	R & P	Disc/drum	155-13	158	2160	86	16.6	20.6	£979
IHydroL	IHydroL	R & P	Disc/drum	155-13	158	2160	89	15.8	20.2	£1103
IHydroL	IHydroL	R & P	Disc/drum	165-13	158	2216	97	13.2	19.4	£1375
IC	Beam1/2E	Worm	Drum/drum	5.90-15	151	2150	103	10.3	17.5	£1064
IC	Beam1/2E	Worm	Disc/disc	5.50-15	148	1924	119	7.8	16.1	Special Order
IC	Beam1/2E	Worm	Drum/drum	5.90-15	158	2435	103	12.9	18.8	£1144
IC	Beam1/2E	Worm	Drum/drum	5.90-15	158	2435	111	11.2	18.1	£1159
IC	Beam1/2E	Worm	Disc/drum	5.90-15	158	2460	114	11.4	17.9	£1168
IC	Beam1/2E	Worm	Disc/drum	5.90-15	158	2460	112	11.5	18.8	£1168
IC	Beam1/2E	Worm	Disc/drum	5.90-15	158	2460	117	10.4	17.8	£1184
IC	Beam1/2E	Worm	Disc/drum	5.90-15	158	2548	121	9.8	17.2	£1106
IC	Beam1/4E	R & P	Drum/drum	5.20-13	137	1328	86	20.5	21.8	£679
IC	Beam1/4E	R & P	Drum/drum	5.20-13	138	1525	86	20.0	22.0	£670
IC	Beam1/4E	R & P	Disc/drum	5.20-13	138	1525	89	16.9	21.0	£587
IC	Beam1/2E	R & P	Disc/drum	5.20-13	138	1566	92	14.7	19.8	£611

Make and model	Production Figures	Years Built	Body Styles	Mechanical Layout	Engine Make (if not own)	Capacity/(cc)/Layout/Valves	BHP/rpm	Torque (lb.ft)/rpm	Transmission gearbox/automatic transmission
						1275/4IL/OHV	65/6000	72/3000	4-spd/-
Autobianchi									
Bianchina	N/A	1958–1969	Cpe Conv	R/R	Fiat	499/2IL/OHV	18/4400	26/3500	4-spd/-
Auto Union									
1000	171,008	1958–1963	Sal	F/F	—	980/3IL/2-Str	45/4500	62/2250	4-spd/-
							50/4500	62/2250	4-spd/-
							55/4500	65/3000	
1000 SP	6,640	1958–1965	Cpe	F/F	—	980/3IL/2-Str	55/4500	65/3000	4-spd/-
Bedford									
Beagle	N/A	1964–1973	Est	F/R	—	1057/4IL/OHV	40/5200	55/2600	4-spd/-
Bentley									
Mk VI/ R-Type	7,521	1946–1955	Sal	F/R	—	4256/6IL/IOEV	N/Q	N/Q	4-spd/-
						4556/6IL/IOEV	N/Q	N/Q	4-spd/Auto
							N/Q	N/Q	4-spd/Auto
R-Type Continental	208	1952–1955	Cpe Spl	F/R	—	4556/6IL/IOEV	N/Q	N/Q	4-spd/Auto
S1/SII/SIII	6,347	1955–1965	Sal Spl	F/R	—	4887/6IL/IOEV	N/Q	N/Q	4-spd/Auto
						6230/V8/OHV	N/Q	N/Q	Auto/-
S-Type Continental	1,131	1955–1965	Cpe Conv	F/R	—	4887/6IL/IOEV	N/Q	N/Q	4-spd/Auto
			Spl			6230/V8/OHV	N/Q	N/Q	Auto/-
T1/T2	2,280	1965–1980	Sal	F/R	—	6230/V8/OHV	N/Q	N/Q	Auto/-
						6750/V8/OHV	N/Q	N/Q	Auto/-
Corniche Continental	1,280	1966–1994	Cpe Conv Spl	F/R	—	6230/V8/OHV	N/Q	N/Q	Auto/-
						6750/V8/OHV	N/Q	N/Q	Auto/-
Berkeley									
B60 - B105	2,000 Est	1956–1961	Spts	F(Tr)/F	Anzani/ Excelsior/ Royal Enfield	322/2IL/2-Str AirC	15/5000	16/3500	3-spd/-
						328/2IL/2-Str AirC	18/5250	22/3000	3-spd/-
						492/3IL/2-Str AirC	30/5500	35/3500	4-spd/-
						692/2IL/OHV AirC	40/5500	43/4000	4-spd/-
							50/6250	45/4000	
Foursome	Incl. above	1958–1961	Spts	F/F	Excelsior	492/3IL/2-Str AirC	30/5500	35/3500	4-spd/-
						692/2IL/OHV AirC	40/5500	43/4000	4-spd/-
							50/6250	45/4000	
BMW									
501/502/3.2	22,750 Est	1952–1961	Sal	F/R	—	1971/6IL OHV	65/4400	95/2000	4-spd/-
							72/4400	96/2500	
						2077/6IL/OHV	72/4500	100/2500	4-spd/-
						2580/V8	90/4800	130/2800	4-spd/-
						V8	100/4800	133/2500	4-spd/-
						3168/V8	120/4800	155/2500	4-spd/-
						V8	140/4800	159/3200	
503	412	1956–1959	Cpe	F/R	—	3168/V8/OHV	140/4800	159/3800	4-spd/-
507	253	1956–1959	Spts	F/R	—	3168/V8/OHV	150/5000	174/4000	4-spd/-
Isetta	161,728	1955–1962	Sal	M/R	—	245/1cyl/OHV	12/5800	11/4500	4-spd/-
						298/1cyl/	13/5200	14/4600	4-spd/-

Suspension Front	Rear	Steering	Brakes (Front/rear)	Wheels/model Tyres	Length (in)	Weight (lb, unladen)	Performance Top speed (mph)	0–60mph (sec)	Standing 1/4-mile (sec)	UK Total Price (£: at Launch)
IC	Beam1/2E	R & P	Disc/drum	5.20-13	138	1575	94	14.6	19.7	£672
IC	IC	Worm	Drum/drum	125-12	117	1100	68 (Est)	N/A	N/A	£581
ITrL	BeamTrL	R & P	Drum/drum	5.60-15	142	1974	80	23.0	22.5	£1241
ITrL	BeamTrL	R & P	Drum/drum	5.60-15	142	2044	81	23.6	23.2	£1259
ITrL	BeamTrL	R & P	Drum/drum	155-15	163	2090	82	23.2	22.4	£1996
ITrL	Beam1/2E	R & P	Drum/drum	4.00-12	150	1680	73	29.1	22.6	£620
IC	Beam1/2E	Worm	Drum/drum	6.50-16	192	4004	100	15.2	20.4	£2997
IC	Beam1/2E	Worm	Drum/drum	6.50-16	192	4004	100	15.0	19.7	£4474
IC	Beam1/2E	Worm	Drum/drum	6.50-16	200	4060	101	13.8	19.1	£4824
IC	Beam1/2E	Worm	Drum/drum	6.50-16	207	3700	115	13.5	19.5	£7608
IC	Beam1/2E	Worm	Drum/drum	8.20-15	212	4480	101	14.2	19.7	£4669
IC	Beam1/2E	Worm	Drum/drum	8.20-15	212	4650	113	11.5	18.2	£5661
							116	10.8	17.7	£6127
IC	Beam1/2E	Worm	Drum/drum	7.60-15 8.00-15	212	4255	119	12.9	18.8	£7164
IC	Beam1/2E	Worm	Drum/drum	8.00-15	212	4225	113	12.1	18.6	£7857
IC	IC	Worm	Disc/disc	8.45-15	204	4659	115	10.9	17.6	£6496
IC	IC	Worm R & P (T2)	Disc/disc	8.45-15 205-15	204	4659	117	10.2	17.5	£9148
				235/70-15	204	4930	119	9.4	17.7	£22,809
IC	IC	Worm	Disc/disc	8.45-15	204	4978	115 (Est)	N/A	N/A	£9789
IC	IC	Worm R & P	Disc/disc	8.45-15 205-15 235/70-15	204	4978	120	9.6	17.1	£11,491
IC	IC	Worm	Drum/drum	5.20-12	123	700	60 (Est)	N/A	N/A	£575
IC	IC	Worm	Drum/drum	5.20-12	123	700	65	38.3	25.6	£575
IC	IC	Worm	Drum/drum	5.20-12	123	850	80	21.8	22.4	£574
IC	IC	Worm	Drum/drum	5.20-12	126/ 131	885/ 950	83	17.2	20.5	£628
IC	IC	Worm	Drum/drum	5.20-12	131	784	80 (Est)	N/A	N/A	£728
IC	IC	Worm	Drum/drum	5.20-12	131	1020	83 (Est)	N/A	N/A	£680
ITor	BeamTor	Worm	Drum/drum	5.50-16	189	2955	84 (Claimed)	N/A	N/A	Special Order
ITor	BeamTor	Worm	Drum/drum	5.50-16	189	2955	90 (Est)	N/A	N/A	£2480
ITor	BeamTor	Worm	Drum/drum	6.40-15	189	3153	100	15.2	20.0	£2458
ITor	BeamTor	Worm	Drum/drum	6.40-15	189	3024	99	16.8	22.2	£2458
ITor	BeamTor	Worm	Drum/drum Disc/drum	6.40-15	189	3241	105 (Claimed)	N/A	N/A	Special Order
ITor	BeamTor	Worm	Drum/drum	6.00-16	187	3308	118 (Claimed)	N/A	N/A	£4801
ITor	BeamTor	Worm	Drum/drum Disc/drum	6.00-16	172	2933	124	9.5	N/A	£4201
IC	Beam1/4E	Worm	Drum/drum	4.80-10	90 93	794	51	N/A	29.8	£415
IC	Beam1/4E	Worm	Drum/drum	4.80-10	90	794	50	N/A	N/A	£399

Make and model	Production Figures	Years Built	Body Styles	Mechanical Layout	Engine Make (if not own)	Capacity/(cc)/Layout/Valves	BHP/rpm	Torque (lb.ft)/rpm	Transmission gearbox/automatic transmission
600	34,813	1957–1959	Sal	R/R	—	582/2HO/ OHV	20/4500	28/2800	4-spd/-
700	174,390	1959–1965	Sal Cpe	R/R	—	697/2HO/ OHV	30/5000 32/5000	37/3400 37/2400	4-spd/-
700 Sport/LS	219	1960–1964	Cpe Spts	R/R	—	697/2HO/ OHV	32/5000 40/5700	37/3400 38/4000	4-spd/-
1500/1800/ 2000	350,729	1962–1972	Sal	F/R	—	1499/4IL/ OHC	80/5700	87/3000	4-spd/-
						1773/4IL/ OHC	90/5250 110/5800	106/3000 109/4000	4-spd/Auto 4-spd/-
						1766/4IL/ OHC	90/5250	106/3000	4-spd/Auto
						1990/4IL/ OHC	100/5500 120/5500	116/3000 123/3600	4-spd/Auto 4-spd/-
2000C/CS	11,720	1965–1969	Cpe	F/R	—	1990/4IL/ OHC	100/5500 120/5500	116/3000 123/3600	4-spd/Auto 4-spd/-
1502/1600/ 1602	349,955	1966–1977	Sal Conv Est	F/R	—	1573/4IL/ OHC	75/5800 85/5700	87/3700 91/3000	4-spd/- 4-spd/-
2002/Tii	409,922	1968–1976	Sal Conv Est	F/R	—	1990/4IL/ OHC	100/5500 130/5800	116/3500 131/4500	4-spd/5-spd/Auto 4-spd/5-spd/-
2500/2800	137,455	1968–1977	Sal	F/R	—	2494/6IL/ OHC	150/6000	155/3700	4-spd/Auto
						2788/6IL/ OHC	170/6000	174/3700	4-spd/Auto
2800CS/ 3.0CS/3.0CSI	28,661	1968–1975	Cpe	F/R	—	2788/6IL/ OHC	170/6000	173/3700	4-spd/Auto
						2985/6IL/ OHC	180/6000 200/5500	188/3700 200/4300	4-spd/Auto 4-spd/-
Bond									
Equipe GT/4S	2,949	1963–1970	Cpe	F/R	Triumph	1147/4IL/ OHV	63/5750 67/6000	67/3500 67/3750	4-spd/- 4-spd/-
						1296/4IL/ OHV	75/6000	75/4000	4-spd/-
Equipe 2-litre	1,432	1967–1970	Cpe Conv	F/R	Triumph	1998/6IL/ OHV	95/5000 104/5300	117/3000 117/3000	4-spd (+O/D)/- 4-spd (+O/D)/-
Borgward									
1500/1800	11,337	1952–1954	Sal Conv Est	F/R	—	1498/4IL/ OHV	80/5500	N/A	4-spd/-
						1758/4IL/ OHV Diesel	42/3400	N/A	4-spd/-
Hansa 2400	N/A	1952–1958	Sal	F/R	—	2337/6IL/ OHV	82/N/Q	116/N/Q	4-spd/-
Isabella	202,862 (all types)	1954–1961	Sal Est Conv	F/R	—	1493/4IL/ OHV	60/4500 75/5200	82/2500 84/2800	4-spd/- 4-spd/-
Isabella TS Coupe	Incl. above	1955–1961	Cpe	F/R	—	1493/4IL/ OHV	75/5200	84/2800	4-spd/-
2.3 saloon	N/A	1959–1961	Sal	F/R	—	2238/6IL/ OHV	100/5100	116/2000	4-spd/-
Bristol									
400	700	1947–1950	Sal	F/R	—	1971/6IL/ OHV	80/4500	96/3000	4-spd/-
401/403	950	1949–1955	Sal	F/R	—	1971/6IL/ OHV	85/4500 100/5000	107/3500 117/3500	4-spd/- 4-spd/-
402 Cabriolet	20	1949–1950	Conv	F/R	—	1971/6IL/ OHV	85/4500	107/3500	4-spd/-
404	51	1953–1955	Cpe	F/R	—	1971/6IL/ OHV	105/5000 125/5500	123/3750 128/4200	4-spd/-
405	340	1954–1958	Sal Conv	F/R	—	1971/6IL/ OHV	105/5000	123/3750	4-spd (+O/D)/-
406	292	1958–1961	Sal	F/R	—	2216/6IL/ OHV	105/4700	129/3000	4-spd (+O/D)/-
406 Zagato	7	1960–1961	Cpe Sal	F/R	—	2216/6IL/ OHV	130/5750	N/Q	4-spd (+O/D)/-
407	300	1961–1963	Sal	F/R	Chrysler	5130/V8/ OHV	250/4400	340/2800	Auto/-
408	300	1963–1965	Sal	F/R	Chrysler	5130/V8/ OHV	250/4400	340/2800	Auto/-
409	300	1965–1967	Sal	F/R	Chrysler	5211/V8/ OHV	250/4400	340/2800	Auto/-
410	300	1967–1969	Sal	F/R	Chrysler	5211/V8/ OHV	250/4400	340/2800	Auto/-

Suspension Front	Rear	Steering	Brakes (Front/rear)	Wheels/model Tyres	Length (in)	Weight (lb,unladen)	Performance Top speed (mph)	0–60mph (sec)	Standing ¼-mile (sec)	UK Total Price (£: at Launch)
					93					
IC	IC	Worm	Drum/drum	5.20-10	114	1213	62	N/A	24.5	£676
IC	IC	R & P	Drum/drum	5.50-12	139	1411	70	33.7	23.9	£894
					152					
IC	IC	R & P	Drum/drum	5.50-12	139	1433	78	23.4	22.8	£1040
					1499					
IC	IC	Worm	Disc/drum	6.00-14	177	2337	92 (Claimed)	N/A	N/A	£1567
IC	IC	Worm	Disc/drum	6.00-14	177	2403	100	13.7	19.0	£1440
IC	IC	Worm	Disc/drum	5.90-14	177	2470	107	11.3	18.4	£1540
IC	IC	Worm	Disc/drum	165-14	177	2492	102	11.8	18.4	£1699
IC	IC	Worm	Disc/drum	165-14	177	2446	104	11.7	17.7	£1777
IC	IC	Worm	Disc/drum	175-14	177	2536	114	9.7	17.3	£1798
IC	IC	Worm	Disc/drum	175-14	178	2646	104 (Est)	N/A	N/A	£2950
IC	IC	Worm	Disc/drum	175-14	178	2646	110	10.4	17.9	£2950
IC	IC	Worm	Disc/drum	165-13	167	2161	97 (Est)	N/A	N/A	£2299
IC	IC	Worm	Disc/drum	165-13	167	2161	99	11.8	18.4	£1298
IC	IC	Worm	Disc/drum	165-13	170	2183	107	10.6	17.4	£1597
IC	IC	Worm	Disc/drum	165-13	170	2227	116	8.3	16.4	£2299
IC	IC	Worm	Disc/disc	175-14	185	2938	121	9.3	17.2	£2958
IC	IC	Worm	Disc/disc	175-14	186	2955	124	8.9	16.7	£3245
IC	IC	Worm	Disc/drum	DR70HR14	183	2845	128	8.5	16.3	£4997
IC	IC	Worm	Disc/disc	195/70-14	183	3030	131	8.0	16.2	£5345
IC	IC	Worm	Disc/disc	195/70-14	183	3030	139	7.5	15.4	£6199
IC	ITrL	R & P	Disc/drum	5.20-13	155	1625	82	17.6	20.8	£822
IC	ITrL	R & P	Disc/drum	5.20-13	160	1834	91	20.0	21.4	£829
IC	ITrL	R & P	Disc/drum	5.20-13	160	1834	95 (Est)	N/A	N/A	£889
IC	ITrL	R & P	Disc/drum	155-13	166	2016	102	10.7	18.6	£1096
IC	ITrL	R & P	Disc/drum	155-13	166	2016	102	10.7	17.9	£1197
ITrL	ITrL	Worm	Drum/drum	5.90-15	175	2520	103 (Claimed)	N/A	N/A	£2415
ITrL	ITrL	Worm	Drum/drum	6.40-15	175	2744	68	42.1	26.9	£1576
ITrL	IC	Worm	Drum/drum	6.70-15	175	3035	93 (Claimed)	N/A	N/A	£2424
IC	IC	Worm	Drum/drum	5.90-13	172	2212	77	21.8	22.1	£1124
IC	IC	Worm	Drum/drum	5.90-13	172	2380	88	19.7	21.7	£1367
IC	IC	Worm	Drum/drum	5.90-13	173	2440	95	17.4	20.5	£1874
IAir	IAir	Worm	Drum/drum	6.40-13	185	2912	100	14.6	19.8	£2395
ITrL	BeamTor	R & P	Drum/drum	5.50-16	170	2464	94	14.7	19.7	£2374
ITrL	BeamTor	R & P	Drum/drum	5.50-16	192	2700	97	15.1	19.9	£3214
ITrL	BeamTor	R & P	Drum/drum	5.75-16	192	2788	104	13.4	N/A	£2976
ITrL	BeamTor	R & P	Drum/drum	5.50-16	190	2632	95 (Est)	N/A	N/A	£3214
ITrL	BeamTor	R & P	Drum/drum	6.00-16	171	2290	115 (Est)	N/A	N/A	£3543
ITrL	BeamTor	R & P	Drum/drum	5.75-16	189	2712	103 (Est)	N/A	N/A	£3189
ITrL	BeamTor	R & P	Disc/disc	6.00-16	196	3010	100 (Claimed)	N/A	N/A	£4494
ITrL	BeamTor	R & P	Disc/disc	6.00-16	185	2469	120 (Est)	N/A	N/A	£4800
IC	BeamTor	Worm	Disc/disc	6.00-16	199	3585	122	9.9	17.4	£4848
IC	BeamTor	R & P	Disc/disc	6.00-16	199	3585	121 (Claimed)	N/A	N/A	£4459
IC	BeamTor	R & P	Disc/disc	6.00-16	199	3527	121 (Claimed)	N/A	N/A	£4849
IC	BeamTor	R & P	Disc/disc	6.70-15	199	3527	130	8.8	16.2	£5997

Make and model	Production Figures	Years Built	Body Styles	Mechanical Layout	Engine Make (if not own)	Capacity/ (cc)/Layout/ Valves	BHP/ rpm	Torque (lb.ft)/rpm	Transmission gearbox/automatic transmission
411	600	1969–1976	Sal	F/R	Chrysler	6277/V8/ OHV	335/5200	425/3400	Auto/-
						6556/V8/ OHV	264/4800	335/3600	Auto/-
Buick									
Special **	—	1961 model	Sal	F/R	—	3528/V8/ OHV	155/4600	220/2400	Auto
Riviera **	—	1965 model	Cpe	F/R	—	6949/V8/ OHV	360/4400	465/2800	Auto
Cadillac									
Fleetwood 75 **	—	1961 model	Limo	F/R	—	6384/V8/ OHV	325/4800	430/3100	Auto
Coupe de Ville **	—	1964 model	Cpe	F/R	—	7030/V8/ OHV	340/4600	480/3000	Auto
Coupe de Ville **	—	1968 model	Cpe	F/R	—	7729/V8/ OHV	375/4400	525/3000	Auto
Fleetwood Brougham **	—	1970 model	Sal	F/R	—	7729/V8/ OHV	375/4400	525/3000	Auto
Chevrolet									
Bel Air **	—	1958 model	Cpe	F/R	—	4637/V8/ OHV	185/4600	N/Q	Auto
Corvair **	—	1960 model	Sal	R/R	—	2295/6HO/ OHV	80/4400	125/2400	Auto
Corvette Sting Ray **	—	1963 model	Spts Cpe	F/R	—	5360/V8/ OHV	360/6000	352/4000	4-spd
Corvette Sting Ray **	—	1964 model	Spts Cpe	F/R	—	5360/V8/ OHV	360/6000	352/4000	4-spd
Impala **	—	1964 model	Sal	F/R	—	4638/V8/ OHV	198/4800	285/2400	Auto
Chevelle	—	1965 model	Sal	F/R	—	3769/6IL/ OHV	140/4400	220/1600	Auto
Corvair **	—	1960 model	Sal	R/R	—	2295/6HO/ OHV	80/4400	125/2400	Auto
Corvette Sting Ray **	—	1963 model	Spts Cpe	F/R	—	5360/V8/ OHV	360/6000	352/4000	4-spd
Corvette Sting Ray **	—	1964 model	Spts Cpe	F/R	—	5360/V8/ OHV	360/6000	352/4000	4-spd
Impala **	—	1964 model	Sal	F/R	—	4638/V8/ OHV	198/4800	285/2400	Auto
Chevelle ** Malibu	—	1965 model	Sal	F/R	—	3769/6IL/ OHV	140/4400	220/1600	Auto
Impala **	—	1970 model	Sal	F/R	—	7440/V8/ OHV	345/4400	500/3000	Auto
Monte Carlo **	—	1970 model	Cpe	F/R	—	5737/V8/ OHV	300/4800	380/3200	Auto
Chrysler (USA/Canada/Australia)									
New Yorker **	—	1957 model	Sal	F/R	—	6250/V8/ OHV	325/4500	N/Q	Auto
Valiant **	—	1960 model	Sal	F/R	—	2786/6IL/ OHV	101/4400	155/2400	Auto
Valiant **	—	1963 model	Sal	F/R	—	3687/6IL/ OHV	145/4000	215/2400	Auto
Valiant **	—	1967 model	Sal	F/F	—	4473/V8/ OHV	180/4200	260/1600	Auto
Chrysler (Europe)									
180/2-litre	N/A	1970–1980	Sal	F/R	—	1812/4IL/ OHC	97/5600	106/3000	4-spd/Auto
						1981/4IL/ OHC	110/5600	118/3600	Auto/-
Citroen									
Traction Avant	759,127 (Incl. Six)	1935–1957	Sal	F/F	—	1911/4IL/ OHV	56/4250	88/2000	3-spd/-
Six (Traction)	(See above)	1939–1955	Sal	F/F	—	2866/6IL/ OHV	76/3800	137/2000	3-spd/-
2CV	3,872,583	1948–1990	Sal	F/F	—	375/2HO/ OHV AirC	9/3500	N/Q	4-spd/-
						425/2HO/ OHV AirC	12/3500	17/2900	4-spd/-

Suspension Front	Rear	Steering	Brakes (Front/rear)	Wheels/model Tyres	Length (in)	Weight (lb, unladen)	Performance Top speed (mph)	0–60mph (sec)	Standing 1/4-mile (sec)	UK Total Price (£: at Launch)
IC	BeamTor	R & P	Disc/disc	185-15 / 205-15	193	3726	138	7.0	15.0	£6997
IC	BeamTor	R & P	Disc/disc	205-15	195	3775	140 (Claimed)	N/A	N/A	£8973
IC	BeamC	Worm	Drum/drum	6.50-13	188	2781	100	12.9	19.2	£2244
IC	BeamC	Worm	Drum/drum	8.45-15	210	4369	122	7.4	15.5	£3639
IAir	BeamAir	Worm	Drum/drum	8.20-15	245	5670	117	11.2	18.1	£7616
IC	BeamC	Worm	Drum/drum	8.00-15	224	5006	122	9.7	17.0	£3700
IC	BeamC	Worm	Drum/drum	9.00-15	225	4952	120	9.9	16.9	£5656
IC	BeamC	Worm	Disc/drum	9.00-15	228	5141	123	9.9	N/A	£6347
IAir	BeamAir	Worm	Drum/drum	7.50-14	209	3696	106	14.2	20.8	£2326
IC	IC	Worm	Drum/drum	6.50-13	180	2492	84	21.4	22.5	£1900
IC	ITrL	Worm	Drum/drum	6.70-15/ 7.10-15	176	3220	147	6.2	14.6	£3323
IC	ITrL	Worm	Drum/drum	7.10-15/ 7.60-15	176	3248	147	6.5	14.6	£3432
IC	BeamC	Worm	Drum/drum	7.50-14	211	3696	107	12.7	19.2	£1989
IC	BeamC	Worm	Drum/drum	7.50-14	209	3696	106	14.2	20.8	£2326
IC	IC	Worm	Drum/drum	6.50-13	180	2492	84	21.4	22.5	£1900
IC	ITrL	Worm	Drum/drum	6.70-15/ 7.10-15	176	3220	147	6.2	14.6	£3323
IC	ITrL	Worm	Drum/drum	7.10-15/ 7.60-15	176	3248	147	6.5	14.6	£3432
IC	BeamC	Worm	Drum/drum	7.50-14	211	3696	107	12.7	19.2	£1989
IC	BeamC	Worm	Drum/drum	6.95-14	197	3071	90	15.1	20.3	£1953
IC	BeamC	Worm	Disc/drum	H70-15	216	4400	116	9.0	16.8	£3371
IC	BeamC	Worm	Disc/drum	G78-15	206	3696	112	9.2	17.0	£3371
ITor	Beam1/2E	Worm	Drum/drum	9.00-14	219	4458	116	11.3	18.2	£3699
ITor	Beam1/2E	Worm	Drum/drum	6.50-13	184	2821	94	17.7	21.1	£2232
ITor	Beam1/2E	Worm	Drum/drum	6.50-13	196	2912	91	13.8	19.9	£1789
ITor	Beam1/2E	Worm	Disc/drum	6.95-14	188	3136	106	11.3	18.0	£2295
IC	BeamC	R & P	Disc/disc	175-14	176	2334	99	13.6	19.0	£1498
IC	BeamC	R & P	Disc/disc	175-14	176	2450	101	12.8	19.2	£1822
ITor	BeamTor	R & P	Drum/drum	165-400	168	2380	73	23.4	22.8	£573
					186	2548	70	29.1	23.3	£1153
ITor	BeamTor	R & P	Drum/drum	185-400	191	2912	82	19.4	21.6	£1087
IC	IC	R & P	Drum/drum	125-400	149	1120	41	N/A	34.4	£565
IC	IC	R & P	Drum/drum	125-400	149	1176	47	N/A	31.1	£598

Make and model	Production Figures	Years Built	Body Styles	Mechanical Layout	Engine Make (if not own)	Capacity/(cc)/Layout/Valves	BHP/rpm	Torque (lb.ft)/rpm	Transmission gearbox/automatic transmission
						602/2HO/OHV AirC	29/6750	29/3500	4-spd/-
DS19/DS21/DS23	1,456,115 (All DS and ID models) (Incl 1,375 Cabriolets)	1955–1975	Sal Est Conv	F/F	—	1911/4IL/OHV	75/4500	101/3000	4-spd/-
							83/4500	105/3500	4-spd/-
						1985/4IL/OHV	84/5250	106/3500	4-spd/-
							91/5900	104/3500	4-spd/-
							99/5500	104/3500	4-spd/-
						2175/4IL/OHV	100/5500	121/3000	4-spd/-
							106/5500	123/3500	4-spd/5-spd/Auto
							125/5500	145/4000	4-spd/5-spd/-
						2347/4IL/OHV	115/5500	135/3500	5-spd/Auto
							130/5250	144/2500	5-spd/Auto
ID19 family	See above	1956–1975	Sal	F/F	—	1911/4IL/OHV	62/4000	92/3000	4-spd/-
							66/4500	98/2500	4-spd/-
							74/4750	98/3500	4-spd/-
						1985/4IL/OHV	78/5250	106/3000	4-spd/-
							81/5500	100/3000	4-spd/-
							89/5500	106/2500	
							91/5900	104/3500	4-spd/-
							99/5500	104/3500	
Bijou	211	1960–1962	Cpe	F/F	—	425/2HO/OHV AirC	12/3500	17/2900	4-spd/-
Ami 6	1,039,384	1961–1971	Sal Est	F/F	—	602/2HO/OHV AirC	22/4500	30/2800	4-spd/-
Ami 8/Super	800,775	1969–1979	Sal Est	F/F	—	602/2HO/OHV AirC	32/5750	30/4000	4-spd/-
						1015/4HO/OHC AirC	54/6500	50/3500	4-spd/-
Dyane 4/6	1,443,583	1967–1984	Sal	F/F	—	435/2HO/OHV AirC	24/6750	21/4000	4-spd/-
						602/2HO/OHV AirC	29/6750	29/3500	4-spd/-
							32/5750	31/3500	
SM	12,920	1970–1975	Cpe	F/F	—	2670/V6/2OHC	170/5500	172/4000	5-spd/-
							178/5500	178/4000	5-spd/-
GS/GSA family	2,473,499	1970–1987	Sal Htch Est	F/F	—	1015/4HO/OHC AirC	56/6500	52/3500	4-spd/-
						1129/4HO/OHC AirC	57/5750	59/3500	4-spd/-
						1220/4HO/OHC AirC	60/6500	64/3250	4-spd/SemiAuto
							65/5750	67/3250	4-spd/-
						1299/4HO/OHC AirC	65/5500	72/3500	5-spd/Auto

Dacia

Make and model	Production Figures	Years Built	Body Styles	Mechanical Layout	Engine Make (if not own)	Capacity/(cc)/Layout/Valves	BHP/rpm	Torque (lb.ft)/rpm	Transmission gearbox/automatic transmission
Denem	N/A	1969–Date	Sal Est	F/F	Renault	1289/4IL/OHV	60/5250	70/3000	4-spd/-

DAF

Make and model	Production Figures	Years Built	Body Styles	Mechanical Layout	Engine Make (if not own)	Capacity/(cc)/Layout/Valves	BHP/rpm	Torque (lb.ft)/rpm	Transmission gearbox/automatic transmission
Daffodil/750/33	312,367	1962–1975	Sal	F/R	—	590/2HO/OHV AirC	22/4000	33/2500	Auto/-
						746/2HO/OHV AirC	26/4000	42/2800	Auto/-
44/46	200,258	1966–1976	Sal Est	F/R	—	844/2HO/OHV AirC	34/4500	51/2400	Auto/-
55/66	310,528	1968–1975	Sal Cpe Est	F/R	Renault	1108/4IL/OHV	46/4600	62/2800	Auto/-
							55/5600	61/3800	Auto/-
						1289/4IL/OHV	57/5200	69/2800	Auto/-

Note : In the UK the Daf 66 officially became the Volvo 66 in 1975.

Daihatsu

Make and model	Production Figures	Years Built	Body Styles	Mechanical Layout	Engine Make (if not own)	Capacity/(cc)/Layout/Valves	BHP/rpm	Torque (lb.ft)/rpm	Transmission gearbox/automatic transmission
Compagno	Est 120,000	1964–1970	Sal Conv Est	F/R	—	797/4IL/OHV	41/5000	47/3600	4-spd/-
F20LK	N/A	1976–1984	Ute	F/4	—	1587/4IL/OHV	66/4800	81/3400	4-spd/-

Daimler

Make and model	Production Figures	Years Built	Body Styles	Mechanical Layout	Engine Make (if not own)	Capacity/(cc)/Layout/Valves	BHP/rpm	Torque (lb.ft)/rpm	Transmission gearbox/automatic transmission
DB18	3,365	1939–1950 (Postwar only)	Sal Conv	F/R	—	2522/6IL/OHV	70/4200	109/2000	4Pres/-
DB18 Sports Special	608	1949–1953	Conv	F/R	—	2522/6IL/OHV	85/4200	120/2000	4Pres/-
Consort	4,250	1949–1953	Sal	F/R	—	2522/6IL/OHV	70/4200	111/2000	4Pres/-
DE27/DH27	255	1946–1951	Sal	F/R	—	4095/6IL/	110/3600	190/1200	4Pres/-

Suspension Front	Rear	Steering	Brakes (Front/rear)	Wheels/model Tyres	Length (in)	Weight (lb,unladen)	Performance Top speed (mph)	0–60mph (sec)	Standing 1/4-mile (sec)	UK Total Price (£: at Launch)
IC	IC	R & P	Drum/drum Disc/drum	125-15	151	1322	67	32.8	24.3	£899
IHP	IHP	R & P	Disc/drum	165-400	189	2464	87	23.3	22.6	£1486
IHP	IHP	R & P	Disc/drum	165-400	189	2780	92	18.4	21.7	£1745
IHP	IHP	R & P	Disc/drum	180-380	189	2811	92 (Est)	N/A	N/A	
IHP	IHP	R & P	Disc/drum	180-380	189	2878	97 (Est)	N/A	N/A	
IHP	IHp	R & P	Disc/drum	180-380	189	2878	105 (Est)	N/A	N/a	
IHP	IHP	R & P	Disc/drum	180-380	189	2878	107	14.4	19.5	£1977
IHP	IHP	R & P	Disc/drum	185-15	189	2960	118	12.3	18.9	£2107
IHP	IHP	R & P	Disc/drum	185-15	189	2904	111 (Est)	N/A	N/A	£2282
IHP	IHP	R & P	Disc/drum	185-15	189	2955	120	10.4	17.6	£2811
IHP	IHP	R & P	Disc/drum	165-400	189	2464	85 (Est)	N/A	N/A	£1498
IHP	IHP	R & P	Disc/drum	165-400	189	2720	87	21.1	22.3	£1498
IHP	IHP	R & P	Disc/drum	165-400	189	2744	97	15.6	21.0	£1499
IHP	IHP	R & P	Disc/drum	180-380	191	2668	99 (Est)	N/A	N/A	£1563
IHP	IHP	R & P	Disc/drum	180-15	191	2668	100	14.2	19.6	£1699
IHP	IHP	R & P	Disc/drum	180-15	191	2668	105	14.5	19.6	£1734
IC	IC	R & P	Drum/drum	135-380	156	1288	45	N/A	33.1	£695
IC	IC	R & P	Drum/drum	125-15	155	1400	68	44.0	25.2	£824
IC	IC	R & P	Disc/drum	135-15	157	1545	72	31.7	24.5	£649
IC	IC	R & P	Disc/drum	135-15	157	1775	88	17.1	20.5	£1025
IC	IC	R & P	Drum/drum	125-380	154	1224	67	63.2	26.0	£549
IC	IC	R & P	Drum/drum	125-15	154	1312	69	30.8	24.3	£610
IHP	IHP	R & P	Disc/disc	195/70-15	193	3197	139	9.3	17.1	£5480
IHP	IHP	R & P	Disc/disc	205/70-15	193	3197	142	8.3	16.5	£6154
IHP	IHP	R & P	Disc/disc	145-15	152	1867	90	18.0	21.5	£1001
IHP	IHP	R & P	Disc/disc	145-15	152	2039	93	16.0	20.2	£2490
IHP	IHP	R & P	Disc/disc	145-15	152	1886	94	14.9	20.1	£1315
IHP	IHP	R & P	Disc/disc	145-15	152	2072	94	15.4	20.0	£1729
IHP	IHP	R & P	Disc/disc	145-15	152	2184	98	14.1	19.5	£4060
IC	BeamC	R & P	Disc/drum	145-13	171	2116	94	12.9	19.3	£3190
ITrL	IC	R & P	Drum/drum	5.20-12	142	1268	50	N/A	29.6	£681
ITrL	IC	R & P	Drum/drum	5.20-12	142	1460	63	50.7	25.4	£778
ITrL	IC	R & P DD1/2E (46 only)	Drum/drum	135-14	130	1646	74	31.2	24.1	£747
ITor	IC	R & P	Disc/drum	135-14	153	1730	80	22.5	22.8	£852
ITor	IC/DD1/2E	R & P	Disc/drum	155-13	153	1725	84	23.0	22.3	£1050
ITor	DD1/2E	R & P	Disc/drum	155-13	153	1875	84	19.4	21.3	£1399
ITor	Beam1/2E	Worm	Drum/drum	5.20-12	150	1715	66	N/A	24.5	£799
Beam1/2E	Beam1/2E	Worm	Drum/drum	6.00-16	137	2337	65 (Est)	N/A	N/A	£3799
IC	Beam1/2E	Worm	Drum/drum	6.00-16	180	3472	72	28.3	25.2	£1183
IC	Beam1/2E	Worm	Drum/drum	6.00-16	180	3584	84	23.3	23.7	£2560
IC	Beam1/2E	Worm	Drum/drum	6.00-16	180	3360	78	26.7	24.3	£1977
IC	Beam1/2E	Worm	Drum/drum	8.00-17	213	5572	79	29.0	23.7	£1400 (Chassis only)

Make and model	Production Figures	Years Built	Body Styles	Mechanical Layout	Engine Make (if not own)	Capacity/(cc)/Layout/Valves	BHP/rpm	Torque (lb.ft)/rpm	Transmission gearbox/automatic transmission
DE36	205	1946–1953	Limo Sal	F/R	—	5460/8IL/ OHV	150/3600	254/1200	4Pres/-
Regency/ Regency II	270	1952–1956	Limo Conv Spl Sal Conv	F/R	—	2952/6IL/ OHV	90/4100	148/1600	4Pres/-
						3468/6IL/ OHV	107/4000	180/1600	4Pres/-
							140/4400	204/2500	4PreS/-
						4617/6IL/ OHV	127/3600	N/Q	4Pres/-
Conquest Century	9,620	1953–1958	Sal Conv	F/R	—	2433/6IL/ OHV	75/4000	122/1600	4PreS/Auto
							100/4400	131/2500	4PreS/Auto
Conquest Rdstr/DHC	119	1953–1957	Spts Conv	F/R	—	2433/6IL/ OHV	100/4600	131/2500	4PreS/Auto
DK400/ Regina	132	1955–1960	Limo	F/R	—	4617/6IL/ OHV	127/3600	N/Q	4PreS/-
							167/4000	260/2800	4PreS/-
104	459	1956–1959	Sal	F/R	—	3468/6IL/ OHV	137/4400	191/2000	4PreS/Auto
Majestic	940	1958–1962	Sal	F/R	—	3794/6IL/ OHV	135/4400	209/2800	Auto/-
Majestic Major	1,180	1960–1968	Sal	F/R	—	4561/V8/ OHV	220/5500	283/3200	Auto/-
SP250	2,650	1959–1964	Spts	F/R	—	2548/V8/ OHV	140/5800	155/3600	4-spd (+O/D)/Auto
DR450 Limo	864	1961–1968	Limo	F/R	—	4561/V8/ OHV	220/5500	283/3200	Auto/-
2½-litre/ V8 250	17,620	1962–1969	Sal	F/R	—	2548/V8/ OHV	140/5800	155/3600	4-spd (+O/D)/Auto
Sovereign	5,700	1966–1969	Sal	F/R	—	4235/6IL/ 2OHC	245/5400	283/3750	4-spd (+O/D)/Auto
DS420 Limo	4,206	1968–1992	Limo	F/R	—	4235/6IL/ 2OHC	245/5500	282/3750	Auto/-
Sovereign SI/SII	45,413	1969–1979	Sal Cpe	F/R	—	2792/6IL/ 2OHC	140/5150	150/4250	4-spd (+O/D)/Auto
						3442/6IL/ 2OHC	160/5000	189/3500	4-spd (+O/D)/Auto
						4235/6IL/ 2OHC	173/4750	227/3000	4-spd (+O/D)/Auto

Datsun (renamed Nissan in the British market from 1984)

Make and model	Production Figures	Years Built	Body Styles	Mechanical Layout	Engine Make (if not own)	Capacity/(cc)/Layout/Valves	BHP/rpm	Torque (lb.ft)/rpm	Transmission gearbox/automatic transmission
Sunny B10	435,877	1966–1970	Sal Cpe Est	F/R	—	988/4IL/ OHV	62/6000	62/4000	4-spd/-
Bluebird (Type 510)	1,696,974	1968–1971	Sal Est	F/R	—	1295/4IL/ OHC	72/6000	76/3600	4-spd/-
						1428/4IL/ OHC	85/6000	86/3600	4-spd/Auto
						1595/4IL/ OHC	96/5600	100/3600	4-spd/Auto
1800 Laurel/	164,985 (Incl. Laurel)	1968–1973	Sal Est	F/R	—	1815/4IL/ OHC	105/5600	115/3600	3-spd/4-spd/Auto
C30 2000	—	1968–1974	Sal Est	F/R	—	1990/4IL/ OHC	114/5600	124/3200	4-spd/Auto
240Z/ 260Z/2+2	622,649	1969–1978	Spts Cpe	F/R	—	2393/6IL/ OHC	151/5600	146/4400	5-spd/-
						2565/6IL/ OHC	162/5600	152/4400	5-spd/-
						2565/6IL/ OHC	162/5600	152/4400	5-spd/-
Sunny B110	1,226,843	1970–1973	Sal Est	F/R	—	1171/4IL/ OHV	68/6000	70/3600	4-spd/-
						1428/4IL/ OHC	85/6000	86/3600	4-spd/Auto

Dellow

Make and model	Production Figures	Years Built	Body Styles	Mechanical Layout	Engine Make (if not own)	Capacity/(cc)/Layout/Valves	BHP/rpm	Torque (lb.ft)/rpm	Transmission gearbox/automatic transmission
Mk I/II/III	500	1949–1957	Spts	F/R	Ford	1172/4IL/ SV	30/4000	46/3000	3-spd/-

Dino

Make and model	Production Figures	Years Built	Body Styles	Mechanical Layout	Engine Make (if not own)	Capacity/(cc)/Layout/Valves	BHP/rpm	Torque (lb.ft)/rpm	Transmission gearbox/automatic transmission
206	152	1967–1969	Spts Cpe	M(Tr)/R	—	1987/V6/ 2OHC	180/8000	138/6500	5-spd/-
246	3,761	1969–1973	Spts Cpe	M(Tr)/R	—	2418/V6/ 2OHC	195/7600	166/5500	5-spd/-

Suspension Front	Rear	Steering	Brakes (Front/rear)	Wheels/model Tyres	Length (in)	Weight (lb,unladen)	Performance Top speed (mph)	0–60mph (sec)	Standing ¼-mile (sec)	UK Total Price (£: at Launch)
IC	Beam1/2E	Worm	Drum/drum	8.00-17	222	5910	83	21.4	22.7	£1700 (Chassis only)
IC	Beam1/2E	Worm	Drum/drum	6.50-16	191	3808	78 (Est)	N/A	N/A	£2335
IC	Beam1/2E	Worm	Drum/drum	6.50-16	196	3920	83	19.1	21.1	£2324
IC	Beam1/2E	Worm	Drum/drum	6.50-16	198	4000 (Est)	95 (Est)	N/A	N/A	£2650
IC	Beam1/2E	Worm	Drum/drum	7.00-16	196	4116	95 (Est)	N/A	N/A	£2778
ITor	Beam1/2E	Worm	Drum/drum	6.70-15	177	3136	82	24.3	23.2	£1511
ITor	Beam1/2E	Worm	Drum/drum	6.70-15	177	3080	87	16.3	20.7	£1661
ITor	Beam1/2E	Worm	Drum/drum	6.00-15	178	2688	101	14.5	20.3	£1673
IC	Beam1/2E	Worm	Drum/drum	7.50-16	217	4964	88 (Est)	N/A	N/A	£4191
IC	Beam1/2E	Worm	Drum/drum	7.50-16	217	4964	94	16.3	20.9	
IC	Beam1/2E	Worm	Drum/drum	6.50-16	196	4144	100	15.4	21.0	£2829
IC	Beam1/2E	Worm	Disc/disc	6.50-16 6.70-16	196	3900	101	15.3	20.2	£2495
IC	Beam1/2E	Worm	Disc/disc	6.70-16	202	4228	119	10.3	17.1	£2995
IC	Beam1/2E	Worm	Disc/disc	5.50-15	161	2090	121	10.2	17.8	£1395
IC	Beam1/2E	Worm	Disc/disc	7.00-16	226	4564	114	11.3	18.0	£3995
IC	Beam1/2E	Worm	Disc/disc	6.40-15	181	3046	112	13.8	19.5	£1786
IC	IC	Worm	Disc/disc	185-15	188	3440	123	9.9	16.7	£2121
IC	IC	Worm	Disc/disc	H70HR-15	226	4706	105 (Est)	N/A	N/A	£4424
IC	IC	R & P	Disc/disc	205-15	190	3388	117 (Claimed)	11.0	18.1	£2356
IC	IC	R & P	Disc/disc	205-15	195	3708	117	10.9	18.0	£4965
IC	IC	R & P	Disc/disc	205-15	190	3703	124	8.8	16.5	£2714
ITrL	Beam1/2E	Worm	Drum/drum	5.50-12	150	1567	76	21.7	21.7	£766
IC	Beam1/2E	Worm	Drum/drum	5.60-13	162	2184	87	18.1	21.4	£889
IC	Beam1/2E	Worm	Disc/drum	5.60-13	162	2075	92	14.6	19.2	£970
IC	Beam1/2E	Worm	Disc/drum	5.60-13	162	2184	91	15.4	20.1	£948
IC	IC	R & P	Disc/drum	6.50-13	171	2172	96	13.1	19.2	£1386
IC	Beam1/2E	Worm	Disc/drum	165-14	177	2262	100	12.6	18.6	£1799
IC	IC	R & P	Disc/drum	175-14	163	2284	125	8.0	15.8	£2288
IC	IC	R & P	Disc/drum	195/70-14	163	2565	115	10.1	16.8	£2896
IC	IC	R & P	Disc/drum	195/70-14	175	2630	120	9.9	17.3	£3499
IC	Beam1/2E	Worm	Disc/drum	6.00-12	151	1590	89	15.3	19.9	£865
IC	Beam1/2E	Worm	Disc/drum	155-13	151	1590	91	15.6	20.1	£970
BeamTRL	Beam1/4E	Worm	Drum/drum	4.50-17/ 5.50-16	136	1344	69	20.3	22.8	£570
IC	IC	R & P	Disc/disc	185-14	162	2173	140	7.5	15.5	£6243
IC	IC	R & P	Disc/disc	205/70-14	167	2609	148	7.1	15.4	£5486

Make and model	Production Figures	Years Built	Body Styles	Mechanical Layout	Engine Make (if not own)	Capacity/ (cc)/Layout/ Valves	BHP/ rpm	Torque (lb.ft)/rpm	Transmission gearbox/automatic transmission

308GT4 – Originally badged **Dino**, this was renamed **Ferrari** in 1975. For all details, see entry under **Ferrari**.

DKW

Make and model	Production Figures	Years Built	Body Styles	Mechanical Layout	Engine Make	Capacity/Layout/Valves	BHP/rpm	Torque/rpm	Transmission
Sonderklasse	230,598	1953–1959	Sal	F/F	—	896/3IL/ 2-Str	34/4000	51/2000	4-spd/-
			Est				40/4250	51/2000	4-spd/-
			Cpe						
			Conv						
Junior/800S/ 800S/F11/F12	350,831	1959–1965	Sal	F/F	—	741/3IL/ 2-Str	34/4300	47/2500	4-spd/-
						796/3IL/ 2-Str	34/4000	53/2500	4-spd/-
						889/3IL/ 2-Str	40/4300	58/2250	4-spd/-
							45/4500	58/2500	
F102	52,753	1964–1966	Sal	F/F	—	1175/3IL/ 2-Str	60/4500	76/2500	4-spd/-

Dodge

Make and model	Production Figures	Years Built	Body Styles	Mechanical Layout	Engine Make	Capacity/Layout/Valves	BHP/rpm	Torque/rpm	Transmission
Custom Royal **	—	1957 model	Sal	F/R	—	5323/V8/ OHV	245/4400	320/2400	Auto
Custom Royal **	—	1959 model	Sal	F/R	—	5916/V8/ OHV	295/4600	390/2400	Auto
Dart Phoenix **	—	1961 model	Sal	F/R	—	5212/V8/ OHV	230/4400	340/2400	Auto

Edsel

Make and model	Production Figures	Years Built	Body Styles	Mechanical Layout	Engine Make	Capacity/Layout/Valves	BHP/rpm	Torque/rpm	Transmission
Ranger **	—	1958 model	Sal	F/R	—	5911/V8/ OHV	303/4600	N/Q	3-spd (+O/D)

Elva

Make and model	Production Figures	Years Built	Body Styles	Mechanical Layout	Engine Make	Capacity/Layout/Valves	BHP/rpm	Torque/rpm	Transmission
Courier	500 Est	1958–1969	Spts	F/R	MG	1489/4IL/ OHV	72/5000	77/3500	4-spd/-
						1588/4IL/ OHV	79/5600	87/3800	4-spd/-
						1622/4IL/ OHV	86/5500	97/4000	4-spd/-
						1798/4IL/ OHV	95/5400	110/3000	4-spd/-

Enfield

Make and model	Production Figures	Years Built	Body Styles	Mechanical Layout	Engine Make	Capacity/Layout/Valves	BHP/rpm	Torque/rpm	Transmission
8000 Electric car	108	1969–1976	Sal	F/R	—	Electric	8hp rating	N/Q	Auto

Facel Vega

Make and model	Production Figures	Years Built	Body Styles	Mechanical Layout	Engine Make	Capacity/Layout/Valves	BHP/rpm	Torque/rpm	Transmission
FVS	352	1954–1958	Sal	F/R	Chrysler	5801/V8/ OHV	325/4600	430/2800	4-spd/Auto
Excellence	145	1958–1961	Sal	F/R	Chrysler	6286/V8/ OHV	335/5000	380/3350	4-spd/Auto
HK500	490	1958–1961	Sal	F/R	Chrysler	5901/V8/ OHV	360/5200	400/3600	4-spd/Auto
						6286/V8/ OHV	355/4800	N/Q	4-spd/Auto
Facel II	183	1961–1964	Sal	F/R	—	6286/V8/ OHV	355/4800	N/Q	4-spd/Auto
Facellia	1,767	1960–1964	Spts	F/R	—	1647/4IL/ 2OHC	115/6400	106/4500	4-spd/-

Fairthorpe

Make and model	Production Figures	Years Built	Body Styles	Mechanical Layout	Engine Make	Capacity/Layout/Valves	BHP/rpm	Torque/rpm	Transmission
Atom	44	1954–1957	Spts Cpe	R/R	BSA	646/2IL/ OHV	35/5750	36/3750	3-spd/-
						(Other motorcycle-type engines also available)			
Atomota	N/A	1958–1960	Cpe	R/R	BSA	646/2IL/ OHV	35/5750	36/3750	4-spd/-
Electron/ Minor	Approx 500	1956–1973	Spts	F/R	Standard/ Triumph	948/4IL/ OHV	38/5000	49/2800	4-spd (+O/D)/-
						1147/4IL/ OHV	63/5750	67/3500	4-spd/-
						1296/4IL/ OHV	75/6000	75/4000	4-spd/-
					Coventry-Climax	1098/4IL/ OHC	71/6500	67/4750	4-spd/-
							83/6800	72/4750	
Zeta	Approx 20	1960–1965	Spts	F/R	Ford	2553/6IL/ OHV	143/5800	162/3500	4-spd/-

Suspension Front	Rear	Steering	Brakes (Front/rear)	Wheels/model Tyres	Length (in)	Weight (lb,unladen)	Performance Top speed (mph)	0–60mph (sec)	Standing 1/4-mile (sec)	UK Total Price (£: at Launch)
ITrL	BeamTrL	R & P	Drum/drum	5.60-15	166	1932	75	28.0	23.5	£981
ITrL	BeamTrL	R & P	Drum/drum	5.60-15	166	1981	88	22.5	23.1	£1036
ITor	BeamTor	R & P	Drum/drum	5.20-12	156	1510	68	31.4	23.3	£800
ITor	BeamTor	R & P	Drum/drum	5.50-13	156	1540	72	29.6	23.3	£898
ITor	BeamTor	R & P	Disc/drum	5.50-13	156	1620	78 (Claimed)	N/A	N/A	£800
ITor	BeamTor	R & P	Disc/drum	6.00-13	173	1895	84 (Claimed)	N/A	N/A	£976
ITor	Beam1/2E	Worm	Drum/drum	8.00-14	212	3920	108	11.5	16.6	£3061
ITor	Beam1/2E	Worm	Drum/drum	8.00-14	217	3999	109	10.5	17.4	£3346
ITor	Beam1/2E	Worm	Drum/drum	8.00-14	209	3535	108	11.8	18.2	£2687
IC	Beam1/2E	Worm	Drum/drum	8.00-14	213	4032	99	11.7	19.7	£2500
IC	BeamC	R & P	Drum/drum	5.20-14	152	1554	98	12.7	18.2	Special Order
IC	BeamC	R & P	Drum/drum	5.20-14	152	1554	105	10.2	17.8	£725
IC	BeamC	R & P	Disc/drum	165-15	152	1515	108 (Est)	N/A	N/A	£966
IC	IC	R & P	Disc/drum	5.60-13	150	1429	110 (Est)	N/A	N/Aa	£1,001
IC	Beam1/2E	R & P	Drum/drum	145-10	112	2150	37	N/A	N/A	£550
IC	Beam1/2E	Worm	Drum/drum Disc/disc	6.70-15	181	4107	134	9.6	16.1	£4726
IC	Beam1/2E	Worm	Disc/disc	6.70-15	207	4230	130 (Est)	N/A	N/A	£6376
IC	Beam1/2E	Worm	Disc/disc	6.70-15	181	4032	130 (Est)	N/A	N/A	£4726
IC	Beam1/2E	Worm	Disc/disc	6.70-15	181	4032	129	8.4	16.3	£4740
IC	Beam1/2E	Worm	Disc/disc	6.70-15	181	4060	133	8.3	16.5	£4879
IC	Beam1/2E	Worm	Disc/disc	5.90-14	144	2184	106	11.9	19.2	£2582
IC	IC	Worm	Drum/drum	5.20-13	132	940	75 (Claimed)	N/A	N/A	£500
IC	IC	Worm	Drum/drum	5.20-13	129	945	80 (Est)	N/A	N/A	£640
IC	BeamC	R & P	Drum/drum	5.60-13	132	1288	75	17.9	20.8	£720
IC	IC	R & P								
IC	IC	R & P	Disc/drum	155-13	137	1000	85 (Est)	N/A	N/A	£700
IC	ITrL	R & P	Disc/drum	155-13	143	1035	90 (Est)	N/A	N/A	£826
IC	BeamC	R & P	Drum/drum	5.20-15	132	1204	90 (Est)	N/A	N/A	£1050
IC	IC	Worm	Disc/drum	165-15	140	1834	117	7.9	15.8	£1482

159

Make and model	Production Figures	Years Built	Body Styles	Mechanical Layout	Engine Make (if not own)	Capacity/(cc)/Layout/Valves	BHP/rpm	Torque (lb.ft)/rpm	Transmission gearbox/automatic transmission
Rockette	Approx 25	1963–1967	Spts	F/R	Triumph	1596/6IL/ OHV	70/5000	92/2800	4-spd (+O/D)/-
TX-GT/S/SS	Approx 50	1967–1976	Spts Cpe	F/R	Triumph	1998/6IL/ OHV	104/5300 112/5300	117/3000 117/3000	4-spd/- 4-spd/-
					Triumph	2498/6IL/ OHV	140/6000 132/5450	152/3000 153/2000	4-spd/- 4-spd/-
TX Tripper	N/A	1970–1976	Spts	F/R	Triumph	1296/4IL/ OHV	75/6000	75/4000	4-spd/-
						2498/6IL/ OHV	132/5450	153/2000	4-spd/-

Ferrari

Make and model	Production Figures	Years Built	Body Styles	Mechanical Layout	Engine Make (if not own)	Capacity/(cc)/Layout/Valves	BHP/rpm	Torque (lb.ft)/rpm	Transmission gearbox/automatic transmission
250GT (Pininfarina)	350	1958–1960	Spts Cpe	F/R	—	2953/V12/ OHC	240/7000	181/5000	4-spd/-
250GT Berlinetta	167	1959–1962	Spts Cpe	F/R	—	2953/V12/ OHC	240/7000 280/7000	181/5000 203/5500	4-spd/-
250GT Lusso	350	1962–1964	Spts Cpe	F/R	—	2953/V12/ OHC	250/7500	188/5500	4-spd/-
275GTB/ GTB4	456/350	1964–1968	Spts Cpe	F/R	—	3286/V12/ OHC 3286/V12/ 2OHC	280/7500 300/8000	188/5500 217/5500	5-spd/- 5-spd/-
275GTS/ 330GTS/ 365GTS	200/100/20	1964–1969	Spts Conv	F/R	—	3286/V12/ OHC 3967/V12/ OHC 4390/V12/ OHC	260/7000 300/6600 320/6600	188/5500 288/5000 268/5000	5-spd/- 5-spd/- 5-spd/-
250GT 2+2/ 330GT	950/1,075	1961–1967	Spts Cpe	F/R	—	2953/V12/ OHC 3967/V12/ OHC	240/7000 300/6600	181/5000 288/5000	4-spd (+O/D)/- 4-spd (+O/D)/ 5-spd/-
330GTC	600	1966–1968	Spts Cpe	F/R	—	3967/V12/ OHC	300/6600	288/5000	5-spd/-
365 California	14	1966–1967	Spts	F/R	—	4390/V12/ OHC	320/6600	268/5000	5-spd/-
500 Superfast	36	1964–1966	Spts Cpe	F/R	—	4962/V12/ OHC	400/6500	350/4750	4-spd/5-spd/-
365 GT 2+2	800	1967–1971	Spts Sal	F/R	—	4390/V12/ OHC	320/6600	268/5000	5-spd/-
365GTC	150	1968–1970	Spts Cpe	F/R	—	4390/V12/ OHC	320/6600	268/5000	5-spd/-
365GTB4 Daytona	1,406	1968–1974	Spts Cpe Spts	F/R	—	4390/V12/ 2OHC	352/7700	318/5400	5-spd/-

Fiat

Make and model	Production Figures	Years Built	Body Styles	Mechanical Layout	Engine Make (if not own)	Capacity/(cc)/Layout/Valves	BHP/rpm	Torque (lb.ft)/rpm	Transmission gearbox/automatic transmission
500C	376,368	1949–1954	Conv Est	F/R	—	570/4IL/ OHV	17/4400	N/Q	4-spd/-
1400/1900	136,115	1950–1958	Sal Cpe Conv	F/R	—	1395/4IL/ OHV 1901/4IL/ OHV	44/4400 59/3700	64/2700 96/2600	4-spd/- 5-spd/-
1100-103	1,019,378	1953–1962	Sal Est	F/R	—	1089/4IL/ OHV	36/4400 50/5200	51/2500 56/3200	4-spd/- 4-spd/-
1100D	408,997	1962–1966	Sal Est	F/R	—	1221/4IL/ OHV	50/5000	56/2500	4-spd/-
1100R	340,000	1966–1970	Sal Est	F/R	—	1089/4IL/ OHV	48/5200	57/3200	4-spd/-
1200	400,066	1957–1960	Sal	F/R	—	1221/4IL/ OHV	55/5300	60/3000	4-spd/-
600/600D	2,452,107 (Incl. Multipla)	1955–1970	Sal	R/R	—	633/4IL/ OHV 767/4IL/ OHV	22/4600 29/4800	29/2800 40/2800	4-spd/- 4-spd/-
600 Multipla	—	1955–1966	Est	R/R	—	633/4IL/ OHV	22/4600	29/2800	4-spd/-
500/500D/ 500F	3,408,000 Est	1957–1977	Sal Est	R/R	—	479/2IL/ OHV AirC 499/2IL/ OHV AirC	13/4000 17/4000 18/4600	18/2500 20/2500 22/3000	4-spd/- 4-spd/- 4-spd/-
500 Giardiniera	327,000	1960–1977	Est	R/R	—	499/2IL/ OHV AirC	17/4600	22/3200	4-spd/-
1800/ 2100/2300	185,000 Est	1959–1968	Sal Est	F/R	—	1795/6IL/ OHV 2054/6IL/ OHV 2279/6IL/	85/5000 97/5300 95/5200 105/5300	93/3000 101/3000 106/3000 123/2800	4-spd/- 4-spd/- 4-spd/- 4-spd (+O/D)/Auto

Suspension Front	Suspension Rear	Steering	Brakes (Front/rear)	Wheels/model Tyres	Length (in)	Weight (lb, unladen)	Performance Top speed (mph)	0–60mph (sec)	Standing 1/4-mile (sec)	UK Total Price (£: at Launch)
IC	BeamC	R & P	Disc/drum	5.60-13	147	1576	99	13.7	18.9	£998
IC	IC	R & P	Disc/drum	155-13	144	1792	110 (Est)	N/A	N/A	£1310
IC	IC	R & P	Disc/drum	155-13	144	1736	115 (Est)	N/A	N/A	£1546
IC	IC	R & P	Disc/drum	165-13	146	1120	85 (Est)	N/A	N/A	£1151
IC	IC	R & P	Disc/drum	165-13	146	1568	112	8.0	16.0	£1412
IC	Beam1/2E	Worm	Drum/drum Disc/disc	6.00-16	185	2815	150	8.0	N/A	£6469
IC	Beam1/2E	Worm	Disc/disc	6.00-16 185-400	164	2804 2112	145	6.6	14.8	£6469
IC	Beam1/2E	Worm	Disc/disc	185-15	174	2889	150	8.0	N/A	£5607
IC	IC	Worm	Disc/disc	205-14	174	2490	153	6.0	14.0	£5973
IC	IC	Worm	Disc/disc	205-14	174	2490	166	5.0	14.7	£7,063
IC	IC	Worm	Disc/disc	205-14	171	2535	145	7.2	15.7	£5973
IC	IC	Worm	Disc/disc	205-14	171	2650	146	6.9	N/A	£6515
IC	IC	Worm	Disc/disc	205-14	171	2650	146	N/A (Claimed)	N/A	£8750
IC	Beam1/2E	Worm	Disc/disc	6.50-15	185	2820	150	8.0	16.3	£6326
IC	Beam1/2E	Worm	Disc/disc	205-15	185	3040	142	7.4	15.5	£6522
IC	IC	Worm	Disc/disc	205-14	173	2860	143	6.8	15.1	£6515
IC	Beam1/2E	Worm	Disc/disc	205-15	193	2911	152	N/A (Claimed)	N/A	£9200
IC	Beam1/2EC	Worm	Disc/disc	205-15	190	3100	180 (Est)	7.8	15.8	£11,519
IC	IC	Worm	Disc/disc	205-15	196	3490	152	7.1	15.2	£7500
IC	IC	Worm	Disc/disc	205-14	173	3195	151	6.3	14.5	£7909
IC	IC	Worm	Disc/disc	215/70-15	174	2825	174	5.4	13.7	£8750
ITrL	Beam1/2E	Worm	Drum/drum	4.25-15	133	1316	60	N/A	28.0	£582
IC	BeamC	Worm	Drum/drum	5.90-14	167	2552	72	N/A	N/A	£1098
IC	BeamC	Worm	Drum/drum	6.40-14	169	2590	84	N/A	N/A	£1389
IC	Beam1/2E	Worm	Drum/drum	5.20-14	148	1736	78	26.4	22.8	£821
IC	Beam1/2E	Worm	Drum/drum	5.20-14	149	1865	81	21.5	22.2	£1064
IC	Beam1/2E	Worm	Drum/drum	5.20-14	154	1911	81	22.5	21.5	£744
IC	Beam1/2E	Worm	Disc/drum	155-13	157	1859	78	21.9	21.7	£682
IC	Beam1/2E	Worm	Drum/drum	5.20-14	154	2023	86	19.9	21.6	£1199
ITrL	IC	Worm	Drum/drum	5.20-12	127	1260	58	N/A	27.7	£585
ITrL	IC	Worm	Drum/drum	5.20-12	127	1351	66	N/A	24.9	£622
IC	IC	Worm	Drum/drum	5.20-12	139	1596	57	N/A	28.2	£799
ITrL	IC	Worm	Drum/drum	125-12	116	1036	51	N/A	31.0	£556
ITrL	IC	Worm	Drum/drum	125-12	116	1113	57	N/A	29.0	£556
ITrL	IC	Worm	Drum/drum	125-12	116	1106	60	N/A	26.6	£483
ITrL	IC	Worm	Drum/drum	125-12	125	1246	59	N/A	27.7	£585
ITor	Beam1/4E/C	Worm	Drum/drum	5.90-14	176	2680	90 (Est)	N/A	N/A	£1475
ITor	Beam1/2E	Worm	Disc/disc	5.90-14	176	2789	90 (Est)	N/A	N/A	£1387
ITor	Beam1/4E/C	Worm	Drum/drum	5.90-14	176	2680	91	15.9	20.0	£1550
ITor	Beam1/2E	Worm	Disc/disc	6.40-14	176	2786	99	12.3	18.5	£1525

Make and model	Production Figures	Years Built	Body Styles	Mechanical Layout	Engine Make (if not own)	Capacity/ (cc)/Layout/ Valves	BHP/ rpm	Torque (lb.ft)/rpm	Transmission gearbox/automatic transmission
						OHV			
1200/1500 Cabrio	Est 37,385 (Incl. 1500S/1600S)	1963–1966	Spts	F/R	—	1221/4IL/	58/5300	61/3000	4-spd/-
						OHV			
						1481/4IL/	72/5200	87/3200	4-spd/-
						OHV	75/5600	87/3200	5-spd/-
1500S/ 1600S Cabrio	—	1959–1966	Spts	F/R	Fiat/Osca	1491/4IL/ 2OHC	80/6000	77/4000	4-spd/-
						1568/4IL/ 2OHC	90/6000	98/4000	4-spd/5-spd/-
1300/1500	Est 600,000	1961–1968	Sal Est	F/R	—	1295/4IL/ OHV	65/5200 70/4200	69/3400 80/3200	4-spd/- 4-spd/-
						1481/4IL/ OHV	72/5200 75/5400	75/3400 79/3200	4-spd/- 4-spd/-
2300 Coupe/ 2300S Coupe	—	1961–1968	Cpe	F/R	—	2279/6IL/ OHV	105/5300 136/5600	123/2800 132/4000	4-spd/- 4-spd/-
1500L	Incl. in 1800/ 2100/2300 figures	1963–1968	Sal	F/R	—	1481/4IL/ OHV	72/5200	87/3200	4-spd/-
850	1,780,000 (Approx)	1964–1974	Sal	R/R	—	843/4IL/ OHV	37/5100 47/6200	41/3400 44/3600	4-spd/Semi-Auto 4-spd/-
	[Later 850s were supplied from Seat in Spain, as re-badged Seat 850s, which were mechanically identical]								
850 Coupe	342,873	1965–1973	Cpe	R/R	—	843/4IL/ OHV	47/6200	44/3600	4-spd/-
						903/4IL/ OHV	52/6500	48/4000	4-spd/-
850 Spider	124,660	1965–1973	Spts	R/R	—	843/4IL/ OHV	49/6200	43/4200	4-spd/-
						903/4IL/ OHV	52/6500	48/4000	4-spd/-
124/124S/ 124ST	1,543,000 (Approx)	1966–1974	Sal Est	F/R	—	1197/4IL/ OHV	60/5600	64/3400	4-spd/-
						1438/4IL/ OHV	70/5400	81/3300	4-spd/-
						1438/4IL/ 2OHC	80/5800	81/4000	4-spd/-
						1592/4IL/ 2OHC	95/6000	93/4000	4-spd/5-spd/-
124 Coupe	279,672	1967–1975	Cpe	F/R	—	1438/4IL/ 2OHC	90/6000	80/3600	4-spd/5-spd/-
						1592/4IL/ 2OHC	108/6000	101/4200	4-spd/5-spd/-
						1608/4IL/ 2OHC	110/6400	101/3800	4-spd/5-spd/-
						1756/4IL/ 2OHC	118/6000	113/4000	4-spd/5-spd/-
124 Spider	178,439	1966–1982	Spts	F/R	—	1438/4IL/ 2OHC	90/6000	80/3600	5-spd/-
						1592/4IL/ 2OHC	108/6000	101/4200	5-spd/-
						1608/4IL/ 2OHC	110/6400	101/3800	5-spd/-
						1756/4IL/ 2OHC	118/6000	113/4000	4-spd/5-spd/-
125/125S	603,870	1967–1972	Sal	F/R	—	1608/4IL/ 2OHC	90/5600 100/6000	94/3400 96/4000	4-spd/- 5-spd/-
Dino 2000/ 2400 Coupe	6,068	1967–1973	Cpe	F/R	Ferrari	1987/V6/ 2OHC	160/7200	126/6000	5-spd/-
						2418/V6/ 2OHC	180/6600	159/4600	5-spd/-
Dino 2000/ 2400 Spider	1,583	1966–1973	Spts	F/R	Ferrari	1987/V6/ 2OHC	160/7200	126/6000	5-spd/-
						2418/V6/ 2OHC	180/6600	159/4600	5-spd/-
128	2,776,000 (Est)	1969–1984	Sal Est	F(Tr)/F	—	1116/4IL/ OHC	55/6000	57/3000	4-spd/-
						1290/4IL/ OHC	61/6000	66/3000	4-spd/-
130	15,000	1969–1976	Sal	F/R	—	3235/V6/ OHC	165/5600	184/3400	Auto/-
Ford (UK and Europe)									
Anglia	55,807	1939–1948	Sal	F/R	—	933/4IL/ SV	23/4000	36/2200	3-spd/-
Prefect	158,007	1938–1949	Sal	F/R	—	1172/4IL/ SV	30/4000	46/3000	3-spd/-
Anglia E94A	108,778	1948–1953	Sal	F/R	—	933/4IL/ SV	23/4000	36/2200	3-spd/-
Prefect E493A	192,229	1948–1953	Sal	F/R	—	1172/4IL/ SV	30/4000	46/3000	3-spd/-

Suspension Front	Rear	Steering	Brakes (Front/rear)	Wheels/model Tyres	Length (in)	Weight (lb,unladen)	Performance Top speed (mph)	0–60mph (sec)	Standing 1/4-mile (sec)	UK Total Price (£: at Launch)
IC	Beam1/2E	Worm	Drum/drum	5.20-14	159	1994	90	19.1	21.0	£1460
IC	Beam1/2E	Worm	Disc/drum	145-14	159	2115	91	14.7	20.1	£1197
IC	Beam1/2E	Worm	Drum/drum Disc/drum	155-15	159	2182	103	15.2	20.3	£1749
IC	Beam1/2E	Worm	Disc/drum	155-15	159	2281	109 (Claimed)	N/A	N/A	£1596
IC	Beam1/2E	Worm	Disc/drum	5.60-13	159	2100	88	19.2	21.4	£1099
IC	Beam1/2E	Worm	Disc/drum	5.60-13	161	2016	89	17.5	19.6	£829
IC	Beam1/2E	Worm	Disc/drum	5.60-13	159	2100	91	15.3	19.7	£1146
IC	Beam1/2E	Worm	Disc/drum	5.60-13	161	2128	94	16.2	19.9	£934
ITor	Beam1/2E	Worm	Disc/disc	165-15	182	2790	100 (Est)	N/A	N/A	£2610
ITor	Beam1/2E	Worm	Disc/disc	165-15	182	2790	120	10.5	18.3	£2944
ITor	Beam1/2E	Worm	Disc/disc	5.90-14	175	2625	88	19.0	21.1	£999
ITrL	IC	Worm	Drum/drum	5.50-12	141	1516	76	26.8	22.9	£550
ITrL	IC	Worm	Disc/drum	145-13	141	1520	80	19.0	21.3	£659
ITrL	IC	Worm	Disc/drum	5.20-13	144	1607	87	18.2	21.0	£850
ITrL	IC	Worm	Disc/drum	155-13	146	1609	91	15.6	20.4	£825
ITrL	IC	Worm	Disc/drum	5.20-13	149	1620	92	N/A	N/A	£1000
ITrL	IC	Worm	Disc/drum	155-13	149	1620	96 (Est)	N/A	N/A	£1089
IC	BeamC	Worm	Disc/disc	155-13	159	1800	83	15.9	20.1	£774
IC	BeamC	Worm	Disc/disc	155-13	159	2040	96	12.8	19.0	£968
IC	BeamC	Worm	Disc/disc	155-13	159	2020	102	12.0	18.4	£1240
IC	BeamC	Worm	Disc/disc	155-13	159	2041	100	10.1	17.6	£1427
IC	BeamC	Worm	Disc/disc	165-13	162	2116	102	12.6	18.8	£1298
IC	BeamC	Worm	Disc/disc	165-13	162	2194	106 (Est)	N/A	N/A	£1942
IC	BeamC	Worm	Disc/disc	165-13	162	2194	109	10.7	17.8	£1797
IC	BeamC	Worm	Disc/disc	165-13	162	2194	107	10.5	17.4	£2047
IC	BeamC	Worm	Disc/disc	165-13	156	2083	106	11.9	18.3	Special Order
IC	BeamC	Worm	Disc/disc	165-13	156	2201	110 (Est)	N/A	N/A	Special Order
IC	BeamC	Worm	Disc/disc	165-13	156	2201	112	12.2	18.6	Special Order
IC	BeamC	Worm	Disc/disc	165-13	156	2201	115 (Est)	N/A	N/A	Special Order
IC	Beam1/2E	Worm	Disc/disc	175-13	166	2191	99	13.4	19.0	£1007
IC	Beam1/2E	Worm	Disc/disc	175-13	166	2218	104	11.9	18.1	£1203
IC	Beam1/2E	Worm	Disc/disc	185-14	178	3042	127	8.1	16.0	£3493
IC	IC	Worm	Disc/disc	205/70-14	178	3042	130	8.7	16.1	Special Order
IC	Beam1/2E	Worm	Disc/disc	185-14	162	2535	127	8.1	16.0	Special Order
IC	IC	Worm	Disc/disc	205/70-14	162	2800	130 (Est)	N/A	N/A	Special Order
IC	ITrL	R & P	Disc/drum	145-13	151	1802	86	16.3	19.8	£871
IC	ITrL	R & P	Disc/drum	145-13	151	1842	91	12.9	18.8	£1111
ITor	IC	Worm	Disc/disc	205/70-14	187	3574	113	11.4	18.4	£3818
BeamTrL	BeamTrL	Worm	Drum/drum	4.50-17	152	1649	57	N/A	27.8	£293
BeamTrL	BeamTrL	Worm	Drum/drum	5.00-16	156	1754	60	N/A	25.9	£352
BeamTrL	BeamTrL	Worm	Drum/drum	4.50-17	152	1649	57	N/A	27.8	£310
BeamTrL	BeamTrL	Worm	Drum/drum	5.00-16	152	1754	60	N/A	25.9	£371

Make and model	Production Figures	Years Built	Body Styles	Mechanical Layout	Engine Make (if not own)	Capacity/(cc)/Layout/Valves	BHP/rpm	Torque (lb.ft)/rpm	Transmission gearbox/automatic transmission
V8 Pilot	22,155	1947–1951	Sal	F/R	—	2525/V8/SV	65/4000	101/1900	3-spd/-
						3622/V8/SV	85/3500	150/1500	3-spd/-
Consul/Zephyr/Zodiac I	231,481	1951–1956	Sal Conv Est	F/R	—	1508/4IL/OHV	47/4400	72/2400	3-spd/-
						2262/6IL/OHV	68/4000	108/2000	3-spd (+O/D)/-
Popular E103	155,340	1953–1959	Sal	F/R	—	1172/4IL/SV	30/4000	46/3000	3-spd/-
Anglia 100E/Prefect	601,496	1953–1959	Sal	F/R	—	1172/4IL/SV	36/4400	54/2150	3-spd/SemiAuto
Escort/Squire Estate	50,943	1955–1961	Est	F/R	—	1172/4IL/SV	36/4500	54/2150	3-spd/-
Consul/Zephyr/Zodiac II	682,400	1956–1962	Sal Conv Est	F/R	—	1703/4IL/OHV	59/4400	91/2300	3-spd/-
						2553/6IL/OHV	85/4400	133/2000	3-spd (+O/D)/Auto
Popular 100E	126,115	1959–1962	Sal	F/R	—	1172/4IL/SV	36/4500	54/2150	3-spd/-
Anglia 105E	1,083,960	1959–1967	Sal Est	F/R	—	997/4IL/OHV/	39/5000	56/2700	4-spd/-
						1198/4IL/OHV	50/4900	69/2700	4-spd/-
Prefect 107E	38,154	1959–1961	Sal	F/R	—	997/4IL/OHV	39/5000	56/2700	4-spd/-
Classic	109,045	1961–1963	Sal	F/R	—	1340/4IL/OHV	54/4900	74/2500	4-spd/-
						1498/4IL/OHV	60/4600	82/2300	4-spd/-
Classic Capri	18,716	1961–1964	Cpe	F/R	—	1340/4IL/OHV	54/4900	74/2500	4-spd/-
						1498/4IL/OHV	60/4600	82/2300	4-spd/-
							78/5200	97/3600	4-spd/-
Cortina I	1,010,090	1962–1966	Sal Est	F/R	—	1198/4IL/OHV	50/4900	69/2700	4-spd/-
						1498/4IL/OHV	62/4700	89/2500	4-spd/Auto
							78/5200	97/3600	4-spd/-
Lotus-Cortina	3,301	1963–1966	Sal	F/R	Lotus	1558/4IL/2OHC	105/5500	108/4000	4-spd/-
Zephyr/Zodiac III	291,899	1962–1966	Sal Est	F/R	—	1703/4IL/OHV	68/4800	94/2000	4-spd (+O/D)/Auto
						2553/6IL/OHV	98/4800	134/2400	4-spd (+O/D)/Auto
							109/4800	137/2400	4-spd/(+O/D)/Auto
Corsair/V4/2000E	331,095	1963–1970	Sal Est	F/R	—	1498/4IL/OHV	60/4600	82/2300	4-spd/Auto
							78/5200	97/3600	4-spd/-
						1663/V4/OHV	77/4750	100/3000	4-spd/Auto
						1996/V4/OHV	88/4850	124/2750	4-spd/Auto
							97/5000	120/3000	4-spd/Auto
Zephyr/Zodiac Mk IV	149,263	1966–1971	Sal Est	F/R	—	1996/V4/OHV	88/4750	116/2750	4-spd/Auto
						2495/V6/OHV	112/4750	137/3000	4-spd/Auto
						2994/V6/OHV	136/4750	181/3000	4-spd/Auto
Cortina II	1,023,837	1966–1970	Sal Est	F/R	—	1297/4IL/OHV	54/5000	71/2500	4-spd/Auto
							58/5000	72/2500	4-spd/Auto
						1498/4IL/OHV	61/4700	89/2500	4-spd/Auto
							78/5200	97/3600	4-spd/-
						1599/4IL/OHV	64/4800	85/2500	4-spd/Auto
							88/5400	96/3600	4-spd/-
Cortina 1600E	55,833	1967–1970	Sal	F/R	—	1599/4IL/OHV	88/5400	96/3600	4-spd/-
Lotus-Cortina II	4,032	1967–1970	Sal	F/R	—	1558/4IL/2OHC	109/6000	106/4500	4-spd/-
Escort I	1,082,472	1967–1974	Sal Est	F/R	—	1098/4IL/OHV	50/5500	59/3000	4-spd/-
							48/6000	54/3000	4-spd/-
						1298/4IL/OHV	58/5000	72/2500	4-spd/#
							71/6000	70/4300	4-spd/-
							57/5500	67/3000	4-spd/Auto
							72/6000	68/4000	4-spd/-
Escort TC	1,263	1968–1971	Sal	F/R	Lotus	1558/4IL/2OHC	110/6000	107/4500	4-spd/-
Escort RS1600	Est. 1,000	1970–1974	Sal	F/R	—	1599/4IL/2OHC	120/6500	112/4000	4-spd/-
Escort	9,382	1970–1974	Sal	F/R	—	1599/4IL/	86/5500	92/4000	4-spd/-

Suspension Front	Rear	Steering	Brakes (Front/rear)	Wheels/model Tyres	Length (in)	Weight (lb,unladen)	Performance Top speed (mph)	0–60mph (sec)	Standing ¼-mile (sec)	UK Total Price (£: at Launch)
BeamTrL	BeamTrL	Worm	Drum/drum	6.00-16	175	3192	65 (est)	N/A	N/A	£748
BeamTrL	BeamTrL	Worm	Drum/drum	6.00-16	175	3192	78	20.2	21.3	£748
IC	Beam1/2E	Worm	Drum/drum	5.90-13	166	2436	73	27.2	24.1	£663
IC	Beam1/2E	Worm	Drum/drum	6.40-13	172	2604	80	20.2	21.8	£842
BeamTrL	BeamTrL	Worm	Drum/drum	4.50-17	152	1624	60	N/A	25.6	£391
IC	Beam1/2E	Worm	Drum/drum	5.20-13	150	1708	70	29.4	23.8	£511
IC	Beam1/2E	Worm	Drum/drum	5.60-13	141	1848	69	34.3	24.2	£622
IC	Beam1/2E	Worm	Drum/drum Disc/drum	5.90-13	172/175	2520	80	23.2	23.0	£781
IC	Beam1/2E	Worm	Drum/drum Disc/drum	5.90-13	179/181	2688	88	17.1	20.9	£871
IC	Beam1/2E	Worm	Drum/drum	5.20-13	152	1708	68	36.4	24.4	£494
IC	Beam1/2E	Worm	Drum/drum	5.20-13	154	1679	76	26.9	22.9	£589
IC	Beam1/2E	Worm	Drum/drum	5.20-13	154	1679	82	21.6	21.5	£599
IC	Beam1/2E	Worm	Drum/drum	5.20-13	154	1764	73	27.2	23.2	£622
IC	Beam1/2E	Worm	Disc/drum	5.60-13	171	1995	79	21.8	21.9	£767
IC	Beam1/2E	Worm	Disc/drum	5.60-13	171	2080	81	20.1	21.8	£723
IC	Beam1/2E	Worm	Disc/drum	5.60-13	171	2055	81	21.3	21.7	£916
IC	Beam1/2E	Worm	Disc/drum	5.60-13	171	2087	83 (Est)	N/A	N/A	£863
IC	Beam1/2E	Worm	Disc/drum	5.60-13	171	2163	95	13.7	19.1	£901
IC	Beam1/2E	Worm	Drum/drum Disc/drum	5.20-13 6.00-13	168	1750	75	25.4	23.0	£639
IC	Beam1/2E	Worm	Drum/drum Disc/drum	5.20-13 6.00-13	168	1887	80	19.8	20.7	£688
IC	Beam1/2E	Worm	Disc/drum	5.20-13	168	1750	94	13.9	18.7	£749
IC	BeamC Beam1/2E	Worm	Disc/drum	6.00-13	168	1820	106	9.9	17.4	£1100
IC	Beam1/2E	Worm	Disc/drum	6.40-13	180	2576	84	19.6	21.4	£847
IC	Beam1/2E	Worm	Disc/drum	6.40-13	180	2744	95 (Est)	N/A	N/A	£929
IC	Beam1/2E	Worm	Disc/drum	6.40-13	182	2800	101	13.4	19.2	£1071
IC	Beam1/2E	Worm	Disc/drum	5.60-13	177	1950	86	17.8	20.6	£653
IC	Beam1/2E	Worm	Disc/drum	5.60-13	177	2000	95	14.3	19.5	£816
IC	Beam1/2E	Worm	Disc/drum	5.60-13	177	2163	88	15.6	20.2	£785
IC	Beam1/2E	Worm	Disc/drum	5.60-13	177	2194	88	14.7	19.6	£909
IC	Beam1/2E	Worm	Disc/drum	165-13	177	2223	97	13.5	18.8	£1008
IC	IC	Worm	Disc/disc	6.40-13 185-14	185	2828	95	17.7	20.3	£933
IC	IC	Worm	Disc/disc	6.70-13 185-14	185	2884	96	14.6	19.6	£1005
IC	IC	Worm	Disc/disc	6.70-13 185-14	185	2912	103	11.0	17.9	£1220
IC	Beam1/2E	Worm	Disc/drum	5.20-13	168	1900	81	21.4	22.2	£669
IC	Beam1/2E	Worm	Disc/drum	5.20-13	168	1890	84	18.2	20.7	£724
IC	Beam1/2E	Worm	Disc/drum	5.20-13	168	1913	81 (Est)	N/A	N/A	£730
IC	Beam1/2E	Worm	Disc/drum	5.20-13	168	1956	91 (Est)	N/A	N/A	£810
IC	Beam1/2E	Worm	Disc/drum	5.60-13	168	1929	88	15.1	19.7	£767
IC	Beam1/2E	Worm	Disc/drum	165-13	168	1994	98	13.1	18.8	£865
IC	Beam1/2E	Worm	Disc/drum	165-13	168	2064	98	13.1	18.8	£982
IC	Beam1/2E	Worm	Disc/drum	165-13	168	2027	105	9.9	17.6	£1068
IC	Beam1/2E	R & P	Drum/drum	5.50-12	157	1641	79	22.3	22.1	£666
IC	Beam1/2E	R & P	Disc/drum	155-12	157	1704	79	19.8	21.6	£853
IC	Beam1/2E	R & P	Drum/drum	5.50-12	157	1674	83	20.6	21.3	£691
IC	Beam1/2E	R & P	Disc/drum	155-12	157	1716	94	14.8	19.5	£765
IC	Beam1/2E	R & P	Drum/drum	5.50-12	157	1674	87	16.9	20.4	£863
IC	Beam1/2E	R & P	Disc/drum	155-12	157	1716	94	13.1	19.2	£966
IC	Beam1/2E	R & P	Disc/drum	165-13	157	1730	113	9.9	17.2	£1171
IC	Beam1/2E	R & P	Disc/drum	165-13	157	1920	113	8.9	16.7	£1447
IC	Beam1/2E	R & P	Disc/drum	165-13	157	1965	99	10.7	18.0	£1150

Make and model	Production Figures	Years Built	Body Styles	Mechanical Layout	Engine Make (if not own)	Capacity/(cc)/Layout/Valves	BHP/rpm	Torque (lb.ft)/rpm	Transmission gearbox/automatic transmission
Mexico						OHV			
Capri I	374,700 (UK prod)	1968–1973	Cpe	F/R	—	1298/4IL/ OHV	52/5000	66/2500	4-spd/-
							64/6000	65/4000	4-spd/-
							57/5500	67/3000	4-spd/-
							72/6000	68/4000	4-spd/-
						1593/4IL/ OHC	72/5500	87/2700	4-spd/Auto
							88/5700	92/4000	4-spd/Auto
						1599/4IL/ OHV	64/4800	85/2500	4-spd/Auto
							82/5400	92/3600	4-spd/Auto
							68/5200	85/2600	4-spd/Auto
							86/5500	92/4000	4-spd/Auto
						1996/V4/ OHV	93/5500	104/3600	4-spd/Auto
						2994/V6/ OHV	128/4750	173/3000	4-spd/Auto
							138/4750	191/3000	4-spd/Auto
Cortina Mk III	1,126,559	1970–1976	Sal Est	F/R	—	1298/4IL/ OHV	57/5500	67/3000	4-spd/Auto
							50/5000	64/3000	4-spd/-
						1599/4IL/ OHV	68/5200	85/2600	4-spd/Auto
						1593/4IL/ OHC	86/5500	92/4000	4-spd/Auto
							72/5500	87/3000	4-spd/Auto
						1993/4IL/ OHC	98/5500	111/3500	4-spd/Auto
Ford (France)									
Vedette	N/A	1951–1955	Sal	F/R	—	2158/V8/ SV	66/4000	90/2500	3-spd/-
Vendome	N/A	1951–1955	Sal	F/R	—	3923/V8/ SV	100/3700	168/1500	3-spd/-
Vedette	N/A	1954–1955	Sal	F/R	—	2353/V8/ SV	79/4600	110/2500	3-spd/-
Ford-Germany									
Taunus 12M	N/A	1952–1962	Sal	F/R	—	1172/4IL/ SV	38/4250	55/2200	3-spd/4-spd/-
Taunus 15M	N/A	1957–1962	Sal	F/R	—	1498/4IL/ OHV	60/4250	82/2000	3-spd/4-spd/-
Taunus 17M	239,978	1957–1960	Sal Est	F/R	—	1699/4IL/ OHV	60/4400	95/2200	3-spd/-
Taunus 17M	669,731	1960–1964	Sal Est	F/R	—	1498/4IL/ OHV	60/4500	83/2700	3-spd/4-spd/-
						1699/4IL/ OHV	67/4500	97/2500	3-spd/4-spd/-
							75/4500	109/2500	4-spd/-
							70/4500	101/2700	4-spd/-
Taunus 12M	672,695	1962–1966	Sal Est	F/F	—	1183/V4/ OHV	40/4500	62/2700	4-spd/-
						1498/V4/ OHV	50/4500	76/2100	4-spd/-
							62/5000	83/2700	
							60/4500	86/2800	
Taunus 17M	516,991	1964–1967	Sal Est	F/R	—	1498/V4/ OHV	60/4500	86/2800	3-spd/4-spd/-
						1699/V4/ OHV	70/4500	101/2700	3-spd/4-spd/Auto
Taunus 20M	193,068	1964–1967	Sal Cpe	F/R	—	1998/V6/ OHV	85/5000	114/3500	3-spd/4-spd/Auto
							90/5000	119/3500	4-spd/Auto
Taunus 12M/ 15M	N/A	1966–1970	Sal Cpe Est	F/F	—	1305/V4/ OHV	50/5000	69/2500	4-spd/-
						1498/V4/ OHV	55/5000	77/2500	4-spd/-
Taunus 17M	N/A	1967–1970	Sal Est Cpe	F/R	—	1699/V4/ OHV	70/4500	101/2700	4-spd/Auto
Taunus 20M	N/A	1967–1970	Sal Est Cpe	F/R	—	1998/V6/ OHV	90/5000	114/3000	4-spd/Auto
						2293/V6/ OHV	108/5100	134/3000	4-spd/Auto
(Ford (USA, Canada and Australia)									
Thunderbird **	—	1956 model	Cpe	F/R	—	5113/V8/ OHV	225/4600	324/2600	Auto
Fairlane **	—	1956 model	Sal	F/R	—	4458/V8/ OHV	176/4400	N/Q	Auto
Fairlane 500 **	—	1957 model	Sal	F/R	—	4458/V8/ OHV	176/4400	264/2400	Auto
Galaxie **	—	1960 model	Sal	F/R	—	5441/V8/ OHV	225/4400	324/2200	Auto
Falcon **	—	1960 model	Sal	F/R	—	2365/6IL/	90/4200	138/2000	3-spd

Suspension Front	Rear	Steering	Brakes (Front/rear)	Wheels/model Tyres	Length (in)	Weight (lb, unladen)	Performance Top speed (mph)	0–60mph (sec)	Standing 1/4-mile (sec)	UK Total Price (£: at Launch)
IC	Beam1/2E	R & P	Disc/drum	6.00-13	168	1940	86 (Est)	N/A	N/A	£890
IC	Beam1/2E	R & P	Disc/drum	165-13	168	1985	96	14.6	19.5	£986
IC	Beam1/2E	R & P	Disc/drum	165-13	168	1982	84	18.8	21.4	£1004
IC	Beam1/2E	R & P	Disc/drum	165-13	168	1985	98 (Est)	N/A	N/A	£1123
IC	Beam1/2E	R & P	Disc/drum	165-13	168	2121	98	12.9	18.9	£1260
IC	Beam1/2E	R & P	Disc/drum	165-13	168	2030	104	11.1	18.4	£1370
IC	Beam1/2E	R & P	Disc/drum	6.00-13	168	1985	92 (Est)	N/A	N/A	£936
IC	Beam1/2E	R & P	Disc/drum	165-13	168	2030	100	12.7	18.8	£1042
IC	Beam1/2E	R & P	Disc/drum	165-13	168	1985	94 (Est)	N/A	N/A	£1074
IC	Beam1/2E	R & P	Disc/drum	165-13	168	2072	99	12.4	18.7	£1042
IC	Beam1/2E	R & P	Disc/drum	165-13	168	2115	106	10.6	18.2	£1088
IC	Beam1/2E	R & P	Disc/drum	185-13	168	2380	113	10.3	17.6	£1291
IC	Beam1/2E	R & P	Disc/drum	185-13	168	2430	122	8.4	16.2	£1484
IC	BeamC	R & P	Disc/drum	5.60-13	168	2083	84	18.1	21.0	£914
IC	BeamC	R & P	Disc/drum	165-13	168	2183	80 (Est)	N/A	N/A	£1732
IC	BeamC	R & P	Disc/drum	5.60-13	168	2115	92	14.7	19.7	£961
IC	BeamC	R & P	Disc/drum	175-13	168	2182	98	13.3	19.0	£1112
IC	BeamC	R & P	Disc/drum	165-13	168	2240	93	15.1	19.9	£1141
IC	BeamC	R & P	Disc/drum	175-13	168	2346	105	10.7	18.1	£1027
IC	Beam1/2E	Worm	Drum/drum	165-400	184	2733	81 (Claimed)	N/A	N/A	£967
IC	Beam1/2E	Worm	Drum/drum	165-400	184	2923	90 (Claimed)	N/A	N/A	£1108
IC	Beam1/2E	Worm	Drum/drum	6.40-13	177	2437	84 (Est)	N/A	N/A	£1340
IC	Beam1/2E	Worm	Drum/drum	5.60-13	160	2008	68 (Est)	N/A	N/A	£1054
IC	Beam1/2E	Worm	Drum/drum	5.60-13	160	1909	78	22.8	21.4	£1146
IC	Beam1/2E	Worm	Drum/drum	5.90-13	172	2268	79	21.4	21.9	£1198
IC	Beam1/2E	Worm	Drum/drum	5.90-13	175	2016	83 (Est)	N/A	N/A	£1135
IC	Beam1/2E	Worm	Drum/drum	5.90-13	175	2082	86	19.7	21.5	£1269
IC	Beam1/2E	Worm	Drum/drum	5.90-13	175	2128	90	15.6	20.3	£1401
IC	Beam1/2E	Worm	Disc/drum	5.90-13	175	2050	88 (Est)	N/A	N/A	£986
ITrL	Beam1/2E	Worm	Drum/drum Disc/drum	5.60-13	171	1904	78	24.8	23.1	£799
ITrL	Beam1/2E	Worm	Drum/drum Disc/drum	5.60-13	171	1904	81 (Est)	N/A	N/A	£N/A
IC	Beam1/2E	Worm	Disc/drum	5.90-13	175	2050	84	N/A (Claimed)	N/A	£1053
IC	Beam1/2E	Worm	Disc/drum	5.90-13	175	2050	90	N/A (Claimed)	N/A	£1126
IC	Beam1/2E	Worm	Disc/drum	6.40-13	181	2170	95	14.8	19.6	£1180
IC	Beam1/2E	Worm	Disc/drum	6.40-13	181	2271	103	N/A (Claimed)	N/A	£1270
IC	Beam1/2E	R & P	Disc/drum	5.60-13	170	1874	81	N/A (Claimed)	N/A	£924
IC	Beam1/2E	R & P	Disc/drum	5.60-13	170	1870	84	N/A (Claimed)	N/A	£1003
IC	Beam1/2E	Worm	Disc/drum	6.40-13	183	2270	90	N/A (Claimed)	N/A	£1197
IC	Beam1/2E	Worm	Disc/drum	6.40-13	186	2380	99	N/A (Claimed)	N/A	£1388
IC	Beam1/2E	Worm	Disc/drum	6.40-13	186	2380	106	N/A (Claimed)	N/A	£1503
IC	Beam1/2E	Worm	Drum/drum	6.70-15	185	3472	113	10.2	17.5	£2536
IC	Beam1/2E	Worm	Drum/drum	6.70-15	199	3500	96	16.4	20.3	£2177
IC	Beam1/2E	Worm	Drum/drum	8.00-14	208	3731	90	15.1	20.0	£2067
IC	Beam1/2E	Worm	Drum/drum	8.00-14	214	4060	107	12.4	18.6	£2691
IC	Beam1/2E	Worm	Drum/drum	6.00-13	182	2436	86	19.5	21.5	£2006

Make and model	Production Figures	Years Built	Body Styles	Mechanical Layout	Engine Make (if not own)	Capacity/(cc)/Layout/Valves	BHP/rpm	Torque (lb.ft)/rpm	Transmission gearbox/automatic transmission
Thunderbird **	—	1961 model	Cpe	F/R	—	6392/V8/ OHV	300/4600	427/2800	Auto
Fairlane 500 **	—	1962 model	Sal	F/R	—	3622/V8/ OHV	145/4400	216/2200	Auto
Falcon Sprint **	—	1964 model	Conv	F/R	—	4261/V8/ OHV	164/4400	258/2200	4-spd
Galaxie **	—	1963 model	Sal	F/R	—	5769/V8/ OHV	220/4300	336/2600	Auto
Galaxie **	—	1964 model	Conv	F/R	—	6390/V8/ OHV	304/4600	427/2800	Auto
Mustang **	—	1964 model	Conv	F/R	—	4727/V8/ OHV	271/6000	312/3400	4-spd
Mustang **	—	1965 model	Cpe	F/R	—	4727/V8/ OHV	271/6000	312/4000	4-spd
Fairmont **	—	1967 model	Est	F/R	—	4727/V8/ OHV	200/4400	282/2400	Auto
Maverick **	—	1970 model	Cpe	F/R	—	3273/6IL/ OHV	122/4000	190/2200	Auto

Frazer Nash

Make and model	Production Figures	Years Built	Body Styles	Mechanical Layout	Engine Make (if not own)	Capacity/(cc)/Layout/Valves	BHP/rpm	Torque (lb.ft)/rpm	Transmission gearbox/automatic transmission
Le Mans Replica	34	1948–1953	Spts	F/R	Bristol	1971/6IL/ OHV	125/5500	N/Q	4-spd/-
Mille Miglia	12	1950–1955	Spts Spl	F/R	Bristol	1971/6IL/ OHV	105/5000	123/3750	4-spd/-
Targa Florio	14	1952–1956	Spts	F/R	Bristol	1971/6IL/ OHV	100/5000 125/5500	118/3750 N/Q	4-spd/-
Le Mans Coupe	9	1953–1956	Spts Cpe	F/R	Bristol	1971/6IL/ OHV	125/5500	N/Q	4-spd/-
Sebring	3	1954–1956	Spts	F/R	Bristol	1971/6IL/ OHV	125/5500	N/Q	4-spd/-

FSO (Earlier named Polski-Fiat)

Make and model	Production Figures	Years Built	Body Styles	Mechanical Layout	Engine Make (if not own)	Capacity/(cc)/Layout/Valves	BHP/rpm	Torque (lb.ft)/rpm	Transmission gearbox/automatic transmission
125p	N/A	1968–1991	Sal Est	F/R	—	1481/4IL/ OHV	70/5400	83/3200	4-spd/-

Gilbern

Make and model	Production Figures	Years Built	Body Styles	Mechanical Layout	Engine Make (if not own)	Capacity/(cc)/Layout/Valves	BHP/rpm	Torque (lb.ft)/rpm	Transmission gearbox/automatic transmission
GT	Est 280	1959–1967	Cpe	F/R	MG	1588/4IL/ OHV	80/5600	87/3800	4-spd/-
						1622/4IL/ OHV	86/5500	97/4000	4-spd/-
						1798/4IL/ OHV	96/5500	107/3500	4-spd (+O/D)-
						948/4IL/ OHV	68/5700	65/3000	4-spd/-
						(Some cars with Coventry-Climax 1216cc engine for £949)			
Genie/ Invader	Est 800	1966–1974	Cpe Est	F/R	Ford	2994/V6 OHV	141/4750	181/3000	4-spd/-

Ginetta

Make and model	Production Figures	Years Built	Body Styles	Mechanical Layout	Engine Make (if not own)	Capacity/(cc)/Layout/Valves	BHP/rpm	Torque (lb.ft)/rpm	Transmission gearbox/automatic transmission
G4	Est 500	1961–1969	Spts	F/R	Ford	997/4IL/ OHV	40/5000	53/2700	4-spd/-
G15	Est 800	1968–1974	Spts Cpe	R/R	Rootes/ Sunbeam	875/4IL/ OHC	50/5800	49/4500	4-spd/-

Glas

Make and model	Production Figures	Years Built	Body Styles	Mechanical Layout	Engine Make (if not own)	Capacity/(cc)/Layout/Valves	BHP/rpm	Torque (lb.ft)/rpm	Transmission gearbox/automatic transmission
Goggomobil	280,379 (Incl. Coupe)	1955–1969	Sal	R/R	—	293/2IL/ 2-Str AirC	15/5000	17/4100	4-spd/-
Goggomobil Coupe	—	1957–1967	Cpe	R/R	—	293/2IL/ 2-Str AirC	15/5000	17/4100	4-spd/-
						392/2IL/ 2-Str AirC	20/5000	24/3900	4-spd/-
T700	87,000	1958–1965	Sal Est	F/R	—	682/2HO/ 2-Str AirC	30/4500	36/3000	4-spd/-

Gordon-Keeble

Make and model	Production Figures	Years Built	Body Styles	Mechanical Layout	Engine Make (if not own)	Capacity/(cc)/Layout/Valves	BHP/rpm	Torque (lb.ft)/rpm	Transmission gearbox/automatic transmission
GT/IT	99	1964–1966	Cpe	F/R	Chevrolet	5355/V8/ OHV	300/5000	360/3000	4-spd/-

G.S.M.

Make and model	Production Figures	Years Built	Body Styles	Mechanical Layout	Engine Make (if not own)	Capacity/(cc)/Layout/Valves	BHP/rpm	Torque (lb.ft)/rpm	Transmission gearbox/automatic transmission
Delta	N/A	1960–1964	Spts	F/R	Ford	997/4IL/	39/5000	56/2700	4-spd/-

Suspension Front	Rear	Steering	Brakes (Front/rear)	Wheels/model Tyres	Length (in)	Weight (lb, unladen)	Performance Top speed (mph)	0–60mph (sec)	Standing 1/4-mile (sec)	UK Total Price (£: at Launch)
IC	Beam1/2E	Worm	Drum/drum	8.00-14	205	4203	118	9.3	16.8	£3797
IC	Beam1/2E	Worm	Drum/drum	7.00-13	197	3136	94	14.8	19.9	£2221
IC	Beam1/2E	Worm	Drum/drum	7.00-13	182	3059	106	11.2	17.8	£2097
IC	Beam1/2E	Worm	Drum/drum	8.00-14	210	4088	105	11.4	18.6	£2055
IC	Beam1/2E	Worm	Drum/drum	8.00-14	209	4347	119	9.5	16.6	£2244
IC	Beam1/2E	Worm	Drum/drum	6.50-14	182	3103	116	8.2	16.0	£1925
IC	Beam1/2E	Worm	Drum/drum	7.00-14	181	2901	128	7.6	15.2	£1922
IC	Beam1/2E	Worm	Disc/drum	7.35-14	192	3397	102	11.6	18.3	£2402
IC	Beam1/2E	Worm	Drum/drum	6.45-14	180	2552	97	14.3	19.8	£2499
ITrL	BeamTor	R & P	Drum/drum	5.50-16	150	1400	110	8.8	N/A	£3074
ITrL	BeamTor	R & P	Drum/drum	5.50-16	150	1862	110	9.6	17.4	£2876
ITrL	BeamTor	R & P	Drum/drum	5.50-16	150	1848	114	10.4	17.8	£3035
ITrL	BeamTor	R & P	Drum/drum	5.50-16	150	1848	125 (Est)	N/A	N/A	
ITrL	BeamTor	R & P	Drum/drum	5.50-16	161	1876	125 (Est)	N/A	N/A	£3188
ITrL	BeamTor	R & P	Drum/drum	5.50-16	161	1736	125 (Est)	N/A	N/A	£3543
IC	Beam1/2E	Worm	Disc/disc	165-13	167	2285	93	14.4	19.5	£1249
IC	BeamC	R & P	Disc/drum	5.90-14	152	1792	94	13.8	19.0	£870
IC	BeamC	R & P	Disc/drum	5.90-13	152	1680	100	N/A (Est)	N/A	£1300
IC	BeamC	R & P	Disc/drum	5.90-14	152	1915	111	12.0	18.6	£1260
IC	BeamC	R & P	Disc/drum	5.20-13	152	1582	96	17.4	20.9	£748
IC	BeamC	R & P	Disc/drum	165-15	159	1990	115	10.7	17.8	£1752
IC	BeamC	R & P	Disc/drum	5.20-13	140	1080	85 (Est)	N/A	N/A	£697
IC	IC	R & P	Disc/drum	5.20-13	144	1105	94	12.9	18.8	£1024
IC	IC	R & P	Drum/drum	4.40-10	114	851	52	N/A	28.6	£495
IC	IC	R & P	Drum/drum	4.80-10	114	994	59	N/A	26.7	£625
IC	IC	R & P	Drum/drum	4.80-10	114	1001	60	N/A	26.0	£644
IC	Beam1/2E	Worm	Drum/drum	4.80-12	135	1344	66	44.4	23.9	£711
IC	DDC	Worm	Disc/disc	6.70-15	190	3165	136	7.5	15.6	£2798
ITrL	Beam1/2E	Worm	Drum/drum	5.20-13	145	1367	80 (Est)	N/A	N/A	£1189

Make and model	Production Figures	Years Built	Body Styles	Mechanical Layout	Engine Make (if not own)	Capacity/(cc)/Layout/Valves	BHP/rpm	Torque (lb.ft)/rpm	Transmission gearbox/automatic transmission
						OHV			

Healey

Make and model	Production Figures	Years Built	Body Styles	Mechanical Layout	Engine Make (if not own)	Capacity/(cc)/Layout/Valves	BHP/rpm	Torque (lb.ft)/rpm	Transmission gearbox/automatic transmission
Westland/Elliott/ Duncan/ Sportsmobile/	227	1946–1950	Spts Sal	F/R	Riley	2443/4IL/ OHV	104/4500	132/3000	4-spd/-
Silverstone	105	1949–1950	Spts	F/R	Riley	2443/4IL/ OHV	104/4500	132/3000	4-spd/-
Tickford/ Abbott	301	1950–1954	Sal Conv	F/R	Riley	2443/4IL/ OHV	104/4500	132/3000	4-spd/-
3-litre	25	1951–1954	Conv	F/R	Alvis	2993/6IL/ OHV	106/4200	140/2000	4-spd/-

Heinkel

Make and model	Production Figures	Years Built	Body Styles	Mechanical Layout	Engine Make (if not own)	Capacity/(cc)/Layout/Valves	BHP/rpm	Torque (lb.ft)/rpm	Transmission gearbox/automatic transmission
Cabin Cruiser	N/A	1957–1965	Conv	R/R	—	204/1-cyl/ OHV	10/5500	N/Q	4-spd/-

Hillman

Make and model	Production Figures	Years Built	Body Styles	Mechanical Layout	Engine Make (if not own)	Capacity/(cc)/Layout/Valves	BHP/rpm	Torque (lb.ft)/rpm	Transmission gearbox/automatic transmission
Minx Ph I/II	N/A	1939–1948	Sal Conv Est	F/R	—	1185/4IL/ SV	35/4100	54/2400	4-spd/-
Minx PhIII– VIIIA	378,705	1948–1956	Sal Conv Est Cpe	F/R	—	1185/4IL/ SV	35/4100	54/2400	4-spd/-
						1265/4IL/ SV	38/4200	58/2200	
						1390/4IL/ OHV	43/4400	66/2200	4-spd/-
Husky	41,898	1954–1957	Est	F/R	—	1265/4IL/ SV	35/4100	55/2200	4-spd/-
Husky SI/SII/SIII	N/A	1958–1965	Est	F/R	—	1390/4IL/ OHV	40/4000	66/1600	4-spd/-
							47/4400	72/2200	4-spd/-
							41/4200	72/1800	4-spd/-
Minx SI/SVI	N/A	1956–1967	Sal Est Conv	F/R	—	1390/4IL/ OHV	48/4600	70/2400	4-spd/SemiAuto
						1494/4IL/ OHV	49/4400	78/2100	4-spd/Auto
							53/4600	83/2000	
						1592/4IL/ OHV	53/4100	87/2100	4-spd/Auto
							58/4000	86/2500	Auto/-
						1725/4IL/ OHV	65/4800	98/2400	4-spd/Auto
							59/4200	92/2200	
Super Minx	N/A	1961–1967	Sal Est Conv	F/R	—	1592/4IL/ OHV	62/4800	84/2800	4-spd/Auto
						1725/4IL/ OHV	65/4800	91/2400	4-spd/Auto
Imp	440,032 (all Imp types)	1963–1976	Sal	R/R	—	875/4IL/ OHC	37/4800	49/2600	4-spd/-
Californian	N/A	1967–1970	Cpe	R/R	—	875/4IL/ OHC	37/4800	49/2600	4-spd/-
Husky (Imp)	N/A	1967–1970	Est	R/R	—	875/4IL/ OHC	37/4800	49/2600	4-spd/-
Rallye Imp	N/A	1965–1967	Sal	R/R	—	998/4IL/ OHC	60/6200	59/3200	4-spd/-
Hunter	Est 470,000 (all Hunter and Minx)	1966–1977	Sal Est	F/R	—	1496/4IL/ OHV	54/4600	73/2500	4-spd/-
						1725/4IL/ OHV	61/4700	85/2600	4-spd (+O/D)/Auto
							72/5000	90/3000	4-spd (+O/D)/Auto
Hillman GT/ Hunter GT/GLS	—	1969–1976	Sal	F/R	—	1725/4IL/ OHV	79/5100	93/3300	4-spd (+O/D)/-
							93/5200	106/4000	
Minx	See above	1967–1970	Sal Est	F/R	—	1496/4IL/ OHV	54/4600	73/2500	4-spd/-
						1725/4IL/ OHV	68/4800	93/2700	Auto/-
Avenger	638,631	1970–1976	Sal Est	F/R	—	1248/4IL/ OHV	53/5000	66/3000	4-spd/-
						1295/4IL/ OHV	57/5000	69/2800	4-spd/-
							69/5800	68/4000	4-spd/-
						1498/4IL/ OHV	63/5000	80/3000	4-spd/Auto
							75/5400	81/3750	
						1599/4IL/ OHV	69/5000	87/2900	4-spd/Auto
							81/5500	86/3400	4-spd/Auto

Note : All surviving Hillman Avengers were renamed Chryslers from September 1976.

Hindustan

Make and model	Production Figures	Years Built	Body Styles	Mechanical Layout	Engine Make (if not own)	Capacity/(cc)/Layout/Valves	BHP/rpm	Torque (lb.ft)/rpm	Transmission gearbox/automatic transmission
Ambassador	In prod.	1959–Date	Sal	F/R	Isuzu	1818/4IL/ OHC	74/5000	N/Q	5-spd/-

Suspension Front	Suspension Rear	Steering	Brakes (Front/rear)	Wheels/model Tyres	Length (in)	Weight (lb, unladen)	Performance Top speed (mph)	0–60mph (sec)	Standing ¼-mile (sec)	UK Total Price (£: at Launch)
IC	BeamC	Worm	Drum/drum	5.75-15	168	2520-2912	102	12.3	N/A	£2335
IC	BeamC	Worm	Drum/drum	5.50-15	168	2072	105 (Est)	11.0	N/A	£1246
IC	BeamC	Worm	Drum/drum	5.75-15	177	2968	104	14.6	19.3	£1854
IC	BeamC	Worm	Drum/drum	6.40-15	174	2772	100	11.4	18.7	£2490
IC	IC	R & P	Drum/drum	4.40-10	106	616	50	N/A	N/Q	N/A
Beam1/2E	Beam1/2E	Worm	Drum/drum	5.00-16	154	1904	59	N/A	26.0	£397
IC	Beam1/2E	Worm	Drum/drum	5.00-16	157	2115	66	46.6	25.3	£505
IC	Beam1/2E	Worm	Drum/drum	5.00-16	157	2115	67	39.7	24.6	£505
IC	Beam1/2E	Worm	Drum/drum	5.60-15	157	2115	73	29.7	23.9	£681
IC	Beam1/2E	Worm	Drum/drum	5.00-15	146	1925	63	27.5	26.3	£565
IC	Beam1/2E	Worm	Drum/drum	5.00-15	150	2080	69	41.4	24.3	£699
IC	Beam1/2E	Worm	Drum/drum	5.60-15	150	2080	73	30.0	23.2	£660
IC	Beam1/2E	Worm	Drum/drum	5.60-15	150	2080	73	35.9	24.5	£587
IC	Beam1/2E	Worm	Drum/drum	5.60-15	161	2185	77	27.7	23.5	£748
IC	Beam1/2E	Worm	Drum/drum	5.60-15	161	2200	78	26.6	23.2	£748
IC	Beam1/2E	Worm	Drum/drum	5.60-15	161	2200	79	23.6	22.8	£727
IC	Beam1/2E	Worm	Disc/drum	6.00-13	161	2200	80 (Est)	N/A	N/A	£723
IC	Beam1/2E	Worm	Disc/drum	6.00-13	161	2200	82	18.6	21.1	£751
IC	Beam1/2E	Worm	Drum/drum	5.90-13	165	2355	83	22.5	22.7	£854
			Disc/drum				82	19.5	21.5	£847
IC	Beam1/2E	Worm		5.90-13	165	2355	83	17.9	20.7	£805
IC	IC	R & P	Drum/drum	5.50-12	139	1530	78	25.4	22.8	£508
IC	IC	R & P	Drum/drum	5.50-12	139	1560	78	22.1	21.9	£647
IC	IC	R & P	Drum/drum	155-12	143	1645	76	24.2	22.8	£622
IC	IC	R & P	Drum/drum	155-12	139	1530	92	14.9	19.8	Special Order
IC	Beam1/2E	Worm	Disc/drum	5.60-13	168	2035	83	17.8	20.9	£838
IC	Beam1/2E	Worm	Disc/drum	5.60-13	168	2035	90	14.6	19.6	£989
IC	Beam1/2E	Worm	Disc/drum	155-13	168	2000	92	14.3	19.7	£838
IC	Beam1/2E	Worm	Disc/drum	155-13	168	2105	96	13.9	19.4	£962
				165-13	168	2114	108	10.5	17.4	£1293
IC	Beam1/2E	Worm	Disc/drum	5.60-13	168	2035	83	17.8	20.9	£733
IC	Beam1/2E	Worm	Disc/drum	5.60-13	168	2035	90 (Est)	N/A	N/A	£838
IC	BeamC	R & P	Disc/drum	5.60-13	161	1895	81	19.8	21.4	£822
IC	BeamC	R & P	Disc/drum	5.60-13	161	1895	85	17.5	20.9	£807
IC	BeamC	R & P	Disc/drum	155-13	161	1882	92	14.4	19.9	£1202
IC	BeamC	R & P	Disc/drum	5.60-13	161	1895	91	15.6	20.1	£942
				155-13	161	1941	96	12.5	18.5	£1073
IC	BeamC	R & P	Disc/drum	155-13	161	1895	96	13.2	19.4	£1051
IC	BeamC	R & P	Disc/drum	155-13	161	1971	100	12.2	19.0	£1156
ITor	Beam1/2E	R & P	Drum/drum	5.90-15	170	2569	87	N/A (Claimed)	N/A	£5895

Make and model	Production Figures	Years Built	Body Styles	Mechanical Layout	Engine Make (if not own)	Capacity/(cc)/Layout/Valves	BHP/rpm	Torque (lb.ft)/rpm	Transmission gearbox/automatic transmission
Honda									
S600/S800	25,853	1966–1971	Spts Spts Cpe	F/R	—	791/4IL/ 2OHC	70/8000	49/6000	4-spd/-
N360/N600	1,165,441	1966–1971	Sal	F(Tr)/F	—	354/2IL/ OHC AirC	27/8500	24/5500	4-spd/Auto
						599/2IL/ OHC AirC	42/6600	40/5000	4-spd/Auto
Z Coupe	N/A	1970–1975	Htch	F(Tr)/F	—	599/2IL/ OHC AirC	32/6600	32/4000	4-spd/Auto
HRG									
1100/1500	187	1939–1955	Spts	F/R	Singer	1074/4IL/ OHC	40/5100	50/2800	4-spd/-
						1496/4IL/ OHC	65/4800	85/2400	4-spd/-
1500 Aero	45	1946–1948	Spts	F/R	Singer	1496/4IL/ OHC	65/4800	85/2400	4-spd/-
Singer-HRG	4	1955–1956	Spts	F/R	—	1497/4IL/ 2OHC	95/5250 108/5750	101/4600 108/4750	4-spd/-
Hudson									
Rambler **	—	1956 model	Sal	F/R	—	3205/6IL/ SV	90/3800	150/1600	3-spd
Humber									
Hawk I/II	N/A	1945–1948	Sal	F/R	—	1944/4IL/ SV	56/3800	97/2000	4-spd/-
Snipe/Super Snipe I	5,149	1945–1948	Sal	F/R	—	2732/6IL/ SV	65/3500	120/1300	4-spd/-
						4086/6IL/ SV	100/3400	197/1200	4-spd/-
Super Snipe II/III	17,064	1948–1952	Sal Conv Limo	F/R	—	4086/6IL/ SV	100/3400	197/1200	4-spd/-
Pullman I	N/A	1945–1948	Limo	F/R	—	4086/6IL/ SV	100/3400	197/1200	4-spd/-
Pullman II/III/IV	4,140	1948–1954	Limo	F/R	—	4086/6IL/ SV	100/3400	192/1200	4-spd/-
						4139/6IL/ OHV	113/3400	206/1400	4-spd/-
Imperial II/III/IV	N/A	1949–1954	Sal	F/R	—	4086/6IL/ SV	100/3400	192/1200	4-spd/-
						4139/6IL/ OHV	113/3400	206/1400	4-spd/-
Hawk II/IV/V/VI/VIA	59,282	1948–1957	Sal Est	F/R	—	1944/4IL/ SV	56/3800	97/2000	4-spd/-
						2267/4IL/ SV	58/3400	110/1800	4-spd/-
						2267/4IL/ OHV	70/4000 75/4000	119/2200 119/2200	4-spd (+O/D)/-
Super Snipe IV/IVA IVB	17,993	1952–1957	Sal Est	F/R	—	4139/6IL/ OHV	113/3400 116/3400 122/3600	206/1400 211/1400 211/1400	4-spd (+O/D)/Auto
Hawk Series I/II/III/IV/IVA	41,191	1957–1967	Sal Est	F/R	—	2267/4IL/ OHV	73/4400	120/2300	4-spd (+O/D)/Auto
Super Snipe/Imperial (S1-VA)	30,031	1958–1967	Sal Est	F/R	—	2651/6IL/ OHV	105/5500	138/2000	3-spd (+O/D)/Auto
						2965/6IL/ OHV	121/4800 124/5000 129/5000	162/1800 160/2600 167/2600	3-spd (+O/D)/Auto 3-spd (+O/D)/Auto 3-spd (+O/D)/Auto
Sceptre Mk I/II	28,996	1963–1967	Sal	F/R	—	1592/4IL/ OHV	80/5200	91/3500	4-spd (+O/D)/-
						1725/4IL/ OHV	85/5500	106/3500	4-spd (+O/D)/Auto
Sceptre Mk III	43,951	1967–1976	Sal Est	F/R	—	1725/4IL/ OHV	79/5100	93/3300	4-spd (+O/D)/Auto
Invicta									
Black Prince	25	1946–1950	Sal Cpe Spl	F/R	—	2999/6IL/ 2OHC	120/5000	158/2300	Auto/-

Suspension Front	Rear	Steering	Brakes (Front/rear)	Wheels/model Tyres	Length (in)	Weight (lb,unladen)	Performance Top speed (mph)	0–60mph (sec)	Standing 1/4-mile (sec)	UK Total Price (£: at Launch)
ITor	BeamC	R & P	Disc/drum	145-13	131	1694	94	13.4	18.8	£779
IC	Beam1/2E	R & P	Drum/drum	5.20-10	118	1119	72	29.3	22.9	£536
IC	Beam1/2E	R & P	Drum/drum Disc/drum	5.20-10	121	1198	85	17.3	19.6	£589
IC	Beam1/2E	R & P	Disc/drum	5.20-10	123	1301	73	32.6	23.6	£755
Beam1/4E	Beam1/2E	Worm	Drum/drum	4.50-17/ 5.50-16	143	1512	75	N/A	21.5	£812
Beam1/4E	Beam1/2E	Worm	Drum/drum	4.75-17/ 5.50-16	143	1624	78	18.4	20.4	£882
Beam1/4E	Beam1/2E	Worm	Drum/drum	5.50-16	162	1708	85 (Est)	N/A	N/A	£991
ITrL/C	ITrL/C	Worm	Disc/disc	5.25-16	N/Q	1624	100 (Est)	N/A	N/A	Special Order
IC	Beam1/2E	Worm	Drum/drum	6.40-15	187	2706	86	18.4	21.4	£1900
ITrL	Beam1/2E	Worm	Drum/drum	5.75-16	178	2968	64	42.1	25.6	£684
ITrL	Beam1/2E	Worm	Drum/drum	6.00-16	178	3332	69	31.2	24.4	£863
ITrL	Beam1/2E	Worm	Drum/drum	6.00-16	178	3360	80	24.5	N/A	£889
ITrL	Beam1/2E	Worm	Drum/drum	6.50-16	188	3696	81	20.6	21.9	£1144
ITrL	Beam1/2E	Worm	Drum/drum	7.50-16	198	4004	76	27.2	N/A	£1598
ITrL	Beam1/2E	Worm	Drum/drum	7.00-16	211	4648	78	26.0	23.3	£2171
ITrL	Beam1/2E	Worm	Drum/drum	7.50-16	211	4870	83 (Est)	N/A	N/A	£1977
ITrL	Beam1/2E	Worm	Drum/drum	7.00-16	211	4648	78	26.2	23.2	£2171
ITrL	Beam1/2E	Worm	Drum/drum	7.50-16	211	4870	83 (Est)	N/A	N/A	£1977
IC	Beam1/2E	Worm	Drum/drum	5.50-15	174	2750	71	30.7	24.1	£799
IC	Beam1/2E	Worm	Drum/drum	6.40-15	174	2750	80	23.8	22.5	£799
IC	Beam1/2E	Worm	Drum/drum	6.40-15	182	3110	83 (Est)	N/a	N/A	£986
IC	Beam1/2E	Worm	Drum/drum	7.00-15	197	4025	90	16.6	20.5	£1482
IC	Beam1/2E	Worm	Drum/drum Disc/drum	6.00-15 6.40-15	185	3080	83	20.6	21.8	£1261
IC	Beam1/2E	Worm	Drum/drum	6.70-15	185	3350	92	19.0	21.0	£1494
IC	Beam1/2E	Worm	Disc/drum	6.70-15	185	3350	100	14.3	19.5	£1512
IC	Beam1/2E	Worm	Disc/drum	6.70-15	188	3415	100 (Est)	N/A	N/A	£1489
IC	Beam1/2E	Worm	Disc/drum	6.70-15	188	3415	100	16.2	20.7	£1512
IC	Beam1/2E	Worm	Disc/drum	6.00-13	166	2455	90	17.1	20.3	£977
IC	Beam1/2E	Worm	Disc/drum	6.00-13	166	2455	92 (Est)	N/A	N/A	£1029
IC	Beam1/2E	Worm	Disc/drum	6.00-13	170	2185	98	13.1	19.3	£1139
ITor	ITor	Worm	Drum/drum	6.00-16	192	3920	90 (Est)	N/A	N/A	£2940

Make and model	Production Figures	Years Built	Body Styles	Mechanical Layout	Engine Make (if not own)	Capacity/(cc)/Layout/Valves	BHP/rpm	Torque (lb.ft)/rpm	Transmission gearbox/automatic transmission
Iso									
Rivolta	797	1962–1970	Sal	F/R	Chevrolet	5359/V8/ OHV	340/6000	344/4000	4-spd/-
Grifo	504	1963–1974	Cpe	F/R	Chevrolet	5359/V8/ OHV	350/5800 365/6200	360/3600 360/4000	4-spd/- 4-spd/-
					Chevrolet	6998/V8/ OHV	400/5400	460/3600	4-spd/-
Fidia	192	1967–1974	Cpe	F/R	Chevrolet	5359/V8/ OHV	300/5800	360/3200	4-spd/Auto
					Ford-USA	5768/V8/ OHV	325/5800	360/3800	5-spd/Auto
Lele	317	1969–1974	Sal	F/R	Chevrolet	5359/V8/ OHV	350/5800	360/3600	4-spd/5-spd/Auto
					Ford	5768/V8/ OHV	325/5800	360/380	4-spd/5-spd/Auto
Jaguar									
1½-litre/ 2½-litre/ 3½-litre 'Mk IV'	11,952 (Postwar)	1938–1949	Sal Conv	F/R	—	1776/4IL/ OHV	65/4600	97/2500	4-spd/-
						2663/6IL/ OHV	105/4600	136/2500	4-spd/-
						3485/6IL/ OHV	125/4500	184/2000	4-spd/-
Mark V	10,466	1949–1951	Sal Conv	F/R	—	2663/6IL/ OHV	102/4600	N/Q	4-spd/-
						3485/6IL/ OHV	125/4250	N/Q	4-spd/-
XK120/140/ XK150	30,357	1949–1960	Spts Spts Cpe	F/R	—	3442/6IL/ 2OHC	160/5000 180/5000 190/5500 210/5750 210/5500 250/5500	195/2500 203/4000 210/2500 213/4000 216/3000 240/4500	4-spd (+O/D)/- 4-spd (+O/D)/- 4-spd (+O/D)/Auto 4-spd (+O/D)/Auto
						3781/6IL/ 2OHC	220/5500 265/5500	240/3000 260/4000	
Mark VII/ VIIM/VIII/ IX	47,190	1951–1961	Sal	F/R	—	3442/6IL/ 2OHC	160/5200 190/5500 210/5500	195/2500 203/3000 216/3000	4-spd (+O/D)/Auto 4-spd (+O/D)/Auto 4-spd (+O/D)/Auto
						3781/6IL/ 2OHC	220/5500	240/3000	4-spd (+O/D)/Auto
2.4/3.4	36,740	1955–1959	Sal	F/R	—	2483/6IL/ 2OHC	112/5750	140/2000	4-spd (+O/D)/Auto
						3442/6IL/ 2OHC	210/5500	216/3000	4-spd (+O/D)/Auto
Mk II 2.4/ 3.4/3.8	83,800	1959–1967	Sal	F/R	—	2483/6IL/ 2OHC	120/5750	144/2000	4-spd (+O/D)/Auto
						3442/6IL/ 2OHC	210/5500	216/3000	4-spd (+O/D)/Auto
						3781/6IL/ 2OHC	220/5500	240/3000	4-spd (+O/D)/Auto
E-Type 3.8/ 4.2	46,300	1961–1971	Spts Spts Cpe	F/R	—	3781/6IL/ 2OHC	265/5500	260/4000	4-spd/-
						4235/6IL/ 2OHC	265/5400	283/4000	4-spd/-
E-Type 2+2	10,930	1966–1971	Spts Cpe	F/R	—	4235/6IL 2OHC	265/5400	283/4000	4-spd/Auto
Mark X/ 420G	24,282	1962–1970	Sal Limo	F/R	—	3781/6IL/ 2OHC	265/5500	260/4000	4-spd (+O/D)/Auto
						4235/6IL/ 2OHC	265/5400	275/4000	4-spd (+O/D)/Auto
S-Type	24,900	1963–1968	Sal	F/R	—	3442/6IL/ 2OHC	210/5500	216/3000	4-spd (+O/D)/Auto
						3781/6IL/ 2OHC	220/5500	240/3000	4-spd (+O/D)/Auto
420	9,600	1966–1968	Sal	F/R	—	4235/6IL/ 2OHC	245/5500	283/3750	4-spd (+O/D)/Auto
240/340	6,840	1967–1969	Sal	F/R	—	2483/6IL/ 2OHC	133/5500	146/3700	4-spd (+O/D)/Auto
						3442/6IL/ 2OHC	210/5500	216/3000	4-spd (+O/D)/Auto
XJ6 SI/SII	152,219	1968–1979	Sal	F/R	—	2792/6IL/ 2OHC	140/5150	150/4250	4-spd (+O/D)/Auto
						3442/6IL/ 2OHC	160/5000	189/3500	4-spd (+O/D)/Auto
						4235/6IL/ 2OHC	173/4750	227/3000	4-spd (+O/D)/ 5-spd/Auto

Suspension Front	Suspension Rear	Steering	Brakes (Front/rear)	Wheels/model Tyres	Length (in)	Weight (lb,unladen)	Performance Top speed (mph)	0–60mph (sec)	Standing 1/4-mile (sec)	UK Total Price (£: at Launch)
IC	DDC	Worm	Disc/disc	185-15	189	3423	142	8.0	15.9	£3999
IC	DDC	Worm	Disc/disc	205-15	175	2826	163	6.4	14.5	£7280
IC	DDC	Worm	Disc/disc	205-15	175	3177	161	7.4	14.9	£5950
IC	DDC	Worm	Disc/disc	205-15	175	3000	170 (Est)	N/A	N/A	£8700
IC	DDC	Worm	Disc/disc	215/70-15	197	3943	130 (Est)	N/A	N/A	£7225
IC	DDC	Worm	Disc/disc	215/70-15	197	3943	133 (Est)	8.1	16.2	£11868
IC	DDC	Worm	Disc/disc	205-15	185	3042	135 (Est)	N/A	N/A	£7725
IC	DDC	Worm	Disc/disc	215/70-15	185	3707	132 (Est)	7.3	15.5	£9945
Beam1/2E	Beam1/2E	Worm	Drum/drum	5.25-18	173	2968	72	25.1	N/A	£684
Beam1/2E	Beam1/2E	Worm	Drum/drum	5.50-18	186	3584	91	17.0	20.6	£889
Beam1/2E	Beam1/2E	Worm	Drum/drum	5.50-18	186	3668	91	16.8	N/A	£991
ITor	Beam1/2E	Worm	Drum/drum	6.70-16	187	3696	90 (Est)	N/A	N/A	£1189
ITor	Beam1/2E	Worm	Drum/drum	6.70-16	187	3696	91	14.7	20.2	£1263
ITor	Beam1/2E	Worm	Drum/drum	6.00-16	174	2856	125	10.0	17.0	£1263
ITor	Beam1/2E	R & P	Drum/drum	6.00-16	174	3136	121	8.4	16.6	£1598
ITor	Beam1/2E	R & P	Disc/disc	6.00-16	177	3190	124	8.5	16.9	£1764
ITor	Beam1/2E	R & P	Disc/disc	6.00-16	177	3248	132	7.8	16.2	£2065
ITor	Beam1/2E	Worm	Drum/drum	6.70-16	197	3864	102	13.6	19.3	£1276
ITor	Beam1/2E	Worm	Drum/drum	6.70-16	197	3892	100	14.3	19.7	£1616
ITor	Beam1/2E	Worm	Drum/drum	6.70-16	197	4032	107	11.6	18.4	£1830
ITor	Beam1/2E	Worm	Disc/disc	6.70-16	197	3980	114	11.0	17.8	£1995
IC	Beam1/2E	Worm	Drum/drum Disc/disc	6.40-15	181	3024	102	14.4	24.6	£1344
IC	Beam1/2E	Worm	Drum/drum Disc/disc	6.40-15	181	3192	120	9.1	17.2	£1672
IC	Beam1/2E	Worm	Disc/disc	6.40-15	181	3192	96	17.3	20.8	£1534
IC	Beam1/2E	Worm	Disc/disc	6.40-15	181	3304	120	11.9	19.1	£1669
IC	Beam1/2E	Worm	Disc/disc	6.40-15	181	3304	125	8.5	16.3	£1779
ITor	IC	R & P	Disc/disc	6.40-15	176	2688	149	7.1	15.0	£2098
ITor	IC	R & P	Disc/disc	6.40-15	176	2856	149	7.4	15.0	£1896
ITor	IC	R & P	Disc/disc	185-15	184	3108	139	7.4	15.4	£2245
IC	IC	Worm	Disc/disc	7.50-14	202	3990	120	12.1	18.5	£2393
IC	IC	Worm	Disc/disc	7.50-14	202	3990	122	9.9	17.0	£2156
IC	IC	Worm	Disc/disc	6.40-15/ Later 185-15	187	3584	120 (Est)	N/A	N/A	£1669
IC	IC	Worm	Disc/disc	6.40-15/ Later 185-15	187	3696	121	10.2	17.1	£1759
IC	IC	Worm	Disc/disc	185-15	188	3696	123	9.9	16.7	£1930
IC	Beam1/2E	Worm	Disc/disc	185-15	179	3192	106	12.5	18.7	£1365
IC	Beam1/2E	Worm	Disc/disc	185-15	179	3360	115	8.8	17.2	£1442
IC	IC	R & P	Disc/disc	205-15	190	3388	117	11.0 (Claimed)	18.1	£1797
IC	IC	R & P	Disc/disc	205-15	195	3708	117	10.9	18.0	£4795
IC	IC	R & P	Disc/disc	205-15	190	3703	124	8.8	16.5	£2253

Make and model	Production Figures	Years Built	Body Styles	Mechanical Layout	Engine Make (if not own)	Capacity/(cc)/Layout/Valves	BHP/rpm	Torque (lb.ft)/rpm	Transmission gearbox/automatic transmission
Jeep									
Wagoneer **	—	1964 model	Ute	F/4	—	3780/6IL/ OHC	140/4000	210/1750	3-spd
Jensen									
PW	17	1946–1951	Sal Conv	F/R	Meadows	3860/8IL/ OHV	130/4300	187/2400	4-spd/-
					Austin	3993/6IL/ OHV	130/3700	212/2200	4-spd/-
Interceptor	88	1950–1957	Sal Conv	F/R	Austin	3993/6IL/ OHV	130/3700	212/2200	4-spd (+O/D)/-
541/541R	419	1954–1960	Sal	F/R	Austin	3993/6IL/ OHV	130/3700 140/3700	N/Q N/Q	4-spd (+O/D)/- 4-spd (+O/D)/-
541S	127	1961–1963	Sal	F/R	Austin	3993/6IL/ OHV	N/Q	N/Q	4-spd (+O/D)/Auto
CV8	499	1961–1966	Sal	F/R	Chrysler	5916/V8/ OHV	305/4800	395/3000	4-spd/Auto
						6276/V8/ OHV	330/4600	425/2800	4-spd/Auto
Interceptor/ SP	6,639	1966–1976	Sal Conv Cpe	F/R	Chrysler	6276/V8/ OHV	325/4600 300/4800	425/2800 380/3200	Auto/-
						7212/V8/ OHV	330/5000 385/5000 287/4800	425/2800 490/3200 383/3200	Auto/- Auto/- Auto/-
FF	320	1966–1971	Sal	F/4	Chrysler	6276/V8/ OHV	325/4600	425/2800	Auto/-
Jowett									
Bradford	40,995 (Incl. vans)	1946–1953	Est	F/R	—	1005/4HO/ SV	25/3500	N/Q	3-spd/-
Javelin	22,799	1947–1953	Sal	F/R	—	1486/4HO/ OHV	50/4100	76/2600	4-spd/-
Jupiter	899	1950–1954	Spts	F/R	—	1486/4IL/ OHV	63/4500	84/3000	4-spd/-
Lada									
1200/1300	N/A	1970-Date	Sal Est	F/R	—	1198/4IL/ OHC	62/5600	64/3400	4-spd/-
						1294/4IL/ OHC	67/5600	69/3400	4-spd/-
Lagonda									
2.6-litre/ 3-litre	1,264	1948–1957	Sal Conv	F/R	—	2580/6IL/ 2OHC	105/5000 125/5000	133/3000 144/2400	4-spd/-
						2922/6IL/ 2OHC	140/5000	166/2500	4-spd/-
Rapide	54	1961–1964	Sal	F/R	—	3995/6IL/ 2OHC	236/5000	265/4000	4-spd/Auto
Lamborghini									
350GT	120	1964–1966	Cpe	F/R	—	3464/V12/ 2OHC	280/6500	227/4800	5-spd/-
400GT	273	1966–1968	Cpe	F/R	—	3929/V12/ 2OHC	330/6500	262/4700	5-spd/-
Miura	775	1966–1972	Spts Cpe	M(Tr)/R	—	3929/V12/ 2OHC	350/7000 370/7700 385/7850	278/5000 286/5500 294/5750	5-spd/- 5-spd/- 5-spd/-
Islero	225	1968–1970	Cpe	F/R	—	3929/V12/ 2OHC	320/6500	262/4700	5-spd/-
Espada	1,217	1968–1978	Sal	F/R	—	3929/V12/ 2OHC	325/6500 350/7500 365/7500	276/4500 290/5500 300/5500	5-spd/- 5-spd/- 5-spd/Auto
Jarama	327	1970–1978	Sal	F/R	—	3929/V12/ 2OHC	350/7500 365/7500	289/5500 300/5500	5-spd/- 5-spd/Auto
Urraco	776	1970–1978	Cpe	M(Tr)/R	—	2463/V8/ OHC	220/7500	166/5750	5-spd/-
						2995/V8/ 2OHC	250/7500	195/5750	5-spd/-
Lanchester									
LD10	3,050	1946–1951	Sal	F/R	—	1287/4IL/ OHV	40/4200	60/2000	4PreS/-
14	2,100	1950–1954	Sal	F/R	—	1968/4IL/	60/4200	N/Q	4PreS/-

Suspension Front	Rear	Steering	Brakes (Front/rear)	Wheels/model Tyres	Length (in)	Weight (lb, unladen)	Performance Top speed (mph)	0–60mph (sec)	Standing ¼-mile (sec)	UK Total Price (£: at Launch)
ITor	Beam1/2E	Worm	Drum/drum	7.50-15	182	3976	92	15.5	20.0	£1994
IC	BeamC	Worm	Drum/drum	6.00-16	197	3248	90 (Est)	N/A	N/A	£1998
IC	BeamC	Worm	Drum/drum	6.50-16	197	3556	90 (Est)	N/A	N/A	£2842
IC	Beam1/2E	Worm	Drum/drum	5.50-16	183	2800	95	13.1	19.0	£1999
IC	Beam1/2E	Worm	Drum/drum	5.50-16	176	3135	116	10.8	18.4	£2147
IC	Beam1/2E	Worm	Disc/disc	5.50-16	176	3260	124	10.6	17.5	£2866
IC	Beam1/2E	Worm	Disc/disc	6.40-15	178	3415	109	12.4	18.8	£3097
IC	Beam1/2E	R & P	Disc/disc	6.70-15	185	3360	131	8.4	16.0	£3861
IC	Beam1/2E	R & P	Disc/disc	6.70-15	185	3514	129	6.7	14.6	£3491
IC	Beam1/2E	R & P	Disc/disc	6.70-15	185	3500	133	7.3	15.7	£3743
IC	Beam1/2E	R & P	Disc/disc	ER70-15	185	3635	126	7.6	15.8	£6744
IC	Beam1/2E	R & P	Disc/disc	ER70-15	185	3950	143	6.9	14.8	£6977
IC	Beam1/2E	R & P	Disc/disc	ER70-15	185	3898	129	7.7	15.9	£8334
IC	Beam1/2E	R & P	Disc/disc	ER70-15	191	4030	130	8.4	15.9	£5340
Beam1/2E	Beam1/2E	Worm	Drum/drum	5.00-16	144	1904	53	N/A	28.5	£320
ITor	BeamTor	R & P	Drum/drum	5.25-16	168	2156	78	22.2	22.7	£819
ITor	BeamTor	R & P	Drum/drum	5.50-16	168	2121	84	16.8	20.7	£1017
IC	BeamC	Worm	Disc/drum	155-13	158	2082	90	14.7	19.9	£981
IC	BeamC	Worm	Disc/drum	155-13	158	2100	86	16.6	20.7	£2148
IC	ITor	R & P	Drum/drum	6.00-16	188	3110	90	17.6	21.7	£3110
IC	ITor	R & P	Drum/drum	6.00-16	196	3615	104	12.9	19.5	£3203
IC	DDTor	R & P	Disc/disc	7.10-15	196	3780	140 (Est)	N/A	N/A	£4950
IC	IC	Worm	Disc/disc	205-15	176	2650	152	6.8	14.9	Special Order
IC	IC	Worm	Disc/disc	205-15	176	2845	156	7.5	15.5	£6444
IC	IC	R & P	Disc/disc	GR70-15	172	2850	170 (Est)	N/A	N/A	£8050
IC	IC	R & P	Disc/disc	GR70-15	172	2850	172	6.7	14.5	£10,860
IC	IC	R & P	Disc/disc	FR70-15	172	2877	177	N/A	N/A (Claimed)	£10,250
IC	IC	Worm	Disc/disc	205-15	178	2795	160	6.2	N/A	£7950
IC	IC	Worm	Disc/disc	205-15	187	3740	150 (Est)	N/A	N/A	£10,295
IC	IC	Worm	Disc/disc	205-15	187	3740	150	7.8	15.7	£9500
IC	IC	Worm	Disc/disc	205-15	187	3740	155 (Est)	N/A	N/A	
IC	IC	Worm	Disc/disc	215/70-15	177	2960	162	6.8	14.9	£9800
IC	IC	Worm	Disc/disc	215/70-15	177	2960	162 (Est)	N/A	N/A	
IC	IC	R & P	Disc/disc	205-14	167	2885	143	8.5	16.6	£5950
IC	IC	R & P	Disc/disc	195/70-14/ 205/70-14	167	2990	158	7.6	15.6	£9975
IC	Beam1/2E	Worm	Drum/drum	5.25-16	158	2464	68	36.8	24.1	£672
ITor	Beam1/2E	Worm	Drum/drum	6.40-15	173	3136	75 (Est)	N/A	N/A	£1144

Make and model	Production Figures	Years Built	Body Styles	Mechanical Layout	Engine Make (if not own)	Capacity/(cc)/Layout/Valves	BHP/rpm	Torque (lb.ft)/rpm	Transmission gearbox/automatic transmission
			Conv			OHV			
Sprite	13	1955–1956	Sal	F/R	—	1622/4IL/ OHV	60/4200	85/2800	Auto/-

Lancia

Make and model	Production Figures	Years Built	Body Styles	Mechanical Layout	Engine Make (if not own)	Capacity/(cc)/Layout/Valves	BHP/rpm	Torque (lb.ft)/rpm	Transmission gearbox/automatic transmission
Appia	98,006	1953–1959	Sal	F/R	—	1090/V4/ OHV	38/4800	52/3000	4-spd/-
Appia Coupe/Sport	2,163	1956–1963	Cpe Conv				48/5200	63/3000	4-spd/-
Aurelia	12,705	1950–1955	Sal	F/R	—	1991/V6/ OHV	90/5000	101/3500	4-spd/-
						2266/V6/ OHV	87/4300	118/2900	4-spd/-
Aurelia GT	2,568	1953–1958	Cpe	F/R	—	2451/V6/ OHV	118/5000	134/3500	4-spd/-
Flaminia	3,424	1957–1970	Sal	F/R	—	2458/V6/ OHV	100/4800	141/3000	4-spd/-
						2775/V6/ OHV	129/5000	169/2500	4-spd/-
Flaminia Coupe	5,282	1959–1967	Cpe	F/R	—	2458/V6/ OHV	119/5100	137/3500	4-spd/-
						2775/V6/ OHV	140/5400	163/3000	4-spd/-
Flaminia Convertible	2,748	1959–1967	Conv	F/R	—	2775/V6/ OHV	150/5400	165/3500	4-spd/-
Flavia/ 2000	79,764	1961–1974	Sal	F/F	—	1488/4HO/ OHV	78/5200	82/3500	4-spd/-
						1800/4HO/ OHV	102/5200	113/3500	4-spd/-
						1991/4HO/ OHV	114/5400	118/4300	4-spd/5-spd/-
							125/5800	127/3700	5-spd/-
Flavia Coupe	26,084	1962–1973	Cpe	F/F	—	1500/4HO/ OHV	90/4500	85/4500	4-spd/-
						1800/4HO/ OHV	92/5200	108/3000	4-spd/-
							102/5200	113/3500	
						1991/4HO/ OHV	114/5400	118/4300	4-spd/5-spd/-
							125/5800	127/3700	5-spd/-
Flavia Zagato Sport	N/A	1962–1969	Spts Cpe	F/F	—	1800/4HO/ OHV	100/5200	120/3000	4-spd/-
Fulvia	192,097	1963–1972	Sal	F/F	—	1091/V4/ 2OHC	58/5800	62/4000	4-spd/-
							71/6000	68/4300	4-spd/-
						1216/V4/ 2OHC	80/6000	77/4000	4-spd/-
						1298/V4/ 2OHC	87/6000	83/4500	4-spd/-
Fulvia Coupe	139,817	1965–1976	Cpe	F/F	—	1216/V4/ 2OHC	80/6000	77/4000	4-spd/-
							88/6000	80/5000	
						1298/V4/ 2OHC	87/6000	83/4500	4-spd/-
							90/6200	84/5000	4-spd/-
							101/6400	96/4750	
						1584/V4/ 2OHC	115/6000	113/4500	5-spd/-

Land-Rover

Make and model	Production Figures	Years Built	Body Styles	Mechanical Layout	Engine Make (if not own)	Capacity/(cc)/Layout/Valves	BHP/rpm	Torque (lb.ft)/rpm	Transmission gearbox/automatic transmission
Series I	Total, SI to SIII, 1,400,000 +	1948–1958	Ute	F/4	—	1595/4IL/ IOEV	50/4000	80/2000	4-spd/-
						1997/4IL/ IOEV	52/4000	101/1500	4-spd/-
						2052/4IL/ OHV Diesel	51/3500	87/2000	4-spd/-
SII/IIA	Incl. above	1958–1971	Ute	F/4	—	2286/4IL/ OHV	77/4250	124/2500	4-spd/-
						2052/4IL/ OHV Diesel	51/3500	87/2000	4-spd/-
						2286/4IL/ OHV Diesel	62/4000	103/1800	4-spd/-
						2625/6IL/ IOEV	83/4500	128/1500	4-spd/-

Lea-Francis

Make and model	Production Figures	Years Built	Body Styles	Mechanical Layout	Engine Make (if not own)	Capacity/(cc)/Layout/Valves	BHP/rpm	Torque (lb.ft)/rpm	Transmission gearbox/automatic transmission
12/14hp	3,137	1946–1954	Sal Cpe Est	F/R	—	1496/4IL/ OHV	55/4700	76/2800	4-spd/-
						1767/4IL/ OHV	65/4700	94/2800	4-spd/-
12hp/14hp Sports	129	1947–1949	Spts	F/R	—	1496/4IL/ OHV	64/5300	79/2800	4-spd/-

Suspension Front	Rear	Steering	Brakes (Front/rear)	Wheels/model Tyres	Length (in)	Weight (lb,unladen)	Performance Top speed (mph)	0–60mph (sec)	Standing 1/4-mile (sec)	UK Total Price (£: at Launch)
ITor	Beam1/2E	Worm	Drum/drum	5.90-15	172	2688	65 (Est)	N/A	N/A	£1228
IC	Beam1/2E	Worm	Drum/drum	155-15	152	1792	76	32.5	25.2	£1772
IC	Beam1/2E	Worm	Drum/drum	155-14	158	2065	81	23.7	22.5	£1588
IC	IC	Worm	Drum/drum	165-400	174	2436	90 (Est)	N/A	N/A	Special Order
IC	DD1/2E	Worm	Drum/drum	165-400	174	2716	91	17.9	20.5	£2863
IC	DD1/2E	Worm	Drum/drum	165-400	172	2633	111	12.3	19.1	£3472
IC	DD1/2E	Worm	Drum/drum	165-400	191	3610	102	15.6	20.2	£3751
IC	DD1/2E	Worm	Drum/drum Disc/disc	6.50-15	189	2750	106	N/A (Claimed)	N/A	£2847
IC	DD1/2E	Worm	Disc/disc	175-400	185	3266	106	13.6	19.1	£3869
IC	DD1/2E	Worm	Disc/disc	175-400	185	3351	112	12.7	18.7	£3888
IC	DD1/2E	Worm	Disc/disc	175-400	177	2999	110 (Est)	N/A	N/A	Special Order
ITrL	Beam1/2E	Worm	Disc/disc	165-15	180	2624	93	18.7	22.0	£2188
ITrL	Beam1/2E	Worm	Disc/disc	165-15	180	2643	103	14.3	19.9	£2075
ITrL	Beam1/2E	Worm	Disc/disc	165-15	180	2756	109 (Est)	N/A	N/A	£2158
ITrL	Beam1/2E	Worm	Disc/disc	175-14	182	2715	115	10.4	17.9	£2121
ITrL	Beam1/2E	Worm	Disc/disc	165-15	176	2558	103	N/A (Claimed)	N/A	£2275
ITrL	Beam1/2E	Worm	Disc/disc	165-15	176	2492	109	13.4	18.9	£2497
ITrL	Beam1/2E	Worm	Disc/disc	165-15	178	2621	109	12.4	18.9	£2989
ITrL	Beam1/2E	Worm	Disc/disc	165-15	178	2624	115 (Est)	N/A	N/A	£2907
ITrL	Beam1/2E	Worm	Disc/disc	165-15	174	2310	113	11.9	18.3	£2736
ITrL	Beam1/2E	Worm	Disc/disc	155-14	163	2170	85	23.5	22.9	£1389
ITrL	Beam1/2E	Worm	Disc/disc	155-14	163	2170	93	18.2	21.1	£1379
ITrL	Beam1/2E	Worm	Disc/disc	155-14	163	2307	95	15.7	20.0	£1251
ITrL	Beam1/2E	Worm	Disc/disc	155-14	163	2318	96	13.9	19.1	£1438
ITrL	Beam1/2E	Worm	Disc/disc	145-14	156	2073	100	15.8	20.0	£1490
ITrL	Beam1/2E	Worm	Disc/disc	145-14	156	1971	103	11.9	18.9	£1548
ITrL	Beam1/2E	Worm	Disc/disc	145-14	156	1971	106	12.7	18.7	£1745
ITrL	Beam1/2E	Worm	Disc/disc	175-13 175-14	156	1874	103	9.4	17.3	£2526
Beam1/2E	Beam1/2E	Worm	Drum/drum	6.00-16	132	2594	55 (Est)	N/A	N/A	£450
Beam1/2E	Beam1/2E	Worm	Drum/drum	6.00-16	132/174	2604/3080	58	N/A	25.7	£N/A
Beam1/2E	Beam1/2E	Worm	Drum/drum	6.00-16	141/174	2935/3275	55 (Est)	N/A	N/A	£N/A
Beam1/2E	Beam1/2E	Worm	Drum/drum	6.00-16	142/175	2900/3886	67	36.1	24.0	£640
Beam1/2E	Beam1/2E	Worm	Drum/drum	6.00-16	142/175	3095/4081	55 (Est)	N/A	N/A	£740
Beam1/2E	Beam1/2E	Worm	Drum/drum	6.00-16	142/175	3044/4030	60 (Est)	N/A	N/A	£N/A
Beam1/2E	Beam1/2E	Worm	Drum/drum	6.00-16	175	3459	73	29.0	23.6	£873
Beam1/2E ITor	Beam1/2E	Worm	Drum/drum	5.50-17	179	2800	70 (Est)	N/A	N/A	£951
Beam1/2E ITor	Beam1/2E	Worm	Drum/drum	5.50-17	179	2912	77 (Est)	N/A	N/A	£951
Beam1/2E	Beam1/2E	Worm	Drum/drum	5.25-17	156	2128	80 (Est)	N/A	N/A	£1266

Make and model	Production Figures	Years Built	Body Styles	Mechanical Layout	Engine Make (if not own)	Capacity/(cc)/Layout/Valves	BHP/rpm	Torque (lb.ft)/rpm	Transmission gearbox/automatic transmission
						1767/4IL/OHV	77/5100	103/3000	4-spd/-
2½-litre Sports	77	1950–1953	Spts	F/R	—	2496/4IL/OHV	95/4000	148/2250	4-spd/-
14hp/18hp saloon	252	1949–1953	Sal	F/R	—	1767/4IL/OHV	65/4700	94/2800	4-spd/-
						2496/4IL/OHV	95/4000	148/2250	4-spd/-
Lloyd (UK)									
650	600	1946–1951	Conv	F/R	—	654/2HO/2-Str	N/Q	N/Q	3-spd/-
Lloyd (West Germany)									
LP600	N/A	1955–1959	Sal Est Conv	F/F	—	596/2IL/2-Str AirC	19/4500	28/2500	3-spd/4-spd/-
Lotus									
[Note : Many optional engine tunes were available on Sevens of all types]									
Seven S1	150	1957–1960	Spts	F/R	Ford	1172/4IL/SV	40/4500	58/2600	3-spd/-
					Coventry-Climax	1098/4IL/OHC	75/6250	N/Q	4-spd/-
					BMC	948/4IL/OHV	40/5000	50/2500	4-spd/-
Seven S2	250	1960–1968	Spts	F/R	BMC	948/4IL/OHV	40/5000	50/2500	4-spd/-
					Ford	1172/4IL/SV	40/4500	58/2600	3-spd/-
						997/4IL/OHV	39/5000	53/2700	4-spd/-
						1340/4IL/OHV	85/6000	80/4000	4-spd/-
						1498/4IL/OHV	66/4600	89/2500	4-spd/-
							95/6000	95/4500	4-Spd/-
Seven S3	1,413	1968–1970	Spts	F/R	Ford	1598/4IL/OHV	84/6500	96/3600	4-spd/-
							120/6200	N/Q	4-spd/-
					—	1558/4IL/2OHC	115/5500	108/4000	4-spd/-
							125/6200	116/4500	4-spd/-
Seven S4	1,000	1969–1973	Spts	F/R	Ford	1598/4IL/OHV	84/6500	96/3600	4-spd/-
					—	1558/4IL/2OHC	115/5500	108/4000	4-spd/-
[Note : Several very limited edition Seven models with different engines were also built]									
Elite	988	1958–1963	Spts Cpe	F/R	Coventry-Climax	1216/4IL/OHC	71/6100	77/3750	4-spd/-
							83/6250	75/4750	4-spd/-
						(More power available to special order)			
Elan (Incl. Sprint model)	Est 12,200	1962–1971	Spts	F/R	—	1499/4IL/2OHC	100/5700	102/4500	4-spd/-
						1558/4IL/2OHC	105/5500	108/4000	4-spd/-
							115/6000	108/4000	4-spd/-
Elan Sprint	—	1971–1973	Spts	F/R	—	1558/4IL/2OHC	126/6500	113/5500	4-spd/-
Elan Plus 2 (Incl. Plus 2S 130)	5,200	1969–1971	Spts Cpe	F/R	—	1558/4IL/2OHC	118/6250	112/4600	4-spd/-
Elan Plus 2S/130	—	1971–1974	Spts Cpe	F/R	—	1558/4IL/2OHC	126/6500	113/5500	4-spd/- 5-spd/-
Europa (All Europa types)	9,230	1967–1971	Spts Cpe	M/R	—	1470/4IL/OHV	78/6500	76/4000	4-spd/-
Europa TC/Special	—	1971–1975	Spts Cpe	M/R	—	1558/4IL/2OHC	105/6000	103/4500	4-spd/-
							126/6500	113/5500	5-spd/-
Marauder									
A/100	15	1950–1952	Spts	F/R	Rover	2103/6IL/IOEV	80/4200	110/2500	4-spd (+O/D)/-
Marcos									
1800/1500/1600	N/A	1964–1968	Cpe	F/R	Volvo	1778/4IL/OHV	114/5800	110/4200	4-spd (+O/D)/-
					Ford	1499/4IL/OHV	85/5300	97/3600	4-spd/-
						1599/4IL/OHV	88/5400	96/3600	4-spd/-
							95/5500	98/3600	
						1650/4IL	120/5400	126/3500	4-spd/-

Suspension		Steering	Brakes (Front/rear)	Wheels/model Tyres	Length (in)	Weight (lb, unladen)	Performance Top speed (mph)	0–60mph (sec)	Standing ¼-mile (sec)	UK Total Price (£: at Launch)
Front	Rear									
Beam1/2E	Beam1/2E	Worm	Drum/drum	5.25-17	156	2457	87	19.2	N/Q	£1276
ITor	Beam1/2E	Worm	Drum/drum	6.00-16	168	2570	95 (Est)	N/A	N/A	£1276
ITor	Beam1/2E	Worm	Drum/drum	6.00-16	181	2912	75 (Est)	N/A	N/A	£1276
ITor	Beam1/2E	Worm	Drum/drum	6.00-16	181	3020	90 (Est)	N/A	N/A	£1946
IC	IC	R & P	Drum/drum	4.00-17	147	1344	55 (Est)	N/A	N/A	£480
ITrL	I1/2E	R & P	Drum/drum	4.25-15	132	1208	62	N/A	24.1	£586
IC	BeamC	R & P	Drum/drum	5.20-15	129	1008	76	17.8	20.8	£1036
IC	BeamC	R & P / Worm (Early)	Drum/drum	4.50-15/5.00-15	129	924	104	9.2	16.4	£1546
IC	BeamC	R & P / Worm (Early)	Drum/drum	5.20-15	129	960	83	12.1	N/A	£511 (Kit)
IC	BeamC	R & P / Worm (Early)	Drum/drum	5.20-13	132	960	85	14.3	19.2	£611 (Kit)
IC	BeamC	R & P	Drum/drum	5.20-13	132	960	80	N/A (Est)	N/A	£587 (Kit)
IC	BeamC	R & P	Drum/drum	5.20-13	132	952	80	N/A (Est)	N/A	£869
IC	BeamC	R & P	Disc/drum	5.20-12	132	966	103	7.6	15.8	£869
IC	BeamC	R & P	Disc/drum	4.50-13	132	1036	90 (Est)	N/A	N/A	£869
IC	BeamC	R & P	Disc/drum	4.50-13	132	1064	103	7.7	15.9	£645 (Kit)
IC	BeamC	R & P	Disc/drum	165-13	133	1210	99	7.7	15.7	£775
IC	BeamC	R & P	Disc/drum	165-13	133	1210	108	7.2	N/Q	£1600
IC	BeamC	R & P	Disc/drum	165-13	133	1258	110 (Est)	N/A	N/A	£1250 (Kit)
IC	BeamC	R & P	Disc/drum	165-13	133	1258	103	7.1	15.5	£1250
IC	BeamC	R & P	Disc/drum	165-13	145	1276	100	8.8	16.0	£895
IC	BeamC	R & P	Disc/drum	165-13	145	1276	116	8.7	15.8	£1245
IC	IC	R & P	Disc/disc	4.80-15	148	1455	112	11.4	18.4	£1951
IC	IC	R & P	Disc/disc	135-15	148	1455	118	11.0	17.5	£1951
IC	IC	R & P	Disc/disc	5.20-13	145	1290	110 (Est)	N/A	N/A	£1499
IC	IC	R & P	Disc/disc	5.20-13	145	1516	114	8.7	16.4	£1312
IC	IC	R & P	Disc/disc	145-13	145	1574	122	7.6	15.7	
IC	IC	R & P	Disc/disc	155-13	145	1590	121	6.7	15.2	£1706
IC	IC	R & P	Disc/disc	165-13	168	1882	123	8.2	16.6	£1923
IC	IC	R & P	Disc/disc	165-13	168	1954	121	7.4	15.4	£2676
IC	IC	R & P	Disc/disc	165-13	168	1960	120	7.5	16.0	£2716
IC	IC	R & P	Disc/drum	155-13	157	1375	109	10.7	17.3	£1667
IC	IC	R & P	Disc/drum	185/70-13	157	1557	117	7.0	15.6	£1996
IC	IC	R & P	Disc/drum	185/70-13	157	1588	121	7.7	15.7	£2370
IC	Beam1/2E	Worm	Drum/drum	6.00-15	166	2576	89	18.4	N/A	£1,333
IC	IC	R & P	Disc/drum	5.90-13	159	1690	115	9.1	16.5	£1645
IC	BeamC	R & P	Disc/drum	165-13	161	1658	106 (Est)	N/A	N/A	£1606
IC	BeamC	R & P	Disc/drum	165-13	161	1658	109	11.4	17.6	£1860
IC	BeamC	R & P	Disc/drum	165-13	161	1658	117	8.7	16.4	£1860

Make and model	Production Figures	Years Built	Body Styles	Mechanical Layout	Engine Make (if not own)	Capacity/ (cc)/Layout/ Valves	BHP/ rpm	Torque (lb.ft)/rpm	Transmission gearbox/automatic transmission
2-litre/	N/A	1968–1971	Cpe	F/R	Ford	OHV 1996/V4	83/4750	123/2750	4-spd/-
2.5-litre/ 3.0-litre/					Ford	OHV 2994/V6	136/4750	193/3000	4-spd (+O/D)/-
Volvo					Volvo	OHV 2979/6IL	130/5000	152/2500	4-spd/Auto
Mantis	32	1970–1971	Spts Cpe	F/R	Triumph	OHV 2498/6IL	150/5700	158/3000	4-spd (+O/D)/-

Maserati

Make and model	Production Figures	Years Built	Body Styles	Mechanical Layout	Engine Make (if not own)	Capacity/ (cc)/Layout/ Valves	BHP/ rpm	Torque (lb.ft)/rpm	Transmission gearbox/automatic transmission
3500GT	2000 +	1957–1964	Cpe Conv	F/R	—	3485/6IL/ 2OHC	220/5500 235/5800	253/3500 232/4000	4-spd/5-spd/- 4-spd/5-spd/-
Sebring	438	1963–1969	Cpe	F/R	—	3485/6IL/ 2OHC	235/5800	232/4000	5-spd/-
						3692/6IL/ 2OHC	245/5200	253/4000	5-spd/-
						4012/6IL/ 2OHC	255/5200	268/4000	5-spd/Auto
Mistral	948	1963–1970	Cpe Conv	F/R	—	3692/6IL/ 2OHC	245/5500	253/4000	5-spd/-
						4012/6IL/ 2OHC	255/5200	267/3500	5-spd/-
Quattroporte	679	1963–1970	Sal	F/R	—	4136/V8/ 2OHC	260/5200	267/4000	5-spd/Auto
						4719/V8/ 2OHC	290/5200	282/3800	5-spd/Auto
Mexico	468	1966–1972	Cpe	F/R	—	4136/V8/ 2OHC	260/5800	268/4000	5-spd/Auto
						4719/V8/ 2OHC	330/5000	290/4000	5-spd/Auto
Ghibli	1,274	1967–1973	Cpe Spts Conv	F/R	—	4719/V8/ 2OHC	330/5000	290/4000	5-spd/Auto
						4930/V8/ 2OHC	355/5500	340/4000	5-spd/Auto
Indy	1,136	1969–1974	Cpe	F/R	—	4136/V8/ 2OHC	260/5800	268/4000	5-spd/Auto
						4719/V8/ 2OHC	330/5000	290/4000	5-spd/Auto
						4930/V8/ 2OHC	335/5500	354/4000	5-spd/Auto

Matra (-Simca)

Make and model	Production Figures	Years Built	Body Styles	Mechanical Layout	Engine Make (if not own)	Capacity/ (cc)/Layout/ Valves	BHP/ rpm	Torque (lb.ft)/rpm	Transmission gearbox/automatic transmission
M530A	9,609	1967–1973	Spts Cpe	M/R	Ford-Germany	1699/V4/ OHV	73/4800	98/2800	4-spd/-

Mazda

Make and model	Production Figures	Years Built	Body Styles	Mechanical Layout	Engine Make (if not own)	Capacity/ (cc)/Layout/ Valves	BHP/ rpm	Torque (lb.ft)/rpm	Transmission gearbox/automatic transmission
1000/ 1200/1300	980,968	1968–1977	Sal Cpe Est	F/R	—	985/4IL/ OHC	65/6000	60/4000	4-spd/-
						1169/4IL/ OHC	73/6000	72/3000	4-spd/-
						1272/4IL/ OHC	69/6200	68/4000	4-spd/-
1500/1800	121,804	1966–1972	Sal Est	F/R	—	1490/4IL/ OHC	78/5500	85/2500	4-spd/-
						1796/4IL/ OHC	100/5500	112/2500	4-spd/-
110S Cosmo Wankel	1,176	1967–1972	Cpe	F/R	—	1964/2Rotor/ Wankel	110/7000	96/3500	4-spd/-
R100 Wankel	95,706	1968–1973	Sal Cpe	F/R	—	1964/2Rotor/ Wankel	100/7000	98/3500	4-spd/-
Capella 616	254,919	1970–1978	Sal Cpe	F/R	—	1586/4IL/ OHC	75/6000	85/3500	4-spd/-
RX2 Wankel	225,004	1970–1978	Sal Cpe	F/R	—	2292/2Rotor/ Wankel	120/7000	100/4000	4-spd/-

Meadows

Make and model	Production Figures	Years Built	Body Styles	Mechanical Layout	Engine Make (if not own)	Capacity/ (cc)/Layout/ Valves	BHP/ rpm	Torque (lb.ft)/rpm	Transmission gearbox/automatic transmission
Frisky	N/A	1957–1959	Spts Cpe	M(Tr)/R	Villiers	325/2IL 2-Str AirC	16/5500 18/5500	18/4000	4-spd/-

Mercedes-Benz

Make and model	Production Figures	Years Built	Body Styles	Mechanical Layout	Engine Make (if not own)	Capacity/ (cc)/Layout/ Valves	BHP/ rpm	Torque (lb.ft)/rpm	Transmission gearbox/automatic transmission
170SV/SD (W136)	153,475 (All W136 types)	1946–1955	Sal Conv	F/R	—	1767/4IL/ SV	45/3600	80/1800	4-spd/-
						1767/4IL/ OHV Diesel	40/3200	75/2000	4-spd/-

Suspension Front	Rear	Steering	Brakes (Front/rear)	Wheels/model Tyres	Length (in)	Weight (lb, unladen)	Performance Top speed (mph)	0–60mph (sec)	Standing 1/4-mile (sec)	UK Total Price (£: at Launch)
IC	BeamC	R & P	Disc/drum	165-13	161	1950	105 (Est)	N/A	N/A	£2114
IC	BeamC	R & P	Disc/drum	175-13	161	1949	125 (Est)	7.8	15.8	£2350
IC	BeamC	R & P	Disc/drum	175-13	161	2028	125	7.2	15.6	£2574
IC	BeamC	R & P	Disc/drum	185-13	187	2300	125 (Est)	N/A	N/A	£3185
IC	Beam1/2E	Worm	Drum/drum	6.50-16	189	2800	130 (Est)	N/A	N/A	£5800
IC	Beam1/2E	Worm	Disc/disc	185-16	189	3100	136	7.6	15.8	£4450
IC	Beam1/2E	Worm	Disc/disc	185-16	176	3330	137	8.4	16.0	£4802
IC	Beam1/2E	Worm	Disc/disc	205-15	176	3330	152 (Claimed)	N/A	N/A	£5581
IC	Beam1/2E	Worm	Disc/disc	205-15	176	3330	158 (Claimed)	N/A	N/A	£5932
IC	Beam1/2E	Worm	Disc/disc	205-15	177	2800	145 (Est)	N/A	N/A	£5980
IC	Beam1/2E	Worm	Disc/disc	225/70-15	177	2866	147	6.8	N/A	£5980
IC	DDC Beam1/2E	Worm	Disc/disc	205-15	196	3810	130	8.3	16.4	£5986
IC	Beam1/2E	Worm	Disc/disc	205-15	196	3810	140 (Est)	N/A	N/A	£6185
IC	Beam1/2E	Worm	Disc/disc	205-15	187	3640	143 (Claimed)	N/A	N/A	£7216
IC	Beam1/2E	Worm	Disc/disc	205-15	187	3640	155 (Claimed)	N/A	N/A	£7893
IC	Beam1/2E	Worm	Disc/disc	205-15	181	2980	154	7.5	15.1	£10,180
IC	Beam1/2E	Worm	Disc/disc	205-15	181	2980	160 (Est)	N/A	N/A	£9849
IC	Beam1/2E	Worm	Disc/disc	205-14	192	3640	140	7.2	15.7	£8320
IC	Beam1/2E	Worm	Disc/disc	205-15 / 205-14	192	3638	156	7.5	15.6	£8890
IC	Beam1/2E	Worm	Disc/disc	205-14	192	3638	165 (Claimed)	N/A	N/A	Special Order
IC	IC	R & P	Disc/disc	145-14 / 165-14	165	1930	95	15.6	19.9	£2160
IC	Beam1/2E	Worm	Disc/drum	6.15-13	150	1654	76	20.0	22.5	£999
IC	Beam1/2E	Worm	Disc/drum	6.15-13	150	1780	86	17.2	20.3	£879
IC	Beam1/2E	Worm	Disc/drum	155-13	152	1806	93	15.1	19.8	£949
IC	Beam1/2E	Worm	Disc/drum	6.45-14	172	2396	91	18.0	20.7	£994
IC	Beam1/2E	Worm	Disc/drum	6.45-14	172	2330	98	13.4	19.3	£1189
IC	DD1/2E	R & P	Disc/drum	165-14	163	2111	115	10.2	17.7	£2607
IC	Beam1/2E	Worm	Disc/drum	145-14	152	1926	105	10.9	18.0	£1650
IC	BeamC	Worm	Disc/drum	165-13	168	2135	102 (Claimed)	N/A	N/A	£1699
IC	BeamC	Worm	Disc/drum	165-13	163	2182	113	9.9	17.0	£1633
IRubber IC	BeamC BeamC	Worm	Drum/drum	4.40-10	110	784	56	N/A	27.2	£450
ITrL	IC	Worm	Drum/drum	5.50-16	175	2538	75	29.0	25.0	£1652
ITrL	IC	Worm	Drum/drum	5.50-16	175	2860	64	47.6	26.8	£1974

Make and model	Production Figures	Years Built	Body Styles	Mechanical Layout	Engine Make (if not own)	Capacity/(cc)/Layout/Valves	BHP/rpm	Torque (lb.ft)/rpm	Transmission gearbox/automatic transmission
220 (W187)	18,514	1951–1955	Sal Cpe Conv	F/R	—	2195/6IL/OHC	80/4850	105/2500	4-spd/-
300 (W186)	11,430	1951–1962	Sal	F/R	—	2996/6IL/OHC	115/4600	144/2500	4-spd/-
							125/4500	163/2600	4-spd/Auto
							136/4500	173/2700	4-spd/Auto
							160/5300	175/4200	4-spd/Auto
300S	760	1951–1958	Cpe Conv	F/R	—	2996/6IL/OHC	150/5000	170/3800	4-spd/-
							175/5400	188/4300	4-spd/-
180/190 ('Ponton')	171,746	1953–1961	Sal	F/R	—	1767/4IL/SV	52/4000	83/1800	4-spd/-
						1767/4IL/OHV Diesel	40/3200	75/2000	4-spd/-
						1897/4IL/OHC	43/3500	74/2000	4-spd/-
							65/4500	94/2200	4-spd/-
							68/4400	96/2500	
							75/4600	101/2800	4-spd/-
							80/4800	103/2800	4-spd/-
						1988/4IL/OHC Diesel	48/3800	80/2200	4-spd/-
						1897/4IL/OHC Diesel	50/4000	80/2200	4-spd/-
220/220S/219 ('Ponton')	109,061 + 7,345 Cpe/Conv	1954–1960	Sal	F/R	—	2195/6IL/OHC	100/4800	119/3500	4-spd/-
							106/5200	127/3500	
							115/4800	152/4100 (220SE)	
							120/4800	152/4100	
							85/4800	116/2400	4-spd/-
							90/4800	123/2400	4-spd/-
300SL	3,258	1954–1963	Spts Cpe Spts	F/R	—	2996/6IL/OHC	240/6100	217/4800	4-spd/-
							250/6200	217/4800	
190SL	25,881	1955–1963	Spts	F/R	—	1897/4IL/OHC	120/5700	107/2800	4-spd/-
190/200/230 'Fintail'	628,282	1961–1968	Sal Est	F/R	—	1897/4IL/OHC	80/5000	105/2500	4-spd/Auto
						1988/4IL/OHC	95/5200	114/3600	4-spd/Auto
						1988/4IL/OHC Diesel	55/4200	86/2400	4-spd/Auto
						2281/6IL/OHC	105/5200	128/3600	4-spd/Auto
							120/5400	132/4000	
						2306/6IL/OHC	118/5400	137/3800	4-spd/Auto
							135/5600	145/4200	4-spd/Auto
220/220SE 'Fintail'	337,803	1959–1965	Sal	F/R	—	2195/6IL/OHC	95/4800	124/3200	4-spd/Auto
							110/5000	127/3500	4-spd/Auto
							120/4800	152/4100	4-spd/Auto
220SE Cpe 'Fintail'	28,302	1960–1971	Cpe Conv	F/R	—	2195/6IL/OHC	120/4800	152/4100	4-spd/Auto
						2496/6IL/OHC	150/5500	159/4200	4-spd/Auto
						2778/6IL/OHC	160/5500	177/4250	4-spd/5-spd/Auto
						3499/V8/OHC	200/5800	211/4000	4-spd/5-spd/Auto
300SE/SEL (W112)	6,748	1961–1965	Sal	F/R	—	2996/6IL/OHC	160/5000	185/3800	4-spd/Auto
							170/5400	183/4000	4-spd/Auto
							185/5500	205/4100	4-spd/Auto
300SE Cpe (W112)	3,127	1962–1967	Cpe Conv	F/R	—	2996/6IL/OHC	160/5000	185/3000	4-spd/Auto
							170/5400	183/4000	
230SL/250SL/280SL	48,912	1963–1971	Spts Cpe	F/R	—	2308/6IL/OHC	170/5600	159/4500	4-spd/Auto
						2496/6IL/OHC	150/5500	174/4500	4-spd/Auto
						2778/6IL/OHC	170/5750	177/4500	4-spd/Auto
600	2,677	1963–1981	Limo Land	F/R	—	6332/V8/OHC	250/4000	369/2800	Auto/-
250S family Series (W108)	325,562	1965–1972	Sal Cpe	F/R	—	2496/6IL/OHC	130/5400	143/4000	4-spd/Auto
							146/5600	157/4200	4-spd/Auto
							170/5600	174/4500	4-spd/Auto
						2778/6IL/OHC	140/5400	166/3600	4-spd/Auto
							160/5500	177/4250	4-spd/Auto
300SEL (W109)	4,888	1965–1970	Sal	F/R	—	2996/6IL/OHC	170/5400	203/4100	Auto/-
						2778/6IL/OHC	170/5600	177/4500	Auto/-
200 family Series (W115) (4-cyl)	1,450,298	1967–1976	Sal	F/R	—	1988/4IL/OHC	95/5000	115/2800	4-spd/Auto
						2197/4IL/OHC	105/5000	132/2800	4-spd/Auto
						2197/4IL/	60/4200	93/2400	4-spd/-

Suspension Front	Rear	Steering	Brakes (Front/rear)	Wheels/model Tyres	Length (in)	Weight (lb,unladen)	Performance Top speed (mph)	0–60mph (sec)	Standing 1/4-mile (sec)	UK Total Price (£: at Launch)
IC	IC	Worm	Drum/drum	6.40-15	177	2970	92	19.5	21.4	£2023
						3168				
IC	IC	Worm	Drum/drum	7.10-15	195	3916	103	14.9	19.9	£3500
IC	IC	Worm	Drum/drum	7.10-15	199	4092	105 (Est)	N/A	N/A	£3301
IC	IC	Worm	Drum/drum	7.10-15	199	4046	96	15.9	20.4	£3301
IC	IC	Worm	Drum/drum	7.10-15	204	4290	107 (Est)	N/A	N/A	£5401
IC	IC	Worm	Drum/drum	6.70-15	185	3880	110 (Est)	N/A	N/A	£5529
IC	IC	Worm	Drum/drum	6.70-15	185	3924	112 (Claimed)	N/A		Special Order
IC	IC	Worm	Drum/drum	6.40-13	176	2596	74	29.5	23.4	£1694
IC	IC	Worm	Drum/drum	6.40-13	176	2684	66 (Est)	N/A	N/A	£1891
IC	IC	Worm	Drum/drum	6.40-13	176	2684	68 (Est)	N/A	N/A	
IC	IC	Worm	Drum/drum	6.40-13	176	2662	87 (Claimed)	N/A	N/A	£1794
IC	IC	Worm	Drum/drum	6.40-13	177	2548	86	18.2	21.4	£1772
IC	IC	Worm	Drum/drum	6.40-13	177	2548	86	17.8	20.6	£1772
IC	IC	Worm	Drum/drum	6.40-13	176	2684	68 (Claimed)	N/A	N/A	£1958
IC	IC	Worm	Drum/drum	6.40-13	176	2750	75 (Claimed)	N/A	N/A	£2083
IC	IC	Worm	Drum/drum	6.70-13	187	2970	101	15.2	20.4	£2123
IC	IC	Worm	Drum/drum	6.40-13	184	2838	90 (Est)	N/A	N/A	£2146
IC	IC	Worm	Drum/drum	6.70-13	185	2800	93	14.2	20.2	£2123
IC	IC	Worm	Drum/drum	6.70-13	175	2720	129	8.8	16.1	£4393
			Disc/disc							
IC	IC	Worm	Drum/drum	6.40-13	166	2388	107	13.3	17.8	£2693
IC	IC	Worm	Drum/drum	7.00-13	187	2816	85	19.5	21.5	£1987
			Disc/drum							
IC	IC	Worm	Disc/drum	7.00-13	187	2882	99 (Est)	N/A	N/A	£1874
				7.00-15	212	3113	99 (Est)	N/A	N/A	Special Order
			Drum/drum	7.00-13	187	2904	80	38.7	25.1	£2050
			Disc/drum	7.00-15	212	3201	80 (Est)	N/A	N/A	Special Order
IC	IC	Worm	Disc/drum	7.00-13	187	2871	105 (Est)	N/A	N/A	£2157
				7.00-15	212	3212	109 (Est)	N/A	N/A	£2395
IC	IC	Worm	Disc/drum	7.00-13	187	2877	108 (Est)	N/A	N/A	£2157
IC	IC	Worm	Disc/drum	7.25-13	192	2975	115 (Est)	N/A	N/A	£2395
IC	IC	Worm	Drum/drum	6.70-13	192	2904	99 (Est)	N/A	N/A	£2249
IC	IC	Worm	Disc/drum	7.25-13	192	2970	105	13.7	19.4	£2490
IC	IC	Worm	Disc/drum	6.70-13	192	3036	105	12.8	19.2	£2690
IC	IC	Worm	Disc/drum	7.25-13	192	3190	106	12.4	18.5	£4288
IC	IC	Worm	Disc/disc	185-14	192	3278	110 (Auto)	14.8	20.7	£3859
IC	IC	Worm	Disc/disc	185-14	192	3388	115	11.2	17.8	£4947
IC	IC	Worm	Disc/disc	185-14	193	3586	125	9.3	17.2	£6995
IAir	IAir	Worm	Disc/disc	185-14	192	3476	107	10.9	18.2	£5660
IAir	IAir	Worm	Disc/disc	7.50-13	196	3591	114	10.4	17.6	£3814
IAir	IAir	Worm	Disc/disc	185-14	193	3520	124 (Est)	N/A	N/A	£4931
IC	IC	Worm	Disc/drum	185-14	169	2800	120	10.7	17.5	£3595
IC	IC	Worm	Disc/drum	185-14	169	2855	120 (Est)	N/A	N/A	£3611
IC	IC	Worm	Disc/disc	185-14	169	3000	121	9.3	17.0	£3850
IAir	IAir	Worm	Disc/disc	9.00-15	218	5445	130	9.7	17.3	£8752
					246	5820	130 (Est)	N/A	N/A	£9796
IC	IC	Worm	Disc/disc	7.35-14	193	3175	106	12.6	19.3	£2575
IC	IC	Worm	Disc/disc	7.35-14	193	3175	114	10.8	17.9	£2575
IC	IC	Worm	Disc/disc	7.35-14	193	3263	120 (Est)	N/A	N/A	£2865
IC	IC	Worm	Disc/disc	7.35-14	193	3175	108	11.2	18.4	£3116
IC	IC	Worm	Disc/disc	7.35-14	193	3270	115	11.2	17.8	£3410
IAir	IAir	Worm	Disc/disc	195-14	197	3616	125 (Est)	N/A	N/A	£5669
IAir	IAir	Worm	Disc/disc	185-14	197	3570	125 (Est)	N/A	N/A	£5410
IC	IC	Worm	Disc/disc	6.95-14	185	2890	95	13.7	19.2	£3475
IC	IC	Worm	Disc/disc	6.95-14	185	2890	102	13.6	19.0	£2388
IC	IC	Worm	Disc/disc	6.95-14	185	2950	84	24.2	22.4	£2438

Make and model	Production Figures	Years Built	Body Styles	Mechanical Layout	Engine Make (if not own)	Capacity/(cc)/Layout/Valves	BHP/rpm	Torque (lb.ft)/rpm	Transmission gearbox/automatic transmission
						OHC Diesel			
						2307/4IL/ OHC	110/4800	137/2500	4-spd/Auto
						2404/4IL/ OHC Diesel	65/4200	97/2400	4-spd/-
230 family Series (W114) (6-cyl)	412,968	1967–1976	Sal	F/R	—	2292/6IL/ OHC	120/5300	132/3600	4-spd/Auto
						2496/6IL/ OHC	130/5300	147/3600	4-spd/Auto
						2778/6IL/ OHC	130/5200	159/3200	4-spd/Auto
						2746/6IL/ 2OHC	185/6000	176/4500	4-spd/Auto
250C/280CE	55,530	1968–1976	Cpe	F/R	—	2496/6IL/ OHC	150/5500	170/4650	4-spd/5-spd/Auto
						2746/6IL/ 2OHC	185/6000	175/4500	4-spd/5-spd/Auto
300SEL 3.5/4.5	12,136	1969–1972	Sal	F/R	—	3499/V8 OHC	200/5500	211/4000	Auto/-
300SEL 6.3	6,526	1968–1972	Sal	F/R	—	6332/V8 OHC	250/4000	369/2800	Auto/-

Messerschmidt

Make and model	Production Figures	Years Built	Body Styles	Mechanical Layout	Engine Make (if not own)	Capacity/(cc)/Layout/Valves	BHP/rpm	Torque (lb.ft)/rpm	Transmission gearbox/automatic transmission
TG500 Tiger	250	1958–1961	Cpe	R(Tr)/R	—	490/2IL 2-Str AirC	20/5000	25/4000	4-spd/-

Metropolitan

Make and model	Production Figures	Years Built	Body Styles	Mechanical Layout	Engine Make (if not own)	Capacity/(cc)/Layout/Valves	BHP/rpm	Torque (lb.ft)/rpm	Transmission gearbox/automatic transmission
1500	84,360	1956–1961	Sal Conv	F/R	—	1489/4IL OHV	47/4100	74/2100	3-spd/-

MG

Make and model	Production Figures	Years Built	Body Styles	Mechanical Layout	Engine Make (if not own)	Capacity/(cc)/Layout/Valves	BHP/rpm	Torque (lb.ft)/rpm	Transmission gearbox/automatic transmission
TC	10,000	1945–1949	Spts	F/R	—	1250/4IL OHV	54/5200	64/2600	4-spd/-
TD	29,664	1949–1953	Spts	F/R	—	1250/4IL OHV	54/5200	64/2600	4-spd/-
TF	9,600	1953–1955	Spts	F/R	—	1250/4IL OHV	57/5500	67/3000	4-spd/-
						1466/4IL OHV	63/5000	76/3000	4-spd/-
YA/YB	7,359	1947–1953	Sal	F/R	—	1250/4IL OHV	46/4800	59/2400	4-spd/-
Magnette ZA/ZB	36,650	1953–1958	Sal	F/R	—	1489/4IL OHV	60/4600 64/5400	78/3000 83/3000	4-spd/Semi-auto
Magnette Mk III/IV	30,996	1959–1968	Sal	F/R	—	1489/4IL OHV	64/4800	85/3300	4-spd/-
						1622/4IL OHV	68/5000	89/2500	4-spd/Auto
MGA 1500/ 1600/Mk 2	98,970	1955–1962	Spts Cpe	F/R	—	1489/4IL OHV	68-72/5500	77/3500	4-spd/-
						1588/4IL OHV	79/5600	87/3800	4-spd/-
						1622/4IL OHV	86/5500	97/4000	4-spd/-
MGA T-C/ De Luxe	2,500	1958–1962	Spts Cpe	F/R	—	1588/4IL 2OHC	108/6700	104/4500	4-spd/-
						1588/4IL OHV	79/5600	87/3800	4-spd/-
						1622/4IL OHV	86/5500	97/4000	4-spd/-
Midget I to IV/1500	226,526	1961–1979	Spts	F/R	—	948/4IL OHV	46/5500	53/3000	4-spd/-
						1098/4IL OHV	56/5500 59/5750	62/3250 65/3500	4-spd/- 4-spd/-
						1275/4IL OHV	65/6000	72/3000	4-spd/-
						1493/4IL OHV	66/5500	77/3000	4-spd/-
1100/1300	189,958	1962–1973	Sal	F(Tr)/F	—	1098/4IL OHV	55/5500	61/2500	4-spd/Auto
						1275/4IL OHV	58/5250 65/5750 70/6000	69/3500 71/3000 77/3000	4-spd/Auto 4-spd/Auto 4-spd/Auto
MGB	513,272	1962–1980	Spts Spts Cpe	F/R	—	1798/4IL OHV	95/5400	110/3000	4-spd (+O/D)/Auto
MGC	8,976	1967–1969	Spts Spts Cpe	F/R	—	2912/6IL OHV	145/5250	170/3400	4-spd (+O/D)/Auto

Suspension Front	Rear	Steering	Brakes (Front/rear)	Wheels/model Tyres	Length (in)	Weight (lb,unladen)	Performance Top speed (mph)	0–60mph (sec)	Standing 1/4-mile (sec)	UK Total Price (£: at Launch)
IC	IC	Worm	Disc/disc	175-14	185	2978	110	13.4	19.2	£3846
IC	IC	Worm	Disc/disc	175-14	185	3058	83	21.3	22.2	£4179
IC	IC	Worm	Disc/disc	6.95-14	185	2945	109	N/A (Claimed)	N/A	£4753
IC	IC	Worm	Disc/disc	6.95-14	185	3000	108	12.7	19.0	£2804
IC	IC	Worm	Disc/disc	6.95-14	185	3063	112	N/A (Claimed)	N/A	£3495
IC	IC	Worm	Disc/disc	205/70-14	185	3169	124	8.5	16.5	£3995
IC	IC	Worm	Disc/disc	185-14	184	3003	118	N/A (Claimed)	N/A	£3475
IC	IC	Worm	Disc/disc	205/70-14	184	3200	124	8.9	16.9	£4275
IC	IC	Worm	Disc/disc	185-14	197	3680	131	N/A (Claimed)	N/A	£6795
IC	IC	Worm	Disc/disc	FR70-14	197	3828	134	7.1	15.5	£7743
IRubber	IC	Worm	Drum/drum	4.40-10	120	847	66	27.8	22.8	£651
IC	Beam1/2E	Worm	Drum/drum	5.20-13	149	1850	75	24.8	22.5	£714
Beam1/2E	Beam1/2E	Worm	Drum/drum	4.50-19	140	1735	75	22.7	N/A	£480
IC	Beam1/2E	R & P	Drum/drum	5.50-15	145	1930	80	19.4	21.3	£569
IC	Beam1/2E	R & P	Drum/drum	5.50-15	147	1930	80	18.9	21.6	£780
IC	Beam1/2E	R & P	Drum/drum	5.50-15	147	1930	85	16.3	20.7	£780
IC	Beam1/2E	R & P	Drum/drum	5.00/5.25-16/ 5.50-15	161	2184	71	28.2	23.2	£672
IC	Beam1/2E	R & P	Drum/drum	5.50-15	168	2465	80	22.6	22.4	£915
IC	Beam1/2E	Worm	Drum/drum	5.90-14	178	2507	84	20.6	21.9	£1013
IC	Beam1/2E	Worm	Drum/drum	5.90-14	178	2507	86	19.5	21.5	£1059
IC	Beam1/2E	R & P	Drum/drum	5.50-15	156	1988	100	15.0	19.3	£894
IC	Beam1/2E	R & P	Disc/drum	5.50-15	156	2015	101	14.2	19.3	£940
IC	Beam1/2E	R & P	Disc/drum	5.50-15	156	1985	101	13.7	19.1	£963
IC	Beam1/2E	R & P	Disc/disc	5.90-15	156	2185	113	9.1	18.1	£1266
IC	Beam1/2E	R & P	Disc/disc	5.90-15	156	2015	101	14.2	19.3	Special Order
IC	Beam1/2E	R & P	Disc/disc	5/90-15	156	2015	101	13.7	19.1	Special Order
IC	Beam1/4E	R & P	Drum/drum	5.20-13	138	1525	86	20.0	22.0	£670
IC	Beam1/4E	R & P	Disc/drum	5.20-13	138	1525	89	16.9	21.0	£682
IC	Beam1/2E	R & P	Disc/drum	5.20-13	138	1566	92	14.7	19.8	£623
IC	Beam1/2E	R & P	Disc/drum	5.20-13	138	1575	94	14.1	19.6	£684
IC	Beam1/2E	R & P	Disc/drum	145-13	141	1700	101	12.3	18.5	£1351
IHydroL	IHydroL	R & P	Disc/drum	5.50-12	147	1820	85	18.4	21.3	£799
IHydroL	IHydroL	R & P	Disc/drum	5.50-12	147	1820	88	17.3	20.7	£813
IHydroL	IHydroL	R & P	Disc/drum	145-12	147	1850	93	15.6	20.0	£845
IHydroL	IHydroL	R & P	Disc/drum	145-12	147	1765	97	14.1	19.6	£911
IC	Beam1/2E	R & P	Disc/drum	5.60-14/ 155-165-14	153/158	2030 to 2260	103	12.2	18.7	£834
ITor	Beam1/2E	R & P	Disc/drum	165-15	153	2460	120	10.0	17.7	£1102

Make and model	Production Figures	Years Built	Body Styles	Mechanical Layout	Engine Make (if not own)	Capacity/ (cc)/Layout/ Valves	BHP/ rpm	Torque (lb.ft)/rpm	Transmission gearbox/automatic transmission
Mini									
Mini 850/ 1000	In prod. (Total (sales over 5 million)	1959–Date	Sal Est	F(Tr)/F	—	848/4IL/ OHV	34/5500	44/2900	4-spd/Auto
						998/4IL/ OHV	38/5250 40/5000 42/5250	52/2700 50/2500 58/2600	4-spd/Auto 4-spd/Auto 4-spd/Auto
						1275/4IL/ OHV	50/5000	66/2600	4-spd/Auto
Cooper	99,281	1961–1969	Sal	F(Tr)/F	—	997/4IL/ OHV	55/6000	54/3600	4-spd/-
						998/4IL/ OHV	55/5800	57/3000	4-spd/-
Cooper S	45,629	1963–1971	Sal	F(Tr)/F	—	970/4IL/ OHV	65/6500	55/3500	4-spd/-
						1071/4IL/ OHV	70/6000	62/4500	4-spd/-
						1275/4IL/ OHV	76/5800	79/3000	4-spd/-
Moke	14,518 [UK assembly only]	1964–1968	Ute Spts	F(Tr)/F	—	848/4IL/ OHV	34/5500	44/2900	4-spd/-
Clubman	331,675	1969–1980	Sal Est	F(Tr)/F	—	998/4IL/ OHV	38/5250 41/4850	52/2700 52/2750	4-spd/- -/Auto
					—	1098/4IL/ OHV	45/5250	56/2700	4-spd/-
1275GT	117,949	1969–1980	Sal	F(Tr)/F	—	1275/4IL/ OHV	59/5300	65/2550	4-spd/-
Monteverdi									
High Speed 375	N/A	1967–1977	Cpe Conv	F/R	Chrysler	7206/V8/ OHV	375/4600	480/3200	Auto/-
375L	N/A	1967–1977	Cpe	F/R	Chrysler	7206/V8/ OHV	380/4600	480/3200	Auto/-
Morgan									
4/4	1,720	1936–1950	Spts	F/R	Standard	1267/4IL/ OHV	40/4300	64/2300	4-spd/-
Plus 4	3,737	1950–1968	Spts Conv	F/R	Standard	2088/4IL/ OHV	68/4000	108/2000	4-spd/-
				F/R	Triumph	1991/4IL/ OHV	90/4800 100/4800	117/3000 117/3000	4-spd/- 4-spd/-
4/4 SII/V	1,294	1955–1968	Spts	F/R	Ford	1172/4IL/ SV	36/4400	54/2150	3-spd/-
						997/4IL/ OHV	39/5000	53/2700	4-spd/-
						1340/4IL/ OHV	54/4900	74/2500	4-spd/-
						1498/4IL/ OHV	60/4600 78/5200	86/2300 97/3600	4-spd/- 4-spd/-
Plus 4 Plus	26	1963–1966	Spts Cpe	F/R	Triumph	2138/4IL/ OHV	105/4750	128/3350	4-spd/-
4/4 1600	3,708	1968–1981	Spts	F/R	Ford	1599/4IL/ OHV	74/4750 88/5400	98/2500 96/3600	4-spd/- 4-spd/-
Plus 8	In prod	1968–Date	Spts	F/R	Rover	3528/V8/ OHV	161/5200 155/5250 190/5280	210/3000 198/2500 220/4000	4-spd/- 5-spd/- 5-spd/-
						3946/V8/ OHV	190/4750	235/2600	5-spd/-
Morris									
8 Series E	120,434	1938–1948	Sal	F/R	—	918/4IL/ SV	30/4400	39/2400	4-spd/-
10 Series M	53,566 (Postwar)	1938–1948	Sal	F/R	—	1140/4IL/	37/4600	53/1800	4-spd/-
Minor	1,303,331	1948–1971	Sal Est Conv	F/R	—	918/4IL SV	27/4400	42/2400	4-spd/-
						803/4IL/ OHV	30/4800	40/2400	4-spd/-
						948/4IL/ OHV	37/4750	50/2500	4-spd/-
						1098/4IL OHV	48/5100	60/2500	4-spd/-
Oxford (MO)	159,960	1948–1954	Sal Est	F/R	—	1476/4IL/ SV	41/4200	65/1800	4-spd/-
Six	12,400	1948–1953	Sal	F/R	—	2215/6IL/ OHC	70/4800	98/1800	4-spd/-
Oxford II/ III/IV	145,458	1954–1960	Sal Est	F/R	—	1489/4IL/ OHV	50/4800	78/2400	4-spd/SemiAuto

Suspension Front	Rear	Steering	Brakes (Front/rear)	Wheels/model Tyres	Length (in)	Weight (lb, unladen)	Top speed (mph)	0–60mph (sec)	Standing 1/4-mile (sec)	UK Total Price (£: at Launch)
IRubber	IRubber	R & P	Drum/drum	5.20-10	120/130	1380	72	27.1	23.6	£497
IHydroL	IHydroL					1400	75	26.2	22.7	£635
IHydroL	IHydroL	R & P	Drum/drum	5.20-10	120/130	1498	78	22.0	21.8	£5457
IRubber	IRubber	R & P	Disc/drum	145-10	120	1375	84	19.7	N/A	£4299
IRubber	IRubber	R & P	Disc/drum	145-12	120/130	1375	87	13.4	N/A	£5753
IRubber	IRubber	R & P	Disc/drum	5.20-10	120	1440	85	17.2	21.1	£679
IRubber	IRubber	R & P	Disc/drum	5.20-10	120	1440	90	14.8	20.0	£568
IHydroL	IHydroL	R & P	Disc/drum	5.20-10 / 145-10	120	1440	92 (Est)	N/A	N/A	£671
IRubber	IRubber	R & P	Disc/drum	145-10	120	1440	95	12.9	18.9	£695
IRubber	IRubber	R & P	Disc/drum	145-10	120	1440	97	10.9	18.2	£756
IHydroL / IRubber	IHydroL / IRubber	R & P	Drum/drum	5.20-10	120	1430	84	27.9	23.5	£405
IHydroL	IHydroL	R & P	Drum/drum	5.20-10	125	1406	75	21.0	N/A	£720
IRubber / IRubber	IRubber / IRubber	R & P	Drum/drum	5.20-10 / 145-10	125	1424	82	17.9	N/A	£N/A
IHydroL / IRubber	IHydroL / IRubber	R & P	Disc/drum	145-10 / 145-12	125	1555	90	13.3	19.0	£834
IC	DDC	Worm	Disc/disc	GR70-15	181	3344	155 (Claimed)	N/A	N/A	£9250
IC	DDC	Worm	Disc/disc	GR70-15	189	3665	152	6.3	14.6	£9250
IC	Beam1/2E	Worm	Drum/drum	4.50-17	136	1624	75 (Est)	N/A	N/A	£455
IC	Beam1/2E	Worm	Drum/drum	5.25-16	140	1876	85	14.1	19.5	£652
IC	Beam1/2E	Worm	Drum/drum	5.25-16	140	1876	96	13.3	18.5	£830
IC	Beam1/2E	Worm	Drum/drum Disc/drum	5.60-15	140	1876	100	9.7	17.5	£1018
IC	Beam1/2E	Worm	Drum/drum	5.00-16	144	1428	75	26.9	23.0	£639
IC	Beam1/2E	Worm	Drum/drum	5.20-15	144	1456	77 (Est)	N/A	N/A	£736
IC	Beam1/2E	Worm	Disc/drum	5.60-15	144	1624	92	10.5	18.1	£774
IC	Beam1/2E	Worm	Disc/drum	5.60-15	144	1516	95 (Est)	N/A	N/A	£683
IC	Beam1/2E	Worm	Disc/drum	5.60-15	144	1516	100 (Est)	N/A	N/A	£659
IC	Beam1/2E	Worm	Disc/drum	5.60-15	152	1820	105 (Est)	N/A	N/A	£1275
IC	Beam1/2E	Worm	Disc/drum	5.60-15	144	1516	100 (Est)	N/A	N/A	£858
IC	Beam1/2E	Worm	Disc/drum	5.60-15	144	1516	102	9.8	17.2	£890
IC	Beam1/2E	Worm	Disc/drum	185-15	147	1979	124	6.7	15.1	£1478
IC	Beam1/2E	Worm	Disc/drum	185/70-14	147	2128	123	6.5	15.1	£5417
IC	Beam1/2E	R & P	Disc/drum	205/60-15	147	2022	120	5.6	14.4	£12,999
IC	Beam1/2E	R & P	Disc/drum	205/60-15	156	2059	121	6.1	15.1	£22,363
Beam1/2E	Beam1/2E	Worm	Drum/drum	4.50-17	144	1704	58	N/A	N/A	£301
Beam1/2E	Beam1/2E	Worm	Drum/drum	5.00-16	158	2044	62	N/A	N/A	£378
ITor	Beam1/2E	R & P	Drum/drum	5.00-14	148	1652	62	36.5	26.3	£359
ITor	Beam1/2E	R & P	Drum/drum	5.00-14	148	1652	62	N/A	26.9	£582
ITor	Beam1/2E	R & P	Drum/drum	5.00-14	148	1652	73	25.9	23.4	£603
ITor	Beam1/2E	R & P	Drum/drum	5.00-14	148	1652	74	24.8	22.8	£587
ITor	Beam1/2E	R & P	Drum/drum	5.25-15	166	2212	71	31.0	24.5	£505
ITor	Beam1/2E	Worm	Drum/drum	6.00-15	177	2688	83	22.4	22.4	£608
ITor	Beam1/2E	R & P	Drum/drum	5.50-15 / 5.60-15	170	2464	73	29.0	24.2	£745

Make and model	Production Figures	Years Built	Body Styles	Mechanical Layout	Engine Make (if not own)	Capacity/(cc)/Layout/Valves	BHP/rpm	Torque (lb.ft)/rpm	Transmission gearbox/automatic transmission
Isis	8,541	1955–1956	Sal Est	F/R	—	2639/6IL/ OHV	86/4250 90/4500	124/2000 124/2000	4-spd (+O/D)/Auto
Cowley	22,036	1954–1959	Sal	F/R	—	1200/4IL/ OHV	42/4500	58/2400	4-spd/-
						1489/4IL/ OHV	55/4400	78/2400	4-spd/SemiAuto
Oxford (Farina)	296,255	1959–1971	Sal Est	F/R	—	1489/4IL/ OHV	52/4350	82/2100	4-spd/-
						1622/4IL/ OHV	61/4500	90/2100	4-spd/Auto
						1489/4IL/ OHV/Diesel	40/4000	64/1900	4-spd/-
Mini – see 'Mini' marque									
1100/1300	743,000 (Approx)	1962–1973	Sal Est	F(Tr)/F	—	1098/4IL/ OHV	48/5100	60/2500	4-spd/Auto
						1275/4IL/ OHV	58/5250 70/6000	69/3000 74/3250	4-spd/Auto 4-spd/-
1800	95,271	1966–1975	Sal	F(Tr)/F	—	1798/4IL/ OHV	80/5000 86/5300 96/5700	100/2100 101/3000 106/3000	4-spd/- 4-spd/Auto 4-spd/-
Moskvich									
407	N/A	1958–1964	Sal	F/R	—	1358/4IL/ OHV	45/4500	64/2600	3-spd/-
408/426	N/A	1964–1971	Sal Est	F/R	—	1358/4IL/ OHV	61/4500	80/2750	4-spd/-
412/427	N/A	1969–1975	Sal Est	F/R	—	1478/4IL/ OHC	80/5800	85/3400	4-spd/-
Nash									
Rambler **	—	1956 model	Est	F/R	—	3205/6IL/ OHV	120/4200	170/1600	3-spd
NSU									
Prinz	94,549	1958–1962	Sal	R(Tr)/R	—	583/2IL/ OHC AirC	20/4800 30/5700	29/2500 31/3000	4-spd/- 4-spd/-
Prinz 4	570,000	1961–1973	Sal	R(Tr)/R	—	598/2IL/ OHC AirC	30/5700	33/3250	4-spd/-
Sport Prinz	20,831	1959–1967	Cpe	R(Tr)/R	—	583/2IL/ OHC AirC	30/5700	31/3500	4-spd/-
						598/2IL/ OHC AirC	30/5700	33/3250	4-spd/-
Wankel Spider	2,375	1964–1967	Spts	R/R	—	500/1 Rotor/ Wankel	64/5000	54/3000	4-spd/-
1000/TT/TTS	261,691	1964–1972	Sal	R(Tr)/R	—	996/4IL/ OHC AirC	43/5500 55/5800 70/6150	53/2000 59/2500 62/4500	4-spd/- 4-spd/- 4-spd/-
110/110S/ 1200C	230,688	1965–1973	Sal	R(Tr)/R	—	1085/4IL/ OHC AirC	53/5000	58/2500	4-spd/-
						1177/4IL/ OHC AirC	55/5200	61/3500	4-spd/-
Ro80	37,204	1968–1977	Sal	F/F	—	1990/2Rotor Wankel	115/5500	121/4500	3-spd/-
Ogle									
1.5	8	1960–1962	Cpe	F/R	BMC	1489/4IL/ OHV	60/4800	81/2400	4-spd/-
Oldsmobile									
Super 88 **	—	1955 model	Sal	F/R	—	5318/V8/ OHV	202/4000	332/2400	Auto
Super 88 **	—	1958 model	Sal	F/R	—	6077/V8/ OHV	305/4600	410/2800	Auto
F85 Estate **	—	1961 model	Est	F/R	—	3528/V8/ OHV	155/4800	210/3200	3-spd
Toronado **	—	1966 model	Cpe	F/F	—	6965/V8/ OHV	385/4800	475/3200	Auto
Opel									
Kadett	2,311,389	1962–1973	Sal Est Cpe	F/R	—	1078/4IL/ OHV	45/5000 55/5400 60/5200	55/2800 60/2400 62/3800	4-spd/Auto 4-spd/Auto 4-spd/Auto

Suspension Front	Suspension Rear	Steering	Brakes (Front/rear)	Wheels/model Tyres	Length (in)	Weight (lb,unladen)	Performance Top speed (mph)	0–60mph (sec)	Standing 1/4-mile (sec)	UK Total Price (£: at Launch)
ITor	Beam1/2E	Worm	Drum/drum	6.00-15	178	2960	86	17.8	21.1	£802
ITor	Beam1/2E	R & P	Drum/drum	5.60-15	170	2464	65	37.5	25.7	£702
ITor	Beam1/2E	R & P	Drum/drum	5.60-15	170	2464	73	27.1	23.9	£799
IC	Beam1/2E	Worm	Drum/drum	5.90-14	178	2473	78	23.6	22.5	£816
IC	Beam1/2E	Worm	Drum/drum	5.90-14	175	2473	81	21.4	21.8	£869
IC	Beam1/2E	Worm	Drum/drum	5.90-14	175	2520	66	39.4	25.9	£868
IHydroL	IHydroL	R & P	Disc/drum	5.50-12	147	1780	78	22.2	22.7	£661
IHydroL	IHydroL	R & P	Disc/drum	5.50-12	147	1780	88	17.3	20.7	£672
IHydroL	IHydroL	R & P	Disc/drum	145-12	147	1900	93	15.6	20.0	£910
IHydroL	IHydroL	R & P	Disc/drum	175-13	164	2645	90	17.1	20.5	£873
IHydroL	IHydroL	R & P	Disc/drum	165-14	164	2645	93	16.3	19.9	£999
IHydroL	IHydroL	R & P	Disc/drum	165-14	164	2645	99	13.7	19.4	£1056
IC	Beam1/2E	Worm	Drum/drum	5.60-15	160	2044	70 (Est)	N/A	N/A	£759
IC	Beam1/2E	Worm	Drum/drum	6.00-13	161	2178	80	23.1	22.0	£667
IC	Beam1/2E	Worm	Drum/drum Disc/drum	6.45-13	162	2005	93	14.5	19.7	£749
IC	BeamC	Worm	Drum/drum	6.40-15	195	3248	75	20.7	22.0	£2266
IC	IC	R & P	Drum/drum	4.40-12	124	1036	63	N/A	27.0	£641
IC	IC	R & P	Drum/drum	4.40-12	124	1120	72	29.6	23.1	£623
IC	IC	R & P	Drum/drum	4.80-12	135	1246	71	32.2	23.7	£729
IC	IC	R & P	Drum/drum	4.40-12	143	1148	76	27.7	23.5	£976
IC	IC	R & P	Drum/drum	4.80-12	143	1148	81 (Claimed)	N/A	N/A	£769
IC	IC	R & P	Disc/drum	4.80-12	141	1510	92	16.7	20.5	£1391
IC	IC	R & P	Drum/drum	5.50-12	149	1365	80	20.5	21.2	£673
IC	IC	R & P	Disc/drum	135-13	149	1365	95	15.1	19.5	£824
IC	IC	R & P	Disc/drum	135-13	149	1465	95 (Est)	12.8	18.7	£1036
IC	IC	R & P	Disc/drum	155-13	158	1584	87	18.4	21.0	£770
IC	IC	R & P	Disc/drum	155-13	158	1579	93	14.8	19.5	£799
IC	IC	R & P	Disc/disc	175-14	190	2688	110	13.1	19.1	£2249
ITor	BeamC	R & P	Drum/drum	5.60-13	165	1975	88	20.1	21.3	£1623
IC	Beam1/2E	Worm	Drum/drum	7.60-15	205	4018	101	12.1	18.3	£2479
IC	Beam1/2E	Worm	Drum/drum	8.50-14	208	4482	114	10.2	17.1	£2604
IC	BeamC	Worm	Drum/drum	6.50-13	188	2898	100	14.2	19.5	£2694
ITor	Beam1/2E	Worm	Drum/drum	8.85-15	211	4670	129	8.1	16.5	£4416
ITrL	BeamC	R & P	Drum/drum	6.00-12	165	1653	75	20.6	21.9	£708
ITrL	BeamC	R & P	Disc/drum	155-13	165	1653	86 (Est)	N/A	N/A	Special Order
ITrL	BeamC	R & P	Disc/drum	155-13	165	1653	88	15.5	20.0	£999

Make and model	Production Figures	Years Built	Body Styles	Mechanical Layout	Engine Make (if not own)	Capacity/(cc)/Layout/Valves	BHP/rpm	Torque (lb.ft)/rpm	Transmission gearbox/automatic transmission
						1196/4IL/OHV	60/5400	70/3900	4-spd/Auto
						1897/4IL/OHC	90/5100	108/2800	4-spd/-
Olympia	80,637	1966–1970	Sal Est Cpe	F/R	—	1078/4IL/OHV	60/5200	62/2800	4-spd/Auto
Rekord	1,280,000	1966–1971	Sal Cpe Est	F/R	—	1492/4IL/OHC	58/4800	76/2500	3-spd/4-spd/-
						1698/4IL/OHC	75/5200 60/4600	94/2500 85/2300	3-spd/4-spd/Auto
						1897/4IL/OHC	90/5100 106/5800	108/2800 116/3500	4-spd/Auto 4-spd/Auto
Commodore	156,330	1967–1971	Sal Cpe	F/R	—	2490/6IL/OHC	115/5200 130/5300	128/3800 138/4000	4-spd/Auto 4-spd/Auto
GT 1900	103,373	1968–1973	Cpe	F/R	—	1897/4IL/OHC	90/5100	108/2800	4-spd/-
Manta	498,553	1970–1975	Cpe	F/R	—	1584/4IL/OHC	80/5200	95/4200	4-spd/Auto
						1897/4IL/OHC	90/5100 156/5500	108/2800 174/4000	4-spd/Auto 4-spd/Auto
Ascona	641,438	1970–1975	Sal Est	F/R	—	1584/4IL/OHC	80/5200	95/4200	4-spd/Auto
						1897/4IL/OHC	90/5100	108/2800	4-spd/Auto

Oppermann

Make and model	Production Figures	Years Built	Body Styles	Mechanical Layout	Engine Make (if not own)	Capacity/(cc)/Layout/Valves	BHP/rpm	Torque (lb.ft)/rpm	Transmission gearbox/automatic transmission
Unicar	200 Est	1956–1959	Cpe	R(Tr)/R	Anzani/ Excelsior	322/2IL/ 2-str AirC	15/5000	16/3500	3-spd/-
						328/2IL/ 2-str AirC	18/5250	22/3000	3-spd/-
Stirling	N/A	1958–1959	Cpe	R(Tr)/R	Excelsior	424/2IL/ 2-str AirC	25/5500	N/Q	4-spd/-

Packard

Make and model	Production Figures	Years Built	Body Styles	Mechanical Layout	Engine Make (if not own)	Capacity/(cc)/Layout/Valves	BHP/rpm	Torque (lb.ft)/rpm	Transmission gearbox/automatic transmission
Clipper **	—	1956 model	Sal	F/R	—	5768/V8/ OHV	275/4600	380/2800	Auto
						5243/V8/ OHV	225/4600	N/Q	Auto

Panhard

Make and model	Production Figures	Years Built	Body Styles	Mechanical Layout	Engine Make (if not own)	Capacity/(cc)/Layout/Valves	BHP/rpm	Torque (lb.ft)/rpm	Transmission gearbox/automatic transmission
Dyna Junior	Est 2,000	1952–1955	Conv						
Dyna 54	N/A	1954–1959	Sal	F/F	—	851/2HO/ OHV AirC	41/5000	47/3000	4-spd/-
PL17	130,000	1959–1964	Sal	F/F	—	851/2HO/ OHV AirC	42/5000 50/5800	51/2500 51/3600	4-spd/-
24CT	24,962	1964–1967	Cpe	F/F	—	848/2HO/ OHV AirC	50/5800	54/2600	4-spd/-

Paramount

Make and model	Production Figures	Years Built	Body Styles	Mechanical Layout	Engine Make (if not own)	Capacity/(cc)/Layout/Valves	BHP/rpm	Torque (lb.ft)/rpm	Transmission gearbox/automatic transmission
Ten/ 1½-litre	N/A	1950–1956	Sal Conv	F/R	Ford	1172/4IL/ SV	30/4000	46/3000	3-spd/-
						1508/4IL/ OHV	47/4400	72/2400	3-spd/-

Peerless (also 'Warwick')

Make and model	Production Figures	Years Built	Body Styles	Mechanical Layout	Engine Make (if not own)	Capacity/(cc)/Layout/Valves	BHP/rpm	Torque (lb.ft)/rpm	Transmission gearbox/automatic transmission
GT	325	1958–1962	Cpe	F/R	Triumph	1991/4IL/ OHV	100/5000	118/3000	4-spd (+O/D)/-

Pegaso

Make and model	Production Figures	Years Built	Body Styles	Mechanical Layout	Engine Make (if not own)	Capacity/(cc)/Layout/Valves	BHP/rpm	Torque (lb.ft)/rpm	Transmission gearbox/automatic transmission
Z102/Z103	100 (Est)	1951–1956	Cpe Spl	F/R	—	2474/V8/ 2OHC	140/6000	135/3900	5-spd/-
						2816/V8/ 2OHC	170/5500	163/3400	5-spd/-
						3181/V8/ 2OHC	220/6000	181/4500	5-spd/-
						4681/V8/ OHV	300/5500	279/4500	5-spd/-

Peugeot

Make and model	Production Figures	Years Built	Body Styles	Mechanical Layout	Engine Make (if not own)	Capacity/(cc)/Layout/Valves	BHP/rpm	Torque (lb.ft)/rpm	Transmission gearbox/automatic transmission
203	685,828	1948–1960	Sal Cpe Est Conv	F/R	—	1290/4IL/ OHV	46/4500	59/2500	4-spd/-

Suspension Front	Rear	Steering	Brakes (Front/rear)	Wheels/model Tyres	Length (in)	Weight (lb,unladen)	Performance Top speed (mph)	0–60mph (sec)	Standing 1/4-mile (sec)	UK Total Price (£: at Launch)
ITrL	BeamC	R & P	Disc/drum	155-13	165	1697	88 (Est)	N/A	N/A	£979
ITrL	BeamC	R & P	Disc/drum	155-13	165	1962	104 (Claimed)	N/A	N/A	£999
ITrL	BeamC	R & P	Disc/drum	155-13	165	1742	85	17.8	20.4	£931
IC	BeamC	Worm	Disc/drum	6.40-13	180	2304	83 (Claimed)	N/A	N/A	£1035
IC	BeamC	Worm	Disc/drum	6.40-13	180	2304	92 (Claimed)	N/A	N/A	£N/A
IC	BeamC	Worm	Disc/drum	6.40-13	180	2380	99	12.3	18.6	£N/A
IC	BeamC	Worm	Disc/drum	165-14	180	2436	105	10.9	17.9	£N/A
IC	BeamC	Worm	Disc/drum	165-14	181	2491	104	11.4	18.5	£1380
IC	BeamC	Worm	Disc/drum	165-14	181	2579	115	12.8	18.6	£N/A
ITrL	BeamC	R & P	Disc/drum	165-13	162	2107	115	12.0	18.6	£1882
IC	BeamC	R & P	Disc/drum	165-13	169	2130	101	12.7	18.9	£1327
IC	BeamC	R & P	Disc/drum	185-13	169	2111	105	12.2	18.2	£1475
IC	BeamC	R & P	Disc/drum	185/70-13	171	2111	125	7.6	15.7	£3500
IC	BeamC	R & P	Disc/drum	165-13	164	2083	93	13.0	18.9	£1263
IC	BeamC	R & P	Disc/drum	185/70-13	164	2135	98	12.5	18.3	£1297
IC	BeamC	Worm	Drum/drum	4.50-12	114	700	59 (Claimed)	N/A	N/A	£400
IC	BeamC	Worm	Drum/drum	4.50-12	114	700	62 (Est)	N/A	N/A	£400
IC	IC	Worm	Drum/drum	4.40-12	129	896	70 (Est)	N/A	N/A	£541
ITor	BeamTor	Worm	Drum/drum	7.60-15	214	4340	106	11.3	18.5	£3867
ITor	BeamTor	Worm	Drum/drum	7.60-15	214	4340	113	10.9	18.2	£3714
ITrL	BeamTor	R & P	Drum/drum	145-380	180	1792	80	24.2	23.1	£N/A
ITrL	BeamTor	R & P	Drum/drum	145-380	180	1848	80	24.2	23.1	£1000
ITrL	BeamTor	R & P	Drum/drum	145-380	180	1805	82	23.1	22.8	£N/A
ITrL	BeamTor	R & P	Drum/drum Disc/disc	145-380	168	1820	89	22.3	22.5	£1330
ITrL	Beam1/2E	Worm	Drum/drum	5.25-16	166	2072	65 (Est)	N/A	N/A	£632
ITrL	Beam1/2E	Worm	Drum/drum	5.25-16	168	2436	72	31.2	24.6	£1014
IC	DD1/2E	Worm	Disc/drum	5.50-15	162	2240	103	12.8	18.6	£1493
ITor	DDTor	Worm	Drum/drum	5.50-16 or 6.00-16	162	2180	120	11.0	18.2	Special Order
ITor	DDTor	Worm	Drum/drum	5.50-16	162	2200	140	8.5	N/A	Special Order
ITor	DDTor	Worm	Drum/drum	6.50-16	162	2800	160 (Est)	N/A	N/A	Special Order
ITor	DDTor	Worm	Drum/drum	6.50-16	162	3360	170 (Est)	N/A	N/A	Special Order
ITrL	BeamC	Worm	Drum/drum	155-400	171	2016	71	N/A	N/A	£986

Make and model	Production Figures	Years Built	Body Styles	Mechanical Layout	Engine Make (if not own)	Capacity/(cc)/Layout/Valves	BHP/rpm	Torque (lb.ft)/rpm	Transmission gearbox/automatic transmission
403	1,214,121	1955–1967	Sal	F/R	—	1468/4IL/	58/4900	75/2500	4-spd/-
	(Incl. Cabriolet)		Est			OHV			
403 Cabriolet	—	1956–1961	Conv						
404	2,416,733	1960–1975	Sal	F/R	—	1618/4IL/	72/5400	94/2250	4-spd/-
	(Incl. Coupe/		Est			OHV	88/5500	101/2800	4-spd/-
	Cabriolet)						80/5400	94/2250	4-spd/-
						1948/4IL/	55/4500	88/2250	4-spd/-
						OHV Diesel			
404 Coupe/	17,224	1962–1969	Conv	F/R	—	1618/4IL/	88/5500	101/2800	4-spd/-
Cabriolet			Cpe			OHV			
204	1,604,296	1965–1977	Sal	F(Tr)/F	—	1130/4IL/	53/5800	61/3000	4-spd/-
	(Incl. Coupe/		Est			OHC			
	Cabriolet)								
204/304	60,937	1966–1975	Cpe	F(Tr)/F	—	1130/4IL/	53/5800	61/3000	4-spd/-
Coupe/Cabriolet			Conv			OHC			
						1288/4IL/	65/5750	69/3750	4-spd/-
						OHC	69/5800	78/3750	4-spd/-
							74/6000	74/4500	4-spd/-
304	1,178,425	1969–1980	Sal	F(Tr)/F	—	1288/4IL/	65/6000	69/3750	4-spd/-
			Est			OHC	69/5800	78/3750	4-spd/-
			Cpe						
504	3,173,191	1968–1989	Sal	F/R	—	1796/4IL/	82/5500	108/3000	4-spd/Auto
			Est			OHV	97/5600	114/3000	4-spd/Auto
			Cpe				79/5100	105/2500	4-spd/Auto
			Conv			1971/4IL/	87/5000	118/3000	4-spd/Auto
						OHV	93/5200	118/3000	4-spd/Auto
							97/5000	124/3000	4-spd/Auto
							106/5200	124/3000	4-spd/Auto
						1948/4IL/	56/4500	80/2000	4-spd/-
						OHV Diesel			
						2112/4IL/	59/4500	86/2500	4-spd/-
						OHV Diesel			
						2304/4IL/	64/4500	95/2000	4-spd/-
						OHV Diesel			

Plymouth

Make and model	Production Figures	Years Built	Body Styles	Mechanical Layout	Engine Make (if not own)	Capacity/(cc)/Layout/Valves	BHP/rpm	Torque (lb.ft)/rpm	Transmission gearbox/automatic transmission
Belvedere **	—	1955 model	Sal	F/R	—	4260/V8/	167/4000	N/Q	3-spd (+O/D)
						OHV			
Savoy **	—	1956 model	Sal	F/R	—	4500/V8/	187/4400	265/2400	Auto
						OHV			
Fury **	—	1959 model	Sal	F/R	—	5212/V8/	225/4400	340/2400	Auto
						OHV			
Fury **	—	1961 model	Sal	F/R	—	5122/V8	225/4400	340/2400	Auto
						OHV			
Fury **	—	1963 model	Sal	F/R	—	5130/V8/	225/4400	330/2800	Auto
						OHV			
Barracuda **	—	1967 model	Cpe	F/R	—	4473/V8/	180/4200	260/1600	Auto
						OHV			
Fury **	—	1968 model	Sal	F/R	—	6276/V8/	294/4400	390/2800	Auto
						OHV			

Polski-Fiat

See **FSO**, above

Pontiac

Make and model	Production Figures	Years Built	Body Styles	Mechanical Layout	Engine Make (if not own)	Capacity/(cc)/Layout/Valves	BHP/rpm	Torque (lb.ft)/rpm	Transmission gearbox/automatic transmission
Bonneville **	—	1959 model	Cpe	F/R	—	6377/V8/	300/4600	420/2800	Auto
						OHV			
Parisienne **	—	1962 model	Sal	F/R	—	4638/V8/	170/4200	275/2200	Auto
						OHV			
Parisienne **	—	1965 model	Sal	F/R	—	4638/V8/	195/4800	285/2400	Auto
						OHV			
GTO **	—	1969 model	Cpe	F/R	—	6375/V8/	365/5200	424/3600	Auto
						OHV			

Porsche

Make and model	Production Figures	Years Built	Body Styles	Mechanical Layout	Engine Make (if not own)	Capacity/(cc)/Layout/Valves	BHP/rpm	Torque (lb.ft)/rpm	Transmission gearbox/automatic transmission
356	7,627	1950–1955	Cpe	R/R	Own/VW	1488/4HO/	55/4400	78/3200	4-spd/-
			Conv			OHV AirC	70/5000	80/3600	4-spd/-
356A	21,045	1955–1959	Cpe	R/R	Own/VW	1582/4HO/	60/4500	81/2800	4-spd/-
			Conv			OHV AirC	75/5000	86/3700	4-spd/-
			Spts			1498/4HO/	100/6200	88/5200	4-spd/-
						2OHC AirC			
						1587/4HO/	115/6500	98/5200	4-spd/-
						2OHC AirC			
356B	30,963	1959–1963	Cpe	R/R	—	1582/4HO/	60/4500	81/2800	4-spd/-
			Conv			OHV AirC	75/5000	86/3700	4-spd/-
			Spts				90/5500	89/4300	4-spd/-
						1587/4HO/	115/6500	98/5200	4-spd/-

Suspension Front	Rear	Steering	Brakes (Front/rear)	Wheels/model Tyres	Length (in)	Weight (lb, unladen)	Performance Top speed (mph)	0–60mph (sec)	Standing 1/4-mile (sec)	UK Total Price (£: at Launch)
ITrL	BeamC	Worm	Drum/drum	165-380	175	2366	76	24.0	23.0	£1129
IC	BeamC	R & P	Drum/drum	165-380	174	2296	84	22.0	21.9	£1297
IC	BeamC	R & P	Drum/drum	165-380	174	2415	100	13.9	18.8	£1495
IC	BeamC	R & P	Drum/drum	6.40-14	174	2300	92 (Est)	N/A	N/A	£1112
IC	BeamC	R & P	Drum/drum	165-380	174	2420	81	25.4	23.1	£1396
IC	BeamC	R & P	Drum/drum	165-380	177	2453	105	12.2	18.8	£2367
IC	IC	R & P	Disc/drum	145-14	156	1874	86	18.1	21.1	£992
IC	IC	R & P	Disc/drum	145-14	148	1960	88	19.9	21.5	£983
IC	IC	R & P	Disc/drum	145-14	148	2015	94 (Est)	N/A	N/A	£1496
IC	IC	R & P	Disc/drum	145-14	148	2052	98	14.7	19.5	£1638
IC	IC	R & P	Disc/drum	145-14	148	2052	100 (Est)	N/A	N/A	£2218
IC	IC	R & P	Disc/drum	145-14	163	2017	93	14.9	20.0	£1195
IC	IC	R & P	Disc/drum	145-14	163	2017	96	14.5	19.6	£1466
IC	IC	R & P	Disc/disc	175-14	177	2645	95	13.2	19.0	£1500
IC	IC	R & P	Disc/disc	175-14	177	2600	106	12.6	18.7	£1676
IC	BeamC	R & P	Disc/drum	165-14	177	2469	96	13.4	18.9	£2609
IC	IC	R & P	Disc/disc	175-14	177	2722	99	12.7	19.1	£1594
IC	IC	R & P	Disc/disc	175-14	177	2667	100	12.0	18.7	£1926
IC	IC	R & P	Disc/disc	175-14	177	2722	103	12.4	18.9	£1705
IC	IC	R & P	Disc/disc	175-14	177	2666	104	11.4	18.3	£2115
IC	BeamC	R & P	Disc/drum	165-14	177	2607	84	21.7	22.4	£2361
IC	BeamC	R & P	Disc/drum	185-14	177	2866	78 (Claimed)	N/A	N/A	£4550
IC	IC	R & P	Disc/drum	175-14	177	2866	87 (Claimed)	N/A	N/A	£4472
IC	Beam1/2E	Worm	Drum/drum	6.70-15	200	3528	100	12.3	19.2	£2200
IC	Beam1/2E	Worm	Drum/drum	6.70-15	205	3612	93	13.7	19.4	£2538
ITor	Beam1/2E	Worm	Drum/drum	8.00-14	208	3934	105	10.8	17.8	£2827
ITor	Beam1/2E	Worm	Drum/drum	7.50-14	210	3976	101	15.1	19.4	£2653
ITor	Beam1/2E	Worm	Drum/drum	7.50-14	205	3556	109	11.5	18.1	£2103
ITor	Beam1/2E	Worm	Disc/drum	6.95-14	193	3219	106	10.9	17.8	£2786
ITor	Beam1/2E	Worm	Drum/drum	8.25-14	213	4067	108	10.7	17.6	£2988
IC	BeamC	Worm	Drum/drum	8.00-14	221	4368	114	9.7	17.4	£3225
IC	BeamC	Worm	Drum/drum	7.50-14	212	3780	96	13.7	19.6	£2796
IC	BeamC	Worm	Drum/drum	7.35-14	204	3797	101	12.3	19.6	£2294
IC	BeamC	Worm	Drum/drum	7.75-14	205	3640	120	7.9	15.3	£2812
ITor	ITor	Worm	Drum/drum	5.00-16	155	1652	87	17.0	20.1	£1971
ITor	ITor	Worm	Drum/drum	5.00-16	155	1652	105 (Est)	N/A	N/A	£1971
ITor	ITor	Worm	Drum/drum	5.00-16	155	1797	102	14.1	19.1	£1891
ITor	ITor	Worm	Drum/drum	5.00-16	155	1797	109 (Est)	N/A	N/A	£1891
ITor	ITor	Worm	Drum/drum	5.00-16	155	1841	125 (Est)	N/A	N/A	£2799
ITor	ITor	Worm	Drum/drum	5.00-16	155	1841	120 (Est)	N/A	N/A	£3331
ITor	ITor	Worm	Drum/drum	5.60-15	158	1848	102 (Est)	N/A	N/A	£1885
ITor	ITor	Worm	Drum/drum	5.60-15	158	1848	109	11.4	18.1	£2215
ITor	ITor	Worm	Drum/drum	5.60-15	158	1848	111	11.5	18.3	£2409
ITor	ITor	Worm	Drum/drum	5.00-16	158	1985	120 (Est)	N/A	N/A	Special Order

Make and model	Production Figures	Years Built	Body Styles	Mechanical Layout	Engine Make (if not own)	Capacity/(cc)/Layout/Valves	BHP/rpm	Torque (lb.ft)/rpm	Transmission gearbox/automatic transmission
						2OHC AirC			
Carrera 2	126	1962–1964	Conv Spts	R/R	—	1966/4HO/ 2OHC AirC	130/6200	119/4600	4-spd/-
356C	16,668	1963–1965	Cpe	R/R	—	1582/4HO/ OHV AirC	75/5200	90/3600	4-spd/-
			Conv				95/5800	91/4200	4-spd/-
911	305,395	1964–1989	Cpe	R/R	—	1991/6HO/ OHC AirC	110/5800	115/4200	5-spd/-
			Targa				130/6100	130/4200	5-spd/-
			Conv				140/6500	130/4500	5-spd/-
							160/6600	133/5200	5-spd/-
							170/6800	135/5500	5-spd/-
						2195/6HO/ OHC AirC	125/5800	131/4200	5-spd/SemiAuto
							155/6200	141/4500	5-spd/SemiAuto
							180/6500	147/5200	5-spd/SemiAuto
						2341/6HO/ OHC AirC	130/5600	145/4000	5-spd/SemiAuto
							165/6200	152/4500	5-spd/SemiAuto
							190/6500	159/5200	5-spd/SemiAuto
						2687/6HO/ OHC AirC	150/5700	174/3800	5-spd/SemiAuto
							165/5800	166/4000	5-spd/SemiAuto
							175/5800	174/4000	5-spd/SemiAuto
							210/6300	188/5100	5-spd/SemiAuto
						2994/6HO/ OHC AirC	165/5800	174/4000	5-spd/SemiAuto
							188/5500	195/4300	5-spd/SemiAuto
							200/6000	188/4200	5-spd/SemiAuto
							204/5900	195/4300	5-spd/-
						3164/6HO/ OHC AirC	231/5900	210/4800	5-spd/-
912	30,745	1965–1968	Cpe	R/R	—	1582/4HO/ OHV AirC	90/5800	98/3500	5-spd/-
914/6	3,107	1969–1972	Spts Cpe	M/R	—	1991/6HO/ OHC AirC	110/5800	116/4200	5-spd/SemiAuto

Rambler

Make and model	Production Figures	Years Built	Body Styles	Mechanical Layout	Engine Make (if not own)	Capacity/(cc)/Layout/Valves	BHP/rpm	Torque (lb.ft)/rpm	Transmission gearbox/automatic transmission
American **	—	1959 model	Sal	F/R	—	3205/6IL/ SV	90/3800	150/1600	3-spd
Super 6 **	—	1960 model	Est	F/R	—	3205/6IL/ OHV	127/4200	180/1600	3-spd
Estate **	—	1961 model	Est	F/R	—	3205/6IL/ OHV	127/4200	180/1600	Auto
Classic **	—	1963 model	Sal	F/R	—	3205/6IL/ OHV	138/4500	185/1800	Auto
770 Six **	—	1964 model	Sal	F/R	—	3205/6IL/ OHV	138/4500	185/1800	Auto
770 vee-8 **	—	1966 model	Conv	F/R	—	4704/V8/ OHV	198/4700	280/2600	Auto
Rebel **	—	1967 model	Est	F/R	—	3802/6IL/ OHV	155/4400	222/1600	Auto
Javelin SST **	—	1968 model	Cpe	F/R	—	5622/V8/ OHV	284/4800	365/3000	Auto
Javelin **	—	1969 model	Cpe	F/R	—	5622/V8/ OHV	280/4800	365/3000	Auto
Ambass- ador SST **	—	1970 model	Sal	F/R	—	5899/V8/ OHV	290/4800	365/3000	Auto

Range Rover

Make and model	Production Figures	Years Built	Body Styles	Mechanical Layout	Engine Make (if not own)	Capacity/(cc)/Layout/Valves	BHP/rpm	Torque (lb.ft)/rpm	Transmission gearbox/automatic transmission
Range Rover/Classic	317,615	1970–1996	Est	F/4	VM	2393/4IL/ OHV Diesel	112/4200	183/2400	5-spd/Auto
					—	2497/4IL/ OHC Diesel	113/4000	195/1800	5-spd/Auto
							119/4200	209/1950	5-spd/Auto
						3528/V8/ OHV	135/4750	205/3000	4-spd (+O/D)/-
							125/4000	185/2500	4-spd/5-spd/Auto
							127/4000	194/2500	5-spd/Auto
							165/4750	206/3200	5-spd/Auto
						3947/V8/ OHV	185/4750	235/2600	5-spd/Auto
							178/4750	220/3250	5-spd/Auto
						4278/V8/ OHV	200/4850	250/3250	Auto/-

Reliant

Make and model	Production Figures	Years Built	Body Styles	Mechanical Layout	Engine Make (if not own)	Capacity/(cc)/Layout/Valves	BHP/rpm	Torque (lb.ft)/rpm	Transmission gearbox/automatic transmission
Sabre 4/6	208/77	1961–1964	Spts	F/R	Ford	1703/4IL/ OHV	72/4400	91/2300	4-spd/-
							90/5000	91/2300	
						2553/6IL/	109/4800	137/2400	4-spd (+O/D)/-

Suspension Front	Rear	Steering	Brakes (Front/rear)	Wheels/model Tyres	Length (in)	Weight (lb, unladen)	Performance Top speed (mph)	0–60mph (sec)	Standing 1/4-mile (sec)	UK Total Price (£: at Launch)
			Disc/disc							
ITor	ITor	Worm	Disc/disc	165-15	158	2249	125 (Est)	N/A	N/A	£3734
ITor	ITor	Worm	Disc/disc	5.60-15	158	2062	109	11.4	18.1	£2063
ITor	ITor	Worm	Disc/disc	165-15	158	1988	113	13.2	18.7	£2277
				[Note: Many different tyres sizes were used on many different 911s. Sizes quoted are for the <u>first</u> derivative of the model]						
ITor	ITor	R & P	Disc/disc	165-15	164	2200	124 (Est)	N/A	N/A	£2745
ITor	ITor	R & P	Disc/disc	165-15	164	2200	130	8.3	16.1	£2996
ITor	ITor	R & P	Disc/disc	165-15	164	2200	130	9.8	17.0	£3992
ITor	ITor	R & P	Disc/disc	165-15	164	2309	137	8.0	15.8	£3556
ITor	ITor	R & P	Disc/disc	165-15	164	2309	137	7.3	15.8	£4663
ITor	ITor	R & P	Disc/disc	165-15	164	2250	129	8.1	16.0	£3671
ITor	ITor	R & P	Disc/disc	165-15	164	2307	137	7.0	15.4	£4585
ITor	ITor	R & P	Disc/disc	165-15	164	2350	143 (Est)	N/A	N/A	£5211
ITor	ITor	R & P	Disc/disc	165-15	164	2250	127	7.6	15.7	£3971
ITor	ITor	R & P	Disc/disc	185/70-15	164	2394	139	6.4	14.4	£4827
ITor	ITor	R & P	Disc/disc	185/70-15	164	2436	145	6.2	14.7	£5402
ITor	ITor	R & P	Disc/disc	185/70-15	169	2370	130 (Est)	7.8	15.8	£6135
ITor	ITor	R & P	Disc/disc	185/70-15	169	2475	135	7.2	15.7	£6249
ITor	ITor	R & P	Disc/disc	185/70-15	169	2443	142	6.1	15.0	£6993
ITor	ITor	R & P	Disc/disc	215/60-15	164	2398	149	5.5	14.1	£5825
ITor	ITor	R & P	Disc/disc	205/55-16/	169	2716	130 (Est)	N/A	N/A	£9999
ITor	ITor	R & P	Disc/disc	225/50-16	169	2716	141	6.5	15.1	£14,100
ITor	ITor	R & P	Disc/disc	185/70/15/ 215/60-15	169	2475	143 (Claimed)	N/A	N/A	£10,996
ITor	ITor	R & P	Disc/disc	185/70/15/ 215/60-15	169	2688	148	5.7	14.3	£16,731
ITor	ITor	R & P	Disc/disc	205/55-16/ 225/50-16	169	2780	151	5.2	13.9	£21,464
ITor	ITor	R & P	Disc/disc	165-15	164	2134	119	11.9	18.2	£2467
ITor	IC	R & P	Disc/disc	165-15	157	2070	125	8.3	16.2	£3475
IC	Beam1/2E	Worm	Drum/drum	5.90-15	178	2562	82	17.7	20.6	£1564
IC	BeamC	Worm	Drum/drum	6.40-15	190	3248	88	17.3	20.6	£1892
IC	BeamC	Worm	Drum/drum	6.50-15	189	3163	91	18.4	21.4	£2078
IC	BeamC	Worm	Drum/drum	7.00-14	189	2884	98	13.9	19.5	£1611
IC	BeamC	Worm	Drum/drum	7.00-14	190	2943	92	14.7	19.9	£1695
IC	BeamC	Worm	Disc/drum	7.35-14	195	3550	105	12.6	18.8	£2258
IC	BeamC	Worm	Disc/drum	7.75-14	198	3436	94	14.2	19.4	£2131
IC	Beam1/2E	Worm	Disc/drum	205-14	189	3395	119	9.4	16.9	£2852
IC	Beam1/2E	Worm	Disc/drum	7.75-14	189	3395	118	8.0	16.3	£3370
IC	BeamC	Worm	Disc/drum	7.75-14	208	3584	110	12.6	18.6	£2914
BeamC	BeamC	Worm	Disc/disc	205-16	176	3880	92	16.5	20.6	£18,109
BeamC	BeamC	Worm	Disc/disc	205-16	176	4525	94 (Est)	16.6	N/A	£27,889
BeamC	BeamC	Worm	Disc/disc	205-16	176	4525	95 (Est)	15.8	N/A	£25,905
BeamC	BeamC	Worm	Disc/disc	205-16	176	3880	99	12.9	18.7	£1998
BeamC	BeamC	Worm	Disc/disc	205-16	176	4249	96	14.4	19.5	£13,505
BeamC	BeamC	Worm	Disc/disc	205-16	176	4300	97 (Est)	N/A	N/A	£13,632
BeamC	BeamC	Worm	Disc/disc	205-16	176	4334	105	11.9	18.4	£18,696
BeamC	BeamC	Worm	Disc/disc	205R-16	176	4379	108	11.3	18.5	£25,506
BeamC	BeamC	Worm	Disc/disc	205R-16	176	4427	107	10.8	18.2	£28,055
BeamAir	BeamAir	Worm	Disc/disc	205R-16	183	4593	110	10.8	18.1	£39,995
IC	BeamC	R & P	Disc/drum	155-15	165	1756	93	14.4	19.9	£1165
IC	BeamC	R & P	Disc/drum	165-15	160	2212	109	9.9	17.6	£1156

Make and model	Production Figures	Years Built	Body Styles	Mechanical Layout	Engine Make (if not own)	Capacity/(cc)/Layout/Valves	BHP/rpm	Torque (lb.ft)/rpm	Transmission gearbox/automatic transmission
Rebel	700	1965–1972	Sal Est	F/R	—	OHV 598/4IL/	25/5250	31/3000	4-spd/-
						OHV 700/4IL/	31/5000	38/2500	4-spd/-
						OHV 748/4IL/	35/5500	38/3000	4-spd/-
Scimitar SE4	1,005	1964–1970	Spts Cpe	F/R	Ford	OHV 2553/6IL/	120/5000	140/2600	4-spd (+O/D)/-
						OHV 2495/V6/	112/4750	146/3000	4-spd (+O/D)/-
						OHV 2994/V6/	136/4750	192/3000	4-spd (+O/D)/Auto
Scimitar GTE	5,127	1968–1975	Spts Htch	F/R	Ford	OHV 2994/V6/	138/5000	172/3000	4-spd (+O/D)/Auto
Renault						OHV			
4CV	1,105,543 (Incl. R1052)	1947–1961	Sal Conv	R/R	—	760/4IL/ OHV	19/4000	33/1500	3-spd/-
						748/4IL/ OHV	21/5000	33/2000	3-spd/-
Fregate	168,383	1952–1960	Sal Est	F/R	—	1996/4IL/ OHV	57/4000	92/2250	4-spd/-
						2141/4IL/ OHV	77/4000 80/4000	121/2200 124/2500	4-spd/SemiAuto
Dauphine	2,150,738	1956–1968	Sal	R/R	—	845/4IL/ OHV	30/4250	43/2200	3-spd/-4-spd/-
Dauphine Gordini	Incl. above	1958–1964	Sal	R/R	—	845/OHV/ OHV	38/5000	46/3500	4-spd/-
Floride/ Caravelle	117,039	1958–1968	Cpe/ Conv	R/R	—	845/4IL/ OHV	36/5000	43/3300	4-spd/-
						956/4IL/ OHV	42/5200	55/2500	4-spd/-
						1108/4IL/ OHV	49/5100	65/2500	4-spd/-
4	8,135,424	1961–1992	Est	F/F	—	747/4IL/ OHV	27/4500	41/2000	3-spd/-
						845/4IL/ OHV	28/4700 30/4700 34/5000	49/2300 48/2300 42/2500	3-spd/- 4-spd/- 4-spd/-
						1108/4IL/ OHV	34/4000	55/2500	4-spd/-
8/8S	1,316,134	1962–1971	Sal	R/R	—	956/4IL/ OHV	42/5200	55/2500	4-spd/Auto
						1108/4IL/ OHV	45/4900 57/5500	65/2500 70/3000	4-spd/Auto 4-spd/Auto
8 Gordini/ Gordini 1300	12,203	1964–1970	Sal	R/R	—	1108/4IL/ OHV	95/6500	72/5000	4-spd/-
						1255/4IL/ OHV	103/6750	86/5000	5-spd/-
10	699,490	1969–1971	Sal	R/R	—	1289/4IL/ OHV	48/4800	72/2500	4-spd/-
						1108/4IL/ OHV	43/4600	57/3000	Auto/-
6	1,773,304	1968–1979	Htch	F/F	—	845/4IL/ OHV	34/5000	42/3000	4-spd/-
						1108/4IL/ OHV	45/5300 47/5500	58/3000 56/3000	4-spd/- 4-spd/-
16	1,846,000	1965–1979	Htch	F/F	—	1470/4IL/ OHV	59/5000	78/2800	4-spd/-
						1565/4IL/ OHV	67/5000 83/5750 65/5100 83/5750	84/3000 87/3500 83/3000 88/3500	4-spd/Auto 4-spd/Auto 4-spd/Auto 4-spd/Auto
						1647/4IL/ OHV	93/6000	95/4000	5-spd/Auto
12	2,865,079	1969–1980	Sal Est	F/F	—	1289/4IL/ OHV	54/5250 60/5800	69/3000 71/3500	4-spd/- 4-spd/-
Riley									
1½-litre	13,950	1946–1955	Sal Conv	F/R	—	1496/4IL/ OHV	55/4500	76/3000	4-spd/-
2½-litre	8,959	1946–1953	Sal Conv Spts	F/R	—	2443/4IL/ OHV	100/4500	136/2000	4-spd/-
Pathfinder/ 2.6	5,536/2,000	1953–1958	Sal	F/R	—	2443/4IL/ OHV	110/4400	134/3000	4-spd (+O/D)/-
						2639/6IL/	97/4750	135/2000	4-spd (+O/D)/Auto

Suspension Front	Rear	Steering	Brakes (Front/rear)	Wheels/model Tyres	Length (in)	Weight (lb, unladen)	Performance Top speed (mph)	0–60mph (sec)	Standing 1/4-mile (sec)	UK Total Price (£: at Launch)
IC	Beam1/2E	Worm	Drum/drum	5.20-12	138	1178	63	N/A	24.6	£525
IC	Beam1/2E	Worm	Drum/drum	5.50-12	138	1211	68	35.9	23.7	£592
IC	Beam1/2E	Worm	Drum/drum	5.50-12	138	1211	72	N/A (Est)	N/A	£845
IC	BeamC	R & P	Disc/drum	165-15	167	2200	117	11.4	18.0	£1292
IC	BeamC	R & P	Disc/drum	6.95-15	167	2305	111	12.3	18.5	£1395
IC	BeamC	R & P	Disc/drum	165-15	167	2305	121	8.9	16.9	£1516
IC	BeamC	R & P	Disc/drum	185-14	170	2500	117	10.7	17.4	£1759
IC	IC	Worm	Drum/drum	4.75-15	142	1344	57	N/A	27.6	£474
IC	IC	Worm	Drum/drum	5.20-15	142	1232	60	N/A	26.0	
IC	IC	Worm	Drum/drum	6.40-15	185	2940	78	26.9	23.2	£1288
IC	IC	Worm	Drum/drum	6.40-15	185	2800	84	22.2	22.3	£1404
IC	IC	R & P	Drum/drum	5.20-15	155	1344	66	45.7	25.4	£769
IC	IC	R & P	Drum/drum	145-15	155	1456	74	28.2	23.7	£898
IC	IC	R & P	Disc/disc / Drum/drum	145-380	168	1708	76	28.7	23.4	£1296
IC	IC	R & P	Disc/disc	145-380	168	1720	80	25.4	22.5	£1168
IC	IC	R & P	Disc/disc	5.30-14	168	1720	89	17.6	20.9	£974
ITor	ITor	R & P	Drum/drum	145-13	142	1275	60	N/A	27.1	£583
ITor	ITor	R & P	Drum/drum	145-13	144	1323	68	40.5	24.3	£539
ITor	ITor	R & P	Drum/drum	5.00-13	144	1393	66	38.1	24.6	£544
ITor	ITor	R & P	Drum/drum	135-13	144	1532	72 (Est)	N/A	N/A	
ITor	ITor	R & P	Drum/drum / Disc/drum	135-13	144	1626	72	25.7	22.6	£3050
IC	IC	R & P	Disc/disc	145-15	158	1568	82	21.9	21.8	£764
IC	IC	R & P	Disc/disc	135-380	158	1652	82	20.6	21.9	£675
IC	IC	R & P	Disc/disc	135-15	158	1652	90	16.5	20.7	£778
IC	IC	R & P	Disc/disc	135-380	157	1753	106	12.3	18.8	£984
IC	IC	R & P	Disc/disc	135-380	157	1881	108	10.9	17.7	£1231
IC	IC	R & P	Disc/disc	135-15	165	1758	86	17.0	20.5	£776
IC	IC	R & P	Disc/disc	135-15	165	1758	80 (Est)	N/A	N/A	£871
ITor	ITor	R & P	Drum/drum	135-330	152	1610	73	29.8	23.8	£735
ITor	ITor	R & P	Disc/drum	135-13	152	1770	81	18.9	21.4	£869
ITor	ITor	R & P	Disc/drum	145-13	152	1636	84	17.2	21.0	£1207
ITor	ITor	R & P	Disc/drum	145-14	167	2156	88	16.7	20.8	£949
ITor	ITor	R & P	Disc/drum	145-14	167	2229	90	15.7	20.5	£1159
ITor	ITor	R & P	Disc/drum	155-14	167	2271	101	12.3	19.2	£1085
ITor	ITor	R & P	Disc/drum	145-14	167	2229	90 (Est)	N/A	N/A	£1269
ITor	ITor	R & P	Disc/drum	155-14	167	2337	101 (Est)	N/A	N/A	£1487
ITor	ITor	R & P	Disc/drum	155-14	167	2237	104	12.4	18.6	£1895
IC	BeamC	R & P	Disc/drum	145-13	171	1940	89	16.5	20.6	£870
IC	BeamC	R & P	Disc/drum	145-13	171	2006	94	12.9	19.3	£1199
ITor	Beam1/2E	R & P	Drum/drum	5.75-16	179	2688	78	25.1	23.0	£710
ITor	Beam1/2E	R & P	Drum/drum	6.00-16	186	3136	95	15.2	19.8	£1125
ITor	BeamC	Worm	Drum/drum	6.70-16	183	3450	98	16.7	20.6	£1382
	Beam1/2E	Worm	Drum/drum	6.00-16						
ITor	Beam1/2E	Worm	Drum/drum	6.70-15	186	3610	93	17.4	20.6	£1411

Make and model	Production Figures	Years Built	Body Styles	Mechanical Layout	Engine Make (if not own)	Capacity/(cc)/Layout/Valves	BHP/rpm	Torque (lb.ft)/rpm	Transmission gearbox/automatic transmission
1.5	39,568	1957–1965	Sal	F/R	—	1489/4IL/OHV	62/4500	83/3000	4-spd/-
4/68 and 4/72	25,091	1959–1969	Sal	F/R	—	1489/4IL/OHV	64/4800	85/3300	4-spd/-
						1622/4IL/OHV	68/5000	89/2500	4-spd/Auto
Elf	30,912	1961–1969	Sal	F(Tr)/F	—	848/4IL/OHV	34/5500	44/2900	4-spd/-
						998/4IL/OHV	38/5250	52/2700	4-spd/Auto
Kestrel	21,529	1965–1969	Sal	F(Tr)/F	—	1098/4IL/OHV	55/5500	61/2500	4-spd/-
						1275/4IL/OHV	58/5250	69/3500	4-spd/Auto
							65/5750	71/3000	4-spd/Auto
							70/6000	77/3000	4-spd/Auto
Rochdale									
Olympic	Approx 400	1960–1972		F/R	BMC	1489/4IL/OHV	60/4800	83/3000	4-spd/-
					Ford	1498/4IL/OHV	78/5200	97/3600	4-spd/-
Rolls-Royce									
Silver Wraith	1,783	1946–1959	Limo Spl	F/R	—	4257/6IL/IOEV	N/Q	N/Q	4-spd/-
						4566/6IL/IOEV	N/Q	N/Q	4-spd/Auto
						4887/6IL/IOEV	N/Q	N/Q	4-spd/Auto
Silver Dawn	761	1949–1955	Sal	F/R	—	4556/6IL/IOEV	N/Q	N/Q	4-spd/Auto
Phantom IV	18	1950–1956	Limo	F/R	—	5675/8IL/IOEV	N/Q	N/Q	4-spd/Auto
Phantom V/VI	1,241	1959–1992	Limo	F/R	—	630/V8/OHV	N/Q	N/Q	Auto/-
						6750/V8/OHV	N/Q	N/Q	Auto/-
Silver Cloud I	2,359	1955–1959	Sal Spl	F/R	—	4887/6IL/OHV	N/Q	N/Q	Auto/-
Silver Cloud II/III	5,013	1959–1965	Sal Spl	F/R	—	6230/V8/OHV	N/Q	N/Q	Auto/-
							N/Q	N/Q	Auto/-
Silver Shadow I/II	27,915	1965–1980	Sal	F/R	—	6230/V8/OHV	N/Q	N/Q	Auto/-
						6750/V8/OHV	N/Q	N/Q	Auto/-
Silver Shadow Coupe/Corniche	7,355	1966–1994	Cpe Conv	F/R	—	6230/V8/OHV	N/Q	N/Q	Auto/-
						6750/V8/OHV	N/Q	N/Q	Auto/-
							N/Q	N/Q	Auto/-
Rover									
Ten/Twelve	26,500	1937–1948	Sal Conv	F/R	—	1389/4IL/OHV	48/4200	N/Q	4-spd/-
						1496/4IL/OHV	53/4200	N/Q	4-spd/-
Fourteen Sixteen	18,750	1937–1948	Sal	F/R	—	1901/6IL/OHV	N/Q	N/Q	4-spd/-
						2147/6IL/OHV	66/4600	N/Q	4-spd/-
P3	9,111	1948–1949	Sal	F/R	—	1595/4IL/IOEV	50/4000	84/2000	4-spd/-
						2103/6IL/IOEV	72/4000	111/2500	4-spd/-
P4	130,342	1949–1964	Sal	F/R	—	1997/4IL/IOEV	60/4000	101/2000	4-spd (+O/D)/-
						2103/6IL/IOEV	75/4200	111/2500	4-spd (+O/D)/-
						2230/6IL/IOEV	80/4500	113/1750	4-spd (+O/D)/-
						2286/4IL/OHV	77/4250	124/2500	4-spd (+O/D)/-
						2625/6IL/IOEV	102/4750	140/1500	4-spd/-
							104/4750	138/1500	4-spd (+O/D)/-
							123/5000	139/3000	4-spd (+O/D)-

Suspension Front	Rear	Steering	Brakes (Front/rear)	Wheels/model Tyres	Length (in)	Weight (lb, unladen)	Performance Top speed (mph)	0–60mph (sec)	Standing 1/4-mile (sec)	UK Total Price (£: at Launch)
ITor	Beam1/2E	R & P	Drum/drum	5.00-14 / 5.60-14	153	2060	84	17.4	20.5	£864
IC	Beam1/2E	Worm	Drum/drum	5.90-14	178	2507	84	20.6	21.9	£1028
IC	Beam1/2E	Worm	Drum/drum	5.90-14	178	2507	86	19.5	21.5	£1088
IRubber	IRubber	R & P	Drum/drum	5.20-10	129	1435	71	32.3	23.7	£694
IRubber	IRubber	R & P	Drum/drum	5.20-10	129	1395	77	24.1	22.4	£575
IHydroL	IHydroL					1456				
IHydroL	IHydroL	R & P	Disc/drum	5.20-12	147	1820	85	18.4	21.3	£781
IHydroL	IHydroL	R & P	Disc/drum	5.20-12	147	1820	88	17.3	20.7	£852
IHydroL	IHydroL	R & P	Disc/drum	5.20-12	147	1850	97 (Est)	N/A	N/A	£852
IHydroL	IHydroL	R & P	Disc/drum	5.20-12	147	1850	97	14.1	19.6	£953
ITor	BeamC	R & P	Drum/drum	5.50-14	147	1540	102	11.9	18.5	£670
ITor	BeamC	R & P	Disc/drum	5.50-14	147	1540	111	11.4	18.1	£775
IC	Beam1/2E	Worm	Drum/drum	6.50-17	206	4700	85 (Est)	24.0	N/A	£3802
IC	Beam1/2E	Worm	Drum/drum	7.00-16	208	5200	90 (Est)	N/A	N/A	£4190
IC	Beam1/2E	Worm	Drum/drum	7.00-16	208	5200	95 (Est)	N/A	N/A	£4695
IC	Beam1/2E	Worm	Drum/drum	6.50-16	200	4060	87	16.2	20.4	£3250
IC	Beam1/2E	Worm	Drum/drum	7.00-17	227	5000	95 (Est)	N/A	N/A	£N/Q
IC	Beam1/2E	Worm	Drum/drum	8.90-15	238	5600	101	13.8	19.4	£8905
IC	Beam1/2E	Worm	Drum/drum	8.90-15	238	6000	105 (Est)	N/A	N/A	£N/A
IC	Beam1/2E	Worm	Drum/drum	8.20-15	212	4480	106	13.0	18.8	£3385
IC	Beam1/2E	Worm	Drum/drum	8.20-15	212	4650	113	11.5	18.2	£5802
IC	Beam1/2E	Worm	Drum/drum	8.20-15	212	4650	116	10.8	17.7	£5517
IC	IC	Worm	Disc/disc	8.45-15	204	4660	115	10.9	17.6	£6670
IC	IC	Worm	Disc/disc	8.45-15	204	4660	117	10.2	17.5	£9272
		R & P (from 1977)		205-15 / 235/70-15	204	4930	119	9.4	17.7	£22,809
IC	IC	Worm	Disc/disc	8.45-15	204	4978	115 (Est)	N/A	N/A	£9849
IC	IC	Worm	Disc/disc	8.45-15	204	4816	120	9.6	17.1	£11,556
		R & P (from 1977)		205-15						
IC	IC	R & P	Disc/disc	235/70-15	204	4816	126	9.7	17.1	£73,168
Beam1/2E	Beam1/2E	Worm	Drum/drum	4.75-17	162	2800	65	N/A	N/A	£589
Beam1/2E	Beam1/2E	Worm	Drum/drum	5.25-17	170	2912	67	N/A	N/A	£646
Beam1/2E	Beam1/2E	Worm	Drum/drum	5.50-17	173	3136	72	41.3	N/A	£704
Beam1/2E	Beam1/2E	Worm	Drum/drum	5.50-17	173	3136	78	N/A	23.0	£742
IC	Beam1/2E	Worm	Drum/drum	5.25-17	169	2950	72	N/A	N/A	£1080
IC	Beam1/2E	Worm	Drum/drum	5.50-17	169	3070	75	29.4	N/A	£1106
IC	Beam1/2E	Worm	Drum/drum	6.00-15	178	3106	77	23.2	23.1	£1163
IC	Beam1/2E	Worm	Drum/drum	6.00-15	178	3265	78	26.5	22.9	£1106
IC	Beam1/2E	Worm	Drum/drum	6.00-15	178	3262	86	21.0	22.5	£1269
IC	Beam1/2E	Worm	Disc/drum	6.00-15	179	3246	86	22.8	23.4	£1365
IC	Beam1/2E	Worm	Disc/drum	6.00-15	179	3287	94	18.0	N/A	£1507
IC	Beam1/2E	Worm	Disc/drum	6.00-15	179	3267	92	17.6	21.1	£1538
IC	Beam1/2E	Worm	Disc/drum	6.00-15	179	3416	100	15.9	20.6	£1382

Make and model	Production Figures	Years Built	Body Styles	Mechanical Layout	Engine Make (if not own)	Capacity/(cc)/Layout/Valves	BHP/rpm	Torque (lb.ft)/rpm	Transmission gearbox/automatic transmission
						2638/6IL/ IOEV	90/4500	130/1500	4-spd (+O/D)/-
							93/4500	138/1750	
							108/4250	152/2500	4-spd (+O/D)/Auto
P5 3-litre	48,541	1958–1967	Sal	F/R	—	2995/6IL/ IOEV	115/4500	164/1500	4-spd (+O/D)/Auto
			Cpe				121/4800	160/2650	4-spd (+O/D)/Auto
							129/4750	161/3000	Auto/-
							134/5000	169/1750	4-spd (+O/D)/Auto
2000/TC	213,890 (Incl. 2200/TC)	1963–1973	Sal	F/R	—	1978/4IL/ OHC	89/5000	108/2500	4-spd/Auto
							110/5500	124/2750	4-spd/-
2200/TC	—	1974–1977	Sal	F/R	—	2205/4IL/ OHC	98/5000	126/2500	4-spd/Auto
							115/5000	135/3000	4-spd/-
3.5-litre (P5B)	20,600	1967–1973	Sal Cpe	F/R	—	3528/V8/ OHV	151/5200	201/2750	-/Auto
3500/3500S	79,057	1968–1976	Sal	F/R	—	3528/V8/ OHV	144/5000	197/2700	-/Auto
							143/5000	202/2700	
							150/5000	204/2700	4-spd/-

Saab

Make and model	Production Figures	Years Built	Body Styles	Mechanical Layout	Engine Make (if not own)	Capacity/(cc)/Layout/Valves	BHP/rpm	Torque (lb.ft)/rpm	Transmission gearbox/automatic transmission
96/95/ Sport/Monte Carlo	250,000 Est	1960–1968	Sal Est	F/F	—	841/3IL/ 2-Str	38/4250	59/3000	3-spd/4-spd/-
							40/5000	60/3000	3-spd/-
							55/5000	67/3800	4-spd/-
96 V4/95 V4	407,500 Est	1966–1979	Sal Est	F/F	—	1498/V4/ OHV	65/4700	85/2500	4-spd/-
99/90	614,021	1967–1985	Sal Htch	F/F	Triumph	1709/4IL/ OHC	80/5300	95/3200	4-spd/-
						1854/4IL/ OHC	86/5200	108/3000	4-spd/-
					—	1985/4IL/ OHC	95/5200	116/3500	4-spd/-
							110/5500	123/3700	4-spd/Auto
							100/5200	119/3500	4-spd/Auto
							108/5300	121/3300	4-spd/Auto
							118/5500	123/3700	4-spd/Auto

Simca

Make and model	Production Figures	Years Built	Body Styles	Mechanical Layout	Engine Make (if not own)	Capacity/(cc)/Layout/Valves	BHP/rpm	Torque (lb.ft)/rpm	Transmission gearbox/automatic transmission
Aronde	1,274,859	1951–1963	Sal Est	F/R	—	1221/4IL/ OHV	45/4400	57/2600	4-spd/-
			Cpe Conv			1290/4IL/ OHV	48/4500	65/2600	4-spd/-
							57/5200	74/2600	4-spd/-
							70/5200	80/2900	4-spd/-
Vedette	166,895	1955–1962	Sal Est	F/R	—	2353/V8/ SV	84/4800	112/2750	3-spd (+O/D)/-
1000	1,642,091 (All 1000-type sales)	1961–1978	Sal	R/R	—	944/4IL/ OHV	35/4800	47/2750	4-spd/Auto
							52/5400	55/3400	4-spd/Auto
							40/5800	47/2200	4-spd/-
						1118/4IL/ OHV	50/5600	61/2600	4-spd/-
						1294/4IL/ OHV	60/5400	71/2600	4-spd/-
1000 Coupe	10,011	1962–1967	Cpe	R/R	—	944/4IL/ OHV	40/5400	47/3400	4-spd/-
1200S Coupe	14,741	1967–1971	Cpe	R/R	—	1204/4IL/ OHV	80/6000	76/4500	4-spd/-
1300/ 1500/1501	1,342,907	1963–1976	Sal Est	F/R	—	1290/4IL/ OHV	62/5200	74/2600	4-spd/-
							70/5400	68/2600	4-spd/-
						1475/4IL/ OHV	81/5400	90/3000	4-spd/-
1100/ 1204S/ 1100 Special	N/A	1967–1979	Htch Est	F(Tr)/F	—	1118/4IL/ OHV	56/5800	60/3600	4-spd/-
							60/6000	62/3200	4-spd/-
						1204/4IL/ OHV	75/6000	70/3600	4-spd/-
						1294/4IL/ OHV	75/6000	76/3000	4-spd/-

Singer

Make and model	Production Figures	Years Built	Body Styles	Mechanical Layout	Engine Make (if not own)	Capacity/(cc)/Layout/Valves	BHP/rpm	Torque (lb.ft)/rpm	Transmission gearbox/automatic transmission
Nine Rdstr/4AB	Est 6,900	1939–1952	Spts	F/R	—	1074/4IL/ OHC	36/5000	48/2800	3-spd/4-spd/-
Ten/Twelve	11,595 (Postwar)	1938–1949	Sal	F/R	—	1194/4IL/ OHC	37/5000	52/2600	4-spd/-
						1525/4IL/ OHC	43/4000	72/2400	4-spd/-
SM1500/ Hunter	22,154	1949–1956	Sal	F/R	—	1506/4IL/ OHC	48/4200	79/2400	4-spd/-
						1497/4IL/ OHC	48/4200	79/2400	4-spd/-
							58/4600	77/2600	4-spd/-
						1497/4IL/ 2OHC	75/5250	85/3000	4-spd/-

Suspension Front	Rear	Steering	Brakes (Front/rear)	Wheels/model Tyres	Length (in)	Weight (lb, unladen)	Performance Top speed (mph)	0–60mph (sec)	Standing ¼-mile (sec)	UK Total Price (£: at Launch)
IC	Beam1/2E	Worm	Drum/drum	6.00-15	179	3200	91	18.4	21.1	£1297
IC	Beam1/2E	Worm	Drum/drum	6.00-15	179	3276	96	15.4	20.4	£1596
ITor	Beam1/2E	Worm	Drum/drum	6.70-15	187	3556	96	16.2	20.3	£1764
ITor	Beam1/2E	Worm	Disc/drum	6.70-15	187	3556	108	14.5	19.8	£1823
ITor	Beam1/2E	Worm	Disc/drum	6.70-15	187	3640	102	17.7	21.5	£1641
ITor	Beam1/2E	Worm	Disc/drum	6.70-15	187	3640	107	15.0	19.6	£1704
IC	DDC	Worm	Disc/disc	165-14	179	2760	104	14.6	19.4	£1264
IC	DDC	Worm	Disc/disc	165-14	179	2810	108	11.9	18.4	£1415
IC	DDC	Worm	Disc/disc	165-14	179	2822	101	13.4	19.4	£2019
IC	DDC	Worm	Disc/disc	165-14	181	2829	108	11.5	18.3	£2139
IC	Beam1/2E	Worm	Disc/drum	6.70-15	187	3498	108	12.4	18.3	£2009
IC	DDC	Worm	Disc/disc	185-14	180	2862	117	9.5	17.6	£1801
IC	DDC	Worm	Disc/disc	185-14	180	2868	122	9.1	16.8	£1988
IC	BeamC	R & P	Drum/drum	5.20-15	158	1764	72	25.6	23.6	£885
IC	BeamC	R & P	Drum/drum	5.20-15	162	1800	76	24.1	22.3	£729
IC	BeamC	R & P	Disc/drum	155-15	164	1904	88	19.1	21.2	£1059
IC	BeamC	R & P	Disc/drum	155-15	166	2275	92	16.5	20.0	£801
IC	BeamC	R & P	Disc/disc	155-15	171	2327	94	15.2	20.2	£1288
IC	BeamC	R & P	Disc/disc	155-15	171	2421	94	12.8	18.7	£1479
IC	BeamC	R & P	Disc/disc	155-15	171	2535	101	12.0	18.5	£1738
IC	BeamC	R & P	Disc/disc	155-15	171	2466	106	10.3	17.7	£1999
IC	BeamC	R & P	Disc/disc	165-15	171	2520	102	11.9	18.8	£2186
IC	BeamC	R & P	Disc/disc	165-15	178	2555	100	14.4	19.7	£3475
IC	BeamC	R & P	Disc/disc	175/70-15	171	2475	107	10.6	17.4	£4147
IC	Beam1/2E	Worm	Drum/drum	5.50-15 5.60-14	157	1914	74	28.6	23.6	£896
IC	Beam1/2E/C	Worm	Drum/drum	5.60-14	157	2044	78 (Est)	N/A	N/A	£799
IC	Beam1/2E/C	Worm	Drum/drum	5.60-14	162	2044	82	19.1	21.0	£925
IC	Beam1/2E/C	Worm	Drum/drum	5.60-14	166	2016	88 (Est)	N/A	N/A	£896
IC	Beam1/2E	Worm	Drum/drum	6.50-15	187	2716	91	18.4	21.0	£1338
ITrL	IC	Worm	Drum/drum	5.60-12	150	1568	74	27.0	23.5	£758
ITrL	IC	Worm	Drum/drum	5.60-12	150	1631	78	22.5	21.8	£640
ITrL	IC	Worm	Drum/drum	145-13	150	1589	81	21.7	22.1	£599
ITrL	IC	Worm	Drum/drum	145-13	150	1631	84	19.6	21.4	£780
ITrL	IC	Worm	Drum/drum	145-13	150	1752	95 (Claimed)	N/A	N/A	£896
ITrL	IC	Worm	Disc/disc	145-330	155	1755	87 (Claimed)	N/A	N/A	Special Order
ITrL	IC	Worm	Disc/disc	245-13	155	1965	107	N/A	18.0	£1493
IC	BeamC	Worm	Drum/drum	5.90-13	167	2116	84	23.3	22.9	£799
IC	BeamC	Worm	Disc/drum	165-13	167	2182	96	16.4	20.9	£1135
IC	BeamC	Worm	Disc/drum	5.90-13	167	2194	90	15.6	20.5	£919
ITor	ITor	R & P	Disc/drum	145-13	156	1962	80	19.6	21.7	£718
ITor	ITor	R & P	Disc/drum	145-13	156	2016	85	15.9	20.4	£899
ITor	ITor	R & P	Disc/drum	145-13	155	2070	95	13.6	19.3	£1039
ITor	ITor	R & P	Disc/drum	145-13	155	2070	95	13.2	18.4	£893
Beam1/2E	Beam1/2E	Worm	Drum/drum	5.00-16	150	1708	65	37.6	24.7	£493
IC	Beam1/2E	Worm	Drum/drum	5.00-16	152	1736	65	37.6	24.7	£620
Beam1/2E	Beam1/2E	Worm	Drum/drum	5.25-16	155	2240	62	N/A	N/A	£576
Beam1/2E	Beam1/2E	Worm	Drum/drum	5.50-16	166	2576	68	37.1	N/A	£768
IC	Beam1/2E	Worm	Drum/drum	5.50-16	174	2520	71	33.7	24.5	£799
IC	Beam1/2E	Worm	Drum/drum	5.50-16	174	2520	74	26.3	24.3	£1129
IC	Beam1/2E	Worm	Drum/drum	5.50-16	174	2688	76	23.5	22.5	£1168
IC	Beam1/2E	Worm	Drum/drum	5.50-16	174	2688	85 (Est)	N/A	N/A	£1218

Make and model	Production Figures	Years Built	Body Styles	Mechanical Layout	Engine Make (if not own)	Capacity/(cc)/Layout/Valves	BHP/rpm	Torque (lb.ft)/rpm	Transmission gearbox/automatic transmission
SM Rdstr	3,440	1951–1955	Spts	F/R	—	1497/4IL/	48/4600	72/2200	4-spd/-
						OHC	58/4600	77/2600	4-spd/-
Gazelle I - VI	83,061	1956–1967	Sal Est	F/R	—	1497/4IL/ OHC	49/4500	77/2000	4-spd (+O/D)/-
			Conv			1494/4IL/	56/4600	83/2300	4-spd (+O/D)/Auto
						OHV	60/4600	83/2300	
						1592/4IL/	53/4100	87/2100	4-spd (+O/D)/Auto
						OHV	58/4000	86/2500	4-spd (+O/D)/Auto
						1725/4IL/	59/4200	92/2200	4-spd (+O/D)/Auto
						OHV	65/4800	98/2400	
Vogue I - IV	47,769	1961–1966	Sal Est	F/R	—	1592/4IL/ OHV	62/4800	86/2800	4-spd (+O/D)/Auto
							78/5000	91/3500	4-spd (+O/D)/Auto
						1725/4IL/ OHV	85/5500	106/3500	4-spd (+O/D)/Auto
Chamois/ Chamois Sport	40,678/4,149	1964–1970	Sal	R/R	—	875/4IL/ OHC	37/4800	49/2600	4-spd/-
							51/6100	53/4300	4-spd/-
Chamois Coupe	4,971	1967–1970	Cpe	R/R	—	875/4IL/ OHC	37/4800	49/2600	4-spd/-
Gazelle	31,482	1967–1970	Sal	F/R	—	1496/4IL/ OHV	54/4600	73/2500	4-spd/-
						1725/4IL/ OHV	61/4700	85/2600	-/Auto
Vogue	47,655	1966–1970	Sal Est	F/R	—	1725/4IL/ OHV	61/4700	85/2600	4-spd/Auto

Skoda

Make and model	Production Figures	Years Built	Body Styles	Mechanical Layout	Engine Make (if not own)	Capacity/(cc)/Layout/Valves	BHP/rpm	Torque (lb.ft)/rpm	Transmission gearbox/automatic transmission
440	84,792	1954–1959	Sal Est	F/R	—	1089/4IL/ OHV	40/4200	51/2800	4-spd/-
450/Felicia Convertible	15,864	1958–1964	Conv	F/R	—	1089/4IL/ OHV	53/5000	55/3500	4-spd/-
						1221/4IL/ OHV	47/4700	63/3000	4-spd/-
Octavia	279,724	1959–1964	Sal Est	F/R	—	1089/4IL/ OHV	40/4200	51/2800	4-spd/-
						1221/4IL/ OHV	47/4700	63/3000	4-spd/-
1000MB/ S100/ S110 series	1,563,175	1964–1977	Sal	R/R	—	988/4IL/ OHV	43/4500	52/3000	4-spd/-
						1107/4IL/ OHV	46/4600	60/3000	4-spd/-
							52/4650	64/3500	4-spd/-
S110R	56,902	1968–1977	Cpe	R/R	—	1107/4IL/ OHV	52/4650	64/3500	4-spd/-

Standard

Make and model	Production Figures	Years Built	Body Styles	Mechanical Layout	Engine Make (if not own)	Capacity/(cc)/Layout/Valves	BHP/rpm	Torque (lb.ft)/rpm	Transmission gearbox/automatic transmission
8hp	53,099 (Post-war)	1938–1948	Sal Conv	F/R	—	1009/4IL/ SV	28/4000	44/2200	4-spd/-
12/14hp	32,188 (Post-war)	1937–1948	Sal Conv	F/R	—	1609/4IL/ SV	44/4000	69/2200	4-spd/-
						1776/4IL/ SV	49/3800	78/2200	4-spd/-
Vanguard I	184,799	1948–1953	Sal Est	F/R	—	2088/4IL/ OHV	68/4200	108/2000	3-spd (+O/D)/-
Vanguard II	83,047	1953–1955	Sal Est	F/R	—	2088/4IL/ OHV	68/4200	108/2000	3-spd (+O/D)/-
						2092/4IL/ OHV Diesel	40/3000	85/1500	3-spd (+O/D)/-
Vanguard III/ Vignale	63,470	1955–1961	Sal Est	F/R	—	2088/4IL/ OHV	62/4000	113/2000	3-spd (+O/D)/Auto/ 4-spd (+O/D)
Vanguard Sportsman	901	1956–1957	Sal	F/R	—	2088/4IL/ OHV	90/4500	122/2500	3-spd (+O/D)/-
8/10	300,817	1953–1960	Sal Est	F/R	—	803/4IL/ OHV	26/4500	39/2800	4-spd/-
							30/4500	41/2800	4-spd/-
							33/5000	42/2700	4-spd (+O/D)/-
						948/4IL/ OHV	33/4500	46/2500	4-spd/-
							35/4500	48/2800	4-spd/SemiAuto
							37/5000	51/2750	
Pennant	42,910	1957–1959	Sal Est	F/R	—	948/4IL/ OHV	37/5000	51/2750	4-spd (+O/D)/ SemiAuto
Ensign/ de Luxe	21,170	1957–1963	Sal Est	F/R	—	1670/4IL/ OHV	60/4000	91/2200	4-spd (+O/D)/Auto
						2138/4IL/ OHV	75/4100	126/2050	4-spd (+O/D)/-
Vanguard Six	9,953	1960–1963	Sal Est	F/R	—	1998/6IL/ OHV	80/4400	116/2500	3-spd (+O/D)/ (+O/D)/Auto

Suspension Front	Rear	Steering	Brakes (Front/rear)	Wheels/model Tyres	Length (in)	Weight (lb, unladen)	Performance Top speed (mph)	0–60mph (sec)	Standing 1/4-mile (sec)	UK Total Price (£: at Launch)
IC	Beam1/2E	Worm	Drum/drum	5.00-16	151	1820	73	23.6	22.0	£724
IC	Beam1/2E	Worm	Drum/drum	5.00-16	151	1820	77	20.2	21.6	£829
IC	Beam1/2E	Worm	Drum/drum	5.60-15	164	2255	78	23.6	22.9	£898
IC	Beam1/2E	Worm	Drum/drum	5.60-15	164	2255	82	21.4	22.4	£898
							84	23.9	22.2	£848
IC	Beam1/2E	Worm	Drum/drum	5.60-15	164	2255	79	23.6	22.8	£840
IC	Beam1/2E	Worm	Disc/drum	6.00-13	164	2255	79	24.9	22.5	£814
IC	Beam1/2E	Worm	Disc/drum	6.00-13	164	2255	82	20.5	21.8	£757
IC	Beam1/2E	Worm	Disc/drum	5.90-13	165	2410	83	20.9	21.5	£929
IC	Beam1/2E	Worm	Disc/drum	6.00-13	165	2410	90	14.1	19.9	£845
IC	Beam1/2E	Worm	Disc/drum	6.00-13	165	2410	92 (Est)	N/A	N/A	£896
IC	IC	R & P	Drum/drum	5.50-12	139	1530	78	25.4	22.8	£582
IC	IC	R & P	Drum/drum	155-12	141	1640	90	16.3	20.2	£665
IC	IC	R & P	Drum/drum	5.50-12	141	1530	78	22.1	21.9	£665
IC	Beam1/2E	Worm	Disc/drum	5.60-13	168	2035	83	17.8	20.9	£798
IC	Beam1/2E	Worm	Disc/drum	5.60-13	168	2035	90	14.6	19.6	£757
IC	Beam1/2E	Worm	Disc/drum	5.60-13	168	2035	90	14.6	19.6	£911
ITrL	ITrL	Worm	Drum/drum	5.50-16	177	2156	71 (Claimed)	N/A	N/A	£841
IC	ITrL	Worm	Drum/drum	5.90-15	160	2009	81	24.5	22.2	£809
IC	ITrL	Worm	Drum/drum	5.90-15	160	1926	87 (Claimed)	N/A	N/A	£639
IC	ITrL	Worm	Drum/drum	5.50-15	160	1960	75	36.6	24.3	£745
IC	ITrL	Worm	Drum/drum	5.50-15	160	1984	78	28.4	22.4	£593
IC	IC	Worm	Drum/drum	6.00-14 155-14	163	1596	75	30.8	23.6	£580
IC	IC	Worm	Drum/drum	155-14	163	1800	82	21.8	21.8	£683
IC	IC	Worm	Disc/drum	155-14	163	1844	83	19.6	21.6	£846
IC	IC	Worm	Disc/drum	155-14	163	1847	86	17.7	21.0	£1050
ITrL	Beam1/2E	Worm	Drum/drum	4.75-16	139	1680	58	N/A	26.5	£314
ITrL	Beam1/2E	Worm	Drum/drum	5.50-16	165	2492	65	36.0	N/A	£480
ITrL	Beam1/2E	Worm	Drum/drum	5.50-16	165	2520	68	32.8	24.5	£576
IC	Beam1/2E	Worm	Drum/drum	5.50-16	164	2654	77	22.0	22.4	£544
IC	Beam1/2E	Worm	Drum/drum	6.00-16	168	2800	80	19.9	21.6	£919
IC	Beam1/2E	Worm	Drum/drum	6.00-16	168	2996	66	68.0	28.4	£1042
IC	Beam1/2E	Worm	Drum/drum	5.50-16	172	2604	77	22.2	22.2	£850
IC	Beam1/2E	Worm	Drum/drum	5.50-16	174	2772	91	19.2	21.4	£1231
IC	Beam1/2E	Worm	Drum/drum	5.20-13	143	1484	61	N/A	25.8	£481
IC	Beam1/2E	Worm	Drum/drum	5.20-13	143	1652	66	39.8	25.2	£616
IC	Beam1/2E	Worm	Drum/drum	5.60-13	143	1680	69	38.3	25.5	£581
IC	Beam1/2E	Worm	Drum/drum	5.60-13	142	1745	66	34.9	25.0	£729
IC	Beam1/2E	Worm	Drum/drum	5.90-15	172	2531	78	24.4	22.5	£900
IC	Beam1/2E	Worm	Drum/drum	5.90-15	172	2660	88	18.2	21.4	£906
IC	Beam1/2E	Worm	Drum/drum	5.90-15	172	2660	87	17.0	21.3	£1021

Make and model	Production Figures	Years Built	Body Styles	Mechanical Layout	Engine Make (if not own)	Capacity/ (cc)/Layout/ Valves	BHP/ rpm	Torque (lb.ft)/rpm	Transmission gearbox/automatic transmission
Steyr-Puch									
650TRII	N/A	1964–1968	Sal	R/R	—	660/2HO/ OHV AirC	36/5500	39/5000	4-spd/-
Studebaker									
Avanti **	4,643	1962–1964	Cpe	F/R	—	4736/V8/ OHV	290/N/Q	N/Q	4-spd/-
Subaru									
1600 Leone	1,269,000	1970–1979	Sal	F/F	—	1595/4HO/ OHV	65/5200	83/2400	4-spd/-
			Cpe	(F/4 on Estate)			70/5200	83/2400	4-spd/-
			Est				77/5600	83/3600	5-spd/-
Sunbeam									
Alpine	3,000	1953–1955	Spts	F/R	—	2267/4IL/ OHV	80/4200	124/1800	4-spd (+O/D)/-
Mk III	Est. 2,250	1954–1957	Sal Conv	F/R	—	2267/4IL/ OHV	80/4200	124/1800	4-spd (+O/D)/-
Rapier	68,809	1955–1967	Sal Conv	F/R	—	1390/4IL/ OHV	63/5000 67/5400	73/3000 74/3000	4-spd (+O/D)/-
						1494/4IL/ OHV	68/5200 73/5400	81/3000 83/3500	4-spd (+O/D)/-
						1592/4IL/ OHV	75/5100 79/5000	88/3900 91/3500	4-spd (+O/D)/-
						1725/4IL/ OHV	85/5500	99/3500	4-spd (+O/D)/-
Alpine	69,251	1959–1968	Spts	F/R	—	1494/4IL/ OHV	78/5300	89/3400	4-spd (+O/D)/-
						1592/4IL/ OHV	80/5000 77/5000	94/3800 91/3500	4-spd (+O/D)/-
							82/5200	94/3800	4-spd (+O/D)/Auto
						1725/4IL/ OHV	93/5500	103/3700	4-spd (+O/D)/-
Tiger	7,066	1964–1967	Spts	F/R	Ford-USA	4261/V8/ OHV	164/4400	258/2200	4-spd/-
						4727/V8/ OHV	200/4400	282/2400	4-spd/-
Imp Sport	Est. 10,000	1967–1976	Sal	R/R	—	875/4IL/ OHC	51/6100	53/4300	4-spd/-
Stiletto	Est. 10,000	1967–1973	Cpe	R/R	—	875/4IL/ OHC	51/6100	53/4300	4-spd/-
Rapier/H120/ Alpine	46,204	1967–1976	Cpe	F/R	—	1725/4IL/ OHV	76/5100 93/5200 72/5500	93/3300 106/4000 90/3000	4-spd (+O/D)/Auto 4-spd (+O/D)/- 4-spd (+O/D)/Auto
Vogue	N/A	1970	Sal Est	F/R	—	1725/4IL/ OHV	72/5000	90/3000	4-spd (+O/D)/Auto
Sunbeam-Talbot									
Ten	4,719	1938–1948	Sal Conv	F/R	—	1185/4IL/ SV	41/4500	58/2700	4-spd/-
2-litre	Est. 1,500	1939–1948	Sal Conv	F/R	—	1944/4IL/ SV	56/3800	97/2000	4-spd/-
80/90	23,881	1948–1954	Sal Conv	F/R	—	1185/4IL/ OHV	47/4800	61/3000	4-spd/-
						1944/4IL/ OHV	64/4100	101/2400	4-spd/-
						2267/4IL/ OHV	70/4000 77/4100	113/2400 113/2400	4-spd/- 4-spd/-
Swallow									
Doretti	250	1954–1955	Spts	F/R	Triumph	1991/4IL/ OHV	90/4800	117/3000	4-spd (+O/D)/-
Tornado									
Tempest	Est 15	1960–1962	Spts Cpe	F/R	Ford	997/4IL/ OHV	39/5000	56/2700	4-spd/-
					Ford	1340/4IL/ OHV	75/5000	79/4000	4-spd/-
Toyota									
Corona	1,788,000 (Incl. 1600S and 1900 Mk II)	1965–1972	Sal Est	F/R	—	1490/4IL/ OHV	74/5000	85/2600	4-spd/-

Suspension Front	Rear	Steering	Brakes (Front/rear)	Wheels/model Tyres	Length (in)	Weight (lb, unladen)	Performance Top speed (mph)	0–60mph (sec)	Standing 1/4-mile (sec)	UK Total Price (£: at Launch)
IC	IC	Worm	Drum/drum	135-12	117	1100	78	20.7	21.2	£699
IC	Beam1/2E	Worm	Disc/drum	6.70-15	192	3360	120	8.8	16.6	£2941
IC	ITor	R & P	Disc/drum	155-13	159	2184	87	16.7	20.7	£2597
IC	ITor	R & P	Disc/drum	155-13	158	1864	97	13.4	19.3	£2726
IC	ITor	R & P	Disc/drum	155-13	158	1885	97	12.1	18.7	£3101
IC	Beam1/2E	Worm	Drum/drum	5.50-16	168	2900	95	18.9	21.1	£1269
IC	Beam1/2E	Worm	Drum/drum	5.50-16	168	2950	91	18.4	21.4	£1127
IC	Beam1/2E	Worm	Drum/drum	5.60-15	161	2280	85	21.7	22.4	£1044
							85	19.4	21.5	£1044
IC	Beam1/2E	Worm	Drum/drum	5.60-15	163	2280	90	20.2	21.1	£1044
			Disc/drum			2340	92	16.5	20.7	£986
IC	Beam1/2E	Worm	Disc/drum	5.60-15	163	2340	90	19.3	21.8	£1000
				6.00-13	163	2300	92	17.0	20.8	£877
IC	Beam1/2E	Worm	Disc/drum	6.00-13	163	2300	95	14.1	19.5	£908
IC	Beam1/2E	Worm	Disc/drum	5.60-13	156	2135	98	14.0	19.8	£972
IC	Beam1/2E	Worm	Disc/drum	5.60-13	156	2135	97	14.8	19.7	£986
				5.90-13		2220	98	14.9	19.8	£840
IC	Beam1/2E	Worm	Disc/drum	5.90-13	156	2220	98	13.6	19.1	£878
IC	Beam1/2E	R & P	Disc/drum	5.90-13	158	2525	117	9.5	17.0	£1446
IC	Beam1/2E	R & P	Disc/drum	5.90-13	158	2525	122	7.5	N/A	£N/A
IC	IC	R & P	Drum/drum	155-12	141	1640	90	16.3	20.2	£665
IC	IC	R & P	Drum/drum	155-12	141	1625	87	17.6	20.5	£726
IC	Beam1/2E	Worm	Disc/drum	155-13	173	2275	103	12.8	18.7	£1200
IC	Beam1/2E	Worm	Disc/drum	155-13	173	2300	105	10.3	17.7	£1599
IC	Beam1/2E	Worm	Disc/drum	6.00-13	173	2220	91	14.6	19.9	£1086
IC	Beam1/2E	Worm	Disc/drum	5.60-13	168	2035	90	14.6	19.6	£1070
Beam1/2E	Beam1/2E	Worm	Drum/drum	5.25-16	156	2184	67	38.7	25.2	£620
Beam1/2E	Beam1/2E	Worm	Drum/drum	5.25-16	159	2492	70	29.1	23.9	£799
Beam1/2E	Beam1/2E	Worm	Drum/drum	5.50-16	168	2605	71	31.4	24.4	£889
Beam1/2E	Beam1/2E	Worm	Drum/drum	5.50-16	168	2830	77	25.0	23.1	£991
IC	Beam1/2E	Worm	Drum/drum	5.50-16	168	2905	86	24.3	23.0	£991
IC	Beam1/2E	Worm	Drum/drum	5.50-16	168	2905	87	20.8	22.2	£1170
IC	Beam1/2E	Worm	Drum/drum	5.50-15	156	2156	100	12.3	19.1	£1102
IC	BeamC	R & P	Drum/drum	5.60-13	150	992	87 (Claimed)	N/A	N/A	£1167
IC	IC	R & P	Disc/drum	5.90-13	150	1250	102	10.1	17.8	£1299
IC	Beam1/2E	Worm	Drum/drum	5.60-13	161	2156	87	17.2	20.3	£777

Make and model	Production Figures	Years Built	Body Styles	Mechanical Layout	Engine Make (if not own)	Capacity/ (cc)/Layout/ Valves	BHP/ rpm	Torque (lb.ft)/rpm	Transmission gearbox/automatic transmission
Corona 1600S	See above	1965–1968	Sal Cpe	F/R	—	1587/4IL/ OHV	95/5800	95/4200	4-spd/-
Corona 1900 Mk II	See above	1969–1972	Sal Cpe	F/R	—	1858/4IL/ OHC	100/5500 124/6000	108/3600 121/4000	4-spd/- 4-spd/-
Crown	352,882	1969–1972	Sal Est	F/R	—	2253/6IL/ OHC	115/5200	127/3600	Auto/-
Corolla 1100	Est. 859,000	1966–1970	Sal Cpe Est	F/R	—	1077/4IL/ OHV	60/6000	62/3800	4-spd/-
Corolla 1200	N/A	1970–1978	Sal Est	F/R	—	1166/4IL/ OHV	73/6000 83/6600	75/3800 75/4600	4-spd/- 4-spd/-
Carina	1,026,068	1970–1977	Cpe Sal Cpe	F/R	—	1588/4IL/ OHV	75/5200	85/3800	4-spd/Auto
Celica	1,210,951	1970–1977	Cpe Cpe Htch	F/R	—	1588/4IL/ OHV	105/6000	101/4200	4-spd/5-spd/-
						1588/4IL/ 2OHC	124/6400	113/5200	5-spd/-
						1968/4IL/ OHC	95/5000	105/3600	5-spd/Auto
Land-Cruiser	N/A	1966–1980	Ute	F/4	—	4230/6IL/ OHV	135/3600	210/1800	4-spd/-

Trident

Make and model	Production Figures	Years Built	Body Styles	Mechanical Layout	Engine Make (if not own)	Capacity/ (cc)/Layout/ Valves	BHP/ rpm	Torque (lb.ft)/rpm	Transmission gearbox/automatic transmission
Clipper/ Venturer/ Tycoon	Approx 225	1967–1978	Spts Cpe Conv	F/R	Ford	2994/V6/ OHV	138/5000	174/3000	4-spd (+O/D)/Auto
					Triumph	2498/6IL/ OHV	152/5500	158/3000	Auto/-
					Chrysler	5562/V8/ OHV	243/4800	290/3600	Auto/-

Triumph

Make and model	Production Figures	Years Built	Body Styles	Mechanical Layout	Engine Make (if not own)	Capacity/ (cc)/Layout/ Valves	BHP/ rpm	Torque (lb.ft)/rpm	Transmission gearbox/automatic transmission
1800/2000/ Renown	15,491	1946–1954	Sal Limo	F/R	—	1776/4IL/ OHV	63/4500	92/2000	4-spd/-
						2088/4IL/ OHV	68/4200	108/2000	3-spd(+ O/D)/-
1800/2000 Roadster	4,501	1946–1949	Conv	F/R	—	1776/4IL/ OHV	63/4500	92/2000	4-spd/-
						2088/4IL/ OHV	68/4200	108/2000	3-spd/-
Mayflower	34,000	1950–1953	Sal Conv	F/R	—	1247/4IL/ SV	38/4200	58/2000	3-spd/-
TR2/TR3/ TR3A/TR3B	83,572	1953–1962	Spts	F/R	—	1991/4IL/ OHV	90/4800 95/4800 100/5000	117/3000 117/3000 117/3000	4-spd (+O/D)/- 4-spd (+O/D)/- 4-spd (+O/D)/-
						2138/4IL/ OHV	100/4600	127/3350	4-spd (+O/D)/-
TR4	40,253	1961–1965	Spts	F/R	—	1991/4IL/ OHV	100/5000	117/3000	4-spd (+O/D)/-
						2138/4IL/ OHV	100/4600	127/3350	4-spd (+O/D)/-
TR4A	28,465	1965–1967	Spts	F/R	—	2138/4IL/ OHV	104/4700	132/3000	4-spd (+O/D)/-
TR5	2,947	1967–1968	Spts	F/R	—	2498/6IL/ OHV	150/5500	164/3500	4-spd (+O/D)/-
TR6	91,850	1968–1976	Spts	F/R	—	2498/6IL/ OHV	150/5500 124/5000	164/3500 143/3500	4-spd (+O/D)/-
Herald/1200	384,531	1959–1970	Sal Cpe Conv	F/R	—	948/4IL/ OHV	35/4500 45/6000	51/2750 51/4200	4-spd/- 4-spd/-
						1147/4IL/ OHV	39/4500 48/5200	61/2250 62/2500	4-spd/- 4-spd/-
Herald 12/50/ 13/60	135,917	1962–1971	Est Sal Conv Est	F/R	—	1147/4IL/ OHV	51/5200	63/2600	4-spd/-
						1296/4IL/ OHV	61/5000	73/3000	4-spd/-
Vitesse 1600/ 2-litre	51,212 (incl. Mk 2)	1962–1968	Sal Conv	F/R	—	1596/6IL/ OHV	70/5000	92/2800	4-spd (+O/D)/-
						1998/6IL/ OHV	95/5000	117/3000	4-spd (+O/D)/-
Vitesse 2-litre Mk II		1968–1971	Sal Conv	F/R	—	1998/6IL/ OHV	104/5300	117/3000	4-spd (+O/D)/-
Spitfire 1,	148,482	1962–1970	Spts	F/R	—	1147/4IL/	63/5750	67/3500	4-spd (+O/D)/-

Suspension Front	Rear	Steering	Brakes (Front/rear)	Wheels/model Tyres	Length (in)	Weight (lb,unladen)	Performance Top speed (mph)	0–60mph (sec)	Standing 1/4-mile (sec)	UK Total Price (£: at Launch)
IC	Beam1/2E	Worm	Disc/drum	5.60-13	161	2161	103	14.1	19.3	£1077
IC	Beam1/2E	Worm	Disc/drum	165-13	170	2320	99	13.5	19.2	£1196
IC	Beam1/2E	Worm	Disc/drum	165-13	170	2290	102	12.9	19.0	£1559
IC	BeamC	Worm	Disc/drum	6.95-14	184	2888	96	16.0	20.1	£1458
IC	Beam1/2E	Worm	Drum/drum	155-12	151	1624	85	16.3	20.4	£787
IC	Beam1/2E	Worm	Disc/drum	6.00-12	155	1655	90 (Est)	N/A	N/A	£949
IC	Beam1/2E	Worm	Disc/drum	155-12	155	1715	95	14.3	19.7	£1109
IC	BeamC	Worm	Disc/drum	165-13	164	2106	98	12.2	19.0	£1185
IC	BeamC	Worm	Disc/drum	165-13	160	2128	105	11.5	18.2	£1362
IC	BeamC	Worm	Disc/drum	165-13	164	2215	113	9.3	17.1	£2345
IC	BeamC	Worm	Disc/drum	165-14	167	2356	103	12.3	18.4	£2780
Beam1/2E	Beam1/2E	Worm	Drum/drum	7.50-16	183	4301	91	16.3	20.3	£4178
IC	IC	R & P	Disc/drum	185-15	165	N/Q	120 (Est)	N/A	N/A	£2400
IC	IC	R & P	Disc/drum	185-15	165	N/Q	125 (Est)	N/A	N/A	£3232
IC	Ic	R & P	Disc/drum	205-15	165	N/Q	137 (Est)	N/A	N/A	£3456
ITrL	Beam1/2E	Worm	Drum/drum	5.75-16	175	2828	75	29.1	N/A	£889
ITrL	Beam1/2E	Worm	Drum/drum	5.75-16	175	2828	75	25.1	23.8	£991
IC	Beam1/2E	Worm	Drum/drum	5.75-16	175	2828	75	25.1	23.8	£991
				5.75-16	181	2835/3024	74	23.4	23.0	£1440
ITrL	Beam1/2E	Worm	Drum/drum	5.75-16	169	2541	77	25.2	23.4	£889
IC	Beam1/2E	Worm	Drum/drum	5.75-16	169	2828	77	24.8	22.6	£991
IC	Beam1/2E	Worm	Drum/drum	5.00-15	154	2016	63	N/A	26.1	£480
IC	Beam1/2E	Worm	Drum/drum	5.50-15	151	1848	103	11.9	18.7	£787
IC	Beam1/2E	Worm	Drum/drum	5.50-15	151	1988	102	12.5	18.7	£976
IC	Beam1/2E	Worm	Disc/drum	5.50-15	151	1988	105 (Est)	N/A	N/A	£1021
IC	Beam1/2E	Worm	Disc/drum	5.50-15	151	2050	105 (Est)	N/A	N/A	—
IC	Beam1/2E	R & P	Disc/drum	5.90-15	154	2128	105 (Est)	N/A	N/A	£1095
IC	Beam1/2E	R & P	Disc/drum	5.90-15	154	2184	109	10.9	18.1	£1095
IC	IC (Beam1/2E - USA)	R & P	Disc/drum	6.95-15	154	2240	109	11.4	18.5	£968
IC	IC	R & P	Disc/drum	165-15	154	2268	120	8.8	16.8	£1212
IC	IC	R & P	Disc/drum	165-15	159	2473	119	8.2	16.3	£1334
IC	ITrL	R & P	Drum/drum	5.20-13	153	1764 to	71	31.1	24.6	£702
IC	ITrL	R & P	Drum/drum Disc/drum	5.20-13	153	1918	79	23.2	22.4	£731
IC	ITrL	R & P	Drum/drum	5.20-13	153	1771	74	28.6	23.4	£708
IC	ITrL	R & P	Disc/drum	5.20-13	153	1841	77	25.8	22.3	£627
IC	ITrL	R & P	Disc/drum	5.20-13	153	1855 to 1988	78	25.2	22.1	£635
IC	ITrL	R & P	Disc/drum	5.20-13	153	1876	84	17.7	20.9	£700
IC	ITrL	R & P	Disc/drum	5.60-13	153	2004	89	17.6	21.2	£839
IC	ITrL	R & P	Disc/drum	5.60-13	153	2085	97	12.6	18.6	£839
IC	ITrL	R & P	Disc/drum	155-13	153	2044	101	11.3	18.1	£951
IC	ITrL	R & P	Disc/drum	5.20-13	145	1568	91	15.4	20.3	£730

Make and model	Production Figures	Years Built	Body Styles	Mechanical Layout	Engine Make (if not own)	Capacity/(cc)/Layout/Valves	BHP/rpm	Torque (lb.ft)/rpm	Transmission gearbox/automatic transmission
2 and 3						OHV	67/6000	67/3750	4-spd (+O/D)/-
						1296/4IL/ OHV	75/6000	75/4000	4-spd (+O/D)/-
Spitfire Mk IV/1500	165,850	1970–1980	Spts	F/R	—	1296/4IL/ OHV	63/6000	69/3500	4-spd (+O/D)/-
						1493/4IL/ OHV	71/5500	82/3000	4-spd (+O/D)/-
2000 (Mk I)	120,645	1963–1969	Sal Est	F/R	—	1998/6IL/ OHV	90/5000	117/2900	4-spd (+O/D)/Auto
2.5PI	9,029	1968–1969	Sal Est	F/R	—	2498/6IL/ OHV	132/5500	153/2000	4-spd (+O/D)/Auto
2000 Mk II/ 2500TC/S	139,524	1969–1977	Sal Est	F/R	—	1998/6IL/ OHV	84/5000	100/2900	4-spd (+O/D)/Auto
							91/4750	110/3300	
						2498/6IL/ OHV	99/4700	133/3000	4-spd (+O/D)/Auto
							106/4700	139/3000	4-spd (+O/D)/Auto
2.5 PI Mk 2	47,455	1969–1975	Sal Est	F/R	—	2498/6IL/ OHV	132/5500	153/2000	4-spd (+O/D)/Auto
1300/1300 TC/1500	214,703	1965–1973	Sal	F/F	—	1296/4IL/ OHV	61/5000	73/3000	4-spd/-
							75/6000	75/4000	4-spd/-
						1493/4IL/ OHV	61/5000	81/2700	4-spd/-
							65/5000	80/3000	4-spd/-
GT6 Mk I/ Mk II	27,884	1966–1970	Spts Cpe	F/R	—	1998/6IL/ OHV	95/5000	117/3000	4-spd (+O/D)/-
							104/5300	117/3000	
GT6 Mk III	13,042	1970–1973	Spts Cpe	F/R	—	1998/6IL/ OHV	104/5300	117/3000	4-spd (+O/D)/-
Toledo 1300/ 1500	119,182	1970–1976	Sal	F/R	—	1296/4IL/ OHV	58/5300	70/3000	4-spd/-
Stag	25,939	1970–1977	Conv Cpe	F/R	—	2997/V8/ OHC	145/5500	170/3500	4-spd + O/D/Auto

Turner

Make and model	Production Figures	Years Built	Body Styles	Mechanical Layout	Engine Make (if not own)	Capacity/(cc)/Layout/Valves	BHP/rpm	Torque (lb.ft)/rpm	Transmission gearbox/automatic transmission
Sports	Approx 660	1955–1966	Spts	F/R	BMC	948/4IL/ OHV	60/5800	N/A	4-spd/-
				F/R	Coventry-Climax	1216/4IL OHC	75/6000	69/5000	4-spd/-
GT	9	1961–1965	Spts Cpe	F/R	Ford	xx/4IL/ OHV	70/5000	N/Q	4-spd/-

TVR

Make and model	Production Figures	Years Built	Body Styles	Mechanical Layout	Engine Make (if not own)	Capacity/(cc)/Layout/Valves	BHP/rpm	Torque (lb.ft)/rpm	Transmission gearbox/automatic transmission
Grantura I/II/IIA	Approx 500	1958–1962	Spts Cpe	F/R	Coventry-Climax	1216/4IL/ OHC	83/6000	75/4800	4-spd/-
					MG	1588/4IL/ OHV	80/5600	87/3800	4-spd/-
						1622/4IL/ OHV	86/5500	97/4000	4-spd/-
						(Other engines to choice - Ford and BMC)			
Grantura III/IV/1800S	Approx 300	1962–1967	Spts Cpe	F/R	MG	1622/OHV/ OHV	86/5500	97/4000	4-spd/-
						1798/4IL/ OHV	95/5400	110/3000	4-spd (+O/D)/-
Vixen S1/S2/S3	723	1967–1972	Spts Cpe	F/R	Ford	1599/4IL/ OHV	88/5400	96/3600	4-spd/-
Griffith 200/400	Approx 300	1963–1965	Spts Cpe	F/R	Ford-USA	4727/V8/ OHV	195/4400	282/2400	4-spd/-
							271/6500	314/3400	
Tuscan V8/V8SE	73	1967–1970	Spts Cpe	F/R	Ford-USA	4727/V8/ OHV	195/4400	282/2400	
							271/6500	314/3400	4-spd/-
Tuscan V6	101	1969–1971	Spts Cpe	F/R	Ford	2994/V6/ OHV	128/4750	173/3000	4-spd (+O/D)/-
Vixen S4/1300	38	1972–1973	Spts Cpe	F/R	Triumph	1296/4IL/ OHV	63/6000	69/3500	4-spd/-
					Ford	1599/4IL/ OHV	86/5500	92/4000	4-spd/-
2500	385	1970–1973	Spts Cpe	F/R	Triumph	2498/6IL/ OHV	106/4900	133/3000	4-spd (+O/D)/-

Unipower

Make and model	Production Figures	Years Built	Body Styles	Mechanical Layout	Engine Make (if not own)	Capacity/(cc)/Layout/Valves	BHP/rpm	Torque (lb.ft)/rpm	Transmission gearbox/automatic transmission
GT	75	1966–1970	Cpe	M(Tr)/R	BMC	998/4IL/ OHV	55/5800	57/3000	4-spd/-

Vanden Plas

Make and model	Production Figures	Years Built	Body Styles	Mechanical Layout	Engine Make (if not own)	Capacity/(cc)/Layout/Valves	BHP/rpm	Torque (lb.ft)/rpm	Transmission gearbox/automatic transmission
Princess 4-litre	N/A	1957–1968	Limo	F/R	—	3993/6IL/ OHV	120/4000	185/2000	4-spd/Auto
Princess 3-litre	12,615	1959–1964	Sal	F/R	—	2912/6IL/ OHV	103/4750	157/2300	3-spd (+O/D)/Auto
							120/4750	163/2750	

Suspension Front	Rear	Steering	Brakes (Front/rear)	Wheels/model Tyres	Length (in)	Weight (lb, unladen)	Performance Top speed (mph)	0–60mph (sec)	Standing ¼-mile (sec)	UK Total Price (£: at Launch)
IC	ITrL	R & P	Disc/drum	5.20-13	145	1568	92	15.5	20.0	£700
IC	ITrL	R & P	Disc/drum	5.20-13	145	1652	95	14.5	19.6	£717
IC	ITrL	R & P	Disc/drum	145-13	149	1717	90	16.2	20.6	£985
IC	ITrL	R & P	Disc/drum	155-13	149	1750	100	13.2	19.1	£1360
IC	IC	R & P	Disc/drum	6.50-13/ 175-13	174	2576	93	14.1	19.4	£1094
IC	IC	R & P	Disc/drum	185-13	174	2632	106	10.4	17.4	£1450
IC	IC	R & P	Disc/drum	175-13 to 175-14	182	2620 to 2842	96	14.9	19.7	£1412
IC	IC	R & P	Disc/drum	185-13	182	2681	104	11.8	18.7	£2352
IC	IC	R & P	Disc/drum	175-14	182	2609	105	10.4	17.8	£3271
IC	IC	R & P	Disc/drum	185-13	182	2760	106	11.5	18.1	£1595
IC	IC	R & P	Disc/drum	5.60-13	155	2016	84	19.0	21.3	£797
IC	IC	R & P	Disc/drum	5.60-13	155	2016	93	15.9	20.2	£874
IC	BeamC	R & P	Disc/drum	5.60-13	162	2128	85	17.1	20.7	£1113
IC	ITrL	R & P	Disc/drum	155-13	145	1904	106	12.0	18.5	£985
							107	10.0	17.3	£1125
IC	ITrL	R & P	Disc/drum	155-13	149	2030	112	10.1	17.4	£1287
IC	BeamC	R & P	Drum/drum Disc/drum	5.20-13 to 155-13	157	1905	85	17.1	20.9	£889
IC	IC	R & P	Disc/drum	185-14	174	2807	117	9.7	17.3	£1996
IC	BeamC	R & P	Drum/drum	5.20-15	138	1260	94	12.0	17.8	£550
IC	BeamTor	R & P	Disc/drum	5.20-15	138	1372	99	12.8	19.3	Special Order
IC	BeamC	R & P	Disc/drum	5.60-13	154	1568	100 (Est)	N/A	N/A	£1277
ITor	ITor	Worm	Drum/drum	5.00-15	138	1455	101	10.8	18.3	£1426
ITor	ITor	Worm	Drum/drum	5.00-15	138	1570	98	12.0	19.0	£1183
ITor	ITor	Worm	Disc/drum	5.00-15	138	1570	100 (Est)	N/A	N/A	£1291
IC	IC	R & P	Disc/drum	5.60-15	138	1625	100 (Est)	N/A	N/A	£1183
IC	IC	R & P	Disc/drum	5.60-15	138	1625/1790	108	10.9	18.0	£1043
IC	IC	R & P	Disc/drum	165-15	138/145	1680/1735	109	10.5	17.2	£1387
IC	IC	R & P	Disc/drum	185-15	138/145	1905	140 (Est)	N/A	N/A	£1620
IC	IC	R & P	Disc/drum	185-15	145	1905	155 (Est)	N/A	N/A	£1797
IC	IC	R & P	Disc/drum	185-15	145	1905	155 (Est)	7.5	14.1	£2364
IC	IC	R & P	Disc/drum	165-15	145	2000	125 (Est)	8.3	16.2	£1930
IC	IC	R & P	Disc/drum	165-15	145	1625	90 (Est)	N/A	N/A	£1558
IC	IC	R & P	Disc/drum	165-15	145	1970	109	10.5	17.2	£1723
IC	IC	R & P	Disc/drum	165-15	145	1960	111	10.6	17.7	£1927
IC	IC	R & P	Disc/drum	145-10	164	1254	101	12.6	19.1	£950
IC	Beam1/2E	Worm	Drum/drum	7.00-16	215	4810	75	26.0	23.1	£3376
IC	Beam1/2E	Worm	Disc/drum	7.00-14	188	3465	97	17.9	21.4	£1397
						3660	105	16.9	21.4	£1626

Make and model	Production Figures	Years Built	Body Styles	Mechanical Layout	Engine Make (if not own)	Capacity/(cc)/Layout/Valves	BHP/rpm	Torque (lb.ft)/rpm	Transmission gearbox/automatic transmission
Princess 1100/1300	39,381	1963–1974	Sal	F(Tr)/F	—	1098/4IL/OHV	55/5500	61/2500	4-spd/Auto
						1275/4IL/OHV	58/5250	69/3500	4-spd/Auto
							60/5250	69/2500	Auto/-
							65/5750	71/3000	4-spd/-
Princess 4-litre R	6,999	1964–1968	Sal	F/R	Rolls-Royce	3909/6IL/IOEV	175/4800	218/3000	-/Auto

Vauxhall

Make and model	Production Figures	Years Built	Body Styles	Mechanical Layout	Engine Make (if not own)	Capacity/(cc)/Layout/Valves	BHP/rpm	Torque (lb.ft)/rpm	Transmission gearbox/automatic transmission
10-4/12-4 (H-Type)	44,047	1946–1948	Sal	F/R	—	1203/4IL/OHV	31/3600	59/2200	3-spd/-
						1442/4IL/OHV	35/3600	68/2000	3-spd/-
12-4 (I-Type)	6	1945–1946	Sal	F/R	—	1442/4IL/OHV	35/3600	68/2000	3-spd/-
14-6 Six (J-Type)	30,511 (Postwar)	1939–1948	Sal	F/R	—	1781/6IL/OHV	48/3600	80/1400	3-spd/-
Wyvern/Velox	132,328	1948–1951	Sal	F/R	—	1442/4IL/OHV	35/3600	68/2000	3-spd/-
						2275/6IL/OHV	55/3300	106/1100	3-spd/-
Wyvern/Velox/Cresta (E-Type)	545,388	1951–1957	Sal Est	F/R	—	1442/4IL/OHV	33/3400	68/1800	3-spd/-
						2275/6IL/OHV	54/3500	103/1100	3-spd/-
						1508/4IL/OHV	40/4000	71/2000	3-spd/-
						2262/6IL/OHV	64/4000	125/1400	3-spd/-
							83/4400	135/1800	
Victor (FA)	390,747	1957–1961	Sal Est	F/R	—	1508/4IL/OHV	55/4200	84/2400	3-spd/-
Victor (FB)	328,640	1961–1964	Sal Est	F/R	—	1508/4IL/OHV	50/4600	80/2000	3-spd/4-spd
						1594/4IL/OHV	59/4600	84/2400	3-spd/4-spd
VX4/90 (FB)	(Prod. incl. above)	1961–1964	Sal	F/R	—	1508/4IL/OHV	71/5200	87/3000	4-spd/-
						1594/4IL/OHV	86/5200	99/3200	4-spd/-
Victor (FC) (Type 101)	233,263	1964–1967	Sal Est	F/R	—	1594/4IL/OHV	70/4800	94/2800	3-spd/4-spd/Auto
							66/4800	95/2600	3-spd/4-spd/Auto
VX4/90 (Type 101)	(Prod. incl. above)	1964–1967	Sal	F/R	—	1594/4IL/OHV	86/5200	99/3200	4-spd/Auto
Victor (FD)	198,085 (Incl. Ventora)	1967–1972	Sal Est	F/R	—	1599/4IL/OHC	72/5600	90/3200	3-spd/4-spd/Auto
						1975/4IL/OHC	88/5500	116/3200	3-spd/4-spd/Auto
VX 4/90	14,277	1969–1972	Sal	F/R	—	1975/4IL/OHC	104/5600	117/3400	4-spd (+O/D)/Auto
Ventora/Victor 3300	—	1968–1972	Sal Est	F/R	—	3294/6IL/OHV	123/4600	176/2400	4-spd (+O/D)/Auto
Velox/Cresta (PA)	173,764	1957–1962	Sal Est	F/R	—	2262/6IL/OHV	83/4400	124/1800	3-spd (+O/D)/-
					OHV	2651/6IL/OHV	95/4600	139/1600	3-spd (+O/D)/-
Velox/Cresta (PB)	87,047	1962–1965	Sal Est	F/R	—	2561/6IL/OHV	95/4600	139/1600	3-spd (+O/D)/Auto
						3294/6IL/OHV	115/4200	175/2200	3-spd(+O/D)/4-spd/Auto
Velox/Cresta/Viscount	60,937	1965–1972	Sal Est	F/R	—	3294/6IL/OHV	123/4600	176/2400	3-spd(+O/D)/4-spd/Auto
Viva (HA)	321,332	1963–1966	Sal	F/R	—	1057/4IL/OHV	44/5000	62/3000	4-spd/-
							54/5600	60/3200	4-spd/-
Viva (HB)	644,687	1966–1970	Sal Est	F/R	—	1159/4IL/OHV	47/5200	62/2800	4-spd/Auto
							60/5600	64/3600	4-spd/Auto
							69/5800	66/4200	4-spd/-
						1599/4IL/OHC	83/5800	90/3200	4-spd/Auto
Viva (HB) 2000GT	18,123	1968–1970	Sal	F/R	—	1975/4IL/OHC	104/5600	117/3400	4-spd/-
Viva (HC)	640,863	1970–1979	Sal Est Cpe	F/R	—	1159/4IL/OHV	49/5300	63/2900	4-spd/Auto
							62/5500	65/3800	4-spd/Auto
						1256/4IL/OHV	53/5200	65/2600	4-spd/Auto
							68/5750	72/4000	4-spd/Auto
							59/5600	68/2600	4-spd/Auto
						1599/4IL/OHC	70/5100	90/2500	4-spd/Auto
						1759/4IL/OHC	77/5200	104/3000	4-spd/Auto
							88/5800	99/3500	4-spd/Auto

Suspension Front	Rear	Steering	Brakes (Front/rear)	Wheels/model Tyres	Length (in)	Weight (lb,unladen)	Performance Top speed (mph)	0–60mph (sec)	Standing 1/4-mile (sec)	UK Total Price (£: at Launch)
IHydroL	IHydroL	R & P	Disc/drum	5.50-12	147	1950	85	21.1	21.7	£895
IHydroL	IHydroL	R & P	Disc/drum	5.50-12	147	2015	88	17.3	20.7	£1000
IHydroL	IHydroL	R & P	Disc/drum	5.50-12	147	2015	87 (Est)	N/A	N/A	£1185
IHydroL	IHydroL	R & P	Disc/drum	5.50-12	147	2015	97	14.1	19.6	£1087
IC	Beam1/2E	Worm	Disc/drum	7.50-13	188	3530	106	12.7	18.9	£1994
ITor	Beam1/2E	Worm	Drum/drum	5.00-16	159	2016	60 (Est)	N/A	N/A	£371
ITor	Beam1/2E	Worm	Drum/drum	5.00-16	159	2072	63	39.2	24.7	£403
ITor	Beam1/2E	Worm	Drum/drum	5.25-16	163	2050	60 (Est)	N/A	N/A	£403
ITor	Beam1/2E	Worm	Drum/drum	5.50-16	169	2374	67	38.6	24.9	£480
ITor	Beam1/2E	Worm	Drum/drum	5.00-16	165	2184	60	N/A	26.9	£448
ITor	Beam1/2E	Worm	Drum/drum	5.25-16	165	2380	74	22.7	22.4	£550
IC	Beam1/2E	Worm	Drum/drum	5.60-15	173	2206	64	N/A	N/A	£740
IC	Beam1/2E	Worm	Drum/drum	5.90-15	173	2251	77	23.7	22.5	£803
IC	Beam1/2E	Worm	Drum/drum	5.60-15	173	2212	72	37.2	24.9	£772
IC	Beam1/2E	Worm	Drum/drum	5.90-15	173	2324	80	21.4	22.4	£834
IC	Beam1/2E	Worm	Drum/drum	5.60-13	166	2150	74	28.1	24.5	£729
IC	Beam1/2E	Worm	Drum/drum	5.60-13	173	2100	76	22.6	22.1	£745
IC	Beam1/2E	Worm	Drum/drum Disc/drum	5.60-13	173	2128	80	18.2	21.4	£635
IC	Beam1/2E	Worm	Disc/drum	5.60-14	173	2184	88	16.4	20.8	£984
IC	Beam1/2E	Worm	Disc/drum	5.60-14	173	2198	88	15.4	20.2	£840
IC	Beam1/2E	Worm	Drum/drum	5.60-13	173	2150	84	17.1	20.6	£678
IC	Beam1/2E	Worm	Drum/drum	5.60-13	173	2194	81	20.4	21.6	£702
IC	Beam1/2E	Worm	Disc/drum	5.60-13	173	2254	93	16.0	20.2	£872
IC	BeamC	R & P	Drum/drum Disc/drum	5.60-13	177	2321	90	19.3	21.2	£819
IC	BeamC	R & P	Disc/drum	6.20-13	177	2350	95	14.0	19.5	£910
IC	BeamC	R & P	Disc/drum	6.90-13	177	2396	98	13.2	19.2	£1203
IC	BeamC	R & P	Disc/drum	165-13	177	2553	103	11.8	18.4	£1102
IC	Beam1/2E	Worm	Drum/drum	6.40-13	178	2520	87	18.0	20.8	£984
IC	Beam1/2E	Worm	Drum/drum Disc/drum	5.90-14	178	2688	95	15.2	20.1	£929
IC	Beam1/2E	Worm	Disc/drum	5.90-14	182	2744	93	13.8	19.6	£1046
IC	Beam1/2E	Worm	Disc/drum	5.90-14	182	2744	99	11.6	18.2	£859
IC	Beam1/2E	Worm	Disc/drum	5.90-14 7.00-14	187	2796	103	12.5	18.3	£956
ITrL	Beam1/2E	R & P	Drum/drum	5.50-12	155	1564	77	22.1	21.5	£527
ITrL	Beam1/2E	R & P	Drum/drum	5.50-12	155	1750	81	18.2	20.5	£607
IC	BeamC	R & P	Drum/drum	5.50-12	162	1734	78	19.7	21.0	£579
IC	BeamC	R & P	Disc/drum	6.20-12	162	1778	83	17.6	20.4	£663
IC	BeamC	R & P	Disc/drum	6.20-12	162	1778	90	15.1	20.1	£701
IC	BeamC	R & P	Disc/drum	6.20-12	162	1955	88	18.0	20.4	£789
IC	BeamC	R & P	Disc/drum	155-13	161	2070	100	10.7	18.3	£1022
IC	BeamC	R & P	Drum/drum	5.20-13	162	1859	78	20.6	21.8	£783
IC	BeamC	R & P	Disc/drum	6.20-13	162	1844	N/A	N/A	N/A	£823
IC	BeamC	R & P	Drum/drum	5.20-13	162	1800	84	17.6	20.3	£802
IC	BeamC	R & P	Disc/drum	155-13	162	1887	84	18.1	21.2	£1174
IC	BeamC	R & P	Disc/drum	155-13	162	1837	87	15.8	20.1	£1174
IC	BeamC	R & P	Disc/drum	6.20-13	162	2088	86	17.1	20.6	£994
IC	BeamC	R & P	Disc/drum	155-13	162	2085	94	13.1	18.7	£969
IC	BeamC	R & P	Disc/drum	165-13	162	2273	97 (Est)	N/A	N/A	£1305

Make and model	Production Figures	Years Built	Body Styles	Mechanical Layout	Engine Make (if not own)	Capacity/(cc)/Layout/Valves	BHP/rpm	Torque (lb.ft)/rpm	Transmission gearbox/automatic transmission
						2279/4IL/ OHC	110/5200	140/3200	4-spd/Auto
Vespa									
400	Est 34,000	1958–1961	Conv	R/R	—	393/2IL/ 2-Str AirC	14/4700	20/2200	3-spd/-
Volga									
M21/M22	N/A	1955–1972	Sal Est	F/R	—	2445/4IL/ OHV	80/4000	130/2000	3-spd/-
M24	N/A	1969–N/A	Sal Est	F/R	—	2445/4IL/ OHV	112/4700	148/2400	4-spd/-
Volkswagen									
Beetle	21 million + (Incl. all Beetle models)	1945–Date	Sal Conv	R/R	—	1131/4HO/ OHV AirC	25/3300	49/2000	4-spd/-
						1192/4HO/ OHV AirC	30/3400 34/3600	56/2000 65/2400	4-spd/- 4-spd/-
						1285/4HO/ OHV AirC	40/4000 44/4100	64/2000 69/3500	4-spd/SemiAuto 4-spd/SemiAuto
						1493/4HO/ OHV AirC	44/4000	74/2000	4-spd/SemiAuto
						1584/4HO/ OHV AirC	50/4000	78/2800	4-spd/SemiAuto
Karmann-Ghia	Incl. in Beetle statistics	1957–1974	Cpe Conv	R/R	—	1192/4HO/ OHV AirC	30/3400 34/3600	56/2000 61/2000	4-spd/- 4-spd/-
						1285/4HO/ OHV AirC	40/4000 44/4100	64/2000 69/3500	4-spd/SemiAuto 4-spd/SemiAuto
						1493/4HO/ OHV AirC	44/4000	74/2000	4-spd/SemiAuto
						1584/4HO/ OHV AirC	50/4000	78/2800	4-spd/SemiAuto
1500/1500S	941,056	1961–1965	Sal Est	R/R	—	1493/4HO/ OHV AirC	45/3800 54/4800	83/2000 76/3000	4-spd/- 4-spd/-
Karmann-Ghia 1500/1600	42,563	1962–1969	Cpe	R/R	—	1493/4HO/ OHV AirC	45/3800 54/4800	83/2000 76/3000	4-spd/SemiAuto 4-spd/-
						1584/4HO/ OHV AirC	54/4000	81/2200	4-spd/Auto
1600TL/ 1600TE	1,813,600	1965–1973	Sal Est	R/R	—	1584/4HO/ OHV AirC	54/4000 65/4600	81/2200 87/2800	4-spd/Auto 4-spd/Auto
411/412	355,200	1968–1974	Sal Est	R/R	—	1679/4HO/ OHV AirC	68/4500 80/4900	92/2800 98/2700	4-spd/Auto 4-spd/Auto
1302/1302S/ 1303/1303S	Incl. in Beetle statistics	1970–1975	Sal Conv	R/R	—	1584/4HO/ OHV AirC	50/4000	82/3000	4-spd/SemiAuto
181 'The Thing'	Incl. in Beetle statistics	1969–1978	Conv	R/R	—	1584/4HO/ OHV AirC	50/4000	82/3000	4-spd/-
K70	211,100	1970–1975	Sal	F/F	—	1605/4IL/ OHC	75/5200 90/5200	90/3500 99/4000	4-spd/- 4-spd/-
						1807/4IL/ OHC	100/5300	112/3750	4-spd/-
Volkswagen-Porsche									
914S/914SC	115,600	1969–1975	Spts Cpe	M/R	—	1679/4HO/ OHV AirC	80/4900	98/2700	5-spd/SemiAuto
						1971/4HO/ OHV AirC	100/5000	116/3500	5-spd/SemiAuto
Volvo									
PV444	196,005	1947–1958	Sal	F/R	—	1414/4IL/ OHV	44/4000 85/5500 70/5500	69/2200 107/3500 76/3000	4-spd/- 4-spd/- 3-spd (+O/D)/-
PV544	243,995	1958–1965	Sal	F/R	—	1583/4IL/ OHV	66/4500 85/5500	85/2500 107/3500	4-spd/- 4-spd/-
120/ Amazon	667,323	1956–1969	Sal Est	F/R	—	1583/4IL/ OHV	60/4500 85/5500	83/2500 87/3500	3-spd/4-spd/- 3-spd/4-spd/-
						1778/4IL/ OHV	80/5000 68/4500 75/4500 85/5500 90/5000 95/5000 100/5600	105/3500 101/2800 101/2800 107/3500 105/3500 107/3500 107/3500	4-spd (+O/D)/- 4-spd (+O/D)/- 4-spd (+O/D)/- 4-spd (+O/D)/- 4-spd (+O/D)/- 4-spd/- 4-spd (+O/D)/-
P1800/1800S	30,093	1961–1969	Cpe	F/R	—	1778/4IL/ OHV	100/5500 108/5800 115/6000	108/4000 110/4000 112/4000	4-spd (+O/D)/- 4-spd (+O/D)/- 4-spd (+O/D)/-

214

Suspension Front	Rear	Steering	Brakes (Front/rear)	Wheels/model Tyres	Length (in)	Weight (lb,unladen)	Performance Top speed (mph)	0–60mph (sec)	Standing 1/4-mile (sec)	UK Total Price (£: at Launch)
IC	BeamC	R & P	Disc/drum	155-13	162	2085	99	11.5	17.9	£1182
IC	IC	R & P	Drum/drum	4.00-10	113	784	52	N/A	29.7	£N/A
IC	Beam1/2E	Worm	Drum/drum	6.70-15	190	3224	78	30.3	24.1	£1113
IC	Beam1/2E	Worm	Drum/drum	7.35-14	188	3090	90 (Claimed)	N/A	N/A	Special Order
ITor	ITor	Worm	Drum/drum	5.60-15	160	1652	63	N/A	24.6	£690
ITor	ITor	Worm	Drum/drum	5.60-15	160	1568	66	47.6	24.2	£690
ITor	ITor	Worm	Drum/drum	5.60-15	160	1669	72	32.1	23.4	£617
ITor	ITor	Worm	Drum/drum	5.60-15	160	1669	75	23.0	22.1	£650
ITor	ITor	Worm	Drum/drum	5.60-15	160	1669	78 (Est)	N/A	N/A	£799
ITor	ITor	Worm	Disc/drum	5.60-15	160	1736	81	21.9	21.9	£697
IC	ITor	Worm	Disc/drum	5.60-15	161	1850	80	18.3	20.7	£875
ITor	ITor	Worm	Drum/drum	5.60-15	163	1915	72 (Est)	N/A	N/A	£1235
ITor	ITor	Worm	Drum/drum	5.60-15	163	1915	77	26.5	26.5	£1196
ITor	ITor	Worm	Disc/drum	5.60-15	163	1915	80 (Est)	N/A	N/A	£1101
ITor	ITor	Worm	Disc/drum	5.60-15	163	1915	85 (Est)	N/A	N/A	Special Order
ITor	ITor	Worm	Disc/drum	5.60-15	163	1915	85 (Est)	N/A	N/A	£1098
ITor	ITor	Worm	Disc/drum	5.60-15	163	1915	85 (Est)	N/A	N/A	Special Order
ITor	ITor	Worm	Drum/drum	6.00-15	167	1904	80	20.7	21.4	£1099
ITor	ITor	Worm	Drum/drum	6.00-15	167	1928	85	19.1	21.5	£925
ITor	ITor	Worm	Drum/drum	6.00-15	168	1904	87	21.7	21.7	£1330
ITor	ITor	Worm	Drum/drum	6.00-15	168	1928	90 (Est)	N/A	N/A	£1330
ITor	ITor	Worm	Disc/drum	6.00-15	168	1994	90 (Est)	N/A	N/A	£1397
ITor	ITor	Worm	Disc/drum	6.00-15	167	2035	83	20.3	21.3	£998
ITor	ITor	Worm	Disc/drum	6.00-15	167	2227	78 (Est)	N/A	N/A	£1112
IC	IC	Worm	Disc/drum	145-15	178	2249	86	16.5	20.4	£1290
IC	IC	Worm	Disc/drum	155-15	179	2341	97	13.8	19.5	£1308
IC	ITor	Worm	Disc/drum	5.60-15	161	1905	80	18.3	20.7	£875
ITor	ITor	Worm	Drum/drum	165-15	149	1985	68	N/A	N/A	£1996
IC	IC	R & P	Disc/drum	165-14	172	2322	92 (Est)	N/A	N/A	£1570
IC	IC	R & P	Disc/drum	165-14	172	2360	93	12.9	18.8	£1571
IC	IC	R & P	Disc/drum	165-14	172	2322	100 (Est)	N/A	N/A	£1790
ITor	IC	R & P	Disc/disc	155-15	157	1900	102	14.8	19.9	£2261
ITor	IC	R & P	Disc/disc	165-15	157	1900	119	10.3	17.8	£2799
IC	BeamC	Worm	Drum/drum	5.90-15	177	2128	76	28.0	23.2	Special Order
IC	BeamC	Worm	Drum/drum	5.90-15	177	2128	95	14.5	20.1	Special Order
IC	BeamC	Worm	Drum/drum	5.90-15	177	2128	85 (Est)	N/A	N/A	£1101
IC	BeamC	Worm	Drum/drum	165-15	177	2062	87 (Est)	N/A	N/A	Special Order
IC	BeamC	Worm	Drum/drum	165-15	177	2062	96 (Est)	N/A	N/A	Special Order
IC	BeamC	Worm	Drum/drum	5.90-15	173	2240	90 (Est)	N/A	N/A	£1201
IC	BeamC	Worm	Drum/drum	5.60-15	173	2491	94 (Est)	N/A	N/A	£1399
IC	BeamC	Worm	Disc/drum	5.90-15	173	2352	95	14.2	19.8	£1293
IC	BeamC	Worm	Drum/drum	5.90-15	173	2435	85 (Est)	N/A	N/A	£1197
IC	BeamC	Worm	Disc/drum	6.00-15	173	2324	91	76	20.7	£1023
IC	BeamC	Worm	Drum/drum	5.90-15	173	2352	94	14.0	19.9	£1372
IC	BeamC	Worm	Disc/drum	5.90-15	173	2387	96 (Est)	N/A	N/A	£1372
IC	BeamC	Worm	Disc/drum	6.00-15	173	2400	98 (Est)	N/A	N/A	£1214
IC	BeamC	Worm	Disc/drum	165-15	173	2448	100 (Est)	N/A	N/A	£1145
IC	BeamC	Worm	Disc/drum	5.90-15	173	2490	106	13.8	19.2	£1837
IC	BeamC	Worm	Disc/drum	165-15	173	2500	109 (Est)	N/A	N/A	£1651
IC	BeamC	Worm	Disc/drum	165-15	173	2500	112 (Est)	N/A	N/A	£1845

Make and model	Production Figures	Years Built	Body Styles	Mechanical Layout	Engine Make (if not own)	Capacity/ (cc)/Layout/ Valves	BHP/ rpm	Torque (lb.ft)/rpm	Transmission gearbox/automatic transmission
						1986/4IL/ OHV	118/6000	123/3500	4-spd (+O/D)/-
1800E/ 1800ES	47,600	1969–1973	Cpe Cpe Est	F/R	—	1986/4IL/ OHV	120/6000	123/3500	4-spd (+O/D)/Auto
140 Series	1,205,111	1966–1974	Sal Est	F/R	—	1778/4IL/ OHV	75/4700 100/5600	108/3000 107/3500	4-spd/Auto 4-spd(+O/D)/-
						1986/4IL/ OHV	82/4700 100/5600 120/6000	119/3000 123/3500 123/3500	4-spd/Auto 4-spd (+O/D)/- 4-spd/Auto
164 Family	155,068	1968–1975	Sal	F/R	—	2979/6IL/ OHV	130/5000 160/5500	152/2500 170/2500	4-spd (+O/D)/Auto 4-spd (+O/D)/Auto

Wartburg

Make and model	Production Figures	Years Built	Body Styles	Mechanical Layout	Engine Make (if not own)	Capacity/ (cc)/Layout/ Valves	BHP/ rpm	Torque (lb.ft)/rpm	Transmission gearbox/automatic transmission
312	Est 150,000	1962–1966	Sal Est	F/F	—	991/3IL/ 2-Str	45/4200	71/2200	4-spd/-
353 Knight/ Tourist	N/A	1966–1988	Sal Est	F/F	—	991/3IL/ 2str	45/4200 50/4250	71/2200 69/3000	4-spd/- 4-spd/-

Warwick

Make and model	Production Figures	Years Built	Body Styles	Mechanical Layout	Engine Make (if not own)	Capacity/ (cc)/Layout/ Valves	BHP/ rpm	Torque (lb.ft)/rpm	Transmission gearbox/automatic transmission
GT	39	1960–1962	Spts Cpe	F/R	Triumph	1991/4IL/ OHV	100/5000	117/3000	4-spd (+O/D)/-

William

Make and model	Production Figures	Years Built	Body Styles	Mechanical Layout	Engine Make (if not own)	Capacity/ (cc)/Layout/ Valves	BHP/ rpm	Torque (lb.ft)/rpm	Transmission gearbox/automatic transmission
Farmer	N/A	1969–1974	Ute	F/R	—	246/2IL/ 2-Str	12/4400	N/A	4-spd/-

Wolseley

Make and model	Production Figures	Years Built	Body Styles	Mechanical Layout	Engine Make (if not own)	Capacity/ (cc)/Layout/ Valves	BHP/ rpm	Torque (lb.ft)/rpm	Transmission gearbox/automatic transmission
Eight	5,344	1946–1948	Sal	F/R	—	910/4IL/ OHV	33/4400	45/2400	4-spd/-
Ten	2,715 (Postwar)	1939–1948	Sal	F/R	—	1140/4IL/ OHV	40/4400	55/2200	4-spd/-
12/48 (SIII)	5,602 (Postwar)	1938–1948	Sal	F/R	—	1548/4IL/ OHV	44/4000	72/2000	4-spd/-
14/60 (SIII)	5,731 (Postwar)	1939–1948	Sal	F/R	—	1818/6IL/ OHV	58/4200	77/2400	4-spd/-
18/85 (SIII)	8,213 (Postwar)	1939–1948	Sal	F/R	—	2321/6IL/ OHV	85/4000	111/2000	4-spd/-
25 (SIII)	75	1947–1948	Limo	F/R	—	3485/6IL/ OHV	104/3600	166/2500	4-spd/-
4/50	8,925	1948–1953	Sal	F/R	—	1476/4IL/ OHC	51/4400	72/2900	4-spd/-
6/80	25,281	1948–1954	Sal	F/R	—	2215/6IL/ OHC	72/4600	102/2200	4-spd/-
4/44 and 15/50	42,197	1952–1958	Sal	F/R	—	1250/4IL/ OHV 1489/4IL/ OHV	46/4800 50/4200	58/2400 78/2400	4-spd/- 4-spd/SemiAuto
6/90	11,852	1954–1957	Sal	F/R	—	2639/6IL/ OHV	95/4500 97/4750	133/2000 135/2000	4-spd (+O/D)/Auto
1500	100,722	1957–1965	Sal	F/R	—	1489/4IL/ OHV	43/4200	71/2600	4-spd/-
15/60 and 16/60	87,661	1958–1971	Sal	F/R	—	1489/4IL/ OHV 1622/4IL/ OHV	52/4350 61/4500	82/2100 90/2100	4-spd/- 4-spd/Auto
6/99 and 6/110	37,209	1959–1968	Sal	F/R	—	2912/6IL/ OHV	103/4500 120/4750 120/4750	158/2000 163/2750 163/2750	3-spd (+O/D)/Auto 3-spd (+O/D)/Auto 4-spd (+O/D)/Auto
Hornet	28,455	1961–1969	Sal	F(Tr)/F	—	848/4IL/ OHV 998/4IL/ OHV	34/5500 38/5250	44/2900 52/2700	4-spd/- 4-spd/-
1100/1300	44,867	1965–1973	Sal	F(Tr)/F	—	1098/4IL/ OHV 1275/4IL/ OHV	55/5500 58/5250 60/5250 65/5750	61/2500 69/3500 69/2500 71/3000	4-spd/- 4-spd/Auto Auto/- 4-spd/-
18/85 & 18/85S	35,597	1967–1972	Sal	F(Tr)/F	—	1798/4IL/ OHV	85/5300 86/5300	99/2100 101/3000	4-spd/Auto 4-spd/Auto

Suspension Front	Rear	Steering	Brakes (Front/rear)	Wheels/model Tyres	Length (in)	Weight (lb, unladen)	Performance Top speed (mph)	0–60mph (sec)	Standing 1/4-mile (sec)	UK Total Price (£: at Launch)
IC	BeamC	Worm	Disc/drum	165-15	173	2500	112 (Est)	N/A	N/A	£1983
IC	BeamC	Worm	Disc/disc	165-15	170	2492	108	9.6	17.4	£2026
IC	BeamC	Worm	Disc/disc	165-15	183	2735	96 (Est)	N/A	N/A	£1354
IC	BeamC	Worm	Disc/disc	165-15	183	2735	101	12.6	18.6	£1415
IC	BeamC	Worm	Disc/disc	165-15	183	2625	90	13.9	19.8	£1465
IC	BeamC	Worm	Disc/disc	165-15	183	2548	99	12.9	18.8	£1569
IC	BeamC	Worm	Disc/disc	165-15	183	2640	105	11.6	18.3	£1974
IC	BeamC	Worm	Disc/disc	165-15	186	2856	106	11.3	18.5	£1791
IC	BeamC	Worm	Disc/disc	165-15	186	3013	113	8.8	16.9	£2488
ITrL	BeamTrL	R & P	Drum/drum	5.90-15	170	2002	75	23.2	22.6	£539
IC	IC	R & P	Drum/drum	165-13	167	1952	74	22.8	22.0	£612
IC	IC	R & P	Drum/drum	165-13	167	1952	84	18.7	21.0	
IC	DD1/2E	Worm	Disc/drum	5.50-15	162	2240	103	12.8	18.6	£1666
ITrL	Beam1/2E	R & P	Drum/drum	4.00-10	82	728	45	N/A	30.6	£794
Beam1/2E	Beam1/2E	Worm	Drum/drum	4.50-17	145	1904	60 (Est)	N/A	N/A	£416
Beam1/2E	Beam1/2E	Worm	Drum/drum	5.50-16	147	2061	69	38.1	25.1	£474
Beam1/2E	Beam1/2E	Worm	Drum/drum	5.75-16	163	2968	63	N/A	26.4	£569
Beam1/2E	Beam1/2E	Worm	Drum/drum	6.00-16	172	3080	70	36.2	24.0	£614
Beam1/2E	Beam1/2E	Worm	Drum/drum	6.25-16	172	3108	75	25.4	23.3	£680
Beam1/2E	Beam1/2E	Worm	Drum/drum	7.00-16	212	4816	85 (Est)	20.4	21.3	£2568
ITor	Beam1/2E	Worm	Drum/drum	5.50-15	169	2576	74	31.6	24.3	£704
ITor	Beam1/2E	Worm	Drum/drum	6.00-15	177	2688	77	27.8	23.8	£767
IC	Beam1/2E	R & P	Drum/drum	5.50-15	173	2445	73	29.9	24.2	£997
IC	Beam1/2E	R & P	Drum/drum	5.60-15	173	2490	78	24.3	23.4	£961
ITor	BeamC Beam1/2E	Worm	Drum/drum	6.00-15	188	3220	94	18.1	21.2	£1064
ITor	Beam1/2E	R & P	Drum/drum	5.00-14 5.60-14	152	2060	78	24.4	22.1	£796
IC	Beam1/2E	Worm	Drum/drum	5.90-14	178	2473	77	24.3	22.6	£991
IC	Beam1/2E	Worm	Drum/drum	5.90-14	175	2473	81	21.4	21.8	£993
IC	Beam1/2E	Worm	Disc/drum	7.00-14	188	3415	98	14.4	20.4	£1255
IC	Beam1/2E	Worm	Disc/drum	7.00-14	188	3470	102	13.3	19.4	£1343
IC	Beam1/2E	Worm	Disc/drum	7.50-13	188	3470	101	16.2	19.8	£1179
IRubber	IRubber	R & P	Drum/drum	5.20-10	129	1435	71	32.2	23.7	£672
IRubber IHydroL	IRubber IHydroL	R & P	Drum/drum	5.20-10	129	1395/1456	77	24.1	22.4	£557
IHydroL	IHydroL	R & P	Disc/drum	5.50-12	147	1820	85	18.4	21.3	£754
IHydroL	IHydroL	R & P	Disc/drum	5.50-12	147	1820	88	17.3	20.7	£825
IHydroL	IHydroL	R & P	Disc/drum	5.50-12	147	1820	87 (Est)	N/A	N/A	£999
IHydroL	IHydroL	R & P	Disc/drum	5.50-12	147	1850	97	14.1	19.6	£903
IHydroL	IHydroL	R & P	Disc/drum	175-13	166	2576	90	18.0	21.2	£1040
IHydroL	IHydroL	R & P	Disc/drum	165-14	166	2576	97	15.2	20.4	£1273

APPENDIX B

Ownership of British marques from 1945

Although the British motor industry was already dominated by the Big Six in 1945, there was still plenty of space for individual enterprise to flourish:

AC: The Thames Ditton company had been rescued from receivership by the Hurlock brothers, Charles and Derek, in 1930. By 1945 they had rebuilt the company, taking in some public capital, and eventually sold out in the 1980s.

Allard: London motor trader Sydney Allard had built a series of Allard Specials for motorsport in the 1930s, then set up a new business, the Allard Motor Co Ltd, to build production cars in 1945. The business was always controlled by Allard family interests, but closed down when the cars went out of production in 1960.

Alvis: Alvis Ltd of Coventry had replaced an earlier Alvis company in 1937, and was still independent in 1945. By making cars and particularly aerospace engines and military vehicles, it thrived until 1965, after which it was taken over by Rover (see below). Rover was absorbed by Leyland Motors in 1967 and became part of British Leyland in 1968, by which time the last Alvis private cars had been built.

Armstrong Siddeley: This Coventry marque emerged after the fusion of Armstrong-Whitworth and Siddeley-Deasy in 1919, but by 1945 car-making was only a minor activity in a Hawker-Siddeley Group which also produced aircraft engines and aircraft in huge numbers. By the end of the 1950s Armstrong Siddeley had merged with the Bristol Aeroplane Company to become part of Bristol-Siddeley, but car manufacture ended almost immediately afterwards. From 1959 to 1962 Armstrong Siddeley also manufactured Sunbeam Alpine sportscars for the Rootes Group.

Aston Martin: Until finally taken over by Ford-UK in 1987, this marque had effectively been a 'rich-man's toy', kept afloat by a variety of benefactors. In 1945 it was still owned by R G Sutherland, but it was bought in 1947 by David Brown, whose Yorkshire-based business was famous for building tractors and transmissions. Having merged Aston Martin with Lagonda a few months later, Brown then sold out to Company Developments Ltd in 1972. There was a period of receivership in 1974/75, a decade of sometimes confused ownership culminating in control by Victor Gauntlett, followed by Ford's rescue in 1987.

Austin: The Austin Motor Co Ltd, founded in 1906, had become Britain's second-largest car-maker by 1945, though the founder, Lord Austin, had died in 1941. Austin merged with the Nuffield Organisation (Morris, MG, Riley and Wolseley being that concern's car marques) in 1952 to form the British Motor Corporation (BMC).

BMC bought the Jaguar Group in 1966 to found British Motor Holdings (BMH), but all were then subsumed into the British Leyland Motor Corporation (BLMC) in 1968 when BMH joined forces with Leyland. Austin remained alive as a marque until the late 1980s.

Austin-Healey: This marque was invented in 1952 on the whim of BMC's chairman, Sir Leonard Lord, who liked the Austin-powered Healey 100 prototype so much that he offered to build it in large quantities, with a name-change. Although all Austin-Healeys were designed by the Healey family (notably Donald and his son Geoffrey), they were always built by BMC/BMH/BLMC.

Bedford: This marque was really a truck-building subsidiary of Vauxhall, the name only being applied to one small Vauxhall Viva-based estate car in the 1960s. Vauxhall had been absorbed by the American giant General Motors in the 1920s, and Bedford trucks had been developed under that ownership.

Bentley: Established by W O Bentley in 1919, the several-times bankrupt maker of sportscars had been rescued from the receiver by Rolls-Royce in 1931. By 1945 it was a completely integrated part of Rolls-Royce, the cars being ever more closely derived from Rolls-Royce designs. That situation persisted into the 1990s, even though the car-making side of Rolls-Royce was split from the larger aircraft engine-making colossus in 1973. Along with Rolls-Royce, Bentley was taken over by the Vickers Group in 1980.

Berkeley: This marque was created by a Biggleswade caravan manufacturer, who had hired Laurie Bond (see Bond, below) to design a sportscar. When the caravan business hit financial trouble in the early 1960s the sportscar side went down with it.

Bond: Although Laurie Bond designed the three-wheelers which carried his name, he had no connection with the Triumph-based four-wheelers which followed. Bonds were always produced in Preston, by Sharps Commercials Ltd, until 1969. Reliant (see below) then took over the Bond business, which Sharps had hived-off, but the only new Reliant-inspired Bond venture to go on sale was the Bug three-wheeler, the last of which was produced in 1974.

Bristol: The prestigious Bristol Aeroplane Co Ltd started building cars in Bristol in 1947, using designs 'liberated' from BMW as unofficial war reparations. Later, in 1960, the car-making business was hived-off to Sir George White and Anthony Crook (both of whom had been connected with Bristol for some time), and a few years later Anthony Crook became the sole proprietor, which he remained in the 1990s.

Daimler: After a turbulent corporate beginning in the 1890s, Daimler had been absorbed by the BSA Group in 1910, who added Lanchester (see below) to its clutch of concerns in 1931. Both marques continued in production, in Coventry, after 1945. BSA then sold the Daimler/Lanchester business to Sir William Lyons of Jaguar in 1960. Although the Lanchester marque was already moribund, the Daimler marque prospered under Jaguar ownership.

Jaguar, of course, merged with BMC in 1966, became a part of British Leyland in 1968, was sold back into private ownership in 1984, and was then taken over by Ford in 1989. Daimler therefore became a Ford-owned marque at that time.

Dellow: These specialized little Ford-based sportscars were produced by Dellow Motors, of Alvechurch, near Birmingham, a business owned by K C Delingpole and R Lowe (hence the derivation of the name). The marque's life was a brief one, and it died where it had begun.

Elva: Frank Nichols designed the first of these cars (Elva was a diminution of the French phrase Elle va! – 'She goes!'), making them in Bexhill, Sussex. Nichols later sold out to Trojan Ltd in 1962, but the final batch of Couriers were produced by Ken Sheppard Customised Sports Cars from 1965.

Enfield: Sponsored by the British Electricity Council, these battery-powered runabouts were built in London by the Enfield Automotive Co, which was finally bought out by a Greek entrepreneur, who moved the business to Cowes, Isle-of-Wight, without success.

Fairthorpe: The brainchild of World War Two hero Air Vice-Marshal Donald Bennett, these were originally kit-cars, later to be joined by fully built-up cars, built firstly in Chalfont St Peter, later in Gerrards Cross, and finally in Denham. The AV-M handed over control to his son Torix in the 1970s, but the business died in the late 1970s.

Ford-UK: Set up by Henry Ford as a personally owned subsidiary of the Ford Motor Company of Detroit, Ford-UK was always family-controlled, especially after minor shareholdings were repurchased in the early 1960s. Over the years share ownership widened considerably, but Ford, one of the world's largest car-makers), has remained independent of any other group.

Frazer Nash: The Aldington family had taken control of this company from Archie Frazer Nash in 1929, and controlled it throughout its life as a car-maker. Car production ended in the mid-1950s as the company's other business – importers of Porsches – expanded.

Gilbern: This Welsh company, based at Llantwit, near Pontypridd, was set up by Giles Smith and Bernard Frieze, who held control until financial problems struck in the early 1970s. There was an attempt to restart production under new ownership, but this came to nothing.

Ginetta: Founded by the Walklett family – no fewer than four brothers were involved in running the company – Ginetta cars were first made at Woodbridge in Suffolk, and later at Witham (Essex) and Sudbury (Suffolk). The Walkletts sold out to businessman Martin Pfaff in the late 1980s, but financial problems followed during the early 1990s. In the mid-1990s Pfaff was still in control, but Ginetta car production had moved to the North of England.

Gordon-Keeble: Technically, and in its personalities, G-K was a descendant of the Peerless, later Warwick (see below) project, for the car was the work of John Gordon and Jim Keeble. Initial assembly was at Eastleigh, near Southampton, but after financial trouble struck in 1965, the company was bought up by London motor trader Harold Smith, but this venture also failed. An attempt to restart production under the De Bruyne name, at Newmarket in East Anglia, was also unsuccessful.

GSM: Originally built in South Africa, this car (the initials stood for Glass Sports Motor, incidentally) was built by GSM Cars at West Malling, in Kent, in the early 1960s.

Healey: Donald Healey set up his own business, the Donald Healey Motor Co Ltd, in Warwick in 1945, building cars with Riley, Nash and Alvis engines until the early 1950s. After this the new Austin-Healey business took up so much of his time (see above) that the Healey car-making side was rapidly run down, though the business name survived as a BMC car dealership in Warwick until the 1970s.

Hillman: Hillman of Coventry had been absorbed by the Rootes Group in the 1930s, and was the most important marque in that multi-headed business from 1945. Rootes eventually sold out to Chrysler of Detroit in the 1960s, after which the Hillman marque was overshadowed by Chrysler, and surviving Hillmans took Chrysler badges from the mid-1970s.

HRG: A small engineering business in Tolworth, Surrey (set up by E A Halford, G H Robins and H R Godfrey) built sportscars from the late 1930s until the mid-1950s. By that time the business was controlled by Stuart Procter, and car production gradually faded away.

Humber: Like Hillman, Humber of Coventry had been taken into the Rootes Group in the early 1930s, and was still a most important part of Rootes until the 1960s, the cars latterly being little more than 'badge-engineered' Hillmans. Humber sales were buoyant until Chrysler took over the Rootes business, and the last Humber of all, a Sceptre, was not made until 1976.

Invicta: This was a small, privately-financed concern, based in Virginia Water, Surrey, after the Second World War. After it closed down in 1950, the moribund company and its assets were bought by the Aldington family (who also produced Frazer Nash cars), but this was no more than an asset-stripping exercise, and no new cars came out of it.

Jaguar: Jaguar of Coventry had been a public limited company since the mid-1930s, but the founder, William Lyons, had always held majority control. Jaguar bought up Daimler (and Lanchester) in 1960, then speedily added Coventry Climax, Guy Motors and Henry Meadows. In 1966, though, Sir William merged his company with BMC, the new holding company being BMH (see Austin, above).

Jaguar became a part of British Leyland in 1968, then a part of the nationalized concern, but was then sold off ('privatized') in 1984. After five years of independence, it was taken over by Ford, and by the mid-1990s was nominally controlled by Ford-USA.

Jensen: The Jensen brothers had set up their own company in the 1930s, but after a financially troubled postwar period they partly sold out to the Norcros Group in 1959. By the late 1960s all had ceded control to the merchant bank William Brandt, but in 1970 a consortium headed by the American motor dealer Kjell Qvale, with Donald Healey alongside him, took over the company. Qvale's company then held control until series production ended in 1976. Attempts to restart Interceptor production in the late 1980s by an offshoot of the old service and parts business were only barely successful.

Jowett: Jowett was a public limited company which had been making cars in West Yorkshire since the 1900s. After World War Two, business was brisk until the early 1950s, when sales of Javelins slumped badly, and the company then closed down. The factory site, but not the company itself, was taken over by International Harvester.

Lagonda: Rescued from receivership in 1935 by Alan Good, Lagonda was in the doldrums in 1945, despite having W O Bentley as technical director, and a promising new car design. David Brown (see Aston Martin, above) bought the much reduced business in 1947 and speedily merged it with Aston Martin. By the 1970s Lagonda had been reduced to little more than an Aston Martin model name, and was therefore part of the package acquired by Ford in 1987.

Lanchester: Lanchester had lost its independence in 1931, when BSA had bought up the loss-making business, then merged it with Daimler. After the Second World War, Daimler built a succession of Daimler-engined Lanchesters, the last of all being the Sprite of 1956. The Lanchester name was bought by Jaguar in 1960 (see Jaguar, above), and so is now in the Ford-owned cupboard of Jaguar assets.

Land-Rover: Rover was a public limited company which found itself with an under-used factory at Solihull in 1945. The Land-Rover 4x4 marque was therefore developed to flesh-out the Rover range. Land-Rover always went along with Rover in the corporate manoeuvrings of the 1960s (see Rover, below), which meant that it was owned by Leyland from 1967, British Leyland from 1968, and finally by the Rover Group. From 1988, therefore, it was owned by British Aerospace, and from 1994 by BMW.

Lea-Francis: The moribund Lea-Francis marque had been revived in 1948, and the small limited company struggled on into the 1950s with a series of old-fashioned cars. The company stopped making cars in 1960 after the Lynx failed to gain any orders, and many years later the rights to the name were sold to Barry Price. Attempts to revive the marque failed.

Lloyd (UK): This Grimsby-based company was small, precariously financed and totally independent of any other car-maker. It was *not* related to Lloyd of West Germany. When the last Lloyd car was produced in 1951, the company disappeared.

Lotus: Colin Chapman and his wife-to-be, Hazel, founded Lotus Engineering in Hornsey, north London, in 1952. The company later moved to Cheshunt, Hertfordshire, and with a single change of name the marque prospered under the Chapman family's control until the 1980s. By that time it had expanded mightily, 'gone public' and moved to Norfolk. After Chapman's untimely death in 1982, when much of the family shareholding had to be sold and a scandal emerged in connection with DeLorean (see Volume 2), there was a troubled four-year period for the public limited company before General Motors took control in 1986. GM persevered until 1993, when it sold Lotus to Bugatti (see Volume 2). By 1995 Bugatti was also in deep financial trouble, but Lotus somehow survived.

Marauder: This was a tiny private venture company set up in 1950 in Dorridge, Warwickshire with George Mackie and Peter Wilks as major personalities. The cars were based closely on Rover chassis, but sold very slowly indeed. The business was closed down in 1952.

Marcos: Jem Marsh and Frank Costin got together in the 1950s to produce specials based on marine-ply chassis, and although Costin soon withdrew, Marsh continued with Marcos into the 1970s, when financial trouble struck. The business was sold in 1971 to the Rob Walker Group, but stopped making Marcos cars during the 1970s. Eventually Jem Marsh bought back the rights to his original company, revived manufacture of the sportscars, and carried on into the 1990s.

Meadows: The Frisky was a short-lived offshoot of the Henry Meadows commercial engine manufacturing business of Wolverhampton, with the separately-financed Frisky Cars Ltd being hived-off in 1958. Sales were always slow, and following a move to Kent, the project collapsed in 1962.

Metropolitan: This was a 'manufactured' marque of BMC (see Austin, above) built at Longbridge, near Birmingham. Originally, BMC had built an Austin A40-engined car for the Nash Corporation for sale exclusively in the USA. Rebadged as the Metropolitan, but still mechanically the same as the previous USA-only car, it was marketed in the UK from 1957 to 1961.

MG: Originally set up in William Morris' Morris Garages premises in Oxford, and developed from there, MG was subsequently handed over by Morris (who by then had become Lord Nuffield) to the Nuffield Organisation. Thereafter, it followed the fortunes of Morris (see below), becoming a part of BMC, then BMH, then British Leyland and finally the Rover Group. This means that it was controlled by British Aerospace from 1988 to 1994, after which it became one of BMW's clutch of marques, a brand-new MGF model (see Volume 2) following in 1995.

Mini: Originally, in 1959, there were both Austin Minis and Morris Minis, but from 1969 British Leyland repositioned Mini to become a marque of its own. Mini, therefore, was controlled by British Leyland and its successors, including the Rover Group, until 1988, thereafter by British Aerospace and from 1994 by BMW.

Morgan: The Morgan car has always been made by a company based in Malvern Link and controlled by the Morgan family. That was the situation in 1935 when the very first Morgan four-wheeler was announced, and it was still the situation 60 years later.

Morris: The Morris marque had been established by William Morris in 1913, and the Cowley (Oxford)-built cars were always to be the most important marque of the Nuffield Organisation which was founded in 1935. By 1945 Morris also controlled MG, Riley and Wolseley, and when Nuffield merged with Austin in 1952, Morris became a constituent of BMC (see *Austin, above*). Over the years, therefore, it became a member of BMH, then British Leyland, but the last Morris cars were produced in 1984 before the Rover Group was officially inaugurated.

Ogle: This very limited marque was an indulgence of David Ogle Design, a design/styling company based at Letchworth, in Hertfordshire. The marque died soon after Ogle himself was killed in a car crash, though Ogle Design continued (most notably to provide Reliant with many styles) into the 1990s.

Oppermann: S E Oppermann was an engineering company based at Elstree/Borehamwood, north of London, which produced the glassfibre-bodied Unicar, then the Stirling models, but there was no connection with any other car-maker.

Paramount: The first Paramounts were produced by a small Derbyshire-based company, but after much financial upheaval the business was taken over by a company controlled by Camden Motors, a thriving motor trade group. However, the project was closed down in 1956, the stock of unsold cars being bought up by Welbeck Motors, another London-based motor trade group.

Peerless: Peerless Cars Ltd, of Slough, featured Bernie Rodger and Jim Keeble among its sponsors, buying all its running gear from Standard-Triumph. After the first business failed in 1960, the car was briefly revived as the Warwick (see *Warwick, below*).

Range Rover: The new-style '100-inch Land-Rover' (see *Land-Rover, above*) was named Range Rover when launched in 1970, becoming a separate marque which has been retained ever since. Range Rover, therefore, was a British Leyland marque, then a Rover marque, being controlled by British Aerospace from 1988, and by BMW from 1994.

Reliant: Established by Tom Williams in 1935, the company first built three-wheelers, then moved ahead to building four-seater sportscars in 1962. By that time Reliant had been taken over by the Welsh-based Hodge Group, but although the Bond marque (see *Bond, above*) was added to the assets in 1969, there was no lasting financial stability. Hodge sold Reliant to Nash Securities, of Kettering, in 1977. Reliant finally descended into major financial chaos in 1990, but was rescued by Beans Industries in 1991, which carried on making cars and three-wheelers.

Do not be confused by the sale of Scimitar GTE manufacturing rights to the Middlebridge concern in the late 1980s, for this did not include the Reliant company itself.

Riley: A Coventry-based, family-controlled car-making company, Riley had been absorbed by the Nuffield Organisation in 1938, and by the early 1950s the cars were being produced in Morris factories. Thereafter Riley followed Morris (see *above*) into BMC, BMH and British Leyland before being killed-off in 1969. Because it was still one of Rover's moribund trademarks in 1994, when the group was taken over by BMW, there was talk of it being revived in the late 1990s...

Rochdale: These cars were always made by a very small, privately-financed company based in Rochdale, Lancashire.

Rolls-Royce: Originated by Charles Rolls and Henry Royce in 1904, the company grew enormously into cars and aeroplane engines, taking in Bentley along the way in 1931 (see *Bentley, above*). By that time it was a large public limited company. After hitting financial trouble in 1971 (spiralling aero-engine development costs were the culprits) it was rescued by the British Government, and the car-making subsidiary was hived-off ('privatized') in 1973. Vickers, the engineering giant, took over in 1980 and have controlled Rolls-Royce (and therefore Bentley) ever since.

Rover: First pedal cycles, then motorcycles, then cars had all been produced by Rover in its early days, this public limited company then expanding strongly after the Second World War by developing the Land-Rover. Rover bought up Alvis in 1965, but was then absorbed into Leyland in 1967. Thereafter, Rover followed Leyland into British Leyland, becoming part of the nationalized remains of that group, but then gave its name to the retitled Rover Group in the late 1980s. British Aerospace took control from the Government in 1988, after which BMW bought Rover in 1994.

Singer: Once one of Britain's largest car-makers in the 1920s, Singer gradually fell back in the 1950s until taken over by the Rootes Group at the end of 1955. Thereafter Singer became one of the several marques owned by Rootes, its final models being based on Hillmans. Rootes sold out to Chrysler in 1967, and the final Singer car was made in 1970.

Standard: By 1939 Standard had become one of Britain's Big Six car-makers, and at the end of 1944 it also bought the remains of the Triumph concern. Having built Ferguson tractors for the Irish tycoon until the late 1950s, the company then struck financial trouble and was taken over by Leyland Motors in 1961. The Standard marque died in 1963, for by this time Triumph had become a more important badge at the Coventry factory.

Sunbeam: Once an independent car-maker, Sunbeam had been rescued from receivership by the Rootes Group in 1935. Killed-off in favour of Sunbeam-Talbot (see *below*), Sunbeam was then revived in 1954, and was thereafter an important Rootes, later Chrysler UK, marque. The last Sunbeam car was produced under Chrysler control in 1976, after which Sunbeam became a model badge for Chrysler and Talbot. The residual rights are now owned by Peugeot.

Sunbeam-Talbot: Having rescued both Sunbeam (see *above*) and Talbot from receivership in 1935, the Rootes Group used both the names, but nothing else, to invent the Sunbeam-Talbot marque in 1938.

From 1945 to 1954 Sunbeam-Talbot was the badge applied to the most sporting, high-performance Rootes Group cars, using running gear mainly developed for Hillman and Humber models. Sunbeam-Talbot gave way to Sunbeam in 1954, and the hyphenated name was never used again.

Talbot would be revived as a new marque badge in 1979 (see *Volume 2*) after Peugeot had taken over the ex-Rootes, ex-Chrysler-Europe businesses in 1978.

Swallow: This car, using all-Triumph TR2 running gear, was produced by the Swallow Coachbuilding Co (1935) Ltd of Walsall, which had originally been an offshoot of the old Swallow business of the 1930s which had produced car bodies. There was, however, no connection with Jaguar (which had grown out of Swallow), for Swallow's modern business was building caravans.

Tornado: These were built by Tornado Cars, of Rickmansworth, a small concern which began by producing glass-fibre bodyshells for kit-cars. Although Tornado tried to set up alliances with established British car-makers, it failed, and faded away in the early 1960s.

Trident: Bill Last was a Woodbridge (Suffolk)-based TVR dealer, who somehow emerged with the ex-TVR Trident prototype styles when the Blackpool firm went through one of its periodic financial crises in 1965. Trident redeveloped the style and added it to proprietary Austin-Healey 1000 chassis and different engines. The enterprise failed in the late 1970s.

Triumph: Proud and independent from 1923 to 1939, Triumph lapsed into receivership and was eventually bought by Standard in 1944. Henceforth, Triumph became an upmarket Standard badge. The TR3A, and latterly the Herald, were so successful that Triumph strangled its Standard parent in 1963. In the meantime, Leyland had taken over management, so Triumph followed Leyland into alliances with Rover, then into British Leyland. The last Triumph car was a Japanese-inspired Honda, and was built in 1984. In theory, at least, BMW could build new-generation Triumphs in future, for it now owns all the rights.

Turner: John Turner set up Turner Sports Cars of Wolverhampton in 1951 to build racing engines, and later sportscars which used proprietary engines and running gear. The last Turners were produced in 1966.

TVR: The original TVR sportscar was produced by Trevor Wilkinson's Layton Engineering in Blackpool. In the next decade, financial turmoil was normal and there were several changes of company name and entrepreneurial ownership before the motor trading TVR dealer-owning Lilley family — father Arthur and son Martin — bought the business in 1965. Recovery followed, and the Lilleys eventually sold out to self-made millionaire Peter Wheeler in 1981. In the mid-1990s Wheeler was still the sole proprietor of what had become a much larger operation.

Unipower: This was a small high-quality GT car produced by Universal Power Drives Ltd, of Perivale, Middlesex, of which racing driver Andrew Hedges was a major personality. This concern was a precision engineering business, later with closer connections with aerospace, but car manufacture ended in the late 1960s.

Vanden Plas: Having started as a car body coachbuilding concern in northwest London (it supplied sporting shells to companies like Bentley and Alvis), VDP was acquired by Austin (see above) immediately after the Second World War. Thereafter it provided bodies for upmarket Austin, later BMC, cars, eventually becoming a marque badge of its own on the front of much-modified mass-market BMC, BMH and British Leyland cars. Vanden Plas also produced the Daimler DS420 Limousine for some years (see Daimler, above), but the business was closed down as part of British Leyland's rationalization in 1980.

Vauxhall: Once an independent car-maker, Vauxhall had been absorbed by General Motors of the USA in 1925, and is still a subsidiary of that car-making colossus. During the 1960s and 1970s its operations were ever more closely merged with those of Opel of West Germany (another GM subsidiary), so that by the 1980s Vauxhall cars had become no more than rebadged and mildly facelifted Opels, though still manufactured in the UK.

Warwick: This was a short-lived and unsuccessful attempt to revive the Peerless GT project (see Peerless, above), still using premises near Slough, Buckinghamshire, its company being known as Bernard Rodger Developments Ltd. After it had closed down, Rodger and his designers John Gordon and Jim Keeble went on to promote the Gordon-Keeble car (see Gordon-Keeble, above).

William: Briefly imported from France and rebadged, this was an Italian Lawil design, which was marketed in the UK by Crayford, who had already become noted for producing factory-approved convertible conversions of cars like the Mini, the Ford Cortina and the Ford Corsair.

Wolseley: William Morris had bought the Wolseley car-making business in 1927 and (as Lord Nuffield) had bequeathed it to the new Nuffield Organisation in 1935. From then on it became one of various upmarket relations of the Morris marque (see Morris, above), following Morris into BMC, then BMH and finally British Leyland. As part of the never-ending rationalization of BL, Wolseley was killed-off in 1975, the surviving cars being rebadged as Princess.

[A similar survey of all British marques which existed after 1970 (including new marques not surveyed above) is provided in Volume 2.]

APPENDIX C

Production figures, registrations, exports and imports, 1945 to 1970

(With grateful thanks to the SMMT for permission to quote official figures.)

Year	Sales of cars in the UK	Private car production in the UK	Car exports from the UK	Car imports into the UK
1945	7,767	16,938	N/A	N/A
1946	121,725	219,162	84,358	63
1947	147,767	287,000	140,691	222
1948	112,666	334,815	224,374	221
1949	154,694	412,290	257,250	1,868
1950	134,394	522,515	397,688	1,375
1951	138,373	475,919	368,101	3,723
1952	141,037†	448,000	308,942	1,876
1953	301,354	594,808	307,368	2,067
1954	394,362	769,165	372,029	4,660
1955	511,420	897,560	388,564	11,131
1956	407,342	707,594	335,397	6,885
1957	433,171	860,842	424,320	8,828
1958	566,319	1,051,551	484,034	10,940
1959	657,315	1,189,943	568,971	26,998
1960	820,088	1,352,728	569,889	57,309
1961	756,054	1,003,967	370,744	22,759
1962	800,239	1,249,426	544,924	28,610
1963	1,030,694	1,607,939	615,827	48,163
1964	1,215,929	1,867,640	679,383	65,725
1965	1,148,718	1,772,045	627,567	55,558
1966	1,091,217	1,603,679	556,044	66,793
1967	1,143,015	1,522,013	502,596	92,731
1968	1,444,770	1,815,936	676,571	102,276
1969	1,012,811	1,717,073	771,634	101,914
1970	1,126,824	1,640,966	690,339	157,956

† Original tables quote a UK sales figure of 191,037 for 1952, which was clearly too high. I have assumed a simple misprint.

NOTES:

These figures have been assembled from two separate statistical charts, which explains why it is not possible to correlate every figure. Where the home market is concerned, because of the 'pipeline effect' there is always a significant difference between 'cars delivered' and 'cars sold'.

Production

It took a long time to recover from the war. The prewar UK production record of 379,310 (achieved in 1937) was not beaten until 1949.

The first 'one million' year was 1958. The nearest to a 'two million' year would be reached in 1972 – 1,921,311.

Imports

The market share of imported cars did not exceed 1 per cent for the first time until 1949. The market share of imports first exceeded 10 per cent in 1969, then rose rapidly – to 25 per cent in 1972 – and would reach 50 per cent in 1977. The peak import penetration figure recorded so far has been 61 per cent in 1979.

Only 27,206 cars were imported during the first 10 postwar years. It took a total of 25 postwar years (until 1971) for the first million to be reached – a figure that was exceeded almost every year in the 1980s!

Exports

Britain's exports were high in the 1940s and early 1950s due to Government policies and supply restrictions; 69 per cent of all British cars were exported in 1946, 67 per cent in 1948 and no less than 77 per cent in 1951. This figure dropped below 50 per cent two years later, below 40 per cent in 1961 and would reach a low of 17.3 per cent in 1988.

APPENDIX D

Price comparisons – now and then

No-one needs to be told that prices have been rising continuously since 1945. However, when comparing car prices 'then' with 'now' it helps to know how much prices in general have changed over the years.

Thanks to the Central Statistical Office, I have been able to assemble the following table *which has been reformulated, and is specific to this book*. Taking January 1946 as my base point (no accurate figure is available for 1945), it shows how the Retail Price Index has changed over the years:

Calendar year (1946 = 100)	Retail Price Index	Calendar year (1946 = 100)	Retail Price Index
1946	100	1971	276
1947	107	1972	295
1948	115	1973	322
1949	119	1974	374
1950	121	1975	465
1951	133	1976	542
1952	140	1977	627
1953	143	1978	680
1954	146	1979	771
1955	151	1980	909
1956	158	1981	1,017
1957	163	1982	1,105
1958	168	1983	1,156
1959	170	1984	1,213
1960	172	1985	1,287
1961	176	1986	1,331
1962	183	1987	1,386
1963	186	1988	1,454
1964	192	1989	1,567
1965	201	1990	1,716
1966	209	1991	1,816
1967	215	1992	1,884
1968	225	1993	1,914
1969	237	1994	1,960
1970	252	1995	2,008

Thus, in 1994/95, the Retail Price Index was at approximately 20 times its 1946 level. Accordingly, the cost of a 1946 Morris 8 would convert to about £6,900 in the mid-1990s. Similarly, the £2,098 Jaguar E-type of 1961 would cost about £42,000 in 1995.

One has to ask the question: Have relative values – prices compared with incomes – changed out of all proportion?